Vil S. Mirzayanov
STATE SECRETS

AN INSIDER'S CHRONICLE OF THE RUSSIAN CHEMICAL WEAPONS PROGRAM

Outskirts Press, Inc.
Denver, Colorado

The opinions expressed in this manuscript are solely the opinions of the author and do not represent the opinions or thoughts of the publisher. The author has represented and warranted full ownership and/or legal right to publish all the materials in this book.

State Secrets
An Insider's Chronicle of the Russian Chemical Weapons Program
All Rights Reserved.
Copyright © 2009 Vil S. Mirzayanov
V3.0

Cover design by Ratmir Akhiyarov

This book may not be reproduced, transmitted, or stored in whole or in part by any means, including graphic, electronic, or mechanical without the express written consent of the publisher except in the case of brief quotations embodied in critical articles and reviews.

Outskirts Press, Inc.
http://www.outskirtspress.com

Paperback ISBN: 978-1-4327-2566-2
Hardback ISBN: 978-1-4327-1923-4

Library of Congress Control Number: 2008927116

Outskirts Press and the "OP" logo are trademarks belonging to Outskirts Press, Inc.

PRINTED IN THE UNITED STATES OF AMERICA

Introduction

This book, while autobiographical and in many places entirely personal in character, is also a firsthand chronicle about the secrets of chemical weapons development in the Soviet Union and in Russia. I worked as a chemist for more than 26 years in the premier center for the development of chemical agents in the Soviet Union - GOSNIIOKhT (State Scientific Research Institute of Organic Chemistry and Technology), during its major developmental period and the pinnacle of its bloom. As an insider in the military chemical complex, I witnessed and participated actively in the laboratory research, development, testing and mass production of modern Russian chemical weapons. Like hundreds of other scientists, I gave my work my best effort, applying all of my energy and capabilities, in order to make sure that these weapons were powerful and effective.

The ruling Communist elite spared nothing - neither resources nor people - to ensure success for its military chemical complex. In order to maintain the highest level of secrecy, in 1974 the Central Committee of CPSU placed this entire complex with all of its scientists, engineers and workers, entirely beyond the bounds of the laws and regulations existing at that time, pretending that it didn't exist. This deprived everyone working under the regime of any elementary rights to defend their own interests. This was a hypocritical effort to create an image of a USSR which was outside of the chemical arms race. That was allegedly solely the activity of the Western aggressors.

For a long time Russia simply reproduced the chemical weapons of Western countries; however, in the beginning of the 1970s Russian scientist Petr Kirpichev and his team created a new class of chemical agents which are many times more lethal than anything known up to this time. Moreover, the chemical agent known to us as A-232 was not a traditional phosphoorganic nerve agent of known structure. For that purpose, GOSNIIOKhT expressly synthesized a pesticide with an analogous structure. This opened up the possibility of using agricultural chemicals as components of binary weapons. Russia profited from this deception and set traps during the time of negotiations of the Convention on the Prohibition of Chemical Weapons (CWC), especially in connection with the advancement of their binary weapons program. When two relatively harmless components react with each other during the flight of a rocket and produce a deadly chemical agent, the binary weapon eliminates most of the expense and danger of the production and storage of chemical agents. It also makes them extremely difficult to monitor and control.

Even when the CWC was being negotiated, Russia secretly and persistently pressed forward with its program of development and testing of the new class of binary chemical agents under the code name *Novichok*, which means "newcomer" in Russian. According to the Wyoming Accord, both the United States and Russia were required to declare their stores of chemical weapons, but Russia lied about the quantity stockpiled and has never acknowledged the *Novichok* program to this day.

As a scientist and as a human being, I went through a long soul searching process and came to the heart wrenching realization that not only were chemical weapons useless for the country's defense, but their main purpose is the mass slaughter of civilians. I could not bear to continue to participate in the deception of the world community by Russia's ruling class. They just wanted to exploit the loopholes written into the CWC in order to destroy their old and useless chemical weapons, while trying to keep the development and stockpiling of new deadly binary weapons a secret.

Even though the concept of Democracy was beginning to catch on fire in Russia, nothing was fundamentally changing. I became involved with the Democratic Movement at my institute and tried to persuade people to stop producing chemical agents, and I appealed to the Moscow's Mayor Gavril Popov, but there were no results. Reluctantly at first, then resolutely, I became a whistleblower. Even now, after all I went through, I do not regret this. If I hadn't spoken up, who would have? Probably no one in the rest of the world would have known about Novichok.

I appealed to the world community to pay attention to this problem in my first article published in the Moscow newspaper *Kuranty* in 1991, but there was no reaction. Then two more articles appeared in September of 1992 issues of *Moscow News* and *The Baltimore Sun* which resulted in my arrest for "divulging state secrets". This was the beginning of my persecution by the Federal Service of Security of Russia – the successor to the KGB. These actions of the Chekists ignited a firestorm of protest in Russia and abroad, preventing the customary reprisals against dissidents. Still, in the year and a half that followed my first arrest and time spent in Lefortovo Prison, the investigation dragged on, and I was prevented from leaving Moscow, except under special approved circumstances. At first the authorities found they could not properly prosecute me, because all the previous laws on state secrecy passed out of existence, when the Soviet Union split up. A new and retroactive decree was drawn up, with the goal of prosecuting me and doling out exemplary punishment for the publication of an article without any technical or state secrets. My case went to trial. It was a secret trial, and no observers were permitted. After the first day in this kangaroo court, I decided I could not ethically allow myself to continue to participate in my own trial. Once more I was arrested and sent for a month to Matrosskaya Tishina, a maximum security prison with a nasty reputation. Ultimately the decision rested in the hands of the Attorney General of Russia, who dropped my case for lack of *corpus delicti*.

In the end, the Chekists' investigation of my case played out badly for them. They attached more than 60 secret and top secret documents, related to the development of chemical weapons in Russia, to my case for the indictment. I copied these out legally during my study of the case materials in the Russian equivalent of the discovery process. Fifty one of them are attached to this book in the Annexes. From these documents it is possible to get some idea of how the *Novichok* program for the development of binary chemical weapons was going in the Soviet Union, then in Russia.

After his nomination for the Nobel Peace Prize and Russia's signing of the Agreement on the Nonproduction and Elimination of Chemical Weapons (CWC) on September 23, 1989, by Edward Shevardnadze, Mikhail Gorbachev, the President of Soviet Union and First Secretary of the Central Committee of the CPSU signed Resolution no 844-186 of the Central Committee of CPSU and Council of Ministers of USSR on October 6, 1989, sanctioning the start up of the binary weapons program. Already a Nobel Peace Prize laureate, Gorbachev on April 23, 1991 awarded the Lenin Prize to the leaders of the military chemical complex for the successful development, testing and production of these arms. Despite the fall of the Communist regime, the *Novichok* program continued up until the end of 1992, and possibly after that.

Despite of my revelations and the ratification of the CWC by Russia, the *Novichok* program was not put under international control, and agents A-230, A-232 and their precursors and the binary components are not on the list of controlled compounds of CWC. This is very troubling because there are no guarantees that Russia isn't continuing such secret programs. These are all extremely compelling reasons for amending the CWC to include these chemicals, but nothing has been done about it. I am sure I am not the only person who has noticed that these loopholes that were written into the CWC could very well have been built in intention ally.

I have struggled with my past over the last eighteen years. As a result of my actions, the lives of a great number of people have been affected, especially at my institute where thousands lost their jobs. A lot of people are not going to be happy to hear my story come out, especially those who are politically motivated, both here and in Russia. Even so, it is time now for the full truth to be heard.

Acknowledgements

There are many people and organizations that helped me during the time of my case and trial, and without their help I certainly would have spent years in a Russian prison. In retrospect, I am also indebted to President Boris Yeltsin, who allowed a modicum of democracy to flourish in Russia at the time of my case. Without that, I would have met with the same fate as Igor Sutyagyn, Valentin Danilov, Alexander Nikitin, Mikhail Trepashkin and Grigory Pasko, who all spent or still are spending time in prison for political reasons.

Foremost, I would like to thank my wife, Gale Colby Mirzayanov and her friend Irene Etkin Goldman for their valuable help during this period of time. They collected information on my case and distributed it to many people who informed scientists, legislators and prominent individuals, who kept constant pressure on the Russian government. Also, I am greatly indebted to my lawyer Aleksander Asnis, who worked tirelessly on my case without receiving any payment. I am indebted to the late Dr. Joshua Lederberg and Dr. Matthew Meselson, for their support during my struggle in Russia, and for their kind letters supporting my immigration petition.

The following organizations worked strongly to support me by writing letters to the Russian and American Governments, and by keeping track the developments in my case from the fall of 1992 until March of 1994, when my case was dropped: the American Association for the Advancement of Science (which sent an

Amicus brief on my behalf to the Russian court in 1994, and which awarded me with their 1995 AAAS Scientific Freedom and Responsibility Award), the American Chemical Society, the American Physical Society, the American Press Center in Moscow, the Andrei Sakharov Foundation, the Arms Control Association, the Carnegie Endowment for International Peace, The Cavallo Foundation (which awarded me with their special Award for Moral Courage in Business and Government in June of 1993), Central Asia Associates, the Committee of Concerned Scientists, the Federation of American Scientists (which was the first scientific society to support me in 1992), the Government Accountability Project (which arranged meetings between helpful people and organizations who wanted to help with my case in 1993), Greenpeace (the Moscow office helped me keep in touch with people in the United States), Helsinki Watch (sent people to try to cover my trial and helped in many other ways), Human Rights Watch, the International Science Foundation, The Kennan Institute, the Kentucky Environmental Foundation, Lawyers Alliance for World Security, Lawyers Committee for Human Rights, the National Academy of Sciences, the New York Academy of Sciences (which awarded me with the 1994 Heinz R. Pagels Human Rights of Scientists Award), Physicians for Social Responsibility, Russian Center for Human Rights, Russian Center for Glasnost, the Union of Councils for Soviet Jews, and Tugan Tel.

I would also like to gratefully acknowledge the following legislators who supported me with their letters and research in my case: Senator Bill Bradley, Congressman John Conyers Jr., Senator Dennis DeConcini, the Greens of the French Delegation to Europarliament, Congressman Stenny Hoyer, Senator Frank Lautenberg, the late Senator Daniel Patrick Moynihan, Congressman Dana Rohrabacher, the late Senator Strom Thurmond and Senator Robert Torricelli.

The following individuals were also extremely helpful in supporting my case and I am most grateful to them: Kenneth Anderson, Academician Georgi Arbatov, Joseph L. Birman, Elena Bonner, Dr. Rainer Braun, Dr. Ronald Breslow, Matt Bryza, Colonel Nikolai Chugunov, Louis Clark, Ken Coates, Ambassador

James F. Collins, Rachael Denber, Dr. Ernest L. Eliel, Dr. Daniel Ellsberg, Will Englund, Sebia Hawkins, Dorothy Hirsch, Kathleen Hunt, Dr. Vladimir Iakimets, Deborah E. Klepp, Dr. Joel L. Lebowitz, Dr. Irving Lerch, Dr. Zafra Lerman, Dr. Fang Lizhi, Academician Viktor Maslov, Patrick F. McManamon, S.J., Dr. Dieter Meissner, Valery F. Menshikov, Andrei Mironov, Micah H. Naftalin, Academician Oleg Nefedov, Dr. Rodney Nichols, the late Leonard Nikishin, Valeria Novodvroskaya, Vladimir Petrenko, Ambassador Thomas Pickering III, Dr. Paul H. Plotz, Valery Rudnev, J.R. Ryan, Academician Roald Sagdeev, Alexey Simonov, Morton Sklaar, Academician Boris Sokolov, George Soros, General Vadim Smirnitsky, Dr. Amy Smithson, Dr. Jeremy Stone, Svetlana Stone-Wachtel, Vladimir Uglev, Dr. Frank von Hippel, Dr. J. Michael Waller, Dr. Torsten Wiesel, Craig Williams, David Wise, Jonathan Wise, Academician Alexei Yablokov, Grigory Yavlinsky, Mark Zaharov, Academician Sergey Zalygin, Academician Nikolai Zefirov and the late Andrei Zheleznyakov. I would like to also thank anyone who is not mentioned here who worked on my case or in supporting me. I understand how important the support letters, as well as the role of the press were in keeping my case under the spotlight of public scrutiny.

Finally, I would like to thank my daughter Elena Orlova and her husband Oleg Orlov who supported me strongly during this period in every possible way, and my two sons Iskander Mirzayanov and Sultan Mirzayanov for their endurance, patience and support. All of their lives were deeply affected by my decisions and actions.

I am dedicating this book with love to my children
Elena, Iskander and Sultan

Table of Contents

Introduction iii
Acknowledgements vii
Chapter 1 – Who Am I? 1
Chapter 2 – My Background 5
Chapter 3 – My Student Days 29
   Can Your Russian Language Take You Everywhere? 29
   In Moscow 35
Chapter 4 – I Become a Person from "The Box" 55
Chapter 5 – My Chemical Career 63
Chapter 6 – Into Supersecrecy 75
Chapter 7 – GOSNIIOKhT's Tangled Bureaucracy 89
   Deputy Director for Science Aleksander Shchekotikhin 89
   The GOSNIIOKhT Party Committee and Deputy Director Konstantin Guskov 99
   The Start-up of the Novocheboksary Factory and the Downfall of Semeyon Varshavski 105
   The Directorate of GOSNIIOKhT 108
Chapter 8 – Science and Scientists in GOSNIIOKhT 119
   Russian VX gas – Substance 33 and the Basics of Russian Binary Weapons 119
   A New Class of Chemical Agents "Novichok" and Binary Weapons 142
   A Successful Binary Weapon Based on Substance 33 151
Chapter 9 – Fight Without End and Evgeny Bogomazov's "Discovery" 169

Chapter 10 – Safety While Working with Chemical Agents is it Possible? 195
Chapter 11 – Struggling With Spies 205
    The Geneva Negotiations 205
Chapter 12 – The Torment of Insight 225
Chapter 13 – I'm Quitting the Party 239
Chapter 14 – I Break the Silence 247
Chapter 15 – Challenging Poisoned Policies 259
    The KGB Arrests Me 259
    Lefortovo Prison 269
    The Downfall of Lev Fedorov 272
    In a Prison Cell for the First Time 274
    I Move to Another Cell 278
    My Cellmates – My Lawyers 280
    The Indictment is Ready 285
Chapter 16 – The Crash of the KGB's Plans 291
    The Court Releases Me from Prison 291
    The KGB vs. Asnis 299
    The Generals do Some "Brainwashing" 301
Chapter 17 – Captain Shkarin Fabricates the Case 307
    The Expert Commission 307
Chapter 18 – I am not Alone 315
Chapter 19 – Boycott of the Investigation 321
    A Person from Volsk and Petrenko's Patriotic Impulse 325
    How the Tatars Became the "Enemies of Democracy" 330
    The Discovery of the Chekists 335
    The Expert Commission: Mirzayanov Told the Truth, Therefore he is Guilty 337
    The Russian Government Comes Running To the Aid of the KGB 341
Chapter 20 – Revenge of the Communists 349
Chapter 21 – The KGB Prepares for a Closed Trial 363
Chapter 22 – Trial and Prison 377
    Prosecutor Pankratov and the Judges 377
    My Second Arrest 386
    "Matrosskaya Tishina" 390
    In the Dungeon 413

Back to the Courtroom 419
Witnesses Ruin the Case 422
Prosecutor Pankratov Rejects the Work of the Chekists,
    Judges Cancel the Trial 431
Killer Koshelev and Biological Weapons 436
Chapter 23 – The Acquittal 445
    The Decision of the Attorney General 445
Glossary 449
Notes 453
Annexes 483
Index 589

Chapter 1
Who Am I?

"**A**re you a spy?"

"Are you working for foreign intelligence?"

These questions struck me like lightning. Never in my life had anybody asked me questions like these. Even my KGB interrogator, Captain Viktor Shkarin, was never so brazen as to insult me in this way. I couldn't understand it. Where was I? What was I doing there?

Slowly it came back to me. I was sitting in a big second floor suite of the Nassau Inn, which is next to Princeton University. Some people were standing around, looking at the signals put out by some kind of a primitive polygraph. My translator, who assaulted me with these horrible words, was someone I had met once before at a meeting with a very respectable and world-renowned scientist, in the Radisson Hotel in Moscow in 1994.

"Go fuck yourself! Just fuck off!" I kept repeating in Russian. No one tried to calm me down. Slowly I became aware there was a door in the room, and I pulled myself through it.

My translator followed me and asked me why I was insulted. All these questions and procedures are routine, he said, for anyone who is trying to get a government job, including the Secretary of Defense.

"I am not going to be the Secretary of Defense! I am sad that I

1

was trying to help the American people. Probably you don't know me," I replied.

"Right now we know who you are," he calmly replied.

Even in my worst nightmares, I couldn't have imagined that someone could insult me some day in this nasty way, in this paradise of liberty. I asked myself - why didn't even one of the famous American scientists or statesmen I had met warn me that in order to serve humanity, I had to go through this humiliating process?

Before that I was in very high spirits, first when I became the first foreigner to receive the 1993 Cavallo Foundation Special Award for Moral Courage. Then in 1994, George Soros personally presented me with the Heinz R. Pagels Human Rights of Scientists Award of the New York Academy of Sciences. In 1995, I was awarded the Scientific Freedom and Responsibility Award of the AAAS, a professional association of more than 100,000 members, at its annual meeting in Atlanta. This very special award was presented to me by the renowned scientist Dr. Francisco J. Ayala. Later that year, I testified at a special hearing on terrorism and the Aum Shinrikyo cult, held by the U.S. Senate Permanent Subcommittee on Investigations. After my testimony, Senator Sam Nunn told me respectfully that I should call him directly, if I had any problems.

Then this nightmare began.

I was feeling crazy. I was cursing my whole life. Probably even my love for Gale, who later became my wife, was not enough to calm me. I told her I probably had to leave the United States of America immediately. It had become a disgusting country, where the KGB was celebrating power. Only naïve people could believe that the spy Aldrich Ames was the only single agent working for the Soviets. Certainly his followers were trying to prevent anyone from helping the United States understand about the Russian "Novichok" program.

When they were negotiating for my assistance with these problems, they asked me to take a lie detector test. It was quite strange that I had to go through these procedures, when they supposedly wanted to get information about a whole new generation of the most deadly chemical weapons ever produced. To reconstruct any chemical agent, would probably have cost no more than a few thousand dollars. But, I think these people already knew that. Afterwards they tried to explain to me that I could devastate America financially (with misinformation), as someone had before.

I had already heard about this polygraph machine and was very curious about it. When I came into the room at the Nassau Inn, and I saw this equipment, there were no words to express my disappointment. It was so primitive and had nothing to do with my scientific background. Mechanically, I asked if Ames had passed his polygraph tests on this kind of equipment. They replied "Yes, but we have improved it since. Right now it is a very reliable machine." Certainly it was reliable enough to produce an entirely questionable result, which could be used to compromise and control me later on.

I am still asking myself why all this happened to me, and so I am trying to put my past into some order with this story. I am sure of this though. Many people in power, both in Russia and in the US, do not want you to know about my story.

Nobel Prize laureate and President of New York Academy of Sciences Dr. Joshua Lederberg is greeting me. February 1995.

Dr. Ayala presents me the AAAS Scientific Freedom and Responsibility Award at the annual 1995 conference in Atlanta.

Chapter 2
My Background

When I try to understand what inspired me at the beginning of the 1990s to publish articles about Russian chemical weapons and the secrets of the military-industrial complex, which drastically changed my whole life, I inevitably come to the conclusion that there was nothing accidental about this. Undoubtedly many people asked, "What did this scientist - this chemist need? Surely, he lived a good life under that regime." Were my actions an impulsive emotional outburst and recklessness?

Not at all. I look back at my life and I see that the whole chain of events in the history of my country and my people made me challenge the lies that littered the state. I became completely entwined in the fate of the country and my people....

I come from a family of village teachers. My father was born in 1902. He was the son of the village mullah, Mirzazhan, from the Kazakov clan. His grandfather and great grandfather were also mullahs, according to the archival documents. Legend has it that the Kazakovs are descendants of the Orenburg Tatars. Some members of his kin were engaged in trade, and others became Muslim clergymen. We know that one of the Kazakovs built a mosque in Kazan which was turned into a warehouse during Soviet times, and in 1975 it was demolished.

Although Muslims had no last names before the revolution, the Cossack "kushamat" (a peculiar nickname that was often added to one's name in Tatar villages) stuck with them after they participated in the rebellion of Emeliyan Pugachev, an Orenburg Cossack, against the Tsar.

My grandfather died after returning from a pilgrimage to Mecca when he was less than 30 years old. My father was only one year old at that time, and my grandmother Minyamal was left a widow with five young children; the eldest was only seven. Still, my father's humble origins remained a blemish for him until his last days and hindered his education and career advancement. Before and a few years after the revolution, my father studied in the madrasseh, a Muslim religious school. Following the family tradition, he was preparing to become a mullah. I think many of my father's actions could be attributed to his efforts to prove that your origins mean nothing, when it comes to loyalty to the new regime. He was ready to be faithful to it. My father became a staunch Communist. I'm not going to blame him or excuse him, because he had no choice. It was the only way for him to survive, because in every respect he was an enemy of the regime in power. At that time, it didn't matter that my father grew up an orphan, practically in poverty. In 1916, his older brother, 22-year-old Fazliakhmet, perished on the German front of First World War.

My father's ancestral roots made him an outsider. His mother came from the Valitov family, whom people considered to be members of the nobility. The Valitovs, on a par with the Russian gentry, enjoyed all the rights of land ownership and property. In return, they had to serve in the Tsar Guards, reporting for duty with their own horses and equipment. As we know, during the endless wars in Europe, the Tsarist military leaders ordered Bashkir cavalrymen to attack first, which often resulted in a change for the better for the Russians. However, many of our people perished and the male population of Bashkortstan began to dwindle away. All signs point to the fact that this was the deliberate policy of the Tsarist regime, which sacrificed their age-old enemies, the Tatars and the Bashkirs. Both groups realized how desperate their situation was, and they regularly rebelled against the Tsar. However, they lost every time, since the powers were not equal. I am not going to debate historical themes here - that is not the point of this book. However, a certain sojourn back into history is still necessary to understand my path to the truth.

Nowadays, there are people who idealize the Tsarist autocracy and long for the time when Great Russian chauvinism was in fact the state policy. However, historical facts are difficult to argue with, and they completely deflate any attempt to rehabilitate Russian expansionism, which resulted in so many deaths and hindered the development of non-Russian peoples, unfortunate enough to live near the Russians[1].

You may judge for yourself. Before Ivan the Terrible seized Kazan in 1552, the population of the Tatars and Bashkirs equaled that of the Russians, and there were about 7 million of each. Four hundred years later, the population of Russians grew by 160 million, while that of Tatars and Bashkirs remained at close to seven million. The reader can draw his own conclusions regarding the scope of assimilation and purposeful genocide of Turkic-speaking peoples in Russia.

Our people were pulled down into slavery. The Russian Tsars almost returned the Tatar and Bashkir people to the Stone Age. They prohibited all crafts connected with iron working, so that the enslaved people couldn't arm themselves and rise up against their oppressors. Moreover, Tatars and Bashkirs were forbidden to marry each other, so that these two kindred nations couldn't unite and become a strong body capable of struggling with their common enemy, the Russian autocracy. These prohibitions were abolished only after the February Revolution of 1917. Nevertheless, we still live with the strong echoes of that colonial regime.

Some people try to prove that the Bolsheviks were internationalists, who completely rejected Great Russian chauvinism and made all the nations of the Russian Empire equal. Unfortunately, these statements have little, if anything at all, to do with the truth. I think the truth is that Bolshevism transformed Tsarist Great Russian chauvinism into Communist demagogy, making it more draconian and disastrous for small populations of people[2]. The facts speak for themselves.

In 1927, the Soviet power structure prohibited the use of the Arabic alphabet, which the Tatars and Bashkirs had used for more than 1,000 years. In this way, Bolsheviks were effective in disconnecting these peoples from their rich centuries-old literature, history and culture. This ban had grave consequences for the generations born after the Bolshevik upheaval of 1917. They literally became generations without any roots, who didn't know their past. Like millions of other Tatars, I don't know the Arabic alphabet and so I haven't read any of my national literature written before 1917.

Another classic example of the Bolshevik policy is the national map drawn up by the Bolshevik empire. New borders were carved out between the republics, which resulted in eternal and overwhelming hostility between nations. In 1918, the first autonomous republic appeared in Bolshevik Russia – Bashkortstan. However, the main territories with the majority of the Bashkir population, which are in the Urals and in the Trans-Urals, were not made a part of this republic. So a time bomb was constructed that still has wrenching effects on the lives of Russians, Tatars, and Bashkir people. This kind of groundwork that was laid is currently exploding in the Caucasus region and is the source unsolvable bloody conflicts.

Even so, when the Bolshevik revolution began, "foreigners" didn't support the Tsarist regime. To a large extent this probably accounts for the defeat of the White Army, because non-Russian peoples saw nothing good in keeping a regime in power that they hated. Also, the Bolshevik demagogy, which promised true equality, played an important role in the outcome of the revolution. However, very soon many people realized what was behind this doctrine. I know from my fellow villagers that a group of young men, including my Uncle Akhmetziya, were forced to serve in the Bolshevik army, and to fight in the Civil War of 1918. However, when they found themselves in the regional center Djirtjuli, they swam across the Belaya River and ran back to their village, on the very first night. It would have been strange if they hadn't done that, as the rule of the Bolsheviks began in Djirtjuli with mass robbery and great excesses. Having demolished the wonderful house of a rich merchant, the Reds rolled a lot of barrels of honey out of his cellar and began oiling the axles of their carts. No attempts were made to give the honey to the poor, who the Bolsheviks were allegedly taking care of.

My father became one of the first Communists in the village and organized a collective farm in 1928 together with my maternal uncle, Mirkasim Kamalov. But the most terrible fact was that, together with other Communists, he participated in the dispossession of the wealthy peasants (kulaks) and their banishment to Baika (a remote region of Bashkortstan). Among them there were his Uncle Mirkasim Khasanbikov, a mullah, his cousin Gulim Khasanbikov, and other close relatives[3].

Gulim was forced to live in this settlement for the rest of his life, and he came to the village several times during the 1950s to visit us. He told my father about all the horrors that he had to suffer through, with his family in the forests in the Ural Mountains of Bashkortstan.

"You know, Sultan, I survived only thanks to my diligence and physical strength," said Gulim. "To get an additional food ration, I collected more than 10 cubic meters of wood by hand, working 18 hours a day... Hey, Sultan, what did you start all this for? Look, how you live. You are the director at your school, but you practically live in poverty. I now have more than 30 beehives, four cows, a horse, and a large house - everything that the state allows deportees to have. I can say that now I am much wealthier than I had been before you dispossessed me. The children are settled. They married, all of them have learned to read, and they live quite well. But am I happy in a foreign land? No! My roots are here, but even now I have no right to come to my native village..."

I inadvertently overheard this conversation when I was only 13, but I understood that a kulak or a village baj (rich man), wasn't an exploiter or a bloodsucker, as they wrote in many of the books I had read by that time. He was a hard worker who, under any circumstances, tried to create something of value.

Another "feat" of my father was his active participation in the so-called Cultural Revolution, which sought to introduce the "backward masses" to Communist culture. Everything that didn't contribute to this was proclaimed hostile, and it had to be destroyed. That is why the Communists started the Cultural Revolution by sawing the minaret down and turning the mosque into a club for their numerous meetings and amateur art activities. They held performances which mostly ridiculed our past and the "exploiters". One of the components of the Cultural Revolution was the newly formed names, which were given to children of "highly principled" people. Accordingly, I was given the name VIL, which is composed of the first letters of the name - Vladimir Ilyich Lenin.

However, even this didn't save my father and his children from the very derisive nickname, "ishan", which the village loafers gave us. It hurt me very much to hear it, and I tried to convince people who insulted me that my father was only a very little boy when his father the mullah died, that he grew up an orphan in poverty and now he had completely renounced "the Old World". It didn't help a bit.

With my parents Vaziga and Sultan in Stary Kangysh in the summer of 1969.

State Secrets

With brother Granit in Stary Kangysh in the summer of 1969.

My great grandfather Nazhmetdin deserved the title "ishan", which the Mufti - head of all the Muslims of Russia - gave to outstanding advocates of Islam. It was meant to honor those who excelled in enlightening people and bringing up devoted followers of the Prophet Mohammed's teachings. In a grassy knoll on a high bank overlooking the Belaya River, you can see the white stone top of the grave-vault, which the ishan built with his own hands. He requested that they bury him there, but this was never done. The explanation was that the vault was on the opposite side of the cemetery, and because of that, those who wanted to pray for his soul wouldn't be able to do so. Some old men told me later that the reason was just envy.

It was no accident that some of my fellow villagers, who didn't know their roots, behaved in this way. To some extent, it reflected the class warfare of the "lower classes" with the "upper classes", which had taken root, thanks to the Bolsheviks.

When I was in graduate school, at the Institute of Petrochemical Synthesis at the U.S.S.R. Academy of Sciences, I always went to my village to visit my parents during my vacations. During one of my trips home, I ran into Uncle Salikh, a close relative on my mother's side, who was sitting on the porch of a country store, keeping company with several tipsy men. He was rather drunk himself. He called to me, "Mirzayanov, I need to talk to you!" He looked resolute and aggressive, as if he were going to take revenge for an insult that had just been hurled at him. Salikh was a disabled veteran, with no right hand, and only three maimed fingers remained on his left hand. Like many people, he lived in poverty and "celebrated" the day in the village store, when he received his small disability allowance. He usually bought a quarter liter of vodka, and kept it in the inner breast pocket of his shabby gray jacket, which he never took off, no matter what the weather was like. From time to time he tenderly took the bottle out of this pocket and took a little sip with great pleasure. At that moment, he impersonated a connoisseur of delicate French wines. After this, the bottle was returned to its place.

Salikh quickly got tipsy, and after that he imagined he was a generous rich man who was ready to treat anybody who was fortunate enough to be honored with his attention at that happy moment. "Hi there, Gadelzhan, come here!" he would forcefully but politely address somebody who was passing by. "I decided to serve you, don't be freaking squeamish. Don't you see who you are talking to? So, you should be proud that I personally paid attention to you, bastard, and have invited you. I didn't have to do it, you son of a bitch, you know that damn well..." Having delivered his standard monologue, Salikh would take the bottle out of his pocket with his crooked fingers, and bring it almost vertically to the mouth of his guest, so that the person whom he was treating couldn't possibly take a single sip.

All men in the village were used to Salikh's manner of serving his guests, and everyone understood that it was a game created by the imaginary hospitality of this disabled man. It had never occurred to anyone to be offended. The store was opposite our house, near the school, and like the other boys, I liked to watch grow-ups and listen in on their conversations. However, I remember that one time a rather indecent guy decided to play a joke on Salikh. He distracted the attention of the veteran Salikh, took a few sips from the bottle that was offered to him, and practically emptied it.

You can't imagine what happened next! Poor Salikh was outraged and couldn't stop yelling at him. He wouldn't agree to the compensation that the youth who had insulted him was offering. Tears were running down the old man's cheeks. He was really unhappy. At that time, vodka was brought into the village only once every three months, and it lasted a week or two. Mostly poor old men and women bought it to sell at a higher price later. They also had to use it to pay for firewood, hay or for having something repaired in the house or in the barn. Without vodka, it was almost impossible to accomplish these things in the village. At that time, vodka performed the same function as foreign currency, as the American dollar or the Euro does now.

That is why when Salikh declared that he wished to talk to me, it wasn't unexpected because he often addressed people in this way when he wanted to "serve" somebody. And this is exactly what happened.

"Muscovite, do you want to drink a little with me or are you freaking squeamish?" he asked as usual.

It was a hot July day and, frankly speaking, with so many people around, I didn't want to demonstrate a positive attitude to his offers. I refused and this provoked the usual angry tirade of Russian and Tatar curse-words from Salikh. However, contrary to his usual habit, he quickly calmed down and said sternly:

"Will you be honest? I need to talk with you." I promised him to be honest.

"People say you study in Moscow. Right?" asked Salikh. I confirmed this.

"And what will you be after you finish your studies?" he continued his interrogation with irony. I explained that if I succeeded in accomplishing my goal, I would have a Ph.D. in chemistry. This didn't make a favorable impression on Salikh. I guessed that he simply hadn't understood my answer. He followed with an acid remark, and asked me not to pull the wool over his eyes because, when necessary, he also could speak vaguely and scientifically, no worse than any rogue-commissioner from the regional center, who is sent to the village every spring to put into service some task on the labor front.

The crippled Salikh was one of the first men to come back to the village in 1942 from the front, or rather from the hospital. Then there were almost no men left in the village except for the chairman of the collective farm, the lame Gerey, and the eternal guard of the property of the collective farm, the lame Shaikhutdin. The rest were very old indeed. The women and children lived who in the village ploughed, sowed, mowed, and harvested the crop. Hay and grain were carried in carts to which cows were harnessed, because all the horses had been mobilized into the Red Army.

The ferocious and lame Gerey with his bulging eyes, which were always red from constantly drinking, appeared one morning in the office yard of the collective farm, which was situated near our house. He had a wet white kerchief tied up on his forehead, and he took a deep breath, and as always, started shouting at the women who had gathered there. I remember one of the phrases that he often repeated, which made the poor women tremble, "Do you think I am from Japan?" At that time, very few people in our village had heard about this remote foreign country across the sea. Even if someone had heard about Japan, they only knew that it was an enemy and that the Red commanders gave the Japanese hell near Lake Hasan, in 1939. That is why these words frightened the poor women almost to death. Some old woman always tried to humbly soothe the raging village boss, "Dear Akhmetgereyzhan. Forgive us. We are ignorant and stupid!"

Once, Gerey badly frightened me too. One wintry day, when I was eight years old, I was gathering straw in the street, which was to be strewn in the farmyard. I didn't notice when Gerey's koshevka (a light cart) passed me, but I almost fell down from fear when I heard his thunderous bass, "You! Ishan's mongrel! Do you think that your father left this straw for you?"

It was 1943 then, and my father was out on the front. There was no one to stand up for me. I was paralyzed with fear, and I could neither move, nor say anything to excuse myself. However, when I saw that his short whip, which was made from twisted leather strips, was returned to the cart, I realized that the storm had passed. Probably that time Gerey decided that scolding was enough. Absolutely exhausted, I managed to drag myself home.

As there were no other deserving candidates, the disabled Salikh was immediately appointed as deputy chairman of the collective farm. He quickly adopted Gerey's style and method of roaring at the helpless women and children. More than 200 beehives of the collective farm's bee-garden produced enough honey for malt drink to always to grace the tables of the farm's managers. Finally the stores were depleted, and babaj (beekeeper) had to use up the surplus honey, that was supposed to feed the bees over the winter. This meant the end of the bee-garden, but that didn't make the chairman and his deputy stop drinking. They switched to a home-brew that was prepared for them in the neighboring Russian villages, in return for grain. The end of the war put an end to Salikh's career, because younger men came home from the front, and they, in turn, wanted the same privileges that Gerey and Salikh had enjoyed.

Salikh was standing in front of me, quiet and somehow drained, but he tried to prove that he was still afloat.

"Tell me," he whispered, moving the rolled cigarette of cheap tobacco and newspaper scrap with the tip of his tongue, from one corner of his mouth to the other. "What will you do with your science?"

I explained that I would invent or develop something new.

"And you will be a scientist?!" Salikh blurted out with indignation. I agreed, because it was very close to the truth. (Although I had and still have a different opinion because, according the Russian notion, "scientist" is a high title. It is an acknowledgement of your real place in science, rather than your profession, as is the case, for example, in the United States). The face of my village interrogator trembled and he shouted at me, making no attempt to restrain himself.

"What? You again? Damn you! What did we need this revolution for? We uprooted you! We did, and after this you will be on the top again, while our children will remain where they are! Tell me, Ishan's bastard, am I right?"

I couldn't think of anything better to do than to remain philosophical and to beat a silent retreat - followed by torrents of foul language vomited up by my relative.

God creates us unequally, but unfortunately many people perceive this as malicious intent on the part of the so-called elite.

Not everything is so simple. Even in my small village, there was enough to alienate people from their former way of life. My fellow villagers who thought about their lives were looking for ways to change them for the better.

Over the last few years, we got accustomed to idealizing our former life and denying everything connected with overthrowing autocracy and the revolution of 1917 in Russia. I suppose it would be a serious mistake to think that everything happened solely due to the evil will of Bolsheviks. If only it were that simple! Many people believed in the changes that were coming, and did everything to make it happen as quickly as possible. Neither my father, nor my Uncle Mirkasim could cope with some of the old savage village customs, and they followed those who promised to "change the world", especially since outrageous events took place in the village, which encouraged some young people to take resolute actions.

Terrible hunger broke out in Russia in 1921, which was connected, to a large extent, with the activities of the Bolsheviks. There were millions of victims of hunger, and cases of cannibalism were not rare [4]. Famine laid its hand upon my village as well, and it was combined with the cruelty of the prevalent village customs of that era.

A neighbor of my mother, a woman named Ak-ebi, couldn't endure her suffering from hunger any longer. She caught someone else's unlucky goose, which had strayed into her garden, killed it, and made soup. This misdemeanor couldn't pass unnoticed in the village. When the poor woman came to herself, she tried to redeem her fault by giving her neighbor everything of value she possessed, including a cashmere shawl, which is expensive even now. The neighbor didn't refuse this treasure, but at the same time he decided to act in keeping with most savage village customs. He and a few other aggressive men quickly organized mob law over the poor old woman. They tied the victim up with a thick rope and paraded her along all the village streets. Every living person had to hit her with a whip or a stick. No one could refuse to participate in this terrible execution, because anyone could be tied to the same rope for avoiding his or her responsibility to "Sharia".

The poor frightened Ak-ebi was moving slowly, barefoot and dressed in her ragged white homespun dress. Her long hair was loose and dirty, and her face was black from soot, which she had deliberately smeared herself with from immeasurable grief. She was too exhausted to utter a single word. Only occasionally did she raise her drooping head, in the desperate hope that someone would have pity on her and not hit her so ruthlessly. However, mercy was not to be expected. That was the cruel custom.

The next morning Ak-ebi died without regaining consciousness, on the cold floor of the small and unheated village jail house, built especially for this kind of thing.

The crowd was over-excited by the mob law and also ruthlessly punished her fourteen year old son. The boy tried to barricade himself into a relative's house, by locking the door from the inside, but furious men dragged the silly little boy through the window with hooks. By daybreak nobody had picked up the ruthlessly disfigured orphan. We only know that he disappeared and no one ever saw him again. All this happened in the early spring, when the snow hadn't completely left the streets and yards of my native Stary Kangysh.

Another drama took place that same year, in the hot summer of 1921, when hunger was rampant.

A widow with three sons lived near my mother's home. Two of her sons were grown-up. They ploughed, sowed, and did all the usual peasants' work, but the third one was much younger, only twelve years old. This family was starving like many others, and every morning the mother made a large pot of soup, which was mainly a mixture of herbs, goose-foot, and a little bran. The family ate a little of this broth and then the mother and her adult sons went to make hay or do other fieldwork. They strictly ordered the younger boy not to touch the precious food. Every day the younger brother patiently waited for the adults to come home to satisfy the hunger that tortured him. During the daytime he never even looked at the incredibly tempting "soup". However, on one agonizing day the hungry boy couldn't stand it any more, and he decided to swallow at least a little bit of the life-saving food. Unfortunately, he couldn't stop until he finished up the whole pot of soup.

When the brothers came back in the evening, they first looked into the pot and literally howled with despair, which soon prompted them to ruthlessly punish their own younger brother. First they hit him with their fists, and then they practically turned into beasts and started hitting him with everything within reach. They only stopped after they buried the boy, who was still alive though no longer breathing, at the end of their kitchen garden, under the manure. Then they fell on the ground exhausted, near the grave of their victim.

There was no one in the village to stop this insanity. Only the children from the neighboring houses cried loudly, watching this horrible spectacle.

Some time later a representative of the Soviet administration appeared in the village and told the elder brother to report to him, at the Djirtjuli Volost (Township) center, which he did.

He returned from Djirtjuli in a good mood. He said that the head of customs there didn't say anything bad to him, and even asked him to deliver a package to the canton (regional district) center in Borai, which is thirty kilometers from Stary Kangysh. Not long after that, the brother went on this errand, but we don't know what happened to him, because no one ever saw him again.

It seems to me that my father loved my mother, Vaziga, a young and beautiful girl, when he married her. At that time she was only a little more than 17 years old. Possibly, it was also a good match, because she came from a family of common peasants, and had lost both her parents. This was evidence that she belonged to the class of poor people which the new regime allegedly supported. When her father Minkamal was conscripted to the front in 1914, my mother hadn't been born yet, and her older brother was seventeen year old. My grandmother had six children to take care of, and we can only imagine what ordeals they had to suffer through.

My grandfather Minkamal never returned from the war. He was taken prisoner by the Germans, along with the other villagers, who were hastily clad in soldiers' uniforms. Then, they sent all the captive Russian Muslims to Turkey, so that Turkey could use them in the war against Russia. However, the Russian revolution upset all the plans of Germany and its allies. Turkey agreed to return the Russian captives, but some of them who were in Baghdad (which was a part of Ottoman Empire at that time), including my grandfather, decided to go on a pilgrimage to Mecca. Grandfather managed to visit the Muslim sacred site and to do everything that Muslim pilgrims should do there. Then, he became ill with a severe form of dysentery and died in Baghdad, after returning from his pilgrimage. According to his countrymen, he was buried in the cemetery of "shakhids" (martyrs who perished fighting for Islam). My grandmother died three years later.

My mother's older brother Mirkasim became the head of the family when he was in his early 20s. The slogans of the Bolsheviks and their promises inflamed the imagination of this bright young man, and he became the first Communist in the village. He also organized the collective farm, along with my father. He sold his large family house so that he would not be reproached by villagers for organizing the collective farm, while contributing nothing himself. With this money he bought a horse, which he brought to the collective farm, and a tiny hut.

By the beginning of the Second World War, Mirkasim became Secretary of the Raikom (Regional Committee of the Communist Party) and volunteered to go to the front. He was killed in the winter of 1943 near Don, not far from Novocherkassk. I remember that he dropped by our place late one night in the summer of 1942. My father was on the front then, and I listened to my uncle's war stories with delight, pretending to be asleep. When he went to leave, he kissed me, but I was "sleeping", so I couldn't look at him openly, which was really very silly. Before that I had watched this strong and handsome man through a crack in the partition made of planks which separated children's quarters from the grown-ups' parts of the room. I still feel admiration when I think about him. He gave the impression of the invincible heroic commander, dressed in his splendid new uniform of the political officer, and he carried the aura of certain victory over the Fascists.

Despite his desperate struggle with his ancestral past, my father narrowly escaped jail at the end of the 1930s. He was simply expunged from the party, as an enemy who had penetrated the Bolshevik ranks by fraud. My father took this disgrace very hard. In 1941, on the front, he joined the party again. It seems that my father fanatically believed in Communism, as a lot of the rank and file did. When he was already well advanced in his years, he assured me that to a large extent, our troubles and our poverty have to do with the existence of the two world camps. So, when there is only one left (and it was clear as day to him, which one), all our problems would easily be resolved.

Lenin, Stalin, and the other "geniuses" of world Communism were like saints to him. Of course, his attitude was automatically passed on to us. Right after the war, my mother told my dad that she asked the secretary of the party organization, Khabel Kagarmanov, why Lenin had embarked on the path of Marxism and had decided to struggle against the Tsar. He told her that the leader of the proletariat had avenged the death of his brother, who was hanged for organizing the murder of the Tsar, and had decided to become the Tsar himself. My mother was horrified. Strange as it may seem, my father wasn't shocked by this report, and he just advised my mother not to repeat Khabel's words to anyone else. As far as I know, Khabel had a sharp peasant's mind, but to this day I don't know how such seditious thoughts appeared in his head. Rumor had it that he used to be a member of a faction of Trotskyites-Bukharinists, Stalin's rivals. But what Trotskyites could there possibly be in the god-forsaken village of Stary Kangysh? Who knows? Maybe the deeply hidden hatred that progressive people felt toward the Bolshevik regime took root and grew from time to time. Perhaps this is the reason why some people in my village composed a list of those the German troops should kill, when they were moving towards the East at full speed in 1942. My mother told me this several times as a great secret, and stressed each time that she was on that list, too. Like my father, my mother was a teacher.

She taught me until the fourth grade. I studied without any difficulties, although there were problems with teachers from time to time. Even at a young age, I had already read a lot, mostly fiction, and that is why I constantly had questions that my teachers couldn't always find answers to.

Generally, I had good relations with kids my own age. I was a child during the hungry war years and the post-war years, when each piece of bread and every potato was worth its weight in gold. We village children didn't even know about sweets or ice cream. We had other joys, growing up surrounded by beautiful country. We spent whole summer days on the Belaya River. In the winter, we went sledding and skiing in the high hills. There were plenty of them near our village. I think the delightful natural environment of my childhood encouraged my love of sports, which I have retained to this day.

The war years left a profound impression on us. We felt the frosty breath of the war that was grinding on thousands of kilometers away from us. As children, we watched with horror as the towboats dragged bombed-out, half-burnt, and blackened hulks of barges and ships against the current up the Belaya River, on their way to Ufa. We understood that they came from the besieged city of Stalingrad. There was no radio in our village then, and we only received news about the war from people who traveled to the regional center of Djirtjuli, which was 15 kilometers away.

The boys always went to see off those young men and very young guys, almost boys, who were heading off to the front. They drove around in a cart in all four streets in the village, singing for the last time. Their songs accompanied by the harmonica were so sad that they brought tears to our eyes. The new recruits bid farewell and symbolically asked for our forgiveness, in case they had accidentally hurt someone.

I remember seeing off 17-year-olds who had never been farther than Djirtjuli in their lives. These boys had never seen a real city, a railway station, cars, or tractors. They sang and cried at the same time. None of them returned home - everyone perished.

When I went to visit Stary Kangysh, I always went to the village club, where there is a memorial plaque with names of more than 200 men who died in the war. This is the list of the victims of just one more world slaughter, from a village with hardly more than 150 households.

How could the number of victims have been less, since Stalin and his accomplices threw absolutely unprepared and unarmed children into battle? Now, in Russia, there are many newly hatched "patriots" who try to rewrite the history of the war and deny these facts. But, fortunately, they can't rewrite the testimony of the people and their memories.

My late relative, Gabbas Nugumanov, who served in the railway troops during Whole War II, told me that he met his fellow-countrymen from Stary Kangysh in 1942, at Klin Station near Moscow. The special train (echelon), in which they were taken to the front, stopped there for technical problems. Klin was just a few hours drive from the front line. His fellow villagers told Gabbas that they had only two rifles for seven people. They were not sure that they would be given more weapons after they got off the train. Alas, their doubts were confirmed: it was clear from the very beginning that warehouses with weapons were not to be found anywhere near the trenches.

The war had the most dire consequences for these unarmed people - no sooner were they unloaded from the train than everybody perished.

I remember I couldn't satisfy my curiosity. I wanted to know how many Fascists our soldiers had killed. The front-line soldiers laughed and told me they knew only one thing - that the Germans hadn't killed them. But they hadn't killed anyone. I was totally baffled by their answers, so I asked my father about it when he was a little tipsy and more talkative. Finally he explained to me that a soldier normally shoots when and where he is ordered to. If a German perished, it was impossible to say who had killed him, and nobody thought about it. My father said a soldier was like an automatic machine. You run when you get an order to run. You crawl when you get an order to crawl. The only relevant questions are those of survival - what to eat, where to sleep, and how to wash yourself.

Stories like these deeply disillusioned me, because I already knew all about the great feats of the heroes who had crushed hordes of German soldiers, from the books I read and the movies I had watched. But my father "comforted" me by saying that the people who had written those books and staged the movies simply lied, because none of them had actually taken part in the war. I protested - what about such famous writers as Konstantin Simonov, Aleksander Fadeev, and Michael Sholokhov - weren't they war correspondents on the front line, who issued newspapers and wrote essays? "Yes, of course," he said. "That's true. But the point is that the editor's office (even that of the military division newspaper) is 40-70 kilometers from the front-line. The editor's offices of the bigger army or frontline newspapers are much further away."

I think that must have been true, because over the course of the war none of our "great writers" got even a scratch. However, several lesser-known writers died or had been taken prisoner.

The story of the great Tatar poet Musa Dzhalil comes to mind. My second uncle, Fazil Nugumanov, seems to be one of the last people to have seen him before he was taken prisoner. Uncle Fazil also narrowly escaped captivity, along with the remnants of the army of the "great commander", Lieutenant General Vlasov, who was one of Stalin's favorites. He told us that Musa had come to his mud-hut late at night in the spring of 1942 and introduced himself as a newsman. My uncle understood that he was a Tatar and they started talking. Musa said that the situation was alarming. This was true. My uncle, a First Corporal Commander, gave Musa something to eat and put him to sleep in his own bed. Early in the morning, the poet heartily thanked my uncle Fazil and left.

Then the army was encircled, with no hope for a breakthrough. The enemy's troops methodically, with German meticulousness, and with the help of artillery, crushed the remnants of the army. They were addressing everybody on a radio megaphone, suggesting they surrender. My uncle and a few others in one section of the front were lucky enough to break through the continuous barrage of German mortar fire.

General Vlasov surrendered, along with what was left of his army. The poet Musa Dzhalil was among the captives. Once he was in German territory he started an active campaign among the captive soldiers, urging them not to fight against the USSR in the army of the general-traitor, who had crossed over to the German side. Dzhalil was betrayed and found himself in the infamous Moabit jail in Berlin. He was sentenced to death by beheading, but while he was waiting for his execution, the poet wrote his immortal Moabit Notes - verses full of love for his people. Timmermans, a Belgian whose cell neighbored Musa's, was lucky to survive. He fulfilled the request of the poet and brought these verses out of the jail.

When I am in Kazan, I look at the beautiful monument to the poet with infinite pain, and think about the greatness of my people, who despite all oppression and adversity, preserved themselves and nurtured such heroes as Musa, who the whole progressive world is proud of. Certainly, he was a Communist and looked at many things through the prism of the party philosophy. But his whole-hearted devotion to his people and his love for humanity is an example of genuine heroism, the kind which helped us to hold out and win in the unequal struggle against Fascism.

In addition to the books which my father brought back from the regional center, the radio became a window to the world for me.

In 1947, my father was the first man in the village to buy a battery powered radio-set. Our whole family liked to listen to concerts of Tatar and Bashkir music. Sometimes in the evenings, I would dial the tuner of the radio and listen to voices speaking in different languages. At that time, I studied Russian very hard, though my knowledge of it was weak. Once I heard something unusual through the constant crackle and background noise, and I understood some things. In an anxious voice, the announcer was talking about slavery in the USSR, about the inevitably hopeless position of the peasants and collective farmers, and about the suffering of former Soviet war captives in numerous concentration camps. I was scared by my discovery, but I didn't even tell my parents about it. They didn't suspect what their son's new preoccupation was. Sometimes they reprimanded me, asking what good there was in listening to this noise and crackling.

Very soon, I found out that this was called "The Voice of America". Of course, it was very difficult for me to believe everything that the American radio was broadcasting, considering that I had never been to the city or seen a railway. However, something that was said about the poor and powerless peasants seemed true to me, even though I was just a boy. Probably that was the time when doubt was conceived in my soul, which would guide and shape my behavior later on.

Indeed, I once saw how an old man, who had lost all his sons in the war, was forced to sign up for a huge loan. He asked in despair where he would get so much money from, if he was paid nothing in the collective farm where he worked. The man and his old wife had nothing to live on. Through the open window of the village council building, which was near our house, I heard the commissioner from the regional center, yelling and threatening, "You, son of a bitch! Do you dare to slander the party and the Soviet system? Thank God your sons are dead, or you would damn sure be serving your term in jail. You are a lucky man. Our party is kind and I am just sending you to the storeroom, so that you, bastard, can think over your crime tonight. Probably, I will be satisfied by your signature, for the amount I offered you."

"The Voice of America" was also right about the limitless taxes, which the peasants simply couldn't pay. I remember once that all the fruit trees disappeared from the yards in our village, as if by collusion. Peasants chopped them down to avoid paying a tax for each tree. In the severe continental climate of Bashkortstan, each apple-tree, even if it was simply a wild variety with small apples, was precious and practically the only source of vitamins. For some reason, Tatars and Bashkirs at that time rarely grew vegetables in their villages, and they only started growing potatoes after the war. There was no money to buy grain, and collective farmers received a few hundred grams of rye as payment for a so-called working unit (this was a unit of measuring labor). I remember once, that in the neighboring village of Minishta, people received a whole kilogram of it! This was a real sensation. It was hard to believe. All the milk from the private cows of each collective farmer was given to the state, and as soon as a calf was born, it was taken away as meat tax. Every hen was counted and a collective farmer had to hand over all the eggs.

At that time, the tax agents were merciless. One cruel agent with eyes empty from drinking was especially ferocious. He had a Russian last name, Murov, though he was a Tatar. He would enter the house where a family couldn't pay taxes, make a list of all the things that could be confiscated, and then he took the sheep and goats.

Once he came to the home of a widow, who was our neighbor. At that time, there were only two sons at home, 16-year-old Madikhat and 7-year-old Favaris. Kanifa-apa herself was serving her compulsory "labor minimum" at the collective farm. Each adult had to serve a required number of "working units" there. If anyone failed to do this, for any reason, he or she was inevitably sent to do corrective work collecting wood in the mountainous regions of Bashkortstan.

Cursing away, Murov started collecting things from the house. When that seemed too little for him (what could be precious in poor peasant homes at that time?), he seized an axe and threatened the boys. He told them he would kill them if they didn't tell him where all the valuables were hidden. The heart of the poor Madikhat couldn't stand it and he fainted. My mother and the whole village came running to save the boy. At that time, we couldn't even dream of doctors. There were none in the neighborhood. The villagers managed to nurse the boy back to health.

We were the children of teachers (at that time, we were a family of four, plus my grandmother), but we suffered the same hardships and often we were starving. The salaries of our parents, minus the numerous taxes and the state loan installments, which sometimes amounted to half of your annual salary, weren't even enough to put food on the table, never mind buying any decent clothes. Every day after school, my younger sister Lisa and I grated two large buckets of potatoes with a homemade grater made from a half-rusty piece of iron sheet. Our hands were constantly bleeding and aching because of this monstrous labor. But what could we do if we had no flour and potatoes replaced bread?

The news that "Voice of America" reported about the fate of our war captives terrified me. When my father was sharing his war experiences, he said that he had never used up all his bullets, because he kept the last one for himself. He was planning to shoot

State Secrets

himself, if he was ever surrounded and in danger of being taken prisoner. He knew that any prisoners of war would be considered traitors to Russia, with all the ensuing consequences.

At that time, a soldier who had been taken captive made it back to our village. He told us about the extensive horrors of Fascist captivity, but preferred to remain silent about the conditions in our camps, which were equally atrocious. Each month he went to the regional center to confirm that he was still residing in his native village and hadn't gone off anywhere. He was released from the Soviet camp for former prisoners of war, only on this condition. A few men from my village served ten-year sentences of hard labor in the Donbass mines in Ukraine, and they remained there forever. They were guilty in the eyes of the Motherland, because they had been freed from the Fascist camps by British and American troops. These were our allies, who then handed them over to the NKVD (People's Commissariat for Internal Affairs). Later, it became clear they had returned to their country only to be sent to the Siberian gulags.

I can't help noting the shameful role that Winston Churchill played in all that. In 1945, he betrayed millions of Soviet war captives, by ordering that they should be forcibly sent to the Eastern zone of Germany occupied by the Soviet troops [5].

An acquaintance of mine, a Tatar who now lives in New York, was in German captivity at that time and he knew what to expect in his Motherland. He told me that a lot of people had committed suicide to avoid the Stalinist camps or had crippled themselves, cutting off their hands or even their whole arms. According to him, that caused quite a stir in the West, for example in the U.S. in 1945-1947, and it helped a few lucky men avoid being dispatched to the USSR.

Soon I found someone to talk with, who shared my interest. He was an accountant at the boarding school, where my father had started working as the director. My father bought a radio-set for the boarding school, and it turned out that this accountant had also been listening to "Voice of America" at night. He warned me very sternly that I must not tell anybody about this obsession of mine, because it could result in my imprisonment and a severe penalty for my parents.

I kept my word. Now I am writing about it, when the man I was talking to and my parents are no longer alive, and it seems that "Voice of America" is breathing its last breath, due to the evil scheme of some American politicians [6]. Isn't it too early to dismiss Communism, when millions of believers in this flavor of Fascism openly want to take revenge, not only in Russia, but also in other countries devoted to the ideas of the free market and the pluralism of opinions?

My discovery of America didn't set me against the Soviet regime, nor did it make me a partisan of the West. When I was young, I believed that everything would be fine in our country. We only had to follow Lenin's guidelines. I thought that the enemies of the Soviet state deliberately set people against the party, to return them to their dark past. Nevertheless, the seeds of doubt remained in my soul for years to come, after listening to "Voice of America".

I think it already influenced me, when I was summoned to the regional department of the KGB, during my last year in high school. They suggested I go to their school for Chekists, but I refused. It is difficult to say what prompted me to make that decision then, but I think mostly I was encouraged by the "enemy's" influence, as it was called by officials, "Voice of America."

My refusal to be recruited was a bolt out of the blue for Lieutenant Colonel Nasirov, the regional head of the KGB. At that time, I was the top student not only in my high school, but also among all the high schools in the region. I was the secretary of the Komsomol Committee at my school and a member of the bureau at the Komsomol Raikom (regional committee). Nasirov didn't show any emotion; he only asked me not to tell anybody about our conversation.

The lieutenant colonel was sitting under the portrait of his leader, Lavrentii Beria, and he severely cautioned me about the possible consequences of my insubordination. He added that this was the first time he had met anyone who refused such an honor to serve the party by being a member of the KGB. All of this happened in the middle of March of 1953, soon after Stalin died.

Chapter 3
My Student Days

Can Your Russian Language Take You Everywhere?

Before I had this first contact with the KGB, I had studied for three years in Tatar High School N 1, in Djirtjuli. I am very proud of my school and I remember the names of all my teachers. I am sure that they were really highly professional people. They devoted their whole lives to bringing up students who came from the surrounding villages for their education. That was a very difficult time, when even a single piece of bread was precious.

My favorite subject was mathematics, taught by Gali Zilyaev, a graduate of Kazan University, but the other subjects were not a burden for me. I think this was mostly because of our teachers. When I was sitting in my Tatar literature classes taught by Sag'dat Aglyamova, who masterfully read the verses of Gabdulla Tukay, Khadi Taktash, and other Tatar poets, I even found myself dreaming that I wanted to become a writer.

My Russian literature classes taught by Maria Grigorievna Filippova with the poems of Pushkin, Lermontov, and other famous Russian poets were no less thrilling! She was a brilliant, democratic, and beautiful young lady from Ufa, and an idol for all the boys. Many of us were simply in love with her. Unfortunately, most of us were not at all skilled at writing essays in the Russian language, which was foreign to us and not related to Tatar, which falls into the Turkic group of languages. Still, it didn't discourage anyone from taking Maria Grigorievna's classes. I am grateful to her, because she introduced me to classical music, by encouraging me to listen to concerts that were broadcast on the radio, and tenderly cultivating in me such a love of music as she had herself. At that time, I didn't have a record player, or even records, so the loudspeaker of the local relay system was my only source of this music.

Now, when I listen to masterpieces of opera, artfully performed by the world-renowned singers Anna Netrebko, Ildar Abdrazakov, Placido Domingo, and others, at the New York Metropolitan Opera House, I always remember my teacher with gratitude and admiration.

My other teachers were also very talented, and I owe them a lot. I was especially fond of the headmistress of our school, Gaishagar Gabbasovna Sharipova, who took me under her wing like a mother hen, though she was very young at that time. She protected me from many troubles that I faced, at times when my success made me dizzy.

For a long time, Faina Lvovna Levina, who had been evacuated from besieged Leningrad, was our thoughtful class supervisor. She worked hard so that we country villagers could develop polite manners and receive a good education. When the war was over, Faina Lvovna remained in remote Djirtjuli forever, never returning to her native Leningrad.

I have kept in touch with my school over the years, visiting it on vacations, sending different letters on many occasions. Over the course of time, this connection weakened slightly, but fortunately, it never broke, even though a few generations of teachers have changed over.

As for my promise to the regional KGB chief to keep the secret about their efforts to get me to enroll as a student for their school, I am writing about it in my book for the first time, for reasons that will become clear a bit later. Lieutenant Colonel Nasirov decided to take revenge for my lack of respect towards his "company". I finished high school in 1953 with a silver medal, and that allowed me to enter any institution for higher education without taking the entrance exams. But there was a holdup, as it took me more than a month to get my draft card (a document allowing me to transfer my enlistment to another military office) from the regional military department. The regional commissioner insisted that I should enroll in the Orenburg Artillery School. But I was obstinate.

Every morning in July of 1953, I walked from my village to the military department, and every evening I returned home on foot, since there was no transportation between the village and the regional center in those days. There was no result. Many of my fellow students had already submitted documents to different institutions and I still haunted the doorstep of the military department.

Finally one day, after I had been sitting for the whole day by the door of the military commissioner's office, I declared that I wouldn't leave the building, and I would stay there for the night. It was the end of the workday and the employees looked at me as if I had gone mad. They didn't like my resolute look at all, and threatened to call the police. At the same time, they realized that no threats could stop me now. At that moment, the military commander, Major Bezrukov, came out of his office and with a tone of disgust in his voice, ordered them to give a draft card to "this young whippersnapper". I was so happy! I crossed the Belaya River and I ran the whole way to my house without stopping once.

At home, I announced that I was going to study in Moscow. My parents didn't object, though my departure would cost them a lot of money. I got the money for my travel and for a month of living expenses in the capital. After that I was supposed to live on my scholarship and get a part-time job, so I could buy clothes and other necessities.

The delay with my draft card, which allowed me to enter a university, had its effect. With all the hardships characteristic of any journey at that time, I managed to reach Moscow only on Saturday, July 26. I was traveling in an overcrowded fourth-class train car, where passengers were sleeping on the floor. This journey took two full days and nights, and it was agonizing for me, even though I was a strong young man.

My ordeals were not over at that point. I was planning to enter the Bauman Higher Technical School in Moscow, and I wanted to major in "optical instruments" there. I arrived too late to go to the admission office there, and so I couldn't get a place in the dormitory. I had nowhere to sleep even a little bit. I decided to return to the Kazan train station where I had left my luggage in the office.

I didn't know Moscow at all, and it was difficult finding my way around on the metro. No matter how hard I tried to find the Kazan train station, for some reason I always ended up at the Kiev Station. Probably I didn't have enough practice speaking Russian, since the subjects in our high school were taught in the Tatar. I was always speaking Tatar with other students.

By that time, I had suffered a lot because of my poor Russian language skills. I think it is the main reason why the first love of my youth ended in failure.

Once, when I was passing by the regional photographer's studio, I saw a portrait displayed there of a wonderful young lady in a school uniform. Her large and thoughtful eyes and amazingly beautiful oval face struck me. Her long thick braids made her look like a movie star. This portrait was beautiful and surreal. Then I saw this girl in the street!

At that time and for a long time afterwards, I was extraordinarily shy, and I had to make an incredible effort just to speak to girls. That is why I couldn't even dream of just coming up to a beautiful girl and speaking with her. I felt an insurmountable longing that I did not understand. Soon I learned that she was studying in the Russian school, though I am sure she was a Tatar or a Bashkir, not a Russian.

In those days, it was fashionable among the Soviet and local party officials to send their children to Russian schools, while the children who came from villages usually entered a Tatar high school. Certainly, this reflected the social stratification of the times.

Several months later, I made friends with Rishat Muratov, a decent and kind boy my age from the Russian school, who spoke the Tatar language mixed with Russian words. His father was the Second Secretary of the Raikom of the C.P.S.U. Soon I learned that my mysterious young lady lived in the same house as my new friend. Rishat explained that his neighbor was named Irene, and her father Bainazarov was the chairman of the Regional Council of People's Deputies.

I was completely distressed by this news, because it meant we had absolutely nothing in common. The only thing I could do was to steal secret glances at Irene, when she dropped by Rishat's place for some reason. For a long time, I never managed to utter a single word in her presence. They always spoke Russian there, and even the colloquial version of Russian was beyond me at that time, and for years afterwards.

I rented a flat from a Russian landlady and I tried to master this difficult language by speaking with her. I asked her, and she agreed to correct my mistakes. But speaking Russian with such a young beauty, whose looks deprived me of any ability to think, was out of the question. I frankly envied my friend who could speak so freely and naturally with Irene, as if she were his sister. Meanwhile, I cursed my shyness, and I was perfectly sure that I would never be able to overcome it. There was only one thing left for me to do. I had to make sure that Irene would know me as the top student and sportsman.

I tried really hard, and as I had a serious incentive, my efforts produced results. By winter, I became the top student among the eighth-graders and I was elected to every possible school and Komsomol committee.[7] It was surprising that I was elected secretary of the Komsomol school committee, which was the highest acknowledgement of my new position, although I was only sixteen and we had eighteen-year-olds on the committee.

When our physics teacher was ill (she was the only one in our school who taught her subject in Russian), another teacher from the Russian school replaced her. I knew from Rishat that the teacher spoke very well about me when he went back to his Russian school. According to Rishat, students of my age from that school were intrigued. Probably my friend's news prompted me to take a desperate step. I summoned all my courage and wrote a letter in Russian to the object of my affections. Rishat handed Irene this note with my confessions of love and a proposal to be friends. Soon I received Irene's answer, and she wrote that she had heard a lot about me and she even doubted that she deserved to be my friend. My joy was boundless when I received her reply to my second letter, and she offered to meet me.

We had to meet late at night at the end of one of the central streets of the town. That frosty February evening, Irene and I strolled along the street, and she told me about herself and her girl friends. I understood everything but, unfortunately, I was thinking too slowly to keep the conversation going in Russian. Of course, I could have recited poems in Tatar, or I could have told her about the books I had read; plenty of them were in Russian, but it seemed to me that some heavy weight was hanging on my tongue. I tried to murmur something, but I couldn't say anything sensible. Horrified, I realized that I wasn't making a very good impression. The embarrassment that overwhelmed me at that moment stopped me from even looking at Irene, but at the same time, I was infinitely happy that such a beautiful and bright girl was walking beside me and talking with me.

We met a few more times, but I still behaved as though I were paralyzed. I understood that it was time to declare my love, to hug and kiss Ira, but all of this was beyond me.

My greatest happiness came from an episode connected with my performance at the regional cross-country ski championship. I couldn't participate in the 15-kilometer race because I had broken my skis. Only the gym teacher had a spare pair of good skis, but for some reason he had decided to take part in the race himself, without any training. It was a great pity for me because I was in good shape by then and I had already taken the first place in the 10-kilometer race. But then unexpectedly I got the chance to show what I was made of. My teacher dropped out of the race after the first circle and the judges allowed me to start the race on his skis. Then a snowstorm broke out over us and it was practically impossible to see the ski-track. All the participants stopped racing. But I was inexorable and continued the race because I knew that Irene was among the few spectators.

I finished the race alone and became the champion, but I was happy for a different reason. Right then Rishat handed me a note from Ira with her words of admiration and an invitation for a date.

That date was our last one. Probably my mumbling and unintelligible murmuring in bad Russian dampened her enthusiasm. I failed to turn our budding friendship into love. After all, we were only 16, and at that time there were heated debates in the Komsomol newspapers about whether someone could experience love at such a young age. The answer was always certainly negative. According to the Komsomol directives, love at such an early age distracted young people from their studies.

I met Irene a few more times under different circumstances, but there were no more dates. During the summer following 9th grade, we both worked as counselors in a pioneer camp. Though we had a lot of different opportunities for meeting privately there, I never dared to speak to her. She was silent, too. Still, I was extraordinarily happy to be next to her.

As the years passed, my feeling turned into permanent pain. Though there was no love in the generally accepted meaning of the word, the image of Irene haunted me for a long time, overshadowing my further infatuations with women. There were moments when I cursed her for this and I tried to hate her, but it was beyond me.

We never saw each other again. I remembered her always as I saw her in that portrait on the stand in the photographer's studio.

In Moscow

The Russian language problem haunted me in Moscow as well. Finally, I spent my first night in the Kiev Railway Station. Policemen drove out every suspicious looking character from the overcrowded waiting room. I think my looks didn't really appeal to the police, because I was dressed in my ski tracksuit - which looked like coveralls. On my feet I had worn out old boots. At that time, Moscow was full of internal troops, and the police were struggling with criminals who had been released from the jail and labor camps, through amnesty after Stalin's death. Practically all the released prisoners rushed to the large cities and started terrorizing people.

The people of Moscow hadn't yet recovered from the shock caused by the appearance of the troops and tanks, which were there to prevent a coup organized by Beria and to arrest this omnipotent head of the KGB. I had to spend another day and night near Kiev Station. Fortunately, the nights were relatively warm then.

Early on Monday morning, I was already in the reception of Bauman High Technical School (MVTU) in Moscow. The admissions secretary listened to me and explained that the admission of medal winners was finished, and he had no right to admit me, a medal winner, to the entrance exams on general terms.

Needless to say, I was deeply disappointed because I hoped that I would be admitted and would receive a place in the dormitory. I desperately wanted to sleep, I could hardly stand up, and I couldn't think straight. However, the instinct of self-preservation prevailed. I asked a university entrant to give me a reference book on Moscow institutions for higher education and I started making phone calls. The third Institute I called was the Lomonosov Institute of Fine Chemical Technology (MITKhT) in Moscow. I asked if I could come right away and get a place in the dormitory. The answer was positive, and this settled my fate for many years to come.

I immediately went to 1 Malaya Pirogovskaya Street, and submitted my documents as if I were in a dream. I could hardly understand which department and major I should choose to list in the application. I coped with this task intuitively and made no mistakes. I asked to enroll in the Department of Organic Synthesis, with a major of "artificial gas and liquid fuels", where the scholarship was the biggest in the institute. Even today, I can firmly say that I was never sorry about my choice.

Studies in the college and the life in the dormitory were combined with my constant struggle for survival, because my parents couldn't help me at all financially. My income consisted solely of the scholarship, and it was hardly enough to cover poor meals and pay for a place in the dormitory. Very often, I went to the Kiev

State Secrets

Station to find work unloading train cars. Unfortunately, this job wasn't always available. Sometimes, like some of my fellow students, I managed to get hired for a night shift at the Dorogomilovsky chemical plant.

The work there was hard and hazardous to the health, because safety measures were very primitive. When I was in my fourth year I found a very profitable job. I delivered bottles of distilled water to the laboratories of the institute, and I almost became a prosperous student. I could even dress more decently and buy the first pair of winter shoes I had in my life.

With great difficulty, I managed to scrape together a little money from my poor scholarship to buy tickets to the Bolshoi Theatre. The tickets were the cheapest ones, for the upper circle of the theatre. Even to buy those, I had to go to the Bolshoi Theatre the evening before the tickets went on sale and cue up with other poor opera lovers. Most of us were students, spending a cold winter night together on the street.

They made frequent roll calls in the line, and those who were late were ruthlessly crossed off the waiting list for the tickets. When the ticket offices opened at 10 A.M., the first two hundred names on the list had the best chance of buying tickets for the next ten days of the month. It was cold, and I desperately wanted to sleep and to drink something hot, but this couldn't stop me. Cold nights in lines became a peculiar musical school for me. Among the students there were great connoisseurs of opera music who shared their knowledge with grateful listeners. Since I came from a remote village and I had never listened to live music before, this was always wonderful and enchanting. Soon the following operas became my favorites - "Aida" by Giuseppe Verdi, "Pikovaya Dama" by Petr Ilyich Tchaikovsky, and "Demon" by Anton Rubinshtein.

At that time, everybody loved the singers Nelepp, Lisitsian, and Ivanov. I remember "Aida" performed by Georgi Nelepp (Radames), Irina Arkhipova (Amneris), and Galina Vishnevskaya (Aida), as if I heard it only yesterday. Aleksander Melik-Pashaev conducted the orchestra brilliantly.

By that time, famous the singers Ivan Kozlovsky and Sergei

Lemeshev had already stopped performing on the stage of the Bolshoi Theatre, and I didn't have a chance to enjoy their beautiful voices. But I remember very well the debut of ballerina Maya Plisetskaya in "Walpurgis Night" of "Faust". Of course it was a remarkable show, featuring the wonderfully staged dances of a corps de ballet in a witches' sabbath!

I never expected that my studies in the institute would turn out to be a process, which mainly consisted of performing certain duties. There was little captivating there that could ignite a spark in young minds. Unfortunately, practically everything was a burdensome compulsory routine.

From the first years of my studies, I retained the impression that the teachers deeply distrusted the students. They thought that we were lazy and only trying to cheat them. Most lecturers were completely unable to explain anything and the poor students couldn't force themselves to listen, despite all threats. For example, one time the famous academician Ivan Nazarov was giving a lecture on the basics of organic chemistry. In a monotonous and boring voice, he was trying to explain this subject, which we badly needed. The material was supposed to be interesting and we understood that he was a prominent scientist, but there was no lecture as such. It simply wasn't working out. Fifteen minutes after the beginning of the lecture, the academician started resorting to sanctions. "The third row from the back, the student in glasses! Would you be so kind as to leave the auditorium?" he ordered. "The young man from the second row on the left - this refers to you as well. You, the girl next to him, you are free to go, too. All of you! Come to my office after the lecture to explain yourselves!"

After the lecture, 15-20 students lined up near his office door. Those who were dismissed from the lecture had to answer to Nazarov himself at the exam. It was almost impossible to cope with that ordeal, and many students flunked out because of their poor performance in organic chemistry.

Unfortunately, even though famous scientists were terrible at giving lectures, it wasn't perceived as their flaw. On the contrary, the fault was attributed solely to lack of diligence on the part of students. Sometimes really strange things happened. The famous physicist and chemist Yakov Syrkin was also a poor lecturer. Finally, he was so upset with his students' lack of understanding, that he made a big show of leaving the lecture hall, never to return.

Student at MITKhT in Moscow, 1956.

Vil S. Mirzayanov

Graduate student of the Petrochemical Institute of Academy of Sciences of the USSR. Moscow, 1963.

    I also remember another curious incident connected with him. At that time, it was rumored that the Americans had developed or would soon develop a thermonuclear bomb. A student asked a corresponding member of the U.S.S.R. Academy of Sciences (who later became an academician) if such a weapon was possible. This scientist replied categorically that it was impossible, even theoretically. You can only imagine our disillusionment when, half a year later, the U.S.S.R. announced that the test of the H-bomb had been successful. For the first time, I realized that even corresponding members and academicians could be mistaken. Much later, I learned that in most cases membership to the U.S.S.R. Academy of Sciences had nothing to do with a scientist's talent. It was mostly determined by someone's contacts and his or her devotion to some clan within this organization. The heads of these clans usually arrange deals between themselves and decide who will be "elected" this year, and who would have to wait until the next year.

Many academicians and corresponding members were elected by direct order of the Central Committee of the C.P.S.U., which as "the guiding organization" in the country, fostered certain people connected with science. It artificially provided them with goods unavailable to average hardworking selfless scientists, and it provided career growth for their bosses, the would-be scientists.

My last remark does not reflect in any way on the respected reputation of the late Yakov Kivovich Syrkin, who undoubtedly was a prominent scientist. He made a valuable contribution to the theory of molecular structure.

I won't dwell on the lecturers who were not up to the mark. They were in the majority at MITKhT. At the same time, I want to speak well of such outstanding professionals as Olga Zuberbiller, who was a professor of Calculus and Professor Nisson Gelperin, the chairman of the "Processes and Apparatus" Department. Students who were not required to attend, teachers, and outsiders simply interested in the subject matter regularly attended their lectures, which were thrilling and amazingly easy to understand.

Unfortunately, interesting lectures and seminars didn't constitute a significant part of the overall student schedule. There was an abundance of subjects that literally sucked our souls dry, making our prime years a misery. I am sure that we wasted about 70 percent of our academic time during the first three years for nothing.

Almost every day, there were lectures and seminars on the history of the Communist Party of the Soviet Union, which were followed by the so-called "principles of Marxism-Leninism" course and philosophy. "Military" classes were just as frequent. There was a military department at the institute, which was composed of elderly colonels and lieutenant colonels, graduates of the Voroshilov Academy of Chemical Defense. These old campaigners had snugly settled into the capital, and they took special pleasure in mocking the students. They thought that students should work for the privilege of avoiding military service, by being diligent in their meaningless classes.

There was something sad and at the same time funny about the column of girls and boys in civilian clothing, marching along the embankment of the Moscow River. When a colonel called them up in front of the line, some students had difficulties with the reports that they had to deliver. Either they forgot things and mixed up the word order, or they saluted with their left hand like the German soldiers in war movies. Colonels especially enjoyed themselves when "student K" had to suffer through this procedure. He couldn't coordinate his arms and legs while marching, and that is why this student was considered a persistent slacker in military science and had serious academic problems.

Classes in chemical defense were total dogma. We had to remember all the physical and chemical constants (melting and boiling points, vapor pressure, density, etc.), as well as the chemical and physiological properties of all the chemical agents. God forbid that you attempt to express something in your own words or to elaborate on the definition or answer provided by the textbook. This was considered to be an unforgivable mistake.

"Well, what is the distinguishing effect of nitrogenic mustard gas, compared with the effect of ordinary mustard gas?" asked Lieutenant Colonel Xenia Knyazeva. I explained that the difference is that the poisoning was evident only after a period of time, not immediately.

"Wrong!" she exulted. "This property is called the... c..u..m..u..l..a..t..i..v..e effect. You should read the instructions, young man!"

At that time, it wasn't a laughing matter for me, because I had the highest grades in all my subjects and I was counting on receiving a higher scholarship. In a heartbeat, I had lost this chance by not using the favorite word of a pretty woman in military uniform.

Later, it felt like I got my revenge when I was taking an oral exam in Colonel Aleksander Shvarts' class. He was a great boaster, and he liked to tell us tall tales about his war experience. Although according to his colleagues, Shvarts had spent the whole war in the smoke screens divisions and wasn't in any real battles, he was the classical example of a petty nitpicker. Mostly he taught us how to darn the respirator haversack, while he explained why the gas mask filter held back the fumes of chemical agents. Then he checked on our mastery of the subject.

"Now tell me - thanks to what force does the filter of the gas mask keep back the fumes of various chemical agents?" asked the colonel. Each student explained this quite correctly, describing in his or her own way the adsorption of molecules to the surface of activated charcoal. But the colonel was implacable and dismissed them for failing to properly grasp the academic material. Finally, it was my turn for this torture.

"Well, what keeps the molecules of chemical agents on the filter after all?" he repeated his question.

Something enlightened me at that moment and I solemnly and slowly uttered, "Cohesion forces".

The colonel jumped up with joy, and he almost kissed me. He was beside himself with happiness, because a student had remembered his favorite phrase. He even forgave all the other unlucky students and announced that everyone had passed his test.

Every year, our studies at the Military Department became more and more difficult. We had to study numerous machines for degassing military equipment and military uniforms, including clothes and gas masks. It was downright impossible to remember their characteristics. These machines were absolutely useless because the uniforms were completely spoiled after the neutralization treatment. In the military camps we made sure many times that this was so.

In the summer after our second year, we were taken to the military camps in Florichi, which is not far from Nizhny Novgorod (the city was called Gorky then). This place was very swampy and sandy with a pine forest. We lived in tents - one unit in each. We were dressed in terribly uncomfortable soldier uniforms and had tarpaulin boots, our feet being covered in fabric foot wraps. Sometimes it was more than 35 degrees Celsius, and our feet became swollen.

Young soldiers, who had just finished the regimental school that trained sergeants and lance corporals, gave us the orders. Marshal Zhukov was then the Soviet Minister of Defense. He was notorious for his cruelty and his loud mouth. Soldiers were punished for the smallest offence. Then they were put into the guardhouse, or even sent to the penal battalion. The time that a soldier spent in these "establishments" wasn't included in his term of military service. If he lost some piece of his uniform or equipment, or if it was stolen, he had to pay for that loss. It was his own business where he would find the money. Usually the soldier who was robbed made up for the loss by stealing from others, especially from the rookies.

Soon I experienced firsthand the consequences of this kind of discipline in the glorious Soviet Army.

I entered the soldier's toilet where 8-10 people were doing what they had to at the same time. I took off my belt, hung it on the nail on the wall, and squatted. When I raised my head, I saw that my belt was no longer on the nail. The situation was terrible and I immediately reported the incident to my unit commander, a guy with a vacant herpetic face and foolish blue eyes. He ordered me to pay and promised to give me the new belt after that. I had just enough money for this fine and for a whole month I had no money left to buy cigarettes or any sweets. In the cafeteria, we received only two tiny pieces of sugar for tea.

This kind of discipline was applied to us, the students, with special refinement. The sergeants didn't hide their hatred for those who opted for higher education, and whenever the opportunity arose they demonstrated savage cruelty, so that the students would always remember their pettiness. We were marched to the cafeteria, singing a compulsory song. As soon as we sat down at the table, Sergeant Korytko ordered, "Finish-sh!" For some reason, he pronounced the "sh" sound with a wheeze. I thought I could eat very fast, but I didn't even have time to deal with the soup. Feverishly, and already on the move, I swallowed my millet porridge with a piece of fat pork. The moment we sat down at the table we stuffed two pieces of black bread into our pockets, and this saved us from constant hunger, which we felt as soon as we left the cafeteria.

Thanks to the commander of our unit, one more shocking memory was added to my inventory of impressions of my experience with our "glorious and invincible" army.

Near our tents, there were other tents housing former soldiers who were summoned for re-training. Again, the sergeant made us march near those tents. "Sing!" he ordered. We didn't want to sing. Then he ordered, "Double quick march!" We ran for some time turning back and forth on command. "Quick march!" the next command followed. Then, this dumb-faced commander ordered again, "Sing!" One of the soldiers who had been observing us from his tent, couldn't control himself and said bluntly, "Son of a bitch!" I don't know how this happened, but I reacted automatically, "Even more than that!"

We sighed and at that very instant, a frantic yell startled us, "Stop!!!" The man was pale, and his face quivered with indescribable rage. He didn't dismiss us but rushed to the officers' quarters to complain. We all understood what could follow, but no one sympathized with me. Everyone was glad that it hadn't happen to him.

Soon the commander of the platoon, a young lieutenant, came out. He called me solemnly in front of the line and announced an "emergency event", which had never happened before in their glorious unit. He explained that an insult to a Soviet Army commander might entail up to two years of penalty work. However, he said that taking into consideration the young age and insufficient political and moral awareness of student Mirzayanov, the commander of the battalion decided to limit my punishment to an extra detail in the cafeteria and to washing the floors in the Lenin Room.

Of course, I did all of this without asking any questions. But that was only the beginning. When it was boiling hot, more than 35 degrees Celsius outside, we were ordered to put on rubber overalls, boots, and gas masks. We had to deactivate "the site" contaminated with mustard gas. In order to do this, we had to dig up and turn over the ground, then mix it with bleach, and there was a time limit for all of this. We did everything ahead of schedule, and with satisfied faces we overturned our boots to pour out the sweat. They thanked everybody, but then I heard, "Mirzayanov, go to the commander!"

I ran until I reached the commander's center to see the head of our military department, General Khandozhko. He was sent to MITKhT from the Main Political Directorate of the Soviet Army, where he had received his "training". He was an aide to Lev Mekhlis who, together with Lavrentii Beria exterminated more Red generals than the whole fascist army.

The man was short, with a round face and a black moustache, and somehow he reminded us of our "dear" Iosif Stalin. He openly imitated the leader's manner of putting on an air of importance and majesty. He even spoke with a slight Caucasian accent, though he was Russian.

In a harsh voice, Khandozhko started speaking about the blemish on all students, which presumably was created by my error, and he threatened me with a military tribunal, dismissal from the institute, and other penalties. Oddly, for some reason I felt no fear.

Not everyone found our life in camp so hard. Some guys even liked the meaningless drills, and by the end of our stay there they became aides to platoon commanders, and gave us orders like the sergeants. Later, after graduating from the institute, they soon rose to the top of the administrative ranks.

There was nothing remarkable about my second tour of duty in the military camp, right after my graduation from the institute. In the summer of 1958, we were sent to the chemical battalion in Jykhvi, Estonia. Hardly anyone took any interest in us, and we spent our time paying cards or chess, and missing Moscow.

Another monster that gobbled up students' precious academic time at MITKhT was our exhaustive study of Marxism-Leninism. Lectures were given by former party bosses and "scientists", and this was a very lucrative occupation at that time. Those classes were incredibly boring. We could miss lectures in other subjects without any serious punishment, but the attendance was taken strictly in those classes. Skipping three lectures for an "invalid" reason could result in dismissal from the institute. So, fooling around with party matters was extremely dangerous. There was nothing left but to learn everything by heart, all the dates of endless Bolshevik congresses and conferences, their agendas, Lenin's speeches, and how he struggled with the hateful Mensheviks, etc. There was no guarantee that you wouldn't get confused by all this heresy, so students prepared simple crib sheets.

Once, a man who resembled a human being appeared in this Communist kingdom of almost medieval ignorance. That was Rem Belousov who came to us from Moscow State University. Rumor had it that he was a secretary of the Komsomol committee there, but had been removed because his views were incompatible with the party doctrine.

Soon we learned about the views of Belousov. First of all, he said that not a single one of Stalin's five-year plans for the economic development of the country had been implemented. It was even more terrible to hear that the party's plan, according to Lenin's appeal, to have 100,000 tractors which would secure the victory of socialism, was never fulfilled. "How come?" we asked in a great outburst. Rem Aleksandrovich explained this very simply. In all the reports on implementing the plan, hundreds of thousands of manufactured tractors were mentioned as, "translated into a 15 horse-power tractor". So, each 60 horse-power tractor was counted as four tractors, though it couldn't work in the place of four machines. All this was very strange. Although the views of our new lecturer were very progressive at the time, he didn't aim to go beyond "going back to Lenin's principles".

For a long time after his lectures, we joked whenever we saw a tractor in the street. One student asked another how many tractors he saw. The latter answered that he saw one. "No, dear friend, you are opposed to the party line. There are four tractors there, not one. You should study the history of the party, young man!" added the joker.

The party paid close attention to the institute. Ekaterina Furtseva was a former weaver, who studied at our institute for a year or two. Later she became a member of the Politbureau at the Central Committee of the C.P.S.U. I saw her in 1955. I remembered her resolute, attractive face, her red hair braided on the nape, and her energetic step tap-dancing on the marble floor of the second floor landing, which students traditionally called the "hole" because of the glass dome above it.

The institute's rector, Myshko, was a stout dumpy guy with short legs, who could hardly keep up with the leader of Moscow Communists (at that time Furtseva was the First Secretary of the Moscow City Committee of the C.P.S.U). For a long time, Myshko held "important posts in the Soviet state apparatus", including that of Deputy Chairman of the Moscow City Council. But afterwards he was demoted to rector of MITKhT. We remembered him, because he quoted Sergei Esenin in his speeches. Esenin was proclaimed a bourgeois poet by the official propaganda, and it was forbidden to publish his poetry.

However, Myshko combined Esenin's romanticism with his own roguish habits, which were very far from poetry. For instance, he hired his son-in-law to design the Marxist-Leninist rooms, for which large amounts of money were budgeted. In fact, professional artists did this job for peanuts, while Myshko and his son-in-law divided the money between themselves. At that time, the mischief of the Soviet elite knew no limits.

A storm broke out when it turned out that Myshko had borrowed large amounts of money from some elderly professors, with no intention of repaying them, hoping that these old creditors would soon pass away, departing for a better world where they wouldn't need any money. But the wife of one old man proved to be quite brave. She stirred up such a scandal that Myshko even agreed to be transferred to some department and to write a doctoral dissertation. But this job was too hard for him. The question was settled simply: Myshko was transferred to another "important position in the Soviet administration". After all, it was impossible to cast a shadow on the "pure reputation of a Communist".

A friend of Furtseva's was Lecturer Khokhlova, who was a permanent secretary of the institute's party committee. She was especially noted for keeping up appearances.

When the next rector of the Institute, Professor Xenzenko, divorced his wife and married a student (oh, what a scandal!), Khokhlova organized a crusade for "the purity of Communist morals". As a result, Xenzenko was removed from his position as rector and later, he was driven out of the institute. After this great shock, the scientist fell seriously ill and died.

Lecturer Aleksander Smirnov was another "prominent party leader" who worked at the institute during my studies. I don't know why, but as the Vice Chairman of the Department of Chemistry and Chemical Industry of the Central Committee of the C.P.S.U., he frequently visited the Department of "Artificial Gas and Liquid Fuel" to supervise our group. In class he would just stand there silently, while we carried out experiments on the synthesis of organic compounds or performed differential distillations of the heavy residues of resin pyrolysis. Nothing could bring him out of this inert state. Even the time when I once made the mistake of short circuiting the power grid and plunging the whole laboratory into darkness for a while, seemed to have no effect on him. I think the prospect of a scientific degree attracted Smirnov. In the evenings, he tried to work in Andrei Bashkirov's Laboratory at the Institute of Petrochemical Synthesis, at the U.S.S.R. Academy of Sciences. However, Smirnov's attempts were doomed. In one of the laboratories, he assembled an experimental unit for synthesis based on carbon monoxide (an extremely poisonous gas) and hydrogen. Either he forgot that the gases flowing out from the reactor should be directed into the exhaust hood, or the rubber hose that served this purpose came off, and the whole thing nearly ended in catastrophe. An employee who happened to enter the room found the unconscious Aleksander Sergeevich on the floor and immediately carried him out into the street. The people summoned by the alarm just barely managed to save the unlucky researcher.

None of this prevented him from becoming the chairman of the Department of Chemistry and Chemical Industry of the Central Committee of the C.P.S.U. The fate of six to eight Soviet ministers, who were in one way or another connected with chemistry, depended on him. Additionally, through his department, he managed issues of chemical weapons and often visited the State Scientific Research Institute for Organic Chemistry and Technology (GOSNIIOKhT) — the premiere institute that developed chemical agents in the country, where I later worked for 26 years. His son-in-law, Henri Kazhdan, also worked in this institute and though he wasn't a specialist, he still held a high position there.

Eventually, Smirnov achieved his ambition and became a "famous scientist". Smirnov and Vladimir Gryaznov, a former party administrator at the Institute of Petrochemical Synthesis at the U.S.S.R. Academy of Sciences, received a patent some very dubious discovery (pure Soviet classification).

I still remember quite well a number of other meaningless subjects which students were forced to study, such as the theory of machines and mechanisms, heating engineering, and construction, etc. Sometimes we asked our teachers why a chemist should try to calculate and design thermal boilers that produce steam and electrical energy, if electricity has been transmitted for a long time from electric power stations. There were mechanical engineers who worked there, specialists in this field. The machines and components were also designed by specialists and machinists. There were other institutes in Moscow that trained plenty of engineers, majoring in that area. We didn't receive any answers to our questions. I fear that the same thing still goes on and students have no time to study their major subject areas, for which they entered their institutions of higher learning in the first place.

Each head of every department thought that their area of specialty was the most important one. Even in the Athletic Department, teachers practically terrorized the students who failed to meet the regulation standards for jumping or distance running. It didn't matter if you were good at skiing, for example, or if you played volleyball very well. Our overweight PE teacher, Victoria Naumovna, was concerned only with her test.

In our second year, my fellow sportsmen and I failed the test in physical training, even though we achieved good results in different city competitions. This was because we had problems with an idiotic set of exercises called "GTO" ("Ready for Labor and Defense"), which required bizarre exercises such as standing on your head.

Two days before our exams, I had to train one whole night, learning how to stand on my head. The next day, I took the damn test with an open wound on my forehead, and since I had trained the whole night, there was no time to prepare for my exam. However, the women from the Athletic Department were not interested in that. Our trainers who were also teachers couldn't help, as they couldn't go against the instructions "sent down from above."

After my third year, the student life at MITKhT became merrier. Apart from Marxism and military science, practically all the unnecessary subjects were behind us, and we could focus on our major subjects. The teachers and professors in our favorite subject areas were not so diabolical, and they didn't hate the students. Many students never made it this far, because they couldn't cope with the meaningless drills.

My introduction to the manufacture of chemical products came through my internships at some operating plants. Unfortunately, they were more like excursions, though perhaps a bit more specialized. They didn't help us much in acquiring the skills of a technological engineer.

I was most impressed by my internship at the Novocherkassk Chemical Plant. At that time, it was a huge plant for producing synthetic fuel from carbon monoxide and hydrogen, using captured German technology and equipment. This plant received state subsidies, but it was unprofitable because the gasoline it produced was of such low quality, that it wasn't even good enough to refuel the factory buses. During the war, the Germans solved this problem by using additives such as tetraethyl lead. But this additive, which is also a strongly toxic compound, was produced in small quantities and so the products of the plant were of little use. The situation was the same at the two other large factories that were relocated from Germany to Salavat (Bashkortstan) and Angarsk.[8] By that time, the U.S.S.R. had started developing the rich deposits of natural oil from Bashkortstan and Tatarstan, which produced much better gasoline.

Some time later, a team of scientists led by Andrei Bashkirov, the head of our department, found a better application for the saturated hydrocarbons produced from carbon monoxide and hydrogen.

At that time, the U.S.S.R. had the largest whaling fleet in the world, and it practically wiped Antarctic whales off the face of the earth. Fat was cut off the carcasses of these huge mammals and sent to chemical plants (for example to the Kazan plant), where it was processed and used to produce heavy primary alcohols. These in turn were used to make the synthetic detergent "Novost". Even at that time it was clear that this madness would have to stop some day. Bashkirov proposed a method for oxidizing the product of the Novocherkassk plant, called "synthine", in the presence of boric acid into heavy primary alcohols. This was a revolutionary solution, and we were very proud of our professor.

When Docent Gilyarovskaya suggested that I should conduct

experiments researching the process of synthine oxidation in my fourth year of studies, I happily agreed. Before that I had hardly dreamed about the career of a scientist. At the time, I thought it was better to work at a plant in the field of chemical engineering; however, I quickly realized that my place was in the research laboratory. You are practically alone there, face to face with the unknown, and it is up to you alone whether something new and unexplored is created or not.

This became even clearer to me when I was a fifth-year student during an internship at the Shebekino Chemical Plant, not far from Belgorod, where the first industrial technology for producing primary alcohols was under development. A few students from our department studied the operation of this future plant, with a prototype unit. The performance of this unit was dynamic and full of surprises, but generally I felt it was terribly boring, routine and repetitive from day to day. The few night shifts that I spent with the unit finally and for all time convinced me that there was nothing remarkable about the job of a shift engineer, except the monotony of the technological process. The work is exhausting and it is not compensated by any creative satisfaction.

By that time, I had seriously fallen in love with my fellow student, Rita Skibko, who returned my feelings. She worked diligently at the department for the synthesis and technology of vitamins and drugs, headed by the famous scientist Nikolai Preobrazhensky. Soon we got married, dreaming about a family scientific career.

Bashkirov suggested that I do the work for my degree thesis in his laboratory, and I was very inspired by this opportunity.

Soon I was introduced to my supervisors - Yuli Kagan, a senior scientist, and Nikolai Morozov, a graduate student. When Kagan and Bashkirov went on an extended business trip to China, Morozov became my actual supervisor. We studied the role of proposed carbon complexes with an iron catalyst while different organic hydroxyl compounds were synthesized on it.

Nikolai was a kindhearted person who did everything possible to make me feel free to devote myself to the work. We conducted almost all experiments together and I certainly trusted him completely. I quickly mastered the experimental techniques, and I carried out the kinetic experiments with pleasure, drawing gas samples into adsorption tubes and weighing them. You literally kilometers run, for hours on end, rushing from the laboratory to the weighing room and back again.

Unfortunately, our early work was unproductive. We failed to get reproducible experimental data. All the time, we got different results, which were beyond any logical explanation. Sometimes, we made odd "discoveries", when the catalyst we tested showed more than a 100% conversion of the carbon monoxide. Later it turned out that when we were cleaning the reactor, we had left a few threads of a worn-out cleaning rag behind.

We didn't know what to do. The day when course papers had to be defended was approaching with a disastrous speed, but still we had no reproducible results. As if sensing that we were having problems, Kagan wrote a letter from China, though naturally he couldn't help us from there.

Fortunately, Bashkirov returned from China earlier than planned. Though he didn't know our work in detail, he taught us a valuable lesson. Bashkirov listened to Nikolai, who was just starting his career in science, and rebuked us properly. He demanded that we repeat all the experimental operations with the maximum possible accuracy and observe intervals between selecting the samples and the weighing. After this, things went smoothly, and I managed to finish my work on time.

Chapter 4
I Become a Person from "The Box"

Before we had to defend our theses, the members of our class of 1958 were assigned to various scientific research institutes and plants. I was offered work at "Post Office Box 4019", located on the Highway of Enthusiasts in Moscow. I agreed to this, though I knew nothing about this enterprise or about my future work there. The institute was a secret establishment which was significant for the defense of our country, so my future seemed romantic and thrilling.

I came to work at the beginning of September, after military camp and a trip home to Stary Kangysh with Rita to meet my parents.

I arrived at my appointed time, but I couldn't start working because I had no clearance to access secret documents. That process took a little more than a month. Then it turned out that I was supposed to work in the experimental unit, Workshop 17, for developing the technologies for producing boranes, which are highly explosive and poisonous compounds used in making rocket fuel.

I passed the test on safety measures, and I went to the plant, where there was a continuous line of machines and devices with valves, under a glass hood purged by a powerful stream of ventilating air.

Like all employees, I had to change into cotton work overalls before entering the workshop. They were a whitish-blue color and hung on me like an old potato sack, because of numerous washings with bleach. I was given a gas mask, which I had to carry with me at all times while working in the unit. We wore white cotton caps on our heads, and to be honest, we looked somewhat ridiculous. To top it all off, we had heavy crudely tanned leather boots, and our feet were wrapped in soldiers' foot-wrappings. All this made us look like the prisoners in the movies of that time.

There was a pungent smell in the workshop that almost blew the caps off our heads, despite the powerful ventilation. It was literally killing us, as it slowly but constantly permeated our entire bodies. I was completely nauseated. I asked the assistant foreman Efimych, how long that smell would persist. He flashed me a toothless smile, and said that it would always be so. For some reason, Efimych's eyes were sparkling unnaturally and he was waddling like a boatswain on a ship in stormy weather…

Soon I successfully completed my study at the unit and started working as a shift engineer. From time to time, the work was very intensive and dangerous, because the experimental reactor for producing diborane was leaking occasionally. It was damaged at high temperatures by the corrosive mixture of poisonous and explosive gas. In those days, it was very hazardous and labor-intensive work to trace the leak in time and to replace the reactor. If this happened during the night shift, it was twice as difficult, and of course people got seriously poisoned. We spent an hour in the chamber of this reactor saturated with poisonous diborane, replacing this damned unit.

Though we were in our so-called hose-type gas masks and breathed fresh air pumped in from the outside when we were in this chamber, our clothes absorbed a lot of diborane. When we finished our work and left the chamber, we went through a corridor where other shift workers without gas masks, were standing near the control panel. Then we went to shower and change our clothes. On our way through, we breathed in high concentrations of diborane emitted by our clothes, and the men and women standing around in the corridor were also forced to breathe in this poison.

State Secrets

People with various qualifications and levels of training worked on my shift. Most of them had solid work experience, and they helped me adjust well to this dangerous profession. After a few months, I developed good relations with my workers and they hardly ever let me down. Still, we did have a few accidents, which I will never forget.

During each shift I got about 30 liters of ethyl alcohol on receipt (it smelled strongly of toluene) to wash down the machines and units that were being repaired. We were pretty careful with this liquid, though not entirely. Everyone knew that it wasn't poisonous, and sometimes people even drank it without any noticeable consequences. During one of the night shifts, I told two young workers, Kostya Dzhavadov and Dima Eminov, to wash down the alkaline hydrolysis unit with this alcohol, though I didn't stay to supervise this operation because it was too trivial. Soon I heard Dima's shrill cry, and he ran to his work station, along with some other workers. He buried his face in his hands and moaned with pain, so we dragged him to the water tap and washed his eyes and face. We did everything we had to, according to the safety instructions for cases of eye burns with alkaline solution. I called the ambulance, which immediately arrived and took Dima to a Moscow hospital.

The accident was largely my fault, because according to the instructions, the supervisor was directly responsible for everything that happened on his shift. Still, I was puzzled: how did this accident occur, if there was no alkaline in the unit being cleaned?

Later, during the investigation, we found out that the two young men had finished their job and started fooling around, pouring alcohol over each other. Some of the alcohol got into Eminov's eyes. Fortunately, his burn wasn't serious and he soon returned to work. Of course I was punished for my negligence, and I was deprived of my quarterly bonus.[9]

Another emergency incident occurred on another of my night shifts that literally shocked me. A young worker on my shift was studying journalism by correspondence at Moscow State University, and this was the source of his pride and arrogance. He had the highest worker's category and conducted an important technological operation - the low temperature distillation of diborane. Purity of the product depended on the precision work of the operator. If the quality of the end product was lower than standard, they had to run the distillation over again and the reactor unit had to be stopped.

I started noticing that my aspiring journalist often came to work not quite sober. According to the protocol, I was supposed to dismiss him immediately and send him to the clinic for a medical examination. I decided that a reprimand would be sufficient, but it happened a few more times. I sincerely sympathized with the young man because he would have been fired at once, if I had dismissed him.

One night my "journalist" arrived tipsy again for his shift. Though he assured me that everything would be fine, I decided to stand near him and we would conduct the distillation of the product together. We worked like this until almost midnight, and then I was called to another machine. I had to leave him for just a few minutes, but this was long enough for an accident to take place. I heard the frightened cries of women, who were working nearby on the drainage unit, and ran back. A shaft of flame was bursting from the wall. I immediately understood that the "journalist" had opened the purge valve, which was never supposed to be used under any circumstances, unless all the gas mains had been purged with inert nitrogen gas. The valve had to be plugged immediately, but this hadn't been done. Every second counted. Flames were licking the pipelines filled with diborane and hydrogen, and this could easily have resulted in a powerful explosion. There were two large tanks of pure diborane, only a few steps from the raging fire, behind the door on the landing. If they exploded, only a pile of ashes would be left of our entire Post Office Box institution and its personnel, and a whole block of buildings in Moscow would be seriously damaged. The situation was terrifying.

I acted like an automaton. I grabbed a roll of asbestos cloth, which was hanging on the opposite wall, and threw it over the valve, having no time to unroll the cloth completely. Urgently I covered valve with the cloth, and quickly I began to turn it off. Fortunately, it worked. The fire went out and when I came to myself, I just felt a slight chill. Only then did I notice the silence. There was no one around anywhere. Everyone was terrified and had run away.

Soon they returned to work, and I wrote a report about the incident. I felt confident because I had managed to do everything that was necessary. Privately, I was pleased that I didn't panic in this critical situation. However, my worries were not over. Another worker reported that our "journalist" was nowhere to be found. He had vanished into thin air, but since the guards couldn't let anybody leave the workshop without my written permission, I decided that my hard worker was still around there somewhere. We started looking for him, but to no avail. Suddenly, an idea struck me and I decided to check out my guess. There was a degassing chamber in the unit, which was used for removing poisons from the machines and reactors. It was flatly prohibited to enter this chamber without a hose-type gas mask on. That is where we found our "journalist" stretched out on the floor, sleeping like a log.

Luckily, it turned out that he wasn't poisoned at all and was quite healthy. But this served as a good lesson for me, for my whole life. After that, I tried to be guided by common sense, not just by feelings of sympathy or pity.

My work at Post Office Box 4019 exhausted me. It was especially difficult during the night shifts, because I couldn't sleep properly when I came home. We were living in one room with Rita's parents then, and it was so cramped when our daughter Lena was born that you couldn't even turn around. I quickly came to the realization that the work of a shift engineer required practically no initiative or elements of creativity. This was a real impasse for me. So, despite all the obstacles, I started to prepare to enter graduate school. That was the only way for me to leave my work, because I was obliged to work for three years at the place of my assignment, irrespective of my wishes. Only two years of work experience were required to enter graduate school.

Hard work and bad living conditions had an adverse impact on my health. At my medical exam, the doctors recommended that I start getting treatment immediately, warning that I could be sent to a hospital. Soon my health improved and our living conditions changed for the better.

I wanted to study at the graduate school of the Institute of Petrochemical Synthesis of the U.S.S.R. Academy of Sciences, which I knew well. But when my documents had to be submitted, I discovered a very important paper was missing: the character references from my workplace, signed by the director of the institute, the chairman of the trade union committee, and the secretary of the Party Committee. I quickly collected signatures from the director and the chairman, but there were problems with Sorokin, secretary of the Party Committee. He said that the party thought that young specialists were necessary right there at this important production site, and if I wanted to study I had to do it there. I almost cried from resentment and profound disappointment. However, I decided that I would return to him 10 days later. Probably he would relent and give in.

But the party boss didn't change his mind then either. Instead, he rebuked me as a persistent slacker who was trying to shun his duty to the party and to the people. They had let me study and had fostered me, but apparently it wasn't a success.

When I came on my shift that evening, I was upset and unable to hide my feelings. Of course my workers asked what had happened, so I told them. Then Dima, who became a professor of law in the future, said "Give me that paper!" I gave it to him and was surprised to see that Dima calmly signed it in place of the secretary of the "mind, honor, and conscience of our era". He said that I would be a fool if I let "that idiot Sorokin" stop me.

I had to agree with this dubious method because there was no other choice. I am still sure that nobody ever read this paper - it was simply a formality. After all, I was going to study at my own risk and lose half of my salary. I wasn't looking for some kind of government award or career advancement.

Probably I left Post Office Box 4019 just in time. These days, it no longer has a secret name. It is called the Institute of Organic Silicone Compounds Technology and is close to GOSNIIOKhT, where I would work 26 years…

In 1959, our "Post Office Box" designed a large plant for producing boranes (diborane, pentaborane, decaborane, etc.), which was built in the Redkino settlement, located halfway between the cities Klin and Tver.

Later, my boss and I visited this plant to evaluate its readiness for operation. We found significant defects in the assembly of the gas mains and the layout of equipment, which we reported to Vladimir Rostunov, the chief engineer. He was an energetic and resolute looking middle-aged man.

Twenty years later I met him again at the Novocheboksary Chemical Plant, which produced the chemical agent Substance 33, an analog to the well-known VX nerve gas. By that time, Rostunov had become the chief engineer of the Main Administration "Soyuzorgsynthesis" at the U.S.S.R. Ministry of Chemical Industry, which supervised the production of chemical weapons. He and other bosses were awarded the Lenin Prize, as well as other honors and regalia of the Soviet era, for launching the Novocheboksary Plant. He was a talented engineer and probably would have gone on to achieve more, except for his fondness of alcohol, which hindered his further career advancement.

In the early days, during my business trip to Redkino, I met many of my fellow students who had been "assigned" to this plant, where a branch of our "Post Office Box" was soon organized.

Many years later, I learned that a lot of the people who had worked there got poisoned with boranes. Some of them died, and some remained helplessly crippled for life. This happened to my fellow student, Yuri Bujnitsky. Yuri was a tall handsome man with a slightly swarthy face and a tender chin, which revealed his kindness. Apparently, this feature of his made him a little bit uncomfortable, because he was the appointed head of the workshop and had more than 200 subordinates working under him.

I met him once at the Lenin State Library in Moscow with his slim and pretty wife. I was truly happy for Yuri, and I thought that they made a beautiful couple. A few years later I found out that Yuri had been seriously poisoned. Treatments in different clinics didn't help him, and he was completely paralyzed. His wife left him. Serendipitously, a disabled woman, who had managed to start walking, began taking care of Yuri, and a few years later he started moving a little bit.

Poisoning with boranes had terrible consequences. In addition to their immediate effect on the central nervous system, they had a strong residual effect. The product of their decomposition - water insoluble boric acid - accumulates in the blood vessels of the brain and can't be removed.

My friends and fellow students, Yuri Ermakov and Gena Kolovertnov, who lived and worked in Redkino, were married to Hungarian girls from our group. Soon Yuri and Gena started graduate school at the Karpov Physical Chemical Institute. After graduation, they went to work in the Novosibirsk academic town with their families. Both friends were talented scientists and they made valuable contributions to the theory of catalysis. I remember when their doctoral theses were presented in GOSNIIOKhT in 1976, and the speakers referred to works of Gennady Kolovertnov. By that time, he was no longer alive. He perished in the waters of the Pacific Ocean while scuba diving. After a long flight, he put on an aqualung and dove into the water. Many people now think that long flights and alcohol consumption can lead to dehydration, increasing the chances of decompression sickness, so waiting 12-24 hours after flying before diving is commonly advised. Flying shortly after diving is even more dangerous.

Yuri Ermakov made his career in science very quickly, and he was less than 35 when he defended his doctoral dissertation and became the First Deputy Director of the Catalysis Institute of the Siberian Branch of the U.S.S.R. Academy of Sciences. Yura committed suicide. He couldn't stand the bullying of party committees at his institute and at the Siberian Branch of the Academy of Sciences. Party members organized persecution for him, as they were not pleased that Yura had an affair with a young research assistant, whom he had unfortunately fallen in love with.

Chapter 5
My Chemical Career

In the autumn of 1960, I successfully passed my entrance exams and entered graduate school at the Institute of Petrochemical Synthesis at the U.S.S.R. Academy of Sciences. Still, there was a moment during my exam on the history of the Communist Party of the Soviet Union when I made a crucial mistake. There was a question about the agenda of some Bolshevik congress, and the frail docent who was examining me went out of his way to ask me leading questions, so I couldn't remember what the Bolsheviks were talking about. Offended by my lack of diligence, this dogmatist angrily gave me a "Three" ("C" mark). I feared that a low mark in such an "important" subject would prevent me from entering graduate school, and I would have to go back to my "boranes" for one more year. However, at the institute they were rather sympathetic about my mark. Probably by that time, many people understood that the exam in Marxism-Leninism was useless for a young chemist. Still, a year later, I had to take this exam again. Before that I had to attend some insanely boring seminars at the Academy of Social Sciences, which was located opposite the "Moskva" swimming pool (where the Temple of Christ the Savior has now been built).

The first two years of my studies in graduate school were not very successful. I was sent to work in Professor Vasily Sokolov's laboratory for the analysis and separation of hydrocarbons. The laboratory consisted of two really cramped rooms. The elderly professor was quite friendly when he welcomed me, but he didn't suggest a topic for my dissertation research or even a workplace. However, he promised that there would surely be something when the construction of a new building at the institute was completed. This was supposed to take place two years later, but the problem was that I had only three years to study.

All I could do was to doggedly peruse the scientific literature and to try to find a research topic myself. I had already identified the major direction I wanted my research to take. It had to be connected with chromatographic analysis. At that time, this was a relatively new area of science, and it was rapidly progressing in our country thanks to Aleksander Zhukhovitsky and Nisson Turkeltaub.

I had read almost all the available scientific literature in this field, and I was forming some ideas for my future work. However, I couldn't do anything without instruments and a work area. My scientific supervisor wasn't at all interested in these problems. At that time, he was carefully sowing the seeds of an idea among influential circles to create a new institute called the "All-Union Research Institute of Nuclear Geophysics and Geochemistry" (VNIIYaGG). Actually, such an institute was soon founded and Sokolov became the deputy director, as he had planned.

At the second All-Russian Scientific Conference on Chromatography, I got acquainted with Turkeltaub and told him my story. He invited me to his laboratory, which had moved to VNIIYaGG from a different institute, by that time. He suggested a topic for my dissertation and promised to introduce me to Zhukhovitsky. By then, I had just barely managed to scrape together my chromatograph and I was given a working area in the new building of the Institute of Petrochemical Synthesis.

Soon I met with Zhukhovitsky and he agreed to supervise my work. Meeting and working with Zhukhovitsky and Turkeltaub made an indelible impression on me. They were truly pioneers in the science of chromatography. I remember with gratitude how generously they helped me and many other young scientists. They gave unstintingly of their time and energy.

Sadly, Turkeltaub died of a heart attack at the young age of 44. I think the reason for his early death was too many tragedies in his life. When he was a student in 1939, he was mobilized into the Polish Army and found himself on the front fighting against the Soviet Union. He was taken prisoner and ended up in a prisoner of war camp near Saratov.

During the Second World War, Sokolov's laboratory for gas well surveys was evacuated to Saratov, and they continued working there, sending out field expeditions. Geochemists performed their gas well surveys, and the results were used to predict the locations of oil deposits. Their methods involved the analysis of hydrocarbon gases in the air samples taken from shallow boreholes.

Sokolov had suggested this method at the beginning of the 1930s, and it seemed promising, because it didn't require expensive drilling to discover oil deposits. At that time, there were only two dilapidated oil drilling rigs in the country. The situation in this industry was so desperate that Sergo Ordzhonikidze, the Commissioner for Heavy Industry, even promised to present "his last pair of underwear" to someone who would suggest an alternative solution. Very soon, Sokolov became that person.

The people's commissar kept his word, but he presented the inventor with a dacha near Moscow and a car, instead of his underwear. However, not a single oil deposit in the country was discovered with this method. The most important thing for the Soviet system was to come up with a new initiative, or to assume the obligations of the so-called "socialist labor competition". Soon, Sokolov became a Doctor of Sciences and a professor without having to defend any dissertation. The professor dispatched his first scientific expeditions (at the expense of the state, of course) to his dacha in the Moscow suburbs.

One time, when the geochemists were working on a field trip not far from the camp of Polish prisoners of war, a woman who was working in the expedition noticed that one of the captives, a young handsome brunette, was closely observing their work. They soon got acquainted, as the guards didn't pay much attention to the expedition workers. They had become accustomed to their presence near the camp. It turned out that the captive, Nisson Turkeltaub, was a former student of Krakov University. He knew very well what the scientists were doing there, because he had worked with similar instruments at his university.

Soon Turkeltaub started working with the expedition party, returning to his camp at night. His exceptional talent and diligence impressed the head of the expedition, who asked the higher authorities to release Turkeltaub to his personal custody. However strange as it may seem for that dreadful time, the authorities were lenient, and they met the expedition's leader's request halfway. Sokolov's uncanny ability to find convincing and irresistible arguments played a role in this. He was excellent at that.

After the war, Turkeltaub graduated from Saratov University, and he quickly carved out a brilliant career in science, becoming the favorite scientist of all chromatography specialists in the USSR. His collaboration with the outstanding Russian scientist Zhukhovitsky played a great role in that.

Zhukhovitsky was a world famous scientist who made a serious contribution to the field of molecular structure, adsorption, diffusion, and chromatography. He was awarded a rare international prize for his achievements in the field of chromatography, a gold medal named after Mikhael Tsvet, the founder of chromatography. Zhukhovitsky became a Doctor of Chemical Sciences at the age of 27, which is a rare achievement for a chemist in any country. In his doctoral dissertation, he wasn't afraid to challenge the authority of Michael Dubinin, the official "master" of this science in the USSR. He remarked that Dubinin's so-called volumetric theory of adsorption was nothing but the repetition of the famous theory of Polyani. As a result, Zhukhovitsky had to defend his dissertation for a second time, before the Higher Attestation Committee. The official opponent of the young scientist was Dubinin himself. In spite of this, the committee had to approve the talented young man's work.

But, Dubinin, who was an academician, a lieutenant general, and the head of the Department of Adsorption at the Voroshilov Academy of Chemical Defense, later got his revenge by preventing

State Secrets

Zhukhovitsky from being elected a member of the U.S.S.R. Academy of Sciences. Also in 1948, during the campaign against "cosmopolitanism", Dubinin published a "stinging" article in *Proceedings of Academy of Sciences of the U.S.S.R.* about Zhukhovitsky, who was by then the First Deputy Director of the Karpov Physical Chemical Institute. Unfortunately, by that time Zhukhovitsky had already published his article on problems of molecular structure, in collaboration with the well-known English scientists Heitler and London in an English journal. At that time, this was considered to be a sign of "cosmopolitanism", and Dubinin's article was a direct appeal to the KGB to punish the author.

Zhukhovitsky miraculously escaped the sad fate of many Russian scientists who were sent to the Gulags. During the war and afterwards, he fruitfully served the needs of the military, and that may have made a difference. For example, for many years he studied the questions of adsorption protection from chemical agents, at the Central Military Scientific Research Technical Institute (TsNIIVTI).

Almost 60 years after Dubinin's provocative article was published, I was holding those very *Proceedings of the Academy of Sciences of the U.S.S.R.* in my hands, in the New York Public Library. I can't tell you how mean-spirited and vile it was for me!

I met with Dubinin only once, and I was struck by his "flexibility". While I was writing my doctoral dissertation, I had to study the adsorption dynamics of soman and sarin on carbon adsorbents. I was working with a gas chromatography (GC) method for analysis, in order to avoid mistakes in the calculation of equilibrium concentrations. I selected samples from the gas stream coming out of the adsorption tube, with determined concentrations of soman and sarin in them, and then I recorded the so-called adsorption fronts. When I tried to process the same results using Dubinin's equation, using all the corrections he had suggested, everything was excellent and my data fit this equation, but the final constants were much larger than the author had suggested. Nobody could explain to me what the problem was.

Then I decided to ask Dubinin himself about it. One day, when he was at a meeting of the Science Council of GOSNIIOKhT, I asked him to find some time for me. He agreed and I briefly explained my difficulties. He didn't suggest anything reasonable in response, but he wisely remarked that sometimes an experiment was worth many theories. Professor Nikolaev from the Academy of Chemical Defense overheard our conversation and hurried to rescue his boss. He explained that I had worked with small concentrations, and the equation was meant for large concentrations.

In fact, I had worked with a wide range of concentrations, from large to micro-concentrations. But this argument had no relevance because I had to defend my doctoral dissertation. I had already gone through so many difficulties, that I decided not to acquire an adversary.

It proved to be no easy task for me to part from my former supervisor, Professor Sokolov. It wasn't difficult to get a new scientific supervisor, because it seemed that the directorate of the institute understood the situation very well. At that time, Andrei Bashkirov, who was a corresponding member of the Academy of Sciences of the U.S.S.R., was very well respected among scientists. He advised me bluntly, "Run away from Sokolov before it is too late!"

For some reason, my youthful enthusiasm often tripped me up at crucial moments in my life, and it nearly nipped my scientific career in the bud. Since I had spent long hours in the library with the scientific literature, I also had the time to study the works of Sokolov. In fact, there were quite a lot of them. He had written more than ten books and other publications.

Nevertheless, the more I read, the deeper my feeling of "Deja vu" became. I had already seen it all before somewhere else. Finally, in R.M. Barrer's book "*Diffusion in and Through Solids*" (Cambridge University Press, 1951, in Russian trans.) I found whole pages, with notes from Sokolov, asking his typist to copy out sections without any changes. Sometimes, the professor wrote "let us suppose" above "let us assume" of the original text, or "thus" above the word "consequently". Then instructions followed to copy "from" and "up to", so that they could copy from another book without acknowledging the original author. This was the story behind each of my supervisor's books.

I was shocked and miserable about my discovery, because I knew that I wouldn't be able to keep quiet, when the facts cried out scandalous plagiarism. This was certain to disrupt my "peaceful" life. I shared my discovery only with a few people, who strongly recommended that I remain completely silent, "so as not to ruin my life".

Instead, I went to the editorial office of newspaper *Izvestia* with copies of my "discoveries". At that time they published critical articles about this kind of thing. After a long wait in the reception area, the editor on duty asked me in. He listened to me, laughed, and explained that these kinds of cases were so numerous that if they published them all, the newspaper would turn into a chronicle of plagiarism in science.

At the same time, the editor promised to send my papers to the plagiarist's workplace, so that measures could be taken "on the spot", as he put it.

Some measures were "taken" - an extended attack against me got underway. Sokolov's friends, who were famous scientists, came to the institute to have "talks" with me. Some tried to persuade me, while others threatened me directly, saying that my career in science would be over if I didn't withdraw my petition.

Once I was summoned by the academic secretary of the institute, where I was handed a letter from the USSR Ministry of Geology, signed by the Deputy Minister and sent to me via the Directorate of the institute. It said that I was invited to the ministry to discuss my complaint about Professor Vasili Sokolov. This letter was obviously provocative because I hadn't officially complained about anyone. The fact that it was addressed to the director of the institute, and not to me directly, showed that the authors of the letter wanted to paint me up as a plotter and a scandalmonger. When Minna Khotimskaya, Dean of the Graduate School, handed me this letter, she made it known there was official dissatisfaction with my behavior, and added that Nikolai Nametkin (a deputy director) was very displeased with me.

I decided to see it through, especially since Zhukhovitsky deeply sympathized with me and supported me after my revelation.

I went to the Ministry of Geology, though it was clear to me that the authors of the letter were not going to discuss anything with me. They had a different objective - to discredit me in the eyes of the institute leadership.

The head of the Personnel Department at the Ministry received me, praised Sokolov for a long time, and then recommended that I take my petition back. I suggested in response that the Ministry should say in an official statement that Mirzayanov was wrong. "It is up to the minister to decide!" the official countered arrogantly. Evidently, the minister and academician didn't agree.

In spite of those problems, all obstacles for the appointment of my new scientific supervisor were lifted, and I had the necessary instruments for my experiments, so I went back to work at the laboratory for days on end.

I came to work at 9 A.M., and left no earlier than 11 P.M., in order to get to the metro station before it closed. At that time, graduate students were allowed to work at the laboratory as long as they could. Around 9 P.M., the electrician on duty usually came and warned that he could cut off the power to the whole building. I always had 100 milliliters of ethyl alcohol ready for that occasion. The electrician was quite happy with this arrangement, and allowed me to work on until midnight.

Of course, it was against the rules to work alone late at night, but the circumstances and my youthful enthusiasm made me bend the rules. Fortunately, this never led to any major accidents, but small incidents did occur. During my experiments, I had to prepare gaseous mixtures of hydrogen with admixtures of different compounds such as methane, carbon monoxide, oxygen, nitrogen, etc. in a steel tank. Then, I pumped this mixture into the measuring tank for further experiments.

One evening, when I was quite tired and had decided to finish up the last experiment for the day, a leak materialized at the joint of the valve to the tank. I decided to eliminate it by tightening the connecting nut on the valve. I don't know why, probably because I was tired, I turned this nut from left to right. But it had to be in the opposite direction on the hydrogen tanks. The result was terrifying. Fire ruptured from the tank with a hiss, fortunately not in my direction, but in the direction of the wall covered with ceramic tiles. I made a great effort not to throw the damned tank down. With the same spanner that had helped me "create the flame", I turned the valve to the left and the fire went out. I remember I drank up the alcohol that I had kept for the electrician in one gulp, not even diluting it with water, and I quickly left the laboratory.

Later, my guardian angel saved me once more from real trouble. During my work at night, I used cooling fluid from a Dewar vessel. The concentrating adsorption column had valves that closed at both ends, so that concentrated admixtures in ethylene could be quickly cooled and evacuated, after the regeneration that took place when it was purged with helium at a high temperature.

I had carried out hundreds of these experiments by that time, and all my movements were almost automatic. But that night, I made an awkward movement and a hot steel column touched the glass wall of the Dewar vessel. A deafening explosion resounded and I was covered with glass splinters. Fortunately, my eyes were not damaged, and I just got a few scratches on my face. I was very lucky because I wasn't wearing my safety goggles or a special mask at the time, as the safety measures required.

I finished the experiments for my dissertation on time, and only the writing remained. Zhukhovitsky helped me a lot with that. Following his recommendation, I started working as a senior scientist at the All-Union Scientific Research Institute of Complex Automation of the Oil Industry (VNIIKA NeftGas). Turkeltaub was supposed to move there soon with his laboratory. There were grand plans to create something like a center for chromatographic research, with its design and its experimental and industrial functions based on modern chromatography.

Unfortunately, these plans were never realized. VNIIKA NeftGas still had a Chromatography Department, but only for design purposes. Under these conditions, I had few prospects for work as a specialist in the area of researching and developing modern methods of chromatographic analysis. By the end of 1964, I finished all the technical aspects of my dissertation and submitted it, looking forward to my turn to defend it.

However, fate decided to test my strength again. Alas, this time

I failed the ordeal. When I tell my friends about it, they all collectively assured me that I behaved reasonably, because I had no other choice. But I feel otherwise.

The defense of my dissertation was scheduled for the end of May, 1965. Before the meeting of the Science Council, I finished all the technical work and was going to leave the Institute of Petrochemical Synthesis earlier than usual. One day, I suddenly bumped into Professor Sokolov in the corridor. We greeted each other, and the professor said in his squeaky voice that he knew about my defense and had even read the abstract. Then Sokolov added that my work had made a good impression on him and he was ready to support me at a meeting of the Science Council.

I was amazed at his generosity and openhanded attitude. I had caused so much trouble for my former supervisor. But then Sokolov quickly brought me back down to earth, by asking me to sign just one paper. He took a few sheets of paper out of his briefcase. The text read that some time ago, due to lack of experience and poor knowledge of the scientific literature, Vil Sultanovich Mirzayanov had written incorrectly about the use of sources by Professor V.A. Sokolov, the author of numerous large monographs. Now he deeply regretted it and asked that these allegations be dismissed for having no basis in reality.

The application was addressed to the Minister of Geology. I looked at the blackmailer, considering how I could hit him without crippling him. But I managed to control myself and even asked idiotically if that was all. "Yes, yes, of course, you know, Nikolai Sergeevich doesn't like scandals, and I can arrange this tomorrow if you behave prudently," he concluded.

Instantly, my whole life passed in front of my eyes. I remembered the enormous difficulties that I had to overcome to approach one of the crucial moments of my scientific career. By that time, I had divorced my wife and lost my family. Everyone who knew anything about the Soviet system, was very well aware that the path to research was closed to any scientist, however talented, without an official scientific degree. Usually, the science councils, where a dissertation is defended, evaluate the quality of work, only by official reviews of specifically appointed opponents and speakers on the topic. Among the members of the Science Council, there can be no more than three or four specialists on the dissertation topic under discussion. The rest rely strictly on their intuition or other external factors. Any negative review or comments can produce an unfavorable result in the secret vote. If a candidate for a degree fails to get two thirds of the votes of the council members present at the meeting, the dissertation "is knocked down", and the candidate loses the chance to defend his or her work again. The label testifying "low" qualification of the candidate sticks with him forever and only real luck can help him get rid of it.

I displayed some "prudence", and signed two copies of the appeal. Then I felt smeared with indelible dirt from head to foot. I couldn't overcome this feeling, either during the defense of my thesis or after it. The speech of Professor Sokolov, who supported my dissertation, caused a sensation.

After the results of the voting were announced, I told my supervisors about my degradation. They comforted me in every possible way, but at heart I cursed myself and swore never to bargain with my conscience again.

Chapter 6
Into Supersecrecy

After my divorce, there was nowhere for me to live, because of the housing shortage in Moscow. Rita and I still shared a room and the situation was becoming increasingly more stressful. My only option was to try to buy a new cooperative apartment, and I couldn't afford to continue working at VNIIKA NeftGas on my salary. So I began to look for new work. Unexpectedly, Professor Victor Berezkin, my masters' thesis advisor, offered to help me. He did not explain where he had recommended me for work, but he proposed that I meet with an acquaintance of his, a man he had once worked with who was a representative of one of the Post Office Boxes.

I agreed to this, though I remembered the story of my friend Volodya Shakhrai about how Berezkin had been poisoned during his time working at the Central Scientific Military Technical Institute (TsNIIVTI), researching chemical agents. After a long cure, and it seems a not an entirely successful one, he developed a strong allergy to literally every chemical solvent.

Several days later I met with Aleksei Beresnev, who introduced himself as chairman of the Analytical Department of "Post Office Box 702". We didn't have a professional conversation, but he proposed that I go to his institute and fill out the paperwork necessary to get access to work with secret documents.

I went to the address Beresnev gave me, and there I was stunned by the sight of a gloomy and decrepit old building on the Highway of Enthusiasts. I wondered if I was in the right place. You could get a glimpse of this monstrosity from a bridge that passed over the railway on the way to Post Office Box 4019, where I had worked as a shift engineer for the last 2 years. During that time, I had gone several times to a "night resort", which was located in the Tarasovka Settlement, half an hour's trip from the Yaroslav Train Station on the Northern Moscow Rail Line.

Workers visited this night resort from different Post Office Boxes, and allegedly some of them had worked on the synthesis of chemical agents and on their military applications. I listened to their horror stories and came to the conclusion that they were engaged in a suicidal business. How ironic it was that I willingly agreed to work in this kind of nightmare. I was strongly motivated by the salary, so I could have my own place to live in.

Next, I went to explain the reason for my forthcoming departure to my bosses at VNIIKANeftGas. It was bizarre, but my explanation threw the Secretary of the Party Committee into a rage. He refused to approve my application for withdrawal, and accused me of being egotistical. I was forced to work with an old party hack, a lathe operator.

This man tried to change my mind over the course of several hours, explaining that earnings appeared to be a completely trivial motivation for a party member. In his opinion, the fulfillment of your duty to the party was the most important thing. Of course, it was the same Party Committee at my job, which determined what my "duty" was. This old hand and the "party line" did not succeed in changing my mind, because I was pretty sure I could not continue living in a one-room apartment with my ex-wife. Then, I still had to suffer through another committee meeting of the Party Committee, which wanted to "dress down" their obstinate comrade.

I was given a reprimand, but it was really nothing more than a private assault on me. I was hoping that these people would not

State Secrets

decide to give me a "party penalty". Where could I disappear to if they wanted to do this? How would I be able to "continue to fulfill the party line" as they expected, if they didn't sign off on my withdrawal?

I decided to "shoot the bank". On the advice of a friend who was a lawyer, I refused to go to work. I had the right to do that under the Soviet Labor Code; moreover, the administration of VNII-KANeftGas was required to pay me in full for my absence from work. Apparently, the demagogic Soviet system, in order to prove the omnipotence of the working class, had written some unexpected idiosyncrasies into the law. Then along came a joker - a daredevil, who threw down a challenge, and established a precedent in the area of private issues.

I openly gave notice to the Party Committee and to the director of the institute that I might utilize this law. "Ah, does this mean you want to live by the law, and not by the rules of the party of Lenin, like a lawyer?" my educator, the lathe operator asked me indignantly. This conversation was already becoming more dangerous, and I barely managed to ignore his provocation.

Several days later, I set out to visit the regional magistrate, where an employee drew me aside to explain the essence of the problem. Finally a telephone call was made in my presence, and this resolved the whole problem in a flash. I was free to leave my job.

In the summer of 1965 I started at my new job by filling out specialized forms with lots of questions, including the following: "Where do your parents live, and if they have died, where were they buried?" Another one was: "Where do the brothers and sisters of the person filling out this questionnaire live, and where do they work?" The longer your list of relatives, the more time was required to start your real job because the Chekists have to spend more time to check everything out.

The purpose of the questionnaire was to grant a security clearance with access to classified documents, in exchange for signing an obligatory pledge to keep the secrets which would be entrusted to you in your job. It was necessary to renew this clearance every 5 years. You had to go through the same process all over again.

Since no one made any notes when they filled out the questionnaire the first time, everyone had to be very careful not to allow any discrepancies to appear five years later, when filling out the new questionnaire. It's entirely possible all the questionnaires were fully checked out by officials, since the original verification process took about 3 months.

Then I was given instructions about my duties as a secret holder. I was entirely prohibited from having any contacts with foreigners, from making any trips abroad, and from visiting any restaurants, exhibitions, museums, libraries etc. without a special permit from the Second Department.

I heard nothing from my future employer until after this process had run its course. Then they contacted me to let me know that I could go to a doctor for a medical checkup, to see if I met the requirements of the Post Office Box – the place of my future employment. The checkup was also complicated, with numerous analyses, and these procedures took about 2 weeks. My health turned out to be good enough.

And so, on November 30th 1965, I finally passed through the militarized guard post into the enterprise known as Post Office Box 702 for the first time. From there I went to the Analytical Department, which was in the main laboratory building (GLK), where access was guarded in the same way, and I had to show my pass once more.

On the way there, I was shaken by the appalling view of dirty old one story brick buildings. On the left side of the path, pilot plants which had been constructed in the 19th century or earlier littered a large part of the territory occupied by the Post Office Box (which later became known as GOSNIIOKhT – pronounced ghosnee-okht). Smoggy white clouds puffed up over dirty roofs of these buildings covered by black bitumen, and there was a whistling sound from the escape of compressed air of some unknown gas from numerous exhaust pipes. This gave it all a dangerous and oppressive aura you couldn't shake off.

A revolting smell was leaking from a few open doors and broken windows. You could see people dressed in dirty jumpsuits with white skull caps on their heads inside these rooms and near the doors. From that first time until the last days of my residency at GOSNIIOKhT, I was never able to shake off the unpleasant sensation created by these buildings, which were already half destroyed by time. (Later I heard that some new, but terrible and featureless buildings were built in place of some of them).

The new nine-story administration building, which faces onto the Highway of Enthusiasts, is of necessity a modern architectural devil, but it only covered up the repulsive view of the decrepit ghost structures. All of those which remain standing were once jailhouses for political prisoners or sharashka[10]. Before the Second World War and later there was a factory there for the production of mustard gas. Eyewitness accounts document that in October 1941, the staff buried several metric tons of mustard gas in trenches near what is now the main laboratory building (the GLK), as German troops were approaching Moscow. No steps were taken to destroy or degrade the agent. It was simply dumped untreated into the ground.

The GLK is a three-story brick structure built in 1961. The building extends so that it is butts up to the tramway tracks, and trains are constantly rumbling by, creating a small but audible noise in the building and vibrations, which are a nuisance for those working with highly sensitive physical chemical instruments.

On the short end, the GLK is connected with another old three-story building, by a second story bridge which then turns sharply left and connects to yet another horrible old three-story building. This third building looks out on the Highway of Enthusiasts, and almost connects by cast iron rails with part of a bridge that was built across the rail line, shortly after World War II by German prisoners of war. From this bridge it is possible to get a good view of a large part of the GOSNIIOKhT territory, with its buildings. Numerous ventilation pipes are sprouting out of the roofs, direct evidence that a strong ventilation system is working in these buildings – the specters of the work of a chemical laboratory.

Aleksei Beresnev was the head of the Analytical Department, and he was also head of Chromatographic Laboratory 25. He briefly explained the goal of the work of his department and laboratory. Basically it consisted of developing methods for routine analyses at the experimental manufacturing site, and small scale laboratory analysis of the synthesis of chemical agents and their precursors. He also gave me instructions for compiling scientific research records and the basics of the secrecy regime. I was given two weeks to study the regime requirements and safety technique from numerous manuals and to pass an exam on the safety, medical, fire and other requirements for working independently. The exam was to be given by a commission chaired by Aleksander Shchekotichin, the Deputy Director of Science.

I had to go through numerous safety briefings, on fire and gas-handling technologies in special departments, the heads of which had to sign off on my papers, proving that I had satisfactorily passed through these routine procedures.

Also, I had to become familiar with their system of keeping records in the secret work journals. In the GLK, (as in the other scientific research and experimental corps), this was organized by the local branch of the First Department [11], which controlled every aspect of all systems of paperwork, including sending and receiving secret letters, reports, methodologies, instructions, and various dissertations, the secret library and archives.

Each scientist, coming to the job, was required to pass his "red certificate" (assistants and engineers giving their passes were receiving only notebooks) through a window at the First Department, and in exchange for that he received a briefcase or a suitcase with notebooks for records and accounts. Instructions about working with secret documents were included. All the lines were numbered in every notebook, and it was sewed with strong thread, the end of which was affixed to the last page with a stamped wax seal.

The registration of each notebook in the briefcase was recorded in an "inventory journal", which contained a specialized chart that kept track of the inventory number of the notebook, the number of pages, the date of the start of the notebook, the date of the verification and destruction of the notebook after it was fully used up, and whether or not its text had been typed up.

If at any time the notebook was traveling to a different department, or even to your boss, it was recorded in the appropriate column in the inventory journal.

State Secrets

It was extraordinarily difficult to persuade a scientist to give up his working notebook to storage, after filling only half of it out, since often the notebook contained results that would be needed several years later. But, if the space in the notebook was already used up, then it was already pointless to try to discuss the matter. This complicated everything and created difficulties at work, as each scientist, before writing up reports or scientific articles, had strongly abbreviated all the details and parts of the research process, often giving just the final results. You can imagine how terrible each scientist felt when operatives from the First Department were checking the content of his briefcase.

In this way, the work system in GOSNIIOKhT created great hardship, even for authors who were using their own reports and methods. No more than four copies of these materials were then typed up and approved by the Deputy Director of Science. Then they were stored in the "Special Library".

The author could only take out a copy of "his" report for a strictly limited time period, and you had to apply in writing for special permission to become familiar with the work of others. To get this special permission, you first had to go talk to the head of your department. Then the head of the First Department had to sign off on it, after he verified that the suitability of the applicant corresponded appropriately to the theme of the report (there was a special list for checking this compatibility). Then the approvals of the Deputy Director and the Director of the Institute were routinely required.

Ordinarily, it was practically impossible for a scientist to know the status of any problem, since he was not granted access to the card catalog of materials stored in the Special Library. Access was granted to only a very few people at the institute. Later on, as head of the Department of Foreign Technical Counterintelligence, I was given almost unlimited access. But in all fairness, I must say that I hardly ever used this privilege to familiarize myself with materials far removed from my sphere of professional interests. I think my reticence was based on common sense, since many of us knew that officers in the Special Library routinely kept track of everything that happened within their domain, for the Deputy Director. To bring yourself under the suspicion of the KGB was easier than trying to justify yourself later on.

During working hours, your notebook had to be placed only on the writing desk. Other notebooks, the inventory journal, and your instructions for storage procedures had to be placed in a private executive safe in the workroom. During lunch time, all notebooks were locked in this safe, and the head of the department kept a spare key.

In the evening, at the end of the working day, scientists had to put their notebooks back into the briefcase, which was then sealed in a special way with a personal seal with the inscription of Post Office Box 702 engraved on it. Later that was changed to the name of the institute – GOSNIIOKhT, with a five pointed star. Many years before this it was known as NII-42 (Scientific Research Institute 42), but some people believe that the name was changed to GOSNIIOKhT to mislead Western intelligence agents.

Though it is difficult to describe, this system created such a huge psychological burden on every person with a briefcase for secret material, even though they were compensated by a 15% pay increase.

Occasionally a scientist went home without returning his notebook. The head of the department or his deputy was responsible for compliance with these procedures, from the time he came to work until the last employee on his shift went home. When the duty officer from the First Department anxiously informed this boss that one of his employes went home without turning in the notebook, an alert was declared.

The boss tore the seal off the door and unlocked the room with his spare key. Then he entered the room and unlocked the safe of the negligent worker. All the contents of the safe were extracted and given to the First Department, on receipt. As a rule, the worker remembered about his blunder only when he got home, and suffered through the entire night without any sleep.

The next working day, a commission was established specifically to take up this matter, investigate the "case", and write up a report with the facts (of the worker's guilt).

The minimum punishment for this "crime" was an official reprimand by the institute and withdrawal of the worker's quarterly bonus, which sometimes made up as much as one quarter of his paycheck. Additionally, it was not so rare for all the personnel of the laboratory or department to be punished by cutting their bonuses for such a violation. So, the guilty person was responsible for losing money for everyone else. I think every scientist at GOSNIIOKhT experienced several anxiety attacks, waking up at night in a cold sweat with the sinking feeling that he forgot to turn in his ill-fated notebook. Losing your official GOSNIIOKhT seal brought on the same kind of punishment. Not only would it cost you financially, but you would suffer from nervous strain for no less than an entire month. At the workers' meeting, the department chairman tried to bear down on the guilty worker in every way, and this continued up until someone else was found guilty of the same crime.

There was another strict system for controlling note taking. Writing on anything like a scrap of paper was strictly prohibited. The Department of the Security Regime made routine periodic checks of the rooms of the scientists. If the officers of this department found any paper with notes, a strict punishment was handed out and the guilty scientist could lose a considerable part of his salary. It was sickening to watch some of these officers, who were recruited from the ranks of metal workers, lathe operators and other representatives of the working class, routing through the trash can in the workroom. Writing down any chemical formula, even having something to do with pesticides or water, on a scrap of paper, was considered an especially serious crime.

All waste paper and rubbish from the workroom were burned in a special incinerator, located within the institute territory, which was also used as a crematorium for the corpses of test animals which had been used in experiments with chemical agents. I'm sure they set up the system this way because all people were considered potential traitors by the KGB.

No one had the right to use either the formula of a chemical agent or of its precursors in the text of a report, and you also weren't allowed to use conventional chemical notation. There were several codes for each compound. One code was used for recording the "internal number" in the notebook, a second code was used for writing in scientific reports, and the third was used for recording in letters to other secret institutes or organizations. For example, Substance 33 – the code for the Soviet analogue of the well-known nerve gas VX, had to be written up in GOSNIIOKhT notebooks as M-01 (it also was given a trivial name such as "complex ether"), but in letters or reports it was necessary to write "Substance R-33."

Soman and sarin could be written in notebooks as ordoval-1 and ordoval-2, respectively, and accordingly as M-02 and M-03, but in reports and letters it was necessary to name these substances as R-35 and R-55.

Lachrymators (tearing agents), known in the West as agents CS or CR, were written in working notebooks as "Substance 65" and "Substance 74" respectively, and accordingly in letters renamed as Substance K-410 and Substance K-444.

The typist was not allowed to see any chemical formula combined with a specific code. Therefore, in place of a chemical name or a code, a bracketed blank space was left, which would be filled in later by hand by the author of the report. It was considered a crime if the scientist entrusted anyone else with this business, for example a lab assistant. Since the department chief had his informers in practically every room, violations of these restrictions would always be discovered and punished.

In 1983, Yevgeni Bogomazov, who was a senior scientist in the Physical Chemistry Department, had the misfortune to place his trust in his lab assistant. Someone reported this to the Security Department, and though Bogomazov was not expelled from the institute, he was docked 30% of his quarterly bonus. People thought that the KGB had shown great generosity.

My boss also explained to me the very important daily procedures for entering and leaving your workroom. In each workroom, a specific person was assigned the responsibility of sealing up the room at the end of each day, and had to turn the key in to the duty officer of the department, who checked the rooms and issued receipts for the keys.

The following workday morning, the responsible person was required to check the integrity of the seal on the door of the room and to open it. Workers from the Security Department often violated the door seal and then sealed it back up with another seal. If the person responsible for the room did not notice such a "violation of the internal regime", sanctions were poured out on him accordingly.

From the beginning of my work at GOSNIIOKhT, I was instructed that no one had the right to take any kind of notes on sheets or scraps of paper at any scientific meetings. If the organizer of the meeting specified that you were allowed to take notes, and the types of notes you could take was determined, then you had to go to the First Department to receive a special notebook with numbered pages. At the end of the meeting, you had to return the notebook immediately to the First Department. If you were a visitor attending the meeting from another organization or enterprise, and were given the right to take notes, then you had to give your special coded address. At the end of the meeting your notebook would be sent to the First Department of your organization. There was a special mailing network system (spetzpochta) run by the KGB for these kinds of communications.

The system of handling notes mentioned above is working very strictly throughout all organizations and enterprises which work with classified information. For that reason, it is simply disinformation when some people in the U.S.A. are writing tall tales in their books, describing how people from the former Soviet Union took notes at secret meetings and carried them out in their briefcases, reading them in the car, etc. No such kind of "business conduct" would ever be tolerated by the KGB. Without any hesitation, this person would be sent behind bars forever, as a spy. Every meeting like this was supervised by one or two officers from the Department of the Security Regime, so no one could take away any notes, even by accident.

Additionally, the Foreign Technical Counterintelligence Department was responsible for making sure the meeting room was acoustically and electronically secure. As the former chief of that department, I can tell you that if you attended any meetings outside of your enterprise, a special written invitation was sent to your boss through the special KGB mail service.

There is also a special high frequency telephone system for emergency calls. It is located inside a special room with no windows, in the Special Communications Service Department[12] of GOSNIIOKhT. This room is electronically and acoustically protected. The Director of the Institute, some of his chief deputies, and the chiefs of the so-called special services departments also have alternating high frequency telephones (with the insignia of the U.S.S.R. in the center of the dials), which are slightly less protected than the special phone in the special room. They have a special telephone book for these phones, and I know from personal experience using this system, that all these phones are supervised and controlled by the KGB. It is absolutely impossible to invite someone to a secret meeting, using an ordinary phone, even if you could distort your voice in some way as the aforementioned authors of tall tales are saying, to try to confuse readers. It should be pointed out that scientists and their assistants were strictly attached to their work places and didn't have the right to visit any other laboratories or departments without special permission.

Every person in this secret Post Office Box had his own pass with his photo on it and some coded pictograms showing his permit for entrance to the guardian of the building. On the inner side of the door of each laboratory room a list is posted of people who have the right to enter.

The first time I came into the territory of this Post Office Box I was literally stunned, because before that I couldn't even imagine how all of this is disgusting, insulting and psychologically damaging for normal human beings. I never stopped to think that I sold myself for money. Life behind the doors of GOSNIIOKhT was not free, and everyone there felt himself or herself to be some kind of person who was deprived of some of the most basic rights. Luckily it was only for 7 hours a day, five days a week. The atmosphere surrounding the relationships between scientists and their bosses was doubly totalitarian. It was so oppressive that you had to be lucky and a real survivor to make any progress in your scientific career. Every scientist knew that he had to pay a high price for the relatively high salary and some privileges given by this employment system.

Most workers understood that they were facing a certain amount of danger and agreed to this risky work in exchange for hazard pay. GOSNIIOKhT compensated employees that spent at least three weeks of the month working with chemical agents with a "hazard bonus" that could significantly increase a worker's salary. For the junior analytical and physical chemists who worked directly though less frequently with chemical agents, the extra pay totaled a maximum of 33 percent of their salary. Those working with chemical agents, not precursors, on a daily basis, received a hazard bonus equal to 55 percent of their salary. This bonus was normal for researchers who synthesized new chemical agents or were involved in the associated medical and biological research and testing.

Employees had to log the number of days they spent working with chemical agents, and they also kept consumption logs in which they recorded the dates and amounts of chemical agents used. From time to time, a special commission audited these records in all of the departments. If they were incomplete, the commission publicly punished the heads of the departments for their negligence and omissions and deprived employees of their bonuses. One could often see researchers feverishly filling out work registers and consumption logs on the day before an audit.

More often, employees who had not accumulated enough hazard pay days simply made false entries in their journals and then destroyed the chemicals involved all at once. To deter this practice, officers from the Second Department of the Security Directorate could force the assistants to weigh ampoules with chemical agents in their presence, but these controllers never knew what was in the ampoules. Consequently, scientists working with chemical agents could do anything they wanted with the chemicals and still get paid their bonuses. The hazard pay system also encouraged abuse from senior GOSNIIOKhT officials, who could punish and manipulate employees by assigning them work that did not involve chemical agents and thereby severely curtail their earnings.

Other than the bonuses, work with hazardous substances did have its perks for some. Every employee working in hazardous conditions had a yearly paid vacation of thirty-six working days.

Employees with a master's degree received an additional week of vacation time, and those with a doctorate got an additional two weeks of vacation. They could take their holidays free of charge at a special resort for people in the chemical industry, which was located in Yalta on the Black Sea coast. GOSNIIOKhT employees who regularly worked with chemical agents could also opt for early retirement. Women could retire at the age of 45, if they had worked with chemical agents for at least 8 years, while men could retire at the age of 50 if they had 10 years of hazardous work. GOSNIIOKhT had a lunch cafeteria that was free for all employees except the laboratory and departmental chiefs, though this could hardly be called a "benefit" because the food quality and choice were so poor. GOSNIIOKhT's leadership managed to skim enough funds from the main employee lunch cafeteria to allow themselves their own separate senior staff cafeteria, where the food quality and choice were arguably better.

Chapter 7
GOSNIIOKhT's Tangled Bureaucracy

Deputy Director for Science Aleksander Shchekotikhin

From my very first day on the new job, I shuddered when I thought about the arrangements, because I understood how difficult it would be for me to fit in there.

The important part was to pass the exam on safety technique given by the Deputy Director of Scientific Work, who was also head of one of the divisions at the enterprise.

There were several such divisions. Work connected with the synthesis of new chemicals or physical-chemical and medical-biological research and its associated analytical security work, were all carried out in specialized departments, under the supervision of Deputy Director Aleksander Shchekotikhin. According to the words of several senior scientists, he "committed atrocities" with his exam on safety technique.

When I came to take the exam, I was taken aback by his sad invalid state, which was incongruous with his status as a deputy director. When Shchekotikhin was a colonel working as a senior researcher at TSNIIVTI[13], they were in the process of synthesizing fluoro-ethers, and the retort flask his reaction was running in exploded. He was missing part of his right arm up to his wrist, and in its place was a shining prosthesis. He was also missing two fingers from his left hand. The expression on his face was haughty and sarcastic. He gave the impression of a man who had already decided that anyone who came to him must know that the way things would turn out would depend on his superior will. He seemed pleased by his ability to give an unsatisfactory grade to someone with a higher scientific rank than his – to a doctor of science or a professor.

Shchekotikhin was not lacking in talent. He had graduated from the Military Academy of Chemical Defense with a gold medal and had a master's degree in chemistry. All the same, he was not working at a job engaged in real science, and he understood his vulnerability in this respect very well. In the time I got to know him, he turned into some sort of human weathervane, trying to anticipate the orders of the Director of GOSNIIOKhT, Ivan V. Martynov, providing his boss with an ideological screen.

At the meetings and conferences of the Science Council, where he presided with great pleasure when the director was absent, he squandered his previously prepared witticisms, and made a practice of peppering the text of his speeches with satire. Often it was about people who were falling out of favor or candidates for demotion.

Possibly a science bureaucrat needed these qualities to be successful, and Shchekotikhin certainly had more than his fair share of them. In certain circles, he could blurt out remarks to scientists of well-known ethnicity, such as: "They've turned the institute into a synagogue, you understand." But this did not save him from the caustic gossip of other anti-Semitic types like Aleksei Beresnev, Konstantin Karavanov and others, because they said Shchekotikhin was half Jewish himself, and his wife was also Jewish.

It seems to me that Shchekotikhin was a sincere believer in the greatness of Stalin, and he did not conceal his admiration for the man, to his very last day on the job at GOSNIIOKhT. When he invited me for first time into his office for my formal introduction, his first question to me was: "So, Vil Sultanovich. You're a Tatar. Tell me how you oppressed us all for 400 years under the Tatar yoke!" I was horrified by this taunt. I was educated well enough to know that according to Russian historians Tatars did that[14], but even if it had happened it was so long ago. Weren't all nations supposedly equal under Communist friendship in the USSR, enjoying socialist development?

I could only blurt out, "Sorry. The Mongols destroyed our state first – the Bulgar State". The former colonel was more than satisfied by his offense and my discomfort. He continued, "Right now people began to forget who gave us a great victory and armed us against the imperialists. Surely you know who are responsible for this turmoil. They are pygmies in comparison with our great genius Stalin." After this introduction he took a magazine down from the bookshelf. It was the March 1953 issue of the journal *Proceedings of the Academy of Science of the U.S.S.R.*, in which a large memorial portrait of Stalin was printed, on the occasion of his death. In this very same issue there was an article by the same Shchekotikhin, which was published when he was a graduate student under the Lieutenant General and Academician, Ivan Knunyantz.[15]

Unfortunately, many of the departmental and laboratory heads I was soon to get acquainted with, thanks to my work in the Department of Analytical Chemistry, possessed equal or lesser qualifications than those of their Deputy Director of Science. Many of them admitted that they were engaged in "politics", lobbying for new rooms, laboratories, equipment, instruments and increases in staff and bonuses. For this, it was essential to become a "necessary man" to the director of the institute. At that time, Director Martynov had become a genuine gourmand in his choice of executives.

Almost every future chief had to come to his position through membership in the Party Committee, at whatever the cost might be. For this reason, the struggle for a spot on the Party Committee was surprisingly tough at our Post Office Box. It was not enough for a striving would-be director to place the people he needed there. Other department chairmen, secretly dreaming of pushing upward to even higher positions, pressed forward their own people in turn. You could count on your fingers the science-chiefs who did not participate in this loathsome campaign. Evidently, success depended on how up to date you were on all the behind-the-scenes intrigues relating to new appointments and the allocation of bonuses. Your success also depended on your ability to keep track of your rivals, to get deeply involved in the personal affairs of your victims and to make short work of them without pity, all in the name of the party.

There were several who especially distinguished themselves in this respect, bosses who played so well with other people on this disgusting Communist balalaika. They were Professor Vladimir Zoryan - who became Chairman of the Department of Medical and Biological Research ("MB" Department), his protégé Professor Grigory A. Patrushev- who later became the director of the institute, Vsevolod Dobrianski - the head of the laboratory of the "MB" Department, Victor Shulga- the head of another laboratory in the same department, and Vladislav Sheluchenko - head of Department "D" (Degasification). There was also Evgeni Fokin who, thanks to his tainted academician father, became chief of the laboratory for synthesizing chemical agents. Finally, I would like to mention Mikhael M. Fedyachkin, chief of the laboratory in the Analytical Department, and Professor Mikhael A. Englin, head of the laboratory for synthesizing fluoroorganic compounds.

Each of these people possessed exceptional talent in demagoguery, though they were not particularly flourishing in their scientific affairs. The last of them, Englin, without any embarrassment, held the infra-red spectra of research compounds upside down several times, because he hadn't taken the time to learn about them. Aside from his regular duties, he also served as chairman of the committee that examined and made decisions about the publication of scientific articles in the open press, especially those dedicated exclusively to peaceful problems. Although the decisions of this committee were not definitive and approval by the Central Directorate was also required, the final decision usually depended on this committee.

Under the leadership of Englin, this committee ruined many of my articles, which were dedicated purely to chromatographic problems. The reasoning of this professor was always primitive, and not subject to appeal. Once I brought an article entitled "New Chromatographic Methods for the Separation of Hydrocarbon

State Secrets

Gases" to this committee for scrutiny. "An article about gases?" asked the scientist-Chekist. "Well, no. This kind of business won't work, because you are disclosing the nature of the work of our enterprise. For instance, our laboratory is busy synthesizing gases." Then he peremptorily shot down my article.

Three months later at the next meeting of Englin's committee, when I brought a revised article with the title "New Chromatographic Methods for the Separation of Short-Chain Hydrocarbons" for consideration, the vigilant professor again rejected my work, saying this time: "Aha! This means a new method. Then you must take it through the patent application process and only after that come to me. Do you understand?" In truth, the limits of this veteran's "creativity" were unknown, and it was useless to try to change his mind. He knew very well that he was holding on to his position only by his fervor. At one time Englin had also been "head chemist" on the problems of synthesizing chemical agents capable of breaking through gas mask filters.

Unhappily for Englin, difluoromethylamine was his only "invention", and luckily it was incapable of breaking through the gas mask filters. It could only burn up instantly in the air. However, this was ample reason to award him with a doctoral degree and the title of professor.

Another person mentioned above, Vladislav Sheluchenko, did not go any further in the service of science than Englin. I frequently collided with him in our discussions of my GC methods of analysis of chemical agents. My arrival at Post Office Box 702 corresponded to a period in time when chromatography was beginning to come into its own as a method of analysis. This indisputably progressive method was already widely used in all industrialized countries and in many areas of science and industry, so I was astonished to find that they were only beginning to apply chromatography at GOSNIIOKhT.

Partially, this situation was due to the difficulties connected with the chromatographic instruments used in the area of defense. During the analyses of highly toxic compounds, the instruments themselves became increasingly dangerous, because probes of deadly compounds were injected and forced through them with inert gas from a tank connected to the gas chromatograph. Any breach of hermeticity, spilling of the probe, breakage of the microsyringe dosing the probe, or another mishap could give the operator enormous trouble, even severe poisoning. For example, if we introduced a probe of 10 micro liters of Substance 33 into the instrument, and for any reason that probe made contact with someone, the consequences would be extraordinarily severe for him.

The construction of the lab bench and the chromatographic instruments was such that, there were absolutely no guarantees that an accident could not occur to poison people. However, thanks to the enthusiasm of the young scientists at this time, especially Igor A. Revelski and Yuri Novikov, I was able to find solutions to these problems and make progress on chromatographic methods for creating routine analyses of numerous samples.

Since I was the first person to come to the Post Office Box with a science degree granted for research in the field of chromatography, I wanted to develop methods for the detection of microconcentrations of chemical agents in various media.

Before that, they had used traditional indicator methods for making judgments about the nature and concentrations various chemical agents, by examining the color and intensity of the dyed by-products of the reaction. There was (and still is) a large laboratory at GOSNIIOKhT for researching these methods. In those days Lev Brovkin was the head of this laboratory, and along with Sheluchenko, he blatantly wrestled to keep a monopoly in this important area. Whoever dared to propose an alternative method was treading on their turf and became their personal enemy. They struggled against him in every possible way.

Naturally, my boss warned me about this in advance, when I had proposed researching chromatographic methods for determining the presence of soman and sarin in the air and water.

Receiving the go ahead for this work, I finished the project along with my co-workers relatively quickly and wrote up a report, which had to be approved by the Deputy Director of Scientific Work, Shchekotikhin. He was a clever old hand at this kind of thing, and he decided to avoid the risk of getting drawn into a dispute with Brovkin and his protégé Konstantin A. Guskov, another deputy director in the science area. So, in keeping with the purest tradition of Soviet bureaucracy, he gave my report to Guskov for approval.

Along came the year 1967, and chromatographic methods were universally acknowledged as progressive. They were being widely adapted for solving many problems in industry and scientific research. In our Post Office Box, however, they had decided to arrange a kind of a trial for them, the goal of which was to reject the use of chromatography for all military chemical agents.

Guskov called a meeting in his work office to decide this question. Just in case my boss Beresnev should show up, he sent for his deputy, Vasily Lysenko, who had been schooled for many years by our Party Committee. He had become an expert in these kinds of matters, and always managed to escape from them without defining his position, since he was simply a conformist.

In the course of an hour, I had to explain the fundamentals of chromatographic methods to the deputy, but I saw how they listened to me without any confidence, as though I myself had invented the methods and was trying to foist them off on my audience.

Up to that time I had acquired considerable experience lecturing on the subject of gas chromatography, including a three year period when I taught a course, while trying to increase the qualifications of the engineers and leading staff members of the Ministry of Chemical Industry. I had also taught a few brief courses for interested people at the Post Office Box, since I was trying in every possible way to promote gas chromatographic (GC) methods into areas of analytical chemistry that attracted me.

But in this meeting all my efforts were for nothing, and I saw that they simply didn't want to understand me. This reminded me of another event that many authors wrote about.

In the beginning of 1930 a lecturer came to talk to some peasants about the tractor, how it was built and how well it ploughed. At the end of the presentation, the lecturer asked the men if they understood everything. One of them responded: "Sure, we understand our comrade very well. Only, we don't understand... Where do we harness all this to the horses?"

The difference here was that those attending our meeting were literate, and possibly they understood what they were told. But, the workings of the power structure at the closed Post Office Box gave them the ability to reject any new work with impunity, discredit it, and discredit the researcher, while laughing at any attempts to encroach upon their monopoly. If necessary, they could turn down the very scientific method, and the scientist would think "Thank God! At least this didn't mess up my life."

"Aha! I understand that as a person, you don't know the physical chemical properties of sarin. You have to know that sarin disintegrates before it reaches 150 degrees Centigrade, but in the injector of your chromatograph it was 180 degrees Centigrade!" Sheluchenko happily exclaimed.

"How could you use a flame-ionization detector for the registration of sarin, when it had to have been completely burned up there?" inquired the former secretary of the Komsomol Committee of the Post Office Box.

My replies were simple and obvious for specialists, as say a keyboard of a computer would be for any American student these days. I even tried referring to a classified American source on the use of GC methods at a factory producing sarin.

"You know, Vil Sultanovich, for your information, this is a typical example of disinformation, which the imperialists are using so well!" exclaimed Sheluchenko, emphasizing his special closeness to sources of this kind of information. All that was left for me was to shut up and accept my defeat.

I was only sorry that my work was not used for more than a year, since it was being passed along from one expert to another for second opinions, and this gave Guskov the chance to direct it into the closed library of the institute, without his signature.

Actually, I was pleased with this outcome. "It's good that they can't destroy anything at all," I thought at that time.

But now I think that it wasn't very good for all of us, because this same Sheluchenko became the chief specialist on issues of the destruction of chemical weapons in Russia, and to a considerable degree our safety depended on his level of knowledge. This "chief specialist" has never worked a single day in a laboratory, nor has he ever worked on researching methods of chemical weapons destruction. Instead, he simply became the chief of all those who were working on this problem. If a man in Russia is a boss, then it means he is automatically acknowledged as "smart". The reason for this is that life there flows with difficulty, mirroring the tradition so well communicated in this old adage: "If I'm the boss – you're a fool. If you're the boss, then I'm a fool."

It seems there were no limits to the imagination of someone who was dreaming of being seated on the Party Committee, to be near to the Director and other chiefs at the weekly meetings and to quietly, unobtrusively come closer to this maniacal feeding trough.

Sergei Vtorigin had been working for many long years as a senior research scientist, but he did not see any prospects for further advancement. So he simply went to the secretary and volunteered to take minutes at the Party Committee meetings, or if necessary, to rewrite them. Up to this point, a girl with a high school education had done this job. Anyway, Sergei easily managed to persuade the new secretary of the Party Committee, that he met the requirements, because you had to have a master's degree in chemical science for this important party work.

After a year of rewriting the minutes, Sergei Vtorigin's dream came true, and he became a responsible member of the Party Committee and chief of the laboratory. For this he dispatched a respected and entirely capable specialist, Lev Kaufman, to his retirement and pension.

You should have seen how happy Vtorigin was, sitting in his office, as the head of the laboratory! He didn't consider it necessary to try to conceal his glee, sitting in an armchair behind a table with three telephones and a switch for a loudspeaker for dealing directly with his subordinates.

The secretary of the Party Committee usually was one of the shift engineers from the experimental plant of GOSNIIOKhT. Those engineers were really obtuse. They were not even thinking about anyone's scientific career, because they deeply hated people from science. I believe that in their case the "general line" of the Party was properly reflected – support for the working class.

Although the director of the Institute had considerable power over all business, his fate depended considerably on party affairs and the way in which he could be represented to the Raikom (Regional party Committee), by the Moscow City Party Committee and by the secretary of the Institute's Party Committee.

This secretary had his own direct channel to the Raikom, independent of the director. Additionally, the Institute was supervised by a special representative from the Central Committee of the CPSU, who primarily carried out the party influence through the Party Committee secretary. It was clear that the party organs always had the last word, and the fate of the director and the entire institute depended on them.

In the beginning of the 1970s, Director Martynov's relations with the Ministry of Chemical Industry were not "approved", and several times they registered "unsatisfactory" remarks for him in the "Socialist Competition". This meant that the director could have been entirely swept away from his post. However, his party channels not only protected him from possible dismissal, but also GOSNIIOKhT began to change internally and quickly attained the status of a leading enterprise. Our Institute was given greater funding, in the form of currency, which allowed them to acquire a large consignment of modern instruments from the West, especially those produced in the United States.

Our institute acquired the following instruments – a nuclear magnetic resonance spectrometer (NMR) used to study the structure of chemical compounds and to identify them, electroparamagnetic instruments used for the same purpose, unique x ray crystallography equipment, infra-red and ultra-violet spectrometers, chromatomass spectrometers, and other chromatographs used for carrying out serial elemental analysis and other tasks.

We knew that these instruments were on the list of equipment prohibited for trade to the U.S.S.R., but native ingenuity, and certainly the generosity of our trade agents in the West (who made deals through intermediary firms organized by the KGB), easily allowed us to circumvent all the trade barriers. Since the Western firms could not have written "to GOSNIIOKhT" on the invoices for the instruments, this work continues at the so-called open institutes. We became familiar with Mircotec chromatographs in Laboratory 25, and with Varian at the Institute of Synthetic Alcohols. I was part of a group that worked together with English engineers, to make adjustments to the chromatographs for the first time.

These renovations at GOSNIOKhT were the result of the kind of work they were conducting. Our institute was equipped for modern research and nicely supplied with imported instruments, though not as lavishly as would come to pass in 1972.

My work was stimulated to a considerable extent by the receipt of the new chromatographs, since they made it possible to selectively determinate phosphoorganic chemical agents and their precursors.

The GOSNIIOKhT Party Committee and Deputy Director Konstantin Guskov

Let us return to the question of the selection of the Party Committee secretary, since this will help us to understand more about our work.

Yuri Mochalov, who worked on the start-up section crew in the Kazan Plant for Organic Synthesis that produced ethylene oxide, had learned more than everyone else about the Party Committee secretary's work at GOSNIIOKhT. His only "positive" quality was his naïve and total belief in Communism, which he demonstrated with great expression once during a meeting of his work unit's party group. During his speech, with a passionate oath of loyalty to the ideals of Lenin, he gestured dramatically, even ripping off part of his shirt.

Yuri spoke very poorly while sharing his thoughts, and for this reason he decided to disguise the defects in his thinking with the drama. It was of no use. After this they noticed him and promoted him to the position of secretary of the Party Committee. All the same, Yuri never, until the end of his days as secretary, learned to articulate. However, that didn't stand in his way when he wanted to lecture some poor professor from the party meeting rostrum. "This means, Nicolai Aleksandrovich, you understand, the party can't stand by indifferently….. It means for you, you understand, bedroom business. We, you understand, had to shake out your sheets... it means, you understand..."

Behind this nonsense tirade was the true menacing control of the Communist Party over the lives of the people. The ubiquitous presence and the interference of the Communist Party into the private lives of researchers only intensified the bureaucratic tangles at GOSNIIOKhT. The institute's Party Committee actively engaged in the "moral upbringing" of its employees, which amounted to nothing more than the petty settling of personal scores between individuals. Veterans of GOSNIIOKhT can recall how the Party Committee wrapped its tentacles around Boris Medvedev, a young physical chemist who fell in love with his research assistant. In meeting after meeting, the Party Committee openly subjected him to insults and mockery. When Medvedev couldn't stand this persecution anymore, he deliberately exposed himself to Substance 33, the VX analog. He simply entered his workroom, took the ampoule of Substance 33, poured it into a glass with water and drank the mixture. Medvedev's death was so quick and violent that laboratory colleagues and doctors from GOSNIIOKhT's Medical Department could do little but helplessly watch him suffer and die.[16] No wonder so many scientists at GOSNIIOKhT, stifled by party control and interference into their lives and bureaucratic lies, simply turned to the bottle for escape.

Nevertheless, Mochalov proved to be ambitious and even finished a party school affiliated with the Moscow City Committee of the CPSU. He was even selected to become a member of this committee, but such high ambitions brought him down. One night he drank himself half to death and was lying in the street. He was picked up by the police and sent to the "sobriety station". Mochalov decided to scare the official with his membership certificate to such a high organization. Apparently, they were accustomed to clients who were much higher VIPs than Mochalov, so the supervisor of the drunk-tank reported "where he had to". Shortly after that, our secretary exchanged his party career for a trade union, where he was not able to run away from his swift defeat.

Another Party Committee Secretary, the one who replaced Mochalov, was Nikolai Golosov. He was an incredible colorless dimwit, but he was able to make his way through the apparatus of the Chemistry Department of the Central Committee of the CPSU. Once more, this showed everyone what kind of person was needed in those days, to work in the higher organs of power in the country.

I remember during the height of the battle by the organization "Democratic Russia", for further democratization of the country through the destruction of the CPSU's monopoly of power, that the party bosses came to the institute and Golosov was among them. One of the local members of "Democratic Russia" had said that there were no practical ways for working out alternative decisions and legislation in a one-party system in the country. In response to this comment, Golosov proclaimed "First of all, we prepare several variants for each decision in our department." As they say, it was useless to comment on this.

The advancement of Deputy Director Konstantin Guskov up the career ladder at Post Office Box 702, serves as a good example of how things worked. All departments and laboratories, which were engaged in researching the technological processes that were to be introduced into existing and new start-up factories, were placed under his command. He was also First Deputy Director of GOSNIIOKhT for a long time, and had right to sign the financial documents.

Guskov completed his master's degree at the Mendeleev Chemical Technical Institute of Moscow, while he was studying the technology of chemical agents. After that he came to work at Post Office Box 702, as the head of the experimental plant. He did everything that was required of him and became a member of the Party Committee. Then he became the paid secretary, automatically guaranteeing him the ability to get an even higher appointment, with the agreement of the Central Committee of the CPSU.

Shortly thereafter, Guskov became a deputy director. In all fairness, I must say that he was a rather talented engineer, able to quickly grasp the essence of a problem. He was not afraid of making tough decisions, which required considerable responsibility, because of their potential consequences. I was aware of this soon after the beginning of my work at the Post Office Box.

In the beginning of the 1930s, our enterprise had researched methods of developing ethylene oxide from ethylene, and from that step it was easy to get the military blistering agent known as mustard gas. It is well known that ethylene oxide also serves as a wonderful initial reagent for the synthesis of many chemical products (polymers, anti-freeze and others), and currently more than several hundred thousand tons are produced annually by the industrialized countries of the world. You can also produce ethylene sulfide from ethylene oxide. This can be transformed into diethylaminoethylmercaptan, which is a precursor for the chemical agent Substance 33. A special department existed in the enterprise, known as Technology of Organic Synthesis (TOS), and its goal was to research the technology of the compounds that carry the title "dual use" agents.

Many attempts were made at Post Office Box 702, to master the production of ethylene oxide from ethylene, but none were successful, including the unfortunate start-up of the factory section in the town of Salavat, Bashkortstan.

In 1967, when the Kazan Plant for Organic Synthesis had yet to master the latest improved technology, the annual worldwide production of ethylene oxide exceeded 60,000 tons.

As the creator of the chromatographic methods for analyzing reaction mixtures, I also participated in the long drawn out set-up of the plant in Kazan. The "Government Commission" on the start-up was under the leadership of Oscar Diment, who was the head of the TOS Department. He had been transferred there from the Ministry of Chemical Industry, where he had worked for a long time as Chief Engineer of the Main Administration "Soyuzorgsynthesis", which our Post Office Box was directly subordinate to. The Commission was composed of such ordinary members, that it appeared to me that Guskov suffered greatly since he did not serve as its chairman.

At work they explained that the alleged productivity of ethylene oxide fluctuated greatly, showing a tendency to constantly degrade. Guskov decided to investigate the reason for this, by analyzing the registered indices of the constants involved in the process (temperature of the reactor, maintenance of humidity in the reactant gas and others). He chose me to work as his assistant on this matter, and we worked for 15 out of 24 hours, unwinding the graphing tape that was several hundred meters long and plotted productivity graphs, using various parameters. Finally we found the reason for the declining efficiency of the working reactor. (Incidentally it was loaded with more than 10 tons of pure silver, since at that time in the U.S.S.R. it was not possible to manufacture a catalyst which covered the surface of an inert solid. We had 3 reactors filled with this quantity of silver.)

On the morning of the scheduled start-up, after finishing all the necessary preliminary work, a huge crack was found in the cup (the top) of this reactor. This was a terrible disappointment, since it proved that the reactor cover had been manufactured from ordinary steel, known as "steel 3". Notorious "steel 3" was something between cast iron and simple iron, suitable perhaps for manufacturing our celebrated Soviet tractors, which broke even before they began to plough the fields of the kolkhozes (collective farms).

Someone in the Construction Bureau had decided to "economize" on materials for the reactor cup, although its body was designed and manufactured from high quality stainless steel. In this case, the planning and preparations of the Soviet system meant the loss of almost half a year while waiting for the blunder to be corrected, despite an encouraging speech about the mastery of important matters for "defense" production.

In any case, our group managed to accomplish the production of this important precursor used for manufacturing Substance 33, at the Novocheboksary Chemical Industrial Plant. Guskov learned an important lesson from this: never to give up his place as the chief of a start-up commission, guaranteeing him numerous rewards and a good reputation, which usually rained down on him, purely by luck.

Truly Guskov became more experienced in this kind of business, being able to choose, if a quick victory was in greater doubt, or he could wait a bit if it were more convenient for him. In particular, at the 1971 start-up of the factory division for producing diethylaminoethyl-mercaptan at the Novocheboksary Chemical Plant, he conceded this role to Vladimir Rostunov, Chief Engineer at the Main Administration of the Ministry of Chemical Industry of

Russia -"Soyuzorgsynthesis". Ultimately in 1974 he reached his goal and received this Prize for the "creation of Soviet V-gas".

Now and then, we were surprised by the realization that Guskov managed his duties pretty well, even though he was strongly devoted to alcohol. Once in a while he went on a real bender at work. Sometimes, when he was barely standing on his feet, after drinking a lot of spirits in Brovkin's lab, his younger drinking buddies usually would pull him through the check-point, in order to get him into the company "Volga" car and take him home.

I spent about a year working on the 1971 start-up of the Novocheboksary complex, with my assistants Vladimir Forov and Yury Bugrov. Literally all of the equipment was brought to us from GOSNIIOKhT and assembled there by my assistants and some workers from the Department of Analytical Chemistry. My GC methods of analysis of the reaction mixtures of ethylene sulfide and diethylaminoethyl-mercaptan (and of course the products) were successfully applied at the start-up and later utilized by the section. The start-up brigade from our enterprise, at that time bearing the new name of our institute - State Union Scientific Research Institute of Organic Chemistry and Technology (GOSNIIOKhT), was headed by Vadim Makhlin, an acquaintance of mine from our student days at MITKhT.

Our factory section was stunned by the sight of the huge buildings and apparatuses there. This plant had to guarantee the production of 20,000 tons a year of the final product of the chemical agent known as Substance 33. So, this is how we evaluated the politics of détente in the international arena, operating at that time!

Some heated arguments were inevitable, during that start-up time. Once, when my analysis showed that samples of the end product contained significant impurities, the chemical analysis showed a clean end product. When they finally started to show a purity of more than 100%, it became crystal clear that these results from chemical analysis were simply false, since the methods used to obtain them were not selective.

Our Guskov did not give up control of the end product – chemical agent Substance 33, and he reported only to the bosses. Before that, he did not participate at all in this technological research process. All of the technical methods used in the manufacturing process at the Novocheboksary complex were carried out by Department "T", which was headed up by Professor Semeyon Lvovich Varshavski, who had garnered every imaginable Stalin and Lenin Prize.

Unquestionably he was a talented scientist, but it's unfortunate that Varshavski dedicated himself to such an ignoble business as researching the technical production of chemical weapons. He introduced highly qualified engineers and successful organizers into his group, capable people who were able to use everything hidden from the eyes of those simpletons who sprouted out of the party machine, in order to organize the massive production of chemical weapons in the U.S.S.R. The production of sarin, soman and Substance 33 were organized directly under his scientific leadership.

However, at the time of the Novocheboksary start-up, it was completely obvious, that the top leadership of GOSNIIOKhT was trying in every possible way to limit Varshavski. There were some simple reasons for this. First of all, he had all of those awards and the leadership thought that it was time for him to stop, since as some of them said "the Moor has finished his business and must go away." Also, he was vulnerable because of his answer on the celebrated "fifth point" of his questionnaire concerning nationality, namely he was Jewish.

The Start-up of the Novocheboksary Factory and the Downfall of Semeyon Varshavski

Department "T", which was headed by Varshavski at that time, consisted of two large laboratories. The boss of one of these was Professor Varshavski himself, and the other was run by an energetic and talented man, Igor Sergievski, who died suddenly after the set-up of the Novocheboksary factory. Still, I think the first Soviet industrial-scale production of ethylene sulfide was successful, exclusively thanks to his service. I know he had proposed using potassium rodanide in a reaction with ethylene oxide for the synthesis of ethylene sulfide (a precursor to diethylaminoethyl-mercaptan). The groundwork for the technology of Substance 33 was accomplished by Yury Privezentsev, Igor Sergievski, Veronica Patrikieva and others. I remember how distressed Sergievski was about Guskov. "He's a good man, but it's clear that he is hanging around Novocheboksary only for the awards," he said.

The set-up of this production facility took more than a year. During that time, we lived in apartments in the factory hotel, under highly constrained conditions. Aside from work, there was practically no entertainment other than card games, accompanied by drinking vodka and other strong liquor.

One of the deputies of Varshavski in those days was Yury I. Baranov, who is currently a deputy director of GOSNIIOKHT. He was deeply anti-Semitic, but he was also servile to the point of stupidity. All the same, he did everything he possibly could, in order to dispatch his boss to retirement with a pension, right after the start-up of the Novocheboksary complex.

Varshavski was excluded from membership to the Science Council at GOSNIIOKhT, since Leonid A. Sokolov, the Deputy Director for the Security Regime at that time, had decided that in his opinion, the application which Varshavski had submitted for permission to visit his daughter in Israel, amounted to "insolence." Up until this time, Varshavski had become rather a senior man, and naturally he wished to see his beloved daughter. No judgment was passed on this matter. Then he had a heart attack, but since he was in deep disgrace, they did not find a place for him at the privileged hospital where he and other leading scientists at GOSNIIOKhT usually went. Instead, they placed him in an overcrowded regional hospital, where he had to lie in the cold corridor. He caught pneumonia there and died several days later.

This is how the Soviet system repaid one of its own principal researchers on chemical weapons, a man who showed just a hint of divergence from the iron rules of totalitarianism.

I am thankful to him for his readiness to help young scientists, including myself. When I had difficulty and couldn't even get the theme of my doctoral dissertation approved, although the practical work had already been completed, Varshavski organized a seminar in his department with my report. The seminar under his chairmanship issued a very favorable and complimentary decision about my work, which undoubtedly played a very positive role in my scientific career later on.

The success of the start-up in 1973 of the Novocheboksary Factory for producing Substance 33, brought golden days of triumph to GOSNIIOKhT. The Institute's Director, Ivan Martynov, became a "Hero of Socialist Labor" and Konstantin Guskov received the Lenin Prize. The true author of the technology, Yuri Privezentsev, could have obtained this same prize after a long ordeal, but Martynov "persuaded" him to be satisfied with a medal of Lenin. When the Director asked Yuri which award he would prefer, "the highest award of the Motherland – the Order of Lenin, or simply the Lenin Prize," Yuri answered modestly, "I prefer to have both."

He did not pay such a high price for his audacity in the end though. Yuri Privezentsev was excluded from the list of candidates to be recipients. They found some people, who, under Martynov's leadership, were able to receive the author's certificate (the Soviet patent) for this technology, which was already operating in the Novocheboksary Factory. All this was done openly and with cynicism, in the hope that Privezentsev, would think about the Regime of Secrecy, would not be able to complain to anyone. But thanks to the success of the start-up with his technology, his work became well known to Leonid A. Kostandov, who was the Minister of Chemical Industry of that time. Yuri was granted an audience with the minister, and this meeting decided the fate of the award in favor of the real author of the technology.

It's well known that when the list of candidates for receiving the Lenin Prize was brought to the attention of Mstislav Keldish, who was then the President of the U.S.S.R. Academy of Sciences, he was very surprised not to see any academicians on the list. At that point he said that he did not believe that GOSNIIOKhT could resolve this problem.

Word came back quickly, that the academician Mikhael I. Kabachnik, who was from the Institute of Elemental Organic Compounds of the Academy of Sciences, should be included in the list. They were not embarrassed by the fact that he had no relationship to the problem at hand, other than the fact that he presented himself as a member of the Science Council at GOSNIIOKhT and tried to synthesize VX gas without any success.[17]

The Directorate of GOSNIIOKhT

Clearly GOSNIIOKhT reached its pinnacle under the leadership of Ivan Vasilievich Martynov, a retired colonel and a graduate of the Military Academy of Chemical Defense.

Martynov managed to avoid military service during the war in a very original way. In his army unit, he was fortunate enough to fall under a horse and received a disability certificate that kept him from the battlefront. Regardless of such a military service record, his subordinates, with the silent consent of their master, always introduced him as an honored veteran of WWII.

The "horse injury" didn't prevent Martynov from entering the Military Academy of Chemical Defense, and after graduation, he served at the UNKhV[18], and was monitoring GOSNIIOKhT. This service determined the future career of this vain "warrior".

GOSNIIOKhT was one of the main contractors for UNKhV, which formulated the technical tasks and the terms for conducting scientific research. A lot of the funding for GOSNIIOKhT was based accordingly, and UNKhV even had a special department and a Science Council composed of military scientists, chaired by the Deputy Director of Science for the Chemical Troops. This department was responsible for implementing the terms for conducting scientific research.

Apparently, Martynov's work as a supervisor was rather highly esteemed by this department, and his career was very successful. He successfully defended his master's thesis, supported by professors Leonid Soborovski and Sergey Ivin. Soon after that, he retired and came to GOSNIIOKhT as the Deputy Director for Science.

In 1961 after he had held this post for some time, he became the institute's director instead of Dmitri Kutepov, who then became the Deputy Minister for Chemical Industry of the U.S.S.R. The positions of the institute's Director, several of his deputies, the

State Secrets

Director of Scientific Research and his deputies were given only to a very special group of people. This group, which was known as the "nomenklatura," was the top of the elite ruling class or bureaucrats in the Soviet Union. These people were approved by the Central Committee of the CPSU, and enjoyed the most lavish privileges, including access to special stores, hospitals, resorts and schools for their children. GOSNIIOKhT itself was closely monitored by the Military-Industrial Commission (VPK), which was headed by one of the secretaries of the Central Committee of the CPSU[19].

As the new director, Martynov was energetic, pushy, and he possessed all the qualities necessary for an autocratic and bureaucratic management style. He did not tolerate any independence on the part of his subordinates. Shortly, he managed to change the fundamental direction of GOSNIIOKhT, from an institute with diversified operations into one specializing almost exclusively in the development and testing of new types of chemical weapons.

He shut down the Dzerzhinsky and Borislavsky branches of the institute in Western Ukraine as incompatible with the main thrust of GOSNIIOKhT's activities. Under Martynov's leadership, the Volsk branch in Shikhany was reorganized, and this branch over the course of time became a powerful center for chemical weapons development. Every year, increasing numbers of graduates from colleges and universities in Moscow, Leningrad, Saratov, Volgograd, and other cities came to work there. Many Saratov Military Chemical College graduates came to work at the pilot plant. Industrial products, provisions and goods were supplied directly from Moscow for this branch. The housing situation for employees was decent, and along with the rather privileged salary, it attracted young people.

Martynov rallied practically all of GOSNIIOKhT to help establish and launch the Novocheboksarsk Plant for manufacturing Substance 33 and CS gas. Oddly enough, this coincided with the complete termination of the industrial production of chemical weapons in the United States, and that is unfortunately a typical example of the two-faced policy of the CPSU.

In 1974, every record of every chemical weapons development

program and production was purged from the record, even from the secret lists of state secrets. This meant that GOSNIIOKhT and other institutions of the military-industrial complex found themselves operating outside of the law. For Martynov, moral issues have always been, and I am sure still are, of very little importance.

He was a man of a medium height, a bit swarthy, with dark hair and a decisive chin. His features combined to give the impression of a strong-willed face, and he reminded me of our "illustrious" movie actors – playing military leaders who followed our genius Stalin's instructions on defeating German armies. It seemed that he imitated them, and so his directorate also reminded us of military headquarters. Most of his staffers were former military officers, who played their roles as career military men with marked pleasure.

When any one of the scientists displayed ordinary civilian carelessness or clumsiness, the almighty Martynov did not hesitate to thunder out against him, regardless of who else was present. I am sure that he had practically no sense of humor, and he always took everything too seriously, strictly by the book like soldiers do. This is the reason why people tried to 'tune' him in the right way. They used to say that if someone got him to go in one direction, it was almost impossible to turn him back the other way.

Professor Vladimir Kurochkin told me that it was absolutely necessary to be the first person to get to the director's office and tune him properly. Only those who managed to get to the pompous director first were successful. My classmate from MITKhT, Professor Yuri Zeifman, who worked in Ivan Knunyantz's laboratory, characterized him as a "superman". I'm sure he was partially right.

Martynov was warm and fatherly to people in his inner circle, and anyone who succeeded in getting close to him was assured of a successful career. The director never forgot those people and patronized them like a baron. He had an excellent "nose" for new trends in synthetic laboratory work and always gave them the green light. Probably this was the reason why he supported Petr Kirpichev's team[20] at GOSNIIOKhT's Volsk branch. As soon as he learned about their work and their preliminary results in 1973, he arranged for them to be given top secret clearance, which meant the status "of the highest importance".

According to the senior engineer of this group, Vladimir Uglev[21], the team was provided with first class equipment on Martynov's directive, and was ordered to submit their reports to Moscow immediately, even in handwritten form. It turned out that the director was farsighted, not only because their work was highly important for the state, but also in the area of his personal interests. After Martynov received the highest award possible in the U.S.S.R., the "Hero of the Socialist Labor" for the successful start-up of the Novocheboksarsk Plant for producing chemical weapons, he felt inspired to become a member of the U.S.S.R. Academy of Sciences. A special vacancy was created for him before the next regular election to the academy, thanks to the Council of Ministers. However, he was not elected a Corresponding Member at first, despite excellent official support.

"This whole damn bunch of academicians and corresponding members! They are not bloody organized at all!" complained retired Colonel Foma Gorelov, Martynov's first aide and head of the Scientific Technical Department at GOSNIIOKhT, about the "irresponsible" electors.

Colonel Gorelov knew almost nothing about science, but he liked to recall incidents that had taken place during his service as Commander of the Special Battalion for Chemical Defense. "You see, one of my soldiers was bored to death without women and he became violent. And, you see, he screwed one of the local girls, well something like he raped her. So the case went into full swing. The investigator appeared and ordered us to arrange an identification line-up, presenting all the soldiers on the parade ground, without hats. The victim had to look at them and recognize the rapist. I agreed and asked him to come by with the girl the next day. But as soon as he left, I ordered an unscheduled bath-day and haircuts for the soldiers; they had to shave off all their mustaches.

The next day, you see, the investigator and the girl turned up. She made her way along the line and began to cry out from exasperation. "They all look the same!" she sobbed. "The rapist had a thick head of hair and a mustache," the unmarried girl recalled, in helpless despair."

So this was Colonel Foma Gorelov's way to show his quick

military wit. He savored telling this story with great pleasure, but he did not understand why people who listened to it turned away in embarrassment....

For nearly a year, Foma was busy trying to help his unlucky master become a corresponding member of the Academy of Sciences, and he was very upset about this failure. Apparently he missed the mark, assuming that high-level support would be enough for this undertaking to be successful. As a rule, the Academy of Sciences rubber-stamped the admission of candidates who were governmental people, the directors of the defense-oriented institutes. However, as people say, even a wise man stumbles. Sometimes, even a "superman's" candidacy was steam-rolled during sessions of the U.S.S.R. Academy of Sciences. Usually though, this kind of outcome was an exception, and it was interpreted as "inadequate work" with the influential members and the leaders of the Academy of Science clans.

At the next election, Martynov became a corresponding member, but this time they worked properly. Frequently you could see Volga cars rolling in, bringing different academicians and corresponding members to a house that was used as a hotel by GOSNIIOKhT. There they gathered for friendly, but lavish, dinner parties, with cognac and caviar, so that the guests had no cause to doubt the director's scientific merits.

The governmental decree, which established an institute at the U.S.S.R. Academy of Sciences for fundamental research of new chemical weapons principles, made it possible for Martynov to take a critical step towards getting a "high" scientific rank. According to the code accepted in the military-chemical complex, the term "physiologically active compounds" (FAV) was used as a screen for the forbidden term "chemical agents". So the new institute was called the Institute for Physiologically Active Compounds (IFAV), and Martynov was appointed its director (It is located in Chernogolovka, in the Moscow Region).

We know that the scope of the superman's authority was much too low there, unlike his reign at GOSNIIOKhT. He was unhappy, because he could not order people to accept his authoritarian rule. The young scientists there practically ignored their director for his "backwardness", and they imposed a secret boycott on him.

As soon as the Vice President of the U.S.S.R. Academy of Sciences, Yuri Ovchinnikov, saw that Martynov didn't keep up with his workload, he had a "serious conversation" with him. After that our hero began declining very rapidly and was replaced by a truly prominent scientist, the academician Nikolai Zefirov.

After the GOSNIIOKhT director Grigori A. Patrushev died, Martynov tried to get back into his "native easy chair" – the director's position, but it was already too late. I am not writing about this with malicious intent. I am simply satisfied that Martynov's plan to make the Institute of Physiologically Active Compounds, which belonged to the U.S.S.R. Academy of Sciences, into something similar to GOSNIIOKhT, failed. His lack of talent wasn't the only reason for it. It also happened because young scientists were disgusted with the "special themes" he had proposed.

Some well-known scientists were contacted by my lawyer Aleksander Asnis to become experts in my "case" after the Moscow City Court sent it back for further investigation in 1994. Their reactions showed how strong this disgust and their devotion to democratic ideals were. Academician Nikolai Zefirov, Director of IFAV at the Russian Academy of Sciences, and Oleg Nefedov, Vice-President of the Russian Academy of Sciences, were among those who agreed to participate in the expertise.

The retirement of Martynov unleashed a furious competition for the director's post. Although the Ministry of Chemical Industry backed another candidate, Grigory Patrushev enjoyed the Central Committee's favor and became director of GOSNIIOKhT in 1979. The appointment astonished many people since few had ever noticed that Patrushev had such mighty contacts within the party. He didn't flaunt his connections, but for anyone paying close attention, the signs had always been there. Patrushev headed the Biomedical Department, and he managed to win funds for a new building to house his laboratories. His fiefdom grew so large that people began to speculate that it might separate from GOSNII OKhT and become its own entity. Such growth does not happen on its own.

GOSNIIOKhT was populated mostly by chemists, and most of

the department chiefs resented the appointment of a medical professional to lead GOSNIIOKhT. They had hoped the rival candidate Guskov would get the post, and they regarded Patrushev's appointment as an alarming sign for their careers. I did not feel that way though. I knew Patrushev as a highly cultured person and an excellent specialist, so I was originally pleased when he became director.

The pressures of the job must have weighed on him though. Within just a year, Patrushev was transformed into a short-tempered and impatient administrator. Aside from that, Patrushev had a tendency to be mean-spirited. If he disliked someone he could not resist the temptation to victimize that person using the harshest ploys of Soviet bureaucracy. Patrushev's other shortcoming was his blind faith in Communist ideals. Like many others, I did not share his passion for Stalin, since Khrushchev had by that time revealed the despicable toll that Stalin's autocratic policies had taken on the country.

Personally, I think Patrushev became so unbalanced because his position was tenuous, in part due to his extremely frosty relations with the young Deputy Minister of the Chemical Industry, Sergei Golubkov, who had objected to his friend Konstantin Guskov not becoming the new director. Golubkov never missed a chance to wound Patrushev's pride, so Patrushev had to be careful not to offend the overconfident and capricious deputy minister. Patrushev's attempts to gratify Golubkov damned him. At the end of 1983, Patrushev came down with the flu that was raging through Moscow. Despite his illness and soaring temperature, Patrushev felt obligated to work so as not to incur Golubkov's wrath. His illness became much more dire, and despite intensive treatment, Patrushev died in 1984.

After his death, everyone expected Guskov to fill Patrushev's vacancy since he had powerful Golubkov's backing. On the day that the Board of the Ministry of Chemical Industry was to give its formal approval to Guskov's appointment, the GOSNIIOKhT staff was so confident of the outcome that banquet tables were laid out to toast to Guskov. When a rumor swirled around the institute that Victor Petrunin, the former director of the Volsk branch, was a dark horse candidate, nobody took it seriously. Before the board meeting began, however, the former First Secretary of the Saratov Regional Party Committee and acting Deputy Prime Minister of USSR, Vladimir Gusev, called Vladimir Listov, the Minister of Chemical Industry, on Petrunin's behalf. Listov announced Petrunin's appointment, surprising all members of the Board, demonstrating once again party's control of key decisions.

Petrunin became "wiser" over the years, working for a long time in the provinces in GOSNIIOKhT's Shikhany branch. There he learned the art of managing people Soviet style. Relatively quickly, he understood that his career depended on how well he was able to meet and greet his bosses visiting from Moscow. He had to do his best to indulge his guests in every possible way, arranging trips to the Volga, where they could rollick on the estate of the late Count Orlov.[22] This lifestyle strongly attracted him, because he liked to drink and to please his guests with his singing. Petrunin loved playing the role of a magnanimous baron. And why not celebrate, when hundreds of people from his institute were forced to work on the estate, for a few months out of each year without pay?

Once Petrunin became Director of the Volsk branch, you could often see him riding in a troika (the traditional Russian carriage with three horses) on the neighboring collective farm. Tipsy, happy and rosy-cheeked from the fresh steppe air, he was sitting in the sleigh singing popular Russian folk songs, while he accompanied himself on the Russian accordion.

Once, during one of those trips to the Volga River, the hospitable Petrunin gave his guests a big scare. After toasting to his "dear guests" many times, and after singing numerous Russian romance solos, the not entirely sober host of the party, "Vityusha", disappeared. The guests from Moscow didn't seem to take any notice. It was a beautiful romantic night, with bright stars in the sky. An enormous bonfire was surrounded by tables decked out with salmon, caviar and other scarce gourmet foods from the institute's storage room. No one had any gloomy premonitions, and so nobody began looking for the singer, as the need for folk songs and dances reached its peak. As usual, no one remembered the end of the party. They found themselves in their cozy beds, but their host was not among them.

In the morning, suddenly one of the Muscovites saw something that looked like a human body under the steep precipice of the riverbank, near the estate. He cried out desperately in fear, and the guests immediately understood that this body could only belong to Victor Petrunin. The fearful guests made their way down the steps on the hill, barely dragging their feet, because no one had fully recovered from his hangover.

As they tried to reach their poor "Vityusha", it became clear that this was a silly and absurd death. The steep slope and height of the cliff did not leave any doubts about the tragic outcome. That was why all of the people who were running were amazed to see that one of the guests, who had already reached the high thin grass with the sprawling body, was laughing so loudly and merrily. Those who approached him soon understood that the "body" really did belong to "dear Vityusha", but he was just in a deep sleep. Even the happy cries of the overexcited guests could not disturb his snoring. Suddenly, Vityusha reacted to the suggestion to "have a shot of alcohol", and he sprang to his feet as if nothing had happened. You could see his face quiver only slightly, when he looked up at the steep cliff. Possibly, he remembered his flight off the cliff, the night before.

One of the prudent guests had brought a half-empty bottle of cognac with him (perhaps for the forthcoming commemoration or just from the need to have his precious drink with him at all times). He took it out and gave "Vityusha" a full glass, clinking his glass to the bottle to show that he too would like to have a sip.

Soon everybody was talking merrily and singing the praises of their host for his heroic deed and the strength of his body and spirit. Probably these qualities were not at all important for surviving a fall from such a height. Only the completely relaxed, yet strangely elastic body of a drunk could somehow deflect the shock of all the blows he took in his tumble flight off that cliff, while snagging tree branches, or banging into the compressed red clay protrusions sticking out of the wall. Also, since he was drunk, he never went into shock from the fear. Probably "Vityusha" just passed out and fell into a dream.

To his credit, this episode did not frighten Petrunin, nor did he stop trying to please his visitors from Moscow. He enjoyed meeting and seeing off his guests, until that happy day when he was appointed Director of GOSNIIOKhT. He understood that they held the key to his transfer out of this Hell-hole and into the capital. Until that moment, he had to work under a lot of other directors and continue as the Deputy Director for Science of the Shikhany branch of GOSNIIOKhT.

Chapter 8
Science and Scientists in GOSNIIOKhT

Russian VX gas –
Substance 33 and the Basics of the Russian Binary Weapons

The true author of Substance 33, Sergei Zotovich Ivin and the first person to synthesize it, his graduate assistant Iya Danilovna Shelakova, received only a few minor prizes of little significance for the successful start-up of the Novocheboksary pilot plant which produced it.

I am confident that this was a demonstration of "love" on the part of the Director Martynov, since Ivin was a talented scientist. Military specialists universally recognized his authorship of Substance 33 (O-iso-butyl-S-2 - diethylaminoethyl-methylphosphonothiolate).

Ivin repeatedly claimed that he had laid out the investigation of thiocholine ethers (which was used for creating the chemical agent VX), even before the well-known publication by the Swedish scientist Tammelin (O-ethyl -S-2- di-iso-propylaminoethyl-metylphosphonothiolate).[23]

After this publication about the high toxicity of thiocholine ethers, orders were issued in the U.S.S.R. for large-scale synthesis of this group of compounds at four different locations: TSNIVTI[24] (under S.Z. Ivin and I.D. Shelakova), GOSNIIOKhT (under Gladstein who lagged considerably behind Ivin - apparently this explained his jealousy), the Voroshilov Military Academy of Chemical Defense (in the department headed by Ivan Knunyants, who repeatedly declared his skepticism within his closed circle since he considered thiocholine to be a mistake made by Americans and Soviet specialists), and the Institute of Elemental Organic Compounds of the Academy of Science of the U.S.S.R. (under the leadership of Mikhail I. Kabachnik, though apparently Professor Sergey Godovikov ran the business.) This last group worked without any success, and it was completely dependent on Gladshtein, since the synthesis model was tested in GOSNIIOKhT (then known as Post Office Box 702).

The Administrative Building of GOSNIIOKhT, June 2002.

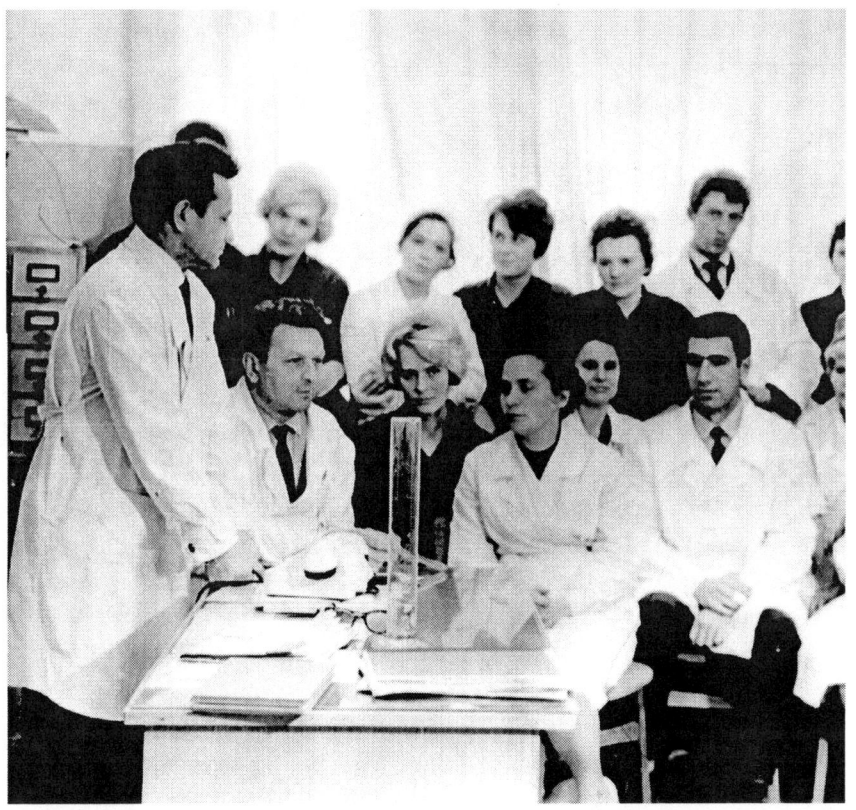

Professor Sergey Ivin (standing) and his laboratory group in Moscow, 1968. Third from the right Iya Shelakova, and first from the right in the second row is Professor Georgi Drozd.

At that time, the leadership of TSNIVTI, under the command of General Knunyants, refused to confirm Ivin's claim about his independent research on thiocholine ethers. The pretext of their argument was that if such a compound had any toxicity, it would have a high boiling point or be a jelly-like product, making it unsuitable for practical applications.

Furthermore, the choice of Substance 33 was an unfortunate one. In summary, the physical chemical properties (compared with VX it had far too low a volatility), the chemical properties (compared with VX it was much too unstable for long term storage), and the toxicity (in contact with air it absorbed moisture like a vacuum pump and quickly lost its active properties, though the toxicity fell only negligibly since the decomposition products were also highly toxic), all made its use practical only for intravenous and intramuscular applications.

The situation was further aggravated by its production technology, which would not permit an active product yield of more than 90%. Therefore, the technical production of Substance 33 in the Novocheboksary chemical plant, was marked by the number 87%, and to a significant extent it was predetermined that its stability in long term storage would be poor.

At the end of 1980, the laboratory of Georgi Drozd was the first to pay attention to these problems. For a long time prior to that, the lab had researched various methods of synthesizing Substance 33, and had compared the characteristics they found to the properties of VX. This comparison looked very unfavorable for Substance 33, as VX could be stored without any appreciable change in its original level of activity for more than 20 years.

A panic literally set in when the results of Drozd's research were formally registered in a scientific report, which was circulated to Guskov and the military representatives for GOSNII-OKhT. Still, they did not forget to give Drozd orders forbidding him to research this problem further.

My good friend, Professor Igor Revelski, was instructed to verify the disturbing facts. He corroborated the sudden change in the chemical composition of Substance 33 and its declining activity in storage. The scientific report of Igor Revelski met exactly the same fate as the report prepared by Drozd. Frequently in the Soviet system of science, researched facts were sacrificed for the sake of the financial and personal interests of the bosses who were in charge of science in the country. Unfortunately, this kind of thing can happen just about anywhere, even in a democratic country like the U.S.A.

In Drozd's opinion, the American scientists had a theoretical blowout in their research program, when trying to use the last stages of their technology of the production of VX gas for its binary version[25].

According to the results of the kinetic research carried out by Valeri Lebedev, a senior researcher at GOSNIIOKhT, VX gas produced by mixing semi-product QL^{26} with sulfur, should disintegrate within 10-15 seconds, since the temperature in the binary reactor would exceed more 300 degrees Celsius in this time interval. This is exactly why the American military chemists, after fifteen years of unsuccessful efforts and expenditures of more than $15 million on this project, were forced to "create holes" in the bodies of their binary reactors for the chemical weapon (CW) "Blue-8". These holes opened with special explosives 10-11 seconds after the startup of the mechanical mixer and at the beginning of the reaction between QL and the powdered sulfur. Clearly the key question became how to store this sulfur in a reactor for a long period of time without developing lumps and caking, so that it could be used effectively.

Ivin was in charge of a large laboratory in GOSNIIOKhT, for the synthesis of newly perspective chemical agents. He was a talented scientist who distinguished himself by his amicable relations with everyone whom he worked with, and he profited from universal respect at the institute and its branches.

The original idea for a binary chemical weapon was proposed and realized in Ivin's laboratory between 1971-1972, on the basis of the thiol ethers (Substance 33 and others of this sort) as well as on the basis of the fluoro ethers (soman, sarin and others). At first it was proposed as a new technological approach for production of sarin and soman.

As would be expected, it looked like a most attractive and simple system for producing sarin. Felix Ponomarenko, who was a graduate student at the time, definitely achieved success in this area. His idea was based on the reaction between the cyanide ether of methylfluorophosphonic acid and iso-propyl alcohol. The rate of the reaction was amazingly high and the yield of final product was more than 80 %. His results became known to some military people from the Directorate of the Chief of the Chemical Troops (UNKhV), who joined with some chemists from Military Unit 61469 in Shikhany, stole his work, and quickly filed for a patent for his invention. Of course this was done entirely without

Ivin's or Ponomarenko's participation.

A really scandalous standoff developed, since Ponomarenko had already included the results of his research in his dissertation, and the fate of the dissertation depended to a considerable extent on UNKhV's judgment of his work. The military specialists came forth with a "compromise". They did not back away from their "invention", but they gave Ponomarenko's dissertation a favorable judgment, and he safely defended it.

Deputy Director Konstantin Guskov was impassioned at that time by this highly promising theme, which was given the code name "Khoryok" (translates as ferret) in different indices. He conducted this work in the Volgograd and Shikhany branches of GOSNIIOKhT. To tell the truth I didn't have any knowledge about this "Khoryok" business until 1977.

One winter day in 1977, Guskov called and asked me to come to him for an urgent discussion. He told me that the binary bomb would be tested in Shikhany, and he personally asked me to help with the analyses of the field samples. Since I had already developed gas chromatographic (GC) methods of analysis for different purposes, including for conducting various tests in Department "RP" (which was in charge of preparation and conducting field tests), my methods could easily be adjusted for analyzing the field tested samples at Shikhany. So, I agreed to go and participate in the testing.

Intermediate non-toxic variants of the binary bomb were being tested. One of the compounds selected was the cyan ether of O-isobutylmethylphosphonic acid, and the other was N, N-diethylaminoethyl alcohol. The resulting reaction produced a non-toxic oxide analogue of Substance 33, O-isobutyl-O-2 - diethylaminoethyl-methylphosphonate according to:

$$\begin{array}{c} O\text{-}i\text{-}C_4H_9 \\ / \\ CH_3\text{-}P\text{=}O \\ \backslash \\ CN \end{array} + HO\text{-}CH_2\text{-}CH_2\text{-}N(C_2H_5)_2 \rightarrow \begin{array}{c} O\text{-}i\text{-}C_4H_9 \\ / \\ CH_3\text{-}P\text{=}O \\ \backslash \\ O\text{-}CH_2\text{-}CH_2\text{-}N(C_2H_5)_2 \end{array}$$

State Secrets

I was told that laboratory studies proved that the reaction between these reagents was going at a high rate and the yield of final product was also more than satisfactory, and so the outcome was not in doubt.

On the appointed day, we drove to the polygon (test site), where we could observe the air and the field from one of the shelters. We waited for an airplane to appear. The military airport was located 15 kilometers away in the town of Beketovka, and we saw the airplane take off, and then rise to gain the necessary altitude. The soldiers accompanying us were ordered to go to the basement so they could not observe the experiment that was about to take place. Then I saw that the transport airplane was practically right over us at a low altitude. Something blasted out just below the plane, and a white mist appeared which turned red, reminding me of holiday fireworks. I knew that dye was added to the mixture in order to make the reaction visible.

They set up little squares in a strict order on the testing field, with metallic trays on which they placed strips of filter paper for adsorption of the drops of the binary chemical agent analog they were testing. The paper strips should have had stains from the red dye that was added to one of the reagents. Specially trained soldiers collected the trays with the filter papers and delivered them to the analytical laboratory. Chemical compounds were extracted from the strips with a solvent. Then my assistant Boris Dubin and I analyzed those samples using a Varian 1800 Gas Chromatograph with a thermionic detector, for the selective determination of the final product, which was the O-analog of Substance 33.

Our analysis showed a very low level of efficiency for the binary bomb, with the yield of the final product being only about 7%. This poor result was disappointing, but no one tried to cast doubt on my results, because there were very few red stains on the filter paper strips, which would have been direct evidence that they had been exposed to a small quantity of the final reaction product. For me it was clear that this was the result of faulty construction design work and a short reaction time between the binary components.

I believe Guskov also understood this and decided not to test a second bomb. To his dismay he was facing huge opposition to this project. Since there were no miraculous results, his bosses lost all interest in it on every level. However, just in case an urgent need should arise, the subject was handed over to (or rather forced upon) Drozd.

This situation clearly reflected the negative mind-set held by the Construction Bureau "Basalt", the Military-Industrial Commission of the Central Committee of the CPSU and the leadership of the army, toward researching binary weapons.

An interdepartmental commission under the leadership of Vladimir Listov, who was then the Minister of Chemical Industry, decided that "the Army doesn't need less effective wares than the mono-variant." The mono-variant was clearly understood as a chemical agent. After this decision, the topic of binary weapons was shelved and existed in practicality, thanks only to the enthusiasm of individual researchers. This very idea seemed intriguing to me.

Ivin was instrumental in helping the synthesis laboratories in Volsk (Shikhany) and in Volgograd get started. I suppose that the appearance of such a talented scientist as Petr Kirpichev, the author of the new and highly effective chemical agent in Shikhany, was a result of his fruitful activities.

After Ivin's premature death at the end of 1980, his laboratory fell under the leadership of Evgeny Fokin, a man who lacked any kind of specialization. Partially, it was also supervised by the director of the institute, since he had to participate in meaningful scientific work in a laboratory in order to become a corresponding member of the U.S.S.R. Academy of Sciences. Later, Evgeny Fokin had to turn over part of his laboratory to Yuri Kondratiev.

Kondratiev willingly worked for a long time at the Shikhany branch of GOSNIIOKhT, where he was able to defend his doctoral dissertation, with the help of Ivin. Thanks to his ties of kinship with one of the members of the Politburo of the Central Committee of the CPSU, Kondratiev quickly became director of a prominent newly organized scientific institute – the All Union Scientific Research Institute for the Chemical Defense of Plant Life (VNIISKhZR) in Moscow.

Since he did not have any kind of specialization in organizational work and was amazingly inarticulate, this scientist from Shikhany, who was promoted to an administrative post, quickly botched his job at the institute. After that, they transferred him to GOSNIIOKhT, where he resides to this day, because there, as nowhere else, he began to feel at home in the world of secrecy, with his lack of talent and his terrifying conservatism.

A more talented student of Ivin's, Yury Gololobov, was forced out of GOSNIIOKhT by the envious director, who didn't want to have anything to do with him. There was another large-scale laboratory at GOSNIIOKhT for the synthesis of new chemical agents headed up by Professor Boris M. Gladstein, a man who I respected professionally and developed a highly positive impression of. In the past some of my colleagues frequently hinted that Professor Gladstein had more than a close relationship with the GRU.

I developed a series of GC procedures for the study of the so-called thion-thiol isomerization (it formed the basis for the American binary weapon), which the workers in Gladstein's laboratory used intensively. It seems to me that this lab did not achieve any particular success, although the staff was comprised of highly talented scientists.

Gladstein used all of his promotional talents to push ahead with "Substance 100-A" and "Substance 100-B", which were analogues of Substance 33. The difference lay in the substitution of O-isobutyl radicals by O-cyclopentyl and O-methylcyclopentyl radicals accordingly. The patent for these compounds belongs to the prominent military chemist, Abram Bruker. The technology of the production of cyclopentyl and methylcyclopentyl alcohols was developed by my longtime friend Professor Yevgeny Yevzirikhin.

Bruker and another scientist of this laboratory Leonid Soborovski developed a method of oxidizing phosphorylization, which was used to easily obtain the precursors needed for the synthesis of phosphoorganic chemical agents on an industrial scale.

Under the energetic support of GOSNIIOKhT Director Ivan Martynov, Substances 100-A and 100-B went through extensive testing. The results of this testing can be found in the text of the doctoral dissertation of Grigory Patrushev, who was then chief of the Department of Medical Biological Research and later became a director of GOSNIIOKhT.

Nevertheless, these compounds appeared to have little promise, considering that the industrial technology for manufacturing Substance 33 had already been mastered at the Novocheboksary Factory, and a new wave of research had begun on the binary weapons. For this reason, the subject of "Substances 100-A and 100-B" became a closed one. There is a real possibility that this theme was originally planted by the American agent Joseph Cassidy, who fed information about a relatively useless chemical agent to General Mikhael Danilin, who was the chief spy for the GRU (General Intelligence Directorate of the Soviet Army)[27].

The laboratory for the synthesis and research of the psychotropic compounds was under the leadership of Professor Nikolai Yarovenko, who came to GOSNIIOKHT from TSNIVTI along with Ivin.

Psychotropic compounds are strong agents affecting the human psyche, based on chinuclidine ethers (one analogue known in the West is BZ).[28] According to Yarovenko's account, such a compound would cause a soldier to smile happily and have beautiful dreams, setting aside his weapon. Yarovenko drew a detailed picture of such hallucinations, after coming from Leningrad, where several students in the Military Medical Academy had voluntarily tested this preparation on themselves.

The activities of this laboratory were considered very successful, since BZ, under the code name of "Substance 78", successfully passed through testing, and its production was achieved on an industrial scale at the Volsk branch (Shikhany) of GOSNIIOKhT. Our own Laboratory 25 participated in this work in a big way during the time of the start-up of the pilot plant.

Also, one of the analogues of BZ was determined to be a good anesthetic (by Doctors of Chemical Science Felix Dukhovich and Elena Gorbatova.) For that reason, the analogue was produced at the experimental plant of GOSNIIOKhT, and sent to the Burdenko Military Hospital in Moscow.

After Yarovenko's death in early 1980, Victor Komarov, a retired colonel and former professor at the Military Academy of Chemical Defense, replaced him. It seems that you can't call his activities successful, since bit by bit the laboratory plunged into a routine, researching basic compounds of a less significant nature. For example, for a long time they seriously researched a compound which stimulated nausea. It was thought that once it had worked its effect on a soldier, he would tear off his gas mask, because the nausea was intolerable, and after that the real chemical agent could kill him. What a nightmare!

What could we Soviets do if double agent Cassidy did a brilliant job, and we spent a lot of resources, without getting any positive results? Nevertheless, I was forced to participate in this work, researching methods for determination of micro-concentrations of this preparation.

Another prominent laboratory, headed by Professor Vsevolod Ginsburg, was devoted for a long time to searching for specialized natural compounds that could kill people. It seems to me that they succeeded in isolating and purifying the strong and naturally poisonous protein of ricin, found in plants of the castor bean family. As far as I know, a large volume of work was performed there by Doctor of Chemical Science Natalya Merzabekova, who studied the amino acid sequence of the protein, after the purification of raw materials and so forth. The technological research, for the completion of an experimental reactor, was authored by my good friend and neighbor, Evgeni Chizhov, who said he had worked closely with Natalia Merzabekova and Valeri Demidyuk. The later had defended his master's dissertation on the theme of the chromatographic isolation of pure ricin.

Demidyuk was notable for his "creeper vine-like" character, being a model orthodox Communist. This trait evidently became crucial in his appointment to the post of Chief Consultant to a new journal pretentiously titled *Chemical Weapons and Problems of Their Destruction*, which came out of Russia, thanks to different sources of American funds.

Under Chizhov's leadership in the beginning of 1970, a pilot plant was opened at the Volsk branch of GOSNIIOKhT, in order to produce the quantity of ricin necessary for field testing.

Ricin is the strongest poison, surpassing all phosphoorganic chemical agents in toxicity. It does not leave any traces in the organism of the victim, making forensic work practically impossible. On the other hand, most specialists know that it possesses almost insurmountable shortcomings in its application, which would prevent it from meeting the standards needed for broad field testing. In particular, ricin loses all its toxic characteristics at only 50 degrees Celsius. Also, it has practically no vapor pressure at the normal temperatures at which its aerosol form would be dangerous for people, since it is a compound with a high molecular weight. For this reason, in order to poison someone with ricin, it is necessary to introduce the poison by injection or by another manner, for example by ingestion.

In the end, a senior scientist in Ginsburg's laboratory, Pavel Gitel, began to intensively research methods for using hollow needles filled with ricin, which could be packed into a bomb or missile. With the explosion of the bomb, thousands of these needles would be thrown around, piercing people's bodies. Such tests were carried out; however, it seems that no particular success was achieved. Yet, there is every reason to suppose that exactly this ricin, produced at GOSNIIOKhT, was used by KGB agents to try to kill Aleksander Solzhenitsyn. Fortunately they were not successful. According to the testimony of General Oleg Kalugin, the Bulgarian Special Services which were trained by the KGB killed the famous Bulgarian dissident Georgi Markov, in London in 1973, with ricin which was injected into him by a special umbrella[29].

Nevertheless, aside from producing ricin for the Science Research Institute of the KGB, Ginsburg's laboratory could not fulfill its principal task – the creation of a chemical weapon based on ricin, thanks to the physical properties of the protein. Up until the middle of the 1970's, variants of CW based on phosphoorganic compounds turned out to be more promising. It's possible that this artificial problem also was implanted, thanks to American double agent Cassidy.

This scientific division was busy synthesizing and researching fluoro-organic compounds up until the mid 1960's. Sergey Makarov, one of the foremost specialists in the world in this field, worked there. He was the scientist who first synthesized and researched many of the basic fluoro-organic compounds, including trifluoronitroso methane, trifluoromethyl amine and a series of stable phosphoorganic radicals. However, because of the closed secret nature of GOSNIIOKhT, Makarov published very little of his work. The leaders of his department (Ginsburg's future lab) were busy with the problems of rocket fuel and heavy inert fluids for spacecraft and other specialized technology.

In the end, the laboratory of Vsevolod Ginsburg was reorganized. The new head man, Professor Yuri Kosarev, arrived from the Military Academy of Chemical Defense. He was a specialist on the degasification of chemical agents and was distinguished by his meticulous attention to triviality.

If Yuri Kosarev attended any meeting, it was fully guaranteed that the meeting could last an additional hour or two, because of his nitpicking and faultfinding with each phrase or letter of the most trivial project decision.

Ginsburg was transferred to the laboratory of Mikhael Englin, where his efforts to resolve the problem of penetrating gas mask filters were very unsuccessful. Also, this laboratory made the most unprofessional efforts to study the dynamics of adsorption of a series of fluoro-containing poisonous agents to gas mask filters. Aside from that, they were busy searching for lachrymators, using information picked up from foreign sources. You can already guess which foreign sources they were getting their information from.

At one point, I began to work with one of the developments of this lab, and I developed GC methods of analysis of the air in white lab rats' cells, as part of the medical and biological testing. For a long time I analyzed the air in experimental animals' cells.

The results of this testing were lamentable for Englin, since the agent under investigation was very unstable and a weak irritant. The professor in charge of these experiments didn't seem to be accusing me of developing poor methods, just of underestimating the results. My analyses showed that the animals only reacted to the irritant if it were given in large "horse size" doses.

When faced with unsuccessful results, every developer of a new technology or agent blamed the person who created the analytical method that was used for its evaluation, and these accusations always found support from the Deputy Director of Science.

In this case, Deputy Director Aleksander Shchekotikhin, who absolutely trusted GRU information, organized a "conference" in his office, inviting those who had malevolent intentions towards the author of the method (me), and as usual he revealed his obstructionism. The "conference" prepared for me was analogous to an execution. They invited people from the Laboratory of Indication, which was under the leadership of the aforementioned Lev Brovkin and Vladislav Sheluchenko, to fill in as my opponents. These people did not have even a rudimentary understanding of chromatography, yet they were ready to lend a hand to their bosses. Their help consisted of exclamations like "Aha! Your analysis showed that at some time there was a low concentration in the chamber, but the animals reacted strongly, judging from the instruments used to measure breathing frequency!" This is exactly what Shchekotikhin cleverly asked me, saying, "You should answer this..." It was clear that they were trying to draw me into an argument in an area that was outside of my expertise.

Englin was obstinate and penetrating, and he arranged for field testing of the substance on the Shikhany military test site. (At the institute we joked that if you used Misha (Englin) instead of a chemical agent in a test, he certainly would succeed in breaking through the gas mask filter.) Up to this point I was hearing "happy talk" at a meeting in the Directorate of the Chief of Chemical Troops (UNKhV) on Frunze Naberejnaya (Moscow), about the "perfect irritant of Englin", from the representative of the Institute of Toxicology in Kiev, where they were conducting some experiments.

In the fall of 1979, I went to the Shikhany Polygon (which was located 120 km south of Saratov)[30] with Rudolph Naberezhnich, a senior scientist from Department "RP", and we began to adjust the gas chromatographs for conducting field testing. At that time, I already felt like one of the group, since I had repeatedly been there on business trips to Shikhany-2, where the military-chemical institute and polygon were situated.

For a very long time Major General Anatoly Kuntsevich was the commander of this entire complex, including the chemical defense battalion which went under the common name of Military Unit 61469. His deputy for scientific work was Colonel Igor Evstafeev, who had once been in charge of the field testing department.

Before this trip, I was generally communicating with the military who were working in the Physical Chemistry Department, where they conducted analyses of all the samples they picked up from the testing on the polygon. This department was under the leadership of Yuri Gorbunov (who had a M.S. in Chemical Science), for a long time. He was a gentle and benevolent man with a pleasant appearance, who had spent several years in Cuba on a business trip, but I never managed to ask him about that. Evidently, our military chemists had found some kind of business at this "outpost" of Communism, butting up to the flank of the United States, which was called "the Citadel of World Imperialism."

From 1966 on, I traveled regularly to this department, and helped them in every possible way to achieve mastery over the chromatographic methods of analysis. Prior to 1973, this department acquired only low-quality U.S.S.R. produced chromatographic instruments, with the help of GOSNIIOKhT. Then in the beginning of 1974, the most modern American scientific equipment began to appear there.

Sergey Pichidze, who was still a young senior lieutenant at the time and a graduate of the Military Academy of Chemical Defense, was the one who organized all of this. Wonderfully cunning and a keen natural psychologist, he could use all the possible channels in Moscow to get a large sum of currency appropriated for massive purchases of laboratory equipment from the West.

I was curious about how he accomplished all of this. Pichidze explained to me that it was necessary to buy two or three boxes of chocolates for this, and to go to Vneshtorg (the Ministry of Foreign Trade) located on Smolenski Naberejnaya in Moscow. Then you needed to appeal to the woman in charge of or working on the purchase of imported instruments. At first, he said, you asked what the procedures were for purchasing foreign instruments and anything else. Then, with the manners of a gentleman you thanked her kindly and handed over a box of chocolate candy, as a tip for the consultation. After this, you confidentially try to find out if there was any hard currency remaining that had been spared during the process of purchasing instruments.

Indeed, while filling the orders for instruments, there often is a difference between the sum of currency budgeted for some organization and the real amount spent on the purchase. This money must, of course, be returned to the customer, and they did this - in Soviet rubles, not in hard currency like American dollars. At this time the hard currency equivalent for rubles was a laughable value: one dollar was equal to 70 kopecks. But just try to get currency appropriated in this ratio! For this reason, the apportionment of currency for any foreign purchasing was tantamount to an act of charity or a present.

Money could always be saved in this way on the numerous purchases made in hard currency. What was left over could be combined again with other sums and saved, to purchase instruments for someone else, let's say for a handsome gentleman like Sergey Pichidze. Naturally, Military Unit 61469 had to pay for this, but only in Soviet rubles. This did not present a particular hardship, since the sum in rubles was ridiculously low. As you can see in this case, this scheme was based on honesty. No crime was committed, and there was no cheating, since money didn't go into anyone's pocket.

The imaginative antics of Pichidze sometimes reminded me of the escapades of Klestakov, from Nikolai Gogol's comedy *The Inspector*. One day in 1986, Pichidze showed up with a friend at the car dealership in the Kujbishevski Military District, where people from Military Unit 61469 shopped for their cars.

Anyone who was familiar with the automobile trade in the U.S.S.R., knew that in order to purchase an automobile, you first had to get on a waiting list at work, and then if you were lucky you could get one 5-8 years later. The cars they "gave" us in this way were models that were becoming obsolete and poor in their technical performance. Good automobiles went to satisfy the demands of the Soviet bureaucracy. They had their own list for that, and the cars that they were "given" were more fashionable, if such a word can be used to describe Soviet automobile construction.

Dropping by the showroom, Pichidze declared to the manager: "I'm here from General Razuvanov."

This statement was not particularly suspicious, if you take into consideration the fact that the military did not name their division number, for reasons of secrecy. The manager of the dealership, who was a colonel himself, knew this military unit, where General Razuvanov was the commander. Right away he understood that Pichidze was someone who came to personally pick up a car for the military commander of Unit 61469.

State Secrets

"Just today we received a car, a Zhiguli-luxe, and you can take that car," answered the colonel-manager of the shop.

Calmly and with a bit of a haughty attitude, Pichidze asked what was required for that. The manager replied "Nothing other than formal confirmation from the military unit that you are working there."

This was already customary business for Sergey and he quickly brought the manager a certified telegram from the office of the commander saying that Pichidze was employed in Military Unit 61469.

"Pay and take your beauty," came the answer. Pichidze and his friend had brought a sum of money with them sufficient to pay for the luxury car.

In the evening of that long June day, as the military people were leaving work, they watched Pichidze with undisguised envy, moving slowly along the main street (there were only two streets) of the Shikhany-2 settlement. Pichidze was smiling happily, proudly seated behind the wheel of the beautiful new Zhiguli-luxe. There were no such automobiles to be found in the settlement, even belonging to the general himself.

Naturally the general decided to check on why he did not "get" the car first. However, when he phoned the manager of the Kujbishev shop to inquire about it, he was told that he had already sent him the car.

A scandal broke out in Shikhany-2, but no matter how the assistants of the military commander tried, they were not able to find any official fault. All of the sales documents were written up in the name S. Pichidze, and he was legally the owner of the automobile.

At one time there were even so many imported physical chemical instruments in the Military Unit 61469, that they could not all be fully put to use. I won't hide the fact that the base was in very short supply of detectors, and some equipment was assigned to me out of friendship, essentially to help me fulfill my doctoral dissertation.

The equipment acquired by Pichidze (mostly American), helped elevate the testing on the Polygon to a new level. It became possible to use these instruments to analyze probes of compounds on the test site, which had been practically impossible to analyze before. Even the analyses of probes with phosphoorganic chemical agents were now speeded up by several times, by using the American on-line cholinesterase equipment. This considerably shortened the work that was done by hand, which had required numerous employees.

Rudolph Naberezhnich came with me to Shikhany-2, and like the majority of the people in Department RP at GOSNIIOKhT, he had been one of the longtime regulars, in the department run by Igor Evstafeev. For this reason we were greeted with great good will and a promise to help us in our work.

At that time, there were many obstacles which complicated our testing. All military bases prepared some kind of exhibition and some kind of sanitary cleaning was conducted at the test site on the base, etc. The chief problem, however, was an American satellite which appeared on fixed days of the month to survey the Shikhany Polygon, and naturally, everything had to wait until it cleared out of the observation zone.

Finally, on one day in September, taking all the proper precautionary measures, we put several kilograms of Englin's substance out on the polygon.

Dressing ourselves in full chemical defense suits with thick rubber gloves and gas masks, we took some of the powdered preparation out of a container and scattered it on an area of a defined size.

We completed all operations according to the instructions for conducting these tests, and were finishing up a ways off from the square, changing into our casual clothes. For some reason I felt I was pulled back closer to the square. I wanted to smell the test preparation. Since I had been developing methods of analyses of different irritants like CS and CR, I had become familiar with some of their functions. This was practically unavoidable since laboratory equipment is very vulnerable and there is no absolute guarantee against leaks of the chemical compounds being tested.

I had not detected any irritating scent on my gloves when I removed them (without my gas mask on), and it was surprising that I did not smell anything on the area closest to the square, where they were still misting the rest of the chemical into the air.

When I went right up to the square, the result was the same. There was no smell, even when I practically inhaled the air right over the preparation. This shook me up, and I asked Rudolph to confirm my discovery. He did the same and satisfied himself that there was no smell.

We were hoodwinked. It was annoying that Englin, Shchekotikhin and the other science bureaucrats had fooled us for so long, subjecting us to insults and all sorts of abuse!

The Deputy Commander of the base, Igor Evstafeev, found out about the results and our experiences from his subordinates, who had been participating in the testing. I think that he was thrilled, because military chemists were always happy when civilian chemists suffered defeat. They believe that only military chemists can do something reasonable in the field of military chemistry.

Soon after this Professor Georgi Sokalski, a retired colonel from the Military Academy of Chemical Defense, replaced Englin, and he was also far removed from the area he had worked in.

I remember how he loved to tell how he had worked as an expert for the Soviet delegation in Geneva, at the negotiations for the Convention for the Prohibition of Chemical Weapons (CWC). I am not convinced that he was capable of inventing "trouble", and later he was replaced by Sergey Maleykin, who was considered a long-time favorite of Ivan Martynov, the Director of GOSNIIOKhT.

One of the more talented scientists working at GOSNIIOKhT was undoubtedly Professor Georgi Drozd, a student of Sergey Ivin. Drozd graduated from the Military Academy of Chemical Defense and served in the army for several years before coming to work at GOSNIIOKhT. He quickly defended his masters' thesis, then his doctoral dissertation in 1972.

As often happens with talented people, the leadership of the institute was not able to find any kind of worthy use for Drozd. It was not profitable for the director of the institute to assign him people and working space for synthesizing new compounds. Georgi was too willful and at times too independent.

I think that to some extent the Deputy Director of the Security Regime, Colonel Sokolov, saved him from his uncertain situation. When a scientist-erudite was needed for the censorship of dissertation work on a subject, in accordance with the system of secrecy symbols (there were three degrees of secrecy), the choice fell to Drozd, who headed up the corresponding commission at the institute.

The symbol of secrecy and the name of the problem that any dissertation deals with, sometimes play a role in its future fate. If the dissertation was written on the topic of "Foliant" (appearing as "F"), then there would be an order for secrecy and instructions for its discussion within a circle of organized specialists. "Foliant" meant the problem of the search for new chemical agents, in accordance with a special directive by resolution of the Central Committee of the CPSU.

Even if someone had additional clearance for other secret work, this did not mean that he could be allowed to become familiar with the material of this subject. A special request must be made by the chief of the department or laboratory, and it had to be signed by the Deputy Director of the Security Regime and the director of the institute himself, agreeing that this "person" was permitted to work on the problem at hand. Even within the area of the problem of "Foliant", there were individual themes that required even more restricted access. All of this was strictly controlled by officers in the First Department, which had corresponding records permitting people access to different themes.

The membership of the Science Council of GOSNIIOKhT that was discussing the theme of "Foliant" was intentionally composed of a narrower group of people than usual. There were even more restrictions in discussing sub-sectional problems of this topic, for example, as in the case of "Novichok" and others.

Only a very few people in the institute had clearance to all information there. Certainly the Director of GOSNIIOKhT and the Deputy Director for the Security Regime had this kind of access. We had 6 deputy directors and as many as 40 chiefs of various laboratories, but almost of all them had only limited access to classified materials, as was needed for their work.

Drozd also played a very central role in helping some people prepare their dissertations. They were officers from the Special Forces of the KGB, who were working to ensure food safety within the Kremlin. He was their scientific leader.

Some of the work carried out under Drozd's leadership was the research of metabolites (the products of destruction or breakdown) of phosphoorganic chemical agents within living organisms, with the help of "tracer" atoms.

On several occasions, a number his assistants grossly violated the rules of fire protection and prevention. The first time, a fire completely burned up all of the equipment in one of the laboratory rooms. The second time, a short circuit started the fire, and around 800 grams of Substance 33 was "lost".

This fire started at night, and it was noticed for the first time by passengers on the tramway, which crossed the bridge on the Highway of Enthusiasts, overlooking a good part of the institute's territory. Passengers from this tram reported the fire to the Moscow City Fire Brigade.

On another day, when I came to work, I saw a security cordon and the institute's fire brigade at the GLK. My boss Beresnev got permission for me to go into my room and organize an analysis of the water on all the floors, where water had spilled out while the fire was being extinguished. At this time, it became known that during the fire, some part of the total store of Substance 33, which was being stored in the thermostatically controlled flask in the burning room, had either burned up or spilled out.

Luckily, I did not detect any residue of Substance 33 in the water probes. At that time, my ability to determinate properly was not yet particularly high (I had an American chromatograph with a flame-photometric detector), and I did not have enough time to make the preliminary selective concentrations which I had developed.

I do not believe, even up to this time, that Substance 33 was missing from the probe. We had to conclude that during the fire, the chemical agent burned up, evaporated or decomposed completely. Part of the chemical agent must have been carried away in the steam or with the smoke of the fire, into the Moscow air.[31]

In 1981 Drozd was instructed to tackle the problem of creating a binary weapon, and as far as I remember he tried to reproduce the scheme of the American version. Apparently, due to his overly critical opinion of the American invention, he abandoned this idea and went back to his old work of searching for new perspective compounds and the isolation of pure chemical samples.

During the whole time I worked with Drozd at GOSNIIOKhT, we were on friendly terms. He tried to support me in every possible way, though my situation was not simple because of my doctoral dissertation. Georgi agreed right away to help me in a concrete way, whenever I needed his help, for example when I asked him to be my official opponent on my dissertation. He wrote a very good review of my dissertation, and this really helped me with a successful defense.

In 1987, the decision was made to work intensively on binary chemical weapons, and Drozd was entrusted to head up that sector. Drozd took Igor Vasiliev as his assistant, and Drozd had helped him defend his long-suffering thesis, so he could become a Doctor of Chemical Science. So much for gratitude! When Drozd's department was shaping up quite successfully, Victor Petrunin, the Director of GOSNIIOKhT decided that it would be better if he headed that department himself. So, Vasiliev ran to get under the wing of the Director, betraying his former protector.

When I was arrested and locked up in notorious Lefortovo Prison, Capitan Victor Shkarin, the investigator, showed me the resolution of the Permanent Technical Commission of GOSNIIOKhT.[32] This body decided that the article "A Poisoned Policy", which was co-authored by Lev Fedorov and me, amounted to the disclosure of state secrets.

At that time though, I was really surprised that the name Drozd was not listed among the members of this commission, who signed the report. He was one of the key figures on this commission. Later I found that he categorically refused to sign this document.

As Drozd was making headway in the development of a new version of *Novichok*, he became embroiled in a scandal involving improper collaboration with the Syrian government. In 1992, Russian Deputy Prime Minister Vladimir F. Shumeiko and Syrian President Hafez Assad signed a memorandum pledging cooperation to create a "Center for Environmental Protection". Lieutenant General Anatoly Kuntsevich, the scientific deputy in the Directorate of the Chief of the Chemical Troops, used this agreement as a cover to help the Syrians with their chemical weapons program. Russian President Boris Yeltsin later appointed Kuntsevich to be his point man on chemical and biological disarmament matters, a job that came with the odd title of "Assistant on the Conventional

Problems of Chemical and Biological Weapons". Kuntsevich was well known as a heavy drinker and a man who was looking for any monetary advantage he could find as Russia's economy hit rock bottom in the early 1990s. The Syrians reportedly asked Russia for certain equipment for an "environmental chemistry laboratory," such as laboratory hoods, compressors, and vacuum machines as well as scientific information about nerve agents.

At Kuntsevich's request, Drozd was defining the physicochemical characteristics of soman and sarin so that this data could be shared with the Syrians. This activity would have brought in badly needed funds for GOSNIIOKhT, if not for Drozd himself. Victor Polyakov, Petrunin's first deputy, pulled the plug on this illicit collaboration by accusing Drozd of stashing a few hundred kilograms of dichloranhydride of methylphosphonic acid, a key precursor for sarin, soman, and Substance 33 that is prohibited from export, amidst boxes of equipment bound for Syria. Even Drozd's former wife, who was a pilot plant engineer, told the KGB he was culpable.

I know that equipment was being shipped, but I do not know whether Drozd was involved in smuggling this key precursor chemical. Anyone could have dipped into the unguarded tank car that usually sat on the grounds of GOSNIIOKhT. It contained several tons of dichloranhydride of methylphosphonic acid, made at Shikhany. As a result of the investigation, GOSNIIOKhT fired Drozd in 1993 and Kuntsevich got the axe in 1994, for "mismanagement."[33] In 2001, the Russian authorities dropped all these allegations because of lack of evidence.

Another remarkable scientist from GOSNIIOKhT was Professor Andrei Tomilov. His laboratory was working with the electrosynthesis of organic compounds. In addition to the technological process for manufacturing pinacolyl alcohol, which is a necessary precursor for soman production, Tomilov successfully developed the original methods for producing tetraethyl lead, adipodinitrile, and others. Tomilov was awarded with the Lenin prize for his work on pinacolyl alcohol.[34]

My group worked with this laboratory for a long time, developing different GC analytical methods for them. Tomilov is one of those talented people, fanatically devoted to science. When I met him, I had the impression that he was hardly interested in anything that did not directly concern his research. Kind and well disposed to everyone, he was always ready to help anyone who wanted to contribute to the field of science. Tomilov had always sympathized with me, and I am still grateful to him for his friendly support in helping me prepare and defend my doctoral thesis.

The GOSNIIOKhT directorate always regarded him as some kind of an alien body, mean-spiritedly victimizing him in every possible situation. It seemed that all these little jabs didn't even touch Tomilov, and he continued his research as if nothing had happened, and was the productive author of numerous monographs and textbooks on the problems of the electrochemical synthesis of organic compounds.

It is not surprising that when it became necessary, Andrei Petrovich created an original method for the electrochemical synthesis of highly pure arsenic from arsenic oxides, the products of the alkaline hydrolysis of lewisite.

A New Class of Chemical Agents "Novichok" and Binary Weapons

From 1971 to 1973, Petr Kirpichev, a senior scientist from the Shikhany branch of GOSNIIOKhT, and his assistants developed a new class of chemical agents which later became known as Novichok agents, and all problems connected with them received this codename. The word "Novichok" translates as "newcomer". At first, Substance A-230 was synthesized and tested, which stands for

$$CH_3-P(=O)(F)-N=C(CH_3)-N(C_2H_5)_2$$

or N-2-diethylaminomethylacetoamidido-methylphosphonofluoridate (Codename A-230 or Substance 84). For the first time, the acetoamydin-radical $(C_2H_5)_2N-C(CH_3)=N-$ (creating P-N –bound) was introduced into the molecular skeleton of sarin or soman, instead of the O-alkyl radical. This was fantastic from standpoint of military chemists, because the toxicity of the new substance was up to 5-8 times higher than was the toxicity of Substance 33. The result depended on whether the skin-resorptive or the intravenous test was used.

According to senior engineer Vladimir Uglev, who was the assistant of Kirpichev, the long time military chemists in Military Unit 61469 didn't believe it. They only started to take this agent more seriously when they conducted their own laboratory tests with animals. Old jealousies didn't allow them to recognize the importance of this discovery. However, Director Ivan Martynov immediately sensed the perspectives of this agent and took measures to support Kirpichev's work, showing his personal interest. With his persistency he prompted the Central Committee of CPSU to take a decision to promote such agents[35].

A group of scientists of Shikhany branch of GOSNIIOKhT. Shikhany, 1978. First from the right is Petr Kirpichev. Victor Petrunin is the third from the right.

GOSNIIOKhT's Shikhany scientists, 1974.
Standing from left:
Vladimir Vasiliev, Sergey Sedov and Sergey Koshelev.
Sitting from left:
Yuri Rink, Valerij Djuzhev-Maltsev and Victor Petrunin.

This work was granted top priority and a few people were given clearance to become familiarized with it. This of course didn't stop the military specialists from trying in every possible way to compromise it or break it. Things became more complicated in the winter of 1977 when they found that this agent was crystallizing in containers at temperatures below -10 Celsius. The problem was solved by adding some N,N-dimethylformamid to the pure agent. Even though this agent was diluted a bit by this solvent, its toxicity was extremely high, and GOSNIIOKhT tried to push it through the standard military field tests, with the goals of developing the technology of its production and getting it formally accepted as a chemical agent of Soviet Army.

Petr Kirpichev's group then synthesized and tested analogs of agent A-230:

State Secrets

```
        F
        /
CH3O-P=O                              Agent A-232
        \
         N=C(CH3)-N(C2H5)2     amidin

        F
        /
C2H5O-P=O                             Agent A-234
        \
         N=C(CH3)-N(C2H5)2
```

The agent A-232 has the same toxicity as Substance 33, though it is much more volatile than Substance 33 and agent A-230. Its stability against moisture is lower than both these agents. Kirpichev synthesized and tested the ethoxy-analog of agent A-234 and ultra highly toxic solid derivatives of agent A-230 and A-232 where the amidin radical was replaced by a guanidine radical. Their codenames are A-242 and A-262, respectively:

```
       F
       /
CH3-P=O                              Agent A-242     guanidine
       \
        N=C-N(R)2, where R – diethyl radical
        \
         N(R)2


       F
       /
CH3O-P=O                             Agent A-262
       \
        N=C-N(R)2, where R – diethyl radical
        \
         N(R)2
```

                    —N=C—N(C2H5)(C2H5)
                        |
                        N
                       / \
                     C2H5 C2H5

At this point jealous Director Martynov decided that enough was enough, and he deprived Petr Kirpichev of the authorship for agent A-232. At that time Petr had to send all materials directly to GOSNIIOKhT, without leaving any copies in the local secret archives or library, so Martynov and his crooks did what they wanted with them. Superman Martynov "presented" this agent to his son Boris Martynov, who had already become chief of Gladshtein's former laboratory. Boris was dreaming about his PhD. Up to that time Ivan Martynov was a Corresponding member of Academy of Sciences of the USSR, and Victor Petrunin the new director of GOSNIIOKhT was keeping an eye on him, hoping that his former boss would help him also become a member of Academy.

For that reason Director Victor Petrunin became enraged in 1987, when Petr Kirpichev had the audacity to submit his proposal about his doctoral dissertation, based on his work to the Science Council at GOSNIIOKhT. Petrunin told him that no single person in Russia would allow him to write such a secret dissertation. (This was a pure lie). "You'd better ask for my advice first" concluded the director. Ironically, this was Kirpichev's ultimate reward by his country, for inventing a principal new class of chemical agents. Not one of the so called leading scientists of GOSNIIOKhT raised his voice in support of this really talented scientist.

It wasn't a matter of dissidence or politics which could endanger their lives. This was a clear demonstration of the real moral cores of these people. They were interested only in their own careers and nothing more. To tell the truth, practically all of them were no longer real scientists. They were simply survivors.

At this time I met Petr near my office in the corridor of 6th floor of the Administrative Building, when he came out of meeting with Petrunin. He told me that he was officially pressured to give up his authorship in favor of Martynov's son but he had refused. This was followed by Petrunin's tirade. Petr was smoking cigarette after cigarette and said: "They are miserable people! They think that a PhD is the ultimate goal of life. They do not understand that there is also human pride and honor. I cannot sell my honor for a PhD."

Theft of professional work by a person or group of people was not entirely uncommon and sometimes routine behind the scenes maneuvers were going on between GOSNIIOKhT and UNKhV.

In the late 1970s, in order move the effort forward, GOSNIIOKhT Director Grigory Patrushev established an interagency commission to oversee the final medical-biological and laboratory tests of A-230. In addition to GOSNIIOKhT personnel, officials from the Directorate of the Chief of Chemical Troops, the Military Academy of Chemical Defense, and Military Unit 61469 observed these tests, which were conducted in the fall of 1981. I was working in the Physical Chemistry Department at that time. Samples were delivered from the test chambers to my laboratory, where I used GC methods to analyze the laboratory tests which explored the fundamental properties of A-230. I did the same type of analysis for the animal testing of A-230. These observers were literally breathing down my neck as I processed the samples through my equipment and calculated the concentration of A-230 present in each sample. The test results showed that A-230 was 5 to 8 times more lethal than Substance 33 and would be an effective chemical agent.

All signs pointed to a success in the making until the initial field tests of A-230 were conducted at Nukus in Kara-Kalpakia, Uzbekistan, since they were not so impressive.[36] At that point, a decision was made to conduct field tests on A-230 under joint GOSNIIOKhT-Army supervision. A special laboratory headed by Yevgeni Bogomazov[37] from Department RP was created to perform GC analysis of the field test samples. The analysis was done at Nukus, running between 300 and 500 samples over the period of a few days. Some of my laboratory assistants participated in this work, and one of my graduate students, Valerij Djuzhev-Maltsev, developed the GC method of analysis that was employed.

The results were so good that the military dropped their objections. Bogomazov also staged a round of live agent field tests with A-230 at Nukus in 1986 and 1987 using bombs and rockets.[38] The successful completion of these tests led to two important events. The first was a victory celebration at a 1987 party meeting in our institute. There, Director Victor Petrunin announced that GOS-

NIIOKhT had achieved the type of sensational accomplishment that only happened once every forty years, namely the discovery of an entirely new weapon, A-230. The second hallmark event came with the Soviet Army's official approval in 1990 of A-230 as an agent that could be used in all types of munitions. After that, the production of experimental quantities of agent A-230 began at GOSNIIOKhT's Volsk and Volgograd branches, and plans were drawn up for the full-scale production of A-230. Designs were prepared, and the ground was cleared for construction to begin on a huge new chemical weapons production factory in Pavlodar, Kazakhstan. With the collapse of the Soviet Union, the funding for a dedicated A-230 production facility evaporated, and Kazakhstan became an independent nation[39].

Since my graduate students and I had developed the GC analysis, my graduate students were also involved with conducting the toxicity and medical biological tests at both locations. Our analytical methods were also employed during the field tests of A-232 at the Shikhany test site. Though the A-232 research was by no means a central focus of my research at that time, I occasionally saw reports that kept me abreast of this agent's development. A-232 was developed and tested in parallel with, though a little later than, A-230.

Chemical agent A-232's major advantages were its ability to withstand cold temperatures and its ability to circumvent the list of chemical agents to be controlled by forthcoming Chemical Weapons Convention (CWC). According to the projected list of controlled chemical agents and precursors listed in the schedules of the CWC, there were no agents or precursors included which were from class of phosphates with the CH_3-O-P – radical, because the majority of agricultural phosphoorganic chemicals (such as pesticides and herbicides) have this radical. Known phosphoorganic chemical agents are phosphonates (with the CH_3-P radical). Since agents A-232 and A-234 were phosphates, they were ideal agents for concealing and cheating the inspectors supervising the implementation of and compliance with the CWC.

In order to accomplish the field testing at Nukus, GOSNII-OKhT constructed pilot plants which made hundreds of kilograms of A-232 for testing. GOSNIIOKhT's Volsk and Volgograd branches performed the scale-up of the production technology and made "experimental" quantities "a few tons" of this agent. Field testing for agent A-232 was just as successful as it was for agent A-230, and the Soviet Army also approved it as a warfare agent.

It was impossible for the Soviet military-chemical complex to hold out against the temptation to create a binary weapon on the basis of agent A-232. Luckily for them, the theme of "Khoryok" was a proper fit for the realization of their dreams.

To that end, an independent scientific sector was organized in 1987, headed up by Dr. Igor Vasiliev, under the direct supervision of Director Petrunin. The basic model of the reaction between cyanide of methoxyflurophosphonic acid and amidin was chosen:

$$CH_3O-P(=O)(F)(CN) + H-N=C(CH_3)-N(C_2H_5)_2 \rightarrow$$

$$CH_3O-P(=O)(F)-N=C(CH_3)-N(C_2H_5)_2$$

Certainly there were many unresolved problems connected with the choice of temperature, the rate of supply of reagents, the mixing regime, the choice of promoters of the reaction and the chemicals for the elimination of hydrocyanide as a by-product of reaction, etc.

Everything was rolling along very well, until a disastrous accident occurred, which delayed development of this version of Soviet binary weapon almost for one full year. During laboratory experiments, part of a rubber tube, through which exhaust gases of the reaction were traveling from the reactor to the on-line IR-spectrometer, ruptured and began leaking poisonous agent A-232 into the laboratory air. This happened right next to the hood where my good friend and research engineer Andrei Zheleznyakov was working. Andrei started to feel dizzy, and he immediately reported to Vasiliev that he was experiencing blurred vision consistent with chemical poisoning. However, Vasiliev couldn't find a better solution than offering him a glass of alcohol. Andrei collapsed next to the Metro station when he left GOSNIIOKhT. He was taken to Skilofosovskaya Emergency Hospital where the doctors had no idea how to treat him[40].

When the KGB started prosecuting me, Andrei was the first to support me. His interviews with the *Baltimore Sun* and the Russian magazine *Novoe Vremya* were critical in helping the world learn about the *Novichok* binaries. We never saw each other again after I was jailed in Lefortovo, but we often spoke on the phone, which we both knew was bugged by the KGB. Andrei was a jovial fellow, a good scientist and an extremely talented wood carver. Before the laboratory accident, a few prominent artists invited him to work in their studios, but the poisoning robbed Andrei of his concentration, his regular job, and his creativity. Journalists who regularly approached him for interviews treated him with indifference, and Andrei gradually stopped communicating. Andrei Zheleznyakov was an honest and thoroughly decent person. It was tragic that he lost his life to the very weapon he helped to create and revealed to the world. Most of those who knew of his poisoning never did anything to help save his life.

Though this accident delayed the completion of the binary weapons project on the basis of agent A-232, it didn't stop it entirely. This theme showed so much potential that the Central Committee of Soviet Union under its First Secretary, future Nobel Peace Prize laureate Mikhail Gorbachev, and the Council of Ministers of the USSR secretly issued a formal resolution[41] for the implementation of the project. Gorbachev signed this document almost immediately after the US and USSR governments signed the Wyoming Memorandum, a special "memorandum of understanding" about chemical disarmament[42], on September 23 1989.

Despite of all the complications caused by the Democratic Movement in Russia and the collapse of the Soviet Union, the military-chemical complex of Russia still managed to accomplish its mission and successfully test a binary chemical weapon based on deceitful agent A-232.

A Successful Binary Weapon Based on Substance 33

The prominent Engineering Department of GOSNIIOKhT was an important place for the development of CW production technology. The main tasks of this department were to maximize the automation of the production of chemical agents and to research and test equipment in order to regulate the technological process. This included the automation of the sampling process and the analysis of probe samples which were collected. I collaborated extensively with the associated lab department on this job, and I often took business trips with the employees I worked with. I worked with Leonid Vishnevski, who was head of the laboratory in 1967, on introducing chromatographic methods of analysis to the Kazan plant "Orgsynthesis", which produced ethylene oxide.

This department was very strong throughout. I think that the well-known scientist and professor Nikolai Bogatkov-Korsakov was to a large extent responsible for this.

Unfortunately, he had a very erratic and independent nature, often clashing with Director Ivan V. Martynov. In 1975, Martynov responded to this behavior with a hotly worded statement, and he fired Professor Bogatkov-Korsakov with great pleasure. In his place, Martynov inserted Henri Kazhdan, who was the son in law of the aforementioned Aleksander Smirnov, chief of the Chemistry Department of the Central Committee of the CPSU.

I remember him only for two scandals, one which almost landed him in criminal court for stealing equipment from the institute.

As a member of the Soviet ruling elite, Kazhdan had access to closed stores with fine imported goods. He decided to grab the attention of the women in his department with the direct delivery of bras and panties, which were in short supply then. He carried all of this across the carefully guarded checkpoint of the institute in his briefcase. Departmental and laboratory heads, who had special permission from the Deputy Director of the Security Regime, could carry their briefcases through the checkpoints at the guard station without being searched.

Apparently, someone who was not happy with Henri reported his activities to the special bodies at the institute, and one day his briefcase was searched without ceremony. Inside they discovered a quantity of women's panties and bras, but the strong backbone of this supplier of women's underwear helped him remain in his post without any consequences.

Another scandal developed after the death of his high-ranking father in law, and that time he had some real problems. Kazhdan had a perfectly equipped workshop with good lathes and metal fitting and tooling equipment, and he secretly organized the production of precision miniature woodworking machines, which surpassed even the well known Japanese ones in quality.

It's not clear to me if he sold them or was getting ready to sell them, but apparently Henri presented some of them to Deputy Director of Science Guskov, to Professor Kurochkin, and others. Workers from his department wrote a series of complaints, and the wheels of justice began to turn. The experienced investigator obtained a confession from Henri, but the case which was brought by the special prosecutor was dropped and did not go to court, because further development of his case would have threatened the regime of secrecy. In all fairness, I must say that these crazy activities of the department chairman did not have much of an impact on the work of the department. He had very good executives and laboratory chiefs, and many experienced and gifted people were working with them, including Natalia Godzhello, Vladimir Goncharov and Mark Stepanski.

Natalia Godzhello (who had a M.S. in Chemical Science) was a veteran in the field of research and production of chemical agents in the U.S.S.R. We lived in the same neighborhood, and she remained my friend, even during the time of my persecution by the KGB. This challenge provoked a reaction by the investigators and the Director of GOSNIIOKhT, in spite of the fact that Godzhello had already retired with a pension at this time. She was summoned to give testimony about my case to the KGB. I learned from our conversations that Godzhello came from a family of chemical engineers, who ran one of the first CW test sites for the Red Army in Kuzminki (this is now a densely populated region of Moscow.)

Her family lived close to this site where CW were tested, and sometimes destroyed. This Polygon continued to operate there until 1960, when its ownership was transferred to Shikhany from TSNIVTI. Godzhello graduated from the Chemistry Department of Moscow State University (MGU) before World War I, and was sent to work at the plant in Chapaevsk, which produced mustard gas and lewisite. After a period of time working there, Natalia Mikhailovna was sent by her boss, against her wishes, to work in the Technical Production Department, where she only had to deal with documentation. Quite possibly this saved her life.

The organized technological production of chemical agents was terrible from the standpoint of technical safety. In Natalia's own words, faces and hands were burned in the mustard gas-producing section. When workers removed their gas masks or gloves, their skin was burned by mustard gas vapors. Also, they unfortunately did not know that the mustard gas vapor in the air percolated through rubber. When the artillery shells were missing some mustard gas and needed topping off, it was customary to refill them from a tea kettle.

There were many victims in such a system. The number of catastrophes multiplied during the war years when work on CW production was intensified, though the technology and the low level of safety standards remained unchanged. In order to make up for the shortage of workers in the plant, they once brought in soldiers from Uzbekistan. Those soldiers had no idea whatsoever about chemical technology, and they were completely unsuitable for work in the factory. Since their only experience was in their kishlaks (small villages in Central Asia), almost all of them without exception became victims of this horrible production process.

Finally Moscow was forced to respond in some way, so they sent a commission to investigate, which was chaired by the Deputy Minister of Chemical Industry, according to Natalia. As usual, they adopted some organizational measures to bring about changes to the leadership. However, they could not bring about the essential changes needed.

Another large laboratory existed in GOSNIIOKhT for the development of the production technology of tearing agents (lachrymators), which was headed up for a long time by Arkady Gribov (M.S. in Chemical Science), who later replaced Sergei Smirnov. I collaborated with this laboratory during almost all of the 26 years I worked at GOSNIIOKhT.

I worked with my assistants Boris Dubin and Olga Golubeva, developing methods for the determination of micro-concentrations of the agents CS and CR in different media. This included analysis of the air and water that had supplied the start-up of the corresponding experimental pilot plants for the production of these agents. We also researched methods of analysis of the precursors of the developed irritants.

Gribov was a good organizer and distinguished himself by his purposefulness, though apparently he was not a researcher in the full sense of the word. He was able to use the specialties of his subordinates to his advantage. Among them, Sergei Smirnov undoubtedly excelled. He specialized in working out the technology of the nitrile derivatives of a series of organic compounds. He started with the development of the technology of obtaining an allyl cyanide monomer for producing highly stable rubber. Later, he successful developed the technology for producing malonodinitrile, one of the principal precursors of ortho-chlorbenzyledenemalonodinitrile, which is known as the chemical agent CS.

A pilot plant for researching the technical production of CS operated on the institute territory for 5 years. Later an analogous pilot plant was opened at the Volsk branch of GOSNIIOKhT. In spite of huge efforts they made there, the technology for producing malonodinitrile was mastered only with great difficulty.

The year 1978 came and the time for the start-up of a large-scale division for the production of agent CS was approaching in earnest, at the Novocheboksary chemical complex. A quantity of malonodinitrile was necessary for this, but it had not been produced by the branch. I believe the reasons for this were the inadequate qualifications of the plant personnel and the absence of appropriate equipment. Though the matter of ortho-chlorbenzaldehyde and other precursors of agent CS was temporarily resolved by purchasing French chemicals through Turkey, the problem of malonodinitrile hung in the air.

Victor Petrunin was the director of this branch at the time, and he resolved the problem quite simply. Petrunin ordered all research labs to stop their activities for several months, and all scientists were ordered to synthesize the ill-fated precursor in glass retorts. Considering the availability of cheap human labor, such a "solution" was not original, though it was effective. When the time came for the start up the Novocheboksary plant, the malonodinitrile supply was ready.

Just a year earlier, the division for producing agent CS had been set up in a local chemical plant in Slavgorod. I was not able to participate in this opening, because I became ill in December of 1976. I had to give away my plane ticket, so my assistants Yuri Bugrov and Boris Dubin went there to introduce the methods and analytical procedures that were needed. Unfortunately, even though I had an official release from a doctor, the director of GOSNIIOKhT, my immediate supervisor Aleksei Beresnev and the aforementioned Sergei Smirnov considered that my illness was not sufficient reason for my refusal to go on this trip. I was given an "official reprimand".

I participated fully in the start-up of the Novocheboksary pilot plant, and my GC method of determination of microconcentrations of agent CS in the air (at the minimum permissible level of concentration) was adopted, practically unaltered. The reason for this was that the other method proposed by Brovkin's laboratory was extremely unselective and disorienting. However, the successful introduction of my methods required a stable working GC with an electron-capturing detector.

Up to this time, the domestically produced Tsvet-100 chromatograph had proven to be a pretty good piece of equipment, but it was running in a very unstable way, with its sensitivity constantly changing. Through my work experience at GOSNIIOKhT, I already knew that this task could only be resolved with the help of an American Varian 1800 chromatograph. So, I ordered this instrument for the job, and I defended my choice, in spite of strong pressure from Guskov and the Volgograd institute "Giprosynthesis", which was designing the pilot plant. They worked in every possible way to dissuade me from my proposal, arguing for a long time that I should use only "domestically produced equipment for the defense industry". I would have been happy to comply, if I had not known about the unstable characteristics of domestic equipment. I insisted on my own way in this case, since I was the author of the procedures. I had the exclusive right to guarantee the trustworthiness of the analysis only with the equipment that I had chosen.

Leonid Kostikin, Deputy Director for Science and Igor Gabov, Deputy Chairman of Main Administration "Soyuzorgsynthesis" of the Ministry of Chemical Industry ran the pilot plant start-up. My American instrument could not be reproached for the way it worked, and we had practically no problems with the analyses of the air probes. Air was sampled from the room where we worked and also from under the roof of the plant.

It was impossible to avoid heated arguments about the concentrations of air that was analyzed. Generally, the results showed us that the concentration of agent CS in the work room exceeded the limit of permissible concentrations (LPC). The boss did not agree with this. However, when we discovered a substantial concentration in the corridor leading from his laboratory in the plant, he was very displeased. This was because these rooms were considered to be located outside the range of the agent's influence. "This cannot be!" exclaimed my opponent.

Such obstructionism was already familiar to me, because I had already collided forcefully with the chief engineer of the experimental plant at GOSNIIOKhT, Victor Zhakov, during the testing of the technology of agent CS production. The levels in the workroom at that time frequently exceeded the LPC. Zhakov was more than happy to try to discredit my methods of analysis, but it turned out that he was a bit ignorant about the adsorption basics.

He tried to compromise my procedures (which the workers were using to check the air) by ordering that the air sampling be taken after a day had passed during which the ventilation in the workroom had been shut down. At this point, we made a surprising discovery: the concentration of agent CS in the still air without ventilation was greater than it was on working days with the ventilation running. This result was simple to explain. Once it had adsorbed on the surfaces in the room - the walls, the equipment and so forth - the irritant, which had a relatively low volatility, was then slowly desorbing. Naturally during intensive ventilation, the concentration of agent CS was diluted by a large volume of air. This concentration of CS was less than that which came from the relatively low volume of practically static air. We were even successful in modeling this phenomenon on the lab bench, demonstrating that our explanation was correct.

Surprisingly, when we made our methods and procedures for analysis of the air more accurate, the ill-will of the top leadership became stronger. This reminds me of an incident connected with the discussion in a section of the Science Council of my patent claim on the GC method of determination of micro-concentrations of agent CS in the air.

At this meeting, Deputy Director Guskov unexpectedly came out against my invention. Without having any knowledge of the essence of the problem, he peremptorily declared that my proposal for concentrating the adsorbent, using small glass beads, could not work because the vapor of CS could not adsorb. I repeatedly had proven the validity of my proposal with positive experimental results. The Deputy Director used his great power, and I found myself in a very delicate situation. However, without any fear, I decided to defend my invention and brought forth a brief report about the basics of the dynamics of adsorption.

After this, the section defended my proposal in an open vote, and a year later I received a patent on my invention. All my documents, including the actual patent carried the code "Top secret", "Series F".

According to U.S.S.R. patent law at that time, the inventor was supposed to be rewarded for his method of analysis. The size of the remuneration was calculated by a complicated method, with numerous correction factors, and was fixed by a special commission. The author of the patent had to demonstrate the validity of the correction factors to this commission, and naturally this is where all the battles developed. Usually the author valued his work on a high level according to the scale of factors, while the rank and file of the science commission, most of whom had never invented anything in their entire lives, often envied the success of the author and came out against him.

In the end, everyone had to compromise and the remuneration was fixed, but it didn't end there. The commission's decision had to be approved by the First Deputy Director, who signed the financial documents. Here he was guided by his own considerations which were clear only to him, and by the amount of money which came in yearly from the Ministry of Chemical Industry specifically for inventions and proposals and for improving production.

After I received an award for the appropriate sum by the commission, I set out for Guskov's office. I was surprised that he approved the commission's decision without any discussion. Now and then you can misunderstand someone you already considered in a negative way. How can you so simply judge someone after that?

In Novocheboksary, we were able to demonstrate experimentally that the poisoning of the corridor was caused by the transport of agent CS on the clothing of people who were working in gas masks in the reaction chamber area, where the concentrations of the agent were extremely high.

My work experience at Post Office Box 4019 on the production of poisonous boranes helped me resolve this complicated problem. We had discovered traces of CS in the snow on the roof of the plant, and also on the ground close to the plant. It was said that complete isolation of the production of chemical agents from the environment was practically an impossible task.

Unfortunately, I must say, that Sergei Smirnov, who was the author of the technology in the plant in Novocheboksary, was most memorable for his negative character traits, such as the tendency to inform on his colleagues for no reason at all. (This was not his worst feature.) Practically no one was really sure that he was not exaggerating a hundredfold when he was informing. His allegations could be brought to a higher boss, or even the Deputy Director of the Security Regime.

Even now, I do not understand why he did this, because he was successful enough and even a talented scientist. Maybe such a character flaw is a sign of some kind of mental illness. Though he was able to act like this with impunity among his scientific colleagues, this practice caused him to be fired from a new position he had been promoted to, the chief of an important scientific-technical department. In his new department, practically each scientist had his own direct access to the top leadership, including the special service of the KGB, so Smirnov simply could not stand up to the competition. Still, he was quite effective in his role in developing the pilot plant for malonodinitrile production in Polotsk, Belarus.

For a long time, a special department, the Department of Ammunition Development, known as "RP", existed in GOSNIIOKhT, and it worked with radiation chemistry and the processing of radioactive waste. It allegedly turned out to be at odds with the principal themes of the institute, but its chief, Nikolai Bogdanov, was a scientist who enjoyed the support of some well known atomic physicists. This practically guaranteed autonomy for his department. He even went to the appropriate international conferences on his own initiative. For us this was a stunning development.

We were baffled by the report that not long before this, Bogdanov had been employed as a military representative of UNKhV at the Volgograd CW pilot plant. Then retired Colonel Bogdanov became a Lenin Prize laureate for the development and introduction of the methods of vitrification (encasing radioactive material in borosilicate glass for storage) into industry.

Two scientists who had worked with Bogdanov for a long time, Oleg Plyushch and Victor Dmitriev (each who had a M.S. in Technical Science), told me how the recipient of such a prestigious prize accomplished this. Scientists from the "RP" Department and their boss were engaged in a collaborative effort with the enterprises of Minatom (Ministry of Atomic Energy) stationed in the Urals. On one of their business trip to the atomic enterprise, the locals told the Muscovites about their research, which could not be realized. Sneaky Bogdanov understood right away that a big catch could be made there, so he offered his help in getting the Lenin Prize for this work, in exchange for listing him among the researchers of the method. Nothing could be done, but to agree to such a "business proposition". Thanks to his connections, the Lenin Prize was not a very difficult achievement for Bogdanov. That is how the former military representative became a famous scientist.

After Bogdanov's sudden death in 1973, Director Martynov secured the breakup of the department. It was transformed into a new department, with a theme that was unfamiliar up to that time, the development of field testing for perspective chemical agents and the conducting of these tests. I think that this was a reasonable step to take, since GOSNIIOKhT depended completely on the military for this important business. Since the military had a monopoly on the situation in those days, they could easily fake the test results, at their discretion. Maybe this didn't happen frequently, but let's just say that scientists at the institute who had participated in field-testing, had confirmed such incidents. The former Deputy Director, Mikhail Kulikov, who had been supervising matters connected with the development of the GOSNIIOKhT branches, was appointed the head of the new "RP" department.

In his previous office, Kulikov had excelled in his very original style of leadership and administration of the branch offices. For example, one of his favorite activities when he was visiting the Volsk branch was to lead the scientists in a fire drill. He declared an alarm in all the offices and settlements where the workers lived, and all day people stopped work for a "fire drill".

During the time of World War II, Kulikov had been a deputy director and the chief engineer of an experimental plant. He loved to tell the circle of people accompanying him on business trips stories about his life, which was rich with events.

"You know, I even cheated Beria," he began his story. This episode was connected with his institute's fulfillment of an important government job, that of researching the organic glass for the armored canopies of airplanes. The canopy produced at the technological institute proved to not be durable and the bullets of German fighters easily pierced it.

One day it was reported that the KGB Chief Marshal, Laverentii Beria, was coming to the institute for "discussions" with the leadership there. An order was given for all samples of aircraft canopies, including American and German ones, to be placed in a special location.

State Secrets

On the appointed day, Beria arrived at the institute and arranged for the testing of these canopies. On the Marshal's order, an officer accompanying him pulled his pistol out of his holster and began to shoot at each of the samples displayed. The German and American samples remained undamaged, but ours were riddled with bullet holes throughout. "How much time do you need to correct your defective product?" the KGB Chief asked in a threatening manner.

Kulikov answered that the institute would rectify the situation in half a year. "I will be here exactly three months from now," announced Beria. It was clear to everyone what the inevitable consequences of the follow-up visit would be: everyone who had any relationship to those who were responsible for this problem would be shot.

It was also clear at that time that any kind of serious study of the problem could hardly succeed in three months. Kulikov decided to gain some time in order to survive, and he took a desperate step. Indeed Beria arrived at the institute exactly on the day promised and dispatched the glass to the location known on the map from the first testing, and the test was repeated. The results this time were amazing: all samples, including the ones made by the institute were bulletproof.

Beria showed no outward reaction and only asked in a somewhat softened tone "How much time do you need to begin the production of these samples in the factory?" Kulikov answered that six months was sufficient for this. He was given a period of 4 months, and everyone felt that the threat had passed. No one would be shot for carrying out their job.

Still, none of those present, including the high-ranking bosses from the Ministry, failed to guess how Kulikov had "corrected" the situation. He simply set up an American glass sample for the test, after having removed all its trademarks. Later on this business became much easier. Quickly a regular supply of American glass was established, on the scale needed for aircraft construction. The production of durable bulletproof glass was achieved in a Soviet factory, but only after a year had passed. Meanwhile, Kulikov's wits saved his life and the lives of many "responsible" people.

In fairness to Kulikov, I must note that he found the people necessary in a short period of time to organize the work in his department. His most important decision in the beginning was to invite Professor Mikhael Baranaev, a strong specialist in CW applications, from the Military Academy of Chemical Defense, to head up the conversion training.

Baranaev was a general who was notable for his in-depth studies of the mass transfer process of chemicals in the atmosphere, under the influence of different factors. Over a period of 30 years he developed mathematical methods of modeling these processes. I repeatedly used his equations and formulas for measuring the concentrations of vapors of chemical agents, after injecting them into air flowing at different speeds, with different temperatures and humidity. There were no cases in which my experimental results did not agree with the theoretical figures obtained by Baranaev's methods.

General Baranaev was wonderfully modest and accessible. He could explain practically all difficulties, which arose in the course of physical chemical research. A legend grew up around him in the 1930s, when the slightest suspicions of political unreliability from anywhere caused senior scientists to be exiled. Baranaev did not hide the fact that he believed in God and continued to attend church. Probably, Baranaev's brilliant talent and his idealistic "head in the clouds" character, forced his boss to protect him in every possible way, since he really was indispensable.

Unfortunately Kulikov was not always so lucky in his selection of employees. One example was the case of Victor Promonenkov, who was appointed chief of the Laboratory for Field Testing. Promonenkov had no understanding whatsoever of the sector of work he was in charge of, having worked on CW synthesis his entire working career, and he compromised GOSNII-OKhT considerably with his incompetence. Perhaps his only positive contribution, from my point of view, was his research work on the synthesis of the cyan ethers of methylphosphonic acid, which was accomplished in the laboratory of Sergei Ivin.

Ivin patronized Promonenkov, since he had married his niece. Later, Promonenkov was transferred to the All-Union Science Research for the Chemical Defense of Plants (VNIISKhZR), as a deputy to the "talented" director Kondratiev, who was mentioned before. There he organized a new secret department on the problem of "FT", which was connected with research on the chemical defoliation of trees, along the lines of the American defoliant "agent orange", which was used to destroy the forest in Vietnam.[43]

I remember Promonenkov as someone who could easily promise unattainable results for his projects, and he was someone who could easily pass himself off as a specialist in any area of chemistry.

When Promonenkov left GOSNIIOKhT, his post was filled by Gennady Kostenko, a retired colonel and World War II veteran, who was once the chief of a department in Military Unit 61469. Kostenko (who had a M.S. in Technical Science) was a sober realist who kept a healthy supply of self-criticism and some skepticism toward all the branches of military chemistry. He did not hide his nihilism or his cynical outlook towards his own prospects. Honestly, Gennady Ivanovich was the man who compelled me for the first time to take a fresh look at the whole problem of research and testing of chemical agents in the U.S.S.R. and in our complex.

During the course of numerous business trips to the Shikhany test site, we spent a lot of time traveling together on the train to Saratov, and on the steamboat on the Volga River that went to the town of Volsk. Sometimes we traveled on a cutter-launch that had underwater wings. During these trips, Kostenko gradually told me the "secrets" of chemical weapons in the U.S.S.R.

Once, during the summer of 1978 we were traveling on an old steamboat named "Azin" after one of the Civil war heroes. We stood on the top deck, and under the protection of the noise of the paddlewheel and the puffing engine of the steamboat, Gennady Ivanovich patiently explained to me that chemical arms were an absolute anachronism in the military business. He corroborated the "news" I had heard from Drozd, that these arms were not tested in maneuvers by scientists or even by a single military corps. Not a single concrete question of their practical application had been worked out, and you could not even speak about their medical aspects, since there were no specialized doctors or hospitals for curing potential poisoning by chemical agents.

I was shaken up by what I heard, and I asked why all this was being done and why were we wasting vast resources on CW research, testing and production. I was curious to know if the highest ranking military people in the U.S.S.R. knew about this. "Of course they know, and they hold the military chemists in contempt," was the answer.

Then he told me how Colonel General Vladimir Pikalov, head of the Chemical Troops, was pestering the Defense Minister asking to award him with the title Marshal of the Chemical Troops. The highest officer answered them with a smile and said that he could do that, but "Where are all these chemical troops?" Indeed this prominent military formation actually consists of some numbers of independent chemical battalions and regiments.

"Chemical agents and their problems in the U.S.S.R.… this is a gigantic feeding trough for the military and civilian generals," concluded Kostenko. Be that as it may, he continued to do his job well. Since Kostenko had a wide network of connections with his former colleagues, he easily settled organizational matters, connected with the typical ordeals that resulted from the regular research at GOSNIIOKhT. Even during the start-up time at Shikhany, he continued to travel there. This was not such a bad place. You could gather mushrooms in nearby fields, or try your luck at fishing on the Volga River.

On one of these furloughs, Gennady Ivanovich injured his hand and the cut became inflamed. He turned to a military hospital known to him from a job in the past at Shikhany, but his appeal was too late and the cure was too unprofessional. The inflammation turned to gangrene and in several days he died.

I worked for a long period of time with Kostenko's laboratory, developing chromatographic methods of analysis of the samples from the test site. Since the preliminary testing of chemical agents was conducted in the laboratory, my methods were also used in those experiments. I was working closely with Oleg Plyushch, who was one of his deputies and his assistant.

Oleg Pavlovich (who had a M.S. in Chemical Science) was an

State Secrets

exceptionally polite and highly cultured man. He was a strong specialist at his job, even though he had been studying issues of radioactive chemistry and the burial of radioactive waste for a long time.

Unfortunately, Oleg, like many talented people, was too principled for his own good at times. He sometimes brought down the fire of envious people on himself, people who were simply untalented and not professional scientists. Once, during a departmental party meeting, he came out against accepting Adolph Zaozerov into the party. Zaozerov was someone who was being promoted intensively by Professor Evgenia Volkova, the head of another laboratory in the department.

Evgenia, being a great lover of art, was charmed by Zaozerov, who was really a wonderful baritone, practically on a professional level. Apparently, the senior scientist's vocal talent was unequaled, but it was absolutely useless for the leadership of scientists and for the area of work that needed to be developed.

Although Plyushch and several other people were warned in advance about the possible unfavorable consequences of such a hasty step, Zaozerov was accepted into the party and soon became a departmental head. When he finished the energetic reconstruction of his office, the new chief strangely began to force Plyushch out. At the time, I watched more with horror than anything else, how GOSNIIOKhT could drive problematic people out of their positions. There was not one conference, departmental meeting, or meeting in Shchekotikhin's office, where Plyushch's name was not mentioned without mocking comments.

Oleg Pavlovich was forced to leave GOSNIIOKhT, because he did not hold up well under such psychological assault. I met him again twelve years later, in 1995, at a conference on ecological problems in the Moscow City Duma. I was very happy to learn that Oleg Pavlovich had successfully defended his doctoral dissertation and had become the director of an important scientific research institute for biological problems of interest to the Ministry of Health. Right away he invited me to come to work for him, promising to give me good terms of employment. Unfortunately, at this time I understood completely that it was unsafe for my children and me to remain in Russia any longer.

Adolph Zaozerov did not put down roots as the new chief of Department "RP". He was not able to adjust to relations with the military, and he understood very little about the direction which his department must be developed in. Having a handsome appearance and a wonderful vocal gift, he was still very far away from science. His success did not progress further than the reconstruction of his office into a luxury chamber.

In 1984, Zaozerov was replaced by Nikolai Kuznetsov, from the enterprise (NPO) "Basalt" - the leading contractor for scientific manufacturing. Basalt was the main designer in the U.S.S.R. of ammunition that contained chemical agents.

Kuznetsov was invited to work by the former director of GOSNIIOKhT, Patrushev and his deputy Guskov, who intended to give the department a more goal-oriented character. Also, it was nice to have someone who could promote the research of the institute directly to NPO "Basalt", and have it realized.

The new director, Petrunin, quickly promoted him to his deputy. In 1991 he was sent by GOSNIIOKhT to the Volsk affiliate, to try to work on an old idea that Guskov's collective had failed to accomplish in 1978. It became Kuznetsov's contribution to successfully complete the testing of a binary weapon there. He understood that the previous failure with testing the binary variant on the idea of the reaction according to

$$CH_3-P(=O)(O\text{-}i\text{-}C_4H_9)(CN) + HS\text{-}CH_2\text{-}CH_2\text{-}N(C_2H_5)_2 \rightarrow$$

$$CH_3-P(=O)(O\text{-}i\text{-}C_4H_9)\text{-}S\text{-}CH_2\text{-}CH_2\text{-}N(C_2H_5)_2$$

was due to the fact that they used an aviation bomb which was dropped from a low altitude. There was not enough time for the components of the binary weapon to mix thoroughly.

All that remained was to design a shell, or better yet a rocket, that intensified the mixing process. This is much easier to describe than to accomplish. But, thanks to their connections with military contractors, the Kuibyshevski Special Design Bureau had already completed all of this work by the end of 1990, and positive results followed.

Engineering a binary rocket is a delicate task. The burster charge used to break the barrier separating the two precursor chemicals has to be sufficient to initiate rapid mixing yet not destroy the precursor chemicals or disturb the ballistic trajectory of the rocket. Kuznetsov's engineers worked to design this mini-reactor in flight, and it underwent preliminary testing at Basalt's facilities in Samara (formerly known as Kuibyshev). A decision was taken to hold the tests at Nukus instead of Shikhany because prevailing opinion held that the US intelligence community did not know about the Nukus test site. The success of field tests of the Substance 33 binary rocket led the Soviet Army to adopt the first binary device as a chemical weapon in 1990.

The Soviet Army's approval of the Substance 33 binary weapon triggered efforts to produce these weapons for the Soviet arsenal. Scaled-up studies and pilot plant production took place at Novocheboksary and probably also at Shikhany. In military circles, being able to produce a few grams of an agent was not significant. Waging war required tons of chemical agent, so figuring out how to produce large quantities of a specified agent was a crucial accomplishment. In the case of Substance 33, proving the ability to mass produce this new binary would qualify this agent's developers to apply for the USSR's highest awards.

As it turned out, this achievement merited the 1990 Lenin Prize, the Soviet equivalent of the Nobel Prize. Protocols for the Lenin Prize specified that it is awarded only for a *great* new development and that the Secretary General of the Communist Party approve of each one bestowed.[44] Lenin Prizes are given out personally by the First Secretary of the Central Committee on April 21st, the anniversary of Lenin's birthday. In 1990, Soviet leader Mikhail Gorbachev, who in 1987 had told the international community that the Soviet Union was no longer making chemical weapons,[45] signed off on the Lenin Prize given to Petrunin and a host of generals for the Substance 33 binary.[46] According to tradition, GosNIIOKhT also hosted parties celebrating this achievement.

Chapter 9
Fight Without End and Evgeny Bogomazov's "Discovery"

During my first years at GOSNIIOKhT, I wasn't completely deprived of contact with my scientific colleagues on the outside, and it was even possible to participate in scientific conferences. I could still publish my articles in scientific journals, but only rarely and with great difficulty. Over the course of time, all of this was systematically blocked in such a way so that there was no longer any opportunity to contact the outside scientific world.

There was the Science Council at the institute, which regularly discussed the topics of both master's and doctoral theses to be defended there. Soon this area became fully autonomous.

Before 1977, all theses defended at GOSNIIOKhT were sent to the Higher Attestation Commission (VAK) of the Government of the USSR for further approval, but after that an expert commission was created at the institute for considering all theses related to the 'Foliant' theme. This made the lives of the candidates for degrees much easier, but it also led to the isolation of all the scientists. The most important part was that it created the possibility to turn "useful" people into scientists, because the number of potential opponents and people making decisions was reduced. Mainly the fate of any thesis was determined in the court of public opinion, which was created by the board of directors and other bosses close to them.

Certainly I was not willing to give up my ambitions of a career as a scientist, and I tried my best to achieve that. The topic of my scientific research was related to the development of chromatographic methods for the determination of small concentrations of chemical agents and their precursors in different media. The methods I developed could be used both for chemical agents and for ordinary compounds. This comforted me to a great extent, because I could consider myself a researcher who was solving problems of general scientific importance. I was tormented by great doubts about the utility of all our work, after conversations with my friends Kostenko, Drozd, and other military specialists, so I tried to solve principle problems.

Prior to my research at GOSNIIOKhT and in the military-chemical complex in general, only the cholinesterase method was used for the determination of concentrations of phosphoorganic chemical agents (POCA). This method was based on using a biochemical substrate, extracted from horse's blood. The horses they used for this were raised in special conditions, making sure that their feed was free of any traces of pesticides. This method was considered universal and was officially used to estimate concentrations of POCA everywhere throughout the military-chemical complex. Nevertheless, even though the method was very sensitive, it was not at all selective. The presence of many pesticides and other chemicals in the samples led to gross errors in the results of the analyses.

I worked with my assistants, Tamara Beregova and Valery Djuzhev-Maltsev, to develop a whole group of chromatographic methods for the determination of low concentrations of POCA. These methods could completely replace the old cholinesterase method, as they were selective and provided objective analytical data. They also cut the cost of the analysis by a factor of ten. At the same time, we developed chromatographic methods for the analysis of micro-concentrations of CS (ortho-chlorbenzyledenedimalononitrile) and CR (dibenz-b,f-oxidiazepine) in different media.

Eventually, my boss began to interpret my success in his own funny way. He believed it posed a threat to his own status and became very unfriendly towards me. I must say that administrative work never did attract me. It only distracts scientists from their real work – the business of doing science, and it wastes a lot of time with numerous meetings and conferences.

Certainly I did everything I could to make my attitude toward becoming a boss and a bureaucrat clear to everybody. But there was a glitch I hadn't anticipated.

The board of directors of the institute drew up a secret list of all the potential candidates for replacing department heads, just in case they retired. Beresnev told me that he accidentally found out that I was on this list, as a possible candidate. This also came as a surprise to me, but I considered this list to be a pure formality. I did not pay much attention to it, and I did not even try to put my boss's mind at ease.

But I should have! After that day I became an unwelcome rival in his eyes, and he openly started to show his disapproval of me in every possible situation. His hostile attitude manifested itself in the worst way possible. It became very difficult for my graduate students to defend their theses.

The Higher Attestation Commission had ground rules that governed the thesis process, along every step of the way. First, every thesis was discussed at the leading laboratory in the specialty area involved, before it was defended at the Science Council. The head of that laboratory had to familiarize himself with the thesis in advance and then make a decision to call an expanded seminar, in which the thesis was discussed. If he decided not to call for that seminar, it would block the progression of the thesis. He also completely controlled the list of people who had the right to participate in this expanded scientific seminar. Then a resolution was passed at the end of the seminar, regarding the compliance of the thesis with the requirements formulated by the Higher Attestation Commission.

This is where my boss created obstacles in every possible case, showing all of his punitive knowledge. Beresnev was a veteran, the former lieutenant of a special "barragefire" detachment, during World War II.

His unit had a very special job. Their orders were to wait well behind the front line, and if our troops were forced to retreat, their job was to shoot them. There was no limit to his resourcefulness at blocking us, but at the end of the day we managed to overcome all his obstacles, though only through a great waste of time and effort. Still, I found it was much easier to support and intercede for others, even if they were my students, than to get help for myself.

Our boss was also battling against my colleague and our senior researcher Igor Revelsky and his graduate students in the same way. Fortunately, Beresnev's scientific ability was not held in high esteem, and GOSNIIOKhT scientists did not support him. Their presence at the expanded seminars, somewhat curbed our boss' irrepressible fantasies.

It was clear that some KGB people supported Beresnev, and we were even sure that Director Patrushev was rather afraid of him.

My graduate student, V.L. Djuzhev-Maltsev was defending his thesis at the Science Council in 1979, and despite Beresnev's attempts to obstruct the process, Djuzhev-Maltsev's defense was rather successful. He answered all the questions thoroughly, showing deep knowledge of the problem. He had good references and recommendations from different institutes and organizations within the military-chemical complex concerning the work he had done and how useful it was. All the scientists who spoke afterwards unanimously approved of the thesis.

Then the time came for the secret voting. According to the Higher Attestation Commission rules, there had to be a quorum (minimum number of the Science Council members present). Although the number of members had exceeded the quorum at the beginning of the session, one person was missing when the voting time came. Deputy Director of Science Guskov, who was also a Science Council member, was urgently called to the Ministry during this session.

Normally, when someone left the Science Council, they signed a register to get a ballot, recorded their vote and put it into the ballot box. And this is exactly how everything was done in this case. But the chairman of the Science Council and director of the institute Patrushev knew what my boss was capable of, so he decided to wait for his deputy to return in order to repeat the whole procedure. When I asked him about it, he dryly reminded me that I knew very well why it was necessary.

After the lunch break, we had to wait three more hours and then repeat everything. Although all the members of the Science Council voted positively, everyone had a nasty aftertaste from this compulsory procedure.

I wrote my doctoral thesis in 1975 with great difficulty, having practically no time for that. In order to do it, I had to stay overtime in a special room of the First Department at GOSNIIOKhT practically every evening and write my thesis. I also understood that I had no chance of breaking through the barricade created by my boss. Still, I always wanted to do my best, and I decided to see it through to the end. I was also inspired by Revelsky's successful defense of his doctoral thesis in 1974. Revelsky succeeded because of his good relations with military specialists and influential people on the Board of Directors, who had arranged for a preliminary discussion of his thesis in the expanded seminar, in the absence of our boss. At the end of the day, Beresnev just refused to go there, and the defense was a success as expected.

Soon after that Beresnev called me to his room, and he asked me in all seriousness, if he could become a candidate for a doctoral degree in chromatography. I answered that he could not, because he was not a specialist in the field.

In this way, I burned my last bridges behind me. The former "barrage fire detachment" lieutenant informed me that this time he wouldn't repeat the mistake he had made in Revelsky's case.

Indeed, he was very inventive. He organized my work in such a way that it yielded only practical results, without any detailed research. I had to do the theoretical part of my work covertly. Like all the other groups, we worked according to approved annual and quarterly plans, so it wasn't that difficult to conceal additional research. When our boss asked a question "What are you doing?" each of my research assistants answered monotonically: "We are developing this analytical procedure."

We had a difficult time though with internal publications, that is with writing reports on our additional research. The boss simply turned them down. No secret document was supposed to be published at the institute's typing bureau without his permission. Sometimes we succeeded in doing that anyway, but our boss did everything he could to correct these "blunders." He had a strong ally, Leonid Kostikin, the Deputy Director for Science who helped him with that.

Kostikin was a consummate Soviet bureaucrat, who saw everything through the prism of "self-serving". To the end he was extremely slippery and unscrupulous. Following the principle "birds of feather flock together," he quickly found a common language with Beresnev and became the next (and the worst) supervisor of the Analytical Department.

One day he called me in with Beresnev and declared that on the recommendation of my boss, he couldn't approve a large scientific report of mine. The reason was that my work was outside the scope of the laboratory's annual plan.

At that moment, I was overcome by a bold desire to disgrace this schemer. I put on an innocent face, and asked him if he had any other objections to my report, possibly connected with insufficient research work that had been done. Or could it be that the material was badly presented or carelessly arranged?

"What are you talking about, Vil Sultanovich? There are no remarks like that and there is no way there can be any, because everything is great in that respect," exclaimed Kostikin. "The only problem is that I can't let the report, which contains subject matter that is different from that of your department, pass to the scientific and technical library", he added in an apologizing tone.

"Well, if my report had been stipulated in the annual plan, would you have submitted it?" I asked, pretending to be a babe in the woods.

"Without any doubt," the deputy stated categorically.

"Can you give me your word on that?" I urged him on.

"If you want to, of course, I can," he agreed in a patronizing manner.

"Then could you please give the order to have the laboratory's annual plan brought here from storage in the First Department," I insisted.

To my astonishment, Kostikin immediately called the Scientific and Technical Department (NTO) at the institute and asked them to send over the plan. A few minutes later, the supervisor of our NTO Department, Antonina Vitchenko, brought the department's file, with the required documents. Immediately I found a clause in the plan, which spelled out this topic for future work in black and white, with a remark attached that it should be completed by submitting a scientific and technical report.

A profound silence set into the office. A few minutes passed, and Kostikin's face dissolved into a foolish smile. He was at his wit's end, and had no idea what to do next.

"Leonid Ivanovich. You know, a few years ago Vil Sultanovich was planning on leaving the party," the lieutenant of the "barrage fire detachment" said, rushing to his buddy's aid. Kostikin forgot to wipe the stupid smile from his face and tried to feign indignation, "You don't say so! Really?"

It is true that I was suffering deeply from discontent, in 1973, both with my "discovery" that people's money was being squandered on our activities, and with the general situation in the country. Political persecutions were becoming rampant. Once we were celebrating someone's successful defense of their thesis in a restaurant, and I mentioned that I wanted to drop out of the party. But it went no further than that, as I decided against this desperate move.

Of course, Beresnev's remark was not by chance, though I was sure that a serious investigation of any charges based on a conversation in a restaurant was not in the best interests of the institute's top management.

"Exposing" a dissident at an institute like GOSNIIOKhT would damage the reputation of the director and other "responsible" people. That is why I indignantly asked to continue this conversation at a Party Committee meeting. No, Kostikin didn't want that! Immediately he found a way out, and suggested that my report should be submitted to our secret library, without his or my boss's signature.

"If you don't agree to that, I will immediately call Leonid Aleksandrovich Sokolov (Deputy Director for the Security Regime) and ask him to destroy the report," he added. There was nothing left, but to agree.

Beresnev also invented a fail-proof system for not letting me defend my own thesis. According to the regulations of the Higher Attestation Commission, candidates for both doctoral and master's of science degrees were required to have positive references, signed by the institute's power triangle – the director, the chairman of the trade union committee, and the secretary of the Party Committee. Also, in order to receive these recommendations, each candidate had to get signatures of the corresponding people at his or her departmental level. This could only be done when the applicant had no administrative or party reprimands.

They started hanging these reprimands on me for every possible reason. For example, my junior assistant Boris Dubin once went to join the civilian militia squad after work. He got drunk, and got into a fight with someone.

"Vil Mirzayanov is to blame," they decided at the departmental party meeting, on the recommendation of its head, Beresnev. I received a party reprimand "for poor emphasis on personal upbringing". Consequently, I could receive no positive character references during the half year period after that.

The reprimands continued for the next five years, until one day I publicly announced that I never, under any circumstances, intended to defend any thesis. It seemed to me that this slightly placated my tormenter. However, just to make sure that I had given up on this idea completely, he decided to deprive me of my group and all my equipment.

This is when I unexpectedly received support from two people who had long sympathized with me, Professor Semeyon Dubov, the head of the Physical Chemistry Department, and Professor Vladimir Kurochkin, the head of the laboratory within Dubov's department.

Dubov graduated from Moscow State University, and before the war began he was sent to one of defense plants producing tetraethyl lead, a highly poisonous compound which increases the quality of gasoline. Professor Dubov didn't like to talk about that terrible plant. People often died there from poisoning, and the number of deaths was comparable to casualties on the battlefront.

Thanks to his good health and more than a bit of luck, Dubov survived in that Hell. When he returned to Moscow, he started working in the military-chemical complex. In the early 1950s, when Jews were persecuted in the USSR, Dubov had to go to Dzerzhinsk and work at the branch there of Post Office Box 702 (GOSNIIOKhT).

In the early 1960s, he was allowed to return to work at the headquarters in Moscow, where he soon became head of the Physical Chemistry Department.

I believe that Professor Dubov, like no one else, was the right person for his job –the head of a scientific division. Amazingly lively and in good shape with handsome features, he was always polite and attentive. He quickly won the sympathy of anyone he was talking with. Although sometimes Dubov could get carried away by some unrealistic ideas, he was very pragmatic for the most part, and always very careful.

Once he confessed to me that sometimes he was mainly concerned with running the trade union, party, and numerous other meetings for our team. These meetings were considered important elements of the so called "personal upbringing work", which was used as a tool to dupe the entire population of our country, in the spirit of totalitarianism.

"While I've been working at GOSNIIOKhT," Dubov continued, "I've never heard that anyone was punished for negligence or any shortcomings in scientific research, but a lot of people were punished for underestimating personal upbringing within the team."

Since Dubov was a good organizer, he quickly attracted many talented young scientists, and made sure his department was supplied with modern scientific equipment. He created a notable team of scientists with the widest possible variety of interests, given the situation at that time. There was not one area of physical-chemical research that did not fall within the domain of his department's development. They conducted fundamental research on the newly synthesized compounds, using methods of nuclear magnetic resonance and electromagnetic resonance, infrared and ultra-violet spectroscopy, X-ray structural analysis, mass spectroscopy, and chromatomass-spectroscopy. They studied the kinetics of reactions between physiologically active compounds and biochemical substrates, and the methods of quantum chemistry were applied to develop the preliminary forecasting of perspective chemical compounds. The results of these studies were applied to different works, on a modern level. Since there was such a wide range of research, they had to divide up the responsibilities of the team leaders and more than 160 people who worked under them.

Professor Dubov asked Vladimir Kurochkin to be his aide. Kurochkin came to GOSNIIOKhT from the Science Research Institute at the General Intelligence Directorate (GRU) of the Soviet Army. In early 1960s, this institute was reorganized and many employees from there came to work at GOSNIIOKhT.

When the war began, Kurochkin volunteered to go to the front, where he was badly wounded. I accidentally learned that he had received a lot of awards, which were evidence of his bravery on the battlefront. Kurochkin was gentle by nature, always friendly and quite talented. When he was talking with someone, he quickly grasped the essence of any problem, and did everything he could to make sure that person he was conversing with felt comfortable, and did not fear being misunderstood. He had excellent skills as an organizer but, he was also a man of his times. He didn't mind wasting his time and energy at the endless meetings of the Party Committee, the trade union committee, and the board of directors of the institute. Kurochkin understood that if he avoided these meetings, he wouldn't be able to provide his team with state-of-the-art equipment, to raise their wages, or to promote talented young people. Dubov and Kurochkin made a good partnership, campaigning for the development of the Physical Chemistry Department.

At first Director Patrushev ignored my requests and wouldn't let me move to another laboratory. However, Kurochkin's diplomatic talents worked wonders and the issue of my transfer was settled quickly. Of course, there were good reasons for that. Shortly before my arrival at the Physical Chemistry Department, a senior staff scientist there, Yevgeny Bogomazov, began research aimed at identifying chemical agents which could break through the filter of a gas-mask.

Bogomazov was a graduate of and then a candidate for a master's degree at the Military Academy of Chemical Defense (MACD).[47] He had just completed his dissertation work in General Mikhael Dubinin's department, and his topic was developing GC methods for evaluating gas-mask reliability. Yevgeny was a typical product of his military educational establishment.

I hope that many of my good friends will forgive me for saying this, but I think that the majority of the MACD graduates are notable for their adventurous and easy approach to all types of problem solving. However, when they use this approach for solving scientific problems, the matter often goes belly-up. Most of them force their way into key positions using all their efforts, and they have no scruples, using people, using bootlicking, hypocrisy and betrayal of their former friends, to achieve their goals. My words may seem harsh and judgmental, but my encounters with people from the MACD have brought me to this sad conclusion. I would advise everyone who has anything to do with MACD graduates (with a few exceptions) to check all of their proposals and research results ten times over, before accepting them as truth.

I don't mean to imply by this description that Yevgeny Bogomazov did not have any talent. Mostly he excelled in his self-aggrandizement, which tainted everything he did. After Bogomazov received his master's degree, he got a job in Englin's laboratory, but he saw no career prospects there, so he quickly moved on to the Physical Chemistry Department.

In a short time, Bogomazov managed to captivate the head of the department with his ideas. Very soon, Bogomazov and two of his junior colleagues, Dmitri Zalepugin and Aleksander Dmitriev[48] (both MACD graduates), made a discovery that all the military chemists of the world could only dream of.

They discovered that the thionic analogs of soman and sarin, $CH_3P=S(F)-OR$, where R is the alcoxy radical - could break through an army gas-mask filter. Then these compounds, which have a comparatively low toxicity, would turn back into their oxygen analogs, $CH_3P=O(F)-OR$ (chemical agents) once they had passed through the filter.

Additionally, according to their results, the same was true for the thionic analog of the neopentyl ether of methylfluorophosphonic acid. The oxygen analog of this ether has toxic features identical to soman. That was a sensational discovery, but it could not be trumpeted to the public - to the deep regret of ambitious Bogomazov. Naturally, Bogomazov's discovery was immediately reported to the headquarters of the Chemical Troops at the Ministry of Defense, and the Central Committee of the CPSU. In the eyes of those organizations, Bogomazov became one of the leading scientists, a man who made a revolution in military science.

With his usual grandeur, he returned to his research, and decided to attract large-scale resources to his discovery. A number of GOSNIIOKhT's subdivisions began working under his scientific leadership.

A special group was organized under the supervision of Aleksander Yakovlev at the Engineering Department, to develop an automated device for the analysis of the adsorption properties of the newly synthesized compounds. According to the project, these new compounds should be brought on line by two groups of chemists who were specializing in synthesizing compounds.

Also, the Physical Chemistry Department started a broad-based study for the deeper understanding of the adsorption processes, which caused the breakthrough of chemical agents mentioned above.

A young graduate student, Aleksander Klochkov, from the X-ray Structure Analysis Group headed by Doctor of Chemistry Efim Galperin, began working on his masters' thesis about the adsorption properties of the thionic analogs. Another graduate student from the group for determining physical-chemical constants, Valery Belikov, discovered that there was a great difference between the compounds that broke through the filter and those compounds which irreversibly adsorbed to the filter, in terms of the thermal effects on adsorption.

A real scientific fever was ignited, which also caused some

new discoveries to be made. For example, one of Dubov's favorite graduate students, Aleksander Tarasov, invented an inhibitor, which blocked the spontaneous ignition of the thionic analogs in the air. Tarasov also found the optimal concentration for the inhibitor, which secured retention of the so-called field or combat concentration of chemical agents in the air. However, everything was being done very incorrectly, because analyses of the mixtures were faulty.

The overwhelming power of the secret regime allows scientific schemers to work miracles, and to pay no attention whatsoever to any analysis. So, Tarasov successfully defended his thesis for his master's degree before the Science Council.

I learned about all this work only two years after it began, when I transferred into the Physical Chemistry Department, to further research the adsorption processes connected with the breakthrough. True, I had seen Bogomazov before I came to the department. Several of my friends had pointed out a tall and heavy young blond man with blue eyes and a plump white face, and whispered in my ear that he was the author of a stupendous discovery.

Following GOSNIIOKhT's principle: never ask about things that do not directly concern you, I did not ask anything about the nature of Bogomazov's discovery then.

After so many years of frustration connected with my doctoral thesis, and simply longing for a team of true scientists, which I believed the Physical Chemistry Department to be, I came to Dubov's office. Kurochkin and Bogomazov were also present.

Dubov, as head of the department, briefly told me about the importance of Bogomazov's project, not only for the institute, but also for the "Foliant" program. Overall, my task was to provide compelling theoretical scientific grounds for Bogomazov's discovery. I believe it was probably some kind of "landscaping job", to give such a magnificent discovery additional grandeur.

Of course I was literally shaken when I heard about Bogomazov's research results for the first time. His discovery would render any person helpless – whether he was a soldier or an innocent civilian. Being sensitive by nature, I was tormented at that moment by the vision of children meeting their painful deaths in gas masks, which became absolutely useless against a chemical weapons attack, thanks to Bogomazov's discovery.

We discussed the details of my transfer into the department, and talked about my American instruments, which Dubov had managed to wangle away from Beresnev for my work. We also talked about the possibility that I would finally be able to defend my doctoral thesis, but I could not recover from the shock of what I had heard.

Sometime later, I went to lunch with the young genius and some of his colleagues, and I couldn't help asking Yevgeny how he felt about it. What if his discovery was ever used against peaceful civilians?

He replied he realized that he might be prosecuted by an international tribunal, as the Nazi war criminals at the Nuremberg trials had been. However, he said, he was only a scientist who had had a great bit of luck. I noticed an undisguised smugness and some kind of bragging on his plump face, probably caused by the presence of Galina Beletskaya, a pretty young laboratory assistant.

By that time, I had almost grown accustomed to shocking talk in some of the seminars run by my colleagues. For example, if they described the lethal properties of some newly synthesized compound as LD 50 (50-percent lethal intravenous dose), that meant that no less than 50 percent of the laboratory animals had to die during tests. I saw rabbits in their agonizing death throes in the test chambers at Department MB. Even after all of that, this young man's obvious cynicism truly stunned me. I understood at once that we would never be on good terms.

However, despite my feelings and my private suffering over this, I had to do the work that I was assigned. I almost never had any assistants in my new department, so I had to do absolutely everything with my own hands. That was according to the wishes of the young genius. Certainly, that meant a lot of routine and unskilled work, but I didn't have any choice. I patiently set up my chromatographs and assembled an experimental dynamic set for adsorption analysis.

By the winter of 1982, I already completely understood the

uselessness of chemical weapons for our national defense. Even worse, I was convinced that they were directed at the helpless civilian population in the first place. I knew from the press that there were ongoing discussions and negotiations in Geneva for a treaty that would ban the development and production of chemical weapons. But wasn't it strange that the new project we were developing would mean a new and dramatic turn for the worse in the chemical weapons race?

Since our military-chemical complex had big plans for developing new methods of breaking through the gas-mask filter, a special interdepartmental council was created for discussions and for coordinating the research related to that. Academician Lieutenant General Ivan Knunyants, a well-known military chemist, was appointed the head of this group.

Once I happened to be present at one of the meetings of that council. I was listening to the reports and papers delivered that morning, and I realized that they weren't up to the job. They seemed like a bunch of dilettantes. I told Bogomazov about my misgivings, and as a result they stopped inviting me to the meetings.

While I was busy setting up my equipment, I was able to observe Bogomazov's colleagues at work. Zalepugin and Dmitriev toiled selflessly, testing everything new and every new chemical compound that came in from the synthesis laboratories.

Soon they discovered that the selenium analogs of soman and sarin, synthesized by Dr. Evgeni Greenshtein's group, could also break through the gas-mask filter. It looked like we would soon be able to meet the demand of the Directorate of the Chief of the Chemical Troops (UNKhV) to reduce the initial concentrations of aerosolized chemical agents to less than a few hundredths of a milligram per liter of air. For some reason the military authorities were stuck on the idea that this concentration of chemical agents would be economically "efficient" for killing soldiers on the battlefield, and those in the command stations and gas-protection chambers.

Meanwhile, I began modeling all the stages of the experiment to study the "breakthrough" effect, as Bogomazov had requested. From my previous experience, I knew only too well that technologists often underestimate the importance of choosing the right analytical method, and of using highly skilled personnel for tests. I decided to look into the analytical process control in much more detail.

At first glance, it looked like everything was being done well enough. Gas samples were taken from the adsorption tube outlet that modeled a gas-mask filter, with a special gas-tight syringe. Then, the samples were analyzed in a Tsvet-100 chromatograph with a flame-ionization detector. There was an instrument that recorded the chromatograms, and the results showed a number of so-called peaks corresponding to different compounds. The distance of the interval from the start point of the chromatogram to the peak is a characteristic parameter of each compound. So once you have measured this interval for each compound (in its pure form or mixed with an inert gas), it can be used for the identification of peaks in chromatograms of unknown mixtures, in order to determine the composition of the mixture.

This is the theory and it's a good one, but in practice everything is much more complicated. Very often a sample contains some additional compounds, which can give the same or nearly identical peak intervals in the chromatogram. When a chromatographic analysis is being conducted using a nonselective flame-ionization detector, the probability of error is rather high, due to several overlapping chromatographic peaks of the organic compounds. It should be said that really experienced specialists almost never used these intervals, because the recorders couldn't move the paper tape at a constant rate. Instead, real specialists used a stopwatch to time the emerging chromatographic peaks (measurement was taken at the maximum value), and they got much more precise and reliable measurements. Modern devices now take highly precise measurements automatically, with the help of computers.

Once I suggested to Aleksander Dmitriev that we use a stopwatch during the experiments. The first result showed chromatograms with registered peak times for various samples of soman. Then, for comparison, we took the same measurements on the same chromatogram using a mixture of inert nitrogen and the thionic analog of soman.

State Secrets

It turned out that the peak time of the compound emerging from the dynamic adsorption set, which Sasha believed to be the peak of the thionic analog, did not coincide with the peak of the same analog in nitrogen. The difference was very significant and it left no doubt that these peaks belonged to different organic molecules.

It quickly became clear to me that we were dealing with a fundamental error. However, my discovery didn't make any impression on the MACD graduate, because he was coached to trust only his boss.

I didn't know whether or not he reported our results to his scientific boss, but I was preparing to analyze the same samples in a Perkin Elmer GC with a flame photometric detector. Deep down inside, I was already sure that all those folks who had made this sensational discovery were in for a huge disappointment. Even though this could adversely affect my career and complicate my doctoral dissertation work, I was thrilled to realize that this terrible menace to people was not real.

On the outside, it seemed that nothing had happened. I continued preparing my experiments and began my own research in the comparative analysis of the kinetics of the adsorption of chemical agents on active carbon and other adsorbents used for concentrating admixtures and the necessary follow-up, along with further chromatographic analysis. Additionally, I was studying the kinetic performance of the catalytic adsorbents used in modern gas masks.

I worked practically alone (only rarely did Bogomazov give me a laboratory assistant for help), and I got tired of the long drawn-out experiments in which I had to take gas samples every 5 minutes and analyze them over a 3-4 hour period. However, some kind of inspiration was pushing me forward and I was getting a lot of satisfaction from my work. I obtained unique data that allowed me to understand what processes were taking place in the concentrating columns and to choose the right adsorbent for them.

The research on the kinetic performance of gas-mask filters also produced very interesting results. For the first time ever, we obtained adsorption fronts for chemical agents on the gas masks used by the Soviet Army.

During the course of that research, I developed a series of methods for concentrating small quantities of chemical agents in the air and in liquids. My developments were registered and I received patents for them.

By that time, I understood that I would not be able to defend my doctoral thesis as it was. I would have to revise and rewrite it. I knew that would be tremendous work, but I was not afraid of it. I began writing my thesis again – at home, in my apartment. For that purpose, I invented a special system of codes for all the chemical agents mentioned in the work. That way, the theoretical calculations, diagrams, and charts did not contain any secret information, and I did not violate confidentiality. I could write late at night and on my days off, without running to the institute's First Department for special permits to work at GOSNIIOKhT in the evenings.

It was time for a more thorough examination of the results showing breakthrough for the thionic analogs of soman and sarin.

To the great regret of the authors of the discovery, and to my greatest joy, the analysis of the samples, carried out with the help of my chromatograph with a selective detector, showed no breakthrough effect for a 10 minute period after the air with the chemical agents began flowing through the filter. Repeating the tests always gave the same result.

By the middle of the summer of 1983, Bogomazov finally acknowledged his mistake, but he continued to play the role of a great inventor saying that it was possible there could have been some experimental error in my work. But there was no error.

You had to give Bogomazov credit for his initiative and enterprising abilities. He soon established good relationships with other research institutes that were working on the "Foliant program" and developing individual means of protection.

Along with Bogomazov, I visited the Elektrostal Technological Research Institute (ENITI) for the first time. It was the leading scientific institution that was developing gas masks and filters for military equipment and installations (command posts, air-raid shelters, and so forth).

ENITI's director, Vladimir Smirnov impressed me favorably with his proficiency in very different areas of the adsorption processes, chromatography, and adsorption material production technology. All the research fellows at ENITI who I later worked with were very well informed. I'm very grateful to them for their help with my research. Although science in Russia is going through very tough times now, I am sure that ENITI will survive and continue doing science, because it makes peaceful products for people's protection.

In 1985, I asked Smirnov to be one of my official opponents, at the defense of my doctoral thesis, and he agreed at once. He wrote a very favorable review, which played a great part in my successful defense.

Dubov and Bogomazov got out of their thorny situation, by putting a positive spin on the failure of the "breakthrough". From what I know, they asked the UNKhV to relax the requirements for the initial concentration of chemical agents, and naturally their request was rejected. This made it look as though GOSNIIOKhT had developed a method for breaking through the gas mask filter, but they could not meet the requirements of the capricious military.

In fact, even if the initial concentration of chemical agents had been 10 times higher, it would not have created the required breakthrough effect. But nobody dared to say anything about that. With his usual brilliance, Dubov substantiated the need to expand in-depth research of adsorption of aerosolized chemical agents in the gas-mask filter.

Anyway, that work was not useless or wasted. Many new facts were discovered in the course of the research. In particular, it was discovered that the vapor of chemical agents remains unchanged on an adsorbent catalyst for a long time. I think this is a rather dangerous discovery for reasons of health protection. Somebody might try to develop a method of displacing toxic agents from the adsorptive catalyst and drive them into the lungs. On the other hand, this discovery creates a number of other disturbing questions about how gas masks can possibly be used again after they have been used for filtering contaminated air, for example at a factory for destroying chemical weapons.

What is the legal status of a contaminated gas mask? Can every used mask be regarded as a carrier of potentially hazardous chemical agents, even in small quantities? I am not ruling out the possibility of using gas-mask filters for the purposes of intelligence and industrial espionage.

Under the circumstances, it is interesting that the aforementioned graduate student, Valery Belikov, "discovered" a peculiar thermal effect in activated carbon, which allegedly took place when a chemical agent was breaking through the gas-mask filter. Of course, that was sheer juggling of the data, because, as my experiments convincingly proved, not one of the tested substances could break through the filter. However, none of this bothered Belikov, or prevented him from completing his work and defending his master's thesis without a trace of embarrassment. I regret that I didn't dare talk about this openly at the preliminary defense of Belikov's thesis. At that time, I really did not want to enter into conflict with my new bosses, who certainly knew about everything.

After he received his degree, Belikov joined the Communist Party. He had to wait for his party membership for several years because of the notorious enrollment quotas set by the Central Committee of the CPSU: three workers to one intellectual.

It's worth mentioning that Belikov was the last secretary of the Party Committee at GOSNIIOKhT. He was elected when the party had already fallen to pieces and only the department heads and Director Petrunin remained. President Yeltsin issued a decree after crushing the coup attempt in August of 1991, and it banned all political parties at enterprises.

Despite all the problems connected with his failed discovery, Bogomazov managed to get the maximum benefit from our collaboration.

Bogomazov was watching me at work with the Varian 3700, an American gas chromatograph, and he noticed that I was using the special tips filled with rubidium sulfate for the thermionic detector very thriftily and carefully. The tips were packaged together with the new chromatograph in small quantities, and when they were used up it was extremely difficult to buy new ones. My friend Sergey Pichidze from Shikhany used to supply me with them occasionally. At that time, however, I only had a very small stock of new ones.

Hard currency at that time was always in short supply in GOSNIIOKhT, and if we ran out of the detector tips, it could have stopped our experiments. Our repeated attempts to refill the used heads by pressing fine rubidium sulfate powder into them did not give us positive results. Maybe we were not persistent enough.

In the early 1980s, the Dzerzhinsk branch of the Special Design Bureau began making rather good gas chromatographs with a wide range of detectors including the one we needed – the thermionic detector with a rubidium sulfate tip. Unfortunately, it was very unstable in work, and its performance was changing all the time, making it practically useless for quantitative analysis of phosphorous-containing compounds.

Once, Bogomazov asked me for a used detector tip, so I gave it to him. I watched as he manipulated the head in some way, with the help of a solution, but I was rather skeptical about his attempts.

The next day, Bogomazov returned the old detector tip to me, but now it was restored and looked like a new one. I was intrigued and both of us stayed to work into the evening to test it out. Our tests showed splendid results. The detector showed a stable zero background and high sensitivity - no worse than the sensitivity guaranteed by Varian. We kept testing the detector for a whole week and results were always good. Our inventor soon restored all of my used detector tips, and solved the problem of purchasing new ones from the American manufacturer.

However, Bogomazov was not content with what had been achieved – his nature longed for grand-scale achievements. On the basis of this success he decided to remodel the thermionic detector of the Tsvet-110 gas chromatograph.

After he had made some changes, the domestic thermionic detector had practically the same sensitivity, selectivity, and stability characteristics as its American counterpart. Bogomazov immediately suggested starting up a plant at GOSNIIOKhT for manufacturing thermionic detectors for sale.

Although Director Patrushev supported Bogomazov's idea, this plan was never realized. The market for these detectors was very limited, and the artificially low prices for chromatographs, fixed by Price Commission of the U.S.S.R. Council of Ministers, did not allow them to sell detectors at a price that would even cover the costs.

Bogomazov would not have been himself, if he allowed that to stop him. He always tried to get the maximum benefit from all his achievements, although that sometimes brought him bitter disappointment. He realized that he would never make a successful career searching for toxic agents capable of breaching the gas-mask filter, so he decided to switch over to thermionic tips.

At that time, Bogomazov's stepbrother was the director of a large precious stone factory in Moscow. Leonid Brezhnev's daughter often visited that factory, and she liked to fill up her handbag with diamond jewelry made there.

Bogomazov made contacts there with some people who provided services to powerful people. In this way, he met the future mayor of Moscow, Yuri Luzhkov, who was then the director of the NPO Khimavtomatika. At that time, Luzhkov enjoyed the personal confidence of the Minister of Chemical Industry, Leonid Kostandov, and ran errands for him.

Khimavtomatika also had a section that participated in the Foliant program. In particular, it designed an automatic line for taking samples of Substance 33, and it arranged for their delivery to a laboratory at the chemical plant in Novocheboksary. Luzhkov was Director of Khimavtomatika and in charge of Khimavtomatika's branch in Dzerzhinsk, so he was directly interested in improving the quality of Tsvet-110 chromatographs.

Evgeni Bogomazov with his innovative ideas came in very handy, and Luzhkov provided him with a laboratory and equipment at Khimavtomatika. Bogomazov began working there without pay, in the evenings and on his days off, mounting thermionic detector tips on new chromatographs.

It wasn't at all difficult for the MACD graduate to arrange to have the new director of GOSNIIOKhT, Petrunin, visit Khimavtomatika. He went along with Luzhkov and "accidentally" visited the room where Bogomazov and his assistant were working. Luzhkov then told Petrunin about Bogomazov and his achievements, and he added that Bogomazov had to work at Khimavtomatika in the evenings because he probably couldn't find understanding at GOSNIIOKhT.

Soon after that, Petrunin sent for Bogomazov and appointed him head of a new laboratory for the analysis of field test samples. That was the hour of Bogomazov's shining glory.

It should be said here that as the head of the field test laboratory, Bogomazov greatly helped GOSNIIOKhT to add a new substance, chemical agent A-230, to the Soviet Army's chemical warfare arsenal.

Actually, the ongoing tests of A-230 on the new test site in Nukus (in Kara-Kalpakia, Uzbekistan) were not particularly encouraging. Possibly it was because the test site, which was built in 1983, had low-skilled personnel and the set-up and technical support were poor. Or maybe there were some other reasons.

At Nukus, the old cholinesterase method was used, and the faulty analysis it gave could well have been the main cause of failure. However, you can't exclude the possibility that the military authorities were opposed to promoting A-230 as a chemical agent.

Before that I was already aware of a number of cases in which the military had some field analysis results adjusted downwards. This information came from a number of sources, including GOSNIIOKhT employees.

The situation dramatically improved in 1986, when Bogomazov was appointed Research Director in charge of all testing carried out by GOSNIIOKhT on the Nukus site. At that time he began working there on a regular basis. With his characteristic energy, Bogomazov had the test site provided with all the necessary equipment and instruments. It was staffed with the best specialists in analytical control, who were using chromatography for the analysis of samples on the highest scale. Sometimes the number of samples reached one thousand. The specialists who were sent to work in Nukus from GOSNIIOKhT and its branches saw their salaries raised.

Bogomazov quickly found a common language with the military people, as he had known many of them since his student days at MACD.

Possibly he could manipulate test results himself and adjust them upwards. However, I knew that the fate of the tests would not be decided by Bogomazov's ability to manipulate the facts, but by more practical considerations. The military-chemical complex was badly in need of a stimulating factor, as Mikhail Gorbachev declared under perestroika.

If some sensational result was achieved by the military-chemical complex, this could engender such a stimulating factor, but that was possible only through close cooperation between civilian and the military leaders of the military-chemical complex.

In 1987, Petrunin announced at a party meeting that GOSNII-OKhT had achieved such a sensational success, one which only could happen once in every 40 years. He said the success could be called ground-breaking without any exaggeration.

At that meeting Bogomazov was sitting solemnly at the presidium, literally shining with happiness. He was so overcome with emotion that he occasionally closed his eyes for a long time. Almost everyone present at the meeting assumed that Petrunin was talking about the successful completion of tests on the new chemical agent A-230.

Still, I think that more than a few of the people present wondered: Why do we need all of that, when our country is suffering from acute shortages and everything is on the slippery slope down to Hell?

My story about Bogomazov would not be complete, if I didn't tell you about his downfall.

Bogomazov achieved the height of his success in those days, but his active nature would not let him rest on his laurels. Time was working against him at GOSNIIOKhT, and his envious colleagues, and especially his boss Nikolai Kuznetsov, could not bear their lucky colleague's success any more. Little by little, Bogomazov was pushed away from other promising research projects, in particular from testing the new binary weapons.

At that time, according to the media reports, the first joint ventures with foreign firms began sprouting up in Russia (though more on paper, than in reality). These joint ventures were developing various business projects for environmental protection, analytical instrument making, etc. Bogomazov was getting ready to work for one of them. This time, his vanity defeated him. By believing strongly in his indispensability and his privileged position at GOSNIIOKhT, Bogomazov completely lost his caution and his orientation.

Once, he came to work, and with obvious pride he began showing off his new business ID card written in English. For GOSNIIOKhT, this was like waving a red cape in front of a bull. He was immediately dismissed from his position as the head of the laboratory, and he was demoted to the position of junior researcher.

Humbled and insulted to his core, Bogomazov soon resigned from GOSNIIOKhT altogether and went into private business. According to the rumors, this did not work out either. Finally in 1994, he suffered a stroke and turned into a helpless invalid. At the age of 40-something, he was all alone. Everyone including his wife had deserted him. After a while Bogomazov recovered a little from his stroke, and decided to return to GOSNIIOKhT, but his days there were numbered and he died as a rank and file employee.

Fortunately, my debunking of Bogomazov's discovery and the disappointment it caused my bosses did not reflect unfavorably on my own work. I continued my research and wrote my doctoral dissertation - "Development and Study of New Methods of Frontal and Elution Chromatography for the Determination of Micro-Concentrations of Chemical Agents."

By the beginning of 1985, I had submitted my thesis work to the Science Council for defense. Most doctoral candidates have problems choosing official opponents for their theses, due to the limited number of institutions and people that can be asked to review their work, but I did not have any problems with that at all.

Long before Petrunin was appointed Director of GOSNIIOKhT, he agreed to be my official opponent. I think he agreed because he appreciated my work that had benefited the Volsk branch of GOSNIIOKhT, which he headed at that time. I gave all the assistance I could to the branch's Physical Chemistry Department and acted as a scientific advisor to the graduate students who worked there. Two talented scientists, Valery Djuzhev-Maltsev and Nadezhda Steklenyova, wrote their master's theses in chemistry under my guidance.

Two other people agreed to be my official opponents, Georgi

Drozd and Vladimir Smirnov, and they also gave my work favorable reviews. Additionally, my work was received favorably by a number of interested scientific institutions that I had sent my dissertation and abstract to. Among those organizations was a department of UNKhV.

I successfully defended my dissertation in June of 1985, and all members of the Science Council unanimously voted "in favor" of it. During the defense, only Sheluchenko, made an attempt to question the validity of my results. He made some kind of a statement, saying that the results presented in the dissertation were obtained only from experimental research conducted in the laboratory, while in practice some of them might not be confirmed. Still, he acknowledged that the regularities revealed were of great importance.

Martynov, the former director of GOSNIIOKhT, was sitting in the front row, and he retorted immediately: "It's great that this work opens up new prospects - as a doctoral thesis should!"

Sheluchenko pulled himself up short, seeing that the seeds of doubt he was trying to sow did not fall on fertile ground as expected. He continued "Despite my remarks, I think that the work meets the demands of a dissertation for a doctoral degree."

Oh my God! People's hearts are so mysterious! I still had a vivid recollection of a serious conversation with Martynov in his director's office, back in 1976. It was immediately following a staff meeting, at which Beresnev blamed Revelsky and me for his own failures in the department, making us the scapegoats responsible. Martynov was infuriated, and after that meeting he openly threatened me with reprisals, saying he could do whatever he wanted with me. He also said then that I would hardly ever be able to defend a doctoral dissertation. After that incident my life became very hard, as Martynov actually gave out carte blanche for any actions against me. I don't know whether Beresnev was telling the truth when he once confessed to me that if it hadn't been for my talent and my ability to get results at work, he would have "handled" me as I deserved a long time ago.

Chapter 10

Safety While Working with Chemical Agents – is it Possible?

The Degasification Department (Department D) had an important place in the scope GOSNIIOKhT's work. This department developed methods for degasification of chemical agents and any equipment contaminated by them. According to the regulations, all the safety manuals had to be evaluated, revised and re-approved every five years. These manuals contained descriptions of degasification methods, checks for completeness, and the safety and first aid rules.

In the beginning, like my co-workers, I believed that the degasification methods described in the manuals were not subject to any doubt. But once I started to question them and began to study their efficiency independently of the planned revision schedule, I began to regret that I started this too late.

Back in the mid 1970s, Department D was reorganized in order to make it more clearly focused, goal oriented and efficient. Retired Colonel Grigori Drell, who had been a senior researcher from TSNIVTI, became the head of this department and one of its laboratories. My good friend and a retired colonel, Imam Yamaleev, became the head of another laboratory.

I collaborated with Drell's laboratory in mastering the methods of chromatographic analysis. They had good American equipment purchased according to my recommendation, but unfortunately this equipment could never produce the results expected. This was due to the bone-headedness of the chief of this department.

Drell distinguished himself by his cruelty to his staff. He was entirely confident that they were making enormous efforts to violate safety rules and were to blame for all the emergency incidents which happened so often in his department. So, when one of his researchers, Olga Kolyada, was badly poisoned by mustard gas, Drell did his best to shift the blame to the victim. In reality, a drop of mustard gas happened to fall onto her glove, but she did not see it in time. Yperite has a highly effective rate of penetration and easily passes through rubber, causing lesions in the form of hard to treat burns and severe inflammation of the skin. If you consider that it is also one of the strongest mutagens, the consequences of contact with mustard gas can be terrible.

Immediately after the lesion was discovered, wet swab samples taken from the glove were brought to me. I analyzed them with the American Perkins Elmer chromatograph with a flame-photometric detector, which could selectively register chemical compounds containing sulfur or phosphorous atoms.

From the resulting chromatogram, you could tell there were several sulfur compounds, but not mustard gas. Surely, the degasification agent must have destroyed the mustard gas when Olga Kolyada decontaminated the glove at the end of the working day, according to safety procedures.

Chromatographic analysis of the control samples taken from a fresh glove surface did not show the presence of sulfur compounds either. So, it was practically proved that an organic sulfur compound got onto the surface of Kolyada's glove, and it had to be mustard gas, as no one in the laboratory worked with any other sulfur-containing compounds.

You couldn't expect anything else from Drell, who was notable for his devil-may-care attitude towards safety. According to one of his senior researchers, Sergei Davydov, he forced his employees to

State Secrets

work with mustard gas, without any protection and even to sniff its vapors, so they could remember the smell. After this unfortunate accident, Kolyada was obliged to retire, and she died a year later of cancer.

Some of the safety violations at GOSNIIOKhT were due to the ignorance or carelessness of its employees. For example, safety procedures required that anyone transporting samples of dangerous chemicals from one part of the facility to another must place the test tubes in portable steel containers with activated charcoal strewn on the bottom, to absorb the agent in case of an accident. This was supposed to offer the carrier some protection. Safety regulations also required small-scale laboratory work with hazardous chemicals to be accomplished in cabinets with exhaust hoods that sucked the air inside the cabinets away from the workers, allowing them to perform many procedures without full gas masks.[49] As I prepared for an experiment connected with transforming Substance 33 into a stable aerosol, a beautiful, young research assistant appeared in my room, but without a container. My jaw dropped when she took three test tubes out of her pocket with her bare hands and quietly placed them in the safety cabinet. To this day, I still reproach myself for not reprimanding her for her carelessness because she died of lung cancer a couple of years later.[50]

Other dangers at GOSNIIOKhT resulted from a misplaced trust in out-dated safety procedures. Every five years, the Decontamination Department was responsible for revising all the safety manuals, which contained descriptions of decontamination methods, checks for completeness of safety precautions, and safety and first aid rules. Instead, the department merely reissued the manuals without making any significant changes, despite real improvements in safety technologies and practices. Misguided trust in the old ways is the reason that the process to sanitize items contaminated by soman was not changed for decades. I personally analyzed the decontamination solutions that GOSNIIOKhT used, and I always found that the decontamination solutions did not destroy significant quantities of agents such as sarin and soman.[51] According to GOSNIIOKhT's safety manuals, glassware and gloves could be used again, unless they were broken or torn after cleaning with these decontamination solutions. Since the administration was too stingy to supply us with fresh gloves, GOSNIIOKhT laboratory workers were compelled to reuse ones that were still contaminated. Safe practice calls for protective gloves to be used only once.

The danger for GOSNIIOKhT's workers was clear, and matters were made even worse by the fact that the waste water, from rinsing the allegedly decontaminated glassware and gloves, ran directly into the Moscow city sewer system, carrying with it the residues of undestroyed chemical agents. When gloves were torn, instructions required the scientist to cut to them up into narrow strips, which were placed in bags that were sent to Moscow's garbage sites. Arguably, such lax safety practices put human health and the environment at risk, both inside and outside of GOSNIIOKhT's territory.

The Soviet Army preached an entire philosophy of reusing previously-contaminated equipment, weapons, and clothing. This approach was deeply wrong, but General Anatoli Kuntsevich, the commander of the military chemical complex at Saratov, had developed his own methods of decontamination. When I applied this decontamination solution on steel test plates to model the use of Kuntsevich's decontamination solution on military equipment, I was shocked to find that all of the samples contained a hundred times more than maximum permissible concentration of sarin.[52] The safety practices in Military Unit 61469 were particularly egregious. Soldiers took unreasonable risks and there were open safety violations. I was horrified to see an officer bring a couple kilograms of soman to his work station and open a container to take samples without using any safety measures whatsoever. When I asked why he was so "brave" and taking such risks, he simply replied that he was "a chemical officer."

Perhaps the most significant safety shortcut that GOSNIIOKhT's hierarchy took was with the very air that its employees breathed. Employees at the main laboratory building at GOSNIIOKhT were constantly breathing an atmosphere partially composed of exhaust air. GOSNIIOKhT had powerful ventilators, but this ventilation system was largely redirecting exhaust air into the workrooms, and on days when the atmospheric pressure dropped, the exhaust air from the safety hoods would spread out close to ground level in the rooms. On such days, it was literally impossible to breath in the laboratories, and it was not uncommon to see people in gas masks rushing out of the main laboratory building.[53]

The same was true on the eve of Soviet holidays, when according to the rules all rooms had to be free of all chemical agents (old and newly synthesized ones) and their precursors. For almost a week all scientists and assistants were busy destroying these hazardous substances in huge quantities under the hoods creating contamination in the ventilation exhausts.

According to the safety rules, the ventilation was shut down at 6 PM and started up again at 8 AM the next day, one hour before the working day began. These requirements were supposed to provide enough time to clear the working rooms of chemical agent vapors that were released during the night, while the ventilation system wasn't working. The Safety Department ordered me to research the dangers posed by these procedures. As a model, I used a non-toxic substance and the tracer sulfur hexafluoride, which has far less adsorption on the walls of the hoods and working room surfaces than any of the chemical agents. I discovered that the tracer was released in significant amounts in the closed hood, diffusing into the room and becoming adsorbed to the walls during the night time. The chemical agents were less volatile than the safer model, so they were more likely to adsorb to the workroom walls and surfaces at night.

After starting the ventilation up at 8 AM, an initial measurement was taken at 9 AM the next day. By 5 PM, the concentration of sulfur hexafluoride was equal to 70% its original value that morning, proving that the model was desorbing slowly. So, the working rooms were never free of any traces of chemical agents, unless the ventilators were operating round the clock.

My findings did not prompt the management of GOSNIIOKhT to take any steps to correct this problem, because they could not afford such a luxury as a permanently working ventilation system.

At that time, the problem of purification of the exhaust air, which was ventilated from the buildings of GOSNIIOKhT, had not been resolved in any way at all. I am not sure that this problem has been solved, even today. Activated charcoal cannot be safely used to purify these emissions, as it is a flammable solid, which is extremely dangerous. It is absolutely clear that a fire at such a plant could have catastrophic consequences.

This was the reason why the exhaust ventilation at GOSNII-OKhT was not equipped with filtering devices, and practically all of the air from the production and laboratory areas was emitted into the atmosphere without any purification.[54]

Certainly they did try to solve this problem by using inorganic adsorbents, aluminum oxide in particular. Victor Aborkin, a senior researcher from the Department D, was obsessed with this idea, which was the topic of his master's thesis.

Having only a very vague concept of the basics of adsorption, this inventor managed to attract the attention of Guskov and Golubkov, the Deputy Minister for Chemical Industry, to his idea. Then he enlisted the help of those two bosses, who became his co-authors, and he aggressively and persistently pushed his idea further along. Aborkin began promoting this adsorbent project in Workshop N 34, in the Volgograd Scientific Production Association where soman was produced.

When I visited this workshop in 1984, I was shown a big adsorber outside the building where aluminum oxide had turned into an absolutely airproof monolith. It turned out to be a lesson on adsorption basics for the unlucky speculators, but they had already received considerable sums of money for their "invention", so they didn't care.

When I returned to Moscow, I decided to make a more thorough check of this adsorbent. As a result of this test, it was proved that after adsorption, soman could exist in its solid state indefinitely without degrading. Moreover, aluminum oxide stopped adsorbing soman after acidic vapor, or just hydrogen chloride gas or clorine, was passed through it. The concentration of hydrochloric acid in the atmosphere of the Volgograd plant exceeded the permissible standards by hundreds of times. So this huge monolith had entirely stopped working as a "filter" a long time before. Still, it contained huge quantities of the dangerous chemical agent.

The plants for producing phosphorous chloride, which was a

State Secrets

precursor for the synthesis of phosphoorganic compounds including soman and sarin, were continuously secreting unbroken clouds of chlorine and hydrogen chloride into the open air.

I went on a number of business trips to our Volgograd branch and to the Volgograd Institute of Toxicology and Professional Pathology. Their buildings were located on the territory of the NPO "Khimprom". Along with the employees of these institutions, I was repeatedly "assaulted" by chlorine gas. In this place it was sometimes even difficult to see each other in the workrooms, due to the extremely high gas content. Only a gas mask could help, and gas masks were provided to all the visitors, who had to wear them until they left the territory of the NPO enterprise.

Sometimes distance could not save you from a gas attack, even if you were far away from the plant. I remember that during one of my first visits to Volgograd, we stayed in the Beketovka settlement, which is 7 kilometers from "Khimprom". In the middle of one summer night, we woke up suffocating. Immediately we understood from the smell that we were being poisoned with chlorine. We could save ourselves only by closing all the windows and covering them with wet sheets and blankets.

The residents of the settlement and of other regions located within the zone of the gas attack could breathe somewhat easily only when the wind shifted direction. If the wind was blowing from the plant, which is on the banks of the Volga River, it was a real disaster. No wonder all this led to massive protests by the inhabitants, even during times of Communist stagnation. Unfortunately, the protests did not produce any tangible results. From time to time, party leaders simply found some scapegoat, leaving the existing production process unchanged.

Aluminum oxide was equally unsuitable as a filtering adsorbent for purifying the emissions from GOSNIIOKhT. In the laboratory rooms, calcium hypochlorite and hydrochloric acid (the solution of hydrogen chloride gas in water) are used almost everywhere on a daily basis to destroy chemical agents, to neutralize chemicals on the laboratory glassware, gloves and other items for individual protection. Since aluminum oxide is very quickly deactivated by acid and chlorine, it would be absolutely useless in a filter.

Additionally, there is another substantial obstacle that prevents the use of any filters in the path of the air vented into the atmosphere.

According to the safety standards for working with chemical agents, the linear velocity of the air sucked by the ventilation into the laboratory exhaust hood should be at least 1.0 meter per second. It is believed that only this air speed, as measured at the hood gate when opened to 40 centimeters above the surface of a table, can guarantee certain safety to people working with chemical agents. Additional airflow is forced into each room through the ventilation with air-blowers located close to the laboratory building, in order not to create a rarefied atmosphere during the constant suction through the exhaust hood. The pressure equilibrium between outgoing and incoming air volumes is maintained in this way. Every room is equipped with its own ventilator fan, which constantly drives air out of the building. The capacity of each ventilator is calculated for maintaining the necessary exhaust air velocity and no more than that.

If some filter with an absorbent is installed in the path of the exhaust air, this would reduce the exhaust velocity from the laboratory chamber to a level below the allowable limit, and this would be intolerable. Every exhaust hood has a chart attached to it where the date and the last measured air velocity are logged.

If these measurements are lower than the standard norms, any operations with chemical agents must be terminated. So, if filters were installed, the existing ventilation units would have to be replaced, requiring an extensive capital investment. Even in good times, the leadership of the military-chemical complex could not afford such a 'luxury' for their scientists.

The Soviet military-chemical complex was also running their factories without proper waste water and exhaust air treatment. In 1986, I decided to introduce my new, highly sensitive, and selective chromatographic methods for the determination of concentrations of soman and sarin at the Volgograd chemical plant, where their previous analytical procedures showed that the exhaust air was meeting permissible standards. Our first analyses of the exhaust air, conducted on February 10th 1987, were made of samples taken after the plant had been closed for maintenance and inspection for one and a half months. The sobering results showed that air containing many times the permissible level of soman was flowing out of the exhaust stacks.[55] I assumed that these already poor levels would increase when the plant was operating.

In addition, the analysis of several samples taken from the tank storing Volgograd's decontamination waste water showed that 100 to 1,000 times the maximum permissible concentration of soman remained in the water.[56] The main reason for this mistake was a flawed cholinesterase-based analytical method of the determination of the residues of sarin and soman in presence of salts such as sodium chloride and others in this waste water. That waste water from the Volgograd plant was mixed with the waste water from the production of pesticides, and it flowed into a nearby lake, which was directly adjacent to the apartment complexes of Volgograd Industrial Association VPO "Khimprom."

This lake was nicknamed the "White Sea". The same defective analytical methods and irresponsible engineering practice at Volgograd Industrial Association VPO "Khimprom" resulted in the disastrous breakthrough of these waters into the Volga River in the spring of 1965. According to eyewitnesses, the entire surface of the Volga River up to Astrakhan was covered with dead fish.[57]

I presented these findings in full detail to Victor Petrunin, Director of GosNIIOKhT, who then calmly reminded me that Sergei Golubkov, the Deputy Minister of Chemical Industry, had once been the Volgograd factory's chief engineer.[58] Presenting Golubkov with this "inconvenient truth" would simply result in the loss of both our jobs, he asserted. Moreover, he warned that environmental and safety analysis at the Novocheboksary plant would reveal a similar state of affairs. I had no doubt that he was correct on both counts. Indeed, the Novocheboksary factory used a dangerously flawed GOSNIIOKhT technology for the recirculation of its waste water, a process in which it was decontaminated by ozonation and redirected for subsequent use, including decontamination procedures and the laundering of protective suits and underwear. Unfortunately, they used the cholinesterase method to monitor and control the effectiveness of this procedure, and I had already proven that it produced gross errors in the Volgograd factory. A similar ozonation procedure was used to "scrub" the air vented from the technological buildings into the surrounding environment, using the same flawed cholinesterase method for evaluating the air.

True to form, nothing came out of my attempt at prompting accountability, except for some flaming rhetoric directed back at me. GOSNIIOKhT Deputy Director Konstantin Guskov said that I had performed this research on my own initiative, and that GOSNIIOKhT did not stand behind my conclusions.

Really, it was impossible to control the fate of all the containers with chemical agents in the working laboratories. According to security regulations, every room had the right to keep up to 200 grams of chemical agents in its iron safe under the hood. The limit was up to 500 g or more for some laboratories (Departments MB, D and RP) which consumed large quantities of chemical agents. At the end of each day, scientists were supposed to lock their box and hang the key up under the hood. Taking into account that there were more than 100 laboratory rooms working with chemical agents in the GLK, this means that at least 20 kg of them were stored in this building alone, and perhaps more than 60kg altogether at GOSNIIOKhT. This is more that I had previously estimated, when I wrote the article "A Poisoned Policy" in *Moscow News*[59], about than dangers posed to Moscow's citizens by storage of chemical agents at GOSNIIOKhT. What could have happened if a major fire had broken out in the GLK and could not be contained?

There was already a huge fire in the Novocheboksary factory on April 28, 1974, during which "several tons of Substance 33 was dispersed within a 30 kilometer radius" of the storage facility for the final chemical agent of Installation 83. According to eyewitness accounts, more than 100 people were poisoned there.[60] The environmental problems created by military chemical complex of Russia is also raised by Judith Perera.[61]

It's actually laughable that they tried to pretend that they were worried about foreign intelligence services picking up information about new chemical weapons in the environment surrounding GOSNIIOKhT and its branches and test sites, since the contamination was so widespread.

Chapter 11
Struggling with Spies

The Geneva Negotiations

At the end of the 1970s, a new division appeared at GOSNII-OKhT with the intriguing name "the Sector for Foreign Technical Counterintelligence". Ivan Sorochkin, who looked like a crook, was its first chief. He came to the institute from an establishment connected with the KGB, and his elusive slippery behavior was striking. The mystery of his mission became a little clearer when he appeared in our laboratory accompanied by an elderly man with a gloomy red-veined face and a skinny middle-aged brunette. They started rummaging through the wastebaskets looking for something, and when they found some scraps of paper, they put them into polyethylene bags and departed with satisfied faces.

I became acquainted with Ivan Sorochkin himself, as he was interested in my technique of analysis of micro-concentrations of chemical agents in different media. It turned out that he was a retired lieutenant colonel with a master's degree in chemistry. His two other employees, who also appeared to be retired military people, spent their time at writing desks in a small room, and they were constantly busy writing something. Later I found out that they were writing reports about analytical work which they had never participated in. They were just copying excerpts from the completed works of others, creating the impression that these works were carried out by their orders and with their participation.

The sector of the institute dedicated to foreign technical counterintelligence (PD ITR) was far from modern. It wasn't involved in developing technical methods for the determination of trace quantities of chemical agents. Sorochkin lived a parasitic life, imitating activity, in the typical Soviet way. As a specialist on the determination of micro-concentrations of chemical agents and their precursors, it pained me to see Sorochkin and his subordinates use my work to cover up their own idleness.

Back in 1984, I drew the attention of Kurochkin to the "specific character" of the activity of PD ITR, and he promised to talk with Grigory Patrushev, who was then the director of GOSNII-OKhT. I wanted my knowledge and experience to be used for creating an experimental basis for that service. However, our conversation achieved nothing, although real changes were still possible at that time.

The conceited Sorochkin had wormed his way into Patrushev's confidence, and he virtually became his main advisor on many important issues. Working with the new Deputy Director in charge of the Security Regime, Sorochkin managed to get the director to hold back some departmental specialists. Soon Sorochkin became the head of one of the key subdivisions of the institute - the Scientific and Technical Department (NTO). However, when Sorochkin started plotting against First Deputy Director Guskov, he obviously didn't properly calculate his own power.

According to an administrative provision on executive personnel, the position of the head of a department is competitive and should be approved by secret voting at the Science Council of the institute. Usually this procedure is a simple formality, because few people dared to vote against him when the director of the institute recommended someone for a position. However, there are always exceptions in life. In fact, everything worked in an atypical manner at that time. In the end Sorochkin became an ignominious failure and was not approved for the position. After that, he decided not to push his luck any further, and he quickly retired from the institute.

After that, Sergei Stroganov, an elderly retired colonel, was appointed the chief of the PD ITR Department. By that time this service had acquired the status of a department. Before that, Stroganov had worked at the Ministry of Chemical Industry. He brought three more people with him, who were also retired military men, who had worked in the technical subdivisions of the KGB. This event coincided with the replacement of Duka, the Director of the Security Regime Department, by Aleksander Martynov, a young KGB major, who had graduated from the Mendeleev Chemical and Technological Institute and had been assigned to GOSNIIOKhT. However, the future KGB officer didn't stay long there. Te was sent to study at the KGB Academy, becoming a Chekist officially.

This was the situation at the institute when an idea occurred to me... to become head of the PD ITR Department, myself. I went with my idea to Nikolai Maslov, a friend of mine, who was head of the Planning and Economic Department at the U.S.S.R. Ministry of Mineral Fertilizers. For a long time, he had worked at different positions in the leadership of the Ministry of Chemical Industry, and at one point he had been the deputy chief of their Main Administration "Soyuzorgsynthesis", which GOSNIIOKhT was a subsidiary of. That is why he knew the industry and the work of our institute reasonably well. I met Nikolai on holidays, along with some of our other colleagues, including Aleksander Ivanov. Later Ivanov started working in a section of the Chemistry Department at the Central Committee of the C.P.S.U., in charge of the military-chemical complex. When General Anatoly Kuntsevich was dismissed in 1994 in his capacity as the Chairman of Russia's Committee for Problems of the Chemical and Biological Weapons Conventions which answered to the president of Russia, Ivanov followed him a year later as the new chairman of that committee.

Nikolai Maslov liked my idea, and he immediately called Ivanov on a high-frequency communication channel. Ivanov quickly understood what we wanted and promised to talk it over with Victor Petrunin, Director of GOSNIIOKhT. This meant that the question was settled. A few days later, Petrunin called me and said that he had decided to appoint me to a very important position, as the head of the Foreign Technical Counterintelligence Department. He added that the formal agreement of the Ministry of Chemical Industry was required, and he hoped that it would succeed without any problems.

I felt that Guskov and Martynov, Deputy Director of the Department of the Security Regime, were not happy with the news about my appointment. Still KGB Major Martynov assured me that he would help out and give me the necessary support.

The next day, I was called to Ministry of Chemical Industry. It turned out that PD ITR answered to the Third Administration of the Ministry of Chemical Industry, in which Mikhael Milyutin, a KGB Lieutenant General, was the director. I was introduced to him by Ivan Tkachenko, head of the PD ITR Department, and a former commander of the division that served at the Semipalatinsk nuclear test site in Kazakhstan.

The KGB general turned out to be a gray, slightly hunched elderly man with a slightly swarthy face imprinted with certain traces of intelligence. He was dressed in civilian clothes, and he seemed to be surrounded by an atmosphere of disappointment which was heightened by the backdrop of his huge gloomy office. There were models of ships, tanks, and some other armaments on one of the tables. These were gifts, and each model had an engraved silver plate.

The general asked me to sit down, and he sat opposite me, asking in a friendly way, "How are you feeling?" I said that I would be much better if I could find support for my plans for providing the department with the modern scientific equipment which I considered necessary for implementing the task at hand.

I briefly stated my understanding of our work, and the general answered that Tkachenko and Krasheninnikov would help me out. When we parted, General Milyutin asked me not to hesitate to contact him directly if I encountered any difficulties.

After this, I met Victor Krasheninnikov, a handsome young man with gray hair and a kind face, which contrasted with his responsibilities. He was the deputy head of the Third Administration, but he in turn answered to another deputy head of the same department, Elena Batova, a woman in her late 50s.

The amiable intelligent manner of Victor Ivanovich won people over, and it was difficult to imagine that he could hurt other people or let someone down. I liked him at once, and this impression lasted for a long time - I was never mistaken about Krasheninnikov. I think that he was a rare exception among the officials of such an odious department. To the end of my days on the job, I couldn't imagine what his responsibilities were. Aside from monitoring the PD ITR at the ministry, he also arranged for the development of different industrial exhibitions. However, as far as I was concerned, his most important responsibility was connected with processing applications for imported equipment.

Scientific research institutes could buy new foreign scientific equipment, for the purpose of evaluating it. This was necessary so that recommendations could be made for its purchase on a large scale. A pretty woman collected these applications at the institutes, discussed them with Krasheninnikov, and decided whether or not they could be submitted for approval at the next meeting of the Military Industrial Commission (VPK) at the Central Committee of the C.P.S.U.

Krasheninnikov was shrewd enough to understand my major objective in my new position. I was primarily interested in scientific activity, and the PD ITR was my second priority. Still, he did everything he could to support my plans.

The Ministry of Chemical Industry, along with the employees from the PD ITR Department, elaborated the one-year plan as well as the long-term plans. These plans included the evaluation of the institutions involved in the development of the "Foliant" project, from the standpoint of their vulnerability to foreign technical intelligence. The next step was the development of a plan to fix the weaknesses in the system. In order to do this, it was necessary to provide the PD ITR Department with a technical basis, and I knew that it was useless to rely on other GOSNIIOKhT departments in that area. Krasheninnikov liked the logic behind my reasoning and he promised to help.

The branch research conference scheduled for November of 1986 fit my plans perfectly. I was very grateful to the predecessor of Stroganov for his efforts to organize this conference. A year later I personally felt very sorry for him when I was forced to suggest he leave his job. Unfortunately, there was absolutely nothing for him to do when we really started working at the PD ITR Department. The qualifications of the retired Colonel Stroganov, a veteran of the front lines who had served at Semipalatinsk Nuclear Test Site for a long time, were just not right for laboratory work. He even had trouble writing because his hands were always shaking.

The bulky "top secret" general instruction manual, approved by the Military Industrial Commission of the Central Committee of C.P.S.U., stipulated the objectives and tasks of the PD ITR, and the rights and responsibilities of its agencies. One of the most important tasks was the development of methods of permanent control over the activities of defense organizations and enterprises, in order to control the activities of foreign technical intelligence. This gave me the right to study all scientific and technical documents and plans of the scientific departments and laboratories.

All planned technical tasks for implementing scientific, technical, and design work were required to comply with a section of the specifications on PD ITR and had to be signed by the head of the PD ITR Department, among others. So there was a lot of paperwork, but I found a good way out of this. Retired Lieutenant Colonel Svyatoslav Sokolov, a senior scientific assistant, was also working in my department. After graduating from Moscow State University, he worked at the KGB Scientific Research Institute, and he was the head of the Physical Chemistry Laboratory there, so he understood scientific questions quite well. Svyatoslav Sergeevich was intelligent, had gentle manners and, therefore, he was the ideal person for communicating with the heads of research subdivisions at GOSNIIOKhT. Unfortunately, he was past his prime and, despite all his efforts, he couldn't work at the laboratory of the department that I soon put into order. Work there required both manual labor and the skills of a specialist. Still, for a long time, Sokolov helped me out by attending numerous committee meetings in my place, as the head of the PD ITR Department, and by inspecting the documentation.

On the sixth floor of the GOSNIIOKhT's modern new administrative building (the picture of this building was published in many articles devoted to my "case"), there was a room near my office that received all the bugged phone calls. All the telephone lines went through there, including the ones for internal use. With the help of the switchboard, it was possible to intercept telephone conversations so that people talking didn't notice anything, and tape-recorders were installed there, too.

One of our employees sat at the control panel and monitored this dirty work. Before I was appointed head of the department, I heard in passing that there was such a service, but I really didn't want to believe that it was true.

I decided to get rid of this unpleasant burden at any cost. The briefs I studied didn't mention the use of such underhanded strategies of the PD ITR. I went to Ministry of Chemical Industry, to Krasheninnikov and Tkachenko, in order to get more precise explanations. They confirmed that tapping telephone conversations was outside our area of responsibility. It was done at the request of local KGB agencies. The head of the PD ITR Department at the Redkino subsidiary of the scientific industrial company (NPO) "Khimavtomatika", who was present during our conversation, said that he had this service transferred from his department to someone in the First Department.

The responsibilities of PD ITR included the technical protection of the telephones from tapping by foreign intelligence services, but that was a very different matter and we took it very seriously and even helped the Main Department of Ministry of Chemical Industry with that.

We had to develop measures against taping conversations, meetings, and scientific conferences, as well as the meetings of the science councils and their sections. According to the recommendations of the department, the office doors of the heads of departments and laboratories were provided with acoustic protection. Additionally, a large part of our work was devoted to protecting GOSNIIOKhT's computer center and the computers from electromagnetic radiation, which could be a source of information for foreign intelligence. It was possible to eliminate information leaks through an electric cable by installing a special transformer. However, it was very difficult to provide protection from external radiation. This work required considerable expense. The walls of GOSNIIOKhT's two-story computer center (with a total area of several hundred square meters) were covered with a fine-steel net. There was another system of steel nets to protect the windows and doors. Together, these nets encased the building.

From time to time, the PD ITR Department checked the efficiency of this protection with special instruments. However, we didn't have the necessary equipment to gauge the leakage of radiation on certain frequencies, so a special service of the PD ITR Department at "Khimavtomatika" at Redkino did this work. It was the only institution in the system of the Ministry of Chemical Industry that had the right to examine rooms with electronic computers.

Such serious protection was required after we found out that information could be read on foreign computers with the help of the specially implanted "bugs", which were practically impossible to detect. According to the rumors, some specialists who were repairing a minor breakdown in the 1980s accidentally found a "bug" in a powerful computer that was made in Japan and installed at Gosplan (State Planning agency of the U.S.S.R.) This "bug" had been transferring information to foreign intelligence agencies for a few years, and according to a certain schedule, it "shot" the accumulated information to a spy satellite.

In principal, it was possible to spy without using a "bug". It was enough just to record the electromagnetic computer radiation from a certain distance with the right equipment. That is why so much attention was paid to protection. Nobody wanted to be counted among the negligent workers.

For protection, we could use "jammers", noise generators which were supposed to make it impossible to use electromagnetic radiation for obtaining computer information. Our industry manufactured such "jammers", but the "noise" they created made the operation of foreign computers impossible. Primitive computers like the "Robotron" made in East Germany could tolerate the noise of a "jammer" and you could work on them with secret information in any specially equipped room.

State Secrets

By a twist of fate, after my arrest in 1992, I saw a "Robotron" computer on the desk of Victor Shkarin, a KGB investigator, when I was brought to his office. It had no "jammer" and I noticed that his office had no special protection. Moreover, from time to time, the investigator opened the window to air out the cigarette smoke from his cramped office. I teased him, saying that he was violating the PD ITR instructions for handling top-secret matters, but the captain was very serious. I got the impression he didn't appreciate my sense of humor.

The question of protecting computers at GOSNIIOKhT was very important, because a number of imported instruments couldn't go through the entire cycle of processing the information they received by themselves. This was the case, for example, at the Physical Chemistry Department, where they couldn't use the computers with the NMR and chromatomass-spectrometer, devices for identifying chemical compounds made in the USA. This was beyond all common sense and I immediately settled this problem. There was a good excuse. The instructions stated that no special protection was required if secret information did not exceed 15% of the total volume of the processed information. But who could check the percentage of secret information, which was processed at facilities with, for example, chromatomass-spectrometers?

It wasn't so easy to settle the question about tapping telephone conversations, because this work was done at the request of the Deputy Director of the Department for the Security Regime, and as I soon discovered, the job was performed with great enthusiasm. This is not surprising, since it allowed the operator to report every day to the KGB major himself, and to keep him well informed about the private lives of the institute employees!

I hurried to Martynov to discuss the fate of the concealed listening unit in the PD ITR Department. I gave him the reasons why this unit shouldn't be my responsibility and asked the major to transfer it to the Department for the Security Regime, where the former blacksmith from the Analytical Department, Boris Churkov, could handle this work very well. I suggested that we provide technical support, making sure that the equipment was maintained at the necessary level and even purchase a more automated recording system, if necessary.

Martynov's face turned red with anger and he said, "So, you start your work by making a mess of ours?!"

He had already become used to almost completely controlling the PD ITR Department, although formally it answered directly to First Deputy Director Guskov. However, before we had our conversation, I had learned that the operator of the concealed listening unit was also intercepting Guskov's conversations. If necessary he could intercept the Director himself, except during his high frequency communications, of course. Several times I noticed Guskov sitting near his office and talking with people who had come to see him. So he understood that not only were the telephones being intercepted, but talks in his office were subject to eavesdropping as well. It was very easy for Martynov's people, who were nominally members of my department, to install the "bugs". They provided protection of information in the offices, and from time to time they checked the telephones and doors. This was funny and a little bit sad, because the people who were supposed to protect the bosses in these offices actually worked against them. Unfortunately, these were the KGB's rules of the game. And I decided to go against the grain!

I explained to Martynov, who could hardly contain his rage, that additional work not stipulated by the provisions for organizing the PD ITR Department, might cost a lot in terms of energy and productivity, not just for me but also for him as Deputy Director in charge of the Department for the Security Regime. "Bugging" distracts us from our main work, which had increased sharply in its significance, on the threshold of finalizing the Chemical Weapons Convention.

Nobody at GOSNIIOKhT doubted that the negotiations for finalizing the CWC had nothing to do with the work of the military-chemical complex.

We had to hide our new developments at any cost. The KGB major certainly understood that my arguments were pure demagoguery. However, he couldn't openly object to my logic, especially since I referred to the opinion of people from the Third Department of Ministry of Chemical Industry, of the USSR. As a result, Martynov promised to think it over.

The struggle for transferring the concealed listening unit succeeded only in 1988, when I handed over all the keys for the room and its equipment to Boris Churkov from the Department of the Security Regime, on receipt. However, these facts didn't prevent the Director of GOSNIIOKhT, Victor Petrunin, from stressing in interviews to different correspondents that my responsibilities included tapping the telephones of the institute employees, as well as looking through their papers.

Concerning this "looking through the papers" business, I can firmly state that from my first days in my position as head of the PD ITR Department at GOSNIIOKhT and of the branch, I prohibited this occupation as useless and offensive to people's dignity. In my opinion, the objectives of the department were different, and I did my best to run the department professionally.

There was also the matter of protecting the secrets involving the production of chemical agents. Part of the work of some Finnish specialists, which addressed the problems connected with technical control issues raised by the Chemical Weapons Convention (CWC), appeared at GOSNIIOKhT. There was nothing there that could possibly surprise me, but the information contained in those reports allowed me to understand to some extent, the Western countries' level of knowledge and experience in identification of chemical agents. And I believed this corresponded to their capabilities of technical intelligence.[62-67]

At the same time, I couldn't refuse Guskov's next request to help the scientific commission conduct an evaluation of the effectiveness of a new radioactive device for detecting a gas attack on Soviet tanks. This device was proposed by scientists from the Military Academy of Chemical Defense, and it was designed and constructed by the Tula Special Design Bureau of Automation (OKBA). I spent a week in Tula testing this device, by "easy" military specialists. Several times OKBA created artificial concentrations of Substance 33 in a huge gas chamber. They injected the required volume of liquid agent into the flow of air directed into the gas chamber, and it was all thoroughly mixed by powerful fans. After that, two parallel streams of air from the chamber were sampled and directed through cells with a biological substrate (cholinesterase) and a radioactive device with an alpha-radiation source.

Whereas the cholinesterase analysis showed an almost constant concentration in the gas chamber model, the radioactive detector showed a decline of the concentration of Substance 33, and within ten minutes only very small concentrations were recorded. We repeated these tests several times, but the result was always the same.

I called the attention of the members of the commission to the fact that, increasing moisture in the air was the reason behind the tendency of the radioactive device's signal to drop to almost a zero level. On the basis of this, I proposed the idea that the molecule of Substance 33 was undergoing a reaction of dietherification and the creation of mobile positive hydrogen ions (H+), which resulted in the formation of complexes of salts with molecules of Substance 33. These compounds have much higher ionization potentials than the original molecules of Substance 33, and under those conditions they cannot be ionized, which caused the drop in the detector's signal.

No one believed me at the time, but I performed experiments with other scientists from the Physical Chemistry Department, and we entirely proved my hypothesis. The fate of this development of the Military Academy of Chemical Defense was solved entirely.

A scientific and technical conference on the problems of the PD ITR of the branch took place in November of 1986 at the Volgograd Scientific Production Association (Khimprom). Representatives of the Novocheboksarsk, Volsk, and Volgograd subsidiaries of GOSNIIOKhT, the Redkino subsidiary of the NPO "Khimavtomatika", and employees of Ministry of Chemical Industry of the U.S.S.R. took part in the conference. Krasheninnikov, Tkachenko, and Kochetkov, a representative of our Main Administration "Soyuzorgsynthesis" with whom I shared a room at the privileged hotel for the regional committee of the CPSU, were also there.

A few years later, Anatoly Kochetkov became a member of the expert commission that the KGB investigator appointed for investigating my case, and he signed a resolution saying that I was guilty. Since then he has been actively promoted and became a member of the Russia's Committee for Conventional Problems of the Chemical and Biological Weapons which answers to the President of Russia. However, I am not going to accuse him, because I know how long it took him to slowly scale the job ladder to a high position. He was terrified to lose his position.

The major topic of the conference was the need for the technical re-equipment of the PD ITR service of the branch. It seemed to me that everybody present realized that. Besides, I agreed with the management of Workshop 34, which proposed that my suggestions should be implemented to discover trace quantities of soman and sarin in the emissions of the vented air and wastewater. Good prospects for purchasing more advanced laboratory equipment began to develop. The department already had three Varian chromatographs, and I could order a new Varian 3600 for capillary chromatography and a Finnigan chromatomass-spectrometer produced in the USA. When I was writing the applications, Krasheninnikov advised me, "Write so that the readers will shed tears of sympathy that we have lived without such necessary equipment for so long." I did my best and soon we were informed that the chemistry section of the Military and Industrial Commission of the Central Committee of the C.P.S.U. had approved the application.

When I became head of the department, I simultaneously became a member of the Science Council and some of its sections. Additionally, I was made a member of numerous committees, including some which were in the same line of business as the Department for the Security Regime and the First Department.

Despite our strained relations, the Deputy Director in charge of the Department for the Security Regime had to put up with me and, if possible, cooperate. I remember he even invited more than ten people from the KGB to the institute, so that they could listen to my lecture devoted to basics of organizing the PD ITR Department.

I had to give in to the pressure from my colleagues and was elected secretary of the primary departmental party organization. Its members were Communists in my department, in the Department for the Security Regime, in the First Department, and in the Department for Special Communications.

This position took up a lot of my time because the endless meetings of the Party Committee and its subcommittees on different occasions, or without any occasion. This seriously complicated my work, but I found a good way out. I had Svyatoslav Sokolov elected my deputy. He was also appointed my deputy at the PD ITR Department. One of the responsibilities of the secretary was the monthly collection of membership dues. Party members, in turn, had to present information about their salaries, so I learned that the Deputy Director in charge of the Department for the Security Regime was a KGB major and received his salary at the Lubyanka Headquarters of the KGB. I also learned from the personnel files about two other members of my organization. One of them was Ivan Surinsky[68], a retired lieutenant colonel who was previously the head of a prison camp in Siberia, and another had been the deputy chief in charge of political work at a prison camp in Altai.

All of this put me in a very negative frame of mind. I started to realize that my attempts to receive equipment, space, and people for research work gradually got me involved with a circle of shady, terrible people, whom I had never respected. I am quite an emotional person, and sometimes it is difficult for me to restrain my emotions. I can't say that rudeness is in my nature, but over the course of time, I often found out that my antipathy became noticeable.

I gradually started thinking about what role I could play, surrounded by these people, the majority of whom could hardly be called decent, and about the role of GOSNIIOKhT and its policies, which were being developed in connection with the CWC negotiations in Geneva.

GOSNIIOKhT took part in this process, by sending its experts to Geneva, but they were selected by only two people - the Director and Martynov. It was a great mystery to me which criteria they used. So, Yuri Skripkin, head of the Analytical Laboratory, and Boris Kuznetsov, head of the Technological Laboratory, became experts.

In 1993 Kuznetsov also became a member of the expert commission that the KGB investigator appointed to consider my case and signed the indictment. Additionally, he spoke on the side of the prosecution in GOSNIIOKhT's lawsuit against me in the period of January-February of 1994.

But in 1988 Kuznetsov, who was a very narrow-minded person, came running to my office after each trip to Geneva and breathlessly told me about his new work.

On a higher level, Igor Gabov was in charge of further confirmation of the position of the experts from GOSNIIOKhT and Ministry of Chemical Industry on technical aspects for the Geneva negotiations. At that time, Gabov was demoted to a senior engineering position at the Main Administration of "Soyuzorgsynthesis" (The Union of Organic Synthesis), but his friends kept him afloat. A few years later, he was also an expert on my case and argued with enthusiasm that I was guilty of disclosing state secrets.

At that time, the question of how the verification of the CWC would work in the future was a great problem in the negotiations. The majority of the delegations, including the U.S. and the U.S.S.R., supported conducting remote inspections, without visiting the actual plants. So the analysis of emissions of the ventilated air, sewage, and other waste became very important. That is why highly precise and sensitive methods of analysis of chemical compounds played a crucial role. Mainly the emphasis was on looking for organic phosphorus compounds that had a direct chemical bond between carbon and phosphorous atoms (C-P bond). But it wasn't difficult to circumvent the inspection process. Chemical products with the same bond could be produced for civilian applications at the same facilities producing organophosphorus-based chemical agents. So, units producing phospoliols with the C-P-connection, which were used as metal-extracting agents, started operating at GOSNIIOKhT and its subsidiaries.

Later on, common sense prevailed in Geneva, and the CWC was signed in the beginning of 1993, stipulating on-site inspections as a normal control procedure.[69, 70]

However, the development of the more toxic chemical agent A-232, in which the carbon atom is bonded to the phosphorous atom through the oxygen atom (C-O-P bond), considerably complicated the control process. My point is that many agricultural chemicals, which are produced at ordinary chemical plants, have the same bonds.

Many people supposed that it would be a great way to get rid of the old junk, while the new developments would be kept secret and would become the basis for a new round of competition in the field of chemical weapons. Nobody doubted that the U.S. would do exactly the same thing.

I am almost certain that the entire policy and strategy of negotiations in Geneva were developed at UNKhV (Administration of the Commander of the Chemical Troops), and General Anatoly Kuntsevich monitored this process. No one should be misled by the fact that he didn't take part in the negotiations personally.

The ruse was based on the "dual-use" compounds which were the precursors for ordinary agricultural and other civilian chemicals, but could also be used as precursors for producing chemical agents. When a new chemical agent is being developed, a corresponding civilian preparation is also being developed, for example a pesticide. That is the game.

The development of binary nerve agents will make it unnecessary to organize the dangerous production of chemical agents, as they do for example at the Novocheboksary plant. It makes the problems connected with producing, equipping, storing, and transporting the warheads much easier. The most important point is that any potential violator of the CWC can use some civilian facilities for production, and those factories could be completely unaware that they are producing precursors for lethal binary weapons.

These ideas became really clear to me when I saw the formula of a new pesticide, which was similar to the formula of agent A-232 on a poster, which was hanging on the wall opposite the Directorate. Boris Martynov who was standing nearby boasted that he was "covering his product" in this way. The poster with the formulas of pesticides developed at GOSNIIOKhT and other institutes was meant as a widespread advertisement of the institute's products. At the same time, the idea was for specialists to "become accustomed" to them as to civilian products.

Quite accidentally, I also soon learned about a strange but significant incident, the meaning of which became clear to me later on.

The typing bureau where secret materials were printed or taped didn't accept a report prepared by our department on the problems of the PD ITR. The explanation was that the bureau was urgently retyping all technical documentation of the Novocheboksary plant that produced the chemical agent known as Substance 33. It turned out that the report was altered to pretend that they were producing VX gas. This was funny and sad, and I had no idea how they could possibly play the international inspectors for such fools. They were supposed to come to the plant and make sure that a specific chemical agent was being destroyed, not some theoretical agent. Apparently there was something in the strategy of negotiations that allowed them to hope that this trick might work.

At that time I didn't understand the main idea behind this whole undertaking. Later on when I was released from the KGB's Lefortovo prison after my first arrest, I called my friend, the late Leonid Lipasov, and he told me about a mistake that I had made in my article "A Poisoned Policy" (*Moscow News* from September 16, 1992). Only then did I realize how far-sighted the masters of the military-chemical complex had been. In my article I said that General Kuntsevich and others had received the Lenin prize in 1991 for the development of binary weapons based on a new substance. Actually, that turned out not to be the case. Instead, they got the prize for binary weapons based on the well-known Novocheboksary agent Substance 33! The tricky juggling and revision of documents from the Novocheboksary plant was a part of that whole operation.

It would be naive to assume that the generals from the military industrial complex (VPK) did all this just to receive prizes. Everything was done according to a plan that had been elaborated beforehand, a plan that was coordinated with the strategy for conducting negotiations on the framework of the CWC. In the summer of 1995, I met with Amy Smithson a Senior Fellow and now PhD, who was working at the Henry L. Stimson Center in Washington, D.C. I was preparing an article for a collection to be published. In my article, I alleged that, according to the Wyoming

Memorandum, the parties were supposed to exchange the formulas of their chemical agents, subject to destruction at the second stage of the implementation of this accord. The well known American, Professor Matthew Messelson rebuked me for an inaccuracy. Actually, the parties were supposed to exchange this information three months before signing the CWC, but Russia didn't come forth with this information.

The main task of the PD ITR Department was made very specific then. It was necessary to keep all new projects a secret. In order to accomplish this, we had to quickly develop more sensitive techniques for the determination of traces quantities of chemical agents in the waste water and air.

In 1989 this work was accelerated because American specialists were soon supposed to visit a number of chemical establishments connected with the development and production of chemical agents. A committee headed by Guskov was formed to prepare for this, and I became a member of this committee.

The necessary techniques were to be developed on an emergency schedule, over the course of about two months. I asserted that it was impossible to develop techniques that were a hundred times more sensitive than the current ones, in such a short period of time. I was puzzled why there should be such a rush before the arrival of specialists, if they were not going to take samples of the water and air. With quite a serious air, Guskov explained that when the foreign specialists came into the room they could take a "swab" from the surface of the wall or floor with their handkerchiefs and then "decipher" the new compounds at home. I made an effort not to burst out laughing. That was how our heads imaged the work of foreign technical intelligence! Science couldn't and still can't disclose secrets in such a fantastic way.

According to the "wise" plan of our bosses, all imported equipment had to be removed from the rooms where the Americans were supposed to visit. But that was all that could be done to prepare for the meeting.

Additionally, Guskov explained that Americans were also supposed to visit Workshop 34 of the Volgograd scientific industrial company "Khimprom" that had produced soman and sarin before

State Secrets

1987. I didn't understand why I had to take care that there was no agent A-230 in the air around this workshop. The deputy director said that behind the fence of Workshop 34 there was a unit of the experimental plant of the Volgograd subsidiary of GOSNIIOKhT, which produced this chemical agent...

Chapter 12
The Torment of Insight

Our operations for protecting the new developments of GOSNIIOKhT didn't correspond with the changes that were taking place in our country at that time, or with the foreign policy directed at making the world a safer place. It turned out that along with hundreds of other scientists, I had participated in a vast conspiracy against the future Chemical Weapons Convention, repeating the role played by the captive scientist from the Stalinist era.

In September of 1994, the management of GOSNIIOKhT filed a lawsuit against me and demanded 33 million rubles, claiming that my public speeches and articles in the press had caused moral and material damages to the institute. The management of the institute accused me of calling GOSNIIOKhT a "sharashka", which is the term coined by Aleksander Solzhenitsyn to mean a jail/science-research institute. This was blatant hypocrisy on their part, as they knew quite well that during the war and even for a long time after that, there was a jail for political prisoners who were chemists at the institute. The prisoner/scientists were escorted to their work in the laboratories and experimental units from their jail cells. Often these people were selfless and very talented.[71] Isn't it the pinnacle of cynicism or even a sin of some sort to call these people "employees of GOSNIIOKhT"? Petrunin did exactly that when he included the victims of this Stalinist labor camp in the list of employees of his institute, in an article he wrote about the 80th Anniversary of GOSNIIOKhT. [72]

Later on, scientists at GOSNIIOKhT continued the sad tradition established by these selfless researchers, in working conditions that were very far from safe. Speaking of "sharashka", I have always been talking about the conditions of labor and "the regime" at that institute, and not the scientists, as among them there were and still are outstanding specialists, such as Professor Andrei Tomilov.

At the same time, it was inexplicable from the point of view of the most basic human rights, that people who were working in the field of chemical weapons in the U.S.S.R. were working outside of the law. It's as though they didn't exist. For example, when someone started talking about raising scientists' salaries or pensions at least up to the level of miners or other people working in dangerous professions, the administration literally replied as follows: "You see. We don't exist for the state. It has never admitted and it never will acknowledge that our country develops and produces chemical weapons." As a result, the bosses concluded it was impossible to raise these questions at all.

Later I confirmed that the ruling clique in the U.S.S.R. distinguished itself with its unparalleled hypocrisy, when it came to the problem of chemical weapons. On the list of information of state secrecy, (my "case" was later fabricated on this basis), there wasn't even a single reference to Russian chemical weapons. That is, it was more secret than the "major secrets of the U.S.S.R". The regime of secrecy in the military-chemical complex was organized precisely to make this hypocrisy and deceit possible. The regime of the "sharashka" allowed them to do this quite brazenly.

Clearly the system of the military-chemical complex was starting to decay. The construction of a large-scale plant in Novocheboksary, for the industrial production of the Substance 33, defied all possible logic. In 1974 it was brought fully on-line. Hundreds of millions of rubles were squandered on this weapon, which was useless, even from the point of view of Russian military specialists.

This happened at a time when the U.S. had completely halted the production of chemical weapons.

There were a lot of pressing questions, which needed immediate answers. In particular, detailed studies of Substance 33 demonstrated its very low level of stability. Sometimes samples were taken from shells filled with Substance 33, which had been in storage for a couple of years. Tests of these samples showed that only about half of the agent was present. No one could explain this phenomenon, because the loss of activity was much greater than expected. After a year of investigating this, the source the problem was finally discovered. The factory workers, who were filling up the shells with the chemical agent, had decided not to waste the precious ethyl alcohol that was used for swabbing the holes of the shells to be filled. Instead, they started to use hydrochloric acid for this purpose, and it is a perfect activator of the decomposition of Substance 33.

At that time, the foremost scientists and chemists started developing some elements of political consciousness, as they were certainly influenced by the words and actions of Andrei Sakharov, Aleksander Solzhenitsyn, and other outstanding leaders in science and literature. But, we could only learn about them by listening to the Western "radio-voices". Sometimes scientists abroad displayed real civic heroism by standing up for the truth, working in the cause of preserving peace. At that time, the deeds of Daniel Ellsberg[73] in the U.S. and Mordechai Vanunu[74] in Israel made an indelible impression on me and many people in the U.S.S.R.

In 1971 Daniel Ellsberg published the Pentagon Papers, 7000 pages of secret Pentagon documents about the Vietnam War, which the military did not want the American people to know about. The Soviet press presented this as some kind of power struggle within the American intelligence community. However, anyone familiar with our newspapers and their propaganda tricks could easily guess what had really happened. I understood that Ellsberg sacrificed himself in the name of civic truth, so that Americans could judge for themselves what the real face of President Nixon's administration was. In accordance with American law, he was threatened with more than a hundred years of imprisonment. Nixon ordered the use of all possible secret illegal channels to investigate Ellsberg's case, but the brave man received a fair deal after all. The judge got acquainted with the criminal case, and when he was certain that it violated the norms of the U.S. Constitution, he decided to terminate it immediately. President Nixon soon resigned from office, because he lost his base of support thanks to the Watergate scandal with its "dirty tricks", and because of the Pentagon Papers. The case against Daniel Ellsberg was one of the supporting arguments during the impeachment of Nixon.

Our press wrote about Mordechai Vanunu in 1986-87. He published information in a British newspaper about Israel's secret nuclear weapons program. Although many people wrote about that before, few believed that this information was trustworthy, because it was based on indirect evidence. Vanunu proved his claim with photos he had taken at the Israeli nuclear installation where he worked, so naturally everyone believed him. The case took a dramatic turn, when Vanunu was kidnapped by Israeli secret agents and brought back to Israel, where he was secretly sentenced to eighteen years of solitary confinement.

I was stunned by the actions of this courageous man, who had decided to let the world know the crazy plans of the Israeli military clique. I never believed those who accused Vanunu of treason to his motherland. Many of those who supported this accusation were under the same kind of propaganda hypnosis that was practiced under the Stalinist regime. The actions of Vanunu had a serious impact on me and it's possible they subconsciously motivated my own actions later on.

Gradually it became clear to me that the chemical arms race was an important element of the Cold War that had nothing to do with boosting the defense potential of the country. It was also apparent that only a narrow circle of interested military and civilian generals benefited from this insanity. It was even difficult to imagine what other sphere they could prosper in, if they could not rely on the slavish and poorly paid labor of scientists working in hazardous conditions!

The KGB played a special role in that. In 1972, a KGB representative became Deputy Director in charge of the Department of the Security Regime. As a result, access to the institute and laboratories was tightened up. Before that all the guards were civilians, and often these were elderly women - grannies who didn't quite know what to do with their weapons. They were replaced with military professionals from a regiment that had been transferred over from a top-secret site in Siberia. So there you have it - this was the real face of the Soviet disarmament policy, not the one that the propaganda declared in the press!

Probably the only crucial role of the KGB at the institute was to work on the problem of keeping state secrets. That is what the Chekists were necessary for. There were four secret departments with numerous personnel, but at best they could only provide for the safety and the movement of secret documents, not for the safety and movement of chemical agents, either new or old. I think instead, they had a symbolical meaning, perhaps for scaring off foreign agents. In fact, I never heard of any incident during the time I was working at GOSNIIOKhT, in which "enemy intelligence" was trying to get a hold of something in the military chemical complex, not even during my years as head of the Department for Foreign Technical Counterintelligence. There was practically no one to "struggle" with.

Still, you couldn't say that the KGB had lost its "vigilance". From time to time KGB representatives ran party meetings, in which some general got up and gave a report about the plots of foreign intelligence agencies, which did their best to steal of our defense secrets. However, this was pure fiction. The speakers' own examples always refuted their allegations. One deputy director of a department of the KGB came up with a story about the deputy director of the Design Institute of the Chlorine Industry. Having allegedly become entangled in his debts and with women, he decided to cash in on "state secrets". When he had accumulated enough "secrets", he started looking for a buyer. Finally, he managed to get acquainted with a Swedish journalist and even agreed to a deal. However, like in the best Soviet movies, he was caught by our glorious Chekists while selling the secrets, and he was exposed as an enemy of our Socialist regime. The speaker said proudly that the "Swedish journalist" was our agent.

What could you expect from those Chekists, whose primary occupation was provocation? I used to work with a former KGB employee who told me about special troops of the NKVD which were organized in the Far East of the U.S.S.R., and trained to imitate German troops. After they finished their training, rookie Soviet agents were parachuted near those "troops", and they quickly ended up in an encounter with the Chekists (who were disguised as German officers). The captured Soviets were tortured and some of them agreed to work for the "Germans", which meant immediate death without any investigation or legal proceedings. However, when it was necessary to be really vigilant and resourceful, KGB employees were careless.

I will always remember the case of the late chief of the Department "D" laboratory, Nikolai Ostapchuk. He was very fond of drinking, even at work. Thanks to the alcohol, or perhaps out of an excessive desire to work with secret documents, Nikolai handled them as ordinary papers and carried them home in his briefcase. The KGB didn't take any measures, even though he fell down drunk several times and slept somewhere in the street, once in a "perehod" (pedestrian underpass) not far from GOSNIIOKhT. One day Ostapchuk suddenly died, and his wife came to GOSNIIOKhT, bearing the top-secret papers safely back to the Department for the Security Regime. Many people in the management of this department were not pleased at all. It seems it would have been better for them if those papers had just disappeared without a trace. Then it would have been possible to hush up the incident without any consequences, but Ostapchuk's widow didn't ask for the help of his friends from the directorate, to make up for her late husband's blunder. This was the way she took revenge on his drinking buddies.

The control over the safety of chemical agents was organized absolutely perfunctorily. First, it was carried out by employees of the Department for the Security Regime, who didn't have even a primitive notion about chemistry. Usually part of the staff of this department was composed of representatives of the working class, like Boris Churkov and Vyacheslav Malashkin, who in this way or otherwise became involved as KGB informers.

Secondly, control was maintained by judging the difference between how much of a substance was received and what was used up. The daily expenditure of chemicals was recorded only by the person who actually did the work. Generally speaking, he could use up nothing and later dispose of the chemicals at his own discretion. It was only important to log an entry in the registrar journal. In order to get extra compensation for working with hazardous materials, an employee had to submit a report, accounting for the number of days he or she worked with chemical agents. Often scientific assistants, who hadn't accumulated enough hazard days, simply made false entries in their registers about the work they presumably conducted. To protect this fraud, they just destroyed the chemicals for the experiments in one go, according to procedures described in special manuals.

Controllers from the Department for the Security Regime could force the scientific assistants to weigh the ampoules with chemical agents in their presence, but it was all the same to them what was in those ampoules. So a potential plotter could do anything he or she wanted with the chemicals. Unfortunately, control at the institute is the same today as it was before.

Probably there were very few workers at GOSNIIOKhT, to whom the ensigns from the militarized security guard hadn't offered their services. I personally knew a few of these lads, who would offer to take anything you wanted out from the territory of GOSNIIOKhT, for a few hundred milliliters of alcohol. They were very conscientious about keeping their word, carrying out different construction materials, paint, iron rods, and other items for building country houses near Moscow. These guys didn't care what was taken out with their direct participation, although they knew that the stuff they took out had been stolen. Actually, the theft of state or collective farm property wasn't considered a criminal offense in those days in the U.S.S.R. Only those who had nothing to steal at work didn't do it. It was very difficult to qualify this as theft, because the Bolshevik state had been constantly robbing and plundering people for several generations, to the extent that the state made it practically impossible for people to survive without theft. So theft didn't cause indignation, and almost no one reported it to the authorities. In this sense, the Soviet people were really united because they were entirely linked by a collective cover-up.

Even in the prewar years, people were dying at GOSNIIOKhT from chemical agents. Healthy young men left home from the villages which were subject to total collectivization, escaping for the cities, including Moscow. According to one veteran, these poor devils were ready for any work, even at the chemical "sharashka". The strongest and healthiest ones were urged to participate in testing the effects of chemical agents. For a few dozen rubles, some careless sturdy youngsters agreed to become guinea pigs. They didn't suspect what kind of torture they would have to endure, before they went to a better world or became hopeless lifelong cripples, for the sake of the crazy reckless plots of the bosses of the military-chemical complex.

After my presentations about the dangerous concentrations of chemical agents in Volgograd to Victor Petrunin in October 1988, the Council on Technical Counterintelligence of the Ministry of Chemical Industry invited me to a meeting. Sergei Golubkov was the chairman of this council. I presented my report there, with all the data collected in the Volgograd NPO "Khimprom" about my findings of the unacceptable concentrations of sarin and soman in the nearby "White Sea" and in the air. After that there was a profound silence. No questions and no comments. Only GOSNIIOKhT's Deputy Director Konstantin Guskov replied, "Vil Sultanovich did this entire job without the endorsement of GOSNIIOKhT, and his presentation is purely an unfinished scientific experiment, which should be checked and verified." After that Golubkov gave a long speech about the importance of technical counterintelligence work, and then he lectured the audience about how to determinate traces of our newly developed substances in waste water and air, with the help of advice given by Academician Nikolai Enikolopov who had never worked a single day in this area in his life.

Some people tried to comfort me after that meeting, saying "Be happy, Vil Sultanovich! Ten years ago, they would have sent you to the camps for that, not quietly home." It was true, but I understood entirely that my work with foreign technical counterintelligence was fiction. It was just one of a variety of Soviet deceptions, because you could easily find soman near the plant in Volgograd. That is, if you were not too lazy to look for it. Moreover, it made me feel like I was sitting at same table with ne'er-do-wells, who were incapable of doing any scientific work. I felt like I was there just to provide them with cover for their crimes against innocent people.

It was a well known fact that these people were really corrupted criminals. Even though Arvid Pelshe was a member of the Politbureau of the Central Committee of the CPSU, he published a report in the party magazine "Party Life" in December of 1987 about the investigation of the criminal actions of these people. [75]

At the same time, these people were continuing with their deceptive games, pretending that they were the real protectors of secrets of Soviet military complex. I already wrote about how they ordered me to develop super-sensitive methods for the determination of Novichok agents in waste water and air. Meanwhile, all the wastes from the destruction of chemical agents (including A-230 and A-232) that were used in laboratory experiments, were packaged in steel barrels, which were shipped by railway to Shikhany. There they were dumped into a hole in an open area next to the forest, where people gathered berries and mushrooms. Wasn't it ironic that my department was ordered to determinate traces of these substances at the level of 1 ppt (part per trillion) within two months?

I tried to explain the real situation and sent Director Petrunin an official report, but there was no logic working in the system. There was a real threat that I would lose my job, on the pretext that I had ruined the State Plan for securing the military chemical complex. I don't think that Petrunin, Guskov and the others were so stupid that they did not to understand the elementary scientific realities. It was trap set against me.

My young senior scientist Vladimir Buzaev came up with a plan to write a fictitious method, in order to placate the bosses, but I categorically refused to accept this machination, because it was impossible for me to cooperate in the destruction of my scientific integrity and personal honor. "That's fine," he replied. "You'll see how they ruin you." He was right. Petrunin called a meeting exactly two months later in late December 1988, when I sent my report to the Directorate of GOSNIIOKhT that my department couldn't fulfill its order.

Right at the beginning, Guskov declared that I had ruined such an important governmental order on the protection our defense capabilities, so our leadership right now was in a very bad situation. There would be severe consequences for all of GOSNIIOKhT.

Deputy Director Aleksander Martynov exploded in response: "Didn't I ask you not to appoint Mirzayanov as the chief of Foreign Technical Counterintelligence Department? You didn't listen to me so you are picking up the harvest!"

Compared with Guskov and Martynov, Director Petrunin knew the real situation with my assignment. He was changing colors - getting red and white without any verbal reaction. Then he asked me how long it would take me to develop this method. I answered that if the entire global scientific community couldn't do that then there would be no time period for it at all. On that note, Petrunin closed the meeting. My assistants and many people were sure that swift retaliation would come, but nothing like that happened. Nevertheless I clearly understood that I was not their man - someone who could play their games, joining in the cheating and manipulations. For them I was the ultimate stranger...

Once in 1988, in the third year of Gorbachev's Perestroika, Petrunin was lecturing to us "stupid" scientists at one of the introductory sessions, "Any Perestroika is purely the internal business of the country. You can't forget for a minute that the nature of capitalism hasn't changed, and imperialism, as before, is still our most evil enemy. That is why our task is to fortify the defense power of our country. Any other attitude plays into the hands of our enemies and is criminal."

By that time there were already many democratically minded scientists and engineers at GOSNIIOKhT. Some of them formed an organization to support Yeltsin's democrats, and they were regulars at meetings and demonstrations against the C.P.S.U. and the opponents of Perestroika. I was one of organizers of these meetings, and this pained the Directorate greatly. Although neither the department I headed nor I were directly subordinate to the KGB, we were considered to be in its domain to a certain extent. That is why my behavior was so provocative to the Chekists. Some well-wishers from the Directorate reproached me for my excessive idealism and my impractical approach to life. However, I had already made the decision to struggle against the reigning system, particularly against the military-chemical complex. It goes without saying that I didn't even allow myself to think about neglecting the regime of secrecy at my job.

By that time I had managed to equip my department with modern imported laboratory instruments. There were some real scientific successes as well. Among them were the preservation of chemical agents intact in solid materials such as brick, concrete, sand and others, and the development of chromatomass-spectrometric methods of analysis of these agents, as well as my special methods of extraction of these agents from solid media.

Since I moved to the U.S., I have answered many questions posed by correspondents on subject of the Gulf War veterans.[76] Many of them are currently ill with an unknown disease, accompanied by symptoms consistent with poisoning by chemical agents. Official statements say that Iraq didn't use the chemical weapons it possessed against the US Army. At the same time we know that Iraq had experience in using chemical weapons in the war against Iran and also against its own Kurdish citizens, shortly before the events in the Persian Gulf. I have no reason not to trust this version because the open use of chemical weapons against the well-equipped US Army could not have passed unnoticed.

Numerous UN inspections in the defeated territory of Iraq showed that there were no more stockpiles of chemical weapons. They stated that they were partially destroyed before the American intervention in Kuwait and the invasion of Iraq in 1991. Ultimately it seems clear that the American military chemists carelessly destroyed a large arsenal of Iraqi chemical weapons in the open air with crude explosions. Such a barbaric way of destroying chemical weapons is not effective, and a considerable fraction of the chemical agents would have remained intact. When chemical agents are exploded in this way, what remains mixes with solid particles (dust, sand, and products of combustion), and results in the strong contamination of the affected area. Adsorbed chemical agents can "live" on the surface of solid particles indefinitely, without changing their chemical composition. Moreover, highly toxic yet very stable pyrophosphonates are produced, at the high temperatures of the explosions of phosphoorganic agents. Given the climatic peculiarities of the Persian Gulf with its dry air, and its plentiful sand and dust which could be carried a long distance from the place of chemical destruction, we may presume that the American troops could have been exposed to the remnants of the "destroyed" chemical agents.

Finally, I would like to note that Human Rights Watch conducted an expedition in 1993 to the Kurdish village where the Iraqi regime had used sarin against peaceful inhabitants. There, they took some samples two years after the gas attack, and almost a year after samples had been taken from the graves of the victims. It was proven that micro-concentrations of sarin were found there. For the first time in the world and in the practice of scientific research, it was demonstrated that even such a relatively unstable chemical compound as O- isopropylmethyphosphonfluaridiate (sarin) could remain intact under the ground for a long time.[77]

Determination of adsorbed compounds is extraordinarily difficult, and it requires special laboratory research. I don't know whether or not such analyses were conducted in the field laboratories of the US Army or what their results might have been. If an ion mobility spectrometer was used, which was the main field instrument of the US Army, it is probable that chemical agents were not discovered in solid micro-particles. This device is designated for the determination of chemical agents in the gaseous phase. It has a relatively low sensitivity and can't record those small concentrations which don't kill people, but still are hazardous to the health.

Additionally, this device has very low selectivity. That means it is difficult to determine which molecule it has finally registered. That is why it had to be preliminarily adjusted for registering known compounds, which appear some time after the device starts operating, if they are present in the analyzed air. Each compound has its characteristic time of display. If the device gives a signal with a characteristic time that doesn't correspond to the time for which it is adjusted, the signal is discarded as interference.

I think that during the Persian Gulf conflict, these spectrometers were adjusted for detecting mustard gas, sarin, and VX gas because there was information that Iraq possessed these kinds of chemical agents. Unfortunately, the US intelligence didn't take into consideration the fact that Iraq couldn't produce the American agent VX gas. It is highly likely that Iraq had the Soviet agent Substance 33, which is analogous to VX gas, but has different physical and chemical properties. It is also important to point out that Substance 33 has a different characteristic time of display on an ion mobility spectrometer. This means that if American soldiers were exposed to Substance 33, chemical specialists from US intelligence agencies couldn't register it in the air. I can't claim with confidence that Iraq had Substance 33, but I do know that modern Soviet chemical weapons were delivered to the Middle East in the 1980s. A retired colonel who participated in this operation told me about it. It is not difficult to guess where these weapons could have been shipped to, especially if we take into consideration which friends the Soviet Union had in this region, at that time.

Another serious problem that the American soldiers who have been to the Middle East may have been subjected to is the possibility of a deferred effect of low level exposure of chemical agents. When concentrations are low, the effect of these substances won't be discovered during immediate exposure, as there are no immediate symptoms consistent with exposure to large concentrations.

The bosses of the military-chemical complex in Soviet Union were constantly pushing their scientists, aggressively giving the impression that chemical war could break out any day. The more successful were the negotiations in Geneva, the more intensive became the testing of new weapons carried out at the test site near Nukus. As a result, the Soviet army officially accepted "Novichok" as a weapon. This means that for the first time in the history of the chemical arms race, the Soviet Union took possession of its own chemical weapon, instead of borrowing one from a probable opponent. By that time the major parameters of the CWC had already been determined, and naturally "Novichok" wasn't on the list of prohibited and controlled substances. If we consider those circumstances, we can better understand Director Petrunin's boastful statement of about the "epoch-making success".

Those were the circumstances under which I finally had to make a decision regarding my future.

And I made a resolute step…

Chapter 13
I'm Quitting the Party

On May 4th of 1990, I submitted my resignation notice to the Party Committee, officially leaving the C.P.S.U. I wrote that the C.P.S.U. is a criminal organization which doesn't have the right to be reorganized, so I was officially severing all my ties with it. It was the first statement of this kind in the history of GOSNII-OKhT.

After this the events evolved rapidly. On June 7th of 1990 a decree was issued about transforming the PD ITR Department back into the PD ITR Sector, with fewer employees. I was transferred to the Laboratory for Elemental Analysis, in the capacity of "leading research scientist". Yuri Skripkin became my immediate supervisor. He had appeared at the institute from time to time, but he was spending most of his time in Geneva at the negotiations. Skripkin was really a narrow-minded sycophant. Petrunin was well aware of my attitude, and he deliberately transferred me to Skripkin's subdivision as retribution for my political activity.

By that time I had become one of the co-chairmen of the Democratic Russia Movement (DDR) at GOSNIIOKhT. Almost every day we issued our agitation leaflets and posted them in prominent places, so people would know the truth about the events that were taking place in the U.S.S.R. Often GOSNIIOKhT supporters of the DDR were sent, under our leadership, to different meetings and demonstrations, in support of the DDR and Boris Yeltsin, whom everybody loved at that time.

At the same time we started struggling to break up the C.P.S.U.'s power monopoly, and to achieve a majority in the workers' councils. People were becoming bolder right before our eyes. They were no longer afraid of expressing their opinions. At one of the general party meetings that took place in March of 1990, contrary to the wishes of the Party Committee and the Board of Director, Edward Sarkisyan (another DDR activist), and I were elected co-chairmen. This was the first serious defeat for the backers of Communist power at GOSNIIOKhT. It was incredible for people to see the Director of GOSNIIOKhT and members of the Party Committee sitting in the hall, and not at the presidium as they were accustomed to. This might seem like an insignificant detail now, but at that time it showed that the power of the C.P.S.U. had cracked and you could successfully battle against it. Sarkisyan and I took turns presiding and gave the floor to the DDR supporters. They delivered speeches denouncing the C.P.S.U. and the corrupted authorities. Still, at that time it was still an internal party struggle, and it became increasingly more intolerable for me to keep my membership.

After work I often went to the country in Luzhniki for meetings of the supporters of democratic reforms. You could see anyone there - newly hatched anarchists with their shocking black flags, monarchists of every stripe, and even ultra-revolutionary democrats, as well as those who supported the separation of the Baltic republics from the U.S.S.R.

Investigators T. Gdlyan and V. Ivanov were the most popular figures in the country at that time. The authorities persecuted them for their excessive zeal in investigating the corruption of the party elite in Uzbekistan. At that time we saw those people who would be at the helm of Russia a few years later. Yuri Afansiev and Gleb Yakunin were the most popular leaders of the DDR.

Almost every day, we watched clashes on television between those who backed the power elite and the supporters of democratic reforms in the Supreme Soviet of the U.S.S.R. and in the Congress of People's Deputies of the U.S.S.R. Everywhere you could feel the excitement. People were getting much more involved in politics, and the country was on the threshold of serious changes. There was change in many people's internal lives everywhere, even at the secret "Post Office Boxes" like GOSNIIOKhT. However, the management of these establishments was deeply ultra-conservative. They owed far too much to the C.P.S.U. and its functionaries. They had received their unlimited power over scientists and others, thanks only to the party. Not one of GOSNIIOKhT's bosses could work as a scientist any longer, and that's why these people feared any changes like the plague. For this reason the supporters of DDR at the institute had become the personal enemies of the management, not just their ideological opponents.

When I began working with the DDR, I clearly understood what the consequences might be. I could be dismissed from my position. Still, my sense of civic responsibility had finally matured and crystallized by that time, and that didn't allow me any compromise.

Actually, I was pleased when people at GOSNIIOKhT expressed their sympathy towards me, as someone who had sacrificed his position for the sake of progress and democratization of the country.

Little changed after our department broke up. The director of GOSNIIOKhT promised that I would hold onto all the equipment and laboratory rooms, but as a formality I would be moved to a different subdivision. Frankly, I didn't really believe this, because I knew that Petrunin was a cowardly person, easily changing his mind if something even hypothetically threatened his position. If he received an order from the higher authorities, he did everything to carry it out.

That is exactly how it happened. Back in the autumn of 1989, there were attempts to tear my group apart. A lot of people were willing to have our group transferred to their subdivisions. Most of them were interested in our equipment, because at that time we had the most modern chromatographs, a chromatomass-spectrometer, and other equipment for physical chemical analysis. In order to preserve the group, I even agreed to the Director's offer to transfer me to a new enterprise with collective ownership, which was set up by Igor Pronin, a former secretary of the Party Committee, under the guidance of GOSNIIOKhT's top management. At that time these enterprises had just started sprouting up. In spite of my infamous attitude toward Party Committee secretaries, Pronin agreed to cooperate with me, because he was well aware of our capabilities and how we had developed analytical methods for ecological purposes. This was the area he was planning to work in with his new enterprise. Soon we established connections with the Moscow Committee for Ecology, and we received numerous requests for investigations of different ecological problems in the city districts.

At that time some people from my group were working on a topic important in civilian industry. We had finalized some agreements on research work aimed at developing a method to determine the onset of the process in which grain becomes moldy in the granary. The method used chromatomass spectrometry to identify certain key components of gasses produced by molds. After a while, we made good progress in this direction. We developed an experimental technique and identified all the volatile components of a few musty cultures grown on grain, in collaboration with a team of scientists headed by Professor Zakladny from the Institute of Grain.

Unfortunately, we couldn't finish this work with specific recommendations, because problems arose within my group. Petrunin, following the advice of Skripkin and Deputy Director Polyakov (by that time Guskov retired), refused to transfer our equipment along with us to Pronin's newly organized enterprise. At first sight, it seemed surprising that the director was unable to settle such a simple question, but on closer inspection, you could see the scheming of the party and executive officials behind the scenes. They couldn't forgive my "treachery", and wanted to make an example of me, to teach me a "lesson".

I made desperate efforts to save my group and the equipment that was so difficult to come by. But my ill-wishers - namely Skripkin, Polyakov, Bogdanov (head of the Research and Technical Department and the son of the odious head of the RP Department), and Vlasov the Chief Engineer - managed to block every one of our suggestions. They had studied together at one department in the Military Academy of Chemical Defense.

I am sure that the notions of honor and decency don't exist even theoretically for these people, so you had to be very careful when talking with them, especially if you were working on the problem of destroying the stockpiles of chemical weapons. They can do anything to preserve their power. In March of 1994, they "handed over" two of their bosses to the KGB - their patron Petrunin, and General Anatoly Kuntsevich who had organized the delivery of the chemical agent precursors to the Middle East. In return, the grateful KGB didn't bother their buddies while investigating the case.

At that time I frequently attended city meetings of the DDR activists, but it was becoming increasingly more painful to watch people waste a lot of their time arguing over questions that were insignificant from my point of view. It had become a simple trade off, and the prize was DDR management and leadership positions. Surprisingly, many DDR members were totally out of touch with reality, and they were completely uninformed about the real situation in the plants and science research institutes, those places where people actually worked.

At the end of June of 1990, I spent a whole day at what was supposed to be an organizational conference of DDR supporters, which took place in the District Council of Moscow Oktyabrsky District. A number of people were there including Victor Zaslavsky, Arkady Murashev, and Nikolai Travkin, who were well-known at the time. Such a barefaced and cynical struggle for management places ensued, that I finally decided to leave, after witnessing this disgusting spectacle for six hours.

During a break I tried to speak with Murashev, but he wasn't available. I was worried that GOSNIIOKhT and other enterprises of the military-chemical complex were still receiving the same governmentally budgeted funds as before, despite a decision by the Supreme Soviet of the U.S.S.R. to significantly cut military expenses. The new allocations were presumably meant for chemical industry, not for defense establishments, but this was a dangerous trick. At that time I wasn't really sure that even Gorbachev or others in high positions knew anything about this. So, I wrote a brief note to Murashev, explaining the situation and asked him to meet with me. He was a popular People's Deputy of the Supreme Soviet and a co-chairman of the "Inter-Parliamentary Group", the first opposition faction in the history of the U.S.S.R.

Unfortunately, Murashev never found the time to meet with me, although I was sitting not far from him. I saw him read my note and look around to see who the author was. When I pointed to the note and to myself, he nodded in response. A few years later the KGB prosecuted me, and my lawyer asked Murashev to testify about my appeal to him as to a People's Deputy, but he "didn't remember" my request.

Back in June of 1990, I realized that my relatively independent life at GOSNIIOKhT couldn't continue forever, and I decided to ask Deputy Director Kurochkin to transfer our group to the Department for Fundamental Research, which he headed. He agreed and started "working on" Petrunin. To his credit, Kurochkin didn't stipulate any prerequisite conditions regarding my activities with the DDR, even though he remained a loyal C.P.S.U. member until it completely collapsed.

During one of our conversations, I candidly told him that I was going to struggle with the ruling clique of the military-chemical complex, which prevented Russia from pursuing a peaceful policy, in spite of the changes taking place in the country and in the whole world. Kurochkin thought my ideas, regarding the complete termination of research work on the development of chemical weapons, were too radical. I was afraid that it would be very difficult in the future for the CWC to control research, because there was no clear interpretation of this process. Also, according to the draft of the CWC, development was to be prohibited, but in my opinion, the terms were not clearly defined. Kurochkin agreed with me, but he said he thought that the problem couldn't be settled completely. We had to be ready for dirty tricks, so we had to continue our scientific research. Naturally, I was absolutely sure that the ruling clique of the military-chemical complex would jump at the opportunities opened up by the lack of precise definitions in the wording of the CWC.

I was impatient to share my misgivings with people openly in the press, but the question was – how to do it. There was no doubt that all matters relating to chemical weapons were top secret. I couldn't just go to the director of GOSNIIOKhT and ask him to let me publish an article that described how he had hindered the process of conversion at the institute. I couldn't expect him to agree to let me state in the press that the institute continued to develop and test new kinds of chemical weapons. Unfortunately, this is exactly what I was supposed to do, according to the standing instructions, which prohibited any independent correspondence stating a personal opinion, and any independent correspondence that qualified as "a personal opinion". Only the director of GOSNIIOKhT and his deputies had this right.

The local DDR organization was especially worried about conversion at GOSNIIOKhT. In our leaflets we openly pointed out that a peaceful policy was only formally pursued at GOSNIIOKhT. We presented our suggestions at our workers' conferences, but it was clear that the director and his confidants were not anxious to move in our direction.

Then several events took place, which became something of a turning point for me. At the end of February of 1991, the director of GOSNIIOKhT signed an order to transfer my group to Kurochkin's department. But the order wasn't put into effect! Polyakov and Skripkin openly ignored it. They prohibited the transfer of any people or laboratory equipment. It was strange to see such overt insubordination on the part of the director's assistants. In this situation all the signs pointed to the fact that the real boss at the institute was Deputy Director Victor Polyakov, not Director Petrunin. The situation was further aggravated by the fact that we had already contracted and started our practical work, conducting ecological evaluations of a number of areas in Moscow.

Two months later the director cancelled his transfer order. I finally realized that my opponents wanted me to give up and be humbled. They acted on the request of Chekist Aleksander Martynov, who had conclusive information about my activities within DDR and my attitude toward chemical weapons.

One day at the end of April 1991, a festive atmosphere set in at

GOSNIIOKhT. Tables were decked out with a banquet in the Directorate, and toasts were loudly proposed. It was the same in a number of departments. My friend Victor Dmitriev said that they were celebrating the Lenin Prizes that had been awarded to Director Petrunin, General Kuntsevich, and other "scientists".

"For what?" I wondered.

"For a binary compound," he replied.

I was really amazed, because this problem was very far from being solved. I thought that Igor Vasiliev was still "lucky" in spite of his love of adventure. I wasn't at all surprised that his name wasn't on the list of award recipients. This was completely in line with Soviet practice, when the real author or inventor was given only the crumbs from the table of the power lords. I thought this was the case again.

However I was mistaken about the cause of all this revelry - which substance this highly touted binary compound was based on.

In his last conversation with me, Kurochkin asked what my objective was. I clearly explained that I saw only one way to solve the problem of chemical weapons - to ban all kinds of work in this area, including scientific research. I thought that GOSNIIOKhT should no longer serve military purposes and I was determined to fight for this with all means available.

My former patron only shook his head in reply. I realized that he disagreed with me completely. "Someone inside this incubator of death should assume the initiative," I encouraged myself. Unfortunately, I started having problems with my health.

Chapter 14
I Break the Silence

With great difficulty, I got permission to take my regular vacation at the end of July in 1991. I went to Baranovskoe, a settlement near Moscow, where I had a little plot of land. I was planning to build a dacha (summer house) there. There was a lot of work and that helped me to recover a bit.

On August 21st, the truck driver who brought us concrete for the foundation said that a lot of tanks were moving along the highway towards Moscow. We ran over to our neighbors' house, where there was a radio and a TV, and that's how we found out that there was a coup in progress against the government in Moscow. The weather was overcast, dull and rainy, but we decided to finish our work. My assistants talked me out of going back to Moscow, and we followed the events in the capital without switching off the radio for a minute.

By that time I was becoming less enthusiastic about the leaders in the DDR. Nobody there was willing to address the pressing problems that were developing. Their main idea was to seize power. Then, they said, they would decide about everything else.

I still sympathized with Boris Yeltsin, but I felt that there were no selfless people around him, no scientists or prominent specialists who had any programs or plans which ordinary people could understand. The nomenklatura in control at the time saw this, and they knew their power was unshakeable. The DDR leaders were mostly dilettantes, former instructors of Marxism-Leninism, representatives of the Soviet press, or just plain rascals. All these people combined presented little danger to the Communist regime. These demagogues couldn't attract sharp young minds and train them to be intelligent and honest politicians. Experts, erudite and otherwise competent people also had no illusions about the economists surrounding Boris Yeltsin. There never was any real science of economics in the U.S.S.R. The primary objective of the Soviet "economists" was to explain the basics of socialism and Communism, from the point of view of Marxist-Leninist "philosophy." If anyone has any doubts about this, let them read the dissertations by these scientists in the Russian State Library.

These were the kind of people who were at the helm of the DDR movement. Many progressive people in Russia pinned their hopes on them, but unfortunately the DDR's leaders let them down, and they compromised themselves entirely in the eyes of the public. Certainly the common members of the DDR like me were responsible, to some extent, for the shattering disappointment people experienced, because we allowed a small group of scoundrels, yesterday's fiery Communists, to abuse the people's trust in democratic ideals.

The defeat of the August of 1991 putsch attempt gave some impetus to the democratic movement in Russia, and it also gave rise to a lot of illusions.

While Boris Yeltsin celebrated his victory and was drinking "like a fish" in the Caucasus Region of Russia, the real power structure which remained in the same hands, had just enough time to shed its old skin. First, the president issued a decree that prohibited political activity in institutions and businesses. This was done under the pretext of banning the activities of the C.P.S.U. However, this document wasn't simply a farce. The decree betrayed the ordinary DDR members who actually helped the people who issued this decree to reach their current positions. They certainly realized that the C.P.S.U. was strong, even without its formal organization. What was the point of prohibiting the activity of these party committees, if the directors and all the top managers still controlled all aspects of the life and work of their employees? After all, how could Sergei Shakhrai, a Komsomol leader at Moscow State University, who became one of the DDR leaders and an assistant to Yeltsin, know anything if he still knew nothing about the life of ordinary people in the country?

At GOSNIIOKhT, we employees were deprived of our last chance to come forward and struggle with the opponents of the reforms and democratization.

Overall, it wasn't all that bad. The mass media became even bolder and the newspapers could write concretely about specific problems. I read through the democratic press attentively, but I couldn't find any serious publications about the military-chemical complex. So, I decided I was ready to speak openly about the problems of the military-chemical complex myself.

I never wanted anyone to think that I did it on the sly, in a cowardly way, hiding behind the back of some journalist. I was suffering from the agonizing burden I carried, feeling personal responsibility for participating in the criminal arms race of chemical weapons. Those thoughts which had been constantly torturing me finally pushed me forward to make a resolute decision to pick up my pen.

However, even before I wrote my first article, I was able to succinctly sum up my concerns in a note to Gavriil Popov, who was then Mayor of Moscow and one of the leaders of the "Democratic Russia" movement. Early in September of 1991, at a meeting of the activists of this organization, I passed him a brief note describing how dangerous the reckless activities of the ruling elite of the VPK were to the life and the safety of Muscovites. I asked Popov to meet with me. He agreed and promised to call me.

Alas, I never received his call. Later, at the urgent request of my lawyer, Popov was asked to come to court as a witness on my behalf. He said that he had difficulty remembering the facts - that we had met or that he had received a note from me. He also didn't remember that he had promised to meet with me.

It took me just one evening to write an article. I quickly typed it and took it to the office of the editor of the popular Moscow newspaper *Kuranty*. There I met Constantine Katanyan, a young and quite well known journalist. The article seemed interesting to him and he promised to publish it without any changes. It was published in *Kuranty* on October 10th, 1991.[78] When I was writing the article I knew that according to the Wyoming Memorandum (an accord which the U.S. and the USSR signed in 1989), the parties had to give each other information about all the compounds that could be classified as chemical weapons. It was clear to me that the U.S.S.R. had no intention of honestly meeting its commitments. This is why I concluded my article with an analogy which compared the actions of the leadership of the military-chemical complex with the behavior of a chemical compound capable of inversion, when it changes from one form to another, without changing its chemical composition.

When the article was published, I was still on vacation. According to witnesses, my article made a stunning impression on the directors of the institute. The Science Council of GOSNIIOKhT was urgently called together to discuss it, but they failed to pass the necessary resolution that would condemn the article. That was not because many people objected to it, but because they had no idea how the decision should be worded. Also, it was a little awkward to make a decision about my article in my absence.

The institute's top leaders wrote to the KGB of course, demanding that I should be immediately arrested for my impertinence. Although I don't know why, criminal proceedings were not brought against me at that time. Many people, including me, supposed that this was connected with the shock that the KGB experienced after the failure of the August coup, which ended with the arrest of its bosses, including Vladimir Kryuchkov, chief of the Chekists. It seemed that in our country, the era of Democracy and Glasnost had finally started to take root.

Later it was proven that we had been sorely mistaken. At that time, there were no formal grounds for prosecution and exemplary punishment. Back in November of 1989, the U.S.S.R. Committee of Constitutional Supervision at the Congress of People's Deputies, chaired by Sergei Alekseev, issued a decree that declared all normative acts relating to human rights to be null and void unless they were published openly in the press within three months. Naturally, nobody decided to publish such acts openly. So, all the lists of state secrets simply ceased to exist legally. The Belovezhskaya Decision on the dissolution of the U.S.S.R. confirmed the legality of the acts adopted by the U.S.S.R. Supreme Soviet and, consequently, this resolution of the Committee of Constitutional Supervision.

My article was the first of its kind, and it threw out a challenge to the powerful military-industrial complex (VPK). But, unfortunately, it didn't reverberate either in our country or abroad. Maybe people didn't pay much attention to it because of the dramatic events at that time connected with the break-up of the U.S.S.R. Everything faded to insignificance against this backdrop. It's a pity my warning call went unanswered. I hoped to hear something about the VPK and my article in the programs of "The Voice of America", the BBC, and "Liberty," but there was nothing.

Still, my article pushed the KGB to issue a new decree about the protection of state secrets, which President Boris Yeltsin signed on January 14, 1992. The decree was secretly adopted and it wasn't published, so the general public knew nothing about it. I only learned about it a year later when I was already sitting in jail. This decree reinstated all the invalidated normative acts and lists of state secrets. In this way, the president illegally cancelled the resolution of the Committee of Constitutional Supervision.

Once again the Chekists had their hands on one of the major instruments of total control over everyone whose profession was connected with the VPK clan.

When I returned to work after my vacation in October of 1991, I faced a vindictive reaction from the bosses on account of my article. I wasn't given a pass, so I couldn't enter the institute grounds. The guards on duty showed me an empty space on the rack for passes. Then I called the Department for the Security Regime, which was responsible for this system. They explained that my pass had been removed by order of Aleksander Martynov, Deputy Director for Security. When I called him, he gave no explanation, and said that my pass would be returned immediately. I entered the institute grounds and went to my room. It was open but people from a different department were working there. I realized they had taken away my workplace and my equipment. It was very unpleasant, but to be honest, I didn't expect anything else.

I told myself that this was just my first reward. The second one would be my dismissal. However, I had no regrets.

Soon my friends from the former Coordination Committee of the DDR movement came to see me and started suggesting different ways to regain what I had lost. I refused because I realized that it would be a nerve-wracking waste of time. So I went to the institute library to read scientific journals. I ran into several people I knew on my way there, and everybody behaved differently. Some people turned away and pretended they didn't notice me. But there were people who silently came up to me, shook my hand, and quickly left. And I felt very good about that. I realized that many people who I respected and appreciated approved of my article. Certainly they were afraid, but that was only natural. If I had already spent years of serious consideration, agonizing over my role in this criminal enterprise, working on the development of chemical agents, then how could I expect people who read my article to immediately re-evaluate their lives and their careers?

Someone should be the first and bear his cross, even if he were threatened. I was even more certain of this after I ran into Victor Zhakov, the former chief engineer at GOSNIIOKhT, who literally hissed at me, "What are you doing? You'll leave people without bread and butter! Be assured, they'll run you through the meat grinder and dump you into the sewer!"

I knew that if they decided to do away with me, there was hardly any way to avoid it. However, I chose to make no changes in my daily routine. In the evening I went for walks outside with my kids, and I went to different meetings of the city DDR organization. I also continued jogging in a park that was not far from my house. By that time I was already an avid jogger with more than fifteen years of experience. Running always calmed me down and helped me remain optimistic, although it was becoming more difficult to be optimistic when there was a general depression in the country, and a scientist couldn't count on normal work. My uncer-

State Secrets

tain situation without a workplace and equipment couldn't stay that way forever. The only thing that saved me at that time was a little work in the evenings and on my days off. I analyzed environmental tests at one of the cooperative societies and was paid a little for that. However, soon I lost this work too, because the cooperative had no more work orders.

The DDR activists from GOSNIIOKhT still hoped that they could change the situation. According to a provision in effect at that time, the director was supposed to be elected at a conference of employees, and the council of this group had to work out a contract with him. Only after that, could the contract be approved by the ministry. Petrunin, however, decided not to tempt his fate by trusting it to a meeting of the employees' collective. So he just ordered each subdivision to elect a representative from their ranks. Then he would convene a meeting of these representatives and finish his business there. However, the elections of the representatives showed that Petrunin had slim chances. He then called upon the members of the old council who were mostly "his people" and they obediently reappointed Petrunin the director.

Outraged by this trick, DDR activists and many other people asked me to intercede and inform the Ministry of Russian Industry about Petrunin's fraud. I couldn't refuse and agreed to go there with Vyacheslav Agureev, another chemist.

Our trip couldn't possibly have had a positive outcome, because the people from the former Ministry of Chemical Industry, who were working there, needed Petrunin more than anyone else, to survive.

The aides of our makeshift director and his deputy, who were closely watching my every step, decided to take advantage of our trip and had our absence classified as truancy. They immediately called a meeting of the employees' collective, from the department to which I was formally assigned.

I went to the meeting purely out of curiosity. I wanted to know how people under the new conditions would react to their own blatant manipulation. In the past I had read in books and had heard a little from witnesses, that in the 1930s the "common people" made decisions at the workers' meetings to savagely punish those with whom they had worked and been friends only the day before. As I expected, everything at the meeting evolved as it had in those earlier years.

On November 13, 1991, a meeting took place in Subdivision 45 that resolved to "abolish the position of the leading research scientist and to leave the question of the employment of Vil S. Mirzayanov, Doctor of Chemical Sciences, who occupied this position, to the directorate." One more step was made towards getting rid of dissenters.

Members of the former Coordination Committee of the DDR issued a leaflet in my support for the occasion.[79]

The leaflet was a bold document for that time. Of course, everybody knew the members of the Coordination Committee, so they were taking a bold risk. The administration could start persecuting them, and could punish them in an exemplary manner along with me.

And this is exactly what happened. First a computer was taken away from Valery Morgunov, a research assistant at the Analytical Department, because he used it to type the text of the leaflet. Then the persecution of other former members of the Coordination Committee began. Many of them were quickly dismissed from their jobs because of "staff reductions." This form of punishing disagreeable people was convenient, and it hardly ever failed.

I kept a copy of that leaflet. Every time I read this simple text, I feel a thrill and unbounded gratitude to my colleagues, who dared to perform a real civic feat when times got tough for me.

At that time, I was still hopeful that the leaders of the Democratic Russia movement would pay attention to the situation I described in my article "Inversion," especially since I soon had a good chance to talk with them about it.

On November 8 of 1991, I was in the staff headquarters of the Democratic Russia movement. All day I was compiling packets of papers for the delegates to the second congress, which was to take place a few days later. I managed to meet with Lev Ponomarev and Gleb Yakunin there.

Unfortunately, they hadn't read my article in *Kuranty*. Then I briefly summed up the publication for them and asked them to take

State Secrets

steps to eliminate the danger created by GRNIIOKhT (GOSNII-OKhT was renamed when the USSR broke up), which threatened the lives of Muscovites.

In response, Ponomarev recommended I take a sample of air near GRNIIOKhT and analyze it somewhere. Then the documentary proof that GRNIIOKhT was really dangerous would make it possible to expose the evil chemists.

I don't know what kind of dreadful advice this was - whether it was downright stupidity or just an ordinary provocation. If I had followed Ponomarev's "advice", I could have legally been arrested immediately on suspicion of espionage. I was reeling from the shock of such a crazy recommendation by one of our "leaders," with whom I had sympathized until then. Truly, he had advised a stranger to commit a crime! This is why I never tried to talk with Ponomarev about it again.

However, at the urgent request of my lawyer, I met with Ponomarev again in January of 1993. By that time he was a deputy of the Russian Supreme Soviet. We hoped he would be a witness for the defense, and confirm that I had met with him in the "Democratic Russia" headquarters and tried to draw his attention to this imminent danger. At that time my lawyer, Aleksander Asnis, was looking at all the different options for defending me in court, and it was very difficult. He hoped that he would be able to prove that I had repeatedly tried to draw the attention of public figures, deputies, and representatives of power to the imminent danger, though in vain. It would mean, according to the Criminal Code of Russia, that I had exhausted all legal means of raising my concerns through the proper channels, and had a legitimate right to take steps, even if my actions violated the current law. My article "Poisoned Policies" could be qualified as one such action.

Asnis and I were received with hospitality when we came to see Lev Ponomarev in his office in Room 1609 in the White House on the Krasnopresnenskaya Embankment. By that time, my "case" was widely known throughout the world and people recognized me everywhere, even in the subway. Many passers-by greeted me and thanked me for what I had done.

However, when Asnis briefly explained what we wanted, a

thick silence fell over the room. It was clear that Ponomarev was dumbfounded and couldn't find the words that would help extricate him from the situation. The deputy's consultant Maximov saved him. According to him, Lev Aleksandrovich was a public figure, and his authority could be seriously damaged if he took part in the proceedings as a witness. "The investigator will certainly ask why there was no feedback and what actions Lev Ponomarev took regarding this issue" he continued. "Probably you, Vil Sultanovich, were not persistent enough and didn't repeat your request," Maximov the lawyer, insisted.

"Indeed, Vil Sultanovich, why didn't you appeal to me again? I always try to help people when they appeal to me, if they can't get an apartment or have problems with their pension, and with many other issues. I most certainly would have tried to help you, too," said the DDR "leader", happily grasping the idea put forth by his aide.

This time my lawyer Asnis and I were the astonished ones. Despite his constant imperturbability and incredible self-control, Asnis was deeply disappointed and couldn't hide his feelings. There at the Krasnopresnenskaya Embankment, I realized for the first time why people had long ago dubbed such politicians "Dermocrats." (This translates literally as "Shitcrats".) Still somehow I found the composure to blurt out that I didn't want to distract him anymore from his great work.

I was really ashamed in front of Asnis about what was going on. I didn't believe that politics was always such a dirty business, or that politicians were necessarily dishonorable people. I don't think so now, either. It seems to me that almost any business can be pure and noble if you do it honestly and professionally. Can the profession of a sanitation worker be "dirty", only because he is dealing with sewage? On the other hand, chemists, surgeons, and people from many other professions have to put up with a lot of unpleasant things too.

Back in 1991, all my bridges were burned behind me, and it was clear that I would soon be fired from GRNIIOKhT.

On January 5th 1992, I was sent to the Personnel Department, where they handed me an order about my termination, of course for "staff reduction" reasons. The Deputy Chief of the Department for the Security Regime, German Mosyakin, also came to see me. He was a short man, amazingly unpleasant and slippery. He asked me to sign an agreement about the non-disclosure of state secrets, which was already familiar to me from my first days at GOSNII-OKhT.

I said that I would be happy to do this if they showed me a Russian law or governmental decree with a clear definition of what the state secrets in our profession were. I explained to Mosyakin that after my dismissal from the institute I had no intention of living by rules invented by people like him. Of course he couldn't show me any document that would explain all the subtle aspects regarding state secrets. He just obsequiously begged me to do him a favor because it was his job. We parted at that.

Unfortunately, my dismissal coincided with the beginning of Yegor Gaidar's reforms in Russia. So, overnight I lost all my savings. These reforms turned my family and me into paupers. I started struggling for survival, which wasn't easy because I had two sons, 5-year old Sultan and 13-year-old Iskander.

The Gaidar reform wasn't a "shock therapy" as it was dubbed then. It proved to be just another revolutionary attack in the history of Russia. As always, the top leaders hoped to solve problems that had existed for centuries, in one round. In principle, I have always supported reforms in Russia, but they shouldn't be so destructive. The authors of the "reform" acted absolutely brutally and inhumanely, even by Russian standards.

Nikita Khrushchev was a cynical and self-confident Bolshevik reformer. However, when he saw that he could no longer extort people by making them sign up for state loans "to restore the national economy," he abolished those loans. At the same time he suspended annual payments on them, but he promised to resume the payments 15 years later. From the psychological point of view, he was right. The newly hatched reformers were not willing to do even this, and they promised nothing to the people they had robbed.

Was it so difficult to try and develop a long-term plan to compensate people's savings by selling state property, natural gas, and resources? I am certain it could have been done, but the "reformers" led by Gaidar, were people with the same Bolshevik background. Bolsheviks never thought about people. They have always considered citizens to be "small screws" in the huge wheel of the state machinery. The very fact that they studied in the U.S. doesn't mean anything. They crossed the ocean, but they came back the same specialists in the economy of developed socialism as they had been before.

Currently, Russia is paying for the great conceit and arrogance of these "specialists", and the future of the development of democracy in this country remains in question, because of their mistakes.

At that time I couldn't afford to indulge in similar reflections. I started working in commercial organizations that found practical application for scientific and technological achievements, but these attempts were also fruitless. All those commercial organizations quickly switched over to the simple operations of "buy and sell", because at that time only those activities allowed them to survive.

Chapter 15
Challenging Poisoned Policies

The KGB Arrests Me

Since there was no public reaction to my article "Inversion", the feeling of dissatisfaction haunted me. From conversations with my colleagues, I realized that they were continuing to test chemical weapons at the Nukus site, even though Uzbekistan had declared independence. This was completely absurd and beyond my comprehension. The leadership of the VPK was wasting money on testing chemical weapons that no one needed, while a lot of military people were being laid off, industrial production was plummeting at a breakneck speed, and people were doomed to struggle for their basic survival.

I was disappointed with the results of my first public statement, so I didn't write a second one. I thought that times were too tough for people to get interested in the problems of chemical weapons. The country had other business to attend to.

I felt that way until one day when I accidentally stumbled across an article devoted to chemical weapons, in the weekly *Sovershenno Sekretno* (translates as "Top Secret") written by Lev Fedorov.[80] The author was a dilettante and there were a lot of mistakes. I immediately realized, judging from the text, that Fedorov had only a vague conception about the fundamental nature of the problem, because he wasn't a specialist in this field.

In any case, the problem was raised again and people began to call me to ask what I thought about it. As a specialist and a person who had put forth considerable effort to create this evil, I understood that I had no right to keep silent. I asked myself, "If not me, then who would speak as a professional to prevent the next deception?" There were and there are scientists in the VPK who are unquestionably more talented and knowledgeable than I am. However, I knew that none of them would ever risk speaking publicly on the problem of chemical weapons, because they had already become part of the totalitarian system.

I asked for Lev Fedorov's telephone number in the editor's office of *Sovershenno Sekretno*, called him, and we agreed to meet in my apartment. Our meeting took place in the middle of August. Fedorov had graduated from Kostroma Military Chemical School, but he had only a weak notion about the problems of chemical weapons. I also had the impression that he was a bit too curious. Probably I told him too much, for example about the essential difference between the new chemical agents and the ones that were known up until that time. We agreed that each of us would prepare for future publication our own version of an article on the problem of chemical weapons in Russia. Then we would work on an agreeable coordinated text and would try to publish the material in one of the popular papers.

Two days later I wrote an article called "The Chemical Sharashka in Moscow Expects Help from America." The day after that, I met with my co-author in the subway and handed him my version of the article. However, Fedorov didn't bring his version, and I wasn't very happy about that. On the other hand, I realized that he simply had nothing to write about.

At the end of August and in the beginning of September, Fedorov had to participate in a conference in Finland. When he returned, he called and said that he had reached an agreement to publish the article in the weekly paper *Moscow News*. We met again shortly after that, and I handed him the manuscript of a different article, one about the ecological aspects of chemical weapons production at the Volgograd plant. This plant had been constructed with materials and equipment brought in from Germany after the Second World War.

This factory was created so that we had something to poison our former allies (like the United States) with, because the U.S.S.R. was already preparing for a war with them. Later that plant started producing soman as well. GOSNIIOKhT opened a branch there for experimental industrial production, and at first it produced Substance 33, then "Novichok," and components of binary weapons. For many years the plant had also been a "training school" for top managers for the VPK. I wrote about this in my article. But this article was never published independently. Later, after I was released from Lefortovo Prison, I was surprised to read it in "The Bulletin of the Social and Ecological Union". It was published in the form of an interview, which I allegedly gave along with Lev Fedorov. However, no such interview ever took place.

In September, Fedorov called to tell me that he had arranged for me to meet Will Englund, a journalist for the *Baltimore Sun*. The interpreter was Andrei Mironov, a famous dissident, who had served a prison term for anti-Soviet propaganda. I told Will Englund what I had written about in my article for *Moscow News*. I had the impression that he had a sharp mind and could quickly grasp the essence of the problem. However, it bothered me a little that Fedorov obstinately tried to impose a discussion of dioxins in Ufa on Englund, and that distracted us from our main issue for a long time.

At the end of our conversation, Englund asked me how I could verify my story, and I replied that the strength of my convictions would never allow me to disclose any secrets - technical or otherwise. I recommended that he get in touch with my colleague Edward Sarkisyan, an activist in the Democratic Russia Movement. Probably he would confirm what I had told Englund. Edward and I didn't discuss this beforehand or have any kind of understanding or preliminary agreement, but I hoped that he could meet with the American correspondent, and he did. Edward told me about it later over the phone. He also added that he had made a recording of the conversation with Englund and they agreed that Englund would show him the material before publication. A few weeks after that I asked him to call to Andrey Zheleznyakov who agreed to answer the reporter's questions.[81]

Just before *Moscow News* released the article, Leonard Nikishin from that paper called to read me the text. Although Fedorov had made a few insertions that did not sit well with me, I agreed to the article's publication, since Nikishin insisted there was little time for changes. *Moscow News* published "A Poisoned Policy" on September 16, 1992 with a joint Mirzayanov-Fedorov byline and dressed it up with a landmark photograph of GOSNIIOKhT's administrative building. That was the first published image of a secret Post Office Box.[82]

From its opening lines, "A Poisoned Policy" left the readers no illusions, asserting that Russia was continuing to test and produce chemical weapons despite international pledges to the contrary. It also stated that this activity threatened the health of Muscovites, and that the generals operating the chemical weapons complex were running amok. The article warned that Russian military authorities had already approved new chemical weapons and stockpiled a large amount of them. GOSNIIOKhT, the article specified, had developed a new toxic agent that was much more powerful than VX and had also successfully developed and produced a new binary variant of that agent. The first production of the binary agent had occurred at Volgograd, and in the spring of 1991 former Soviet President Mikhael Gorbachev had rewarded those involved with the prestigious Lenin Prize. The new binary had been field tested in the first quarter of 1992 at the Nukus test site, perhaps without the knowledge of Uzbekistan's new President, Islam Karimov. The article further pointed out that these binary tests had occurred on President Yeltsin's watch, after his January 29, 1992 statement committing Russia to a 1990 bilateral agreement with the United States to eliminate chemical weapons and no longer produce them.[83] In other words, five years after Soviet leader Gorbachev pledged that the country had stopped making chemical weapons, Russia had just tested the most powerful chemical weapon ever.

"A Poisoned Policy" painted a very grim picture, reporting that GOSNIIOKhT had been literally poisoning Moscow's citizens by releasing toxic agents directly into the air. Furthermore, the article stated that it was nearly impossible to prevent such dangerous pollution, and that the decontamination solutions that GOSNIIOKhT developed and employed were really not all that effective. GOSNIIOKhT was storing toxic chemicals unsafely, even in open barrels, and the barrels were transported on regular trains to the Shikhany test site, where they were dumped into open pits. GOSNIIOKhT's leaders knew but had not informed the public that environmental analyses had proved that the facility's grounds and the water beneath it were contaminated with toxic chemicals. For these reasons, Russians should not trust the important task of destroying chemical weapons to those who made and continued to make them, for these very people had every intention of maintaining their dangerous and deceptive practices.

During an interview with *Novoe Vremya*. October 21 1992.

With my co-author Lev Fedorov. October 21 1992.

From the left to right: Lev Fedorov, Vladimir Uglev and Vil Mirzayanov. Moscow, February 1993.

Even though "A Poisoned Policy" in *Moscow News* did not name any of the binary agents or give any formulas, I felt that the public and the government would surely take notice this time. Serendipitously, Englund's article in the *Baltimore Sun*[84] appeared on the same day, stating that Russia had developed a new chemical agent that was 10 times more toxic than the well-known nerve agent VX. The article also reported that US government officials and independent experts in chemical weapons arms control were surprised and skeptical about these new chemical weapons.[85]

I was preoccupied with trying to feed my family, unaware that GOSNIIOKhT set in motion the process which culminated in my arrest only five days after "A Poisoned Policy" appeared. The institute's Permanent Technical Commission assembled to consider whether my article contained secret information. On September 25th, these five senior officials passed a Top Secret resolution[86] claiming I had revealed state secrets learned during the course of my career. GOSNIIOKhT's Director Petrunin[87] sent this resolution to the KGB with a letter asking it to decide whether or not to initiate criminal proceedings. The KGB, in turn, forwarded a letter which stated that my actions indicated a "criminal offense" along with my case materials to its Investigation Department.[88] Russia's Deputy Attorney General, Ivan Zemlyanushin, issued a warrant for my arrest on October 19, 1992, "for prevention of further divulging of state secrets and possible intervention in an investigation".

The Chekists did a lot of work before I was arrested. Later a well informed Russian newspaper reporter told me that two events preceded my arrest. First, at an executive meeting convened in the office of Barannikov, who at that time was the chief of the MB RF (the Ministry of Security of the Russian Federation - the successor to the KGB), four generals out of seven spoke out in favor of my arrest. Second, President Boris Yeltsin visited the MB RF on October 18, 1992. Brief information about this appeared in the press, mentioning that the president had a talk with employees of the MB RF and this talk grew into an expanded meeting of the ministry's board.

That is why I have reason to suppose that President Yeltsin himself gave "the green light" to the generals for my arrest.

The patience of the Chekists was completely exhausted when, at Lev Fedorov's invitation, I went to the editorial office of a popular Russian weekly magazine to give an interview on the problems of chemical weapons.

On the morning of October 20, 1992, I met with Fedorov at the Pushkinskaya Metro Station, and we went to meet with Oleg Vishnyakov, from the paper *Novoe Vremya* (*New Times*). The handsome young correspondent met us in a cramped room, and he got right to work without wasting any time. At first, it seemed to me that he didn't know very much about the problem of chemical weapons, but during our conversation he got to the heart of the matter quickly, and by the end of the interview we were discussing problems almost on the same level. As we were leaving the *Novoe Vremya* editor's office, I noticed a blond man and a blond woman without any characteristic features, next to the bulletin board which displayed the current issue of this magazine. Both blonds were discussing something in a lively manner, and I also noticed that they attentively looked at me...

The interview was published when I was already in Lefortovo Prison.[89]. Oleg was pressured and even interrogated in the Investigation Department of the MB RF. However, he wasn't afraid to publish this material, although this article wasn't supposed to see the light of day, according to the calculations of the Chekists, because it was confiscated and was among the material evidence exhibits of my "crime." But that was later...

On October 22, 1992, my friend Edward Sarkisyan woke me with an early morning telephone call. Edward said that a few people identifying themselves as KGB agents rang his doorbell and had demanded he open his door. Fortunately, Edward refused and called the police because at that time, criminal gangs roamed the city posing as policemen and KGB. They were forcing Muscovites to open their doors, then robbing and killing them.

Later that morning, with my sons off to kindergarten and school, I was getting ready for my usual trip to the street market near the Sokol Metro Station, where I was selling jeans and sneakers to support my family, when my doorbell rang. I asked who it was, and the answer was devastating, "We are from the Ministry of Security. Open the door!" I remembered Edward's call earlier that morning, and at first I thought that it was a strange coincidence of fate, so I shouted, "Get out of here at once! I am calling the cops!" To sound more convincing, I added that I had an axe and would defend myself. And indeed, I called the police.

Meanwhile, I already guessed that these people really were from the MB RF, and that they had come to arrest me. They were knocking more insistently, and I was dialing up Mironov and Englund.

I had just enough time to call to the journalist Englund from the *Baltimore Sun* and tell him that the KGB had come to get me.[90] From behind the door I could hear these men tell my wife Nuria that they were arresting me because of the article in Moscow News. Outraged, Nuria shouted that they were mad, that someone couldn't be arrested for a newspaper article. At this point, I realized they had already shown Nuria the arrest warrant. As the verbal volleys escalated, the local police arrived and demanded that I open the door immediately. Then they threatened to break it down. They advised me that police in the West would not be so patient. It was clear I could not stall until the media arrived. So, I opened the door because I did not want to have it broken by force.

The apartment was instantly so full that nobody could even move. Some sturdy guys settled comfortably into the kitchen, and one of them handed me an arrest warrant that said my apartment would be searched. I stood calmly, suddenly amazed at the simplicity of the proceedings. My only worry was Nuria, who was very upset and angrily venting at me, telling me they were tearing up the place and that I would have to clean up the mess. Trying to save the apartment from being torn to bits, I complied with a sharp command to produce everything that had to do with the Moscow News article, showing them where my manuscripts, scientific articles, and different papers were kept.[91]

The senior KGB officer ordered me to get dressed, and a few minutes later we left with two agents walking in front of me, two behind, and another two holding me by the arms. I felt like a big-time gangster in a movie. I made a wise crack that the officers shouldn't hold me so tightly, because I could easily poison them all, and to my amusement they loosened their grip. They put me into a yellow Zhiguli that took off along the Highway of Enthusiasts, and then the motor died as the car was crossing the tramway tracks right in front of a tram. Two of the burly escorts jumped out to push the car as I started joking that they weren't even properly prepared to capture a state criminal. Glaring back at me, the lead officer said they had lost their form a bit lately, but he assured me that it would all come back. Looking out the window as the Zhiguli passed GOSNIIOKhT, I knew as it turned to the right near the Aviamotornaya Metro Station that they were taking me to the notorious KGB prison, Lefortovo.

Lefortovo Prison

In Lefortovo I was immediately taken to the second floor of a thoroughly guarded three-story building that housed the Main Investigation Department. A young, tall, and slightly overweight blonde man with bright blue eyes "took me in" upon receipt into one of the offices off the long corridor. He declared that his name was Victor Shkarin and that he would be in charge of my case.

Investigator Shkarin briefly explained the reason for my arrest and solicitously asked me if I had any complaints. He did his best to demonstrate proper and polite behavior. After a brief formal procedure for establishing my identity, I resolutely refused to say anything or give any testimony without the presence of a lawyer. Probably this was a trifle theatrical, but it seemed to me that it was the best way to proceed, since many of our dissidents described their arrests with details like this in their memoirs.

Right away the captain started calling for a legal consultation. It was obvious that the system worked smoothly and everything was anticipated. He told me politely, "We will have time for everything." He made it seem as if we were working for the same company and pursuing some common cause.

I was sitting in Investigator Shkarin's small office for a long time, while we waited for the lawyer. The room was furnished with three chairs, a huge safe, a wardrobe, and a writing table with a squeaky computer.

I didn't know yet what hardships were in store for me. Investigations, another arrest, imprisonment, closed legal proceedings, and long days full of bitter disappointment - all of this would blend into a long terrible ride in the Maelstrom.

I was getting over my original overwhelming apathy and started taking action. First, I asked for a pen and paper to write a declaration and protested against my detention. I wrote that I would go on an indefinite, dry hunger strike until the moment of my liberation.

The investigator read the text, but he didn't react. Once more I declared that I would not answer any questions or participate in the interrogation without the presence of a lawyer. At that time it wasn't easy for me to hire a lawyer, because I had no money. I felt anxious about causing a huge loss to the family finances, when life was so tough and every kopeck counted. I was particularly sorry for my sons, whom I had doomed to perpetual poverty. In despair, I even thought about why it hadn't happened to me before they were born, when I wasn't so vulnerable. Now, I could only count on the free services of the public defender.

The investigator quickly typed up the "detainment transcript", where my rights were mentioned along with the reasons why I was under suspicion. It was written in the transcript that I was detained at 12.15 P.M., on October 22 of 1992.

Later Investigator Shkarin set about finishing up the "transcript of interrogation of the suspect", because an elderly man with a beat-up old suitcase joined us. He introduced himself as a lawyer from Legal Advice Office N 150, Leonid Grigorievich Belomestnykh.

I seized the moment when Shkarin stepped out, to ask the lawyer to call my wife and give her the message that I had gone on a hunger strike. I was certain (how naive I was!) that if the Belomestnykh told my wife about this, I could ask him to defend my interests in the future. Skipping ahead, I can say that Belomestnykh didn't fulfill my request, but I can't rebuke him. At the end of the day, I am sure that he was at least a temporary KGB employee.

Finally, we started with the interrogation proper. I wasn't so detached and unfeeling about it then, as I am these days when I am describing what happened. Probably I was a bit wound up and too obstinate. Shkarin said I was accused of revealing state secrets in the article "A Poisoned Policy," which was in violation of Article 75, Part I, of the Russian Criminal Code. We got down to business after I agreed to answer in Russian (Tatar is my first language) and accepted Shkarin as the interrogator and Belomestnykh as my lawyer, even though I knew that any attorney that the KGB provided would not work in my interests.

From the start, I insisted on my complete innocence. I stated that the article was based on the facts as I knew them from my work at GOSNIIOKhT, given my direct involvement in the binary program. I had wanted to expose the hypocrisy of the leaders of the chemical weapons complex, because they were simultaneously developing new weapons while pretending to work towards chemical weapons disarmament. While I knew that information about the binary weapons program was secret, it was clear to me that the binary program served only the interests of the leaders of the chemical weapons complex. The article dealt conceptually with the binary program, but I gave no specific data about it. In fact, I had not used a single line from any classified document and therefore I believed that I had not disclosed any state secrets in "A Poisoned Policy."[92] Furthermore, I never gave any concrete information about the composition or properties of any of the new chemical agents or the binaries.

Captain Shkarin did his best to create an impression in the transcript, that I had thoroughly confessed and that I had disclosed state secrets entrusted to me at my work. I must admit that sometimes I enjoyed his game, because I eliminated the obstacles he presented, while trying not to show that I had guessed about them. By this time I had already realized that my investigator had no idea about the essence of my research, and I enjoyed leading him on a bit.

Today I can honestly say that I have nothing to reproach myself for. Looking back, it seems to me that I managed to distance myself from the investigator's position, starting with the very first interrogation, in spite of the truly extreme pressure. My position was that my actions were based exclusively on moral considerations and the aspiration to save the world community from danger caused by the hypocritical policy of the leaders of the military-chemical complex. I remember that several times I had to insist on this very wording, although the investigator tried time and again to grossly distort it. I understood immediately what he was getting at. He wanted my very first testimony to lead to the certain conclusion that everything I published in the mass media was known to me through my responsibilities at work.

In reality, the situation was different from what Shkarin wanted to present. For example, I wasn't allowed to work on the development of binary weapons. This is why I made a mistake in the article "Poisoned Policies", when I wrote that the leaders of the military-chemical complex received Lenin Prizes for creating binary weapons based on a new chemical agent.

I couldn't have known that the binary weapon was based on "Substance 33", which had been produced for a long time at the Cheboksary Chemical Plant, and had already been tested and added to the arsenal of the Soviet Army. The investigator, his bosses, and even more so his consultants from GRNIIOKhT knew about this very well, but this didn't prevent them from deliberately hurling false accusations at me. Their scheme was simple: the jailed suspect can't properly defend himself. This is why Shkarin stubbornly stuck to the basis of the accusation - "the conclusion of the Permanent Technical Commission" at GRNIIOKhT.

A little later I understood the tactics of my investigator and made amendments to my answers on binary weapons. As for the rest, I had no intention of renouncing what I had written based on information I knew from GRNIIOKhT. The articles were conceptual and they didn't disclose any technical or other kinds of details.

When Shkarin finished taping the investigation protocol, somebody knocked on the door and in came a lieutenant colonel with the happy face of a man who has accomplished something very important. Later I found out that he was investigator N. Fanin, who had arrested and brought Lev Fedorov to Lefortovo. Fanin told Shkarin that he and his man had "finished the job very well". I discovered from my case materials, events that were some developments which I came to understand as the downfall of my co-author.

The Downfall of Lev Fedorov

The idea of renouncing the articles I published in the press in order to save myself seemed monstrous to me. Theoretically I could do this, especially since the investigator encouraged me to pass the blame to my co-author Lev Fedorov.

I could have claimed that he had written the largest part of "A Poisoned Policy" and a lot of problems would have been settled, but Fedorov, unlike me, didn't work in a secret area, and he wasn't legally liable for that. This was unacceptable because of moral

State Secrets

considerations. Sadly, Fedorov proved to be not quite up to the same high mark when he appeared before his interrogator that same day.

On October 22, 1992, Lev Fedorov was brought to the Investigation Department of the MB RF. Before that, his apartment had been searched, and the report of the search says that he voluntarily produced all the materials that the investigation was interested in, so the Chekists didn't have to search his apartment. These materials were three manuscripts of my articles. Other papers belonging to Fedorov were not confiscated.[93]

It seems that Lev Fedorov was not so uncomfortable with his investigator in Lefortovo. Ten months later, Lev Fedorov renounced his testimony after I showed the transcript of this report to Mironov and distributed it among my friends along with a copy of the entire case materials. Even so, it remained an enigma to me and many others that he didn't do it the day after he was released, right after his interrogation.

According to the transcript of Fedorov's interrogation[94] that day, he refused to have anything to do with the information which was the basis for the main idea of his published articles. In his conversation with the Chekists, my co-author reduced his role to that of a literary editor of the material presented by me.

To top it all off, Lev Fedorov signed a confidentiality contract on the subject of his interrogation, thereby entering into secretive cooperation with the investigation. However, there is some reason to doubt that his cooperation only began at this time.

I can confirm that Fedorov kept his promise in full. After I was released from prison, he never said a word about his confessions at the interrogation. Moreover, for a long time Lev played the role of a hero, who had suffered from persecution by the Chekists.

Unfortunately, I found out about this too late - only after the interrogation phase of my "case" was concluded and I could read through all the materials. No one can ever guarantee that spiritually weak people won't attach themselves to a noble cause, or that they won't prove to be agents of "our valiant Chekists".

Obliging readiness to give such detailed and pejorative testimony shows that Lev was ready to betray everybody. How else can we explain why he even told the Chekists the full name of the secretary of the Editor in Chief of the newspaper *Argumenti i Fakti*? How else can we understand his detailed description of meetings with Starkov, Vishnyakov, and other people? And why did Fedorov tell the investigators that there were two versions of the prepared article in the editor's office of *Argumenti i Fakti*? It all looks like undisguised cooperation with the Chekists. God forbid if they confiscated only one copy of that article!

Lev's coached testimony was in fact followed by searches of the editors' offices of the newspapers *Moscow News*, *Argumenti i Fakti*, and *Novoe Vremya*. In addition, Oleg Vishnyakov from *Novoe Vremya* was immediately brought to Lefortovo for interrogation. It is curious that there is no time registered in the transcript of that interrogation. In summer of 1993 when I was reading over my case materials, I asked Investigator Cheredilov, who had interrogated Vishnyakov, about it. He said that he had forgotten to do this but he added "You can write a complaint about my error". Isn't such forgetfulness a strange oversight for an investigator of special cases? However, I already knew that Vishnyakov was interrogated about 4 P.M., shortly after Fedorov had spoken to the Chekists.

During the following two days, the Chekists processed information received from Fedorov's interrogation, and Lieutenant Colonel Cheredilov toiled away thinking that he was on the right track. After a successful catch in the editor's office of *Novoe Vremya*, he hurried over to the editor's office of *Argumenti i Fakti*, where, according to my co-author, there were two prepared versions of the article about chemical weapons. The investigator, along with other civilian employees from the MB RF who acted as official witnesses, produced an injunction for the confiscation, and as before, he received the papers he wanted without any interference (it never occurred to anyone to refuse to hand over the articles!)

In a Prison Cell for the First Time

After I signed my transcripts of interrogation, Shkarin called a guard who ordered me to get up and follow him, while holding my hands behind my back. I obeyed and we walked down the corridor to a door which a constable opened, after receiving a light signal in response to his ringing of the buzzer.

The prison made no particular impression on me. It smelled of fresh paint and it was quiet. There was not a soul around. We descended to the first floor and came to a door where another guard was waiting for us. He opened the door and we went to the basement, where I was ordered to take off my clothes and have a shower.

After that, they took me to one of the cells on the first floor. It was a narrow room about six meters long and two and a half meters wide. There was a barred window across from the door, at the height of about two meters. Three iron beds were tightly fastened to the floor. On one of the beds there were two sheets, a mattress, and a quilt. In the middle of the cell, a sink was attached to the wall with a pipe and a valve for water. Nearby there was some kind of a lavatory pan without any water tank or similar device. Above the door there was an iron grating, from which protruded the handle of a radio-loudspeaker. I recognized the voice of the announcer as that of *Radio Station Mayak*.

Finally I was completely alone and nobody disturbed me from sorting out my feelings shaped by everything I had suffered through that day. It's remarkable that I wasn't sad there, in that stone sack. Difficult work awaited me, and I knew that the struggle against injustice would drain me of my strength. I started thinking about different options for my defense. Clearly I couldn't consult with anybody in the jail, so I had to rely entirely on myself. I had already started my struggle by declaring a dry hunger strike. When the window in the door opened, and a head in a white cap suddenly popped in and said "dinner," I politely refused.

I didn't sleep at all, the first night in jail. All through the night, a bright electric light in the middle of the ceiling blazed out from behind iron bars. I had no watch, so I simply lost track of the time, which dragged on endlessly. When I heard the call sound of *Radio Mayak* from the loudspeaker, I understood that it was already 6 A.M. Almost immediately, I also heard a command from behind the door, "Get up!"

I spent the whole morning being photographed and "playing the piano." This is what prisoners call the fingerprinting procedure. A lone guard performed this job for all of Lefortovo Prison. He worked under the diligent supervision of a portrait of "Iron Felix" Dzerzhinsky hanging above his desk.

Eventually, it was time for lunch, which I also refused. Soon after that a window in my door opened again and the command was given, "Get ready to exit!" I got ready immediately, but I only had my old lightweight overcoat, a ski cap, and the winter shoes I was wearing when I was brought there.

This time the jailer led me in a different direction. Along the way he was loudly and constantly snapping his fingers. Probably he was giving the signal that he had a prisoner with him.

Investigator Shkarin was waiting for me in the familiar office. He said that Nuria had called and asked him to tell me that everything was fine at home, and that she promised to do everything she could to help me. She also promised to settle the question of a lawyer. I felt relief at once when I saw my little Sultan in my mind's eye.

Shkarin inquired politely about how I was doing. I thanked him for asking and replied that I was continuing with my dry hunger strike. The captain remarked that he didn't recommend this because it was very dangerous at my age. For that reason, they would do everything to keep me from dying of hunger. Then he began his interrogation. I didn't object, because I decided that under those severe circumstances, I could still do without a lawyer. I was curious to test myself in lone combat, especially since at some point during the previous night's reflections, I had decided that it would be a battle of intellects, and I should not be afraid of dirty tricks. Maybe I was overly self-confident, but I felt already that the investigator had only a vague idea about the essence of my case. This particular interrogation was a pure formality, to confirm that the two manuscripts which Lev Fedorov gave to Chekists were mine. Shkarin also asked me whether I gave anyone else information about the topics of those manuscripts.[95]

I realized that the prosecution would work exclusively with my manuscripts in the future, so I couldn't refer to the editor's or other revisions or amendments. I didn't care because I was certain that I didn't give away any state secrets either in my manuscripts, or in the articles.

I read the transcript and was taken back to my cell accompanied by an escort. I was beginning get used to this. Although according to the law, the suspect can only be detained for 72 hours without being shown an accusation, they made an exception for me. The explanation was that weekends didn't count. You might have thought at this time that I was at some spa or resort. A brilliant invention by our Chekists! I now had more than enough time, and I was still on a hunger strike.

Those were the days when the world's super powers were poised to sign the Convention on the Prohibition of Chemical Weapons (CWC). In all clauses of the "resolution" that the investigator showed me, there was nothing serious enough to serve as a basis for the accusation, except for the clause about binary weapons. Did it make any sense to accuse me of allegedly disclosing the locations of the production and testing sites of chemical weapons? Foreign specialists and correspondents had been visiting Shikhany for a long time. The Nukus test site had become the property of the independent country of Uzbekistan. I knew that the operations of chemical weapons production had already been discontinued at the places Russia had declared. It's true, that I had pointed out the places of production of the new weapons in my article, but I thought that under the political conditions that were taking shape then, that this couldn't be considered a serious criminal offense. Therefore, it was only by a great stretch of the imagination that I could be accused of discussing a new chemical agent and binary weapons.

I spent the second night in my three-man cell in the same way, without any cellmates, and I didn't sleep that night, either. When the radio started blaring and the head of the jailer appeared in the window and commanded "Get up!" I was already on my feet.

At some time later "the head" appeared again and asked, "Are you going to eat?" I answered that I wasn't. "It's up to you," said the head and the window closed.

Around 10 o'clock I was taken to Shkarin again. He said that

Nuria had called once more, and was asking him to tell me that the kids were alive and well and that she would hire a lawyer for me. "There is an uproar building in the press on your account," added the Chekist.

I admit I felt my spirits lifting, but I asked no questions. After all, everyone who wished to could read my article and see that the KGB had fabricated the case. However, the captain hadn't called me in there to discuss what the press wrote about. Shkarin handed me the arrest warrant (it turned out that I had only been detained before that) which was signed by First Deputy Attorney General, Ivan Zemlyanushin.

I Move to Another Cell

After all the formalities were completed, the captain pressed a button and an escort entered the room. We went back to my cell following the familiar route. After lunch, which I refused as usual, the door of the cell opened and I was given the command, "Get up! Take the quilt and the sheets and exit!" I understood that I was moving to another cell. I was taken to the second floor, and the escort stopped near cell number 81, opened the door, and told me to enter the cell.

Two young men were standing there. They pointed to an empty bed and I put my things there. One of the inmates said at once, "You are, of course, Vil Mirzayanov. I figured it out. They said on the radio that you were arrested for high treason. I guessed that you would end up here at Lefortovo." The name of this young man was Aleksander Yavitsky. He had been in Lefortovo for more than a year, on charges of illegal foreign currency operations. I immediately recalled a recent television report from Lefortovo Prison. A correspondent was interviewing Yavitsky, who was saying that conditions in the jail were actually quite good. I remember that when Yavitsky was asked how he managed to end up in such "comfortable" conditions, he answered in the same tone as the reporter: "I had to deserve it." Could I have supposed then that I would manage to find myself in the same KGB jail cell with the

State Secrets

hero of a TV report?

Aleksander told me about his "case." It turned out that he was involved in a sensational episode involving the theft of three million dollars from Sheremetyevo Airport. The government of Russia had borrowed this money from some American bank. After the money was brought to Russia, the money bags containing dollars were dumped on the airfield, where they lay for almost two days before airport workers got interested in the contents of the bags.

Aleksander played a part in the handling of these dollars. According to his story, he bought the dollars for Soviet money at a discount, from some people who had successfully "domesticated the money bags" for themselves. He hid some of the dollars at different dachas and decided to take some of them abroad. Everything finished with that. He was caught on the Western border, with his dollars stuffed in gasoline cans. He said he handed over all the hidden dollars to the investigation; however, a few hundred thousand dollars were never found despite the fact that Aleksander cooperated with the investigation.

My other new comrade was called Victor D. He slept on a bed near the head of my bed. Victor was imprisoned in Lefortovo for killing his drinking buddy - a KGB lieutenant colonel - in a drunken brawl. I established reasonably good relations with my cellmates. Aleksander quickly talked me out of continuing with my hunger strike. He explained that nobody would know about it, but within five days I would be force fed, which is a cruel and humiliating procedure.

How could I argue with that? Prisoners locked up in Lefortovo were almost completely isolated. There was no connection with the outside world, and no meetings were allowed. Food parcels could be sent in once a month, and they were thoroughly searched. It was unlikely that anyone could outwit the Lefortovo jailers and send out news about himself, or get news from the outside world.

Later when I was reading up on my case, I came across a report by one of the jailers. He reported to his bosses that he found a note from my son Iskander in the food parcel. It was written on the inner side of the soap wrapper. "Dad, stand firm, we love you," wrote Iskander…

The toughest trial I had to face in the cell was when I had to use the toilet. It was completely out in the open, and I had to sit down before the eyes of my cellmates. Aleksander saw what I was going through and settled the problem quite easily. "Vil Sultanovich!" he said. "Stop being ashamed. This regime which treats us like beasts should be ashamed!"

He was right, but I was never able to get used to such an inhumane attitude toward people under investigation.

My Cellmates - My Lawyers

I am grateful to my cellmates for a few lessons in "life." If not for them, I would probably still be in jail and my life could follow the script written for me by the KGB.

Their situation was no better than mine, but my cellmates supported me as much as they could and tried to help. Although the investigator had shown me the Criminal Code and pointed out clauses that stipulated my rights, I could hardly comprehend what I was reading there.

A few months later, during one of my numerous meetings with Shkarin, he admitted that people under investigation usually gave up about 90 percent of the information about themselves during the first three or four days. At this time they are simply deeply stressed and helpless.

During my entire stay in Lefortovo Prison I had practically no defender. From the very beginning, I realized that the defense attorneys whom the investigator offered me were not real lawyers, though I made a great effort not to tell them to their faces what I thought about them.

I told my cellmates honestly about my "case" and what I was accused of. They immediately advised me to write an appeal to the district court, asking to be released. As neither my "case" nor I were dangerous, there was no need to keep me under detention until my trial. However, it was completely up to me how to write this appeal, and I had no lawyer to help me. So I spent all my weekends (the investigator does not work on weekends or holidays) in creative work. I tried to substantiate the arguments for my release. My friends advised me to send my appeal through the prison administration, because they said I couldn't trust the investigators when it came to any serious business.

I felt uncomfortable about this because the investigator had asked me to give to him my appeal requesting release, if I ever decided to write such a document. Yavitsky, who then advised me like a lawyer, wisely recommended that I write two copies of the appeal. I could send one copy to the People's Court through the Lefortovo Prison Administration and give the second one to the investigator, if he wanted it so much. That is the way I did it.

In the morning we were taken through two corridors for a walk in the yard. A few security guards were sitting at a large table with TV screens, at the intersection. The promenade ground was a large jail cell, 20-30 square meters in size. This room was different from the other cells because there was sky above our heads, although it was screened off with barbed wire. A guard was pacing back and forth on a special platform above the door to the promenade ground. Sometimes the voices of other prisoners from the neighboring promenade ground reached us, but it was impossible to make out what they were saying. Their voices were muffled by the Russian folk songs, which were constantly playing on the radio.

The radio in the cell was terribly obtrusive, but it was our only connection with the outside world. It drove me crazy to have to listen every day from 9 A.M. until our 10 P.M. bedtime, to *Radio Station Mayak* broadcasting the sermons of Asahara Shoko in poor Russian. He was the head of the Japanese religious cult "Aum Shinrikyo", which later gained notoriety for its unspeakable sarin gas attack on Tokyo subway commuters.[96] He was talking such trash that I had to ask my cellmates to let me lower the volume, but my young friends were used to this voice and they even needed this nonsense. Aleksander easily imitated the fanatic preacher's voice and recited his sermons by heart in unison with the radio.

I suppose that introduced some variety into our prison life. Food was brought to us three times a day, and I must admit the food wasn't that bad compared with what my family could afford to put on the table at that time. I remember on the fourth day of my detainment, we were given boiled buckwheat kasha with meat and a meaty borsch soup for lunch. At that time this was a delicacy for most Russians. Alexander remarked that he was eating such a dish for the first time, and he was sure that it was prepared in my honor.

We were given the newspapers *Vechernaya Moskva*, *Sovetskaya Rossiya*, and *Izvestia*, and we took turns reading them. For a few days they didn't give us *Izvestia*. Evidently some materials were published about me during those days. *Vechernaya Moskva* of October 23, 1992 published an article with the title "Detained for Disclosing a Secret that Doesn't Exist", which discussed a report circulated by the Ministry of Security. The newspaper wrote that employees of the MB had arrested one of the authors of Moscow News article "A Poisoned Policy" on charges of divulging state secrets. The Ministry of Security didn't disclose the name of the person detained, but the newspaper wrote that his name was Vil Mirzayanov and he was threatened with a 2-5 year jail term. Also, according to the article, the prisoner was being kept in solitary confinement at Lefortovo. The article concluded with the remark that since according to international agreements Russia didn't produce chemical weapons, what was there to disclose?

Three days later we were brought some more papers, and we read them from cover to cover, because it helped us to pass the time. On the morning of Monday October 26, when a special team from the prison administration was collecting different appeals and letters to the judicial authorities, I submitted my appeal to the People's Court with a request to release me. It was almost an exact copy of my application addressed to the investigator.

Of course my appeal was written incorrectly from a legal point of view, because I was supposed to ask the court to set me free, since I didn't present a danger to the public; holding me under arrest wasn't in the interests of an unbiased investigation, etc. Instead of saying that, I stated the case from my point of view. But what could I do if my cellmate was my only lawyer at that time?

Three more days passed. The investigator kept silent and didn't call me in for any interrogations. My cellmates remarked that it was a tactical move on Shkarin's part, as he wanted me to be in the agony of suspense and relent. However, I found out later that my appeal had caught the Chekists off guard. They hadn't expected me to decide to write my appeal for release from arrest so quickly, so they had to urgently prepare documents for the forthcoming hearing in court. They didn't even have time to show me the official indictment. With a little delay, my cellmates asked the security guard to bring the October 23, 1992 issue of *Izvestia*. I later took that copy with me when I left the prison.

The journalists Andrei Illesh and Sergei Mostovschikov wrote an article titled "Each Journalist Can Now Become a Traitor to the Motherland". They wrote that a month after the article "A Poisoned Policy" was published, the editor's office of *Moscow News* was searched, and copies of the article were confiscated. The authors summarized the original article and analyzed the problem of defining state secrets, which in the end amounted to bureaucratic secrets. They suggested that the specialists from GRNIIOKhT, who they had criticized in their article, had most probably prepared the resolution of the "expert commission" on the article. According to the authors, my arrest gave reason to suppose that I could disclose the creation of stockpiles of binary weapons in Russia, which were completely concealed from the public eye, and probably even Boris Yeltsin had no knowledge of it. Under the sub-title "Arrest-1992" the authors described what happened on October 22, 1992 in the Lev Fedorov's apartment. My co-author told journalists from *Moscow News* in an interview that about twenty employees of the MB RF arrived at his apartment and produced a search warrant. However, according to the journalists, this was useless because all the Ministry of Security found in Fedorov's apartment, was a huge pile of folders with scientific works, mostly in English. The article in *Izvestia* goes on to say, "Finally, the men from the Ministry of Security confiscated two copies of *Moscow News* for a reason that only they know and took Lev Fedorov to the Investigation Department of the Ministry of Security at Lefortovo."

When Fedorov delivered a speech at the annual conference "The KGB, Yesterday, Today, and Tomorrow" in February of 1993, he entertained his audience with an embellished version of this story about how a crowd of stupid Chekists arrived to search his apartment and spent a long time fiddling around with English language books and articles. But since they had to take something, they confiscated two copies of the article "A Poisoned Policy." This colorful story of the fighter against the KGB and chemical weapons received peals of continuous laughter from other conference participants, while Colonel Kandaurov, who was there from the Ministry of Security, turned red and then white. Obviously he had good reason for that. Unlike everybody else, he knew that the reality had been very different from the scene the speaker-actor painted up for his audience.

On the morning of October 28th, I was taken to the investigator, and once more he told me that Nuria had called and said that she and the children were alive and well. She also said that *Moscow News* had hired a lawyer for me, Aleksander Asnis, and they had assumed the financial responsibility for his services, for working on my case.

I was very pleased to hear this. Now I had a defender and my family wouldn't suffer financially from that. However, the investigator added that Asnis couldn't work on my case because he had no clearance for classified documents. Shkarin also stated that Asnis was offered such access, but the lawyer had refused. I understood, however, that he had made the right decision. He didn't want to make any commitments that would limit his freedom in the future. Then the investigator changed the subject and said off the record, "The stir in the press is growing. Today *Moscow News* published Fedorov's and your portraits on the front page."

I asked Shkarin to let me have a look at this issue of *Moscow News*. He replied that he had given it to someone, but he would give it to me as soon as he found it. I saw this colorful issue for the first time, with the wonderful materials of the journalists, only after my release. It still makes me feel excited even today.[97] Then Shkarin started the interrogation. From the beginning, I declined the services of lawyer Leonid Belomestnykh. The investigator's goal was to confirm that all the information in the article "A Poisoned Policy" was given by me. Certainly, he also wanted me to confirm that this information was known to me because of my work.

The transcript of the interrogation[98] was compiled in such a way that they would be able to charge me with disclosing information that constitutes a state secret, according to some secret lists, which I knew nothing about at that time. I guessed about that, but didn't try to change anything before signing the transcript. Why? It was because I had no intention of renouncing what I had written in my articles. All of this was more than obvious. So it wasn't the "psychological gingerbread" of the investigator (his revelation that the press supported me) that made me "compliant." It simply never occurred to me that I could or should deny the obvious facts. Several times the investigator hinted that perhaps I wanted to share the responsibility with someone in this case. This idea was completely unacceptable to me. I assumed all the responsibility, because I deliberately initiated and wrote my articles with the goal that is stated in the transcript of the interrogation (and I insisted on this wording).

At that time I couldn't even dream that one day I would copy and publish this transcript. Back then I imagined my future as imprisonment stretching out for long years. Internally, I was ready for such an outcome. I even told the investigator with emotion, that one day people would know about my actions, and my sons wouldn't turn red with embarrassment because of their father. I must admit that his "psychological gingerbread" inspired me and I became cocky. Shkarin good-naturedly included all of this in the transcript. After all, even in his worst nightmare he couldn't imagine that some time would pass and all his work that was stamped "Top Secret" would be open to public scrutiny.

After I signed the transcript of the interrogation, the investigator asked me to look through the materials that would be sent to the People's Court, to consider my complaint about my illegal arrest. I already knew everything in the transcript about "the suspect getting acquainted with materials to be submitted to the court" (Case N 62, volume 1, p. 186-187), except for the letter of the Investigation Department to the chairman of the court.

The Indictment is Ready

On October 30 the investigator called me in again. There were two other people in the office besides Shkarin. One of them was relatively young, with an intelligent face. He was obviously embarrassed that he had come to such a terrible place, since he was such a well-bred and decent person. I rather liked him. The investigator introduced him as Prosecutor Belash, and it was his job was to monitor and oversee the legality of the KGB's actions.

The second person who appeared was a corpulent elderly man with gray hair and reddish veins on his face, which showed that his life hadn't been boring. The captain said that this was the lawyer Vasiliev, who would be present at that day's presentation of the official indictment, if I had no objection. Vasiliev said that he had served in the military all his life. He had been a military prosecutor, and currently he worked as a defense attorney. Frankly, I can say that right from the start I didn't like him. Even outwardly he seemed to be a strict proponent of Soviet ways. Still, I thought it would be awkward if I objected to his presence at the procedure, since he had come all that way. I would be showing distrust without even knowing him. I knew that in any case I wouldn't use his services. I knew already that any time the KGB was offering me something, it would be necessary to refuse it. Otherwise, I would fall into another one of the Chekists' traps.

At the end of the interrogation, when the investigator was finishing up the transcript, Vasiliev took the latest issue of the Communist newspaper *Pravda* out of his briefcase and started reading it. Then I clearly understood who they were trying to palm off on me.

My lawyer Asnis wasn't allowed to be admitted to my case which dragged on, because he flatly refused to sign any nondisclosure agreement about state secrets. That was obligatory for getting access to classified documents such as my case materials. Shkarin told me about this in a hurt voice, as if he were complaining that Asnis was too capricious. Taking advantage of the presence of a young prosecutor, I delivered a monologue for about five minutes. I said indignantly that it was a serious provocation against the democratic forces in the country and that the disgusting old KGB still reigned in society. I voiced my exasperation about my arrest and imprisonment, which were absolutely unjustified. After all, everything could be investigated without keeping me in jail.

I think it was a good way for me to vent my feelings. The lawyer Vasiliev tried to calm me down by saying that as time passed I would become accustomed to jail, and I would feel better. "Son of a bitch!" I said to myself, and I was sorry that I couldn't say it to his face.

During my monologue, the prosecutor nodded approvingly as if encouraging me to use even harsher expressions. He even took out a notepad from his huge briefcase and wrote something down. Finally he won my sympathy. Later when I was taken to my cell again and told my cellmates about this prosecutor, Yavitsky burst out laughing. He said that I understood nothing about people, as the prosecutor had his job only because he was a good actor. I was shocked! Incredible! Was it possible to win somebody's favor in these jungles of lawlessness without saying a single word, by "talking" only with your gestures? Yes, evidently Belash was a real professional.

Later Shkarin said that he would present me with an indictment that day. Consequently, my status "was elevated", because up to that point I was considered just a detained suspect. The indictment repeated the text of the resolution of the Permanent Technical Commission at GRNIIOKhT almost word for word. This meant that there wouldn't be anything new from the prosecution. In fact, what else could they invent? The investigator had to build my "case" around this resolution. He had nothing else to work with. That's how it turned out in the end. However, at that time Shkarin had been elaborating the formal aspects of my case, to give some weight to his creation. As Professor Kurochkin liked to say, he was "making candy from shit."

I will cite a passage from the transcript of the interrogation that followed after the indictment was pronounced:

"Question: Do you plead guilty to the charges of the indictment?

Answer: **I plead entirely not guilty to the charges of the indictment** [I will write later about how Andrey Arnold "translated" this sentence into English for Gale Colby. **V.M.**]

Question: What explanation can you give concerning the charges brought against you?

Answer: I qualify this indictment as a political indictment that is making an appeal to intimidate everyone who objects to the leaders of the military-industrial complex continuing to pursue their own policy. In particular, the goal of the military-chemical complex is to try to use all possible illegal means to continue their illegitimate activity that violates agreements, even after an agreement was signed between the U.S. and U.S.S.R. governments about the termination of the development, production, and testing of chemical weapons. They would like to continue today what they did yesterday and my article hindered this. I know dozens of scientists working in this area who completely agree with my arguments listed in the article "A Poisoned Policy," but they are afraid to speak out. My arrest will once again reinforce their fears. I think that my explanation in the article - the information about the military-chemical complex continuing its illegal activity in the area of the development of new chemical weapons - doesn't constitute a state secret. As proof of my words, I refer to my article called "Inversion" published on October 10, 1991 in the newspaper *Kuranty*. I warned in this article that although democratic forces had scored a victory over the coup supporters - that is, over the totalitarian regime and the VPK in particular - the VPK is waiting for a return match. It is trying to guard and preserve all the structures necessary to continue its anti-national policy. In this article I called attention to the development of new chemical weapons in our country. I was an employee at GRNIIOKhT at this time, and I wasn't even disciplined for that article. It is true, that at the beginning of January of 1992, I was dismissed because of staff reductions. If on October 22, 1992, I was arrested for disclosing virtually the same information that I cited a year before in the article in "Kuranty," it confirms my forewarning about the attempts of the leaders of the military-chemical complex to try to get their revenge. It also completely supports my arguments that the current indictment was produced for a political purpose."

All the formalities were completed and I could only wait for the scheduled court session that would settle my fate on Monday. By that time I finally realized that if I wasn't released from the prison, my fate had been decided beforehand. There was nothing I could count on without a reliable lawyer and the support of the people. This is why I was agitated, counting the hours left before the court session.

Different jail procedures like morning walks and going to the shower added some variety to the isolation experience and the cramped space surrounded by four walls. Of course you might think that reading would be a welcome diversion from the gloomy surroundings, but for some reason you quickly got tired of it in jail.

The shower rooms in Lefortovo Prison are in the basement. When you are on your way there, it seems as if you are being taken through some passage from which there is no return. Probably almost everyone in Russia has read or heard about the numerous executions by shooting that were carried out on a massive scale in Lefortovo, especially in the 1930s.

My cellmate, Yavitsky once asked a security guard who was taking us to the shower, "Tell me, Kolya, has anyone been shot here?" The guard gently nodded to the right, pointing downward somewhere. Probably the execution basements were on a level even lower than the shower rooms. My cellmate told me some very curious things. In particular, in May of 1991, capital repairs were started at Lefortovo Prison, which were completed by the middle of August. The daily routine and rules of behavior for prisoners signed by the Superintendent of Lefortovo Prison on August 16, 1991, were found posted on the wall. So everything was ready there for large groups of prisoners - opponents of the coup, which took place on August 21, 1991.

If the wheel of fortune had turned just a bit differently, the leaders in power could have found themselves in Lefortovo instead of in the Kremlin.

Chapter 16

The Crash of the KGB's Plans

The Court Releases Me from Prison

Our usual walk was cancelled on the morning of November 2nd, because of the trip to the People's Court. Right after breakfast I was taken to the Investigator Shkarin's office again, and the lawyer Vasiliev was waiting there too. Shkarin noticed that I wasn't exactly pleased to see this "guest", and he rushed to calm me down, saying that the arrangement stood and I was going to the People's Court. But I would need a lawyer there, and he suggested I sign a paper confirming that I agreed to use Vasiliev's services.

I wouldn't stand for that. I almost lost control over myself, and exploded in a passionate fit of rage. The main point, I shouted indignantly, was that I wouldn't let them play with me as an ignorant jailbird.

"If you have decided not to let Asnis participate in my case," I continued. "I won't let you dupe me with a dummy lawyer."

"Ah, why do you insult me so? I gave up everything and came all the way over here for your sake," Vasiliev whined melodramatically.

I answered I would certainly have apologized if I had invited him, and then suddenly refused. Unfortunately, I added, he was forced upon me, instead of the lawyer hired by my wife and the newspaper.

Shkarin again hurried to "calm me down" saying, "OK, OK, Vil Sultanovich. You will return from court and we will discuss everything quietly. Maybe we will find a solution to the problem."

I countered sharply, "Look here, Captain! Did it even occur to you that the court could decide to release me?!"

To his credit, the investigator didn't carry on with the topic any further, but remarked philosophically, "Nowadays everything is possible."

"So you see," I agreed having relaxed a little bit.

We left the investigator's office and followed a route I wasn't familiar with. Soon we found ourselves in the jail's courtyard, where I spotted a few people who seemed vaguely familiar to me. Then I remembered I had seen the blond couple in front of the editor's office at *Novoe Vremya*, before my arrest. It was clear to me they were there, just in case, trained to remember my "scent."

The paddy wagon drove into the courtyard, the rear door opened, and I was told to climb into the "basket". It was full of people, prisoners collected from various Moscow jails, who were to be transported to different Moscow district courts.

On the way I chatted with a few prisoners. It turned out that they had heard about me on the radio and on TV. They were indignant that I was the one in jail, instead of those scoundrels who poisoned people. I was delighted to hear this, because even people who had nothing to do with the problems of disarmament understood that the big bosses were simply punishing a man who dared to speak his mind.

A few prisoners and I were taken in handcuffs to the dark and dirty basement of the shabby old courthouse building. It was damp in there, stinking of urine. There were cages for holding prisoners, waiting to be summoned into the courtroom. I was placed into one of them. The walls were decorated with obscenities and curses addressed to the judges. One of the inscriptions read, "Damn you, Judge Schanin!"

It seemed that an eternity had passed before the door to my

cage finally opened and two escorts took me somewhere upstairs. At last, we reached the right floor and entered a lobby where about a dozen people were gathered.

It had been eleven days since I last saw free people. I was taken by surprise, when I heard a voice full of enthusiasm calling out my name. Immediately, I was blinded by camera flashes. I was quickly escorted into a room with a lot of benches. I understood that I was in the hall of Kalinin District People's Court in Moscow.

I was ordered to sit down on a bench behind a short wooden barrier. Guards were standing on each side behind the barrier. When the door to the hall occasionally opened, correspondents started feverishly snapping photos of me.

Finally, the door closed and we waited for the judge to appear. Just in case, I mentally prepared myself for a stiff sentence. The most important thing was not to humiliate myself. I would not beg them to release me. Since I had started all this, it was important for me to have the courage to keep my dignity. It was encouraging that the press was interested, and I no longer felt forgotten or abandoned.

A young lady appeared on the platform and inquired if the prisoner Mirzayanov had arrived. One of the guards confirmed this and she uttered, "All rise. Court is in order!"

I stood up and saw a lean, bearded young man with a large forehead. He was wearing a beautiful light gray suit and strongly resembled an atomic physicist from one of the Soviet movies. I liked him even before he started talking, because I could feel that he was an intelligent person who could never deliver a demagogic sermon on patriotism. A strange idea popped into my mind - "Even if he does something harmful to me, it won't be very bad."

The name of the judge was Aleksander Schanin. I was no longer agitated and focused completely on what was going on.

The judge inquired about me and asked if I had a lawyer. I answered that the Investigation Department of the MB RF had deprived me of a defense attorney, and therefore I was going to defend myself. Judge Schanin read my application and gave me the floor. I laid out the essence of my case, which was whipped up by forces that wanted to return Russia to its past. Their major concern was preserving the military-chemical potential, in order to continue the devastating and useless chemical arms race, which no one except the leaders of the VPK needed, because it supported their welfare. The Chemical Weapons Convention had already been initialed, and Russia was just about to sign it. This useless waste of people and their resources no longer made the slightest sense, especially when you considered the serious shortages of industry, food, medications, and many other things in Russia.

The judge asked me my opinion about state secrets and asked if I recognized the necessity of keeping state secrets. I replied that all my work at the State Russian Science Research Institute for Organic Chemistry and Technology (GRNIIOKhT) showed that I was honestly fulfilling my duties, and I also taught my subordinates to do the same. I addressed fundamentally important issues in the press, without disclosing any state secrets. I also stressed in my speech that there was not even a single hint about the technology of producing chemical agents or their chemical formulas in my statements. Anyone could read my article and see that it was true.

Then Prosecutor Buivolov spoke. He declared that I had committed a state crime, so I couldn't be released from jail. I asked for the floor again, saying that thanks to this prosecutor I still didn't have a qualified defense attorney and had to defend myself.

"Those who initiated my case, which can't be fairly investigated in the future, want to keep me in jail," I said. "The prosecution is afraid of publicity and wants to unfairly convict me under the guise of secrecy."

The secretary announced that the court would adjourn for a conference, and I remained seated in my place. The door of the hall opened, and I saw the photo-journalists snapping off shots with their cameras again.

The break lasted about 20 minutes. Then Judge Schanin returned to the hall and read out the court's resolution, which agreed "To satisfy the complaint of Vil Sultanovich Mirzayanov and release him from custody into the court hall," and "To secure a written statement from V. S. Mirzayanov not to leave his permanent place of residence. The Resolution is final, not subject to appeal or protest."[99]

State Secrets

Should I even mention what I felt hearing the resolution about my release? I was just happy! Even experienced people couldn't remember that the court ever released anyone from Lefortovo.

I can't judge whether that was true or not. In any case, the ruling of Judge Aleksander Schanin confounded all the plans of the Chekists, who were accustomed to dealing with powerless prisoners under the cover of secrecy. The secretary of the court immediately asked me to come up to the judge, and sign a receipt for a copy of the resolution, and a written statement of consent not to leave Moscow.

The doors of the court hall opened and journalists, many of whom kept taking pictures, asked me for a few words for the press and television. I did this with pleasure, because I knew that, to a great extent, I owed my release to the mass media, which brought my case to light with an obvious sympathy for me.

However, I wasn't freed immediately after signing the statement of obligation with the judge, because there were a few formalities that had to be taken care of with the guard who had brought me to the court. Once more I was escorted to the court's basement, and the head of the guard made a phone call to confirm that no other criminal proceedings had been instituted against me. Having found out that there were no problems of this sort, he gave me a paper to sign, which said that I had no complaints about the guards escorting me.

Front page of *Moscow News*, November 1 1992.

With my son Iskander after my release from Lefortovo Prison.
November 2 1992.

With my family left to right: Iskander is on the left, Sultan and Nuria on the right. November 3 1992.

After that I was free to leave the court basement and go out into the street, where a TV journalist was waiting for me. I gave an interview as if I was in a dream. I was so joyful about my unexpected release that I couldn't even believe that it had happened. At the end of our conversation the journalist asked where I was going to go, and I responded that I was going straight home to my children. Suddenly, I remembered that I didn't have even a ruble in my pocket. The journalist saw my embarrassment and she volunteered to lend me some money for the fare.

Forty minutes later I made it home, where journalists were waiting for me. They took pictures endlessly of my reunion with my children and asked us to repeat this scene again and again.

The next day the phone rang constantly, and I gave numerous interviews to Russian and foreign correspondents explaining the essence of my case. I never forgot for a minute that my case was only in the initial stage and that I had to prepare myself for a difficult struggle.

The KGB vs. Asnis

On November 3rd, the lawyer Aleksander Asnis arrived and we agreed to discuss the details of my defense. The major obstruction for my case was the demand by the prosecution that Asnis get a security clearance for access to classified documents. Naturally, my lawyer couldn't agree to that and insisted that the letter and the spirit of the law should be observed. Investigator Shkarin called and summoned me, and I answered, "It's my duty to come to the interrogation, but our talk will be absolutely useless until my lawyer is present. Before he is allowed to participate, I won't even greet you, to say nothing of signing any transcripts."

The Investigation Department of the Ministry of Security (MB RF) and the Attorney General's Office were in a very awkward position. It was impossible to deny my lawyer participation in the case on legal grounds, when practically every day the press was holding the spotlight on our struggle.

My lawyer made a strong play to resolve the problem. He wrote a letter to the Attorney General's Office, petitioning to legally transfer my case to his office for prosecution. The correspondence between officials from the prosecutor's office and the FSK (another incarnation of the KGB) shows they were quite embarrassed about it.

What can we say? There had never been a clash of this sort between the unlimited freedom of the Chekists' investigation and formal practice of law which the Attorney General's Office had to observe under the circumstances.

The KGB understood that the case would become completely hopeless despite all the efforts of the investigators, without the cover of secrecy. This is why General Balashov, the Head of the Investigation Department of MB RF, acting upon the advice of Investigator Shkarin, wrote a letter imploring the Prosecutor's Office not to ruin the former practice of conducting business. He said it was essential to their work and added "In our opinion, if we let Asnis participate in the case without observing the established requirements, the investigation will find itself in a situation where it will have to disclose information that constitutes a state secret".[100]

He was right, but he had only himself to blame for throwing himself into this hole…

The newspaper *Izvestia* kept the spotlight on the problem of allowing my lawyer access to my case, and on November 5, 1992, it published a bitter response in an article "Selling Motherland is Under Great Secrecy."[101] In this article, journalists made it absolutely clear to the readers that the delay on the part of the KGB was absolutely illegal. They also made another very critical point - that when the investigators looking into the case of the Committee for Organizing the Coup in August of 1991 had demanded a clearance for the famous lawyer Henry Reznik (who defended the coup supporter Plekhanov), they had to give in and allow the defense attorney to take part in the case without this document, because of public pressure.

After another refusal by the Investigation Department to let Asnis take part in my case, he sent another complaint addressed to the Attorney General of Russia. As a result, Deputy Attorney General Ivan Zemlyanushin sent an indignant letter to the Deputy Minister of MB RF demanding that access to my case be given to Aleksander Asnis.[102] The Deputy Minister of the MB RF, Anatoly Safonov, didn't have any choice but to order General Balashov to "…stop violating the Law". So, Chekists suffered a second defeat in my case, when my lawyer was granted access.[103]

Izvestia responded to this episode in the Attorney General's Office with Valeri Rudnev's article "The Scientist Who was Selling His Motherland Finally has a Defender."[104]

The journalist remarked that his newspaper was closely following the Mirzayanov case, which, in his opinion, finally started following normal juridical procedure. He characterized Asnis as a highly qualified lawyer, who was concerned with the approaching selection of the qualified experts, specialists in the areas of state secrecy and chemical production. He thought that my lawyer could, as a last resort, invoke the "dire necessity" defense in my case, stipulated by Article 14 of the RF Criminal Code, which releases the accused from criminal responsibility.

I was skeptical about this approach because the successful accomplishment of such tactics required getting evidence from the so-called "responsible people." And in the end, the "responsible people" cowardly brushed me aside.

The Generals do Some "Brainwashing"

With the goal of misleading public opinion in Russia and abroad, a briefing was held in the Ministry of Security chaired by Colonel Kandaurov, who would soon become Lieutenant General Kandaurov. He was entrusted with the job of conducting dull and irresponsible briefings, at which he would lie about the events in Chechnya. TV viewers who watched this person work, during the time of the freeing of the hostages in Dagestan in the winter of 1996, could appreciate the true worth of this Chekist's "art" of presenting false information. Finally, he would be forced to retire in disgrace, and ultimately he found his true place as a deputy in the State Duma.

On November 5, 1992, Colonel Kandaurov did his best to rationalize the illegal actions of his colleagues who didn't allow my lawyer to participate in my case.[105] Then the floor was given to General Demin, head of Legal Services at MB RF, who expressed his dissatisfaction with the press, which had allegedly distorted information about the Chekists who were working on my case. Of course, this general didn't expect the degree of scrutiny that the public and the press paid to my case, because he and the service that he headed had been accustomed to doing their business under the cover of secrecy. He was the man who had persistently persuaded Minister Barannikov about the expediency of my arrest. This is why the juridical general at the briefing did his best to justify his failure, by referring to lists of secrets that had never been published, but which I had allegedly disclosed.

His reference to the practice of law in Western countries, concerning this problem, was especially comical. The point is that the lists of these secrets are clearly defined abroad and are published openly in the press. The general tried to explain to ignorant TV viewers that the 1989 resolution of the Committee of Constitutional Supervision didn't touch upon lists of state secrets, because they have nothing to do with human rights. This inquisitorial interpretation of human rights doesn't hold up under any scrutiny or criticism. If someone could be arrested based on these secret lists, and criminal proceedings could be instituted against him, and then he had no right to freely leave the country, what kind of documents would these be? This was a real model of absurdity.

At the conference "KGB Yesterday, Today, and Tomorrow" organized by Sergei Grigoriyants in February of 1993, I asked Sergei Alekseev, former chairman of this committee and one of the authors of the new Constitution of Russia, if the resolution passed by his committee abolished the aforementioned lists. Surrounded by many journalists, the professor of law answered simply and unequivocally, "Yes, it does, because they hadn't been published in time."

General Demin, the head of Legal Services of the MB RF, found himself in a funny situation when Aleksei Lukiyanov, a correspondent from *Radio Station Vozrozhdenie*, reminded him of his reference to American laws about secrets and asked about a similar case that had taken place in the U.S. in 1971. Daniel Ellsberg[106] had used the newspaper *The New York Times* to disclose secret Pentagon Papers about the war in Vietnam. The judge had ruled he wasn't guilty. Demin didn't expect such a question and could only awkwardly "explain it" by a difference in laws, a difference in historical periods, and so on. He categorically objected to allowing lawyer Asnis access to my case. As for the law, the general recognized only the illegal "sub-legal norms" about secrets. That was it.

Another colonel from the chemical troops, Aleksander Gorbovsky, who was the son of the former head of the research center in Shikhany and the Military Academy of Chemical Defense, represented the Committee for Conventional Problems under the President of Russia at the briefing. His task was to try and justify the irresponsible actions of leaders of the military-chemical complex. He claimed that military chemists had never violated anything; they had always acted in accordance with international agreements. Listening to Gorbovsky, you would think that saving people from chemical weapons had always been the only priority of the military. But this propaganda didn't work. The journalist Likhanov wasn't a babe in the woods. He caught Gorbovsky with his own words. The colonel asserted that the draft of the Chemical Weapons Convention contained no traps or loopholes. Then the journalist asked him to explain why not one of the components of our binary weapons was included on the list of controlled precursors.

This was a situation that required intelligence and honesty, but the colonel from the committee gave in, and mumbled something about the future and about perspectives. It's a pity that the mass media at this time completely forgot about Resolution N 508-RP of the Russian government, dated September 16, 1992, about the licensing of precursors of chemical weapons, which was signed by President Yeltsin. This resolution was published in the September 30, 1992 issue of *Rossiskaya Gazetta*. Colonel Gorbovsky was one of the authors of this document, and he certainly remembered it during his tirades at the briefing about adherence to international agreements.

This resolution, adopted on the threshold of the signing of the CWC, prohibited the export of precursors of military chemical agents from Russia, according to an attached list. The list included all known precursors for producing chemical agents: soman, sarin, mustard gas, lewisite, and VX gas. However, there were no precursors for agents A-230 and A-232 on the list. The first one, as I wrote above, had been successfully tested and added to the arsenal of the Soviet Army. The situation was the same with Substance 33. However, our country had never produced either VX gas or its precursors. Why did our president end up on the same team with the liars? It was simply because the leaders of the military-chemical complex were certain that no one in the country would ever dare to expose their true faces. This is why all the technical documentation of the Novocheboksary Plant, which produced Substance 33 but not the notorious American VX gas, was re-written. The generals were glad that the Americans really believed their "canard", that the U.S.S.R. allegedly produced VX gas and not something else.

Why was this fraud so important for them? It was because they cared a great deal about the problems involved with stockpiling Substance 33.

After Substance 33 was successfully tested and binary weapons based on it were added to the arsenal of the Soviet Army, the problem of stockpiling and, consequently the related flaws of this chemical agent were magically eliminated.

The generals were planning to keep cheating their American colleagues, because only VX and its precursors would be mentioned in all the international agreements. There were even some people in the U.S. who tried to cast doubt that this suggestion was based only on the facts. Naturally, the Americans were ashamed to admit they had been led by the nose so easily and for so long! I would like to offer them my interpretation of Resolution N 508-RP of the President of Russia, and explain why the technical documentation on the production of the Substance 33 and the development of binary weapons based on it was forged and passed off as documentation for the production of the VX gas. The fact that precursors of the chemical agents A-230 and A-232 are not on this list is entirely natural, since the generals wanted to keep them for the future.

In an interview published on November 11, 1992 in *Rossiskaya Gazeta* [253], General Anatoly Kuntsevich tried to accuse me, saying that my article was an attempt to "slander Russia." He expressed deep satisfaction that the Americans didn't fall for this "provocation." Of course, how could they "fall for it"? They received most of their information from Kuntsevich himself! The general went too far with the publication of the above-mentioned resolution. He hastily sent copies of it to all countries, including the U.S. Even the celebrated U.S. intelligence services swallowed this bait. This took place when Bush senior was president. Bill Richardson, who was the Deputy Assistant to the Secretary of Defense for Chemical Matters and Kuntsevich's U.S. partner in the CWC negotiations, didn't expect such a dirty trick. He said that it wasn't even the threat of the development of new chemical weapons that worried him: "The concern is [that] those conniving bastards aren't dealing with us honestly. How much else are they lying?" That was a very harsh reaction by the former US deputy aide on chemical weapons.[107]

Many Muscovites in the street, passing by the building of the newspaper *Izvestia*, could see a huge photo-poster in the window of the editor's office. In the picture taken by a photo-correspondent of this newspaper, one could see Kuntsevich fraternizing with Richardson during his trip to the U.S.

It seems to me I ran slightly ahead in my narration. However, all this, apart from the last episode, looked more than strange on the threshold of the signing of the Chemical Weapons Convention. However, even today I can't stop thinking about the question, as to why General Kuntsevich lied to them and to others.

Nevertheless, the general authoritatively enlightened a correspondent by saying, "Military chemical work, like all other defense work, has special status. Each department engaged in weapons development creates certain norms to protect secrecy… I am no legal expert. But it is possible that merely by announcing that a particular institute was working on chemical agents one is divulging a state secret." [253]

It is curious that the general was so willing to drone on about the subject of selling secrets, which, according to him, "is not stipulated by democracy, even American democracy." Kuntsevich repeated this assertion, with explicit hints obviously directed at me in a TV interview on Channel One. It looked as though this topic haunted him, inadvertently giving away something lying deep inside of him. Probably by the categorical nature of his statements, he meant to suggest that "democratic types" like Mirzayanov were the ones most likely to sell out their Motherland. Finally, I had to respond to these jabs in several interviews, but unlike Kuntsevich, I didn't use any half-hearted thrusts. I said directly that only our generals could sell out our country. I meant General Kuntsevich, of course, and my words proved to be somewhat prophetic. I don't think that his preparations, for secretly selling precursors of Substance 33 to another country, were what stressed out the general. Obviously he was under the tremendous pressure of a crime that he had already committed.[107, 108]

Chapter 17
Captain Shkarin Fabricates the Case

The Expert Commission

Asnis participated in my interrogation process for the first time on November 24, 1992. Investigator Shkarin tried to create the impression that everything now depended on the decision that the qualified specialists of the "expertise" (an appointed commission of experts) would make after examining my case. Naturally, fundamental questions about the goals of the expertise arose, because everything that I "had committed" was out in the open - written on paper and published, and there was no need for technical experts to look over and to analyze my writings.

In any case, the examination came down to a legal analysis of published articles - a comparison of the texts of my publications and rough drafts with the existing sub-legal norms pertaining to the regime of secrecy, of the institute rules for internal security, and others, which were top secret documents that no one had ever seen with their own eyes. That is why when Shkarin showed us a resolution about the appointment of the "expertise" with a list of instructions for the experts, Asnis and I started to seriously doubt that this commission could objectively carry through with this procedure.

We immediately wrote a petition asking that we be allowed to see all the sub legal acts and lists of secrets, which the "expertise" was supposed to base its work on. Naturally, Shkarin refused to do this, because he understood that if he showed us these lists, he would cut off the branch he was sitting on. He only agreed to show us individual bits and pieces from these acts, which he considered necessary for the work of the expertise. I reminded him that I couldn't agree to play the role of the illiterate monk Varlaam, who was forced to rely on an imposter who could read and write, in the immortal Pushkin drama "Boris Godunov." However, when he was faced with the threat of arrest, even that monk suddenly remembered how to read, and then he understood that it was not he who was mentioned in the Tsar's decree, but Grishka Otrepyev, who was only trying to make a fool out of him and the ignorant policemen.

Understandably, we sent an appeal about Shkarin's decision to the RF (Russian Federation) Attorney General's Office. Another problem was that the expertise commission was composed almost exclusively of people who had conflicts of interest, since they were representatives of the military-chemical complex. Moreover, several of them were personally interested in the outcome of my case, because I had harshly criticized them in my articles. For example, in the manuscript that Fedorov voluntarily gave to Chekists, I had mentioned Igor Gabov, the former head of Workshop 34 of the Volgograd Industrial Association VPO Khimprom, and I had pointed out Gabov's dishonesty in fulfilling his job responsibilities. This man was on the list of experts, so he got the chance to even the score with me for my criticism.

I also mentioned another expert, Boris Kuznetsov, in one of my articles. In "Inversion" I wrote that specialists on questions of chemical weapons did not go to the Geneva negotiations, but instead some proxies of the military-chemical complex were sent there, and these were people who were a long way from understanding the heart of the matter. At that time Kuznetsov was the only representative from GOSNIIOKhT who went to Geneva as an expert for the Soviet delegation. Even though he was extremely obtuse, he could not fail to understand that I was writing about him.

Another expert I rejected was Yuri Karmishin, who I had also criticized in writing. He was a shady character who had spent all of his adult life working in the First Department of the Volsk branch of GOSNIIOKhT, and he also gave out passes. When I went on business trips to Shikhany, I received my passes from him. He had graduated from some kind of institute with great difficulty, and all of a sudden he was given the right to solve the expert-level problems of my case. But Karmishin didn't have the slightest inkling about chemistry or about our specialty! How could he possibly be an expert? That is why I wrote a request to reject this secret KGB agent. Obviously, my objection was ignored. Later, after his "successful" work on the expert commission, Karmishin was appointed Deputy Director for the Regime at his institute. That meant that he was no longer was just an undercover agent; he openly became an official KGB employee.

After all of this, I was somewhat surprised to see Petr Kirpichev on the list of experts, because he was in fact a highly qualified scientist. However, it was even more amazing that he actually agreed to participate in this doubtful expertise. Later, he wrote a refusal to participate in the commission's work, for family reasons, because his son was seriously ill.

Meanwhile, the investigation and the prosecutor's office were energetically searching for new "evidence" of my guilt, because what they had was clearly inadequate. Mayor General Balashov urgently asked for help from the main eavesdropping service of Russia - the Federal Agency for Government Communications & Information (FAPSI).[109]

FAPSI faithfully fulfilled the request of their colleagues at the KGB and sent the transcripts of 35 intercepted transmissions about my case from the radio stations *The Voice of America*, *Freedom*, *BBC*, and others in many languages. I simply didn't have the time to copy all these reports. The recordings were professional and were thoroughly edited. I couldn't detect a single grammatical or stylistic error there, which shows that the level of radio monitoring and specialists involved was very high. As usual, the state spared nothing for total control over its citizens.

At the same time, Senior Prosecutor V. Buivolov without any

requests was sending copies of published articles to Investigation Department.[110] After that, the investigation entered into entirely uncharted waters by divulging state secrets itself, with just with one goal – to indict and punish me and anyone else who chose to follow my example. I don't know exactly why the investigators supposed it could help them, but they started making requests of GOSNIIOKhT for information about the cornerstones of the modern chemical weapons development program in the USSR.[111]

The response was stunning[112]. For first time in the history of Russia one of its sacred secrets was revealed: that a new chemical agent

> *"...was developed at GRNIIOKhT in pursuance to Resolution N 3509-123 dated April 24, 1977 by the Central Committee of the C.P.S.U. and the Council of Ministers. Also, the information that Mirzayanov reveals in the same article about the development of binary weapons at GRNIIOKhT: "...binary weapons were developed based on a new chemical agent" is true. Work on the creation of a binary weapon was carried out at GRNIIOKhT, in pursuance to Resolutions <u>N 1584-434 of December 31, 1986 and N 844—186 of October 6, 1989</u> by the Central Committee of the C.P.S.U. and the Council of Ministers."*

My lawyer continued to actively seek permission to see all the lists of secrets, which the expert commission would be basing its work on. I was also busy writing petitions necessary for my case. In particular, I asked for a report about the fire at GOSNIIOKhT, in which almost 800 grams of Substance 33 were "lost." Either it burned up or it was carried away into the atmosphere with the smoke. Furthermore, we wrote petitions so that we could obtain copies of documentation about the stockpiling and expenditure of chemical agents at the special warehouse of the institute, in order to get information about cases of poisoning of employees at their workplaces, in laboratories, and in experimental units. We also requested a copy of my scientific technical report with the research about the extent of successful degasification of chemical agents, and other documents.

The expertise was supposed to be carried out at the General Staff Headquarters of the Armed Forces[113]; however, my lawyer rejected the General Staff Headquarters because it wasn't an expert establishment. The investigator then passed a resolution rejecting Asnis' petition, referring to an injunction of the U.S.S.R. Minister of Defense dated August 7, 1990. Ultimately the General Staff refused to participate in this investigation.[114]

Naturally, Asnis requested that we be shown the text of the injunction, but as usual, we were stonewalled with a refusal. Frankly speaking, I had no illusions about the work or the conclusions of the expert commission. While I was sure about the trustworthiness of my information, an official confirmation in the form of answers to the petition, would be additional evidence that everything written in my article was true. The investigator didn't allow Yevgeni Chizhov and German Dmitriev, former employees of GOSNIIOKhT, to work on the expert commission under the pretext that their qualifications were allegedly not sufficient. Certainly my friends Chizhov and Dmitriev had enough knowledge to handle that job honestly and professionally. On the other hand, the KGB knew about my good relations with them, and obviously they didn't want them to look into the matter professionally and objectively.

I didn't quite understand why Boris Kosmynin, a former GOSNIIOKhT employee, had earned the trust of the KGB and was allowed to act as an expert. I had known Boris for a long time, and together we had founded the local organization of the Democratic Russia Movement at GOSNIIOKhT. Kosmynin was noted for his appeals that never clashed with the management of the institute; he just approached them with requests. Boris was not an advocate of any kind of concrete action, and it was often extraordinarily difficult for us (the remaining members of the Coordination Committee of the Democratic Russia Movement) to make any progress in situations when Boris almost always blocked all of our suggestions. Still, we patiently argued and tried to come to a consensus.

My lawyer Asnis suggested that famous Russian democratic figures should be members of the expert commission – such as

Georgi Arbatov, Oleg Kalugin, and Peter Nikulin. He had contacted these people and asked for and received their consent before we proposed them.

A real legal battle broke out around the last two candidates, because they were people from the KGB, though they openly struggled against its anti-national activities. This outraged all the powerful chiefs of the Chekists. It was really obvious from the correspondence between different sections of the KGB.[115-120]

The Investigation Department rejected both of them, but one year later Peter Sergeevich Nikulin became the Deputy Chairman of the Commission for the Reorganization of the KGB, and the lives of those who had dismissed him from the expert commission with a mocking reply came to depend on him greatly. What can you say? Sometimes our fate suddenly takes some very sharp and unexpected turns.

Later I met Peter Sergeevich several times at different press conferences. He made a strong impression on me. It was obvious that he was an intelligent and reasoning person, deeply devoted to democratic ideals. This was extremely rare for someone from the KGB. Apparently that was the reason why he, like Kalugin, became such an embarrassment to the old Chekists. As a member of the working group of the Committee on the Problems of Defense and Security at the RF Supreme Soviet, Nikulin gave an interview to the magazine *Novoe Vremya* in which he broached the fundamental questions of keeping state secrets. He didn't leave a stone unturned, when it came to the old outdated system of "keeping" secrets, in which each department prepared its own lists of secrets and included in the lists whatever popped into their minds "from the health of the general secretary to the buttons on the soldier's overcoat."[121] This system proved to be much worse than simply ineffective, incurring serious losses to the state, on the level of something like 60 billion rubles annually. So, the program "Secret" was developed, which stipulated changes in the regime of secrecy and the preparation of a law about state secrets, on the initiative of the NII (scientific research institute) for Problems of Security of the KGB.

In his interview Nikulin reminded his readers, that on November 29, 1989 he had acted as an expert at a session of the Committee of Constitutional Supervision, and after that all unpublished "sub-legal norms" became invalid.

Nikulin openly criticized the decree Yeltsin signed, which reinstated and made these acts valid again, because this document didn't take into consideration the changes that had taken place in the country. Many of Nikulin's statements later became the basis of a law about state secrets, which the Supreme Soviet had adopted shortly before it was dissolved in 1993.

Later I also had a chance to meet General Kalugin. I never managed to have a good talk with him, but his statements in the press and on TV made a strong impression on me. I am certain that he is an outstanding individual.

I think that I was resolute and decisive in my struggle against the hypocritical policy of the leaders of the military-chemical complex, because to a great extent I was influenced by the actions of this courageous and resolute man. Actions of such individuals are precious little seeds that later grow in the minds of thoughtful rational people, encouraging them to take resolute actions against the old system that hinders the democratic development of Russia and prevents it from joining the civilized world community. Academician Georgi Arbatov was not accepted as an expert on the pretext that he already expressed his opinion in his publication.[122]

Chapter 18
I am not Alone

Investigator Shkarin faced more and more difficulties, but he recklessly held his line. His objective was to produce the resolution that the Chekists needed from the expert commission. To be honest, I didn't take it as seriously my lawyer Alexander Asnis did. I didn't believe that I could be vindicated by the court or the investigation. I felt that only the pressure of public opinion could save me and make the KGB and the authorities retreat.

The press closely followed the progress of my case, and journalists interviewed me practically every day, calling and asking how the investigation was going. This instilled some kind of optimism in me. I still keep a lot of the articles published during that time in my archive.[123-143]

In the middle of November, Dr. Vladimir Iakimets, an activist with the Nevada-Semipalatinsk Antinuclear Movement called me and said that his organization was interested in my case and ready to give me some practical help. He also said that the secretary of the U.S. branch of the movement, Gale Colby, had already been working on this. Gale had learned about my case, from an article in the *New York Times*[143, 144] and from Dr. Frank von Hippel, shortly after my arrest. In early 1993, her friend Irene Goldman joined her in this work. Over the next year and a half, the two women worked long days, tirelessly, privately and at their own expense, meeting people and keeping contact with many American legislators and policy makers, prominent individuals and organizations, committees of scientific organizations and others that protect human rights and support scientists, by phone, e-mail and fax. They kept me posted on how my case was supported and reported abroad. This gave me precious moral support. I can't put into words what I felt when I found out once again that people abroad were interested in my case, sympathized with me, and conducted various campaigns in my defense.

This is how I found out about the appeal by the Federation of American Scientists (FAS) to Russian President Boris Yeltsin. This organization was founded in 1945 by members of the Manhattan Project on the development of the first atom bomb. The objective of this organization was to struggle for peace and universal security. This organization is sponsored by about half of the surviving laureates of the Nobel Prize (45 scientists). In its first address the Federation of American Scientists asked the president of Russia to show generosity and release me from jail. Doctor Jeremy Stone, from the Federation of American Scientists, remarked in his letter to Yeltsin dated October 30, 1992, "Many of our scientists believe that Doctor Mirzayanov acted responsibly."

Another special statement in the form of a resolution was adopted by the FAS on December 5, 1992—signed by Robert Solow, Nobel Prize laureate for peace, Chairman of the FAS, Doctor Jeremy Stone, President, Doctor Frank von Hippel, Chairman of the FAS Fund, and other scientists. It reads as follows:

"*IN DEFENSE OF VIL MIRZAYANOV*

RESOLVED: The Federation of American Scientists hereby recognizes the unquestionable sincerity, courage, and Russian patriotism, with which Dr. Vil Mirzayanov has acted to fulfill his higher civic responsibilities by publishing an article in the Russian journal Moscow News, about Russian development of more devastating chemical weapons and the safety and environmental hazards of the chemical weapons program of the former Soviet Union.

FAS recognizes the critical importance to Russia of a free press with the independence of mind necessary to publish such articles.

Dr. Mirzayanov is acting much in the tradition of the late Academician Andrei Sakharov: in his decision to defend the interests of Russian citizens over the interests of a military bureaucracy; in his decision to raise policy questions while refusing to divulge technical secrets; and in his decision to speak out openly rather than clandestinely.

Accordingly, much as the Federation supported Andrei Sakharov, and defended him for a decade, we recognize Mirzayanov as a scientist of conscience and will support him in confronting the consequences of these responsible disclosures."

I was shocked when I read this resolution. I had never expected such a response to my actions. By nature I have always been rather shy in my relations with people. My family brought me up to value modesty, and that was always what I aspired to. Like millions of other inhabitants of the U.S.S.R., I had internalized the principle at an early age, which was preached by the totalitarian regime - "Keep a low profile." All of this prevented me from believing that I could be appreciated as an individual. Everything that I went through before I wrote those articles was part of a very deep inner process. It was so deep and private that it never even occurred to me to ask anyone for advice. Unfortunately, my wife wasn't close enough to me in spirit to try to understand my actions.

In the middle of December 1992, it became known that the famous scientist Frank von Hippel was coming to Moscow and wanted to meet with me. One December evening, I met with Frank in his hotel room, which was located on the grounds of a former school for the higher training of Communist Party officials.

We talked for about an hour, and I felt that the American scientist tried to understand what prompted me to take such a resolute step. He did it with great tact, and I felt that he was a man of great intellect. I still feel that way about him. I am grateful to Frank for his energetic support. When he was already the top science advisor to U.S. President Bill Clinton, he published an article about my case.[144]

At the end of our conversation Frank gave me a collection of excerpts from reports in the American press devoted to my case and a letter to President Boris Yeltsin from Ernst Eliel, president of the American Chemical Society, and a Nobel Prize laureate.

Support from my colleagues in the U.S. was totally unexpected for me and very valuable. I was extraordinarily pleased with the concern and attention of my foreign colleagues, and I am proud of it to this day.

Dr. Eliel said in his letter that the Board of Directors of the American Chemical Society, which has a membership of more than 145,000 people worldwide, had asked him to express the organization's serious concern about the fate of their colleague, Vil Mirzayanov. It said that many chemists are certain that Mirzayanov acted responsibly when he was disclosing information connected with the development of chemical weapons in the open press. In conclusion, on behalf of the American Chemical Society, Dr. Eliel asked the Russian president for clemency. Dr. Eliel sent three more letters to the president of Russia.

Later after my arrest, I learned that the Subcommittee on Science and Human Rights of the Committee on International Activity at the American Chemical Society, with the energetic and tireless Professor Zafra Lerman, Dr. John Malin, Dr. Joyce Torio and others, had quickly organized a large-scale and powerful campaign in my support.

Even a number of members of the European Parliament were preoccupied with my case. In a letter dated November 19, 1992, addressed to the Attorney General of the Russian Federation, Valentine Stepankov, 24 deputies of the Greens of European Parliament who represented different factions from eight countries wrote:

> "We ask you to undertake all that is in your power to guarantee the moral right of scientists to warn the world

about development of new chemical weapons, and thus to withdraw the charges against Vil Mirzayanov."

The appeal was signed by E. Kvmstrop. K. Rot, Kh. Breher, U. Meizel, F. Gref (deputies from Germany), B. Buasier, M.-A. Isler-Begen, Zh.P. Raffin, M.-M. Dengiran, Zh. Onesta, M. Simeoni (France), P. Staes, P. Lannoi, B. Ernst (Belgium), A. Langer, V. Bettini, J. Amendola, E. Melandri (Italy), E. Newman and Morris (Great Britain), F. Versen (Denmark), N. Van-Dyke (Netherlands), and K. Martins (Spain).[145]

I was especially touched when I learned about the appeal of my fellow countrymen - Tatars from Society "Tugan tel" (Native Speech) to the president of Russia, the Attorney General, the Chairman of the Supreme Soviet of Russia, etc. signed by the president of the Society, R. Galimov, board members N. Garipov, R. Medvedev, and A. Musin, and Professor A. Burganov.

In their appeal they stressed that "future generations of mankind will be grateful to a scientist who bravely supported in the press the draft of the convention for the prohibition, development, production, stockpiling, and use of chemical weapons, and for the destruction of chemical weapons..." At the end of their appeal the authors expressed confidence that "humanism and respectability will prevail in the Russian leadership, and Vil S. Mirzayanov, a member of the board of "Tugan tel," will be free on that glorious day."

For me the biggest surprise was the support I received from the democratic deputies of the RF Supreme Soviet. Deputy Valery F. Menshikov, Head Deputy of the Committee for Energy, Natural Resources, and Ecology, was especially energetic. He spoke at a meeting of the Chamber of the Republics, and called for a notice about the question of the illegal arrest of Mirzayanov to be included in the agenda of the regular meeting of the RF Supreme Soviet. Nikolai Ryabov, Chairman of the chamber, put this suggestion to a vote and the chamber made a decision to include this question on the agenda of the meeting of the Supreme Soviet. According to the regulations, the decision by one of the chamber houses to discuss some question automatically included this question in the agenda of the meeting of the RF Supreme Soviet but its Chairman Ruslan Khasbulatov did everything to block the appeal.[146]

Finally, 35 deputies of the Supreme Soviet sent an official inquiry to V.G. Stepankov, the Attorney General of Russia asking to have the grounds and legitimacy of the proceedings that were instituted against me evaluated. They also asked him "to explain your official position regarding the resolution of the Committee of Constitutional Supervision at the USSR Supreme Soviet, according to which all unpublished secret departmental regulations have become invalidated."

Apart from Valery Menshikov, the following people's deputies signed the inquiry: L. Ponomarev, G. Zadonsky, V. Volkov, L. Gurevich, S. Zasukhin, Gorelov, M. Salie, N. Surkov, V. Urazhtsev, V. Sheinis, N. Yakimenko, A. Kopeika, V. Vermchuk, N. Vershinin, V. Komchatov, A. Shabad, M. Molostvov, S. Sirotkin, V. Varov, S. Yushenkov, G. Yakunin, A. Nasokhin, Yu. Luchinsky, K. Evtushenko, S. Umetskaya, R. Gun. B. Denisenko, Yu. Khrulev, V. Varukhin, Yu. Eltsov. S. Shestov, and S. Kovalev.

The answer came in December 18, 1992 from Deputy Attorney General Ivan S. Zemlyanushin. He stated *"Criminal proceedings were instituted against Vil S. Mirzayanov based on Article 75 of the RSFSR Criminal Code and in accordance with a functioning decree issued by the president of the Russian Federation, N 20 dated January 14, 1992 "About protecting state secrets of the Russian Federation," according to which until new legislative acts are issued that will regulate the safekeeping of state secrets of the Russian Federation, we should be guided by the normative acts adopted in the past on this issue.*

The proceedings were instituted without any violation of the law."

Unfortunately nobody asked why this decree is a secret and wasn't published.

After this letter, it finally became clear that the authorities would judge me by the rules of the totalitarian regime.

Chapter 19
Boycott of the Investigation

Despite all the obstructions, my lawyer Aleksander Asnis followed his clearly outlined plan. This included an attempt to have the sub-legal acts and secret lists of secrets acknowledged as null and void. We were playing to gain time, and could benefit only from dragging the investigation procedure out as long as possible. It was very tough for me, but the main point was that I was free and could endure those hardships.

Nonetheless, it soon began to get on my nerves. The investigator just ignored all of our petitions aimed at a full and objective investigation of the case.

At first, the prospects for the plan we had outlined seemed pretty good. Asnis was negotiating with the RF Supreme Soviet, with the heads of the Committee on Human Rights and the Committee on Legislative Matters. According to procedure, if two committees make a similar decision on a particular problem, it practically becomes the decision of the Supreme Soviet. The Committee for Human Rights had made the decision that the resolution passed by the U.S.S.R. Committee on Constitutional Supervision, which invalidated unpublished sub-legal acts, was lawful. My lawyer also had an agreement with the deputy head of the

Committee for Legislative Matters about a similar decision; however, Professor Mintyukov, the chairman of that committee, returned from his vacation and didn't agree to make such a decision. His primary concern was that such a decision might create problems for his career.

According to our plan for the defense, at an interrogation on December 1, 1992, which lasted for only 25 minutes, I repeated my previous position that I couldn't name my candidates for the expert commission until I was shown the lists of secrets. I informed the investigator that I would again appeal his refusal to show me these normative acts.

Apparently, Shkarin realized that he wouldn't receive any new information from me. So he didn't summon me for interrogation for almost a month and a half, and refocused all his efforts on trying to get "damning evidence" from other people, and on trying to have his version confirmed by the expert commission.

On November 24, 1992 Captain Shkarin called in Dr. Natalya Godzhello for an interrogation. The results of this interrogation were disappointing for the interrogator. Natalya stated "...I think that Mirzayanov didn't disclose any state secrets in publishing information about the creation of a new chemical agent and the development and testing of binary weapons, because he didn't indicate either the class of the compound or its chemical formula, the method of its synthesis, or the technology and equipment used for its synthesis, or the initial precursors from which it is produced. In my opinion, specific concrete information constitutes a state secret, the disclosure of which could allow another state to create the same compound. I think that Mirzayanov published this article, guided by the best intentions, in order to rule out the possibility of an arms race in the area of chemical weapons."[147]

The interrogation of my former deputy, Svyatoslav Sokolov, also proved to be disappointing for Investigator Shkarin. He only stated that "...We took samples of water, air, and solid waste for research both on the institute grounds and at the Volgograd PO Khimprom, where compounds developed at the institute were produced. Mirzayanov personally went to Volgograd to introduce his techniques, which was why he knew the place of the production of

State Secrets

chemical agents very well...".[148]

Even during the investigation with the trial pending, I wasn't going to put an end to my activities directed against chemical weapons. At my request Andrei Zheleznyakov gave an interview to the magazine *Novoe Vremya*.[149] I also gave an interview to this magazine about the danger of testing chemical weapons on the open test site, because the remnants of chemical agents adsorb to dust particles which travel great distances, and can damage people's health.[150]

On January 12, 1993, Shkarin summoned me to his office once more. As I expected, he showed Asnis and me a bundle of resolutions-refusals to all our petitions. They were written pro forma and openly demonstrated arrogance and contempt for my lawyer and me. On the surface, everything was done correctly: I participated in the interrogations, wrote numerous petitions, and signed the transcripts. This created the impression that the investigation was proceeding along an entirely legal course. That was the goal of the investigator. He wanted to sculpt the indictment quietly and calmly. Of course, that didn't suit me. I warned Asnis before the interrogation began that if the investigator once more showed me piles of refusals to our petitions, then I would stop testifying and signing the interrogation transcripts. My lawyer said that it might make our defense more difficult, but he respected any of my decisions, and therefore he didn't object.

When we came for an interrogation on January 12, 1993, and the investigator, as expected, showed us refusals to all our petitions, I wrote an appeal in which I protested against the arbitrary investigation that systematically violated my rights to a defense. Then I refused to participate in the interrogations. I also pledged to respond appropriately to all summons by the Lefortovo Investigation Department.

The investigator tested me by asking me a question about some papers that had been confiscated during the search in my apartment. Of course, I didn't answer and he recorded this formally in the transcript.

The same scene played out again on January 13th and 14th. In this way Shkarin probably goaded me on to use stronger forms of protest. If I refused to come to the Investigation Department for the interrogation, he would arrest me with pleasure and would continue fabricating my case, without any fear that the public might find out about his actions. I decided not to play into the hands of the sneaky captain.

Under the circumstances, the investigation worked solely with my lawyer. Shkarin showed us an enactment about the appointment of the expertise. Since the General Staff Headquarters of the Armed Forces refused to take charge of the expertise, Shkarin added new people to the expert commission and decided it would have to work at Lefortovo. The details of the problem of the investigation were well laid out in *Izvestia*.[151]

After a long ordeal, the investigator complied with one of our requests and seated the two people we had suggested as members of the commission. The first was Reserve Major General Vadim Smirnitsky, former Commander of Military Unit 64518. He was the head of a special subdivision at the U.S.S.R. Ministry of Defense, which dealt with questions of special weapons. Also they seated Reserve Colonel Nikolai Chugunov, who had a master's degree in science, and was the chief specialist for special weapons at the U.S.S.R. Ministry of Defense. He had been an advisor to the Soviet delegation at the Soviet-American negotiations leading to the CWC.

Unfortunately, I didn't know these people, though I had heard about them when I was working at GOSNIIOKhT. Still, I completely trusted my lawyer's judgment and didn't doubt that Smirnitsky and Chugunov would be decent and honest experts.

The results of their work showed that these two people entirely justified our hopes and thoroughly shattered the "findings" of the expert commission prepared by the investigator. I met with General Smirnitsky and Lieutenant Colonel Chugunov for the first time at the judicial proceedings. They both impressed me deeply with their professionalism and logical testimony, which was notably different in nature from the statements of other members of the expert commission.

A Person from Volsk and Petrenko's Patriotic Impulse

The legal battles in the investigator's office in Lefortovo coincided with the signing in Paris of the Convention for the Prohibition of Chemical Weapons (CWC) in January of 1993. At that time I harshly objected to the signing of this convention, because I saw its flaws, which the opponents to chemical disarmament could use to their advantage. First of all, I couldn't catch the logic behind the usage of a very unclear term in the convention "prohibiting the development of chemical weapons," while allowing scientific research work in this field was, at the same time. All my attempts to receive a comprehensible answer, about where the clear distinction between these two notions lay, were fruitless. Moreover, at the level of scientific development at the time, there was absolutely no necessity for the technologically dangerous production of chemical agents. These days and even then, chemical weapons could exist primarily in a binary form, with non-toxic binary components. There was no need to carry out the dangerous and expensive testing of binary weapons. All this could be done in a laboratory, where practically any kind climatic conditions can easily be modeled.

The text of the convention had obvious loopholes that dishonest generals could exploit for their own selfish ends. I gave numerous interviews to the press, on the radio, and on television trying to explain these dirty tricks which were embedded in the convention. Almost no one tried to refute my arguments. The Russian authorities and specialists on chemical weapons kept their dead silence and didn't comment on my statements. I received no answer from foreign specialists, either.

Still I continued to explain that such a convention was far from the best instrument for struggling against chemical weapons. This is why I harshly criticized the convention in my speeches on French TV, on radio station "Echo Moskva," and others, and spoke against its signing. Soon I realized I was no longer alone. Suddenly I found an unexpected ally, a senior engineer at the Volsk branch of GOSNIIOKhT, Vladimir Uglev, who was also a deputy of the Volsk City Council at that time. He was responsible for the ecological issues on this city council and spoke out against the activities of military chemists, who frequently exploded chemical shells at the military testing site, posing a threat to the safety and health of the local population.[152] Also, it turned out that he had worked for a long time with Petr Kirpichev, the creator of chemical agents A-230 and A-232.

When we first met at the beginning of January 1993, Vladimir made a good impression on me, with his determination to struggle against chemical weapons and against the barbaric destruction of the stockpiles at the Shikhany military test site.

Several of his remarks about new developments made it clear that he was a highly qualified specialist who understood the questions of the synthesis and testing of new chemical agents very well. He was well informed about the events that unfolded around the invention of Agent A-232 and how former director of GOSNII-OKhT, Ivan Martynov, was giving the patent authorship for Substance A-232 to his son Boris.

I was very pleased that Uglev was ready to support me. It was extremely important at that time, because there were few people either in our country or in the U.S., who believed in the existence of a secret program for the development and testing of a new generation of chemical weapons. However, along with such positive impressions, I also heard something that was for me an alarming confession. Vladimir told me that some time ago he had been recruited by the KGB to spy on Petr Kirpichev, who was his scientific supervisor. According to his story, he had told Kirpichev everything, and justified his decision to become an informer because he believed that otherwise some other unknown person would have been in his place. Oh, blessed naiveté! You see the KGB made sure its informants had understudies, to exclude the possibility of a "monopolization" of information sources. However, I can't strictly judge those who agreed to be informers, because the KGB was truly omnipotent. Reporting was rampant and very few could resist the suggestion to "become useful to the Motherland." Suspicion practically paralyzed any communications and any discussions, including scientific ones. I tried to avoid suspicions as much as possible, even if I didn't know people well, but

State Secrets

sometimes it seemed to me that there were always at least a few informers among the people who surrounded me. Sometimes I got irrefutable evidence confirming my intuitive guesses, but I always pressed myself not to be tempted to retaliate. Unfortunately, I didn't always succeed and that resulted in conflicts.

I asked Uglev to be extremely careful in his dealings with Lev Fedorov. As I understood, Fedorov's major objective in his relations with Uglev and me was to obtain any kind of information, which he would later use for writing his articles, and for passing himself off as a prominent specialist in chemical weapons. It was more than a provocation at that time, when my lawyer and I were trying with all our might to prove that I hadn't disclosed any state secrets connected with the technical side of the problems of chemical weapons.

A vivid illustration of this is Fedorov's article in which he deliberately and nonchalantly described the formula of Substance 33 and the principle of binary weapons based on it, passing himself off as an outstanding specialist in the sphere of chemical weapons.[153]

Of course it was no big secret to the FSB (the KGB), where this information was really coming from. Uglev was soon under the threat of being charged with disclosing state secrets, and the Saratov department of the FSB started an investigation. Before that Vladimir Uglev gave a sensational interview to *Novoe Vremya*. In this interview, he confirmed my account about the toxicity of the new chemical agents and spoke about the history of their development at the Volsk branch of GOSNIIOKhT. He said that precursors of these agents were not included on the lists of substances controlled under the Chemical Weapons Convention. Moreover, he claimed that a batch of the components of binary weapons was stockpiled at a secret base in the Bryansk Region. Uglev shared my apprehensions that the components of binary weapons, based on the new agent, could be disguised as civilian products, which would make international control much more difficult.[154]

I don't doubt a bit that Uglev's position was sincere. He always adhered to it when he gave interviews to the press. It was extremely important to me that one more person from the military-chemical complex was earnestly struggling against chemical weapons and wasn't afraid of persecution.

We developed rather good relations and met from time to time when he came to Moscow. During these meetings, which took place in my apartment, we openly discussed the problems connected with the prohibition of the development and production of chemical weapons and the destruction of their stockpiles. I was certain that the KGB recorded our conversations because I knew its surveillance techniques. However, this didn't worry me because we didn't discuss any technical secrets.

Vladimir was a courageous person, and he didn't hesitate in the face of impending danger. He was driven by his adamant belief that it was necessary to take such actions for the good of the people.

In the middle of January 1993, a hearing was held at the RF Supreme Soviet on the problem of destroying the stockpiles of chemical weapons. It took place in the While House on the Krasnopresnenskaya Embankment, which less than a year later would be shot up by tanks, driving out coup supporters headed up by adventurous Russian Vice President Aleksander Rutskoi, and the Chairman of the Supreme Soviet and specialist in Marxist political economy, Ruslan Khasbulatov.

I went to this hearing at the invitation of Valeri Menshikov, Deputy Chairman of the Committee for Ecology, with whom I had established good relations. There I met many active participants in the ecological movement who were worried that chemical weapons would be destroyed without the necessary safety precautions.

Vladimir Petrenko stood out among this group because of his picturesque beard. It turned out that he had served in Military Unit 61469 in Shikhany. There the young officer, along with others, was recruited as a guinea pig for the testing of chemical weapons. These experiments were very cheap for the military unit. The officers participating in the experiment each received an insignificant bonus. However, Petrenko almost totally lost his health due to his patriotic impulse, so he was transferred to the reserve. His attempts to receive some kind of compensation resulted in his being charged with slandering the chiefs of the military unit. For a long time he couldn't even receive his small disability allowance. Attempts to address the public were even more costly. His wife was fired from her job at the same military unit, and they started to evict the Petrenko family from their apartment in Shikhany. Later Petrenko's "case" became widely known[155], and he devoted the rest of his life to struggling against the barbaric destruction of chemical weapons at the military test site.

All of the official speakers at the meeting appeared completely insipid and couldn't bring any arguments in support of their projects, other than promising "we will do it." Critical statements by activists from the ecological movement, who arrived from the regions where chemical weapons were stockpiled, added fuel to the fire. They were talking about inadequate storage conditions and barbaric methods of destruction that threatened the safety and health of the surrounding populations.

For example, activists from Novocheboksarsk criticized the military-chemical complex's project for destroying stockpiles of chemical weapons at the chemical plant that used to produce chemical agents. The plant's proximity to the city's densely populated districts was already the reason for the deterioration of the health of the local people, and the generals wanted to keep poisoning people, while destroying the stores of chemical weapons. Even from a purely psychological standpoint, people didn't want to hear that chemical weapons would be destroyed near their homes. However, this never occurred to the functionaries from the Committee for Conventional Problems.

Despite the ongoing investigation and endless interrogations, I tried to participate in various public events as much as possible. In particular, I went to the conference "The KGB Yesterday, Today, and Tomorrow" organized by Sergei Grigoriyants. The conference participants, including many former dissidents who had endured all the horrors of the Soviet concentration camps, greeted me warmly, saying that they supported me in my struggle against the KGB. Of course I was very glad that these people considered me an insider.

Vil S. Mirzayanov

How the Tatars Became the "Enemies of Democracy"

In 1992 a ruthless and bitter campaign unfolded in the Russian press and television against the Republic of Tatarstan, when it announced its intention of conducting a referendum on the independence of the republic. At this time the Tatar Nation saw the prospect of freedom somewhere on the horizon for the first time in many centuries of slavery. Many representatives of our nation were optimistic about it, but by the end of the 20th century, the Tatar Nation found itself in a very thorny situation. Lenin's national policy wasn't the only reason for the degradation of my people as these "democrats" were saying. They claimed that 70 years of the sins of Communism were to blame for everything. Mostly the problems of the Tatar Nation were the result of imperial policy aimed at forced Russification of their colonies and the ruthless plunder of the Tatar national resources – namely oil.

Oddly enough, the U.S.S.R. Communist leaders managed to use the UN to protect the integrity of their colonial empire, while they were demagogically struggling to deprive their Western partners (England, France, Belgium, etc.) of their own colonies. A certain peculiar but interesting thesis was invented and circulated stating that colonies were only those (conquered) territories that were located across the ocean. When even the "Slavic brothers" (Belarus, Ukraine) bordering on the Motherland managed to escape from it, the partial break-up in 1991 of the Russian Empire (called the U.S.S.R.) ended all the demagogic arguments in the international arena overnight. However, this collapse didn't solve the major problem of Russia – the decolonization of the colonies that in their time weren't able to receive the official status of "union republics." I should note that the absence of this legal status – and the preservation of the colonial regime - doesn't make any more legal sense than it makes sense to think that colonies are only to be found across the ocean. The US Congress approved Public Law 86-90 "Captive Nations Week" on July 17, 1959, which pointed out that among the captured nations of Russia were the people of Idel-Ural who are mostly Tatars and Bashkirs. The awakening of the Tatar national identity after the collapse of the totalitarian regime pushed the Tatars to struggle for basic freedom, which mainly came down to the right to decide independently how they should live in their own republic.

Some leaders from the All-Tatar Public Center supported full independence for Tatarstan, up to its full separation from Russia. However, the geopolitical situation of Tatarstan, which is surrounded by regions mostly inhabited by Russians, didn't leave room for any illusions. At the same time, the status of independence could become the basis for building new relations with Russia, to try along with other newly liberated nations of the former empire, to find a fundamental solution to the problem of economic and political integrity of the country, based on a federation or confederation built from the bottom-up.

In my opinion the referendum about independence was largely symbolic, but it was an extremely important step towards real independence. I know for a fact that no one in Tatarstan thought about organizing any military groups to try to solve the problem by force. However, such a ruckus broke out in the press on this account! All the newspapers, both democratic and pro-Communist, were stirring up supercharged anti-Tatar hysteria. I couldn't get rid of the impression that all these actions were well coordinated, especially considering who controlled the so-called free press in Russia. My friends, who were quite well educated and democratically minded people, were surprised at the "impertinence" and "black ingratitude" of the Tatars.

It took a lot of effort to explain the simple truth to these people. Nevertheless, the referendum took place, and its results caused jubilation among the Tatar people. But, everything ended at that.

Although, later the governments of Tatarstan and Russia conducted negotiations on concluding some kind of agreement, it couldn't change anything, except one thing. Before that Tatarstan was the only single colony conquered by the Russians which didn't have a formal agreement confirming that it had voluntarily joined the Russian Empire. Probably even the Tsarist high officials found it extremely hypocritical to pretend that Tatarstan voluntarily joined the empire like the other colonies. The collective psychic wound inflicted on the Tatars by the massive slaughter of mostly innocent women and children after the siege of Kazan in 1552, was carried out by Russian troops led by Ivan the Terrible, and it remains unhealed to this day.

After negotiations in Moscow between the administrations of the presidents of the Russian Federation and Tatarstan, a non-binding agreement was signed about mutual relations that served as a pressure valve, that is, for comforting the Tatar people and for keeping the colonial status of Tatarstan.

In March of 1993, at the invitation of the All-Tatar Public Center, I participated in the congress of this organization. To do so I had to write an appeal to my investigator asking for permission to go to Kazan, because I was still under a written court order not to leave Moscow. Shkarin was happy about this turn of events, because after I had refused to take part in the investigation, I had completely ignored him and refused to sign any papers.

Unfortunately, I soon found out that many people in Kazan were still strongly under the influence of their Communist leaders, who had only one enemy - President Boris Yeltsin, who they felt had to be defeated at any cost. Early in 1991, it was Yeltsin who had offered the Tatars as much independence "as they could swallow". I am certain that as a natural politician, Boris Yeltsin knew that the Russian Empire was an unstable form of governing colonies, and that it had become obsolete, both economically and politically. So a new federal system was necessary that would take into consideration the colonized peoples' hunger for independence. It's not surprising that after such a suggestion, President Mintimer Shaimiev [156-158] of Tatarstan, viceroy of the Russian Empire, and the former First Secretary of the Regional Committee of the C.P.S.U., zealously participated in the Bolshevik coup in August of 1991. The Tatar people, led by their usual short-sighted and naive activists-idealists, saved the unlucky coup supporter from becoming a cellmate of Vladimir Kryuchkov (chief of the KGB), the U.S.S.R. Prime Minister Valentin Pavlov, and others in the infamous Matrosskaya Tishina Prison.

What elements of freedom offered by Boris Yeltsin did the ruling elite in Kazan make use of? Perhaps it was only the "market" possibility - to use the wealth and resources of the Republic of

Tatarstan without any control and to secure permanent places at the top for themselves, trampling on what remained of the system of democratic elections. As for the rest, they didn't even bother to change the names of the streets and the cities which still bear the names of the Bolshevik butchers. Lenin's beloved bronze scarecrow is still displayed in the center of Kazan. It was Mr. Shaimiev, President of Tatarstan, who instructed the people's deputies from Tatarstan like Renat Mukhamadiev to form a bloc in the Supreme Soviet of Russia with extremists like Vladimir Rutskoi, Ruslan Khasbulatov, and Sergei Baburin, inveterate enemies of the democratic development in Russia. In my speech I reminded my audience about this fact, and my appeal to the congress was welcomed with long applause.

After that, I had to calm down a nervous BBC correspondent for a long time, who was asking if I wasn't afraid that Tatar nationalists and separatists would use my authority for bad purposes. I replied that I know my people very well. Tatars distinguish themselves as hard working people. No matter where they settle, they start by building a house and a banya (bath house), but they never buy weapons, even if someone threatens their lives. However, this doesn't mean that Tatars are cowardly. Tatars are among the first of the peoples of the U.S.S.R., who hold the greatest number of the highest award for heroism in the Second World War – the title of "Hero of the Soviet Union". I also said I was certain that after the Tatar people became truly independent, they would live in real friendship with the Russian people.

Less than two years later, a new Russian-Chechen war broke out.

I deeply condemn any war, since I think that no wars are waged to achieve noble goals - not liberation wars, and not wars waged to bring "civilization" to people. I am against solving any problems with the help of military force, no matter whose initiative it is, because in the end innocent people die, although nobody ever asks for their opinions. For this reason, I can't imagine, even theoretically, my people fighting the Russian people. Both peoples are still in a state of poverty and slavery, and they can't be liberated from these problems on their own, because civilized peoples have left them far behind. Any possible conflict will only drag them backwards, which in turn will lead to their natural wasting away. Finally they will just disappear from the historical scene as has happened to many other nations…

However, when the Chechen Republic claimed independence, the behavior of the democratic public and press changed drastically! Long before the armed conflict, nobody ever thought to censure the separatist demarche of General D. Dudaev. Such "tolerance" by itself probably wasn't that bad, because it said something about the maturation of the democratic outlook of our society. Now I am convinced that the statement of the Chechen leader was a concentrated expression of protest of a colonial people of the Russian Empire against keeping their colonial status at the end of the 20th century, but it took on the form of extremism. However, nobody in the press or in the Supreme Soviet thought to speak out against the colonial nature of Russia, nobody supported its quick decolonization, and nobody suggested that negotiations with all the colonies should be started.

Then almost everybody started struggling against the Russian-Chechen war, but on the side of Dudaev. There were even some "democrats" who were sitting in the besieged palace of the rebel general, when fire from there was killing young Russian soldiers. Everybody extracted political dividends from this struggle, even the Communists, many of whom had clearly Fascist views about the non-Russian population.

For some reason, I think that most of those who censure this senseless war of annihilation are sincere, but I can't understand why people have a double standard regarding different peoples. It looks like the Tatar people are the enemy, even if they conduct a peaceful referendum. They asked "How did they dare to do this while they oppressed us for more than 400 years?" However, from the point of view of democrats, "our" nation, which irresponsible politicians have involved in armed escapades is right and should be defended.

I am greatly sorry, but there is nothing else I can do except contemplate the source of such a double standard. I suppose the phenomenon of a defective slave mentality that subconsciously sanctions the creation of a common enemy - the Tatar - is responsible. Another point is that the Russian Nation, which agreed to relinquish control over "Kiev Russia" in the form of Ukraine, doesn't want to understand that Kazan, that is Tatarstan, has exactly the same rights to be the master in its own republic as the Russians do in Moscow. So far the concept of equality doesn't go any further than allowing a Tatar surgeon to operate on the Russian president's heart and to providing the Black Sea Fleet with oil. I don't think it is just by chance that during the past 400 years not a single Tatar has ever been Prime Minister, Minister of Foreign Affairs or has held any other important position for Russia affairs. At the same time many Jews, Ukrainians, and representatives of other nations have held these positions. Doesn't it mean that Russians do not have a more bitter enemy than the Tatar?

In this way, the colonial status of my people is as obvious today as it was yesterday. There is no hope of overcoming slavery until my people come to terms with their never-ending habit of leaving the successors of Sheikh-Gali [159], a well known traitor to Tatar interests, at the helm of power, and gain control over the situation.

The Discovery of the Chekists

Meanwhile, Shkarin toiled away preparing to bring the indictment to its logical conclusion. The expert commission was working, and they found additional material at GOSNIIOKhT that allegedly proved my involvement with the development of binary weapons.[160, 161] Shkarin hurried over to GOSNIIOKhT to conduct the so-called personal inspection and wrote up a report with great satisfaction. He was certain that this time fortune had smiled upon him. He just forgot the saying that ultimately the person who is celebrating is somebody who has last word to say.

Of course GOSNIIOKhT immediately forwarded the document to the Chekists. However, the investigator handled these papers quite irresponsibly, because attaching this document to my case materials meant its complete declassification in the future. On the other hand, even in his wildest nightmare, Shkarin couldn't imagine that I would dare to copy this top secret material along with other documents. It leaves no doubts regarding Gorbachev's deceitful statements that the military presumably "were cleaning up unfinished business."[162]

Shkarin painstakingly prepared for the interrogation. He planned to produce all documents that would prove that I was informed about the development of binary weapons. This is why he summoned me on March 25, 1993, for an interrogation and produced the "Technical Order." At that point, I was still using the tactic of not participating in the interrogations, and I didn't read the documents, but right away I understood everything. It was all true. There was my official stamp on the document. I remembered that the senior research assistant Savkin had brought it to me and asked me to put my stamp on it. I didn't refuse, although I wasn't allowed to be included in that work. In spite of all his efforts, Shkarin had failed to find a list of employees allowed to work on the topic of binary weapons that included my name. The lists existed, but my name wasn't on a single one of them. So now the captain was satisfied to some extent, although he realized that there was very little information in this paper that could be used to formulate the conclusion that I had participated in this work.

Everything in the document was so vague that only a knowledgeable insider could understand what it meant. Not even the words "binary weapon" were on the paper, not to mention the components. Evidently another attempt to interrogate my former deputy, Svyatoslav Sokolov, didn't help to prove my direct involvement in the development of binary weapons. This is why the investigator had to compose the transcript of his interrogation as if he were interested in how informed I was on the toxic properties of the compounds. This was just funny, because the investigator had more than enough information about what I knew regarding the properties of all old and new chemical agents. However, a Chekist wouldn't be a Chekist if he didn't try to take anybody who read this document for a fool…

The Expert Commission: Mirzayanov Told the Truth, Therefore he is Guilty

I was summoned for the next interrogation on April 12, 1993. A surprise was waiting there for my lawyer and me - the lists of secrets[163, 164] and the results[165] of the work of the expert commission. On that day I wasn't ready to change my tactics for my behavior at the interrogations, which is evident from the following passage from the transcript of interrogation, which I also refused to sign. However, after that I changed my mind, following the advice of my lawyer Asnis, because we had already partially reached our objective. First, the expert commission was split in its decision, and the respectable and authoritative specialists, General Vadim V. Smirnitsky and Colonel Nikolai I. Chugunov, didn't agree with the "opinion" of other members, which completely matched the resolution of the Permanent Technical Commission at GOSNII-OKhT[166], with the exception that from it I disclosed "...the cooperation of designers and manufacturers..." naming test sites and locations of production of chemical weapons.

What is more, Asnis and I found another of their declarations most useful for my defense: "The commission has no information (documents) at its disposal at this time about any negative consequences that Mirzayanov's actions caused." In other words, the KGB's vaunted experts stated that my ostensible crime was a victimless one. Also, the investigator finally produced all the lists of secrets that we had been requesting, for such a long time. Nonetheless, at a later date, in violation of all the norms of the Criminal and Procedural Code, Investigator Shkarin did not include these materials in my case (he included only extracts of them), and this is why I couldn't copy them and make them public. However, I managed to copy some of the necessary excerpts regarding the essence of state secrets in the area of scientific research work on weapons. This is why during the next interrogation that took place on April 14, 1993, I worked very hard, reading everything attentively, and copied the parts I found most interesting. Upon the recommendation of my lawyer, I also wrote a petition in which I asked to submit a request for clarification of the terms used on the lists for interpreting chemical weapons. I remember that on all the lists of information that constitute state secrecy, there was not a single word about chemical weapons, or their development and testing. Instead of this the experts and the investigator used general terms such as "ammunition". The situation was exactly the same with the notion of the "special purpose program" for the development of weapons, the information from which I had allegedly disclosed. For these reasons I insisted on my arguments at the interrogation on April 15, 1993. In particular, in answering the usual question of the investigator about what "explanations I could give regarding the materials that were shown to me", I declared:

"I read the resolutions and Lists of Information of state secrecy that were presented to me, and I am submitting a request about elaborating on the question about specifying whether all the lists shown to me - and in particular clauses which the experts refer to in their resolution - are aimed at protecting information about scientific research in the area of the development of chemical weapons in our country, because in the texts of the lists there are no terms "chemical armaments," "chemical weapons," or "military chemical agents." The list of the Ministry of Chemical Industry only contains the terms "model chemical agents of the probable enemy," "objects of chemical weapons destruction," and "means of chemical defense." Additionally, I request that expert Nikolai I. Chugunov be interrogated and asked what, from the point of view of the requirements produced, falls into the notion "special purpose program for scientific research" and whether it is possible to say that I disclosed the final results of some specific program for scientific research. I also request that the experts who signed the general findings be interrogated about their conclusions about the precise wording of Clause 56 of the Temporary List of Information of State Secrecy. I consider it necessary to state that the list of the Ministry of Chemical Industry dated January 1, 1993, is no longer valid because, since according to Clause 1 of this list, it is based on the

State Secrets

List of Information of State Secrecy (compiled in 1980), which became invalidated on January 1, 1993."

I should mention that beginning in January 1, 1993, the new List of Information of State Secrecy, which practically repeats the words of the old one, was introduced in Russia, and it also lacks any kind of wording about chemical weapons.

This conclusion came as no surprise to me, because the majority of the members of the expert commission were representatives of the military-chemical complex. These people were much more guided by their official responsibilities than by their feelings of civic duty. The fact that the experts Major General Vadim V. Smirnitsky (whose military rank was not listed in the document) and Colonel Nikolai I. Chugunov refused to sign this conclusion confirms this. Each of them wrote his own personal conclusion, in which each denied that I had disclosed any state secrets. Their conclusions could be summed up as follows from the resolution written by Nikolai Chugunov[167]:

> *"If the indicated information is true, it can't constitute a state or a work-related secret because it doesn't contain specific facts about the structure of the new chemical agent; therefore, its disclosure can't have a negative impact on the quality of the military and economic potential of the country or have any other grave consequences for the defensive capability, or the state security, or seriously damage the political interests of the state, or damage the state in any other way."*

General Smirnitsky stressed in his conclusions[168] that the information about the newly synthesized chemical agent didn't disclose:

   -its name (conventional or chemical);
   -its physical or chemical properties, which are indispensable characteristics of any synthesized product;
   -the name and quantitative ratio of the components of

the binary system, without this the notion "binary bomb" makes no sense;

-information about what types of ammunition the new chemical agent is intended for;

- or information about whether the chemical agent was adopted by the army.

Victor Shkarin tried to lessen the significance of the conclusions written by the respectable veterans of the Chemical Troops, and he conducted additional interrogations[169-171] to "clarify" their positions, which were already quite obvious. They didn't change their minds, which of course was a serious blow for the carefully concocted "findings" of the Investigation Department. During the interrogation on April 23, 1993 Nikolai Chugunov entirely destroyed one of the main accusatory tricks of Shkarin. When he asked Chugunov about my alleged disclosure of the results of the "goal-oriented program" he said, "It's difficult for me to answer the question as to whether Mirzayanov revealed the results of some kind of concrete program of scientific research work, because the materials presented to the Expertise don't contain any information about a concrete program of scientific research and its elements". Defiant Shkarin tried to save the situation by using the term "goal-oriented program" and immediately sent a letter to Director Petrunin[172] asking for clarification, but the director[173] was almost helpless to respond because there was no real goal-oriented program, except for the General Directives for the creation of a new chemical agent. I was certain that such a "special purpose program" for the development of chemical weapons had never existed and does not exist today. After this crash, Captain of Justice Shkarin simply erased all references to a "goal-oriented program" from all copies of the lists of state secrets quoted in the case and edited their items as if they never ever contained any of those words. He also deleted this from all the other documents and transcripts of interrogations attached to the case except for the letters.

Trying to repair the damage, Shkarin also interrogated the members of the expert commission Anatoly Kochetkov[174], Boris Kuznetsov[175] and Igor Gabov.[176] The first two of them surprisingly "admitted" that Mirzayanov meant the new chemical agent A-232 in the article "A Poisoned Policy". I had never used this codename in my publications and interviews, and I didn't mention the term "Novichok" either. Before these experts testified, Andrei Zheleznyakov and Vladimir Uglev[177, 178] had publicly disclosed them. I didn't understand why Shkarin created this perfidy, until the case went to trial.

There was already a greater blunder in the works, apart from the mistakes mentioned above regarding the arbitrary interpretation of the terms on the lists of secrets, where even the words "chemical weapons" weren't to be found. We also insisted that if all lists of state secrets didn't contain any definition of chemical weapons or chemical agents, then it would not be legal to apply them to my case. The definition "ammunitions" from any reasonable point of view cannot be applied to chemical weapons or chemical agents. Certainly the Investigation Department was in an awkward situation to argue with this logic. To try to save the situation, the Investigation Department of the MB RF sent a letter to General Staff Headquarters of Russia.[179] The answer was confusing[180], though it slightly comforted the investigator. I consider it my duty to say that both the request and the answer are highly provocative.

Those who compiled the new list of secrets and those who interpreted it supposed that the development of chemical weapons would continue in the future. This is despite the fact that by September of 1992, when the new list of secrets was compiled and the term "chemical weapons" still wasn't to be found there, the Chemical Weapons Convention had been initialed and Russia was one of the major participants of the negotiations. However, the signatories participating counted on secrecy and were certain that their secrets would never be made public.

The Russian Government Comes Running to the Aid of the KGB

Evidently, there was more than enough juridical "evidence" of my guilt, from the point of view of the investigation, to justify conducting closed legal proceedings.

On the other hand, the lists of secrets did not contain even an indirect reference to the development of chemical weapons, and it was impossible to ignore this deficit any further. General Balashov and his subordinates understood that if another specialist repeated my actions, they would have practically no legal basis for conducting a legitimate investigation. That is why General-Chekist Demin[181] initiated the urgent adoption of an amendment to the Temporary List of Secrets.[182] The new Russian definition included "information that discloses the content of former or current works in the area of chemical or biological weapons, or the essence of those works, the results achieved, as well as information on the protocols of synthesis, production technologies, or articles of production equipment." On March 30, 1993, it was issued in the form of Resolution N 256-16, signed by Prime Minister Viktor Chernomyrdin.

This was already quite a different story. Finally a real document was issued, in which for the first time in history Russia legally admitted that chemical weapons were being developed. I can say without any exaggeration that it appeared thanks to me.

Hopefully, after this resolution was passed my colleagues, the specialists in chemical weapons, finally got their chance to appeal to the authorities and ask to have their pensions increased to the level of other employees working in especially dangerous and hazardous conditions. However, they probably don't know that such a document exists. This is another reason why I am disclosing this document. Of course the KGB didn't have these noble objectives in mind when it composed this document. It was designed to accuse me by retroactively creating a quasi-legal base to prove my guilt. A number of U.S. human rights organizations, politicians, representatives to the United Nations and others immediately started paying attention to this after I sent the "Resolution" on to my friend Gale Colby, who is now my wife, along with other excerpts from my case.

The "experts" Anatoly Kochetkov[174] and Boris Kuznetsov[175] and others started constantly referring to this resolution during their additional interrogations in the Investigation Department. So then, there it was. There were no doubts left about how and why this hurriedly adopted government document appeared. With a goal of intimidating the American journalist Will Englund in April 9 1993, the Investigation Department summoned him for interrogation as a witness.[183-186] Will Englund categorically refused to testify against me and didn't sign the transcript of interrogation. Unfortunately his interpreter Andrei Mironov made a mistake and signed the interrogation transcript as the interpreter, which could be taken as Will's refusal to sign this document - just because of his lack of knowledge of Russian.

The investigator had no clear legal grounds on which to base my indictment, and so he tried to compensate for this gap by speaking about the alleged serious damage that my publications caused to interests of the state. The List of Major Information of State Secrecy contained the definition of secrecy. Information was considered secret if its revelation resulted in damage to the defense capability, state, military, political, or other interests of the country. For this reason Shkarin appealed to a number of departments with respective inquiries.[187-192]

The response of the military[188] didn't leave any doubt as to what their attitude toward my actions was.

This document became eloquent evidence of how "originally" our military leaders interpreted the Convention for the Prohibition of Chemical Weapons. Probably there is a general style of stating the objectives of the Convention that escapes me. But still, I couldn't get rid of the thought: our military people are certain that the prohibition of the development of chemical weapons is not subject to any control - not only for them, but also, as they expressed, for other countries involved in the development of chemical weapons. I don't know what other people would say, but I think this is more than alarming! Still, I felt slightly better because I knew that, to a considerable extent I had helped to prevent this perversion of the Convention, which hadn't yet been ratified and or entered into force.

General Kolesnikov's attempt to insert his overall contribution into the substance of my indictment proved less fruitful, except for exposing himself with the military's "flexible" interpretation of the Convention.

The investigation asked the general whether I had damaged the defensive capabilities of Russia, which is the primary concern of the Head of the General Staff Headquarters. However, in response, the general refers to politics and some strange "military damage" without deciphering what it involved. Kolesnikov was openly deceitful when he accused me of disclosing the "...conventional names of these new substances and the overall development programs." I have tried to cite all my articles in this book, so that the reader can independently judge what I wrote. It is very easy to see that there was no trace of "conventional names," and even more so no "overall development programs."

The answer of the Ministry of Foreign Affairs put everything into its proper place.[192] In its response, it precisely indicated that the factor which precipitated the Mirzayanov case and all the ensuing scandal, was the dangerous actions of the Russian military-chemical complex.

On May 13, 1993, I was summoned for the last interrogation, at which Senior Prosecutor Buivolov from the Attorney General's Office, was present. The investigator showed me and my lawyer a resolution to drop the charges against me for my part in "disclosing information about the system of organizing promising applied scientific research work, carried out in the interests of the defense of the country, and about the cooperation of specific designers and the producers of chemical weapons..."

Evidently this clause was too absurd, even from the investigator's point of view, because at that time there was enough information in the press regarding this, even without my articles. However, all the charges that I mentioned above, which the expert commission had obligingly rubber-stamped as expected, still stood in force. They were just reformulated in a new indictment. The interrogation that followed, after I was shown this new indictment, was a rather formal procedure. However, it didn't prevent the investigator from sticking to his line and asking questions that had already become stereotypical. Such as the following excerpt from the transcript of the interrogation of May 13, 1993[193]:

"Question: Do you plead guilty to the charges filed against you in the indictment?

Answer: ***No, I am absolutely not guilty of the charges brought against me in the indictment.*** [bold type and italics by me—V.M.].

Question: What explanations can you give concerning the indictment that was shown to you?

Answer: The charge I was shown today appears to be an exact copy of the ones I was shown before, and I regard it as a political provocation performed by the Attorney General's Office and the RF Ministry of Security with the goal of discrediting the democratic transformation in our country. This is an attempt to scare democratically minded scientists by my example. The indictment is a crime against the country that signed the Convention for the Prohibition of Chemical Weapons. This is an attempt to undermine the trust of the whole world community in Russian foreign policy. I think that as neither the form, nor the essence of the indictment corresponds to the current Temporary List of Information of State Secrecy, this fact discredits this criminal case. I am not going to give any explanations regarding the indictment."

On that day the investigator decided to record one more transcript of an interrogation to fulfill some kind of plan he had. He was interested in my attitude toward the General Staff Headquarters. In particular, he wanted to know what I thought about the assertion that the term "ammunition" also covered chemical weapons. He asked what I thought about the additional clarifications of the "experts" Gabov and Kochetkov.

Here are my answers to these questions:

"I looked though the transcripts of the experts' interrogation and the letter, and I am claiming that the experts didn't answer the essence of the question I had posed, because neither of them referred to any special purpose program, the results of which I had allegedly disclosed. Let each of them show me a specific program and point out the statements in my articles that are completely identical with the wording of the results of the aforementioned program. Then I will consider that the experts did their job conscientiously. Otherwise, I will have to consider the conclusion of these experts biased and unscrupulous. For this reason I request an additional expert commission. I think that the answer of G. Funygin, Deputy Head of Department Eight of the Administration of the General Staff Headquarters, is incompetent. It discredits the policy of our country after we have signed the Convention for the Prohibiting of Chemical Weapons. This answer means that the new list adopted on January 1, 1993 provides for the protection of secrets in the area of the development and testing of chemical weapons.

On these grounds I request that the RF government, which issued an addendum to the aforementioned List for protecting secret information in the area of chemical weapons, N 256-16 of March 30, 1993, answer my petition submitted previously, in which I asked that they clarify which clauses from all of the three lists protect the development and testing of chemical weapons."[193]

Naturally, the investigation rejected this petition too, because it was obvious that the adoption of the above-mentioned government amendment confirmed, as clearly as could be, that there was nothing specific about chemical weapons on the above-mentioned lists. Therefore, the indictment had absolutely no legal basis to it. Of course, this wasn't a problem for Captain Shkarin alone. It was the product of the hypocritical policy of the ruling elite of the U.S.S.R., which didn't want to admit, even in the lists of top secrets, that it developed and produced chemical weapons. A perfect analysis was given by Valeri Rudnev of all these aspects of my case.[194]

However, I didn't think then and I don't think now that the investigator failed to understand all this. Of course he understood it, but it was important for him to formulate the indictment, and the judges were supposed to do the dirty work. In the course of their lives, the judges had their reliability tested many times by various district and city committees of the C.P.S.U. They always knew what they were doing, and the overwhelming majority of them faithfully served Lenin's party, and still serves it, even though that party no longer exists. Many have convictions that are so steadfast that judicial reform in Russia is unlikely to occur in the foreseeable future.

Skipping ahead a little, I would like to explain why I underlined my words in the passage from the transcript of the interrogation. In answering the investigator's question, I responded that "No, I am absolutely not guilty of the charges brought against me in the indictment." I said the same at the interrogation on October 30, 1992. However, when I came to the U.S. several years later and saw the English translations of these transcripts made by Andrei Arnold, at the request of Gale Colby, I was literally shocked. My answer to the interrogator's question in both transcripts was translated as "I plead partially guilty." This translation was used to report my case in the U.S. to the State Department, senators and others. The reader can draw his own conclusions. However, the fact that some people in the U.S. were extremely dissatisfied with an audacious Tatar and were trying to compromise me is quite obvious to me. Otherwise, why did CIA use its disgraceful and provocative tactics against me?

Chapter 20
Revenge of the Communists

It was time for me to look through my case materials. According to the Procedural Code, I had to become familiarized with my case and to confirm this before it was brought to court. Day after day I was planning to copy down everything that could be used to expose the methods of the Chekists. Enough material had accumulated in my case, that I could understand the plans of the leaders of the military-chemical complex for carrying out their implementation of the Chemical Weapons Convention.

I believed that the day would come when I would be able to present all this to the general public. Of course, I wasn't at all certain that the court wouldn't send me to jail for many years to come. However, that was already not so important to me, since I got the chance to publish the secrets of the military-chemical complex and the KGB. That is why I concentrated fully on the mind-numbing activity of copying these lengthy transcripts and materials stamped "Secret" and "Top Secret", right under the nose of Investigator Shkarin. He was powerless to do anything about it, and could only resign himself to tolerating my impertinence. Still, I wasn't quite certain that the KGB could forgive my conduct. Even so, I had made up my mind and this meant that I would carry on to the end, and put my decision into action.

Every day, after the long and tiresome job of copying my case materials at the Lefortovo Investigation Department, I went home to my apartment in the "Ivanovskoe" residential housing complex. That summer my family was in the village Baranovskoe near Moscow. Until late at night, I typed up what I had copied during the day. I was completely alone and open to anyone who might have wanted to get rid of me. However, strange as it may seem, I was not afraid at all, and I calmly accepted whatever was to come. Just in case though, I tried to hide the typed texts and, whenever possible I sent them by the fax of the Moscow Greenpeace organization to Gale Colby in Princeton, New Jersey.

By that time the situation in Russia had become very tense. A struggle was in full swing between the supporters of Democracy and the Communists, whose puppets at that time were the Chairman of the Supreme Soviet, Ruslan Khasbulatov, and Vice President Aleksandr Rutskoi. The latter was a former pilot who had served in Afghanistan and received the title of "hero" after he was shot down and taken prisoner three times. Rutskoi was exchanged each time for weapons, which the Mujahedeen then used to kill our soldiers. Even at the very beginning of his political career, when he nominated himself as a candidate for the U.S.S.R. Congress of People's Deputies, this "hero" demonstrated his undisguised contempt for people. Once when it was his turn to speak at a meeting near one of the Moscow cinemas, he remarked to his assistants, "Now I will say a few words to this herd of animals!" Rutskoi didn't notice that the microphone was switched on, and all the people around heard very well how this adventurer appraised them. As a result, the "fighter" for people's happiness was an ignominious failure in the elections. Unfortunately, people in his hometown, where his mother was running a brisk beer trade, later came to believe that the "soldier from Afghanistan" had become a reformer, and they elected him deputy, to their own detriment.

When he became Vice President of Russia after the elections in 1991, Rutskoi managed to cheat not only his friends the Communist deputies, but even Boris Yeltsin. By spring of 1992, the Communists decided that the right moment had come, and they doggedly started attacking the supporters of democracy and market reforms in Russia. When I heard incoherent, hysterical statements from the mustachioed pilot attacking reforms, I couldn't get rid of the thought that the "Evil One" had appeared in Russia.

Every day they showed a different demagogue on TV, the specialist in Marxism, Ruslan Khasbulatov. His unnaturally glittering eyes gave away his addiction to drugs, and I felt disgust and great alarm when I watched him. I saw that no moral barriers existed for this person. Looking straight into the television camera, he could assure people that he was more Russian than any of them. The only little problem was that he was a Chechen, according to his passport. He was fishing for compliments which non-Russian citizens would find insulting: "You don't say so, Ruslan Ivanovich! You don't look like a member of a national minority at all." Unfortunately, all the Bolsheviks, like the Fascists, are the same - they are "international." I felt almost sick listening to the speeches of the frenzied Communists. I clearly saw that they were preparing for a new civil war.

At that time, I felt uncomfortable distracting people by asking them to solve my problems. Inadvertently my case played out against the supporters of Boris Yeltsin, because a lot of people saw not the plots of the KGB in it, but an error in reckoning of the modern reformers. To be honest, if I hadn't prudently linked my fate to the ruling elite of that time, the idea of the Communists coming to power would have been even worse for me. While Yeltsin was at the helm, a hope still flickered under the pressure from the international community, especially from the democratic countries, that the authorities in Russia could listen to common sense and concede. However, if the Bolsheviks returned, it would undoubtedly mean many years in jail for me. I did my best trying to help the democratic forces hold up in this brutal struggle, emphasizing in my numerous interviews and articles published in Moscow, Bashkortstan, and Tatarstan, that the development of democracy in our country was a necessary condition for the fight against chemical weapons.

In the spring of 1993, a referendum was scheduled to take place on the people's confidence in the policy of democratic and economic reforms in the country. At that time a broad range of ecological organizations in Udmurtiya, Chuvashiya, and the Saratov region were actively protesting the planned barbaric destruction of chemical weapons stockpiles in their regions. The local populations were very anxious about this prospect and felt that it meant that the authorities were unwilling to consider the interests of ordinary people.

The policy of the Presidential Conventional Committee for Problems of Biological and Chemical Weapons was provocative and played into the hands of the Communists. Under these circumstances, it was extraordinarily convenient from everyone's point of view to fire General Anatoly Kuntsevich, the odious chairman of that committee, in disgrace. Then the people from the affected regions could decide to vote for the policy of President Yeltsin, because they would see this gesture as a portent for the safe destruction of the chemical weapons stockpiles. I expressed this idea to the democratic leaders in the RF Supreme Soviet, Sergei Yushenkov and Valery Menshikov. Unfortunately, they couldn't or didn't want to take resolute action.

The same fate befell my initiative to revive the Sunday Tatar concerts in Kazan which were broadcast on short wave radio. Numerous radio stations for jamming the foreign "voices," had become useless in the onslaught of the era of Glasnost. In 1989 the U.S.S.R. government decided to put them to better use for developing cultural links between nations. Regular broadcasts of Tatar music started on the weekends, and the Tatar Diaspora living in Moscow finally got a chance to know their own music better. It was at a time when the U.S.S.R. leaders were interested in negotiating a signed agreement with Tatarstan, which had justly demanded the same rights for itself that the so-called union republics enjoyed.

When the U.S.S.R. collapsed and Russia was transformed into a sovereign state, it seemed that the process for granting Tatarstan the right to make independent decisions and to have a real government was evolving more rapidly. I have already written about what happened later, when Tatarstan decided to conduct a referendum on the issue of sovereignty. Then democrats of every shade,

State Secrets

Communists, and nationalist-chauvinists united against this "impudence" of the Tatars. There were no limits to the defamation of my people in the press, on radio, and on TV.

In April of 1993, after lengthy reflection, I called the secretary of Mikhail Poltoranin, who headed the Committee for Radio and Television at that time. I briefly explained the objective of my proposed visit and asked him to spare me 10 minutes to lay out my plans. I wanted famous Tatars - democratically-minded scientists, public figures, and writers to speak on the radio and on TV and call for voting in favor of Boris Yeltsin's policy at the coming referendum. A gesture of good will was necessary in order to do so – a sign of readiness for cooperation and the resumption of the Tatar concert broadcasts on weekends, which had been cancelled. Poltoranin's secretary responded that his chief was very busy, and I had to call his deputy Sergei Yushenkov about it. Yushenkov agreed to meet me and I arrived at the appointed time. In the past I had briefly met with him, to state my position regarding the destruction of chemical weapons stockpiles, so I didn't have to introduce myself.

I thought that President Yeltsin ought to make a special statement on this subject. Yushenkov got interested in this idea, and he promised that he would immediately talk it over with Sergei Filatov, Yeltsin's Chief of Staff. Yushenkov also said he would help put into operation the idea of having the Tatar language broadcasts resumed, and he immediately phoned several of the chief producer's offices at TV and radio stations. As far as I understood, they promised to help and asked me to call. However, in Russia it is difficult to ensure any kind of real and positive result, no matter what you do, without a direct order...

I am sorry that I wasn't more persistent and didn't ask Yushenkov to use this method. The result was the proverbial "football," when you are thrown around with your initiative like a ball. But I decided to do what little I could, and I endlessly dialed the numbers that Yushenkov had given me. The people I called were constantly "out" or "in a meeting." Finally my patience was exhausted.

Fortunately, as Yushenkov told me the next day, Filatov had

approved of my idea of having the Russian President make a statement on chemical weapons. To implement this idea I had to meet with Aleksei Yablokov, the Presidential Advisor for Ecology.

I met him back in January of 1993 in his huge office on the third floor of the Kremlin palace. The vast windows opened up on the Square of the Cathedral of Ivan the Great, where the Tsar-cannon, which has never fired a single shot, is displayed.

When Yablokov learned the reason for my call, he immediately agreed to have a talk with me. Another day I met him and explained my proposal for the Russian President to make a statement regarding the destruction of stockpiles of chemical weapons. Aleksei Vladimirovich agreed with this idea and gave a number of recommendations about how I could develop my project further. The next morning I brought a revised version of the President's statement to him. Three days later he called me at home to say that he had managed to produce a compromise version of the statement and to get the approval stamps of all the respective services, including the Committee on Conventional Problems, and that the President was just about to sign it. After the statement was signed (five days before the referendum), Yablokov called me again. I went to the Kremlin to see him and he gave me a copy. I cite this statement below and can say that to this day it has fundamental significance connected with the issue of the destruction of chemical weapons stockpiles in Russia.

REPORT OF THE PRESS SERVICE OF THE PRESIDENT OF THE RUSSIAN FEDERATION

We are distributing the text of the statement of President B. N. Yeltsin of the Russian Federation on the issue of chemical weapons.

Statement made by the President of the Russian Federation on the issue of the destruction of chemical weapons

In the past few months the public in a number of regions has been seriously concerned about the issue of the destruction of chemical weapons.

In the preceding decades, tens of thousands of tons of military chemical agents have been produced and stockpiled in Russia. The world has changed, and Russia's position in the world has changed: we are not going to attack anybody. The time has come to rid ourselves of chemical weapons which we have inherited from the past legacy. This is not only Russia's view, but also the opinion shared by the one hundred and thirty eight countries which have signed the Convention on the Prohibition of Chemical Weapons this year in Paris.

We must begin the destruction of chemical weapons, proceeding from the requirements not only of international, but also of national security; as the shells and containers are steadily deteriorating and can't be stored indefinitely. These weapons were produced over the course of many years at several plants. The destruction process will be difficult and a substantial period of time will be required for its implementation. However, it has to be started. A government program for the destruction of chemical weapons is currently being prepared. It will be based upon the following principles:

- *Unconditional guarantee of the safety of the life and health of the population, as well as of the condition of the surrounding natural environment;*
- *Unconditional fulfillment of all the social needs of the population living in the zone of influence of the chemical weapons destruction facilities;*
- *Use of the latest technologies, making it possible to minimize the risk and also, in cases where feasible, to extract valuable chemical substances as a result of the destruction;*
- *Reduction to the minimum of the volume of transportation of chemical agents, within the Russian territory.*

The work on the destruction of chemical weapons will begin only after positive conclusions [have been reached] by state environmental-protection experts regarding the Program as a whole and at each individual facility. Such an expert evaluation will definitely involve the participation not only of scientists and specialists, but also of representatives of public organizations, including environmental organizations, on both the all-Russian and regional levels.

I am requesting the executive bodies of Udmurtiya, Chuvashiya, and the Saratov Region to ensure their active involvement in development of this program, in the determination of the priorities and terms of its preparation and in carrying out the work of the destruction of chemical weapons. Such participation will help transform this endeavor – an unavoidable step for Russia – into a powerful lever for the socio-economic development of significant territories of the country, while strictly ensuring the observance of guarantees for the safety of the population. A substantial part of the funds under this program will be channeled towards solving regional issues of public health protection, the protection of motherhood and childcare, as well as towards the construction of housing accommodations, social and community services, roads, and other infrastructure.

The mountains of now useless and dangerous weapons are a heavy burden inherited from the legacy of our past. Russia must be saved from it, in the interests of its own security and in the interests of the security of the whole world.

B. Yeltsin
April 20, 1993

In April of 1993, Gale Colby let me know that the Cavallo Foundation was going to award me a Special Recognition Award for Moral Courage, for defending the interests and security of mankind.

The award was supposed to be presented early in June 1993. Doubtless, I was very glad to receive it. It was heartwarming that people who were completely unknown to me thought and cared about me. The awarded sum of three thousand dollars literally meant salvation for my family at that time, because I had practically no earnings and my family lived off the aid provided by a Norwegian charity organization. I couldn't even think about going abroad to accept the award. This is why an invitation followed for my wife Nuria, so she could go to the U.S. in my place and accept the award.

Despite all of our efforts applying to get a foreign passport, we failed to accomplish this in time to go to the U.S. for the awards ceremony.

In the summer of 1993, another event took place that left an indelible impression on me. At the end of May, a famous journalist, environmental activist and former deputy of the U.S.S.R. Congress of People's Deputies, Aleksander Emelianenkov, called to let me know that Dan Ellsberg, the famous American human rights advocate, was coming to Moscow and he wanted to meet with me. Of course I agreed to meet him without any hesitation.

We met on the evening of June 1, 1993 in a small hotel on Arbat Street. The legendary American was an amazingly modest and lively person. With a slightly stooped posture, like all tall people, thin, with thick gray hair and blue eyes, he gave the impression of a university science professor. It was difficult to imagine that such a man could display the model of civic heroism he had. However, this impression vanished as soon as he started talking. He started asking questions, and I couldn't help but conclude that a huge will and intellect were behind his simple appearance, which he used to immediately draw the person he was talking with into the discussion. However, he showed no signs of obsession that could even hint at an inclination towards fanaticism. We talked for a few hours and I felt that Dan understood me completely and shared my views.

The meeting left a very positive impression on me at a time when I was facing total uncertainty regarding the outcome of my case. I felt at ease and free. If the man I was talking to hadn't flinched in the face of a threat of more than 100 years of imprisonment, and had acted for the people's benefit, then the 5 years of imprisonment that I could face seemed a trifle.

I met Dan again at a press conference held with Russian and

foreign correspondents, where we answered numerous questions.[195-197]

Will Englund[196] gave a brief update my case, recalling that the Russian government even issued a special amendment to the law on March 30th, in order to convict me. According to the journalist, Daniel Ellsberg said, "Russia is fortunate and honored to have a citizen like Dr. Mirzayanov…" I think this was an exaggeration; however I must admit that I was very pleased to hear such an appraisal coming from such a grand person as Dan Ellsberg.

Meanwhile Lev Fedorov got his passport and went to the U.S. to attend the ceremony at which I was awarded the Cavallo Foundation prize. Gale gave a brief speech, accepting the award on my behalf. Although I had already read transcripts of Fedorov's interrogation and knew that he had voluntarily turned over my manuscripts to the Chekists, I decided against demonstrating my contempt for him. I thought: "Let him go and exploit my case. Who knows, maybe his conscience will bother him later…" Alas, I was too naive.

On May 22, 1993, I met Dmitry Ryurikov, the Presidential Aide on Foreign Policy Issues. Ryurikov was forthright in stating his objective for meeting me. He was going to travel to the U.S. and could be asked questions there regarding my case, so he decided to get first hand information.

I stated my position on the issues of chemical weapons for the presidential aide and stressed the ugly and improper role the leaders of the military-chemical complex and the Conventional Committee headed by General Kuntsevich had played. They had misinformed President Yeltsin, compelling him to sign the deceitful government resolution of September 1992, regarding the licensing of chemical weapons precursors.[198] Ryurikov listened to me, asked some questions, and didn't try to enter into any discussion with me. We talked for about 40 minutes, and at the end of our conversation I asked him to help Nuria get her passport. He promised assistance and later did his best to help, though everything was in vain, either because of the confusion that prevailed in OVIR (the bureau in charge of issuing foreign travel passports), or because of the unwillingness of officials to help this notorious Tatar "troublemaker".

State Secrets

The summer flew by without any special episodes. On the weekends I went to spend time with my children in Baranovskoe, and on other days I sat in the Investigation Department and copied my case materials, which already had bloated up to five volumes. At night I typed these materials and sent them off to Gale Colby and Irene Goldman in the U.S. Gale was anxious after she read the transcripts of the interrogation and search of Lev Fedorov[199], because she thought my co-author might try to take some kind of action against me in the future. I didn't suppose that Fedorov would dare to do it, because that would mean his final degradation in the eyes of the public. I don't know how and with what pressure my co-author was persuaded, but at the end of August he applied to the Investigation Department to renounce his testimony.

In early September of 1993, one of the coordinators of the ad hoc international movement for my defense, Gale Colby, came to Moscow. She was a plump middle-aged woman with wavy chestnut hair and large brown eyes on her beautiful oval face, and she made a strong impression with her energy and American efficiency. It was a little unusual that she was so simply dressed. It didn't fit in with my conception of American women. It turned out that she knew some Russian, but she was embarrassed about her pronunciation and constant difficulty with Russian grammar forms, genders, cases, etc. We dropped into a cafe on Old Arbat Street and talked for a long time about my case and all the possible scenarios of its development. Gale again expressed her concern about Fedorov's behavior and wondered what he might try to pull at the upcoming trial. I comforted her, because I was certain that my co-author had already exhausted his potential for harmful action, and it made no sense for him to act openly against me. However, it was crucial, in my opinion, that there be an open trial. Gale had brought a selection of related news articles on my case and another invitation for Nuria, so that she could visit the U.S. and receive the prize money from the Cavallo Foundation.

At the end of September, Nuria went to the U.S. and on her way back, she spent a few days in Germany, at the invitation of the organization "Scientists for Global Responsibility." The heads of this organization, Drs. Dieter Meissner and Reiner Braun, had organized a campaign among scientists in Europe for my defense. Their organization had also started providing some much needed financial assistance for my family.

By the end of September, the political situation became extremely edgy in Russia. The Communist opposition was using its typical tactics once more, causing mass disruptions, and they openly started organizing parallel power structures. Rutskoi and Khasbulatov, who were sitting in the Parliament building, started to establish an armed detachment, following the example of the Bolsheviks in 1917. Barannikov, one of the initiators of my case and the KGB chief, became their "Minister of Internal Affairs" and created a squadron of soldiers from the criminal element. Finally, at the beginning of October, when Rutskoi proclaimed himself "President" of Russia and openly called for "smashing" the existing power structure, Boris Yeltsin decided to act decisively against these mutineers. At the time it began, I was home with my two children watching everything that was happening on TV. I won't describe the world famous scenes of the shootout at the White House and capture of the insurgents. Millions of TV-viewers around the world watched these scenes thanks to the courageous staff of CNN.

I was really suffering strongly about the fate of democracy in our country and was greatly pleased that the criminal adventurers were defeated. However, it never occurred to me or to millions of others, that less than a year later these same people would start their subversive activities again, taking advantage of the humanity of the Yeltsin regime. Finally, Rutskoi even became a regional governor...

Soon I saw with my own eyes what strict measures had been taken at the Investigation Department of Lefortovo Prison to reinforce security. Two military men, armed with small machine-guns, sat near the guard who checked the documents of people summoned to the Investigation Department. It was widely known that there were not enough people in the Lefortovo Investigation Department to investigate the coup. I asked Captain Shkarin if he was also in charge of the rebels' case. He said he wasn't.

Next, a lot of information about the rebels' case appeared on television. It turned out that in contrast with ordinary prisoners, these gentlemen were treated with great indulgence. Their lawyers were allowed in to visit them immediately. They started receiving fresh newspapers, food parcels, and many other things. All of this sharply contrasted with the strict regime for ordinary inmates in Lefortovo, for example, for me and my cellmates. I spent 11 days there and never saw my lawyer once. He wasn't even allowed to work on my case. However, the situation was completely different for the mutineers. When one of the frantic deputies was only considering going on a hunger-strike to protest his arrest, the whole country knew about it right away. His wife was shown on TV, with tears in her eyes, as she theatrically described how the health of her insurgent husband had deteriorated. As for the mustachioed Russian Air Force General, the newspapers were saying that this prisoner was about to die from despair and depression.

One of my well-informed acquaintances told me that a lot of these "former" criminals had psychotic fits just because there was no vodka in their food allowances. They had become so very addicted to vodka, while zealously "serving" the Russian people with their lavish drinking sprees in the White House. I am certain that even this "deprivation" was only a temporary inconvenience, because prisoners and jailers were, as they say, cut from the same cloth, and they couldn't let their friends "suffer" too badly. I will return to this theme later, while describing my confinement in "Matrosskaya Tishina" Prison. Any mention of this maximum security facility makes a good many Russians tremble, because it is notorious for its inhumane conditions.

Intuitively I felt that despite all the protests and letters, my case would move along unchanged, because the old system of justice and investigation in Russia was still practically a separate function inside the state. Still, there was hope that the draft of the new Russian Constitution would be approved in the upcoming referendum, and would eliminate all the legal grounds for my case. Article 15 Clause 3 directly proclaimed, "Laws are subject to official publication. Unpublished laws are not to be applied. Any normative legal acts that touch upon the rights, freedom, and responsibilities of a person and citizen, cannot be applied unless they have officially been published for everyone's information."

This was a real hymn to the glory of human freedom. It seemed to me that we only had to wait a bit, and after the new Constitution was adopted, the Attorney General's Office would have to dismiss my case because of the lack of "corpus delicti". There were other pre-conditions for that as well. First, the law about state secrecy which the Supreme Soviet of Russia had adopted during the last days of its existence required that all lists of information of state secrecy be approved by the President of Russia. The law also abolished numerous departmental lists. Secondly, after the Supreme Soviet was dissolved, Valentin Stepankov, the Attorney General of Russia, who by that time had become a pawn in the hands of the leaders of the October coup, was finally dismissed from his position. Aleksei Kazannik, who was famous for his democratic views and honesty, was appointed in his place. Back in 1989 he did not falter in turning over his position in the former U.S.S.R. Supreme Soviet, to the leader of the opposition and the future President of Russia, Boris Yeltsin.

In my heart I was certain that Aleksei Kazannik knew about my case and that he would personally dismiss it as soon as the guilty verdict arrived at the Attorney General's Office. Of course, as a scientist who was used to handling numbers I realized that such an outcome wasn't 100% guaranteed. However, it seemed to me that any other outcome in my case would be unnatural, considering the complex political situation taking shape at the time.

I was very worried and nervous about the wording of the Convention on the Prohibition of Chemical Weapons and the potential for circumventing it. It also seemed to me that although my case became widely recognized because of the violation of basic human rights, the essence of my concerns as expressed in my public statements had not received adequate coverage. I thought about making another statement to the press and drawing the attention of specialists in the West to the issue of chemical weapons. Looking back, again I see how naive I was.

Chapter 21
The KGB Prepares for a Closed Trial

After the November holidays I was summoned once more to the Investigation Department. A document was waiting for my signature, confirming that I had read the case in its entirety. Leaving the department, I bid farewell to Investigator Shkarin (he had been awarded the rank of major by that time), and I offered him my hand for the first time. I even told him that he wasn't the worst investigator, because I had never heard any insulting words from him, and there had been no attempts to provoke me to take irresponsible actions. He seemed pleased, and I tried to imagine how disappointed he would be when the Attorney General didn't sign off on his work, but cancelled it with a flourish.

At the end of November of 1993, Aleksander Asnis called to say I was to go with him to a department of the Attorney General's Office on Kuznetsky Most (Bridge). I thought that would be the long-awaited end to my ordeal. I was sure that we had been summoned so they could hand us the decision about the termination of my case. We met near the Kuznetsky Most Metro Station and quickly reached the Attorney General's Office. I noticed that my lawyer didn't look particularly triumphant, but Aleksander Asnis was always serious. His face seldom expressed any emotions at all.

We entered the hall of the beautiful building, and Asnis made a call on the internal phone. Soon Prosecutor Vladimir Buivolov found us, we greeted each other, and he handed me the text of the final indictment, which had many pages. At that point I realized that nobody had terminated my case, and the KGB flywheel fashioned by Lenin many years ago was still revolving. However, I had no time for further reflection, because Buivolov persistently repeated his request for me to sign for the receipt of this document. I did so automatically, because I must admit I was simply shocked at what was happening. On the street I quickly recovered and gave my full attention to my lawyer, who was describing the scenario of the events to come. A closed session of my case would take place in the Supreme Court of Russia, and the trial was unlikely to start before next year. The court would consist of either a judge and two jurors, or three independent judges, depending on which we chose. I was shocked at what I heard. "Closed trials have been cancelled, haven't they? How it is possible these days that they want to return to the past?" I asked. Asnis explained to me that closed trials had in fact been cancelled, but not closed hearings. The only difference is that the first session and the last one, when the verdict is made public, would be open. I told my lawyer that I would not participate in such monkey business, and he explained that if that was the case I would be arrested, and the trial would be closed anyway.

After I studied the indictment[200] carefully, I came to the conclusion that the trial would be purely a formality, because the general framework for the final indictment had been prepared to rubber-stamp the lists of state secrets and the conclusion of the so-called expert commission. The only real task of the trial was to determine the length of my imprisonment based on Article 75 of the Criminal Code.

Soon I received a copy of the letter that the Supreme Court had sent to the Attorney General's office, which said that there would be a hearing of my case in Moscow City Court on December 6, 1993. Aleksander Asnis told me that he had met with Judge Nikolai Sazonov who would consider my case. He made a reasonably good impression on Asnis. The judge told my lawyer that even though he was still very busy, he was going to read through the case before the New Year, and after that he would schedule a trial date. I was filled with apprehension that my case was just rolling along by itself. It seemed to have a life of its own, and who could stop it? Anyone who thought they could should refer to the letter of the law, and the general advice that those who are dissatisfied should work to make changes in the law, and not complain about those who are just carrying out their duties. I was certain that I had to do something extraordinary to step off this path of destruction. I was sure that my actions would inevitably drag me under the wheels of the tank of the Soviet system of justice, which had not changed much at all when it became the Russian system of justice.

The news from the U.S. showed that many influential public and state figures there were beginning to become a bit alarmed about my case. One of the first letters from this time period is the one written on October 14, 1993 by the U.S. Senator from New Jersey, Bill Bradley, to Strobe Talbot the Ambassador Plenipotentiary to Russia and Special Advisor on issues of the Newly Independent States[201]. In the letter, he stressed that my trial must be open to the public in accordance with Russian law, and he asked Talbot to raise these concerns with the Russian government at a senior level.

On October 19, 1993 John Conyers, Jr., Chairman of the Congressional Legislation and National Security Subcommittee of the Committee on Government Operations sent a letter to Warren Christopher, the U.S. Secretary of State.[202] He wrote, "Dr. Mirzayanov courageously revealed that the Russian government's public call for the elimination of chemical weapons was deceptive, since new chemical weapons research was being secretly funded... The persecution of Dr. Mirzayanov stands in direct contradiction of the Clinton Administration's commitment to strengthen democratization efforts in the former Soviet Union, and halt the proliferation of weapons of mass destruction. I am confident that you share my deep concern over the treatment of this courageous scientist, and I call on you to personally appeal for his release."

Senator Daniel Patrick Moynihan in his letter to the Secretary of State Warren Christopher, on December 23, 1993,[203] expressed his "deep concern regarding Dr. Vil Mirzayanov, a Russian chemist who has been arrested for publishing an article in *Moskovski Novosti* [Moscow News] alleging that the Soviet Union developed and that Russia subsequently tested a new class of organophosphorous nerve gases, which are highly toxic and when are absorbed through the skin or lungs shut down the nervous system, for use as chemical weapons". "If true", continued the senator, "it means Russia may have disingenuously negotiated and signed a treaty on chemical weapons which does not prohibit its newly developed weapon because it is not listed on the detailed schedules appended to the convention." He finished with the conclusion "... President Clinton will be meeting with President Yeltsin in January. Would you not think it appropriate to raise this issue at that time? I look forward to hearing your views."

Dr. Wolfgang Hirschwald a professor of Berlin Free University, wrote an open letter on December 27, 1993, on behalf of the International Network of Engineers and Scientists for Global Responsibility (INES), the largest association of scientists in Germany and Western countries, addressed to Frederico Mayor, the Director General of UNESCO, regarding the violation of human rights and possible violation of the CWC by my trial.[204]

From the fall of 1993 through January 1994, a number of U.S. scientific societies kept their members current on the developments of my case, and they wrote frequently to President Boris Yeltsin and to Attorney General Stepankov and then to Kazannik who replaced him and others, urging that my case be dropped. Especially vigorous among them were the American Chemical Society (ACS), the American Association for the Advancement of Science (AAAS),[205] the Committee of Concerned Scientists,[206] and the New York Academy of Sciences (NYAS).[207] I am pointing out just some of these documents, which show the high level of solidarity of scientists who defended the right of their colleague to speak out on issues of vital global importance.

The New York Academy of Sciences, which I joined in September of 1993, put forth its full effort to make sure the U.S. press reported more actively on my case. On December 6, 1993, Nobel

Prize Laureate Dr. Joshua Lederberg, who was the president of the NYAS wrote a letter to the Executive Director of *The New York Times* Max Frankel.[208]

Human Rights Watch and its sister organization Helsinki Watch, as well as other organizations supporting human rights wrote letters to Russian officials. I was also supported by the Andrei Sakharov Foundation in the United States, which issued a statement on September 15, 1993. They have many famous individuals and political figures and those of whom the world of culture and science is proud, in their membership and on their advisory board and Board of Directors. The statement was signed by Sakharov's step son Aleksey Semyonov.[209]

The mass media was continuing to cover my case[210-252] sympathetically, with very few exceptions.[253, 254] Authors of those few papers were trying to compromise my articles. Surprisingly there was also a pro-Communist reporter in Kazan, who was working to mock and slander me.[255] That was in striking contrast to so many papers expressing huge support for my case in Tatarstan and Bashkortstan.[256-266]

On the eve of my trial, the Moscow media was extremely busy with the upcoming elections of the State Duma and the referendum on the new Constitution. The daily shows on all TV channels droned on about how the rebel chiefs of the failed putsch "suffered" in their cells in Lefortovo. Ruslan Khasbulatov had grown pale. Rutskoi had shaved off his moustache, and he was going to write his memoirs. These were the highlights of the press reports. *Moscow News* was a happy exception, when it published a statement by world-famous Russian public figures Sergei Alekseev, Georgi Arbatov, Yuri Afansiev, Vitali Goldansky, Tatiana Zaslavskaya, Len Karpinsky, Viktor Loshak, Aleksander Pumpyansky, and Grigory Yavlinsky.[267] It's text was striking, expressing anxiety that Russia was trying to back away from democratic principles:

> "During the whole period of the investigation the public was trying to stop the persecution of Vil Mirzayanov, who was saying nothing at all in the press about technical or

other secrets of the new weapons, though he only spoke out about the danger posed to the world by the double standards which were involved in their development, which has continued, even after the Soviet and Russian politicians were mouthing off that work in this area had been terminated... Bitterness and bewilderment are aroused, not only by the fact of such a trial process, but also because it will be a closed one, in a country which was establishing the principles of democracy."

My defenders in America were troubled with the developments of my case, and they energetically worked for my support at a high level. As a result, on January 4, 1994, the Chairman of the U.S. Congressional Committee on Government Operations, John Conyers, made another special statement[268] in which he stated that:

"Secret star chamber proceedings are completely inconsistent with the open democratic society that Russia claims it is in the process of building. The continuation of closed and secret trials in Russia is very disturbing, especially on the eve of the upcoming Summit. Indeed, the treatment of Dr. Mirzayanov stands in stark contrast to the most important purpose of the upcoming summit – the strengthening of Russia's democratic institutions. I have asked Secretary of State Christopher to personally appeal for the release of Dr. Mirzayanov. Whistleblowers on both sides of the now defunct Iron Curtain deserve protection, not prosecution."[269]

Before the New Year, I received a written summons which ordered me to appear for a hearing in the Moscow City Court as a defendant on January 6, 1994 at 11.30 A.M. However, the hearing couldn't begin because my lawyer Aleksander Asnis couldn't attend it. In the middle of December he was in a car accident and suffered a serious concussion. At the beginning of the year, Asnis was still on sick leave, although he was no longer in the hospital. He gave me advice over the phone regarding my strategy in court and said that I should ask to postpone the hearing because of his illness.

State Secrets

On the morning of January 6, Kathleen Hunt, a National Public Radio correspondent from the U.S., who had continuously reported on all the developments of my case in the past, came to see me. She was accompanied by Andrei Mironov and Nazifa Karimova, from the Tatar broadcast "Azatlyk" of "Radio Liberty". We went by trolley bus to the "Novogireevskaya" Metro Station and then quickly reached "Komsomolskaya."

On the way I read an article by Sergei Mostovschikov titled "Chemistry and Life" in the January 6th issue of *Izvestia*.[270] He presented a detailed analysis of the past investigation and its groundlessness, which made the case without merit in his opinion. Judge Nikolai Sazonov declined to comment on the forthcoming trial, saying only that it would be held behind closed doors. The surprised journalist challenged the fact that none of the six witnesses that had to participate in the trial had yet received a subpoena from the court. He also suggested that the trial would be delayed because of the defense attorney's illness. He wrote further that I was apprehensive about the whole situation. If the Ministry of Security brought the case to court, showing such an enviable obstinacy, and even managed to get away with a secret closed trial, it could easily declare that some grounds had been found sufficient for imprisoning me for 2-5 years.

We rose from the metro underground up to Komsomolskaya Square, where Building 43 housed the Moscow City Court.

The morning was frosty, but it had thawed a bit the day before, and so there was a lot of snow and ice under our feet. The entire time we risked falling under the city transport that was briskly weaving between the snowdrifts. We fell down several times, but didn't injure ourselves, and safely reached the doors of the gloomy and rather dirty yellow three-storied house of justice. Although it was still half an hour before the trial, there were quite a lot of reporters on the street with TV camera crews, photojournalists, and microphones. The telegenic leader of the Democratic Union movement, Valeria Novodvorskaya, stood out among the rest. She was famous in the country for her courageous actions against Bolshevik totalitarianism, and had written several highly expressive essays on my case[271-273]. I gave one of them to Investigator

Shkarin, at her request. He had known her when she was a prisoner at Lefortovo.

Although I tried, I still didn't have enough time to answer all of the correspondents' questions. Mostly they were asking about how I was doing, what forecasts I would give regarding the outcome of the trial, and what I felt right before going to the closed trial. Despite serious doubts and the suffering connected with them, I was resolute and didn't feel any traces of fear or regret. I understood that I had a great moral responsibility, and I realized that I must not show any weakness at the trial. Otherwise my behavior would offend the memory of many thousands of fighters against the Fascist-Communist regime.

Apart from correspondents, there were a lot of ordinary people and former veterans and dissidents who had served their terms in the Bolshevik concentration camps. They came up to me, shook my hand, and asked me to believe that I had their support. It was extraordinarily touching, and I will be grateful to them for their warm words and support until my last day.

Then it was time to go inside the court building, up to the second floor, to Room 30, where two policemen stood by the doors. Surrounded by the constant flashes of the photo cameras and the rattling chatter of the TV cameras, I produced my summons, and a policeman went into the room with it. He returned with a young woman, the court secretary. She checked my passport, opened the door, and I entered the room. On the left was the seating for the judge and the two jurors. Opposite there were two rows of benches for the defendants. I went to the front bench, sat in the middle, and waited for the judge to appear. A middle-aged man was sitting near the armchairs of one of the jurors. I decided he must be the prosecutor. There was nobody else in the room. At 11.30 A.M. sharp the secretary coming into the room announced, "Rise, court is in order!" Immediately, the judge and two jurors, a man and a woman, entered.

The judge was a thickset middle-aged man, who had well groomed black wavy hair. He pretended to be an intellectual, but that didn't match up with his poorly concealed expression of conceit and signs of treachery and slyness. The judge announced the beginning of the hearing of my case and added that he, Nikolai Sazonov, would conduct the session. He announced the names of the two jurors. I remembered that people called them "the nodders", because they always nodded their heads as a sign of certain agreement. The judge's tone of speech wasn't flat. I would say that it had the intonations of a participant in a scientific debate. That was how he started his interrogation about my parentage, year of birth, educational background, etc., which was obviously a trivial introduction to the court session. I answered these questions, trying not to give the impression of an ingratiating defendant, and at the same time trying to respond appropriately. The judge asked who would defend me at the trial. I answered and asked for a two week postponement of the trial, in order to give my lawyer the time to recover his health. Then the prosecutor took the floor and said that he represented the Moscow City Prosecutor's Office, however, another prosecutor, Leonid Pankratov, had prepared for the trial, but had caught a cold. The latter become familiar with my case at the request of the City Prosecutor, and he advised that it could take a considerable time to replace him. So he also asked the court to postpone the hearing until the State Prosecutor recovered.

Then the judge asked me what my preference would be for the composition of the court panel, and I answered that I would like to have the three independent judges to conduct the hearing. My choice was unexpected, but it seemed to me that three judges could have different opinions, which could give me some advantage in the long run. After this, the court adjourned for a short recess. Then the judge appeared, accompanied by "the nodders" and read their decision to comply with the request to have three independent judges and to postpone the next court session until January 24, 1994. That concluded the day's business.

I remember that after the conclusion of that session, numerous correspondents entered the courtroom (the judge had dismissed security), and they interviewed Judge Sazonov. He answered their questions with apparent pleasure. In answering a question by Soni Efron from the *Los Angeles Times*, I said that I wasn't going to remain mute during the trial process, and that I wasn't happy at all about the hearing being conducted behind closed doors, because it created a bad precedent for potential dissidents who disagreed with the current regime. However, I didn't know what I personally could do about it.[274]

The radio stations *Mayak, Echo Moskva, Molodezhny Kanal,* [The Youth Channel] and the TV channels *NTV* and *All-Russia Channel Two* reported on the beginning of the trial. Some newspapers published articles during the weeks that followed the beginning of the trial[275-287] and expressed concern about having a closed trial. The majority of them classified the goal of upcoming trial as an attempt by the Chekists to retaliate against me for telling the truth.

Of course, those in power in the U.S. couldn't ignore such statements. Additionally, Gale Colby and Irene Goldman continued to actively inform the American public, the scientific societies, and senators and congressmen about my case. On the evening of the day that the trial process started, Gale called me and asked whether she should come to Moscow and try to do something for my defense. I replied that she would be more effective and helpful by staying in the U.S., and I asked her not to come. She agreed with my arguments, and Gale's and Irene's work helped accelerate the activities of scientific and other organizations working to support me. Almost every day before the trial, which was scheduled for January 24th, I received new statements in my defense by fax.

Prior to January 6, 1994, some people doubted that a closed trial process was possible at all. However, the press clearly saw after the first session, that the old system was very much alive, and it fully intended to ignore the protests against the closed hearing. This put a lot of people strongly on their guard, both in Russia and abroad, because they felt that the events were unfolding in the same sad and familiar ways as they had in Soviet times. Letters addressed to the Russian powers-that-be show this.[288-296]

A letter was sent on January 13, 1994, from the American Association for the Advancement of Science (AAAS) To the Attorney General of Russia, Aleksei Kazannik[288] which insisted that foreign observers be allowed to witness the trial and stressed that "the Mirzayanov prosecution and secret trial is an unfortunate and very surprising throwback to past practices under the totalitarian regime." The Federation of American Scientists (FAS) in its letter emphasized that my case had become a famous one now in the American scientific community, and had been discussed at the highest levels of our two Governments. The FAS asked Attorney General Aleksei Kazannik to ensure that I received a fair trial and expressed hope that the case could be resolved in a respectful way.[289]

The National Academy of Sciences of the U.S. sent a letter to President Boris Yeltsin on January 19, 1994 asking the Russian Government to drop the charges against me "because they are in clear violation of the Russian Constitution."[290] "If the charge is not dropped", they wrote "we would expect the Russian government to grant Dr. Mirzayanov a fair trial, and we would appeal that it be open in accordance with the U.N. Universal Declaration of Human Rights. Dr. Mirzayanov acted on the dictates of his conscience and, if accorded due process, he would be exonerated on the grounds that he exercised his right to the free speech and did not reveal information that was, at the time, officially recognized as a state secret."

The New York Academy of Sciences in its statement on January 20, 1994 said that it "has received notification that Dr. Vil Mirzayanov will be brought to trial for actions protected under international agreements and required under ethical standards of scientific responsibility. We ask that charges against Dr. Mirzayanov be dropped and that international observers be permitted to attend the trial on January 24, 1994."[291]

The influential Committee of Concerned Scientists appealed to Attorney General Aleksei Kazannik once more on January 19, 1994 and asked him to avert a closed trial. "If this trial takes place in camera, it will suggest that Russia has indeed created a new group of binary chemical weapons. We therefore urge in the strongest possible terms to stop this prosecution lest it cast a pall on your country's declared intent to join with other nations in banning the development of chemical weaponry."[292]

I'm very proud that Roald Sagdeev, the famous scientist, physicist and deputy of the USSR Congress of People's Deputies, who together with Andrei Sakharov and Boris Yeltsin took part in organization of the first opposition bloc of deputies in the history of the USSR, sent an appeal to Attorney General Aleksei Kazannik. He wrote: "If we were able to defeat the Cold War and start the complete destruction of chemical weapons what kind of secrets should be hidden from the world public? ... It is not so much guilt, but the tragedy of a whole generation of scientists and engineers forced to spend their talents in making the weapons of mass destruction. The voice of Mirzayanov - the voice of the conscience of a whole generation – must be heard and not strangled." [293]

The Lawyers Committee for Human Rights of the U.S. sent a letter to the President of Russia[294] in which they said that "Mr. Mirzayanov's case is an important test of the Russian government's commitment to respect human rights and build just legal institutions. We urge you to ensure that the courts act as a truly independent branch of government, according to the rule of law and free from government pressure."

The authors of the appeals were well informed about the legal details and meanings of the resolutions of the Russian government, concerning the lists of state secrecy. Gale and Irene helped a lot in this respect, by distributing excerpts from my case materials to many individuals and organizations who could be advocates for me. Individuals who were working on the scientific freedom and responsibility committees of different scientific societies were for the most part unremitting in their support, sending out frequent updates to their vast membership by e-mail. On January 21, 1994, the American organization "Physicians for Social Responsibility" addressed an appeal to Attorney General Kazannik, which was signed by Dan Ellsberg.[295]

A no less legendary man who is rightfully called the "Chinese Sakharov," the famous scientist Fang Lizhi, signed a letter addressed to the President of Russia on behalf of the Committee on the International Freedom of Scientists of the American Physical Society on January 24, 1994.[296] This courageous scientist was one of the leaders of the democratic movement in China and took part in the well-known events in Tiananmen Square in 1989. The Chinese military were going to arrest him for this, but the U.S. Embassy in Beijing saved him, giving the scientist sanctuary in its building. For several years the Chinese authorities prevented Fang Lizhi from leaving the country. However, under pressure from the international community they had to yield and let him emigrate to the U.S. A short review of protests of the American scientific community is given by *Chemical and Engineering News*.[297]

The time remaining before the beginning of the next court session flew by like a shot. Every day there were a few telephone calls requesting me to give interviews, to speak on the radio, or just to comment on the forthcoming trial.

I don't remember turning down any of these requests. Despite great nervous tension, I met with the journalists and these meetings helped me to focus and better articulate my ideas about banning chemical weapons, and to identify what I saw as potential attempts to circumvent the Chemical Weapons Convention.

At that time in my life, before my trial, I read the whole package of international human rights acts for the first time in my life, and I thoroughly studied the new Constitution of Russia.

Everything in these papers indicated that there were no legal grounds for the prosecution of my case. I already wrote that not one of the lists, on which the prosecution was based and conducted, mentioned even a single word about chemical agents or chemical weapons. The situation was supposed to remain exactly the same as it was before, in the newly democratic Russia. The new list of information of state secrecy, adopted by resolution of the Council of Ministers number 733-55 of September 18, 1992, entered into force on January 1, 1993 and is not fundamentally different from the previous document. However, it turned out that my actions interfered with tradition in this area. As a result, this document was amended with a secret resolution- number 256-55 of the Council of Ministers dated March 30, 1993.[298] In this document, things were called by their true names, directly and clearly, as befits a serious legal document. Although Investigator Shkarin didn't directly cite this amendment in the indictment as a basis for my legal proceedings, the very fact that this resolution was included in the criminal case materials shows that it was meant to be used during the trial.

The question remained open: can previous lists, as well as the new list of secrets with amendments be used in a trial? They must be published to come into effect legally. That was the requirement of the new Constitution. This one thought, aside from everything else, literally caused me to burn with indignation. It turned out that the Chekists and the court wanted to carry out an instructive lesson, by using my example, "You can write and adopt various constitutions, but we will manage without them, and we will judge you according to our former rules."

Someone had to try and break this endless vicious circle. But who could do it? We had become accustomed to waiting for someone else to do this for us. This mythic "someone else" is probably smarter than we are, more self sacrificing, has no children or old parents to care for…

My resolve to take action was slowly but surely ripening. I didn't share my vague and still maturing plans with anybody. Unfortunately, at that time I didn't have anyone close to me, with whom I could discuss and consider my intentions. I didn't know how the public, the ordinary people, would react if I threw out a challenge to the "new" system of the Soviet justice.

By that time, my lawyer Aleksander Asnis was rapidly recovering. Soon he was back at work full time, and we often talked on the phone. He was planning to petition the court to appoint a new expert commission, and he was looking for new candidates to be experts. A number of famous scientists agreed to take on that role.

Meanwhile, it seemed that everything in the country and in the world followed its proper course. President Clinton's long-awaited visit to Moscow took place. The State Duma, where supporters of Zhirinovsky and Communists prevailed at that time, gave amnesty to the putsch ring-leaders and participants of the bloody revolt, which had claimed hundreds of victims. The democratic deputies literally sobbed into their microphones, demagogically urging people to stop "dividing everybody into red and white camps." Translated into normal language, this was an appeal for honest and decent people to join forces with the criminals. Social demagogy had never reached such a pinnacle, even during the times of the Communist regime. The new Attorney General was completely preoccupied with solving this "nationwide" job. It was clear that nobody had time to attend to my case…

Chapter 22
Trial and Prison

Prosecutor Pankratov and the Judges

My day in court began on January 24, 1994 at 10.30 A.M. Nobody accompanied me this time, and I reached the courthouse alone. There was a lively group of Russian and foreign correspondents and television reporters milling about outside the courthouse, and my lawyer Asnis was already answering their questions. Valeria Novodvorskaya was there with her lads from the Democratic Union movement. We warmly greeted each other and posed for the photojournalists. I told the reporters that this day was a test for the new Russian Constitution, which had been developed with such difficulty. A great number of people in Russia and the rest of the world placed their hopes on this document.

Two policemen were standing by the doors of the courtroom, and we went inside and took our seats. I sat down on the defendants' bench and Asnis took a seat in the lawyer's section, not far from me. The prosecutor's place was occupied by an elderly man of retirement age, with sparse gray hair, who was missing his left arm. He was dressed in a prosecutor's uniform, and as you could tell from his medals and ribbons that he was clearly a disabled veteran of the Great Patriotic war (WW II). Soon we heard: "Rise. Court is in order!" Judge Nikolai Sazonov appeared, followed by a light-haired woman, and a tall powerful man, stooped over under the weight of seven thick volumes which he carried under his arm. I was surprised and wondered why there were seven volumes, instead of the five that I had read.

Quickly, I got it. The investigator was trying to make the case seem more weighty and significant, by adding two more volumes. Judge Sazonov proclaimed the opening of the hearing of my criminal case, which would be heard before a judicial panel consisting of Nikolai Sazonov, Valentina V. Laricheva, and Victor G. Yudin, Court Secretary T.V. Pankratova, and with the participation of Prosecutor Leonid S. Pankratov and lawyer Aleksander Ya. Asnis.

When the judge asked if I had any questions or petitions, I stood up and delivered a prepared speech listing my petitions. I declared that the investigation was putting an accusatory spin on my case, and it was obviously biased with the clear goal of putting me - the defendant - in jail at any cost, and in this way frightening possible future opponents of the leaders of the military-chemical complex. Departmental lists of information of state secrecy were being used for that, as well as the so-called List of Major Information of State Secrecy. I added that these are classified documents and were not attached to my case, so my lawyer and I didn't have any way to dispute them. However, the major point was that these normative acts had not been published. This is a direct violation of the Paragraph 3 of Article 15 of the Constitution of the Russian Federation, which gives the precise definition, "Any normative legal acts that touch upon the rights, freedom, and responsibilities of a person and a citizen, cannot be applied unless they have officially been openly published for everybody's inspection."

In my first petition I asked the court to recognize these normative acts and the secret lists of state secrecy as null and void on constitutional grounds. Additionally, I asked the court to cancel the closed hearing of my case, because it contradicted Article 14 of the Universal Declaration of Human Rights and Articles 9-10 of the International Covenant on Civil and Political Rights. My lawyer Alexander Asnis and I filed numerous petitions, including one in which we asked the prosecution to show us the "special purpose program" in the interests of the defense of the country and its results, which I had allegedly disclosed information about. Up to that time, it had not been done, so I asked the court to comply with my second request to show me that program, so that I could finally find out what it was that I had disclosed. Also, since a majority of members of the expert commission formed by "the investigation" were representatives of an interested party, I asked the court to appoint a new, and this time independent, commission.

As a long-time lecturer, I usually tried to observe the reaction of the audience while I was delivering my speech. The face of Judge Sazonov expressed a mixture of deep indifference, along with a dash of undisguised disgust. He obviously thought that I was speaking for the sake of propaganda, like a demagogue who was accustomed to rattling on, no matter who was listening. Judge Yudin tried hard to show the magnanimity and condescension of a prominent individual toward some feeble man. The face of Judge Laricheva openly expressed disapproval, as if she wanted to say, "We'll see what tune you'll sing when we throw the whole book at you." The face of the prosecutor was the most animated one. It clearly expressed exasperation that in this hall of justice, and what was even worse, in his - the prosecutor's - presence, someone dared to challenge the system, that pursued only one objective, that of protecting his sacred State from criminal actions. "We are the bosses here, and you will be very sorry about your eloquence!" Pankratov's expression cried out.

The judge gave the floor to my defense attorney. Aleksander Asnis insisted that a new expert commission be appointed because the current one, in his opinion, hadn't researched the technical aspects of the case. Since the findings of this commission were the basis for the indictment, Asnis asked the court to send the case back to the Attorney General's Office for additional research. He also submitted a petition to summon General Smirnitsky and Colonel Chugunov as witnesses for the defense.

My lawyer's speech was precisely well reasoned, with references to various articles of the Russian Criminal and Procedural Code and to explanations and elaborations that we received from the Scientific Research Institute for Legal Expertise, in response to a request from my lawyer.

The judges and the prosecutor listened to Aleksander Asnis's speech with open scorn, taking advantage of the fact that there were no auditors in the room. However, my lawyer was used to scenes like that, and he wasn't confused by it. The prosecutor took the floor. In contrast with Asnis' speech, there was no logic at all in his words. It was perfectly clear that he hadn't read the case, and he had no clue about the laws protecting state secrecy or the lists of secrets, etc. You can judge for yourself.

"Dear comrades," began Pankratov. "The main point of the petition of the defendant and his lawyer appears to be a request to return the present criminal case for additional investigation. In the name of evaluating all of the materials of the investigation, they have focused their attention on the findings of the expert commission. They say, this is not good, that is not good. Why isn't it a subject for discussion?" grumbled the war veteran sullenly as if he were actually quoting us. "The prosecution believes that this is a flawed approach," he whined. "We are only in the preliminary stage of the trial process. We can't produce objective evidence. Our task is to evaluate everything in the process."

In the words of the prosecutor, all our petitions about compliance with principles of constitutionality and about "the experts" were none of my damn business. Then he recited his ritual mantra, which had nothing to do with my case, but which probably had always served him well in the past. "The defendant and the lawyer are ahead of the schedule. We haven't heard from the expert commission. Have we invited the experts? No, we haven't. How can we go ahead of the schedule? How can we talk about it?" the prosecutor kept grumbling incoherently. "I don't see any reasons to claim that the preliminary investigation has violated any fundamental principles of preliminary investigation. Let us go further!" Our arguments didn't exist for him. "Special purpose programs and Mirzayanov!" the prosecutor was terrified. "This is at least immodest."

I realized then that a simple loud-mouthed bossy soldier stood before me, poorly educated and, therefore dangerous. Then, he touched upon a subject that was much closer to his heart. This had to do with the numerous correspondents and the public, who had assembled in the hallway in front of the courtroom. He didn't like that at all. "How can it be possible that they take pictures so freely and without any permission, and they even express their indignation?" questioned the prosecutor. Still, his train of thought was as clear as could be. He presumed and implied that the defendant was obviously under some "alien" influence, if he jabbered on so freely about the Constitution, democracy, and the UN.

That is why Pankratov stubbornly decided to cut short any of Aleksander Asnis' or my attempts to call into question the actions of the Ministry of Security, the Attorney General's Office, and the court. "I understand what caused this - in the press, outside in the hall. I observed the press people - democrats who are always going everywhere and looking for violations of the law in the Prosecutor's Office, in the Ministry of Security, and in the court. Well there are none - period! We are fighting crime and protecting the State."

Then he started giving out directives, "The President must approve the lists as required by the "law on state secrets." These are the President's functions according to the law. He must also determine the list of officials who must think about this. However, I can say that this law practically repeated everything that existed before October of 1992." These were orders for the judges, so they didn't have to rack their brains over some questions concerning legality. He finished his incoherent speech with the categorical pronouncement, "Russia exists, not the Soviet Union. The President said that secrets are also important for Russia, as they were for the U.S.S.R. I mean his decree of 1992. So we proceed from that; we dance to that. Not one of the petitions can succeed, except for [the one about] the two witnesses. I don't see."

Nothing unexpected took place. Everything was completely familiar, as if I had stood trial and listened to the prosecutor for my whole life. I felt something welling up inside of me, stifling me, and tearing my heart to pieces. The judge announced a recess and we went out into the hallway. A lot of correspondents met us and swamped us with their questions, which my lawyer answered. I had probably spent too much of my energy in the courtroom and couldn't answer their questions adequately. I was only thinking about how to respond properly to everything that had taken place in the courtroom.

For that reason I wasn't attentive to the journalists or to Valeria Novodvorskaya, who came up to me. It was a different matter for Asnis who, with his usual merciless and precise manner, was spewing out acid and sarcastic commentary about everything that was going on. However, when Vladimir Uglev appeared in front of me with a pale face, and said in a nervous voice that he was ready to disclose the formulas of the chemical agents A-230 and A-232, if "these beasts" didn't cancel the trial, I quickly recovered myself. No. I had never disclosed state secrets, and I did my best in every way to avoid being accused of that. Could secret information really be disclosed? No, this was absolutely unacceptable to me. I immediately told Uglev that I would never agree with such an action. From the very beginning I always tried to show that it was possible to talk about the issues without disclosing the essence of the matter. However, I saw that I didn't convince Uglev. His mind was made up, and so I asked that he not refer to me or involve me in any such actions, not because I was afraid of the consequences, but because in my opinion, it would be a dishonest move, in my efforts to get my point across.[299]

I tried going outside to get a bit of fresh air and privacy, and to think about what I could do that day to stop the tank of the Soviet "justice" system that was about to roll over me. But I heard the voice of the court secretary again, announcing that the break was over and the trial session would resume. As we were entering the courtroom, I heard Valeria Novodvorskaya exclaim, "Look, prosecutor! How many people have you sent to their execution?" Probably this was the most terrible question for prosecutors and she knew it. I was certain that the court would reject all our petitions, and I wasn't mistaken. Everything played out exactly as the prosecutor expected. The court secretary started reading the indictment in a woeful tone. Although I had studied this document many times before, I heard it quite differently this time, with some threatening intonations.

State Secrets

The prosecutor was perched at his post with an inert expression. From time to time, when he was turning over the pages of my case with his right hand, the empty left sleeve of his service jacket quivered. Judge Nikolai Sazonov personified absolute indifference during the reading. Judge Yudin was attentively reading the newspaper *Moscow News* with my article. However, Judge Laricheva couldn't restrain her emotions. From time to time she shook her head, which evidently meant, "Aye, aye, aye! How could he stoop to such a low level in life?" When the indictment had been read, Sazonov announced a lunch break until 2.30 P.M.

There were few people in the hallway outside the courtroom. Almost all the journalists had left, as they no longer expected a sensation. I was asked to give an interview for the *Youth Channel* radio, and for some foreign newspaper. I talked with the journalists and then went outside with Asnis to see where we could have a bite to eat.

I didn't really want to eat, so I contented myself with a glass of tomato juice in the nearest grocery store. Suddenly I realized that my decision had crystallized and I would act without hesitation because I had no illusions left. The judges and the prosecutor shouldn't hope that I would submissively wait for their decision, which they had already prepared ahead of time. I decided that I would not willingly participate in their shameful game, while they demonstratively trampled on the Constitution of the country. In essence, they were criminals themselves if they openly ripped apart the *fundamental law* of Russia, for which a lot of blood had already been spilled, in Moscow's streets during the October 1993 events.

I had to put an end to the overt contempt for the law in the courtroom. Sure, the U.S.S.R. Constitution was a demagogic document, and everybody in our country knew that it was all empty words. But now, when we began creating new laws to live by, for life itself, not for propaganda purposes, they were making a scapegoat out of me - a scientist and a confirmed democrat. They used my case to mock everything that I was fighting for, and I could not tolerate that. I had two small sons, and there was no one besides me who could feed them and raise them. When I thought about it, tears welled up in my eyes, and I stopped and tried to calm my disobedient heart which was pounding violently. Still, I managed to keep it all under control and soothe my pain by pressing the little finger on my left hand, as experienced doctors recommended.

I was already calm when I met Asnis, who was hurrying back to the courthouse after his lunch. I thought that he would try to talk me out of my decision, though I would be steadfast. I told him about my decision and added that it was final. Asnis saw that I was really suffering, and he didn't bother me with any unnecessary questions. He was amazingly sensitive and probably realized that I was adamant. He only told me that he respected my position, although he didn't share it. He added that of course it was my decision and his duty was to act in accordance with my wishes. I found myself in total solitude. Possibly my decision was a bit crazy. I felt totally detached from the outside world. Fortunately, my strength hadn't left me, and I even tried to smile when I entered the courtroom.

The judges showed up and returned me to reality. Judge Sazonov asked if anyone had questions regarding the court proceedings, and I stood up and asked to be allowed to make a statement. "Please!" replied Sazonov condescendingly.

I hadn't prepared a written statement. I decided that I could manage without that. I will remember my brief speech and statement for the rest of my life. I was in total control of myself while I was speaking, and I managed to hold the emotions that were surging inside of me in check. This is what I said:

> "Sirs and Madame Judges and Mr. Prosecutor!
> Today you have rejected all of my and my lawyer's petitions. You even declined the request to look into the unconstitutionality of the secret lists of information of state secrecy. I am an ordinary citizen, who has for his whole life observed the law and has lived honestly. But, today you have involved me in a process which has only one name - lawlessness. The fact that you rejected our petitions clearly demonstrates overt contempt for the *fundamental law* of the

Russian Federation - the Constitution. Maybe it was possible to debate its strong and weak points, before the referendum took place and it was signed by the President of Russia. But, today you are openly ignoring the Constitution. You have showed that your Communist convictions come first above everything else. In the situation which has developed, I can't be an accomplice to the criminal activity that you commit together with the prosecutor, whose duty it is to oversee the observance of the laws of the Russian Federation. That is why I refuse to take part in this criminal process of my own free will, so as not to become a party to it. I am announcing that I will not come to any more of its sessions."

The expression of Judge Laricheva showed that she was about to explode from the anger that was overwhelming her. The prosecutor was full of hatred towards me. If he could have had his way, he would have had me shot on the spot. Sazonov was unflappable. However, he summoned his strength and asked sarcastically, "Is that all?" I answered that it was. Then he announced that he was cutting short the session and asked me to sign a notice. The secretary immediately filled out the form of the notice and I signed for its receipt.

Everything became very clear. If I didn't show up for court the next day (on January 25, 1994), then I would be arrested and brought there by force. That is, of course, if I didn't take off. But such a thought didn't even occur to me. My statement proved to be a sensation for the journalists. A few of them were still waiting around for the session to finish. They asked me if I knew what the consequences of my decision would be. Asnis was a bit upset, and it seemed to me that he still thought that my non-participation could take a different form. For example, I could simply refuse to answer any questions. No, I was firmly resolved not to come to the courtroom of my own free will, and I told the reporters about it. At home that evening, I answered the telephone calls from journalists of various publications, explaining my position. I stressed that I wasn't showing disrespect to the court as an institution of justice.

My decision was forced upon me, because I had no other means at my disposal to defend myself as a citizen, in facing people who openly flouted the *fundamental law* of the country - its Constitution. I tried to explain this by referring to the decision of the U.S. judge who had immediately thrown out Dan Ellsberg's case, when he discovered that the Constitution had been violated. The U.S. judges respect the *fundamental law* of their country, and so must it be in our country, in Russia, which is building a democratic society.

That evening Asnis called to tell me that a press conference would take place on January 26th, with our participation in the building that housed the Russian American Information Press-Center on Khlebny Pereulok. I called Nim Naum, the assistant of Aleksei Simonov, who had to be the chairman, to learn the details of the upcoming meeting. I realized that it could be my last meeting with the press, and I decided that I shouldn't be arrested before that time.

My Second Arrest

I spent that evening and the night at home. On the morning of January 25th I got up early and hurried to the kiosk for the latest newspapers. Unfortunately, I didn't find any articles in them about the beginning of my trial. However, I found out later that Fred Hiatt had responded to my case with an article in *The Washington Post* on January 25, 1994.[300] The journalist informed the American public about the beginning of my closed trial and briefly stated the underlying reasons for it, including my claim that the court was violating Russia's Constitution, by using unpublished and therefore not legally valid laws, to prosecute me. He also said the case had already awakened concern in the U.S. about the regression of democracy in Russia. He told that according to my lawyer, I had refused to answer questions, after the judge rejected my appeal about the court's violation of the Constitution of Russia. Hiatt said that Prosecutor Leonid Pankratov surprised many people when he appeared in court in a "military-style three-star uniform" and declined to answer reporters' questions. When human rights activists who waited for him in the hallway of the courthouse asked him questions, Pankratov, according to the journalist, replied, "Get out of my way. Keep your stupidities to yourself."

Fred Hiatt also reported that members of the US legislature, including Senator Daniel Moynihan and Congressman John Conyers, had appealed to the Clinton administration seeking to raise a discussion of this case in the bilateral negotiations. He reported that my lawyer Aleksander Asnis had stressed that he was refused access to some relevant documents in the case, though he was shown others for only a short time, without being allowed to take notes. "'This violates Mr. Mirzayanov's right of defense and significantly impinges on my ability to defend him,' Asnis said."

After breakfast I went for a walk near the house with my younger son Sultan. He was a little sick and didn't go to kindergarten that day. Asnis called and told me about the court session, which had been brief because I hadn't appeared. The judge passed a resolution requiring me to be brought to the court by force. Then Asnis and I agreed to meet that evening in the legal advice office where he worked.

However, our meeting never took place. Around 5 P.M., when I was getting ready to go meet with my lawyer, the doorbell rang again. I looked through the peephole and saw two OMON (a SWAT-like police squad) officers armed with automatic weapons. The policemen said that they were from Moscow Police Department 139. I opened the door without further question, because the futility of the situation was clear, and I was prepared for this outcome. They entered the apartment and one of those large men said that I should get ready to proceed to the police department, and showed me the order of the Moscow City Court, which said that I should be brought by force to the Courtroom #30 at 10:30 A.M. on January 26, 1994. I started to get dressed, but then my wife Nuria intervened. She demanded to see the paper and exclaimed, "It says here that he should be brought to the courtroom by 10.30 A.M. on January 26, and not to the police department. What is the date today and what time is it now? This is an obvious violation of the order and willfulness!"

Then I also realized that I would have to pass the night in the police department, in some stinking, filthy and overcrowded cage, without food or drinking water. This is why I immediately exclaimed, "Guys! They will expose you and everybody will ask you how legal your actions were. Besides, I doubt you are the ones you pretend to be. Why don't you have written instructions from your boss?" A shadow of doubt immediately crept into the ruddy, round and mustachioed face of the OMON officer. He went to the telephone in the kitchen, called his boss, and explained our arguments. He also added that I had demanded written orders from the head of the police department. Probably the boss had also started doubting his actions and backed off. The OMON officer nodded to his cohort, "Let's go!" I got a reprieve to think about the situation that was developing. I realized that I would be arrested in any case. However, I had promised to go to the press conference and I didn't have the heart to ruin it. I decided to leave the house immediately and go see my lawyer. Everything would become clear after that. Sergei Mostovshchikov colorfully described this in the January 26, 1994 evening edition of the newspaper *Izvestia*. According to Sergei, the police came to my apartment at 6.15 A.M. and at 8 A.M. the next day, but failed to find me at home.[301]

So I went to the legal advice office at 6 P.M., but Asnis wasn't there. His secretary asked me to wait. Finally, my lawyer came back at about 7 P.M. and told me the news. First, the court was literally shocked by my decision. Second, Asnis had met with Aleksei Kazannik, the Attorney General, who had warned my lawyer that a meeting of the Attorney General with the defense counselor during the trial was extraordinary. This is why Alexander Asnis asked me to tell no one about this meeting. I kept my word about it for many years. Asnis said that he saw my case on the Attorney General's desk. Kazannik was concerned about my case, which he hadn't yet read. He promised to read it quickly in order to be able to say something specific about it.

When Asnis was leaving Kazannik's office, he saw Prosecutor Pankratov, who in his opinion wasn't there by chance. All of that was reassuring, but there was nothing specific there to encourage me. I made up my mind to be firm and consistent with my decision. I had to act in such a way so as not to disgrace myself, but to intensify pressure on the powers that be of this world, in order to have my case thrown out. Asnis asked me to reconsider and think everything over again. However, I had made my decision and I wasn't going to deviate from my course. We agreed to meet at the press conference, if I hadn't yet been arrested by that time.

Then I called my daughter Elena from the law office, and said that I would go to her place, which was on Leninski Prospect, and spend the night in her apartment. Just in case, I gave her phone number to my lawyer, so that he could give it to any interested journalists and other people I knew well. Of course I knew that the office telephone was tapped by the Chekists, but I was sure that they would cooperate with the local police only in exceptional cases - for instance in an escape attempt or something like that.

Early the next morning reporters started calling and asking for interviews, and soon some of them showed up at my daughter's apartment. The American journalist Kathleen Hunt asked how I was feeling before being arrested. I said that it reminded me of the wait before a surgical procedure.

I went to Khlebny Pereulok with my son-in-law, businessman Oleg Orlov and his two sturdy associates. We had to be very vigilant about possible provocations in that situation. I arrived an hour before the appointed time and met Asnis. He told me about his trip earlier that day to the court, which had made a decision regarding my behavior. Sergei Mostovshchikov wrote about it in *Izvestia*.[302] According to the journalist, it was clear that significant positive changes had taken place. In particular, when the question of my arrest was discussed, and some felt that I should be brought to the courtroom by force, but Prosecutor Pankratov, who had long ago insisted on this measure, abruptly changed his mind and no longer supported this idea. Referring to the Moscow human rights activist, Andrei Mironov, Mostovshchikov wrote that this metamorphosis in the prosecutor was a result of the fact that Attorney General Aleksei Kazannik had been informed about the trial in detail. The journalist thought that information concerning the dubious quality of the compromising material found by the former Ministry of Security, hadn't made it through to Kazannik, and had been blocked by his subordinates. It is difficult to say, Sergei Mostovshchikov ironically continued, how one could be ignorant of a case which was reported in all the newspapers of the country. Still, it was so and even the court was in a state of confusion. The next court session was scheduled only for February 3rd, providing support for Mostovshchikov's theory. I must add that Nikolai Sazonov, as an experienced judge, reckoned the defendant would become "prudent" after he had spent more than a week in jail.

There were many people at the Russian American Information Press Center for the press conference, and there were no vacant places in the hall. Representatives of various information agencies, radio, and television, as well as numerous newspapers, constantly asked questions and took pictures. Aleksei Simonov presided over the meeting. Everything seemed extremely clear: my closed trial was a challenge to the new Constitution of Russia and a test of the emerging democratic society as well. My lawyer reported that earlier in the day Judge Sazonov had decided to have me arrested for contempt of court, and this made the press conference more dramatic. Asnis also thought it was possible that I could be arrested right at the doors of this building, though I thought that was unlikely, because OMON officers really don't like having their pictures taken by the press.

I went home after the press conference. I had decided to let them take me from my home. My son-in-law and his lads accompanied me to 4 Stalevarov Street, to the porch of my apartment.

"Matrosskaya Tishina"

At home, I had a good night's sleep and was calm the following morning. Nuria was suffering from her usual migraine attack, so I had to content myself with tea instead of breakfast. My elder son Iskander went to school early in the morning, and young Sultan stayed at home. Out of the habit I went to the kiosk, read the newspapers on a bench near our apartment building, and then I came back to the apartment, planning to call some people. As time dragged on, the wait was extremely aggravating, but nobody came to arrest me. I read children's fairy-tales to Sultan, and then he started drawing his race cars and space ships... Nuria was prostrate with a white kerchief binding up her head.

Around midday, we heard the doorbell ring, and this time everything was routine: an arrest warrant was produced, with an order to prepare for the trip to jail. The policemen didn't know which jail. They only knew that they had to take me to bedraggled Police Department 139, which had certainly seen better days. It was very close to my apartment block. I was very ashamed in front of Sultan, because he had watched plenty of movies in which various criminals and bandits were arrested. If his father was arrested, there was something wrong. As we say in Russia, they don't throw people in jail for good deeds. Thanks to television every child knows that, and of course my son was no exception. He watched with horror as finely muscled young men with automatic weapons came to take his father away.

It would be a good idea to take some underwear and clothes, I thought mechanically. However, I realized that I was causing my child psychological trauma, so it would have been an inexcusable cruelty to prolong the scene he had to witness. I quickly put on a ski sweater, a light overcoat, a ski cap, and old winter boots that had already lost their original lining a long time ago.

"Hands!" ordered the OMON officer. I didn't understand. However, when he barked the word out again, I saw the unmistakable threat and the resolve in his eyes to knock me down with a shattering blow. Then it dawned on me - he wanted to handcuff me. I dutifully obeyed. My son's eyes were wide open and full of terror. Tears were running down his cheeks. He cried without a sound like old men do.[303]

Finally, Nuria got a bit of control over her migraine and got up to close the door after us. I purposefully went to the door, trying not to look back at Sultan any more. I didn't even have any strength left to tell him, "I'm sorry." Probably I cried, too, but without tears or sobbing. When we were descending the stairs, one policeman with an automatic weapon went ahead of me and the other behind me.

A small paddy wagon was waiting for us in the street. Mechanically, involuntarily, my gaze went up to the kitchen window of my apartment on the fourth floor. I saw my Sultan's little face and quickly turned away. I wasn't able to wave good-bye to him. A lot of residents of my apartment building were watching all this from a distance.

I was glad that the policemen didn't bow my head down, while I was getting into the car as police in the U.S. sometimes do in the movies.

The car stopped in the yard of the Police Department 139, and I was ordered to get out. I was taken through a first floor corridor, which reeked of rats and urine, to the officer on duty, who was sitting behind a barred window. The OMON officer who had escorted me gave the duty officer some paperwork and opened the door to a room screened off from the corridor by glass squares covered with white oil paint.

A drunken middle aged man was crying in the room there, saying that he was the former hockey player "K". I could hardly recognize the famous sportsman who used to play so well on the trade union team. After that he was a hockey referee for a long time. However, the cruel twists of fate in this sportsman's life finally broke him. He had become an inveterate alcoholic, although something remained of his appearance that showed he wasn't an ordinary citizen. His clothes were clearly made abroad and were of a very high quality. You couldn't just go into a store and buy them in Russia. Also, he smoked Camel cigarettes. Soon one of the sportsman's relatives came and took him away. I was left alone.

I could hear the duty officer calling someone and asking what he should do with "this Mirzayanov." However, the jail mechanism worked slowly, and nobody was in a hurry to "place" me anywhere. The wait was long and agonizing, and no one offered me anything to drink or a chance to use the restroom. About five hours passed. Finally, the officer opened the cell door and commanded, "Hands!" They handcuffed me, which meant that they would take me to a prison. I didn't even ask which jail. What was the difference, as it no longer depended on me? We drove around Moscow for a long time and, the car finally stopped near a red building. One of the guards went up to the building and soon he came back and explained some-

State Secrets

thing to the driver. I realized that neither the driver nor the guard knew their way.

Eventually, the car stopped near an arch with large iron-clad gates. We drove a few dozen meters further, stopped again and I was ordered to get out. Somewhere people were loudly and constantly shouting, like at a construction site. However, here the voices were anxious. They were taking some kind of a roll call, calling out names. Construction debris and some other trash was scattered about near the walls of the building. The OMON officer opened the iron door and showed a paper to the sentry inside. We went a few meters down the corridor, and I saw many men dressed in dirty military uniforms sitting behind a poorly illuminated wooden barrier. The room was full of gray tobacco smoke and the stench was a mixture of foul odors and vodka.

The ceiling was of an uncertain color, with some hints that it could have once been white. The walls were once painted green, but there was almost no paint left, and you could see the yellowish lime of peeling plaster. On the remaining surfaces there were huge patches of mold. Drunken eyes were glittering in the dim light, and I realized that I was in the famous jail with the lyrical name, Matrosskaya Tishina. This prison was probably originally constructed as a rest home for sailors, and the name translates as "Sailors' Silence", though its official name is "Investigation Isolator IZ-48/1." Isolators are special prisons constructed during Soviet times, which were used mainly for detaining political prisoners and espionage suspects. This maximum security prison in recent years has also held its share of chronic and extremely violent criminals.

The OMON officer gave my papers to the officer on duty and took off my handcuffs. I was ordered to follow a guard along the corridor. He took me to a cell where there were already a few people, and ordered me to take off all my clothes and to give them to the security guards who were sitting behind a window. I understood that they wanted to make a search. I had few clothes on and hadn't taken anything with me. This was a great blunder. Quickly I removed my clothes and handed them through the window, with my boots. Soon they gave me everything back except my scarf, belt, a little money and the keys to my apartment. I got dressed. It was cold and reeking of sweat and sewage.

Soon I was taken to a different cell which was about 30 square meters. Almost all the window panes behind the iron bars were broken, and a few benches stood near the walls, firmly fastened to the concrete floor, which was black with coagulated dirt. The toilet was near the door on a small platform. A few people were sitting on the floor of the cell enjoying a lively conversation. They paid no attention to my "hello." I sat down on one of the benches and waited to be taken to a different cell. Officers from Police Department 139 had kept my watch, so it was difficult to say what time it was.

More and more people were brought into the cell. Soon it grew warmer, and it became incredibly stuffy. After a while, the cell was completely full of people! A small Chinese man, who didn't know a word of Russian, was sitting on the floor near me, yet a fidgety snub-nosed fellow was loudly trying to explain something to him, by mispronouncing Russian words, so that they sounded like Chinese. A young Korean was lying not far from me, and a young man from the Caucasus Region, with a swollen hand, was continuously rushing around. Groaning with pain, he was squeezing between the other prisoners, who were standing, sitting, and lying around. Judging by appearances, all the prisoners were young, mostly in the 20-35 year age range.

Soon three people made themselves comfortable on the floor near my seat and animatedly discussed their stories of murders, which they asserted they were not guilty of. "Of course, I did them in, those assholes. What else could I do?" one was saying to another. "And it is not the first time, either. So what? I did my time for the last one. OK, let me do my time now. You know, I didn't do it on purpose, it just happened. Something is wrong with my nerves and my head."

Another fellow spoke in turn, about his murders, which were a mere trifle, in comparison with what Stepa had done.

"You know who I am talking about," he added. Then he concluded with a hint of envy, "And Stepa got off, escaped a death sentence because they recognized he was crazy."

I tried not to listen to these heart-rending confessions, but there was no place to disappear to. I realized that if I got up from my seat I would lose it forever.

Soon it became so crowded in the cell that it was no longer physically possible to walk or lie down. I understood that a lot of prisoners among us were brought to Moscow for forensic psychiatric examinations. These people were sharing their experience, about how to pass those exams successfully, in order to avoid execution.

Despite the lack of space, a group of young people formed a circle on the floor, pulled a few tea packages out of their large bags, and put the tea into a large mug. One of them moved between the human bodies, making his way to the toilet. There was no waste tank there, and water was just pouring continuously from the pipeline into the toilet. The young prisoner wasn't bothered by that at all. He put his tin mug to the outlet of the pipe and scooped up dirty water with a habitual movement. Meanwhile, another man was tearing his towel into strips and braiding long wisps from the shreds. They poured the water from the toilet into the mug with the tea and set fire to the wick. The cell filled with terrible smoke which was extremely irritating to my eyes. It became impossible to breathe at all in the cell. "Thank goodness, the window glass is broken," I thought.

Soon the water started crackling and gurgling. It was leaping up, over the brim of the mug, burning the hand of the prisoner who was holding it. They exclaimed in excitement, "That's it! Oh, Baby!" Through the smoke and burning, I smelled an unusual odor that reminded me of strong tea. They wrapped the mug in the towel, let it stand for a while, and then started drinking. They were slowly taking tiny sips, holding the liquid in their mouths for a long time. This was the famous "chefir" (a very strong brew of tea used as a drug).

Soon the eyes of these chefir drinkers started to sparkle, and they started laughing and talking, interrupting each other, telling about their conquests of sluts. It was clear that they didn't care about this jail, the incredibly stuffy and cramped cell, or the strange people around them. One of them turned in my direction and exclaimed, "My goodness! What are you doing here, Father?

People of your age don't go to jail!"

Apologetically I tried to explain the essence of my case. They got interested. Probably they remembered something. One of them muttered that he had heard about some chemist.

"Well, then it is all wrong!" he concluded. Our cell door opened and a stocky elderly bald man appeared. The prisoners immediately gave him a spot on the bench and were very attentive to him. My neighbor saw my surprise and explained that this was famous Nikolai K., who had spent 29 years in jail. Now he "had come back" to jail after a few years "on the outside", because he failed to adapt to a life of freedom. He had killed his mistress with a knife in a drunken brawl. She had also served a few terms in prison. When Nikolai looked at me with almost reptilian indifference, I closed my eyes unable to turn away from his experienced glance. It seemed to me that he understood who I was, and his practiced eye had determined that I was a first-timer and an intellectual. He didn't need to disguise his disdain. I had heard a lot of stories about fierce criminals who bullied intellectuals in jail, and I was expecting something horrible. Maybe they would test me, then beat me. Time stretched out forever, and I was terribly thirsty. I didn't move from my place. My feet had become numb a long time ago, and I tried to rub them. I had to get up and try to stomp them. It helped a bit, but my place was immediately occupied. I thought that, after all, other people were standing around and nobody had fallen down yet, so somehow I would get through this ordeal.

One guy had managed to keep his watch and told his neighbor that it was 3 A.M. I was appalled that it was so early and that we would have to wait so long before we could be moved to our cells, get a bed, and get a little rest. Most of the prisoners around me were sleeping. Some slept sitting or stretched out on the floor, and some slept standing up. The electric light wasn't dimmed at night, so it was very difficult to determine the passage of time. The only difference was that at night the voices in the yard were more audible. The prisoners explained to me that the cells exchanged the latest prison news with each other – about who was placed in which cell, when, and whether there were untrustworthy people or "authorities" around. Later Aleksei Kostin explained it to me in detail.

During his preliminary four-year confinement in Matrosskaya Tishina, Aleksei had become familiar with the full details of prison life.

Finally, the door opened and security guards appeared. They looked very sinister and were holding batons and handcuffs in their hands. The eyes of the first guard who entered were red, and along with his unshaved mug this was evidence that he hadn't yet recovered from a drinking spree the day before.

"Stand up!" he bawled out, although without exception we were all on our feet as soon as we heard the door with the iron bars opening. The man from Caucasus Region, whose hand was wracked with pain, was closer to the door than everyone else. He was just getting ready to ask something when the baton came crashing down on his head with crippling strength. The man crashed to the concrete floor without a sound. "Bastards! Damned bandits! Fuck you all! I will shoot you all. Lie down!" the guard shouted, flying into a rage and grasping at his automatic pistol. I had no doubt that he would open fire upon us. We instantly lay down, sometimes on top of each other, because there wasn't enough floor space for everybody. "Mongrels! Live for the time being!" the red-eyed one finally relented, enjoying our implicit obedience. He paused for a few minutes, then turned and opened the door. The other security guards left with him, and the door closed. The storm had blown over for the time being, and the morning rounds were over. The slumped-over man was groaning near the door. One of the prisoners tried to stop the blood that was trickling from a dark spot under the wretched fellow's shiny black hair.

An hour later the door opened again, and some people dressed in dirty white overalls appeared, accompanied by a guard. One of them announced, "Breakfast!" They started scooping pearl-barley porridge onto the tin plates. They had also brought water. When my turn came, I drank some water and got a plate of porridge, but there was no spoon. Probably they supposed that a decent prisoner should have brought his own. One of the other prisoners saw that I was at a loss and offered me his own. I accepted it with gratitude and tried to eat something. The porridge was utterly loathsome, disgusting, and it was absolutely impossible to eat it. I saw that many people took margarine or some seasoning out of their bags and put it into the food, trying to turn the mash into something edible. Since I had nothing of the kind, I quickly gave it back to the men who were dishing it out, after a few spoonfuls of porridge. I wanted to use the toilet, but I was warned that no one, not even a sick man, was allowed to go there until the last man in the cell had finished his breakfast. So I waited patiently. I went only after one of the murderers had finished his meal with gusto. He was the last obstacle on my way to the toilet. This time I wasn't nearly as ashamed as I had been in Cell 81 of Lefortovo Prison, in October 1992. "I am making progress!" I thought bitterly.

The people in the cell revived, started talking, and drinking more chefir. However, it didn't last long. The cell had to be cleared for the arrival of new prisoners. There were about 50 of us (in 30 square meters!) They divided us into groups of 10 prisoners and sent us for medical examinations, one group at a time. I was in the third group. We moved along the filthy corridor in the direction of the passage I came through the day before. Then we entered a side corridor where someone in white overalls was sitting at a table. Near him a security guard was sprawled in a chair, with a gun round his neck and a baton in his right hand. However, we were told to continue on farther, to a dark room where we had to remove our clothes and go through an examination, one by one. It was damp and cold. We had to go when we heard the order, "Next!" Finally, it was my turn. I came up to a man in white overalls. Another man in white was bustling about. He looked less important, and I understood that he was a low level medic or an orderly.

"Well, bandit, how are you feeling?" the doctor addressed me.

"I am not any kind of bandit. I am a scientist and a chemist," I answered as politely as I could.

"Wha-a-a-a-a-at? Shut up, you mangy dog!" the command rang out and I felt a jab in my back with the baton. It didn't hurt that much, but it was enough for me to instantly "grow wiser." People talked to you here only to make you understand that henceforth you were nobody and your duty was to obey and agree with servility, so as not to get a crushing blow from the baton on your head. I turned to the security guard whose eyes were sparkling with anger.

"Remember, mongrel, once and for all. Decent people don't come here. This is why you are a bandit to me, just like all the rest, you damned bastard!" my jailer lectured me.

Yes, after such a lesson it made no sense to react in a human way to anything that happened. So when the medic stuck a needle from a suspiciously unclean syringe into my vein to withdraw blood (apparently they were checking us for HIV), I was terrified but said nothing. The doctor asked with a smirk: "Any complaints?"

I nodded, "No."

"Next!" shouted the orderly.

We were sent to be fingerprinted and photographed. I was one of the last to go through this procedure. I thought I knew what to expect from my experience at Lefortovo Prison, but there was a big difference between the large empty rooms of the KGB jail and the cramped cell for fingerprinting at Matrosskaya Tishina.

It was already about 2 P.M. when they gathered us together in the holding cell again. From there we were taken through a dirty corridor and upstairs to the baths on the second floor. Newspapers, wrapping paper, potato peels, and pieces of plaster mixed with broken glass were strewn about everywhere. It was damp and chilly on the second floor. Steam seeped out from somewhere, and women's voices could be heard. The "veterans" immediately explained that we were waiting for the women to finish their baths.

Finally, we all got undressed. Most of the men displayed unique jail tattoos. I forced myself not to gawk at this artwork. I was very curious, but I was sure it wasn't safe to stare.

The concrete floor was horribly cold. You could stand only in your shoes. We had to jump around quite a bit, not to become totally numb and frozen.

The bath was a spacious cell with lots of pipes running along the ceiling. Water was continuously trickling from the pipes. First they gave each of us each a piece of dark disinfectant soap, but no wash cloths. There were no towels, either. It reminded me of my childhood, when as boys we quivered terribly and couldn't stop our teeth from chattering, after swimming in the almost frozen Belaya River in early spring. After a little time had passed, we got right back into the water, so we could boast to the other boys about how many times we had been in after the breakup of the ice.

Many prisoners were standing on newspapers that they had brought with them. It proved that experience was a great thing, and there was always a way out of any situation. After the bath, we pulled our clothes back on our wet bodies and were ready for whatever came next. We were escorted back to the first floor and found ourselves in a winding corridor. We were taken to a woman sitting behind a window. She asked a few questions - the year of my birth and other personal details such as my educational background, which article of the Criminal Code I had been arrested under, etc. When I told her I was a Doctor of Chemical Science, she looked at me attentively and marked something on her papers. Then we went to a crowded stockroom on the second floor, where all of our so-called bedding and dishware was being dispensed through two windows. The line near the windows was long and didn't move. Most of the prisoners had already made friends, and they stuck together in groups by cell, like a collective. One of the prisoners took a place in line, and didn't let anyone get to the window before the other members of his collective. I stood and waited patiently until everyone received their mattresses, blankets, mugs, spoons, and plates. Then I realized that I had made a serious blunder. I was given only an aluminum plate and a spoon. There were no pillows, mattresses or blankets left...

I was one of the last to be taken to a cell on the third floor. When the door opened, I saw a few people standing around, (the rule was - prisoners had to stand up every time the doors opened and the supervisor came in), and they looked me over with curiosity. A small television set was standing on a long table in the middle of the cell. It was switched on. A set of iron bunk beds stood on one side of the cell and another was near the washbasin. I quickly counted that I was the eighth person, but there were only four beds. It was strange that one mattress was on the floor, lying almost in the door, opposite the toilet. I saw a young blond man with blue eyes standing near that mattress, and I understood that it was his place. I was surprised but didn't ask about it, because I had realized by then that excessive curiosity wasn't welcome here. Later, when I was transferred to the other half of the jail with better conditions, I found out that the blond guy was an outcast who was turned into a passive homosexual by his cellmates. They had sent him to sleep on the floor near the door. All seven prisoners recognized me.

"Wow, so, it is you, Vil Mirzayanov! What a surprise for us. We already heard about you several times on television. We even knew that you had been arrested. We thought you would be sent to Lefortovo or somewhere, but here you are with us, common criminals,"[304] said a man over forty, with an unnaturally black face and dark eyes with reddish-yellow circles. We became acquainted, and everybody asked me to relax and speak up if I needed anything. They would try to do anything to help me. Since I had nothing with me, they suggested I use their toothpaste, soap, and a safety razor. They had food that their relatives had sent them, and they offered to share it with me. Right after my arrival, food was brought to the cell, consisting of porridge mixed with leftovers of some incredibly fetid fish, bread, and muddy hot water that was supposed to be tea. My cellmates had some dry seasoning, and after we added it the disgusting porridge didn't reek quite so much.

After dinner I had no strength left at all and could day dream only about sleep. My cellmates suggested I lie down on a bed with a mattress, but I was uncomfortable about depriving someone of his turn to sleep, and so I refused. I thought I would put my old light overcoat on the bed as padding and it would be quite enough, but I couldn't get to sleep for a long time because I was suffering from extreme fatigue. The bed was an iron rectangle with thick woven strips of iron sheeting, welded crosswise, and it was extremely uncomfortable to sleep on. The strips were far apart, so they stuck into my body and it hurt. My coat didn't save me from this torture. My cellmates were constantly smoking and the ventilation window was always open, so it was chilly and noisy. There was a constant buzz from the exchange of words between the cells. The "jail mail" was working tirelessly.

Soon I watched my neighbors write something; then they rolled and wrapped their letter in polyethylene film. They sealed the edges of the roll together with the flame from a match, making a capsule. This was tied it to a string, and the other end was attached to something in the cell. Then Victor N., the prisoner with the swarthy face, thrust his hand out through the bars of the ventilation window, shouted out an address. Then he threw the letter-capsule upward. We heard a cry of approval, which meant that the message reached its destination, or one of the transfer points of the jail mail system. All this was new to me and very different from Lefortovo Prison.

Finally I fell asleep, but only for a short while. I woke up because it was cold and my whole body ached from those damned iron strips. My cellmates noticed my suffering and encouraged me to take a bed with a mattress. I did so, but only later. It was time to get up and have breakfast. It smelt of thick tea. It turned out that my cellmates had prepared a generous portion of chefir, which they immediately offered to me. Curiosity got the better of me, and I tried this concoction. However, I didn't feel the euphoria that you might feel after a glass of wine or vodka. Still, there was something about the chefir. My heart was beating faster and my head cleared up, but drinking normal tea had the same effect.

I thought that this prison drink had no effect on me, as for example diethyl ether, because the longtime exposure to chemicals weakens the body's reactions to these substances. Still, to keep company, I joined my cellmates from time to time when they were drinking chefir. When they sipped this drink, they got very excited and began ardently discussing their stories, coming up with various theories about their upcoming prosecutions and trials.

My cellmates treated me with respect. The rumors that "first-timers" were always subjected to humiliating trials proved to be completely wrong.

My cellmates also told me that when the jail regime was toughened and the security guards started beating prisoners half to death for no reason, they had made a collective decision that under no circumstances should any prisoners fall for these provocations by coming to the defense of someone who was being beaten. The security guards were only waiting for such an excuse to start shooting, and to shift the blame for their outrageous treatment of the prisoners. However, the prisoners explained to me that the only ones who returned to jail were those who hadn't learned to be smart and rich enough to avoid further arrest and investigation. Even if someone found himself back in jail, the money made his life there less onerous, and possibly quite tolerable. He always had something to drink and good food to eat. He even had women...

I thought this sounded like thieves' bragging and doubted their words, but they assured me that in jail, just like in the world outside everything could be bought and sold, only it cost much more inside, because the people who provided "all this" charged for the increased risk. They even described some ways of obtaining this "heavenly" life, which I won't go into. It has nothing to do with my emotions; the point is that it is true. Criminals in the armchairs of power joined with criminals who supervise the thieves' world. This is completely logical, because the nature of the criminal Communist regime cannot operate differently.

After lunch the door to the cell opened and the security guard who appeared commanded, "Mirzayanov, get ready to exit!" This meant that I was being summoned to meet with my lawyer. We took a winding route through many corridors, and finally, the guard led me into a room with a table and two chairs that were welded to the floor. Aleksander Asnis was sitting at the table. He couldn't hide his agitation when he saw how worn out and exhausted I was. I must admit I was also excited to see my lawyer. I was very glad that he had found me in this terrible prison. I made an effort to suppress a brazen attitude that was beginning to rise up in me, and I started to answer his questions. Naturally, Asnis asked about my present situation and was deeply disenchanted that they kept me under such terrible conditions. I comforted him, by saying that these conditions were not the worst, although I didn't have a mattress. I had left home as an inexperienced "first-timer" without warm clothes, soap, tooth paste, tea, and other necessities.

I told Asnis about the prison cells where, according to my cellmates, they packed 70-120 people into 30 square meters. Despite the ventilation window and the window in the door which were always open, there simply wasn't enough air to breathe. People went to the door vent to light a cigarette, since it was the only place where the match didn't snuff out because of lack of oxygen... Regardless of the season, those prisoners stripped down to their underwear, because their clothes were always wet from constantly oozing sweat and the high humidity. The heat made the situation worse in the summer, and most people would just lie around on the concrete floor in a state of prostration. Sometimes a towel hanging on the wall would ripple, because the prisoners finally gave up struggling with the lice which propagated so quickly. Prisoners in those cells slept in four shifts, because of the shortage of space, mattresses, and pillows.

It turned out that my lawyer knew all about it, because he often dealt with prisoners from such cells. I felt that I was probably in a relatively "privileged" cell and we could suppose that I was lucky.

My lawyer told me about what was going on in the world "at large." My arrest had created a storm of protest in our country and abroad. Gale Colby and Irene Goldman had called a few times to tell what measures different people had taken in the U.S. to try to help secure my release. Asnis had brought along two issues of the newspaper *Izvestia* with articles about my case. He had also called my wife to learn that everything was fine and the children were healthy.

The next court session was scheduled for February 4, 1994. Asnis asked if he should petition the judges to release me from prison, but I replied that I wasn't going to ask anybody about it, especially not the judge who was an inveterate hypocrite.

Our meeting finished with that, and we said good bye to each other until the next court session. The guard took me back to my cell by a different route. Jailers had their own original, though naive, tactics.

I arrived and told my cellmates about our meeting. Soon porridge and bread were brought and we started our dinner. On the *NTV* channel, Tatiana Mitkova reported that Vil Mirzayanov had finally been found in Matrosskaya Tishina Prison, in a cell with criminals and murderers. I was horrified. I had told my lawyer about my first night in the cramped holding cell with such people. Evidently my story had evolved a bit, before it reached the *NTV* anchorwoman.

My cellmates were not offended and didn't demand any explanations from me, though they certainly guessed that I was the source of the information in this report. I was ashamed and told my cellmates that I was very sorry about Mitkova's words. They began to comfort me, and said that surely I would be transferred the next day to the other half of Matrosskaya Tishina, where they kept the "political prisoners."

The next day was Sunday and it would have been naive to hope that anyone would arrange for my transfer. That proved to be the case. Meanwhile, nothing had changed in our typical prisoners' life: we spent long hours lying around on the bed, in deep and endless speculation, interrupted by sad outpourings of the heart.

I was fortunate that the press responded with significant and unrelenting pressure after my arrest. The wire services *Reuters*, *Agencé France Presse* (AFP), *Associated Press*, and others published reports about my arrest on January 27th. They stressed that the underpinnings of my case were political, which provoked a wide protest in the public and scientific circles of different countries. The U.S. administration reacted immediately. While answering a correspondent's question at a press conference in the Russian-American Center on January 28, 1994, Thomas Pickering, the U.S. Ambassador in Moscow, summed up the official American position:

> "With respect to Vil Mirzayanov, it's a case in which we have taken a great deal of interest and in which we continue to be interested and which I have discussed a number of times with senior officials of the Russian Federation government... We will continue to follow this case with a great deal of interest..."[305]

The *New York Times* gave a brief history of my case on January 28, 1994 and the arrest that followed.[306]

On January 29, 1994 *Izvestia* published two articles[307, 308] about my case: an editorial and an article about the conditions I was treated to in prison. The editorial piece was an attempt to evaluate my case from the point of view of the general socio-political developments in Russia. It stressed that everyone had long understood that the case was absolutely groundless. The judges must have understood the whole absurdity of their actions and of "the Mirzayanov case" as such.

Then the newspaper analyzed possible reasons for why the case was continuing, and it came to the conclusion that a despotic regime and despotism in general were becoming established on the absurdity of the Mirzayanov case. Despite the alarms that the press was sounding, the authorities didn't hear the warnings and continued with my "case," throwing out a challenge to the whole society. So the press would have to find out who was behind all this. However, the newspaper doubted that any such person could be found. *Izvestia* further wrote[307], that

> "...the motherland put the scientist on an equal basis with a murderer. Thus, before the next session of the Moscow City Court, scheduled for February 3, Vil Mirzayanov could be fully morally crushed and humiliated by his time in jail. Aleksander Asnis just wants to have a positive effect on the mental state of his client, and so he regularly meets with him in the investigation isolator cell. However, according to the defense attorney, it is not easy to get a meeting with a prisoner because Matrosskaya Tishina is probably the only single place left in Moscow where there is still a line - a line many hours long for lawyers who want to meet with their clients..."

Another article by Sergei Mostovshchikov[308] on February 1st precisely reflects the impressions of my lawyer came away with from our meeting:

> "Aleksander Asnis met his client and told him that on February 3, at the next session of the Moscow City Court he would raise the question about changing the unnecessary interruption. But, the court could agree to that only if Vil Mirzayanov promises to attend the proceedings. However, the chemist responded that he couldn't voluntarily participate in a closed trial process that is violating the Constitu-

tion of his country. In the first place, the scientist doesn't consider himself to be guilty, and secondly, he is certain that he cannot be convicted based on secret documents, because that is prohibited by Russia's Primary Law. This is why he prefers to stay in jail and appear in the courtroom only if taken there by force."[309]

My meeting with Asnis probably didn't put him in a cheerful mood. He had to brief foreign journalists about my sad predicament. An article by Carey Scott, in the February 1, 1994 issue of *The Moscow Times*, discusses this.[310] The journalist reported that, according to the human rights activist Andrei Mironov, I was being kept under cruel conditions deliberately, especially to humiliate me. Scott also quoted a statement made by "Russia's Choice" at a press conference which took place on Monday, January 31, regarding my case. The statement read that the party "hoped the Moscow court will finish hearing the Mirzayanov case in the shortest time possible in strict accordance with the Constitution and the law."

Then Scott remarked that Nikolai Vorontsov[311], a spokesman for "Russia's Choice" who read the statement, said that I was charged based on a law that "didn't exist before and does not exist now." The article also noted that the human rights organization Helsinki Watch had published a statement, which said my case qualified as "fundamentally unjust" and stated that the case itself was violating "not only the Constitution of Russia, but also basic human rights." Many western papers informed the public about my arrest.[312-313]

One opinion which probably reflected the sentiments of a large part of the American public was expressed more eloquently in an editorial of *The Wall Street Journal Europe* and an article by J. Michael Waller there.[314, 315] He writes:

> "A good way for Mr. Yeltsin to address the problem would be to order Mr. Mirzayanov freed and the circumstances of his arrest and prosecution investigated by responsible authorities. The world is very much in need of that kind of concrete reassurances that Russia is not slipping back into its nasty old days."

My arrest literally caused a firestorm of protest from numerous scientific and human rights organizations. The German scientific society "International Network of Engineers and Scientists for Global Responsibility" (INES) made a sharp protest against my arrest on January 28, 1994, in which it accused the Russian authorities of reverting to the old practices of the totalitarian regime, and it called for a quick end to the practice of persecuting scientists who listened to the voices of their consciences and acted for the sake of all people of the Earth.

The late Dr. Joshua Lederberg, President of the New York Academy of Sciences, sent a fax addressed to Yuri Baturin, the Presidential Assistant for National Security, on January 31, 1994. He called on the Russian government to drop the charges against me, because they were in clear violation of the Russian Constitution.

Additionally, the following organizations expressed their strong protest against the actions of the Russian authorities towards me in numerous letters addressed to President Boris Yeltsin, Attorney General Alexei Kazannik, and Yuri Baturin, the Presidential Advisor for National Security and others: the U.S. Committee of Concerned Scientists, the American Association for Advancement of Science, the Union of Councils of Soviet Jewry, the international human rights organization Helsinki Watch, the National Academy of Sciences, the Federation of American Scientists, the Lawyers Committee for Human Rights, the American Physical Society, the American Chemical Society and others.

Many of these organizations also sent letters addressed to U.S. Ambassador to Russia Thomas Pickering asking him to intervene personally in this case. On February 1, 1994, Senator Bill Bradley addressed Baturin in a special fax, asking him to take measures to stop the closed trial. On January 29, 1994, the International Science Foundation founded by Mr. George Soros, published a statement in my support.

On February 2, 1994, *Agencé France Presse* reported (with a reference to *ITAR-TASS*) that the widow of Andrei Sakharov had urged the authorities to open up the Mirzayanov trial. Elena Bonner said that the closed trial violated my legal rights, and she also denounced the so-called "non-intervention" of the Russian Academy of Sciences and its inertia in not defending me. She said that she had called the president of the Academy twice and asked him to intervene, but she got the impression that the organization "had adopted the same position... that the Soviet Academy of Sciences took when Andrei Sakharov was persecuted."

January 30th was Sunday, and nobody was in a hurry to transfer me anywhere. Time passed in endless conversations, sprinkled with the television news. This time I agreed to take my turn sleeping on the mattress, and it seems to me it was a very wise decision. Finally, I managed to have a good sleep, and on the morning of January 31st life in jail didn't seem so unbearable to me. After breakfast the window in the door opened and I heard the command, "Mirzayanov, take your stuff and head for the exit!" This meant that I had a total of five minutes to get ready. All my cellmates decided that I would be transferred to the other half of Matrosskaya Tishina. Soon the doors of the cell opened and the guard ordered me to follow him.

We spent a lot of time trying to find our way through various corridors and underpasses. Finally, we arrived in a completely different building, where the guard handed me over to the local security guards. One of them ordered me to follow him. We went up to the third floor of the building where there were some small holding cells. He left me there and ordered me to take off all my clothes. The security guard was examining all my clothes carefully, especially the seams.

They kept me there for more than an hour and then took me to the shower. I washed myself with pleasure using my undershirt as a washcloth. So I washed it at the same time. After this I was taken back to the cold holding cell.

Finally, the door opened and I was ordered to enter a room that smelt of some chemicals. They would photograph me and take my fingerprints again. Then I was taken to the fifth floor. I found myself in a short corridor with cells on each side. We stopped at one of them, and the security guard opened the door. A tall and likeable young man with an intelligent face was standing in the cell.

His face was a little yellowish, which showed that the prisoner hadn't been in the sun or in the fresh air for a long time.

There were four beds in the cell and three of them were empty. We got acquainted, and I found out his name was Aleksei Kostin.

I took a place near the barred window opposite Aleksei's bed. Between our beds there was a table with benches firmly attached to the concrete floor. The cell was freshly painted and clean, and the walls were roughly finished with coarse concrete for noise reduction. There was a toilet and a washbasin near the door, behind a short concrete barrier. In the middle of the cell there was a refrigerator with a small television set on it. There was a small nightstand next to each bed for underwear and toilet articles, and we had mattresses and small black pillows. In fact, the conditions here were much better than in my previous cell.

I mentally thanked my lawyer that for having me transferred there. Soon Aleksei told me about his case. He had already been waiting for his trial for almost four years. He had been in almost all the cells of Matrosskaya Tishina, both in this part and in the other half of the jail. Aleksei had been the head of the personnel department of the U.S.S.R.'s first Soviet-American joint venture in St. Petersburg. He had been in this cell with Anatoli Lukiyanov, former Chairman of the U.S.S.R. Supreme Soviet, Yuri Plekhanov, head of security for the U.S.S.R. President Mikhail Gorbachev, and former U.S.S.R. Prime Minister Valentin Pavlov, whose bed I was going to occupy. I was curious about how the coup supporters were treated. Alexei said that ringleaders of the Committee for Emergency Situations were kept under good conditions and under constant medical supervision. Food was brought in for them from a neighboring café, and of course, Alexei enjoyed these privileges, too.

Former Prime Minister Pavlov, who was dead drunk even when he was arrested, enjoyed his favorite pastime here as well. His lawyer brought him vodka and cognac, and prisoner Pavlov hid the bottles under his clothes and brought them to the cell. I think that the guards simply turned a blind eye to this. On someone's order, of course.

Aleksei said that from time to time heated political discussions flared up in the cell, for example, about the true face of the Communist leader Lenin. Plekhanov, the former senior bodyguard for Mikhail Gorbachev, worked himself into such a state of excitement, that he cried and asked them not to offend the memory of the "leader." Nowadays where could a person with such orthodox thinking appear from? Plekhanov was relatively young. When he was a young Pioneer on one of Moscow's streets, Plekhanov saw a camera dangling from under the unbuttoned coat of some foreigner. The young Leninist immediately ran to the policeman on duty. There was a secret institute in the vicinity, and the foreigner was arrested. Nobody knows what happened to him; however, the Chekist career of the future bodyguard of our last Soviet General Secretary started at that moment. First, Plekhanov went to the school for young Chekists where he studied his favorite subject - radio engineering and other subjects important for his future profession. Then he was lucky enough to catch the eye of Vladimir Kryuchkov, the future head of the KGB, who later became his mentor and promoted him in a career that finally led to his important position near the body of Gorbachev. It wasn't surprising that at a critical moment he betrayed him, since he had been trained to serve his master Kryuchkov, not Gorbachev.

As for the origins of the refrigerator, Aleksei said that his enterprise had delivered 15 refrigerators free of charge to the jail, so he was allowed to keep one in his cell. Aleksei mostly ate what his relatives had been bringing for him. Parcels were allowed once a month, but they couldn't exceed seven kilograms, so experienced Aleksei asked his relatives to bring mostly dry products and food concentrates. They were not very tasty, but they were a hundred times better than the food they served in jail.

There was other good news that day too. In the evening I received a parcel from my wife and my daughter Elena, who had stood the whole day in the line so they could hand it through the cherished window just before the service closed. This was great luck because, as Aleksei explained to me, next month I had the right to receive another parcel, but not earlier than 15 days after the previous one. The security guard who had brought the parcel explained that he would give me only one disposable safety razor, and he would give me the new ones as I returned the used ones. I had to submit a written application addressed to the head of the jail for this. Things turned out to be not so bad. I had a good cellmate, there was enough air in the room, and I had my own bed and could sleep. I also had a refrigerator, a television set, and the newspaper *Izvestia*. All this lifted my spirits somewhat.

There were no negotiations through vent window panes in this part of Matrosskaya Tishina, and nobody sent jail mail. I decided that obviously there must be other channels for communication here. My cellmate said that the local authorities often pressured prisoners by threatening to send them to the first half of the jail, to the cells with a hundred or more prisoners. Yes, such threats will surely make you unwilling to establish open contact with other cells. However, from time to time I heard someone knocking on the radiator, and my cellmate sometimes answered. Unfortunately I didn't have a clue about how this alphabet worked.

Another pleasant change was the morning walk. We went up to the roof of the jail accompanied by a security guard. There were isolated walking areas on the roof. We could see roads through the crack between the concrete slabs, so we could figure out where the jail was located.

On February 2nd my lawyer came to see me. He understood from my appearance that my situation had improved, and I expressed my warm gratitude for all his efforts on my behalf. We talked about the court session that was scheduled for the next day. Asnis again asked my permission to petition for my release from jail. Natalia Gevorkyan, the famous journalist from *Moscow News*, told him confidentially that Zoya Korneva, Chair of the Moscow City Court, was completely puzzled by my reluctance to file this petition and exclaimed, "Just what is he doing?"

According to my defense attorney, many journalists and democratically-minded lawyers disapproved of my actions and thought of them as showing overt disrespect for the court. This is why he asked me to consider everything and to make a reasonable decision, especially since he thought I had achieved the effect I had wanted.

Unfortunately, I couldn't do that. The judges needn't feel that I was beginning to cave in and had changed my opinion of them. It was difficult in jail, but it would be much worse later, when they hid me away in a prison camp for many years. We parted, expecting to meet in court on February 3rd. However, something happened that changed our plans.

In the Dungeon

Right after breakfast on February 3rd, I was ordered to prepare for the trip to court. After the search and a long wait I was put into a vehicle which greatly resembled a bakery delivery van. Inside there were iron cages on both sides divided by a narrow walkway. I was put into one of them. I'm not a large man, but I could barely squeeze into it, back-end first. There was an iron seat. It was terribly cold and I could only stand up bent over half way, because my head touched the top of the cage. As we left the prison, I felt that the day was exceptionally cold. Later I was told that the temperature outside was minus 28 Celsius (about minus 18.5 Fahrenheit). The van remained there for about 20 minutes, and then it moved out. By that time I had become completely frozen. The whole cage was made of iron sheeting and a killing cold was seeping in through the walls and the floor, penetrating and percolating throughout my body. The knitted woolen socks I brought with me didn't help at all. I tried to move in some way and it helped a little, but not for long. In such a predicament only valenki (felt boots), a sheepskin coat, and fur-lined mittens could help. That is how the security guard, who was sitting with his gun near the door, was dressed.

Our van stopped in at some places along the way, and we collected new prisoners from various Moscow jails to transport them to the courts.

Finally, it was our turn and we approached Kalanchevskaya Street, not far from Kazan Train Station, where the Moscow City Court was then located. By that time I had only one wish left. I wanted to find myself anywhere where it was warm, and as fast as possible, because I had grown entirely numb. The van made a sharp turn to the left and stopped. I heard a lot of voices. People were shouting, "Mirzayanov – the pride of Russia! Shame on the Communist tyrants! Free Mirzayanov!" I could see people through the van door holding placards.

I couldn't read them, but I did see my last name on one of the placards. One of the security guards cried hysterically at the top of his voice, "Get your cameras out of here! Take them away, I am telling you, or I will break them!" Judging by the outcries, there were a lot of people there and nobody was going to give in. Apparently many security guards kept their workplace a secret and didn't want to be recognized in pictures published in newspapers or in television broadcasts. There were also some more serious reasons, which I will write about a bit later.

About five minutes passed and the guard didn't allow me to be taken out. Finally, the senior guard commanded, "Close the door. Let's go!" I understood that they were supposed to take me back to prison. The car drove around somewhere for a while, and then it turned back sharply. I realized that the security guard had decided to trick the people who were waiting for me, and we were going back to the court again. In fact, we soon entered through the back courtyard of the building. No voices could be heard this time. The security guards' trick had worked.

I was told to leave the cage, and they immediately handcuffed me. There were no steps to get down to the ground. With handcuffs on and feet that I could hardly control because they were completely frozen, it was incredibly difficult to descend from a height of about a meter to the slippery ice that covered the yard near the court. I fell, hitting my right side and my head. When I stood up, they immediately dragged me to the door, which led to the basement of the building. A guard with an automatic rifle was standing at the place where the staircase made a bend, and he examined me fiercely. I walked along the corridor past the guardroom, and through an open door I could see the captain in a dirty uniform with a red armband on his sleeve talking on the phone. A few military men sat smoking on the sofa. I was ordered to turn to the wall and stand there. The officer came up to me and bawled, "Last name?" I answered. A guard took off my handcuffs and commanded, "Let's go!"

State Secrets

We went along a corridor with a lot of shabby gray doors, and I found myself in the little holding cell of the Moscow City Court. It was freezing there too, but not so dreadfully cold as in the iron cage of the van. I took off my shoes and started jumping to get my feet warm. Soon they were burning hot and started hurting terribly. In my student days in Moscow, I used to travel back and forth every day between my institute and the dormitory on the trams which were really cold in the winter. From those times I remembered that the burning pain was a good sign. It meant my feet were not frostbitten.

It got a bit better and I was no longer shivering. My teeth stopped clattering. Someone looked through the peephole and said something. I saw that it was a young soldier who was asking, "Need some weed?" I didn't understand, but just in case, I answered "No." I also added that I wanted to go to the toilet. But the soldier moved away and I heard him asking someone else his strange question. Soon he returned, opened the door, and told me to follow him. The guard was standing in front of some open doors. I could smell the peculiar stench of a public toilet. The guard gave me a sign that I should go inside this dark and unspeakably dirty room. When I came out of the toilet, he took me to the headquarters where an officer told me to stand with my face to the wall as he handcuffed me. Then I was taken somewhere upwards accompanied by four guards. Two young soldiers were holding my hands by the handcuffs, while the other guards were in front of and behind me.

We moved along the corridor on the first floor, and when we reached the spacious front stairway leading to the second floor, I saw a large crowd of people with placards, photo journalists, television crews, and reporters. I had met some of them several times before. People were shouting, "Shame! Free Mirzayanov!" "Mirzayanov, we are with you!" "Why don't you struggle with the bandits?" The guards stopped in the middle of the stairs, bewildered by the deafening cries of the demonstrators and blinded by endless photoflashes. Both young soldiers grabbed my hands with all their might, and it hurt like hell. I couldn't control myself and said to one of them, "Whimperer, stop squeezing my hand or you will get a smack in the face!" Of course I would never be able to do that.

A few more military men showed up, who had apparently been summoned to help out. I was dragged back down the staircase to the basement, and they locked me in the same cell. For a long time I heard the guards cursing the demonstrators. I also received my share of abuse. I could only sit and wait for whatever would happen next. But nothing happened, and I just sat on the cold stone floor because there was nothing else in the cell to sit on. From time to time I stood up and tried to stretch my numb and swollen feet. Time dragged on very slowly and I finally lost track of it completely. I was thirsty, but I forced myself to be patient and bear it. I tried not to think about food, because I knew that there was no water or food there. From time to time it grew quiet in the basement, and I heard a radio somewhere far away. I understood by its signals that it was 4 P.M. It meant I had already been in the cell for more than four hours.

Finally, I heard a voice from the opposite cell, "Where are you from? What jail and according to which code [were you arrested]?" I started answering, but we immediately heard the order, "Silence!" The guard opened the door of my cell and ordered, "To the exit!" He took me along the same corridor as before to the wall opposite the headquarters where more than ten people were already standing around. We were handcuffed in pairs and then joined to form a single chain. In chains we went along the corridor and then up to the courtyard where the same prison van was waiting for us. It was past 6 P.M.

It turned out that the transport van came only after the last trial was over. All prisoners had to wait for this moment.

Before putting us into the van, they took off our handcuffs, and one by one we awkwardly clambered onto the high platform of the van. Then we were locked in the cages again. In the evening it was even chillier, and I started freezing again right away. After prisoners were taken to numerous Moscow jails, it became very quiet in the van. When we stopped near some gates and entered a yard, I guessed that it was Matrosskaya Tishina and that I soon would be in a warm place. I saw through a crack in the door that a young solder in sheepskin coat, black valenki, and fur-lined cap with earflaps turned down was sitting in the van. His hands in large furlined mittens rested on his machine gun. Time dragged on dreadfully slowly. It seemed that everybody had just forgotten about me. The damned frost had penetrated my heart. I was enveloped in panic. It would be so easy to come to such an absurd end! I started knocking on the door to remind them of my existence. The soldier roared, "You there, shut up! Or you will suffer in solitary confinement!" However, even this nightmare ended. I heard voices, and the van doors opened, as did the doors of my cage. I was semiconscious when I got out of the van and walked along the prison corridors in a state of exhaustion.

When we finally stopped I couldn't recognize the old place where they searched me. It was also cold there, and I didn't stop shivering. My teeth were chattering and hurt so much it wasn't funny. My gums always became inflamed when I caught a cold. The guard ordered me to disrobe, and I tried to be quick, hoping I would be taken to my cell faster. However, the jailer deliberately felt all the seams of my clothes very slowly. I stood on my boots that time trying to hold out in that "deep-freezer." It seems to me I got dressed quickly, although I had almost completely lost control over my arms and legs. Only after that when I found myself in a cramped holding cell, where there was a warm radiator, did I remember the prisoner who said during my first night in Matrosskaya Tishina that jail was the wrong place for someone my age. Probably he was right. Even some young prisoners couldn't stand such cruel trials. So it was no wonder that some prisoners cooperated with their jailers, became informers, or even provocateurs in exchange for lightening the burden a bit. But very often they were unmasked. Then the jailers hid them in the solitary cells. After their trials and verdicts for a certain term in jail, "the stoolies" refused to go to labor camps (where the conditions were better), because they could be killed even during the transfer. Then jailers turned them into servants for dirty work in the kitchen, delivering food to the cells, etc.

When I was finally taken to my cell, it was about 9 P.M. Aleksei saw how I felt, immediately understood what the problem was. He quickly made tea with an immersion coil. After a few cups, I recovered. My neighbor saw nothing unusual in my treatment. It turned out this was one of the psychological methods for treating prisoners. He advised me to take newspapers with me next time and spread them out under my feet.

Next day the Moscow and the Western press reported about my court saga with a lot of attention to the details.[316-325] The Bashkir and Tatar papers published articles in which they blamed the government for a biased trial, expressing admiration for my actions.[326-328]

It seems to me that many observers abroad, particularly in the U.S., correctly understood the essence of my case and the underlying reasons for the closed trial.[329] Reflecting on it, the American edition of *The Wall Street Journal* also published an insightful editorial, where it pointed out:

> "Maybe the world is watching the wrong Russian reform. The economic side is troubling; the political side is seriously disturbing.... Compliance with chemical weapons treaties aside, the Mirzayanov trial raises questions about the integrity of Russia's legal processes, about the role of the former KGB in Russia today and about who controls the military complexes."[330]

U.S. government officials were also concerned about my fate. On February 1, 1994 Senator De Concini took the floor in the Senate and expressed deep concern about my trial, because it involved more than the fate of one man. He rhetorically asked

> "Who is in charge here? Civilians operating under the rule of law, or a military-industrial complex that can pull secret regulations out of a hat when challenged?" Furthermore, he cited Ambassador Pickering's remarks at the Russian-American Press Center made on January 28th, saying that "It seems more than strange to us and more than usual that someone could be either prosecuted or persecuted for telling the truth about an activity which is contrary to a treaty obligation of a foreign government."[331]

State Secrets

It seems that the Russian authorities, under the weight of international pressure, started to consider the possible negative consequences of my trial. On February 4, 1994, *Reuters* reported (with a reference to *ITAR-TASS*) that the Russian authorities were allegedly ready to drop my case. Similar information appeared in *The Moscow Times*. [332] The newspaper reported that Baturin had briefed Boris Yeltsin in detail about the Mirzayanov trial process. The President reacted properly and said that the investigation appeared to be unconstitutional.

Back to the Courtroom

On February 5, 1994, after breakfast, I was again taken to the place where I was searched following the usual route, and waited to be taken to the Moscow City Court. This time I had taken Aleksei's newspapers with me to put under my feet in the cage of the jail van. They came in handy because the morning was once more frigid.

This time they unloaded me almost without incident. When I was out of the van I saw a few photo-correspondents hanging on the fence. The guards hurried to drive them away, but these experienced and clever fellows were constantly snapping off shots, and they only jumped down from the fence after the guards threatened them with their batons.

Once more they kept me for a long time in the same holding cell, in the basement of the Moscow City Court. Then six guards, accompanied by two huge German shepherds, handcuffed me and took me upstairs. When we reached the ground floor I saw many people at the end of the corridor behind the iron bars taking pictures and shooting film footage for television. The dogs began to bark loudly. I raised my shackled hands and tried to greet the journalists, but the guards immediately dragged me to the nearest door trying to hide their faces from the cameras.

We entered a large cold hall with heavily frosted windows. At the side, there was a cage for dangerous criminals, which made the gloomy view of the hall even more menacing.

In the front, on the platform, there were seats for the judges. Not far from them my defender Asnis was sitting in his coat, and Prosecutor Pankratov was sitting on the left. His cold blue face matched his usual blue uniform with the epaulettes. The guards put me into the cage, took off my handcuffs and bolted the door with a crash. Only two soldiers and an officer, who sat near the doors, were left in the hall. Asnis came up to me and told me about my family and what efforts he was making to help me. The judge wouldn't allow my wife a meeting. This was his way of retaliating. Once more I flatly refused to petition the court to release me from prison, but I agreed to the suggestion of my lawyer that we file two petitions, one about rejecting the current composition of the court (three judges), and the other asking to hold an open trial.

Soon the court secretary commanded, "Rise. Court is in order!" The judges appeared in the doorway behind the platform, with Judge Sazonov at the head. Everyone was dressed in coats.

Nikolai Sazonov, the chairman, asked everybody to sit down and shouted indignantly to the guard, "Why have you locked him in there? Set him free immediately!"

They let me out of the cage and I sat in the first row facing the judges. Two young soldiers sat close to me, one on each side.

The judge asked me sympathetically if I had any complaints about the conditions under which I was being kept. I answered cheerfully that everything was just great, but I still refused to cooperate with the court that didn't respect the Constitution established by our country.

Prosecutor Pankratov started to whine about how unfair it was that he had to wear just his uniform in that cold room, where the temperature hardly reached 10 degrees Celsius (about 50 degrees Fahrenheit), while everyone else was sitting in their coats…

Asnis took the floor and read his petitions, and then Judge Sazonov announced that the court would adjourn for a meeting. I almost burst out laughing when I saw how Judge Yudin bent over carrying all seven volumes of my case back with him. Apparently he had been told that he should not leave my case materials unattended for a moment, since they carried the sinister "top secret" stamp.

It probably never occurred to the judge that my lawyer was sitting just a few meters from him, with almost a full copy of my case materials on his desk. For the rest of my trial I struggled with the temptation to make a statement and request that Judge Yudin needn't strain himself carrying such a heavy load, because a copy of my case was available for everyone who wanted it. One copy was on the lawyer's table, and the other was in the U.S., because I sent it to Gale Colby. I don't know why, but I felt it was a pity to disappoint these people. I am certain that my case hasn't been declassified to this day. It is still a state secret...

After a short break the judges took their places again, and Sazonov read the decision of the court to reject my lawyer's petitions. Then he announced that the hearing of the case would continue, and started reading transcripts of my interrogations, droning on for a long time in a boring voice. Steam puffed out from his mouth, creating the impression that there was a cooking pot inside of the judge, and something was boiling in there.

Time dragged on slowly. Sometimes I tried to observe the reactions of the judges, the prosecutor, and my lawyer. However, it was routine business for them and no one listened to Sazonov. Both my soldiers clung closely to me like kittens to their mother and slept peacefully. The one on the right with his head on my shoulder started snoring a little. The officer at the door slept too, but he opened his eyes from time to time to glance at his soldiers. They were sitting with their side to their commander and a little bit ahead of him, so he contented himself that they were there, next to me. It seemed that military men, like cats, spent most of their lives sleeping. Suddenly I asked myself, "How many days will I have to listen to this bullshit?" As if in response, Judge Sazonov failed to pronounce some very simple chemical term in the transcript of an interrogation. I raised my hand and corrected him. At once the judge asked me, "Maybe you will help us speed up the hearing? After all, we are all in a difficult situation."

"All right," I answered. "But first I must make a statement about why I addressed the press and published my articles about chemical weapons."

The judge agreed. In a period of about six minutes I presented my statement, explaining the motives behind my actions, and I warned the judges that they, like all citizens, as well as their children, were equally helpless before weapons of mass destruction. In the international situation that had developed, chemical weapons were very dangerous for our country because their development, production, and testing caused harm to people's health, and posed the threat of unpredictable consequences for future generations.

The judges didn't display any emotions. They were deeply indifferent to everything I said. Then they started asking me questions about separate episodes of my case. I answered truthfully, without worrying that my testimony could later be used against me. After a while, Judge Sazonov announced a break.

I was taken to the basement again, and I sat there until the lunch break was over (food for me was out of the question). Then I was escorted along the usual route back into the cold and gloomy courtroom.

Witnesses Ruin the Case

It turned out that some witnesses had been summoned on that day to give their testimony: my former subordinate Anatoly Ryskal, whose low qualifications and laziness had disappointed me, and Leonard Nikishin, from *Moscow News*. However, Ryskal wasn't in Moscow, and even his relatives didn't know when he was coming back. I am certain that he simply got cold feet. His absence disrupted the plans of those people who were counting on an "accusatory" testimony from my former employee.

Nikishin, on the other hand, had arrived and was prepared to give his testimony to the court. Leonard suffered from his excessive weight and was very short winded. He tried to be calm, but he was anxious from time to time and it showed.

He spoke about his acquaintance with Lev Fedorov and how he had obtained the manuscript of the article that was called "A Poisoned Policy." His testimony completely concurred with the transcript of his interrogation in Lefortovo, and he was clear on the point that I hadn't read the final text. The day before the article's publication, Leonard read me the text prepared for publication over the phone, and I agreed with it. Nikishin stated that he hadn't seen any state secrets in this article when he worked on it in 1992, and he didn't see any now. The prosecutor and judges asked him a few more formal questions, and the journalist was dismissed.

Finally, Judge Sazonov announced that the day's session was over. Poor Judge Yudin, looking like a martyr, struggled to lug the heavy volumes out of the courtroom again. I was taken back to my cell in the basement, which I was becoming accustomed to, and from there I was driven back to prison.

News awaited me there. There was a new prisoner in our cell. He was a stocky middle-aged man, with a slightly swarthy and tired, but pleasant, face. It was clear from his black hair and his black eyebrows above black eyes that he wasn't a Russian. We got acquainted, and it turned out he was a Tatar named Ravil Sitdikov. He told us how he ended up there, and I remembered a report in one of Moscow Newspapers about the arrest of a high-ranking employee of the Bank of Russia. Sitdikov was charged with unlawful operations associated with falsified letters of credit.

Between our conversations, I saw a report on the *NTV* channel from the Moscow City Court about the events surrounding my case. Television crews managed to film me through the bars on my way to the courtroom, surrounded by the guards and the dogs. The correspondent Mitkova also reported on President Yeltsin's statement that they had "carried the Mirzayanov case too far." However, the President thought that he shouldn't intervene or pressure the court. Then the telegenic Asnis appeared on the screen and spoke about some details of the trial process. In particular he stated that I had started giving testimony.

I spent Saturday and Sunday in front of the television screen. It was good at the time that we had two television sets. Ravil had brought his portable one. The Saturday newspapers published materials about the trial, based on information that Asnis had presented in between court sessions.[333, 334]

The next court session took place on February 8th. General Smirnitsky and Colonel Chugunov, who was a longtime member of the Russian delegation at the CWC negotiations in Geneva, were summoned to the court as witnesses for the defense. As I mentioned before, they had both refused to sign the findings of the commission prepared by the MB RF's Investigation Department and GOSNIIOKhT, and they had expressed their opinions independently. They clearly pointed out that my articles didn't disclose any information of state secrecy, and in their opinions I hadn't disclosed any chemical or technical information about the new weapons, showing once again that the charges against me were absurd. Both experts spoke lucidly and persuasively.

The judge asked if someone could reproduce the new chemical weapons based on information I had presented in the press. Both experts answered that it was impossible. The prosecutor wanted very badly to hear something negative from the experts, so he even asked if my article could motivate foreign intelligence to look for this information. Smirnitsky calmly answered to Pankratov that this question was outside the area of competence of a specialist on chemical weapons. Pankratov also wondered what damage the information I published had caused to the defense capability of the country. The general was laconic again, "It couldn't cause any damage."

"Do you think that publishing conventional names and codes of new chemical agents openly in the press means disclosing information of state secrecy?" continued the prosecutor. The general said that it was certainly intolerable.

I should note that I had never used any terms defining codes or codes of scientific and research topics or chemical compounds. However, I decided against clarifying this question because it seemed to me that such action would be misinterpreted as an attempt to justify myself. When Colonel Chugunov was asked how he rated the information that I had published, he answered that there were grounds for resorting to administrative sanctions for violating work instruction manuals, but no more than this. He thought that the whole problem of the information disclosed in my articles no longer made any sense, including the violation of the above mentioned work instruction manuals, because of the signing of the Chemical Weapons Convention.

The truth is that I saw Chugunov and Smirnitsky for the first time in that courtroom. I hadn't known them before, but each man left a great impression on me, both by the level of his knowledge and his ability to properly present his point of view. Apparently not only orthodox-minded people studied at the Academy of Chemical Defense, but also some people who could think independently...

Their testimony was in complete contrast to that of Boris Kuznetsov, who was summoned by the prosecutor. He had memorized and rehearsed his testimony, which was written down by Captain Shkarin in the transcript of his interrogation at Lefortovo. Then he reproduced it almost exactly word for word in the courtroom. I had a suspicion that the transcript had been prepared in advance at GOSNIIOKhT by better-educated people, because Kuznetsov's level of knowledge and his amazingly confused articulation gave serious grounds for such doubts. His answers to the questions were straightforward and terribly obtuse, as if he were one of the sergeants on special duty at Matrosskaya Tishina Prison. When he finished with his testimony Kuznetsov asked Sazonov, "Comrade Judge, do you have a latrine here?" Sazonov didn't understand at first, but then he asked him, "Do you mean the toilet? Well then, please ask the sergeant at the door," and happy Kuznetsov bolted for the bathroom.

Will Englund from the *Baltimore Sun* was also summoned on the same day. However, according to Judge Sazonov, he hadn't come to the trial because he was on an extended business trip. This wasn't quite correct, to put it mildly. Alexander Gordeyev[335] quoted Englund as saying that he wasn't inclined "to testify unless he could do so in an open session." Additionally, Englund who had been interrogated at the Ministry of Security in April of 1994 said, "'The essence of a free press is to maintain an atmosphere of trust, and I feel that if I attended a closed trial, it would be a betrayal of that trust.'" Referring to his experience of interrogations in the Lefortovo Investigation Department, the American said that he would abstain from giving testimony because his words could be distorted. "I emphasized repeatedly that Mirzayanov had given me no formulas of the chemicals, but that was deleted from the charging papers,'" the American journalist said to Gordeyev. Unfortunately it was the usual practice of the KGB. Amy Knight wrote a good article[336] about that called "Back to the Old Bad Days in Moscow?" A similar question was raised in *The Moscow Times*.[337]

The court cut short its work until February 10th. When the guard in the basement ordered us to stand up with our faces to the wall, so they could handcuff and lock us in pairs, a prisoner of about forty with an intelligent face happened to be near me. He was constantly scratching himself and killing lice under the collar of his shirt. He greeted me and said he was Nikolai Koltsov, the former chairman of one of the first cooperatives in the north of the U.S.S.R. He was arrested back in 1989, but the trial of Koltsov and his colleagues had only just started when I was in court. He had no time to tell me about his case. But I learned that he was in one of those cells meant for 35 in Matrosskaya Tishina, where they kept 120 people. I was appalled when I saw a louse on him - a sad symbol of the notorious Matrosskaya Tishina cells. I met Koltsov a few days later and we were able to talk about his case.

In the evening I read an article by Valery Rudnev in *Izvestia*.[338] He was both a lawyer and a journalist, and I had met with him several times. After I read his publications I was convinced of his highly professional erudition. That is why his article was extremely valuable for me. Rudnev started his article by saying that my trial could end without a verdict because Article 6 of the Criminal and Procedural Code could be applied. It stipulated that even if the defendant were guilty, circumstances could bring the case to a close. This decision was ambiguous according Rudnev, and he insisted that the court pass its verdict.

However, I didn't trust the court, which pushed with all its strength to reach an unjust verdict in my case. For that reason, I hoped that the Attorney General's Office would drop the case as being illegally instituted.

On February 10, 1994 the court session started with a surprise that Prosecutor Pankratov had prepared for me. He said that Victor Petrunin, Director of GOSNIIOKhT, had been summoned to the trial. The judge also reported that he had summoned Lev Fedorov and Andrei Mironov as witnesses.

Petrunin was the first to testify. When he entered the courtroom and saw the conditions I was sitting in there, he couldn't conceal his embarrassment. Then he regained his composure and even greeted me before he was about to give his testimony. I don't know whether it was his confusion or his usual hypocrisy, but Petrunin started his testimony ...with a complimentary tirade directed at me. He said that he had known me for more than 25 years as a gifted scientist, and that he had always helped me as much as he could. He was my official opponent at the defense of my doctoral dissertation, and had given it a positive review. Then he had appointed me as the head of the Department for Foreign Technical Counterintelligence. Petrunin told the court that he had never had a personal grudge against me, if you didn't take into account the articles in which I had disclosed so many secrets which had caused irreparable damage to the defense capabilities of the country. Petrunin complained that enormous expenses and the labor of many thousands of scientists, engineers, and workers were wasted because of my articles.

When he was answering the prosecutor's question about what the consequences of my articles were for the regime of keeping state secrets, Petrunin exclaimed pathetically, "Comrade Prosecutor! Before Mirzayanov's articles we didn't have any big worries about security, and everything was calm and quiet. Nobody was interested in our institute. But now we don't know what to do: we are literally besieged by the intelligence services of foreign states! You yourself understand how dangerous it will be for everybody if our new research ends up in the hands of people like Hussein!"

I immediately envisioned the picture that Petrunin was painting for the judges: tall concrete walls with barbed wire and roguish spies with binoculars, climbing these fences to penetrate a building stuffed with various test-tubes and fluorescent electronic instruments, wanting to steal the secrets of our beloved motherland... Just like in a Soviet movie with our glorious intelligence officers and the impudent spies from imperialist countries.

Petrunin broke out into a sweat as he finished giving his testimony, and his face became red, although it was freezing cold in the courtroom. He answered questions obsequiously, demonstrating his full loyalty with endless bows in the direction of the judge. Obviously he was afraid that he would also be ordered to sit on the defendant's bench near me. It seemed that his zeal made him shrink a bit, even though he wasn't very tall to begin with. I felt really sorry for him.

Judge Sazonov probably wasn't able to stand the shock he had experienced and declared a break before the witness Fedorov arrived. Asnis came up to me during the break. He was vexed. "I don't understand why the prosecutor is procrastinating," said my lawyer. "He was given instructions to terminate the trial."

Of course this news greatly excited me, but I tried not to kindle any hopes ahead of time (who knows, they could change their minds!), and I answered that if this campaigner was given "instructions", then he was certain to implement them.[339]

My co-author Lev Fedorov was the next to testify. Before his turn, I asked my lawyer not to react to his testimony and not to ask him any questions. I thought: "Let him say whatever he wants for as long as he wants, until they stop him."

There were an extraordinary number of lies and a swagger to Fedorov's speech. To begin with, he decided for some reason to share the details of his glorious biography, how he had graduated from Moscow State University with honors, how he quickly had defended his master's thesis, and then had successfully contended with his doctoral dissertation. Fedorov said defiantly that he had written all the articles, and that Vil Mirzayanov had only signed them. Then, in a very arrogant tone, he started talking about his work on a book about chemical weapons. He mentioned that this process was very difficult and added casually, "Of course, you can't imagine it." At these words Sazonov couldn't restrain himself any longer and burst out from the indignation that overwhelmed him, "Good God! Perhaps I can imagine a little. I write books, too."

Later I learned that Sazonov had published a few law books.

When Lev Fedorov was asked how he had received such detailed information about the new chemical weapons and binary weapons, he said without any embarrassment that he had read about all this in the foreign press, although he had never worked in the area of chemical weapons! The mouths of the judges and the prosecutor, who had had plenty of life experience, twisted sarcasti-

State Secrets

cally because his assertion was so ridiculous. It meant that Fedorov considered them to be complete fools. Judge Sazonov finally decided to put the witness in his place, "Witness Fedorov, could you tell us where and when this information was published? Then we could read all that, too."

No. Fedorov couldn't quite say now precisely, but it seemed to him that such information had been published in many sources, for example, in the proceedings of the Stockholm International Peace Research Institute (SIPRI).[340] However, there was no way to calm down Judge Sazonov, because Fedorov had toyed with the self-esteem of this author of published works. "Tell us, exactly in what year was the edition published with such information? However, I am again warning you in advance, that according to Article 181 of the RSFSR Criminal Code, perjury by a witness is punishable by up to 2 years of imprisonment."

These words took Lev down a notch, and he wilted. Jail just wasn't a part of his grandiose plan. He started explaining pitifully that he couldn't remember, and you know it wasn't so very important. He said it was easy to guess anyway, because, for example Americans openly wrote that they had developed binary weapons. And our country always responded to such things with a mirrored reaction, and reproduced the same kinds of weapons.

Sazonov decided to strike Fedorov a final blow and asked acidly why he hadn't answered in the same way to the investigator during his interrogation in the Investigation Department.

"Here is the transcript of your interrogation from October 22 1992, according to which you claim that the defendant had provided all the information about the development of chemical weapons and you only edited it, giving it a literary treatment," the judge pressed on. "What is more, you testified that Mirzayanov had given information about the new chemical weapons when you and the defendant met with the American correspondent Will Englund."

Fedorov faded out completely and answered that he renounced his former testimony. The judge immediately asked the reason for this decision. Lev obscured the issue and explained that he had been inexperienced, and he was frightened when the Chekists had burst into his apartment early that morning.

After these words I felt squeamish about Fedorov who had perjured himself for the second time. I knew the real reason why he renounced his testimony. He did it only after I had distributed a copy of the transcript of his interrogation, which exposed his own behavior! However, I don't think that my former co-author could justify his words. Lev wanted to make everybody doubt me. He did his best to convince everybody (but the judges, of course!) that I wasn't the person I pretended to be. Later he probably wanted to impart substance to his testimony and share it with the public, so they would admire how bravely and selflessly he had assumed the entire responsibility of "protecting" me. While thinking about this, I probably unwittingly winced and shook my head. The judge noticed it and asked me, "What's the matter with you, defendant? Do you feel bad?"

I answered, "No, I'm all right, but this is totally repulsive. I would be grateful if you could spare me this extremely disgusting spectacle."

"Do you have comments, remarks, or additions?" he asked readily. He obviously wanted Fedorov and me to enter into a verbal battle. But that was even more loathsome for me. I answered that I didn't wish to argue with the witness, and this was why neither my lawyer nor I had any questions for him.

Strange as it may seem, the judge showed leniency toward me and stopped the interrogation of Lev Fedorov.

When Fedorov left the courtroom, he told the correspondents, as if nothing had happened, that he had given testimony which could break open the whole hearing…

Andrei Mironov was the next to testify. He had been the interpreter during the interview I gave to Will Englund that was published in the newspaper the *Baltimore Sun* on September 16, 1992. Mironov also accompanied Englund as an interpreter when he was interrogated in the Investigation Department of the RF Ministry of Security. So, Mironov was well informed about all the events. However, the experienced former dissident who had spent many years in a Soviet prison had made a blunder after the interrogation of Will Englund. The American had refused to sign the transcript of the interrogation, but thuggish Shkarin managed to get Andrei Mironov to sign it. That signature confirmed that the testimony of his American friend was translated in exact correspondence with the original. This allowed the investigation to do without the signature of Will Englund, because he didn't have to sign a transcript in a language that he didn't know.

Evidently this is why Mironov said that he denounced his signature, which had presumably made Englund's refusal to sign the transcript worthless at the very beginning of his testimony. Mironov persistently stressed that I hadn't given Englund any technical or any other detailed information when I made a statement about the new weapons during the interview. Then Andrei said that the American journalist knew about the development of new chemical weapons from other sources as well. He didn't specify these sources, referring to a law about Russian mass media practices. When he was talking about "other sources", I am certain that he meant the interview with Andrei Zheleznyakov.[341]

At that time I noticed that Prosecutor Pankratov was furiously writing something down. Andrei then argued a little with the judges, answered their questions, and finally said that he thought that my prosecution and the closed trial were illegal. I could see by the faces of the judges that they were not well disposed towards Mironov. However, their faces also expressed some confusion. Something hadn't gone as they had planned.

Prosecutor Pankratov Rejects the Work of the Chekists
Judges Cancel the Trial

After Andrei Mironov left, the prosecutor took the floor. He said that the trial had gone on for a long time, but new circumstances had been brought to light in the case. The experts clearly had a difference of opinion, so it was impossible to depend on their conclusions. This is why it was becoming more doubtful that the court could resolve all these contradictions objectively and impartially, based solely on material provided by the investigation. With pathos, the prosecutor further concluded that in his opinion the preliminary investigation was insufficient. Therefore, he had to ask the court to stop investigating the case and to send it back for repeated investigation, with a newly appointed expert commission. New witnesses should be called, especially regarding the allegation by witness Andrei Mironov.

At a reception in Washington, February 1994. From the left to right: Semeyon Reznik, Gale Colby, Irene Goldman, Jonathan Wise, Vil Mirzayanov, David Wise, Louis Clark

With Will Englund. Princeton, summer of 1997.

With Michael Cavallo. New York, February 1995.

That old veteran nicely and effectively performed the task assigned to him by Attorney General Aleksei Kazannik. It turned out that when he received an order from above, he could be objective after all and use all the bungling and blunders that Investigator Shkarin had made while he was fabricating my case.

I closely observed the reactions of the judges while I was listening to the speech of the prosecutor. Not one of them concealed their bewilderment. They were shocked by the prosecutor's statement. I also saw how my lawyer reacted to Pankratov's speech. It seemed to me that Asnis was triumphant, although he was usually imperturbable and didn't show his emotions. He smiled slightly and cast glances in my direction. Of course I understood what colossal efforts Asnis had made leading up to this prosecutor's speech. I admired the talent of my lawyer. Alexander managed to put everything that had been expressed in the numerous public campaigns for my defense, into legal order so that such an opinion had formed. He gave numerous interviews to foreign and Russian

State Secrets

reporters, sparing no effort or time. My friends Gale Colby and Irene Goldman - organizers and coordinators of the U.S. movement in my defense - constantly called on him at any time of the day to get information about my case and to ask advice about further action. Asnis was always clear and concise. And he worked for only a token fee from *Moscow News*.

As soon as the prosecutor finished his stunning speech, the judge announced that the hearing was closed. The next court session was scheduled for February 11th. My lawyer came up to me before the guard took me away, and said that he would file his motion to have me released from jail, along with the prosecutor's written appeal to send the case for additional investigation. I agreed.

It wasn't so cold on my way to jail. I even started imagining that I would be released the next day. I would come out to meet with a lot of journalists who had been writing about my case and people who had come to support me, and I would express my warm gratitude to them. However, my life experience as a scientist and experimenter has taught me not to prepare myself for victory ahead of time. Often disappointments are caused by unpredictable circumstances. I returned to the cell and told my cellmates about the events in court without any special excitement, and it wasn't due to any artificial restraint.

The February 10th issue of *Izvestia*, which had been brought to our cell, contained an article published by Valery Yakov.[342] He gave a review of readers' letters supporting me. Among them, was a letter by a group of Russian scientists (20 professors, PhD's, and master's of science) that was also categorical in its judgment. Although it wasn't addressed to President Yeltsin, they signed a statement which reads, "We consider the prosecution of V. Mirzayanov to be an illegal attempt on the part of the military-industrial complex to hide their inhumane actions."

Three renowned academicians of the Russian Academy of Sciences, Sergei Zalygin, Victor Maslov, and Boris Sokolov, presented concise, logical and convincing arguments for their protest. First of all, they asserted that secrets of any technical problem are specific formulas and blueprints, diagrams, and other technical indices. I hadn't disclosed anything like this. Second, by considering the case about disclosing state secrets, the court confirmed that I told the truth, and that the information I disclosed had truly been concealed from the public. Third, when scientists and specialists sign a non-disclosure agreement they assume definite obligations, but they must be relieved of them, if such fundamental issues as ecological violations connected with life and human health are at stake. In this way, the games played with state secrets during the Chernobyl tragedy led to irreparable calamity for many thousands of innocent citizens, and nobody was held responsible for this.[342]

Killer Koshelev and Biological Weapons

On the morning of February 11th, I was taken to the basement of the court as usual. However, after I arrived in the courtroom, Alexander Asnis said that the hearing would not take place that day. Judge Sazonov was either ill or busy with more important business. The next hearing was scheduled for Monday, February 14, 1994. I was very upset, but I tried to comfort myself.

When I was taken back to the basement and my handcuffs were removed, they asked me which cell I was from, and I pointed to the nearest one where the voices of prisoners were coming from. This wasn't my cell, but I was a little curious and wanted to see some inmates. I entered a long narrow cell where a few young people under 25 were smoking and animatedly discussing prisoners' issues. I understood from their conversation that one of them was a member of the Lyuberetskaya gang which had defiantly murdered a few people. There was also a Muscovite there, a recently discharged soldier who had shot a few policemen while resisting arrest. I just listened and didn't ask any questions. Finally, one of the young prisoners got interested in me and asked, "What's your name, Father, and how did you get here?"

I briefly tried to explain it to him, but my story didn't move him at all.

He said condescendingly, "Well, you are a Doctor of Sciences. How much did you make? I suppose 500-600 rubles," he answered right away instead of me. I confirmed that his answer was very close.

"You know I dished out much more for one night in a restaurant with my chicks than you were paid for several months," he boasted. "Don't worry, I worked, too. Only you were sitting in your laboratory and I was a janitor. I cleansed the society of those who rob people blind," philosophized the young prisoner. However, it was obvious he didn't believe what he was saying.

I noticed that all the prisoners were adamant about their innocence, and all of them justified their crimes in every way possible, by some self-invented theories.

How simple everything in the world is! And it is the same everywhere. Everybody behaves in this way, from Fascists and Communists to God-seekers and murderers. But what could I say, for example, to this young and healthy fellow with eyes drowsy, as if he were drunk? He was saying indignantly that everyone in court was lying, including the victims.

"Just imagine, the victim says that I took his money and valuables without his consent. But these are just lies. He gave all of this to me willingly," complained the bandit. Then he added with a grin, "How could he not, if I kept him hanging upside down from the ceiling for half an hour?"

Then a soldier came up to the doors of the cell and the young people rushed over to him. I heard them bargaining for "weed", and it turned out that it was a name for marijuana. They swore terribly, saying that these bastards had no conscience and they were robbing them blind. However, they did come up with the money and bought the stuff. The weed was packed in matchboxes. A prisoner, who didn't have enough money for it, quickly scribbled a note and asked the guard to give it to a woman who he described in the courtroom. She was to hand over the money. Strange but true! A while later another soldier came up to our cell and gave the prisoner his weed and the change. It was clear that the soldiers were just carrying out the job, but it was the officers and guards, who desperately want to avoid being photographed by journalists, who managed this "business." As soon as the soldier went away, everyone started smoking. The young cop-killer was also offered a smoke. Before this he had stared at a spot on the ceiling, obstinately silent and deep in his thoughts. Finally, the marijuana made him relax, and he started telling me his horrible story.

His name was Alexander Koshelev. He was born in Moscow and lived near Taganka before serving in the Army. When he was 18, he was drafted into military service and was sent to one of the top-secret units that worked with biological weapons on the island of Vozrozhdenie in the Aral Sea. As I understood it, the production and testing sites for biological weapons were located there. Colonel Zaritovsky was the commander of this unit, and Koshelev served there from 1990 to 1992. Along with his friends, he guarded some strange warehouses with a lot of monkey cages, located behind a high barbed wire installation.

Experiments were conducted on these animals on the island. They were given injections of some liquid substance, and the people who did this were dressed in protective rubber suits and gas masks, despite the terrible heat.

The working conditions were extreme. They were isolated, far from the mainland, far from people, and it was terribly hot, which made life unbearably tough on the soldiers. In addition, the sergeants and soldiers who had spent some time on the island cruelly abused the new recruits. They beat them up for anything that seemed like disobedience or lack of respect for their whims.

Once during the summer 1992 an alarm went off in the unit. A few monkeys had escaped from their cages. The bosses were at a loss about how it could have happened. Everybody was sent to search for them and shoot them, because the animals were infected with an unknown disease, which made them very dangerous. Koshelev said in a trembling voice that these monkeys strongly resembled people who were hunted-down, and he felt terrible when he had to shoot a poor stray devil that had hidden among the reeds.

He was discharged from his service two years before that, but he didn't take to life.

"I don't understand how I could get to be so cruel. I never suspected that I could be like that," he lamented. The police took revenge for the inhumane killing of their police colleagues and beat him especially hard. Despite that he still seemed quite strong, as he was only 23.

I advised him to tell his lawyer about his tough service at the test site for biological weapons. Probably one of the reasons for his crimes was the irreparable psychological damage that he had suffered during that damned service.

Having heard Koshelev's story, I realized again that I was right not to trust military men who, despite repeated oaths that our country had discontinued the production and testing of biological weapons, continued with their dirty business, deceiving not only the people of the world, but the President of Russia as well. So, I told myself, it was my duty to carry through with what I had started, so that chemical weapons were no longer either produced or developed.

Meanwhile, the other prisoners hid their marijuana cigarettes in a special way so that the prison security wouldn't find the drugs during their search. However, only one trick guaranteed that the weed they had bought would safely make it through all the checks. One of the prisoners wrapped the marijuana in polyethylene film, and then he sealed all the edges with a match flame, making a capsule. I didn't want to irritate the inmates who were "getting high", so I observed their manipulations from the corner of my eye. Then I saw that the owner of the homemade capsule stuffed it into his rear end. I was quite shocked at such wildness. Probably the young man noticed that and said that a "buddy" in their cell had a birthday that day, and they had to celebrate it. And how could they celebrate anything without weed?

Soon we were taken to the jail transport van that shuttles prisoners to Moscow jails. I was in high spirits because by Monday I could be free, but the tales of the young prisoners in the van made me grow sad again. "Seri, I was given only 8 years. I just wrapped those judges around my little finger. And you?" I could hear a voice from the cage. Seri answered that probably he would be put on probation. "They have no evidence to pin on me," he boasted.

The one sentenced to eight years remarked that his sister would be 18 and she would probably be married by the time of his release. "And I will be 30," he concluded sadly. Seri started comforting him by saying that the most important thing was to make it to "the zone" (labor camp). They say the people there and life are "good."

The weekend dragged by excruciatingly slowly. Even continuous television coverage of the winter Olympic Games didn't help. Although I was almost certain that I would be released on Monday, as my cellmates were telling me, I admitted that the judges would probably still try to take revenge on me and keep me in jail until the second trial. The fact that Judge Sazonov didn't allow my wife to have a meeting with me was a bad omen. He didn't even consider it necessary to explain the reason for his decision.

On the morning of February 14, 1994, when the court session began, Prosecutor Pankratov took the floor as expected. He read his statement, which repeated his speech from the previous session almost word for word. I could clearly see that the judges were nervous, because the decision to drop the charges clearly meant that they had failed to make their actions seem impartial and objective. Now, following the instructions of their former ally the Attorney General, the state prosecutor claimed that their charges were groundless, but camouflaged it by saying that the case should be sent for additional investigation. The judges were obviously not ready for such a somersault on his part and found themselves in a rather delicate position.

After the prosecutor spoke, my lawyer submitted a petition, requesting my release from prison. Then the judges announced a break so the court could compose a resolution.

Forty minutes later the judges returned and Sazonov read the decision of the court, which said that my case should be sent for additional investigation, but I had to stay in jail. It was only unclear for how long. I was disappointed and couldn't think straight. However, I tried to convince myself that we had won a really huge, though not a final, victory. I believed the additional investigation, which the Attorney General's Office had to conduct, not the KGB, would establish the full groundlessness of the charges.

Roald Sagdeev and Dan Ellsberg. February 1995.
Washington, February 1995.

With Gale Colby and Irene Goldman. Atlanta, February 1995.

Of course, I was upset that I would have to remain in jail. But, at the same time I believed that the pressure of the international community wouldn't let them keep me incarcerated for long without any grounds.

Outwardly I was perfectly calm and I even tried to comfort my lawyer who couldn't conceal his disappointment this time. Obviously, the tension of the few last days showed. He had worked tirelessly and had made all possible efforts to ensure the positive outcome of my case. We had no chance to talk because the guard was putting handcuffs on me to take me out of the courtroom.

On the way out, Asnis ran into *Associated Press* reporter Sergei Shargorodsky, who quoted him the February 15th issue of *The Moscow Tribune* as saying: "I am amazed. I simply cannot find the words to express my disappointment with this decision."[343] Vladimir Nazarov wrote about it also in *Kuranty*.[344] *The New York Times*,[345] *The Baltimore Sun*[346] and *Chemical and Engineering News*[347] posted information about latest events connected with my case. Wendy Sloane of *The Christian Science Monitor* symbolically titled her article with Andrey Mironov's words "Mirzayanov's case is the first test of the new Constitution".[348] A more detailed analysis of the legal aspects of my case was perfectly showcased in an article by Valeri Rudnev.[349]

Two days later Asnis came to visit me once more in jail. He told me about my status. It turned out that until the resolution of the court was properly recorded and sent to the Attorney General's Office by special mail, I would remain at the disposal of the court. In other words, I was still a captive prisoner of vengeful Judge Nikolai Sazonov.

When my case and the court's resolution arrived at the Attorney General's Office and the jail received notification of it, I would become the ward of the Attorney General's Office, which would be free to decide my fate. I had only to wait. I was very pleased, because both Asnis and I believed that Aleksei Kazannik would immediately release me. I felt fine when I said good-bye to my lawyer, and I carried back a pile of newspapers with materials about my case.

I prepared myself for the possibility that I would be released

State Secrets

only by the end of the following week. Fortunately, it happened earlier. On Tuesday, February 22, when we were boiling food from concentrates for lunch, the head appeared in the door of the cell, and in keeping with the established rules, asked "Who is Mirzayanov?"

"I am Mirzayanov!" I shouted.

The head snapped, "Quiet! Get your stuff ready to head for the exit!"

I got ready quickly and said farewell to my cellmates. I was glad that I was leaving this damned jail but a little sad that my cellmates remained there.

Fifteen minutes later the cell door opened and the guard ordered me to follow him. We followed the usual route to the place where they searched me. Then I was locked in a solitary cell, and I waited for what seemed like an eternity for the guard to come back.

He returned a few hours later and ordered me to undress. Then he started carefully examining all my belongings and all the folds of my body. There was nothing suspicious there. In my notebook I had the telephone numbers of my cellmates, but it was written as part of a mathematical equation. He didn't notice my trick. However, the guard kept me in the solitary cell for yet another hour.

Finally, he came back and said that he had not been able to get some of my things from the jail storeroom because the keeper had finished his work and left for the day. Then he took me to the prison warden, A. Podrez.

A young and energetic man was sitting in a spacious office behind a long table. According to the inmates, he had inherited his job from his father, and he treasured his position a lot. I immediately decided that he looked like a typical secretary of the Komsomol Raikom. He was so well groomed, well nourished, and pleased with himself because his prospects for the future were simple and bright. If he didn't become a party boss, he would be a VIP in trade or education. Or maybe he would even represent the country abroad, and "stand up for the interests of the proletariat" all over the world, while his efforts would be compensated in foreign currency.

Podrez showed me the resolution of the Attorney General about my release and asked me to sign that I had read it. I did so immediately. Then the warden asked me if I had any complaints or requests. I answered that I couldn't get my stuff from the storeroom, and I didn't have the fare to get home. I asked him to lend me 50 rubles for the metro ticket. Podrez gave me this money and I promised to return it the next day.

I kept my word and I handed 50 rubles through the window for parcels with a note "to be handed to the prison warden." However strange it may seem, the money was received without any questions.

My family was waiting for me at home, because Aleksander Asnis had told my wife about my arrival in advance.

Later I found out that he had practically launched a ground support operation to release me. As soon as my case arrived at the Attorney General's Office along with the official court decision, my lawyer sent a special courier to take the court resolution regarding my release to Aleksei Kazannik's summer house, because he didn't feel well and wasn't at work. He signed a resolution and immediately sent it to the prison.

The first thing I did after my release was to call various organizations and tell them about the terrible conditions in which the prisoners of Matrosskaya Tishina were kept. I got in touch with the Red Cross office in Moscow, and some of their employees came to see me. I told them in detail about this prison, but it turned out that they had heard all of this before. Furthermore, they had even visited the prison, but so far their efforts hadn't been rewarded with any positive results.

I also called Lord N. Bethel who was a very active member of the Commission for Human Rights in the European Parliament. Finally, I decided to send a detailed letter about inhuman conditions in Matrosskaya Tishina to Mr. Sammaruga, president of the Red Cross organization in Geneva.

The newspapers published an interview with me on this topic.[350-354] They also posted reports about my release from jail and gave comments on some possible solutions of my case.[355-359]

Chapter 23
The Acquittal

The Decision of the Attorney General

Although I was released from custody, not everything was clear about my case. Aleksei Kazannik, the Attorney General of Russia, retired immediately after my release.

According to a special resolution of the Duma, he was obliged to sanction the release of the participants of the October 1993 coup. Many people in the Kremlin hoped Kazannik would not submit to this decision and would show "revolutionary consciousness." Kazannik couldn't do that, since he was an exceptionally honest man, even though I am certain that he didn't have any sympathy at all for the mutineers.

The President appointed Aleksei Ilyushenko in his place, a man who had worked in the Russian Presidential Legal Department before that. My lawyer Asnis was preparing for the additional investigation, and at the same time he was doing everything that he could to get my case dismissed altogether. Frankly, I had no idea how he was doing all this. Still, I think my lawyer was justified in being cautious and not hurrying to describe his efforts to me in detail.

First of all, he knew that my telephone conversations could be tapped, and they could also listen in to my private conversations at home. Journalists were often able to fish out information ahead of time, which complicated his work. Neither then, nor later after the case was finished, did I ask Aleksander Asnis about the details of his activities.

That is why when Petr Mukshin, a reporter from the *Interfax* wire services, called me at 11:35 A.M. on March 11, 1994 and said that he had just received a fax from the Attorney General's Office stating that my case had been dismissed, it was an enormous and very pleasant surprise for me.

Soon Asnis called and asked me to come to the Attorney General's Office on Pushkin Street to receive an official copy of the resolution about the termination of my case for "lack of corpus delicti."[360]

I was incredibly excited by this call. It took me a few minutes to get ready. Then I rushed off to the trolley-bus stop. An hour later I was in the Attorney General's Office. A crowd of television reporters and photo journalists has gathered, waiting for us there with their questions. Mostly my lawyer answered them. Indeed, he was now the main character in focus, and the journalists received thorough and detailed explanations from him.

We got our passes and went to see Lev Baranov, the head of the department. He was extremely polite to me and said that he highly esteemed my convictions, which prevented me from acting outside of the framework of the law and from disclosing any secrets. I signed a receipt for the resolution [361] and we said good-bye to Baranov.

Although the termination of my case was expected, it was a sensation, and not just for me. The wire services and newspapers widely reported it.[362-366] I was and am still proud of the conclusion of the editorial in *Moscow News*, which said that my "case had united scientists from many countries, human rights activists." [366]

The termination of my case was also the cause of a pleasant episode at one of the sessions of U.S. Senate on March 15th.[367]

I did not have enough time to give journalists interviews or to answer the telephone calls. Not only famous people congratulated me, but also many that I hadn't known of before.

Gale Colby called from Princeton to let me know that I was awarded the distinguished 1994 Heinz R. Pagels Rights of Scientists Award of the New York Academy of Sciences, "in recognition of his courage and his singular demonstration of the moral responsibility of individual scientists in upholding the integrity of scientific knowledge in an emerging democratic society". Professor Joshua Lederberg, a Nobel Prize laureate (who Gale only half-jokingly dubbed as "one of the gods of science"), and the President of the NYAS, called to confirm this and congratulated me.

The famous philanthropist and billionaire George Soros and another renowned Nobel Prize laureate James Watson awarded me the distinguished prize at a reception in the Radisson-Slavyanskaya Hotel, located near the Kiev Railway Station in Moscow. Mostly it was Americans who accompanied George Soros on his trip across Russia, who were present at the ceremony.

Was I happy? I can say I definitely was. My head was full of sunshine. Despite that, almost none of the problems that I raised have yet been solved. Novichok was unmasked then, and there was no real chance for that yet. My personal problems were also mounting, no job, and no real opportunities. I was still a Russian secret-bearer, and because of that, I didn't have any chance to go abroad and to try to start my new life. Simultaneously I was defiant and recalcitrant, yet full of energy to struggle for my future…

The End

Glossary

AAAS	American Association for the Advancement of Science	
A-208	$\begin{array}{c} \text{O-i-C}_4\text{H}_9 \\ / \\ \text{CH}_3\text{-P=O} \\ \backslash \\ \text{S-CH}_2\text{-CH}_2\text{-N(C}_2\text{H}_5)_2 \end{array}$	Substance 33
A-230	$\begin{array}{c} \text{F} \\ / \\ \text{CH}_3\text{-P=O} \\ \backslash \\ \text{N=C(CH}_3)\text{-N(C}_2\text{H}_5)_2 \end{array}$	Substance 84
A-232	$\begin{array}{c} \text{F} \\ / \\ \text{CH}_3\text{O-P=O} \\ \backslash \\ \text{N=C(CH}_3)\text{-N(C}_2\text{H}_5)_2 \end{array}$	A-232
A-234	$\begin{array}{c} \text{F} \\ / \\ \text{C}_2\text{H}_5\text{O-P=O} \\ \backslash \\ \text{N=C(CH}_3)\text{-N(C}_2\text{H}_5)_2 \end{array}$	A-234

A-242

$$CH_3-P(=O)(F)-N=C-N(R)_2$$ with $N(R)_2$ branch, A-242, where R – diethyl radical

A-262

$$CH_3O-P(=O)(F)-N=C-N(R)_2$$ with $N(R)_2$ branch, A-262, where R – diethyl radical

A-235	Russian code name of sarin
A-255	Russian code name of soman
Complex ether	GOSNIIOKhT's code name of Substance 33
C.P.S.U	Communist Party of the Soviet Union
CW	Chemical weapon
CWC	Chemical Weapons Convention
DDR	Democratic Russia Movement
FAPSI	Federal Agency for Government Communications and Information
FAS	Federation of American Scientists
Foliant	Soviet/Russian nerve agents program
FSB	Federal Service of Security
GC	Gas chromatograph(ic)
GOSNIIOKhT	State Scientific Research Institute of Organic Chemistry and Technology
GRNIIOKhT	State Russian Scientific Research Institute of Organic Chemistry and Technology
GRU	General Intelligence Directorate of the Soviet (Russian) Army
K-410	Russian code name of CS-tear gas
K-444	Russian code name of SR-tear gas

State Secrets

KGB	Committee of State Security
Khoryok	Russian binary chemical weapon program
M-01	GOSNIIOKhT code name of Substance 33
M-02	GOSNIIOKhT code name of sarin
M-03	GOSNIIOKhT code name of soman
MB RF	Ministry of Security of the Russian Federation
MCAD	Military Academy of Chemical Defense
Military Unit 64518	Directorate of Chief of Chemical Troops of Russia
Military Unit 61469	Scientific Research Military Institute and Independent Chemical Battalion in Shikhany-2
Military Unit 26382	Scientific Research Military Polygon and Independent Chemical Battalion in Nukus, Uzbekistan
MITKhT	Moscow Institute of Fine Chemical Technology
NII	Scientific Research Institute
NII-42	Former code name of GOSNIIOKhT
NII-94	Former code name of GOSNIIOKhT
NIOKR	Scientific Research Experiment Design Work
NKVD	People's Commissariat for Internal Affairs
Nomenklatura	the top of the elite ruling class or bureaucrats in the Soviet Union
Novichok	Soviet/Russian nerve agents program
Novichok-5	Russian binary weapons program for A-232
NPO Basalt	Scientific Industrial Association for warfare design
OKBA	Special Design Bureau of Automation
OMON	Special Purpose Police Detachment
Ordoval-1	GOSNIIOKhT code name of sarin
Ordoval-2	GOSNIIOKhT code name of soman
Post Office Box	Part of code name of all secret scientific research institutes
Post Office Box 702	Former code name of GOSNIIOKhT
Post Office Box M-5123	Code name of GOSNIIOKhT for business mailing

Ppt	Part per trillion
R-33	Russian code name of analog of Substance 33
R-35	Russian code name of sarin
R-55	Russian code name of soman
Sharashka	Prison for scientists-political prisoners
S	Secret
SS	Top secret
SS/khf	Top secret/ Foliant program
Substance 33	Russian code name of VX-analog
Substance 65	Russian code name of CS- tear gas
Substance 74	Russian code name of CR-tear gas
Substance 78	Russian code name of BZ-hallucinogen agent
Substance 84	GOSNIIOKhT codname of A-230
Substance 100-A	O-cyclopentyl analog of Substance 33
Substance 100-B	O -methylcyclopentyl analog of Substance 33
TSNIIVTI	Central Scientific Research Military Technical Institute
UNKhV	Directorate of Chief of Chemical Troops of Russia
USSR	Union of Soviet Socialist Republic
VF GOSNIIOKhT	Volgograd Branch of GOSNIIOKhT
VKhK	Military Chemical Complex
VP MO	Military Representative of Russian Defense Ministry
VPK	Military Industrial Commission
"White Sea"	Nickname of lake in Volgograd contaminated by residues of chemical agents and phosphoorganic pesticides

Notes

Chapter 2 My Background (pp. 5 – 28)

1. Geoffrey Hosking, *Russia, People and Empire* (London: HarperCollins, 1997); Dominic Lieven, *Empire: The Russian Empire and Its Rivals* (New Haven, CT: Yale University Press, 2001, London: John Murray, 2000).
2. On Soviet policies to quell ethnic differences and increase their hold on power, see Robert Conquest, *Stalin: Breaker of Nations* (New York: Penguin, 1991); Ronald Grigor Suny, *The Revenge of the Past: Nationalism, Revolution, and the Collapse of the Soviet Union* (Stanford, CA: Stanford University Press, 1993); Terry Martin, *The Affirmative Action Empire: Nations and Nationalism in the Soviet Union, 1923-1939* (Ithaca, New York: Cornell University Press, 2001); Harry W. Hazard and Robert Strausz-Hupe, *The Idea of Colonialism* (New York: Fredrick A. Praeger, 1958), especially chapter 4, "Russian Colonialism: Tsarist and Soviet Empires."
3. In December 1929 Stalin called for the "liquidation of the kulaks as a class" because he claimed they were wealthy and the class enemy of the state, which led and exploited the peasantry to deliberately thwart the government's Five Year Plan. In reality, most kulaks only owned one or two pieces of livestock and had managed to employ a few other peasants. Kulaks were forced into state run collective farms or sent to brutal labor camps. See Robert Conquest, *The Great Terror: A Reassessment* (Oxford: Oxford University Press, 1990); John Thompson, *A Vision Unfulfilled: Russia and the Soviet Union in the Twentieth Century* (Lexington, MA: Heath Publishers, 1996): 261-4.
4. For more on the civil war and famine, Richard Pipes, *Russia under the Bolshevik Regime* (New York: Vintage Books of Random House, 1994); Fisher, H. H., *The Famine in Soviet Russia (1919-1923): The Operation of the American Relief Administration* (New York: MacMillan, 1927).

5. On the fate of Soviet prisoners of war, see Nikolai Tolstoy, *The Secret Betrayal: 1944-1947* (New York: Scribner, 1978); Mark Elliot, "The United States and Forced Repatriation of Soviet Citizens, 1944-1947," *Political Science Quarterly* 88, No. 2 (June 1973): 253-75; Mark Elliot, *Pawns of Yalta: Soviet Refugees and America's Role in Their Repatriation* (Urbana, Ill: University of Illinois Press, 1982); John Whitley, "Countless Prisoners Of War Handed Back To Stalin By Churchill," at http://www.rense.com/general47/butch.htm ; Aleksey I. Briukhanov, "Vot kak eto bilo: O rabote missii po repatriatsii sovetskikh grazhdan" *Vospominaniia Sovetskogo Ofitsera* (Moscow, 1958): 38.
6. The Tatar version of Radio Liberty – Radio Azatlyk right now is broadcasting from Prague (Czech Republic) paid for by American taxpayers' dollars, but its journalists are working under the supervision of the Russian Government and this radio has nothing to do with its very title and the distribution of real information about American democracy and American values.

Chapter 3 My Student Days (pp. 29 – 53)

7. The Communist Party sponsored an organization, the Komsomol, or Communist League of Youth, for those between age fourteen and early thirties, so that they could learn the proper things to become party members. Komsomol members provoked political activity, completed social projects (e.g., planting trees along urban roads), and supposedly served as role models for socialist behavior. John Thompson, *A Vision Unfulfilled: Russia and the Soviet Union in the Twentieth Century* (Lexington, MA: Heath Publishers, 1996): 261-4.
8. One plant was situated in Salavat, in Bashkortstan, and the other in Angarsk, which is located on the Angara River in the Irkutsk region, about 30 kilometers north-west of the city of Irkutsk and 50 kilometers north of the western tip of Lake Baikal.

Chapter 4 I Become a Person from "The Box" (pp. 55-62)

9. Thirty years later, in 1994, I was happy to run into this same man at an international meeting, devoted to the role of mass media in the democratization of society. I was very glad to see him. He was a Doctor of Jurisprudence, a professor, and the head of the Department of Criminal Law at the Moscow Law Institute. I realized then that my old colleague was very embarrassed about his worker's past.

State Secrets

Chapter 6 Into Supersecrecy (pp. 75-88)

10. The term "sharashka"was first introduced by Aleksandr I. Solzhenitsyn, *The Gulag Archipelago, 1918-1956, An Experiment in Literary Investigation I-II* (New York: Harper & Row, Publishers, 1973). Also see Ann Applebaum, *Gulag: A History* (New York: Doubleday, 2003).
    The renowned scientists Rudolf Udris, Peter Sergeev, Michael Nemtsov, and Boris Kruzhalov, who were the first to develop the hydro peroxide process for producing phenol and acetone in 1946, were working in such a chemical *sharashka*. Udris ultimately committed suicide. Sergeev was barely released from this *sharashka* when his son, Andrei P. Sergeev, who was also a chemist, was jailed there on charges of anti-Soviet agitation. See M.S. Nemtsov, "At First We Were Four People," *Chemistry and Life*, no. 2 (1989); Andrei P. Sergeev, "How I Participated in Operation 'Yprit,'" *Izvestia*, 11 August 1992, which chronicles the dumping of around twenty tons of bombs containing mustard gas.
11. The First Department was operating under the control of the Deputy Director of the Security Regime, a KGB officer who only formally was subordinate to Director of GOSNIIOKhT. The Second Department was also operating under the supervision of the Deputy Director of the Security Regime.
12. The Third Department was also operating under the control of Deputy Director of the Security Regime.

Chapter 7 GOSNIIOKhT's Tangled Bureaucracy (pp. 89-117)

13. In the 1950s, the Soviet military directed the chemical weapons pipeline by controlling the research and development efforts, which took place at the Central Military Scientific Research Technical Institute in Moscow. At that time, GOSNIIOKhT was a civilian organization and its only military work was related to developing production technologies for the agents that the military's central research institute discovered. In October 1960, Nikita Khrushchev, General Secretary of the Communist Party, decided that the research of chemical agents was too dangerous for a major metropolitan area and moved the Central Military Scientific Research Technical Institute to a town near the Volga River in southern Russia called Shikhany. Most of the military's senior scientists, which included civilian as well as military researchers, were reluctant to relocate to Shikhany and instead "retired" to GOSNIIOKhT.
14. According to Western historians, there wasn't any Tatar Yoke after the Tatar-Mongols were conquered at the beginning of 13th Century. The opposite is true: the Tatars are the real founders of the united Russian State.

See, for instance, Donald Ostrowski, *Muscovy and the Mongols. Cross-Cultural Influences on the Steppe Frontier, 1304-1589* (Cambridge, UK: Cambridge University Press, 1998); Boris Ischboldin, *Essays on Tatar History*. (New Delhi India: New Book Society of India, 1963); Janet Martin, *Medieval Russia 980-1584* (Cambridge, UK: Cambridge University Press, 1995).

15. I.L. Knunyants, A.I. Shchekotikhin, A.V. Fokin, *Izvestia AN SSSR*, otdelenie khim.nauk, no. 2 (1953), p. 282-289.
16. Within seconds to minutes after exposure to a lethal dose of nerve agent by ingestion, skin exposure, or inhalation, a person will begin vomiting violently and go into seizures, eventually losing consciousness. Even when antidotes are available, these factors can make medical treatment much more difficult. U.S. Army Medical Research Institute of Chemical Defense, *Medical Management of Chemical Casualties Handbook*, 3rd ed. (Aberdeen Proving Ground, MD: Chemical Casualty Care Division, 1999): 105-37.
17. In 1974 the following people received the Lenin Prize for organizing the production of Substance 33: A.V. Fokin, K.A. Guskov, M.I. Kabachnik, Ju.V. Privezentsev, V.M. Romanov, V.F. Rostunov, E.M. Zhuravski. Like Kabachnik and Fokin, Zhuravski didn't have any relationship to this work except that he had been the chief of a department of UNKhV.
18. The Administration of Chief of the Chemical Troops
19. It is necessary to point out that the role of the VPK has been exaggerated in some literature sources. Its role overall was limited to distribution of funds, especially currency etc. Some people named it the fifth wheel of the car.
20. I'll write further about Kirpichev's discovery.
21. Oleg Vishnyakov, "Interview with a Noose Around the Neck", *Novoe Vremya*, No 6, 1993, p. 40. (English version, Oct. 1993, p. 22-23.)
22. Count Grigory G. Orlov (1734-1783) was a lover of Empress Catherine II of Russia. In 1762 he organized the *coup d'état* that placed Catherine on the Russian throne and subsequently was her close adviser. John Alexander, *Catherine the Great: Life and Legend* (New York: Oxford Univ. Press, 1989): 56-7.

Chapter 8 Science and Scientists in GOSNIIOKhT (pp. 119-167)

23. On the initial discovery, L.E. Tammelin, "Dialkoxyphosphorylthiocholines, alkoxymethyl-phosphorthiocholines, and analogous choline esters," *Acta Chemica Scandinavica* 11(1957): 1340-9. For a brief history of "V" agents, Stockholm International Peace Research Institute, *The Problem of Chemical and Biological Warfare: A Study of the*

Historical, Technical Military, Legal, and Political Aspects of CBW and Possible Disarmament Measures, The Rise of CB Weapons, vol. 1 (New York: Humanities Press, 1971): 74-5.
24. *See* ref.13.
25. The Bigeye bomb was developed to mix diisopropyl aminoethylmethyl phosphonate with sulfur to make VX. Frederick R. Sidell, Ernest T. Takafuji, and David R. Franz, *Medical Aspects of Chemical and Biological Warfare, Textbook of Military Medicine, Warfare, Weaponry, and the Casualty: Part I* (Office of the Surgeon General: US Army 1997): 65-6, 70-1.
26. Di-isopropyl-aminoethylmethyl-phosphonate.
27. David Wise. *Cassidy's Run: The Secret Spy War Over Nerve Gas.* (New York: Random House, 2000).
28. BZ is short for 3-Quinuclidinyl benzilate. BZ is an anticholinergic, a category of drugs that includes antihistamines, antidepressants, and antipsychotics. Depending on the dosage, the effects of BZ range from mild drowsiness to loss of coordination, dulled thought process, confusion, paranoia, delirium, and hallucination. These symptoms generally appear several hours after exposure to BZ and can last for up to 96 hours. For more information, see James Ketchum and Frederick R. Sidell, "Incapacitating Agents," *Textbook of Military Medicine*, pp.296.
29. On Markov's murder see, Richard H. Cummings, "The Murder of Georgi Markov," *Intelligencer* 10, no. 1 (Feb. 1999): 9-11.
30. This facility was initially code named Tomko and worked in secrecy under a 1927 Russo-German pact to make chemical weapons. Not far from there, the so-called Tankodrom for training tank crews for German troops was located in Shikhany-1.
31. *See* ref. 82.
32. *See* Annex 5
33. According to Kremlin spokesman Alexander Orofyonov, Kuntsevich was fired because of "a single grievous violation of his work responsibilities." Alexander Gordeyev, "Yeltsin Fires Top Chemical Weapons Official," *The Moscow Times*, 8 April 1994.
34. *See* ref. 56.
35. Resolution of Central Committee of the CPSU and Council of Ministers of USSR from April 24 1977 N 3509-123. *See* Annex 21.
36. The tests could have gone very well, but the old cholinesterase method of analysis that the scientists at Nukus used did not allow the results to be interpreted accurately.
37. Read about his "discovery" in Chap. 9
38. Modeling was used to see how the agent would perform with other types of delivery systems.
39. The factory design was completed by NII Khimproject in Volgograd. GOSNIIOKhT deputy director Guskov told me about the planned move

of A-230 production to Pavlodar, where a commercial chemical plant was already located. At that time, sarin and soman were being produced at the Volgograd plant, which is in a city. Decisions had been made to move chemical weapons production operations to this more remote location. Not only were multiple agents to be produced at Pavlodar, but also the plant's production capability was to exceed that of Novocheboksarsk. For more on the Pavlodar plant, see Gulbarshyn Bozheyeva, "The Pavlodar Chemical Weapons Plant in Kazakhstan: History and Legacy," *Nonproliferation Review* 7, no. 2 (Summer 2000): 136-45.

40. For more on this accident, Will Englund, "Russia still doing work on chemical arms", *The Baltimore Sun*, October 18 1992; Oleg Vishnyakov, "I Was Making Binary Bombs," *Novoe Vremya* 50, December 1992, 46-9, trans. in FBIS-SOV-92-242, 16 November 1992, 25.

41. The work was done under the Central Committee and the Council of Ministers Resolution no. 844-186, 6 October 1989 and Ministry of Industry Decree no. 22-2, 9 December 1989. In Annex 21, see Top Secret Letter no. 1846 ss from Martynov to Shabunin, 24 November 1992; in Annex 31 see also "The Technical Order for the Compound Part of the Experimental Design Work of 'Substance A-232' On the Basis of the System of Components; The Code 'Novichok-5,'" Top Secret Document 2187 ss/khf, signed on 4 May 1990 by GOSNIIOKhT Director V.A. Petrunin, on 27 April 1990 by Chief of 4984 VP MO E.A. Umbliya, on 16 May 1990 by Chief of 458 VP MO N.G. Ragulin, and on 16 May 1990 by NPO Basalt Director A. S. Obukhov. (Moscow: Russian State Scientific Research Institute for Organic Chemistry and Technology, 4 April 1990).

42. *See* the 23 September 1989 Wyoming Memorandum of Understanding between the United States and the USSR, which provided for data on their respective stockpiles to be exchanged in two phases and for a joint verification experiment.

43. There is every reason to believe that the dioxin which was used for poisoning in 2004 Viktor Yushchenko, that time presidential candidate of Ukraine, was produced in this institute.

44. To qualify for this Lenin Prize, Petrunin and his cohorts had to have solid proof that they had designed, tested, certified, and begun mass production of the Substance 33 binary, complete with the signatures of the relevant factory managers. Otherwise, the application for the award would not meet the standard of being a great accomplishment worthy of the Lenin Prize. See also the comments of Vladimir Uglev in Oleg Vishnyakov's article, "Interview with a Noose Around the Neck," *Novoe Vremya*, No 6 (1993): 41-2

45. On 10 April 1987, Mikhail Gorbachev announced during a visit to Prague that the USSR was no longer making chemical weapons and had never deployed chemical weapons outside of its own territory. Jackson Diehl,

"Gorbachev Proposes New Missile Talks; Short-Range Rockets Would Be Negotiated," *Washington Post*, 10 April 1987, A1.
46. In addition to V. Petrunin, the Lenin Prize was given to S.A. Arzhakov, A.V. Gaev, A.V. Kisletsov, A.D. Kuntsevich, S.V. Petrov, E.S. Severin, V.I. Sichevoi. It is not surprising that not one of these "laureates" really worked on this problem. Such was Soviet style of life.

Chapter 9 Fight Without End and Evgeny Bogomazov's "Discovery" (pp. 169-194)

47. For a long time it was known as Voroshilov Military Academy of Chemical Defense.
48. Later he was transferred to the KGB and even participated in the search of the apartment of Lev Fedorov, my co-author of the article "A Poisoned Policy". *See* Annex 8.

Chapter 10 Safety While Working with Chemical Agents - Is it Possible? (pp. 195-204)

49. According to these regulations, the linear velocity of the air sucked by the ventilation into the laboratory exhaust hood had to be at least 1.0 meter per second to guarantee the safety of personnel. Every exhaust hood has a chart attached to it where the date and the last measured air velocity are logged, and if these measurements are lower than the standard norms, any operations with chemical agents must be terminated.
50. Some people in the U.S. are telling me that Substance 33 or VX-gas could not cause cancer, but they are forgetting that Substance 33 never was a pure product. It was a chemical agent of about 80% purity, contaminated with a lot of other compounds. Among them there were also some products of composition with three and more sulfur atoms.
51. These solutions were so ineffective that they did not even destroy the chemical agents to the level of permissible concentration, and that is a major safety shortcoming.
52. I was not the only chemist to note the deficiencies of the decontamination solution that the Russian Army continues to employ. General Nikolai Antonov, the former commander of Military Unit 61469, has also written about this problem. See N. S. Antonov, *Khimicheskoe oruzhie na rubezhe dvukh stoletii, Progress* (Moscow: 1994): 64. These terribly insufficient decontamination methods caused me to publicly oppose the plans of Ministry of Chemical Industry, which was planning to use the factory at No-

vocheboksarsk to destroy chemical weapons. Unit 83 in this factory produced Substance 33, and the walls of this facility remain irreversibly contaminated with Substance 33. Nevertheless, V. P. Ivanov, the Minister of Chemical and Petrochemical Industry accused me of significantly increasing the costs of Russia's chemical weapons destruction program if the Novocheboksarsk facility could not be used. *See* Annex 51 for the full text of secret letter no. 629 from V.P. Ivanov, Chairman of Committee for Chemical and Petrochemical Industry to S.D. Balashov, Head of the Investigation Department at the Ministry of Security of The Russian Federation, pertaining to case no. 62 (Moscow: 13 April 1993).

53. In collaboration with Dr. Igor Revelsky, I conducted research that demonstrated the hazards of GOSNIIOKhT's ventilation system. The reports that our two laboratories produced on this problem were ignored because an entirely new ventilation system would have to be designed to fix the problem. The cost of this monumental task was more than the system could bear.

54. The Main Laboratory Building was constructed in 1961. In 1987, I performed chromatomass-spectrometric analysis of water samples from the artesian well beneath the pilot plant facility. This well supplied many buildings of GOSNIIOKhT with water. My analysis showed the presence of many sulfur-containing decomposition products of mustard gas in significant quantities. Workers operating the excavating machines to prepare the site for new buildings experienced symptoms of poisoning from unknown substances. At last several events with serious poisoning of workers convinced the chief engineer to order the excavations to proceed under the supervision of experienced chemists, sometimes in gasmasks.

55. For example, four air samples were taken from chimney stack number 606A. The first contained 10 times the maximum permissible concentration, the second 50, the third 57, and the fourth 80 times the maximum permissible concentration.

56. After decontamination operations, water was kept in this tank for a fixed time, in a medium of excess alkali solution, to destroy the chemical agents entirely. After that, the contents of the tank were mixed with waste effluents from the production of agricultural chemicals and were thrown outside the plant. I have to mention that for this flawed technology of sarin, V.D. Belyaev, A.V. Bruker, S.L. Varshavski, S.N. Kosolapov, L.A. Kostandov, B. P. Kuchkov, B.Ja. Libman, V.V. Pozdnev, S.N. Potapov, L.Z. Soborovski, and N.N. Yukhtin received Lenin Prize in 1961. From that time, nothing changed in relation to the production of these extremely poisonous waste waters, but it didn't prevent others from receiving the next Lenin Prize. This time: S.V. Golubkov, I. L. Knunyants, I.V. Martynov, I.M. Milgotin, A.P. Tomilov, V.N. Topnikov, and V.M. Zimin were awarded it for production of soman.

State Secrets

57. More detailed information was published in: *Vechernij Volgograd,* June 1 and 3, 1993; *Izvestia,* December 2, 1993.
58. Certainly he reminded me that Golubkov was also one of Communist bosses of Volgograd - Secretary of the Volgograd Gorkom - before he was promoted to Deputy Minister.
59. *See* Annex 3.
60. Vladimir Shcherbak, "They hid the fact of the fire at the Factory but discovered "A method of incineration of chemical agents", Megapolis-Express, February 17 1993; Vladimir Shcherbak, "Where to destroy the chemical weapons", Moscow News, March 14 1993.

    I have no doubt about Vladimir's credibility. For a long time he worked as the chief of the department for the development of technologies of production of the precursors of chemical agents in the Shikhany affiliate of GOSNIIOKhT. Then he became director of GOSNIIOKhT's Novocheboksary affiliate, working on the problems of utilization of precursors at the Novocheboksarsk Factory.

    Childhood illness rates in the areas surrounding the Novocheboksary plant are almost 40 percent higher than in other cities of the Chuvashiya Region. Birth defects near Novocheboksary run at roughly 90 percent. D. Frolov, "A Secret still remains A Secret", *Segodnya* (30 December 1993); I. Nikonov, "What the reporter from Stern Magazine could not know", *Cheboksarskie Novosti* (19 November 1992).
61. Judith Perera, "Environment: Wounds of war – Can Russia combat the deadly legacy of chemical production?" *Guardian,* 23 April, 1993.

Chapter 11 Struggling with Spies (pp. 205-223)

62. *Identification of Potential Organophosphorous Warfare Agents: An Approach for the Standardization of the Techniques and Reference Data* (Helsinki: The Ministry for Foreign Affairs of Finland, 1970).
63. *Identification of Degradation Products of Potential Organophosphorous Warfare Agent. An Approach for the Standardization of Techniques and Reference Data* (Helsinki: The Ministry for Foreign Affairs of Finland, 1980).
64. *Air Monitoring as a Means for Verification of Chemical Disarmament. C.2. Development and Evaluation of Basic Techniques, Part I* (Helsinki: The Ministry for Foreign Affairs of Finland, 1985).
65. *Air Monitoring as a Means for Verification of Chemical Disarmament. C.3. Field tests, Part II* (Helsinki: The Ministry for Foreign Affairs of Finland, 1986).
66. *Air Monitoring as a Means for Verification of Chemical Disarmament. C.4. Further Development and Testing of Method, Part III* (Helsinki: The

Ministry for Foreign Affairs of Finland, 1987).
67. *International Inter-Laboratory Comparison (Round-Robin) Test for the Verification of Chemical Disarmament. F.1. Testing of Existing Procedures* (Helsinki: The Ministry for Foreign Affairs of Finland, 1990).
68. In October 22 1992 he participated in a search of Lev Fedorov's apartment by the KGB. *See* Annex 8.
69. Ralph Trapp, *Verification under the Chemical Weapons Convention: On-Site Inspection in Chemical Industry Facilities* (Oxford University Press, Stockholm International Peace Research institute (SIPRI), 1993).
70. *International Inter-Laboratory Comparison (Round-Robin) Test for the Verification of Chemical Disarmament. F.4. Validating of Procedures for Water and Soil Samples* (Helsinki: The Ministry for Foreign Affairs of Finland, 1993).

Chapter 12 The Torment of Insight (pp. 225-238)

71. See ref. 10.
72. Victor Petrunin, "To the 80th anniversary of GNTC NII Organic Chemistry and Technology – GOSNIIOKhT", *Chemical and Biological Safety* (in Russian), N 5, 2004, pp. 5-10. http://www.cbsafety.ru/rus/saf17_02.pdf
73. Ellsberg is renowned for preparing and releasing the Pentagon Papers to the *New York Times* in 1971. These documents contained secret and incriminating information about US conduct in the Vietnam War. Robert Reinhold, "Ellsberg Calls Decision 'Great,' But Says Ruling on Vietnam Papers is not Surprising," *New York Times,* 1 July 1971. Daniel Ellsberg, "Secrets: A Memoir of Vietnam and the Pentagon Papers (New York, 2002: Penguin Putnam Inc.), pp.498.
74. In October 1986, Mordechai Vanunu, who had worked at the Dimona nuclear facility, told the *London Sunday Times* about Israel's secret nuclear weapons program, which he had documented with photographs. Vanunu must have also been aware of the risks he was taking. Even before the story hit the press, Israeli secret agents kidnapped him and brought him back to Israel, where he was secretly sentenced to eighteen years of prison. He spent eleven and a half years in solitary confinement. Jonathan Randal, "Israeli Troops Kill 4 West Bank Palestinians; Vanunu Is sentenced to 18-Year Term for Revealing Nuclear Secrets," *Washington Post*, 28 March 1988, A21.
75. Director of Volgograd NPO Khimprom V.V. Pozdnev along with his accomplices Sergei Golubkov, Igor Gabov and Konstantin Guskov organized a lucrative underground business which produced civilian wares that were sold in stores. Cash from this scheme was flowing directly into a huge safe installed in the office of Director Pozdnev. They spent part of

this money for providing "a good time" to selected people from Moscow in a special resort built for these purposes. An investigation was started, but only the head bookkeeper was sentenced to prison, and Pozdnev died of a heart attack.

76. For instance, Howard T. Uhal, ex-Clemson University, Clemson, SC, USA, "Soviet Chemical Warfare Agents Novichok and Substance 33: Were They Used During the Persian Gulf War?"
http://www.nbcdefence.net/nore/novi_1.htm

77. Human Right Watch President Ken Anderson's private letter to author, 1996.

Chapter 14 I Break the Silence (pp. 247-258)

78. Vil Mirzayanov, "Inversion", *Kuranty*, October 10, 1991. See Annex 1.
79. The leaflet of the Committee of Democratic Movement of Russia in GRNIIOKhT, "Witch Hunt" at GRNIIOKhT, September 1991. *See* Annex 2.

Chapter 15 Challenging Poisoned Policies (pp. 259-289)

80. Lev Fedorov, "The Delayed Death", *Sovershenno Sekretno*, 12 August 1992.
81. Before that I had a telephone conversation with Andrei. He knew about the article "A Poisoned Policy" and he approved of it. I asked him whether he could give an interview to the American journalist Will Englund. I hoped at the same time that after his history was known by some responsible agencies in the US, perhaps they could give him the chance to be cured in an American hospital. Unfortunately at that time, I didn't know there are not any such responsible agencies, and the ones that exist are mostly busy trying to compromise people like me. Anyway Andrei agreed to give an interview, and I immediately called Will. As a result the whole world became familiar with his history and the history of the development of Russian Novichok agents and a binary weapon based on them. *See* ref. 40.
82. Vil Mirzayanov and Lev Fedorov, "A Poisoned Policy", N 39, September 16, 1992. *See* Annex 3.
83. Letter Dated 30 January 1992, from the Representative of the Russian Federation Addressed to the President of the Conference on Disarmament, Transmitting the Text of the Statement Made on 29 January 1992 by B .N. Yeltsin, the President of the Russian Federation, on Russia's

Policy in the Field of Arms Limitation and Reduction," CD/1123 (Geneva: 31 January 1992).

In an interview with the US television show "20/20," Yeltsin was asked directly whether Russia was still producing chemical and biological weapons. He responded as follows: "It's a very difficult question. Therefore, I want to save this for my one-on-one talk with the US President. I can give only one promise. In the next few months we're going to take steps to discontinue this kind of activity in accordance with international agreements on chemical and biological weapons." Transcript from "20/20," ABC News Division, 31 January 2002.

84. Will Englund, "Ex-Soviet Scientist Says Gorbachev's Regime Created New Nerve Gas in '91," *Baltimore Sun,* September 16, 1992. My quote in the piece was: "Americans should know about it."
85. Most of the experts that Englund spoke to declined to comment on the record. However, Dr. Lora Lumpe from the Federation of American Scientists commented that "it is unlikely that a nerve agent could be 10 times more lethal than VX gas."
86. Resolution of the Permanent Technical Commission at GRNIIOKhT September 25, 1992. Top Secret. *See* Annex 5.
87. Letter of Director GOSNIIOKhT V.A. Petrunin to A.I. Tselikovsky, Head of the Department for Economic Security of the Security Ministry of the Russian Federation , October 1, 1992, N 1594ss. Top Secret. *See* Annex 4.
88. Letter of Major General A.I. Tselikovsky to Major General S.D. Balashov, Head of the Investigation Department at the RF Ministry of Security. Top Secret. *See* Annex 6.
89. O. V. Vishnyakov, "The Binary Bomb has Exploded", *Novoe Vremya*, N 44, p. 4, 1992.
90. When Englund and Mironov went outside to drive to my apartment they couldn't find Englund's brand new car. It was stolen, despite the special police checkpoint with a guard for this compound where mostly foreigners were living.
91. Neither these items nor my doctoral dissertation contained any classified information, chemical formulas, or codes.
92. "Transcript of the Interrogation of the Suspect Vil Sultanovich Mirzayanov," Investigation Department, Case 92, (Moscow: Ministry of Security of RF, 22 October 1992. Top Secret). Later, I had the opportunity to copy this document verbatim, as well as many others assembled in the case against me. *See* Annex 7
93. "Report of the search", Committee of Governmental Security [KGB] of the USSR. Top Secret. *See* Annex 8. Surprisingly the Chekists wrote this document on the paper with title of former title of their Agency.
94. "Transcript of the Interrogation of the Witness", Investigation Department, Case 92 (Moscow: Ministry of Security of RF, 22 October 1992,

State Secrets

Top Secret). *See* Annex 9.

95. "Transcript of the Suspect's Interrogation", Investigation Department, Case 92 (Moscow: Ministry of Security of RF, 23 October 1992, Top Secret). *See* Annex 10.

96. This 20 March 1995 attack killed a dozen, severely and critically wounded 54, mildly injured 980, and frightened thousands of other subway commuters. B.W. Brackett, *Holy Terror: Armageddon in Tokyo* (New York: Weatherhill, 1996); David E. Kaplan and Andrew Marshall, *The Cult at the End of the World* (New York: Crown Publishers, Inc., 1996); Sadayoshi Obu, Tetsu Yamaguchi, "Japanese Medical Team Briefing," in *Proceedings of the Seminar of Responding to the Consequences of Chemical and Biological Terrorism*, Office of Emergency Preparedness (Washington, DC: US Public Health Service, Department of Health and Human Services, 11-4 July 1995): 2-12 to 2-29.

97. There are articles: Interfax Agency about the MB RF report of my arrest; "Statement of Editorial Office of Moscow News"; Victor Loshak, "The State Lie as a State Secret"; Natalya Gevorkyan, "To be prisoner according to Law which doesn't exist"; Aleksei Pushkov, "Really Russia didn't violate anything?" *Moscow News* N 44 (639), October 28-Nowember 1, 1992.

98. "Transcript of the suspect's interrogation", Investigation Department of MB RF, Case 92, 28 October 1992. Top Secret. *See* Annex 11.

Chapter 16 The Crash of the KGB's Plans (pp. 291-305)

99. "Resolution Kalinin District Court of Moscow", November 2, 1992. *See* Annex 12.

100. Annex 13: Letter of Head of the Department for Supervision of the Implementation of the Laws on Federal Security and International Relations State Justice Counselor of the Third Class Leonid M. Syukasev to Major General S.D. Balashov; October 30, 1992 N 13/2-1040-92. Top Secret; Annex 14: Letter of Major General S.D. Balashov to Leonid Sykasev, November 4, 1992. N 6/2753. Top Secret.

101. Andrey Illesh and Valeri Rudnev, "Selling the Motherland is Under Great Secrecy," *Izvestia*, 6 November 1992; Valeri Rudnev, "Without my lawyer I'll not tell you even "Hello"", *Izvestia*, 13 November 1992.

102. Letter of First Deputy Attorney General of the Russian Federation State Justice Counselor of the 2nd Class I.S. Zemlyanushin to Deputy Minister of the MB RF Major General A.E. Safonov. December 10, 1992 N 13/2-1040-92,Top Secret. *See* Annex 15.

103. Letter of Head of the Department, Major General S.D. Balashov to Deputy Attorney General of RF I.S. Zemlyanushin. October 17, 1992 N

6/280. Secret. See Annex 16.
104. Valeri Rudnev," The Scientist who was Selling his Motherland Finally has a Defender", *Izvestia*, 17 November 1992.
105. Press Briefing in the RF Security Ministry, *Federal News Service, Kremlin Package,* 5 November 92
106. *See* ref. 73.
107. Michael Satchell, "Death rattle of poison gas" U.S. News and World Report/September 13, 1993.
108. In 1996 in the US, one of my good American acquaintances told me that General Anatoly Kuntsevich during his visit got quite drunk in the hotel where he was staying and started to sexually harass service woman. Along came the police and started an investigation for this crime, but the case was settled. What was the price was paid by Kuntsevich?

Chapter 17 Captain Shkarin Fabricates the Case. (pp. 307-313)

109. Letter of General Major S.D. Balashov to Major General V.N. Markomenko to the head of the Third Main Department at the Federal Agency for Government Communications and Information under the President of Russia (FAPSI). *See* Annex 17.
110. See Annexes 18 and 19.
111. Letter of the head of a section at the Department, A.A. Shabunin, to Director of GRNIIOKhT V. Petrunin, November 12, 1992 N 6/2835. Top Secret. *See* Annex 20.
112. Letter of Deputy Director of GRNIIOKhT A.V. Kuznetsov to the head of a section at the Investigation Department of MB RF Colonel A.A. Shabunin. November 24, 1992, N 1846 ss. Top Secret. *See* Annex 21.
113. Letter of Head of Investigation Department of MB RF Major General S.D. Balashov to Lieutenant General V.N. Zemlyanitsyn, Head of 8th Department at the General Staff Headquarters of the Armed Forces of the Russian Federation. Top Secret. *See* Annex 22.
114. Letter of the acting Head of the 8th Department Colonel G.I. Funygin to Mayor General S.D. Balashov. December 8, 1992, N 317/5/836. Top Secret. *See* Annex 23.
115. Letter of Mayor General S.D. Balashov to E.M. Primakov, Director of the Foreign Intelligence Service of the Russian Federation, December 10, 1992, N 6/03240. Secret. *See* Annex 24.
116. Letter of the Deputy Director of the SVR [Foreign Intelligence Service] of Russian Federation Major General V.M. Rozhkov to Major General S.D. Balashov, Head of the Investigation Department of the Ministry of Security of Russia, December 17 1992, N 153/5-13265. Secret. *See* Annex 25.

117. Letter of Major General S.D. Balashov to Major General Yu.N. Lukonin, Head of the Personnel Department at the Ministry of Security of the Russian Federation, December 10, 1992, N 6/03238. Secret. *See* Annex 26.
118. Letter of the Deputy Head of the Personnel Department of MB of Russia Colonel E. Soloviev, December 29 1992. Secret. *See* Annex 27.
119. Letter of Major General S.D. Balashov to Major General A.I. Gurov, Head of NII [the Scientific Research Institute] for Problems of Security of the Russian Federation, December 10, 1992, N 6/03239. Secret. *See* Annex 28.
120. Letter of the Head of the Institute Major General A.I. Gurov to Head of the Investigation Department of the Ministry of Security of the Russian Federation Major General S.D. Balashov. December 16, 1992, N 5/NII/76. Secret. *See* Annex 29.
121. Peter Nikulin, "The Secret of the Old Greatcoat", *Novoe Vremya*, N 46, 1992, p. 44.
122. Georgi Arbatov, "Whom does our military-industrial complex deceive?" *Moscow News*, N 47, 22 November 1992.

Chapter 18 I am not Alone (p.p. 315-320)

123. Igor Ermakov, "The Ministry of Security Detained the Author of "Kuranty", *Kuranty*, October 24, 1992.
124. Dmitri Frolov, "Chemical Armament is Continuing!" *Nezavisimaya Gazetta*, October 23, 1992.
125. Dmitri Frolov, "The MB RF is Seriously Worried about Chemical Secrets", *Nezavisimaya Gazetta*, October 24, 1992.
126. Natalya Gevorkyan, "It is the Privilege of the Author to be Imprisoned According to a Law that Doesn't Exist", *MN*, November 1, 1992.
127. Igor Tsarev, "The Case about the Disclosure of a State Secret", *Trud*, October 28, 1992.
128. Oleg Utitsyn, "The Case of the Chemist", *Kommersant*, N 39, October 26-November 1, 1992.
129. P.A. Kochkin, "Moscow has Turned into a Prison", *Ekonomika I mui*, November 1992.
130. Sjifra Hershberg, Hella Rotenberg, Ruslland produceert nieuw en giftiger zenuwgas, *De Volksrant*, N 20749, October 24, 1992.
131. Fred Hiatt, "Russia Jails Scientist over State Secrets", *Washington Post*, October 27, 1992.
132. Will Englund, "Russian Whistle-Blower Denied Visit With Lawyer He Unmasked Plan For Chemical Arms", *Baltimore Sun*, October 29, 1992.
133. Amy Smithson, "Russian Nerve Gas", *Baltimore Sun*, October 30, 1992.
134. Will Englund, "Russian Who Exposed Chemical Arms Is Freed From Jail Pending Trial", *Baltimore Sun*, November 3, 1992.

135. "Wachen umstellen "Izwestija", *Suddeutsche Zeitung* nr. 249, October 28, 1992.
136. "Eine neue Kaltperiode?", *Seuddeutsche Zeitung*, 249, October 28, 1992.
137. Lawrence Uzzel, "The Scientist and the Security Forces", *Crossroads*, November 15, 1992. According to Mr. Lawrence Uzzell, Director of Jamestown's Moscow office, "On November 4, Crossroads called the U.S. Embassy in Moscow to ask if the State Department had issued any statement of protest about this case. The answer: No."
138. Ravil Karamov, "Gafu it, Vil Mirzayanov (Frogive us, Vil Mirzayanov)", *Vakyt* (Bashkortstan), N 10, 1992.
139. Favziya Khairutdinova, "Vilne kotkarik (Let's Save Vil)", *Vatanym Tatarstan*, December 6, 1992.
140. Nanette van der Laan, "Scientist: Russia Won't Come Clean", *The Moscow Times*, December 12, 1992.
141. "Scientist's Lawyer Gets Case File", *The Moscow Times*, November 19, 1992.
142. Betsy McKay, "Scientist to Be Put on Trial", *The Moscow Times*, November 2, 1992.
143. Serge Schmemann, "K.G.B.'s Successor Charges Scientist," *New York Times*, 1 November 1992.
144. Frank von Hippel, "Russian Whistleblower Faces Jail," *Bulletin of Atomic Scientists* 49, no. 2 (March 1993): 7-8.
145. Valeri Menshikov, Vladimir Yakimets, "The Europarliament is against the KGB", *Moscow News*, N 49, December 6, 1992.
146. "Transcript of one Meeting", *Moscow News*, November 15, 1992.

Chapter 19 Boycott of the Investigation (pp. 321-347)

147. "Transcript of the interrogation of the witness N.M. Godzhello", November 24, 1992. Investigation Department of MB RF. Case 62, vol. 1, pp.262-266. Top Secret.
148. "Transcript of interrogation of the witness S.S. Sokolov", January 14, 1993. Investigation Department of MB RF, Case 62, vol. 1, pp. 271-273. Top Secret.
149. *See* ref. 40
150. Vil Mirzayanov, "Testing of Chemical Weapons: Thoughtlessness or Crime", *Novoe Vremya*, N 50, December of 1992.
151. Valeri Rudnev, "'State Criminal" up to now doesn't know what his crime is", Izvestia, January 19, 1998.
152. Vladislav Borovitski, "Over all Saratov is poisoned sky", *Saratov*, October 22, 1993; Vitaly Zemljak, "The poisoned secrets", Interview of Vladimir Uglev and Vladimir Petrenko by Correspondent of Radio Lib-

erty Dmitri Volchek, *Saratov*, August 17, 1993; Lydia Malash,, "When they are shutting up scientists in Moscow explosions are clattering in Shikhany", *Megapolis Express*, February 16, 1994; Anatoli Mikhailov, "The City-Hell, Would " The Chemical Reactor" of Volsk-17 explode?", *Trud*, April 19, 1994; Olga Nikitina, "The Shikhany Syndrome. There is a smell of impending disaster", *Saratov*, May 14, 1994.

153. Lev Fedorov, "Chemical Weapons or Chemical Warfare?", *Khimia i Jizn*, N 7, 1993, p. 67.
154. Oleg Vishnyakov, "Interview with a Noose around his Neck", *Novoe Vremya*, N 6, 1993, p. 40.
155. Gordeyev, Alexander, "Chemical Arms: Russia's Human Guinea Pig", *The Moscow Times*, March 18, 1994; Will Englund, "Chemical Weapons Shadow Moscow. Russia prosecutes whistle-blowers of secret research", *Baltimore Sun*, February 14, 1993; J. Michael Waller, "Post-Soviet Sakharovs: Renewed Persecution of Dissident Scientists and the American Response", *Demokratizatsiya, The Journal of Post-Soviet Democratization*, v. II, N 1, Winter 1993/94, p. 138-147.
156. Geoffrey York, "Islam in Tatarstan", *Globe and Mail* (Canada), May 5, 1998.
157. Celestine Bohlen, "Regions Wary as Putin Tightens Control", *New York Times*, March 9, 2000.
158. Midkhat Farukshin, *The Face and Mask*, Kazan, 2005.
159. Boris Ischboldin, *Essays on Tatar History*, New Deli: New Book Society of India, Second Ed., 1965.
160. "Transcript of the Inspection, Moscow", February 24, 1993, Investigation Department of MB RF, Case 62. Top Secret. See Annex 30.
161. "TECHNICAL ORDER FOR THE COMPOUND PART OF THE EXPERMIENTAL DESIGN WORK OF "Substance-232" ON THE BASIS OF THE SYSTEM OF COMPONENTS", Investigation Department of MB RF, Case 62. Top Secret. See Annex 31.
162. In a mid-January 1996, in an interview with BBC correspondent Mark Urban, Gorbachev insisted that Russia was doing everything according to its arms control agreements with America. He literally said: "I don't know anything about these works. Maybe military people were cleaning their tails in some way." Transcript of "Chemical Weapons News Night," Correspondent Mark Urban (*British Broadcasting Company*: London, 16 January 1996).
163. EXTRACT from "The List of Major Information Constituting State Secrets", confirmed by resolution N 1121-387 of USSR Counsel of Ministers on December 3, 1980. Top Secret. *See* Annex 32.
164. EXTRACT from the "The List of Information to be Qualified as Secret by the USSR Ministry of Petrochemical Industry" confirmed by order N 234-19 of the USSR Ministry of Petrochemical Industry on May 27 1991. Top Secret. *See* Annex 33.

165. FINDINGS OF THE EXPERT COMMISSION Moscow March 16, 1993. Top Secret. *See* Annex 34. The refusal of experts Vadim Smirnitsky and Nikolai Chugunov entirely destroyed this job of Shkarin. Moreover, their conclusions and testimonies didn't leave any chance for the Findings of the Expert Commission to be used in the final Indictment.
166. *See* ref. 86.
167. "CONCLUSION OF THE EXPERT Nikolai Chugunov", March 18, 1993 Moscow. Top Secret. *See* Annex 35.
168. "CONCLUSION OF THE EXPERT Vadim Smirnitsky", March 17, 1993 Moscow. Top Secret. *See* Annex 38.
169. "TRANSCRIPT of the interrogation of the expert Nikolai Chugunov", April 8, 1993 Moscow. Top Secret. *See* Annex 36.
170. "TRANSCRIPT of the interrogation of the expert Nikolai Chugunov", April 23, 1993 Moscow. Top Secret. *See* Annex 37.
171. "TRANSCRIPT of interrogation of the expert Vadim Smirnitsky", March 22, 1993 Moscow. Top Secret. *See* Annex 39.
172. Letter of Head of the section at the Department of Investigation, A.A. Shabunin to V. A. Petrunin, Director of the State Russian Science Research Institute for Organic Chemistry and Technology April 22, 1993 6/001580. Top Secret. *See* Annex 44.
173. Letter of Deputy Director of GRNIIOKhT N.A. Kuznetsov to A.A. Shabunin, Head of the Section of the Investigation Department at the Ministry of Security of the Russian Federation. Top Secret. *See* Annex 45.
174. "TRANSCRIPT of interrogation of the expert Anatoly Kochetkov", March 30, 1993 Moscow. Top Secret. *See* Annex 40.
175. "TRANSCIRPT of interrogation of the expert Boris Kuznetsov", April 8, 1993, Moscow. Top Secret. *See* Annex 41.
176. "TRANSCRIPT of interrogation of the expert Igor Gabov", April 29, 1993, Moscow. Top Secret. *See* Annex 42.
177. *See* ref. 154.
178. *See* ref. 128.
179. Letter of Head of the Investigation Department MB RF, Major General S.D. Balashov to Colonel General M.P. Kolesnikov, Head of the General Staff of the Armed Forces of the Russian Federation, April 22, 1993 N 6/01584. Top Secret. *See* Annex 46.
180. Letter of Colonel G. Funygin, Deputy Head of the 8th Department of the General Staff Headquarters of the Armed Forces of the Russian Federation to Major General S.D. Balashov, Head of the Investigation Department, of the Ministry of Security of the Russian Federation, May 12, 1993 N 317/5/0 397 in response to N 6/01584. Top Secret. *See* Annex 47
181. He was one of initiators of my persecution who awkwardly tried to justify it at a press-conference in November 5 1992. *See* ref. 83.

182. "RESOLUTION of the Council of Ministers", Moscow March 30, 1993, N 256-16. Top Secret. *See* **Annex 43**.
183. Pavel Gutiontov, "Let's Begin with the American to Teach Others", *Moskovski Komsomolets*, N 65, April 7 1993; Maksim Gun, "The American Journalist was interrogated in Lefortovo", *Izvestia*, April 10, 1993.
184. Kim Gamel, American Journalist Interrogated in Lefortovo, *Moscow Tribune*, April 9, 1993.
185. Justin Burke, "US Reporter Called For Questioning By Russia's KGB", *Christian Science Monitor*, April 9, 1993.
186. Jon Auerbach, "US reporter refuses to testify in Russia", *Boston Globe*, April 8, 1993.
187. Letter of the Head of Investigation Department Mayor General S.D. Balashov to Colonel General M.P. Kolesnikov, Head of the General Staff Headquarters of the Armed Forces of the Russian Federation, 6/01341/April 5, 1993. Secret. *See* **Annex 48**.
188. Letter of Head of the General Staff, Colonel General M. Kolesnikov to Major General S.D. Balashov, Head of the Investigation Department at the Ministry of Security of the Russian Federation, April 29, 1993 N 312/10/053. In response to N 6 01341 of April 5, 1993. *See* **Annex 49**.
189. Letter of Head of the Department Major General S.D. Balashov to V.P. Ivanov, Chairman of the RF Committee for Chemical and Petrochemical Industry, 6/01342 April 5, 1993. *See* **Annex 50**.
190. Letter of Chairman V.P. Ivanov to S.D. Balashov, Head of the Investigation Department at the Ministry of Security of the Russian Federation. Secret. *See* **Annex 51**.
191. Letter of Head of the Department Major General S.D. Balashov to G.V. Berdennikov, Deputy Minister of Foreign Affairs of the Russian Federation, 6/01343//April 5, 1993. Secret. *See* **Annex 52**.
192. Letter of Deputy Minister of G.V. Berdennikov to S.D. Balashov, Head of Investigation Department at the RF Ministry of Security, May 11, 1993 N 61/drk. Secret. See Annex 53.
193. Transcript of interrogation of accused V.S. Mirzayanov, May 13 1993, Investigation Department of Ministry of Security of RF, Case 62, v. 1, p. 223-224. Top Secret.
194. Valeri Rudnev, "The Secrets of Chemical Weapons in the Materials of a Criminal Case and the International Conference Reports", *Izvestia*, May 20, 1993.

Chapter 20 Revenge of the Communists (pp. 349-362)

195. Wendy Sloane, "Ellsberg Supports Russian Chemist", *The Moscow Tribune*, June 2, 1993.

196. Will Englund, "Ellsberg Embraces Russian Chemist who Exposed Secret Nerve Gas", *Baltimore Sun*, June 2, 1993.
197. "Press Conference by Vil Mirzayanov and US Professor Daniel Ellsberg", *Federal News Service Kremlin Package*, 1 June 1993.
198. *See* Presidential Directive N 508, published in *Rossiskaya Gazetta* on 16 September 1992, and Government Decree N. 734, published in *Rossiskaya Gazetta* on 18 September 1992.
199. *See* ref. 93 and 94.

Chapter 21 The KGB Prepares for a Closed Trial (pp. 363-376)

200. "INDICTMENT Concerning Criminal Case N 62, about the indictment of Vil Sultanovich Mirzayanov for committing a crime according to Part 1 of Clause 75 of the Criminal Code (UK) of the RSFSR", November 1993. Top Secret. *See* Annex 55.
201. Senator Bill Bradley, letter to Strobe Talbott, 14 October 1993. *See* Annex 56.
202. Letter of John Conyers, Jr., Chairman of the Congressional Legislation and National Security Subcommittee of the Committee on Government Operations, to Warren Christopher, the U.S. Secretary of State, October 19, 1993. *See* Annex 57.
203. Letter of U.S. Senator Daniel Patrick Moynihan to the Secretary of State Warren Christopher, December 23, 1993. *See* Annex 58.
204. Letter of Dr. Wolfgang Hirschwald a professor of Berlin Free University, on behalf of the International Network of Engineers and Scientists for Global Responsibility (INES), to Frederico Mayor, the Director General of UNESCO, December 27, 1993. *See* Annex 59.
205. Letter of the American Association for the Advancement of Science to President Boris Yeltsin, March 30, 1993. *See* Annex 60.
206. Letter of the Committee of Concerned Scientists (in the U.S) to President of Russia Boris Yeltsin, October 25, 1993. *See* Annex 61.
207. Letter of the New York Academy of Sciences to President of Russia Boris Yeltsin, August 25, 1993. *See* Annex 62.
208. Letter of the president of the New York Academy of Sciences, Nobel Prize Laureate Joshua Lederberg to the Executive Director of the newspaper "The New York Times" Max Frankel. *New York Times*, December 6, 1993. *See* Annex 63.
209. Statement of the Andrei Sakharov Foundation in the United States on September 15, 1993. *See* Annex. 64.
210. Mark Champion, "Scientist Says Russia "Dishonest" in Treaty", *The Moscow Times*, January 12, 1993.
211. Olga Kienko, "Mirzayanov's case: Scientist is confident that Chekists re-

vealed themselves", *Kommersant-Daily*, May 14, 1993
212. Valeri Rudnev, "State Criminal" Still Doesn't Know What he Violated", *Izvestia*, January 19, 1993.
213. Olga Shlyapnikova, "Scientist Refused to Answer Questions of the Investigation", *Kommersant-Daily*, January 13, 1993.
214. Igor Tsarev, "Poison", *Trud,* 29 January, 1993.
215. Natalya Gevorkyan, "Mirzayanov's Case is Not Cancelled Even Though we Officially Cancelled Chemical Weapons", *Moscow News*, January 24, 1993.
216. Leonard Nikishin, "Toxic Fruit of Poisonous Policy", *Moscow News*, January 24, 1993.
217. Vladimir Uglev, "To Teach Others", *Moscow News*, January 31, 1993.
218. Svetlana Serkova, "The American Physicists are Looking for Lawyer for the Scientist", *Kommersant-Daily*, February 23, 1993.
219. Olga Shlyapnikova, "The Scientist's Wife refused to go to the Investigation", *Kommersant-Daily,* 24 February, 1993.
220. Vladimir Yakimets, "Mirzayanov's Case on the Mirror of Professor Ellsberg's Fate", *Russia*, N 9, February 24 – March 2, 1993.
221. Karl-Heinz Karish, "Russische Forscher nach Entüllung über C-Waffen in Bedrängs", *Frankfurter Rundschau*, March 15, 1993.
222. SPECTRUM, "Moskau entwickelt neue Kampfgase", *Süddeutsche Zeitung*, 1 April, 1993.
223. *See* ref 219.
224. Valeri Rudnev, "Secrets of the Chemical Weapons in the Case Materials and in the Reports to the International Conference", *Izvestia*, May 20, 1993.
225. Will Englund, "Two Russian Papers Investigated after New Disclosures on Chemical Arms", *Baltimore Sun*, June 11, 1993.
226. *See* ref 219.
227. Andrei Malykh, "The Mirzayanov Case: The Most Important Documents in the Case are Absent", *Kommersant-Daily*, July 8, 1993.
228. S. Fomichev, A. Alekseev, V. Petrov, V. Gergel, S. Kamensky, "The Opinion: It is Impossible to Hold an International Conference in Moscow until the Authorities Stop Persecuting People who are Against Chemical Weapons", *Moscow News,* April 11, 1993.
229. Leonard Nikishin, "Vil Mirzayanov: The Goal is to Develop New Binary Weapons", *Moscow News*, May 28, 1993.
230. *See* ref 218.
231. Thomas W. Lippman, "Russian Scientist Appeals for Colleague. Co-Worker Is Charged With Disclosing Chemical Weapons Secrets", *Washington Post*, June 21, 1993.
232. *Chemical and Engineering News*, June 21, 1993, p. 8.
233. Georgi Arbatov, "Who needs noisy scandal?" *Moscow News*, July 25, 1993.

234. "The Ministries are Already Accused", (Editorial) *Moscow News*, July 11, 1993.
235. Terje Langeland, "Russian Threatens to Reveal Secrets", *The Badger Herald*, N 27, October, 1993.
236. Vladimir Uglev, "To Reveal the Secret of a "Binary", *Moscow News*, October 31, 1993.
237. Michael R. Gordon, "Moscow is Making Little Progress in Disposal of Chemical Weapons", *New York Times*, December 1, 1993.
238. Gale Colby, "Fabricating Guilt", *Bulletin of Atomic Scientists*, October 1993.
239. "Human-Rights Support Sought for Russian Weapons Scientist", *The Sciences*, September/October 1993, p.48f.
240. Manfred Ronzheimer, "Moskauer Chemiker droht Prozeß. Er hatte von der Entwicklung chemischer Waffen berichtet", *Süddeutsche Zeitung*, December 23, 1993.
241. Carey Scott, "Despite Opposition, Trial Of Chemist Pushed Ahead", *The Moscow Times*, December 29, 1993.
242. Vladimir Voronov, "Destroy the Constitution with Instruction", *Stolitsa*, N 51, 1993, p. 10.
243. Gale Colby, Irene Goldman, "When Will Russia Abandon its Secret Chemical Weapons Program?" Demokratizatsiya, *The Journal of Post-Soviet Democratization*, Winter 1993/1994, p.p. 148-154.
244. J. Michael Waller, "Post-Soviet Sakharovs: Renewed Persecution of Dissident Scientists and the American Response", *The Journal of Post-Soviet Democratization*, Winter 1993/1994, p.p. 138-147.
245. Leonard Nikishin, "In the Eve of Trial on the "Case" of Mirzayanov", *Moscow News*, N 50, December 8, 1993.
246. Pat Janowski, "Speak No Evil", *The Sciences*, November/December, 1993, pp. 4-5.
247. Von Dietmar Ostermann., "The Russian Arms Centers have Developed Highly Toxic Chemical Weapons", *Hannoversche Allgemeine Zeitung*, January 6, 1994.
248. An open letter of the Association of German Scientists for Global Responsibility to the German Minister of Foreign Affairs, Klaus Kinkel, *Frankfurter Rundschau*, January 3, 1994.
249. J. Michael Waller, "U.S. may be Funding Russian Secret Weapon", *Houston Chronicle*, January 11, 1994.
250. J. Michael Waller, "Novichok: Russia's Secret Weapon", *San Diego Union-Tribune*, January 11, 1994.
251. J. Michael Waller, "Russia's Terrible New "Secret Weapon", *Indianapolis Star*, January 13, 1994.
252. Sonni Efron, "Russian Scientist Faces Trial for Chemical-Arms Report", *Los Angeles Times*, January 5, 1994.
253. Michael Gusev, "State Secrets Without Protection. Sure, They Should be

Protected but on the Basis of the Law", *Rossiskaya Gazetta*, November 11, 1992., Interview with Michael Gusev, "CBW Aide Quizzed on Program Secrecy Rules Questioned", *Rossiskaya Gazetta*, November 11, 1992

254. Vitali Kaysin, "Let's Wait for the Destruction of Moscow. Reporting from a Top Secret Institute, Which Recently was Busy with the Development of Chemical Weapons and Chemical Agents", *Pravda*, N 4 (25958), January 1993.
255. Ida Schneerson, "Scientist is Trying to Scare People", *Kazan Telegraph*, N 45 (7130), 22-29 March, 1993.
256. Fausia Khajrutdinova, "To Save Vil", *My Fatherland Tatarstan*, November 11, 1992.
257. Radis Nugmanov, "Is Vil Mirzayanov a Traitor or a Patriot?" *Kyzil Tan*, December 23, 1992.
258. Vil Mirzayanov, "I Didn't Divulge any Secrets and Didn't Sell the Motherland", *Bashkortstan*, November 13, 1992.
259. Vil Mirzayanov, "We are Victims of what Kind of Secrets?", *Youth of Tatarstan*, December 19, 1992.
260. Vil Kazikhanov, "Interview with Mirzayanov: I Fulfilled my Patriotic Duty", *Yuldash* (Sojourner), August 12, 1993.
261. Ayaz Gilyazov, "About The Chemical Secrets with a Big Secret (Interview with Vil Mirzayanov)", *Izvestia of Tatarstan*, March 24 1993.
262. R. Minhazh, "Who will Fight for Tatar if not Tatar?" *My Fatherland Tatarstan*, March 23, 1993.
263. Fausia Khajrutdinova, "Well Done!" *My Fatherland Tatarstan*, September 15, 1993.
264. Fausia Khajrutdinova, "For Telling the Truth", *Bulletin of Arsk*, February 2, 1994.
265. "Review of Readers Letters (Editorial): We are Admirers, Proud, and Ready to Defend him", *Youth of Tatarstan*, N 21, February 15, 1993.
266. Vil Mirzayanov, "Maybe I Really Have to Reveal State Secrets?" *Youth of Tatarstan*, N 49, February 15, 1994.
267. Sergei Alexeev, Georgi Arbatov, Yuri Afansiev, Vitali Goldansky, Tatiana Zaslavskaya, Len Karpinsky, Viktor Loshak, Alexander Pumpyansky, and Grigory Yavlinsky, "Mirzayanov will Face a Secret Trial",. *Moscow News*, January 2, 1993. See Annex 65.
268. Statement of the Chairman of the U.S. Congress Committee on Government Operations, John Conyers, January 4, 1994. See Annex 66.
269. On January 12-15, 1993 US President Clinton met President of Russia Yeltsin, in Moscow.
270. Sergei Mostovshchikov, "Chemistry and Life", *Izvestia*, January 6 1994.
271. Valeria Novodvorskaya, "Up to now we have: whips, dungeons, axes", *Khozyain (Owner)*, N 45, December 1992.
272. Valeria Novodvorskaya, "We have Such Secrets that Would Make you

Enjoy Laughing", *Ogonyok*, N 2, 1994, p. 38.
273. Valeria Novodvorskaya, "The Damned Winter", *Moskovskaya Pravda*, February 10, 1993.
274. Sonni Efron, "Chemist Fears Trial will Not Be Fair", *Los Angeles Times*, January 6, 1994.
275. Sergei Mostovshchikov, "There will be Three Judges Instead of One at Vil Mirzayanov's Trial", *Izvestia*, January 13, 1994.
276. Semen Kontsov, "The Counterintelligence Agent Faces a Secret Trial", *Inostranets*, January 12, 1994.
277. Vladimir Voronov, "The Chemists from Lubyanka against the Chemist Mirzayanov", *Sobesednik*, January 27, 1994.
278. See ref. 249.
279. See ref. 250.
280. Richard Seltzer, "U.S. Scientists Protest Against the Trial of the Russian Chemist", *Chemical and Engineering News*, January 24, 1994.
281. Sonni Efron, "Whistle-Blower in Russia Calls Closed Trial "a Crime"", *Los Angeles Times*, January 26, 1994.
282. "IM WORLAUT, Rußlands neue Chemiewaffen. Solitaritätsaufruf für kiritische Wissneschaftler", *Frankfurter Rundschau*, 3 January, 1994.
283. Von Dietmar Ostermann, "Russische Rüstungszentren entwickelten hochgiftige Chemiewaffen, *Hannoversche Allgemeine Zeitung*, 6 January, 1994.
284. "Chemiewaffenprozeß in Moskau. Wil Mirzayanov wird Geheimnisverrat vorgeworfen", *Frankfurter Rundschau*, January 5, 1994.
285. Dina Verchenko, "Vil Mirzayanov's Arrest", *Express-Chronika*, January 28, 1994.
286. Aleksander Protsenko, "What are they Trying Vil Mirzayanov for?",*Megapolis Express*, January 12, 1994.
287. L. Nikitinsky, "The Secret of a State Secret", *Izvestia*, January 22, 1994.
288. Letter of the American Association for the Advancement of Science to the Attorney General of Russia, Aleksei Kazannik. January 13, 1994. *See* Annex 67.
289. Letter of the Federation of American Scientists to the Attorney General of Russia, Aleksei Kazannik, January 14, 1994. *See* Annex 68.
290. Letter of the U.S. National Academy of Science to President Yeltsin, January 24, 1994. *See* Annex 69.
291. Letter of the President of New York Academy of Science Joshua Lederberg to the Attorney General of the Russian Federation Alexei Kazannik, January 20, 1994. *See* Annex 70.
292. Letter of the Committee of Concerned Scientists to the Attorney General Aleksei Kazannik, January 19, 1994. *See* Annex 71.
293. Roald Sagdeev, "This Trial can Cause Damage to our Fatherland," *Izvestia*, February 1 , 1994. *See* Annex 72.
294. Letter of the Lawyers Committee for Human Rights (of the U.S.) to the

President of Russia. *See* Annex 73.
295. Letter of the, the American organization "Physicians for Social Responsibility" to Attorney General Kazannik, January 21, 1994. *See* Annex 74.
296. Letter of the Committee on the International Freedom of Scientists (CIFS) at the American Physical Society to President Yeltsin. *See* Annex 75.
297. "U.S. Scientists Protest Russian Chemist's Trial", *Chemical and Engineering News*, January 21, 1994, p. 8-9.
298. *See* ref. 182

Chapter 22 Trial and Prison (pp. 377-444)

299. In 14 years following these events, the CWC has been signed and ratified by 184 countries and signed though not yet ratified by 4 more, without any mention to the Novichok agents. I believe that it is time to share information with people about their real nature. I also believe that it is my obligation to reveal this information and make it a part of the scientific data, like information about other chemical agents such as sarin, soman and VX-gas.
300. Fred Hiatt, "Russian Court Opens Unprecedented Secrets Trial", *Washington Post*, January 25, 1994.
301. Sergei Mostovshchikov, "Mirzayanov is Arrested", *Izvestia*, January 26, 1994.
302. Sergei Mostovshchikov, "Moscow City Court Decided to use the Force of Police Department 139 Against Vil Mirzayanov", *Izvestia*, January 27, 1994.
303. After that he suffered from a nervous tic for a number of years, and no pediatrician could cure him. Even the "Holy water" that Nuria bought for a tidy sum from non-traditional healers didn't help. At night, in bed, he threw his small thin body from side to side, bumping against the wall, and pleaded in despair, "Mama, this is not my body. It is jumping. Help me please!"
304. Even for very experienced journalists, this was unexpected. See: Sergei Mostovshchikov, "Prosecution of Russian Scientist is seen as 100 a Percent Political Trial", *Izvestia*, January 28, 1994.
305. Excerpt with remarks by US Ambassador Thomas Pickering, from the transcript of the press conference held on January 28, 1994 in the Russian-American Press Center. Formally cited: Extract from the Congressional Record – Senate. (February 1, 1994. S.S 543-544) *Library of Congress*. http: //thomas.loc.gov/cgi-bin
306. "Russian in Chemical Arms Exposé Arrested", *New York Times International*, January 28, 1994.

307. "Editorial: The Mirzayanov Case: Folly of the Authorities or the Establishment of Despotic Power", *Izvestia*, January 29, 1994.
308. Sergei Mostovshchikov, "The Authorities put Scientist Vil Mirzayanov into One Cell with Criminals", *Izvestia*, January 29, 1994.
309. Sergei Mostovshchikov, "Vil Mirzayanov is Sitting in a Cell with Seven Criminals and Four Mattresses", *Izvestia*, February 1, 1994.
310. Carey Scott, "Activists Protest Jailing of Chemist", *The Moscow Times*, February 1, 1994.
311. He was the former First Minister of Ecology of the USSR, a renowned scientist-biologist and academician.
312. "Russian Chemist Jailed after Refusing to Attend Trial", *Chemical and Engineering News*, January 31, 1994.
313. Judith Perera, "Russian Whistleblower Lands in Jail", *New Scientist*, February 1, 1994.
314. "Review &Outlook: Russia on Trial", (Editorial) *Wall Street Journal Europe*, February 2, 1994.
315. J. Michael Waller, "Soviet Redux: Secret Weapons and Poisoned Justice", *Wall Street Journal Europe*, February 2, 1994.
316. Vladimir Nazarov, "Folly is Impossible to Conceal. It will Come out and the Press will Know about it. Maneuvers on Kalanchevskaya", *Kuranty*, February 4, 1994.
317. Svetlana Gannushkina, "First, you Have to be Brought up Properly, and Then you can Ask Questions. Do you Understand?", *Express-Khronika*, February 4, 1994
318. Carey Scott, "Dissident Chemist Moved to Better Cell", *The Moscow Times*, February 2, 1994.
319. Natalya Khmelik, "The Costs of Upbringing", *Express-Khronika*, February 4, 1994.
320. Alexander Gordeyev, "Court Adjourns Chemist's Trial, Blames Protest", *The Moscow Times*, February 4, 1994.
321. Editorial: "Mirzayanov As Prisoner : Scandalous", *The Moscow Times*, February 2, 1994.
322. Olivia Ward, "Ghost of Stalin Haunts Scientist's Trial. Meet Vil Mirzayanov – the First Dissident of the Post-Soviet Era", *The Toronto Star*, February 6, 1994.
323. Ann McElvoy, "Injustice at "Toxic Trial", *South China Morning Post*, February 4, 1994.
324. Soni Efron, "Trial Halted Over Calm Reporters "Circus-Like" Behavior", *Los Angeles Times*, February 4, 1994.
325. Igor Ryabov, "The Chemical War" with an Invisible Enemy", *Novoe Vremya*, N 5, February, 1994.
326. Fausia Khajrutdinova, "Stand Strong, Mirzayanov", *My Fatherland Tatarstan*, February 4, 1994.
327. "The Collective Letter of the Participants of Mass Meeting in Ufa City

(Bashkortstan) to Boris Yeltsin", *Kyzil Tan*, February 3, 1994.
328. Muddaris Aglam, "We Know Right Now (verse)", *My Fatherland Tatarstan*, February 4, 1994.
329. Michael Waller, "Trials of a New Russian Dissident", *Wall Street Journal*, February 4, 1994.
330. Review & Outlook: "Timidity's Price", *Wall Street Journal*, February 4, 1994, A9.
331. Extract from the Congressional Record – Senate. (February 1, 1994. S.S.543-544). *Library of Congress*. http: //thomas.loc.gov/cgi-bin
332. Alexander Gordeyev, "Kremlin Sees Trial of Chemist As Flawed", *The Moscow Times*, February 5, 1994.
333. Vladimir Nazarov, "Behind Closed Doors..." *Kuranty*, February 5, 1994.
334. Sergei Mostovshchikov, "The Case of Vil Mirzayanov: the Trial has Begun After All", *Izvestia*, February 5, 1994.
335. Alexander Gordeyev, "Reporter Refuses a Role in Closed Chemist Trial", *The Moscow Times*, February 9, 1994.
336. Amy Knight, "Yeltsin's KGB. Back to the Bad Old Days in Moscow?" *Washington Post*, February 13, 1994.
337. Carey Scott, "Chemist Evidence "Falsified"', *The Moscow Times*, February 10, 1994.
338. Valeri Rudnev, "Sentence should be Passed on the Mirzayanov Case", *Izvestia*, February 9, 1994.
339. As a typical Soviet bureaucrat, he was not in any rush to fulfill a given order. This could be explained by the state of turmoil in the Attorney General's Office in those days. Duma began discussing amnesty for all the participants of the October 1993 Coup attempt against Yeltsin. President Yeltsin and his administration were furious about this action by Duma, and they prompted Alexey Kazannik to declare that he would not disobey Duma's resolution, which he was obliged to enforce. As an honest individual, Kazannik refused to violate Russian law, and decided to immediately resign after executing Duma's Resolution N 65-1G about amnesty, on February 23, 1994. My trial and Kazannik's saga coincided, creating some options for Pankratov to procrastinate with his order. Nevertheless, one of Kazannik's last decisions was to order me to be freed from jail.
340. SIPRI was established in 1966 as a tribute to Sweden's peaceful history. This venerable international research organization focuses on various ways to curtail warfare and keep the peace, including numerous publications on the development and use of poison gas and methods to eliminate chemical weapons. For more, see www.sipri.org.
341. The KGB intentionally omitted Will Englund's article from my case materials, "Russia is Still Doing Secret Work on Chemical Weapons," *Baltimore Sun, October 18, 1992,* in which he gave information about the development of a series of Novichok agents, and details about Andrey

Zheleznyakov's poisoning, with comments by Dr. Yevgeny Vedernikov, who prolonged his life. Moreover, Shkarin didn't even mention Andrey's name in any documents, despite the telephone conversations taped from my home phone (8 big cassettes were attached to my case), in which I asked him to give an interview to Will Englund, and then later to Oleg Vishnyakov, the reporter from *Novoe Vremya*. Another colleague of mine, Dr. Eduard Sarkisyan was brought to Lefortovo on October 22, 1992 for interrogation. He didn't give any information about the Novichok program. According to one of well informed reporter, it was exactly Andrey's first interview which pushed the KGB to arrest me trying to prevent further revelations about the plot of the Chemical Military Complex. *See* also ref. 40.

342. Valery Yakov, "The Mirzayanov Case Continues to Arouse Protest", *Izvestia*, February 10, 1994.
343. Sergei Shargorodsky (The Associated Press), "Court Halts Trial of Weapons Whistle Blower", *The Moscow Tribune,* February 15, 1994.
344. Vladimir Nazarov, "The Case – to the Additional Investigation, Vil Mirzayanov – to Jail", *Kuranty*, February 15, 1994.
345. "Jailed Scientist Awaits a 2d Trial in Moscow", *New York Times International*, February 16, 1994.
346. Deborah Stead, "Prosecutors File Motion to Halt Scientist's Trial", *Baltimore Sun*, February 11, 1994.
347. Richard Seltzer, "Charges Against Russian Chemist Undergo Review", *Chemical and Engineering News*, February 21, 1994.
348. Wendy Sloan, "Trial of Russian Scientist Provides First Test for New Constitution. Chemist Tried for Divulging Military Secrets, but Under What Set of Laws?", *Christian Science Monitor*, February 15, 1994.
349. Valeri Rudnev, "Mirzayanov's Case was Sent for Additional Investigation and Scientist – to the Jail", *Izvestia*, February 16, 1994.
350. Vil Mirzayanov, "There are no Hellenes or Jews in Jail", *Moscow News*, February 27, 1994.
351. Konstantin Katanyan, "Jailers at "Matrosskaya Tishina Beat People Half to Death. Vil Mirzayanov Discloses Secrets of the Investigation Isolator Cell Number 1", *Golos*, March 7-13, 1994.
352. Leonard Nikishin, Leonid Sharov, "Vil Mirzayanov: Jail Brings you Closer to the Truth", *Obschaya Gazetta*, March 4-10, 1994.
353. Adam Tanner, "Chemist Blasts Jail as "Hitlerite", *The Moscow Times*, February 24, 1994.
354. Marie Jego, "Des Prisons Russes Toujours Sovietiques", *Le Monde*, April 30, 1994.
355. Valeri Rudnev, "Non-Judicial Resolution was Enforced", *Izvestia*, February 23, 1994.
356. "Russia Released Scientist Imprisoned for Disclosure", *Washington Post*, 24 February, 1994.

357. Michael S. Serrill, "Exposing a Devilish Gas", *Time* (International Edition), February 21, 1994.
358. Richard Stone, "Russia Seen Poised to Drop Prosecution of Chemist", *Science*, 25 February, 1994, vol. 263, p. 1083-1084.
359. Kathy Lally, "The KGB's Power: In Some Ways, Little has Changed", *Baltimore Sun*, March 6, 1994.

Chapter 23 The Acquittal (pp. 445-447)

360. Merriam Webster's dictionary defines *corpus delicti* as the facts constituting a crime.
361. "RESOLUTION on the termination of the criminal case", Moscow, March 11, 1994. *See* Annex 78.
362. Sergei Mostovshchikov, "The Mirzayanov Case was Terminated for Absence of Corpus Delicti", *Izvestia* March 12, 1994.
363. Vladimir Nazarov, "The Investigation is Over - Forget About it, Mr. Mirzayanov?!" *Kuranty*, March 12, 1994.
364. Richard Seltzer, "All Charges Dropped Against Russian Chemist", *Chemical and Engineering News*, March 21, 1994, p. 6.
365. David Wise, "Novichok on Trial", *New York Times*, March 12, 1994
366. Editorial: "Chemistry and the Life of Mirzayanov", *Moscow News*, March 13, 1994.
367. Congressional Record. Proceedings and Debates of the 103d Congress, First Session. March 15, 1994, v. 140, N 28. S. 2958. *See* Annex 77.

Annexes

Annex 1

"*Responsible workers of the military-industrial complex love to babble on about conversion. It's a popular theme. In reality, a terrible monster continues to devour our economy. Chemists have a different name for this process -*

Inversion

When our press reports about the successful conversion of enterprises of the military-industrial complex (VPK), and about what great benefits this is going to bring us, this often reminds us of similar announcements, not so long ago, about the success of a century of achievements. Fortunately for them, no one has tried to check up on the real progress, and now hardly anyone is likely to do so in the future. They just won't allow it, that's all.

Who won't allow it? The very same ruling elite of the VPK, which hasn't been rendered harmless. Omnipotent directors with their devoted teams still reign at many enterprises and research institutes, and they enjoy unlimited power without any higher control. And so, as before, initiative and dissent are punished here.

The first, second, and third departments, which are headed up by KGB officers, are still constantly exercising their control over the employees. The very same barbed-wire fence along the perimeter, the checkpoints with guards, a special prosecutor's office, a special police force, a special court, and a center for tapping telephone conversations, as allowed by the implicit agreement of the trade union leaders, all ensure absolute obedience to the powerful directors. If an employee shows initiative or disagrees with them, they always find some sort of compromising material to morally destroy the disagreeable employee. And when this unfortunate person is thrown out onto the street, he can forget about a suitable job anywhere in this country, or even more so about a job abroad—he won't be allowed to leave the country because he knows state secrets.

Vil S. Mirzayanov

Since V. Bakatin came to work at the KGB, the situation hasn't changed for employees of the VPK, and change in the future seems unlikely. I am asserting this from my own "Post Office Box", which is located almost in the center of Moscow. It present itself as a secret structure only to naive Muscovites, who were unaware for decades that it had been killing them with real chemical agents, and that even today it poses a mortal danger. And as for the West... In the autumn of 1967, when preparations were being made for the first exhibition of abstract painters in the U.S.S.R., at the "Druzhba" Club [translates as "friendship"], which was located at this "postal address," BBC Radio called this enterprise "a factory of death."

Six years after the beginning of perestroika, when the Convention on the Prohibition of Chemical Weapons was practically ready, the U.S. and other countries stopped developing chemical weapons, and our press was making a big fuss about the upcoming campaign aimed at converting the VPK [to civilian production]. At that time, at the end of 1990, our director V. Petrunin declared "The nature of capitalism hasn't changed; our potential enemy remains the same, and that is why it is our duty to keep strengthening our defense power."

I am not so naive as to think that his opinion is unique. People like our director are disciplined and do exactly what their bosses tell them to do. It is a characteristic feature. Rumor has it that under his glorious leadership at the former enterprise, they had some problems and could not produce a single precursor. So, he forced all his employees, including the graduate students, to synthesize it in laboratory flasks. Let slaves do it. After a month or two they had synthesized the same amount an industrial unit could produce in one or two days. After that, the director was "riding high" [on his success]. Perhaps no one will investigate how he achieved his "success".

It's not surprising that he tried similar strategies in Moscow. In all sorts of ways he tried to imitate conversion, uttering fine phrases about self-financing and setting up training, but he never forgot about the "savage nature of capitalism." During the time of the negotiations in Geneva, they built a plant for destroying chemical weapons near Chapaevsk. The state squandered over 300 million rubles on it, and in the end, it was closed due to a massive protest by the residents of the city, because it didn't meet even elementary safety requirements.

In connection with this fiasco, not a single hair fell from the heads, either of our clever director, or of his superiors. And what were they to blame for? They unflaggingly supported each other, following the basic policy of the VPK which was focused on taming this very "savage nature." They were busy developing a more modern type of chemical weapon, and its testing was carried out at an open test [site] in one of the most ecologically unsafe regions.

Finally, the work was completed successfully, and in April of that year the director and his bosses received Lenin Prizes. The heroes of the VPK are not particularly worried that more than 70,000 [metric] tons of chemical agents are kept in warehouses, which is extremely dangerous, and that the state is too

State Secrets

impoverished to finance their destruction. Most likely they will not be destroyed in this century. Perhaps, we can expect help from the West...

The representatives of the VPK have started to actively study the West, and they are not at all self-conscious about their status as top-secret VIPs, because they know perfectly well that the regime of secrecy was invented for slaves, to scare them and to subjugate them. That is why they [VPK representatives] can easily go on business trips to the U.S., England, West Germany, and other countries. This would mean nothing, if we didn't know the true face of the VPK and its representatives. No, specialists hardly ever go to the West, since the bosses usually think that they can't be trusted. Those trips are for the director and his closest associates, who you can't call specialists even your wildest imagination. These are the same people who are running around at the negotiations in Geneva, once more trying to make fools out of their Western partners. On the other hand, I think they [the West] have already realized who they are dealing with.

Today, the director, who was a member of the regional bureau of the C.P.S.U. and a permanent member of the Party Committee, resigned from the party. How convenient it is for him this way. However, just a month or two ago, he called together the heads of the laboratories who had resigned from the party and branded them traitors. Emphatically and cynically, he gave his order about an agreement with the Party Committee, under which he was obligated to provide free transportation, work space, etc. in exchange for supervising ideological work.

Our director, who presents himself as a true patriot, is ready for any fraud. Here is a typical example that I witnessed myself in 1988. At one of the operating plants, I discovered that the concentration of chemical agents vented into the air, as well as those released into the waste water, which formed a lake near a densely populated region exceeded the norms of maximum permitted concentrations by more than a hundred times. The director prohibited me from reporting this to higher authorities.

The question is: Why are we misleading the West again? The real power in the VPK is concentrated in its enterprises, which have no desire to convert because their directors with their numerous aides don't want to. They are just waiting for their time to come, simply procrastinating. In chemistry there is a term - inversion. It means that a chemical unnoticeably changes from one form into another, without changing its chemical formula. This phenomenon can only be detected with the help of special instruments. However, sometimes inversion can be reversible. Aren't we witnessing a similar process with our so-called conversion?

If, by any chance, this is not true, we can sooner suppose that the dawdling with conversion is a prelude to the creeping privatization of enterprises by the top leadership of the VPK. I got this idea from the fact that just the other day our enterprise received eight brand new Mercedes from the Ministry of Petrochemical Industry. Two of them were given to our director. All of this is taking place while the country lacks the money to buy food and medications, and while our chemical industry is in a deep crisis because of the shortage of imported raw materials.

How long are we going to put up with it?

Vil Mirzayanov,
Doctor of Chemical Sciences"

Annex 2

"Witch Hunt" at GRNIIOKhT

"*On May 5 of 1990, Vil Sultanovich, head of Department 11, dared to resign from the ranks of the C.P.S.U. and to give a rather unflattering evaluation of the criminal essence of the party in his notice. That is where it all started. Could our administration, which faithfully served the interests of the totalitarian system and its own, leave this heresy unpunished? Of course, not. Soon on June 28, 1990, Order N 531 appeared about breaking up the department headed by Mirzayanov. On August 13 of the same year, another decree was issued (N 664) about appointing the rebellious chief to Department 45 in the capacity of leading research scientist. Then, for some reason, another order followed (N 129 dated February 1, 1991), transferring him to Department 20. Then, due to some circumstances of which we know nothing, on April 30th 1991, the management cancelled this order by a different one (N 332).*

Finally, after all these tribulations Vil S. Mirzayanov was returned to Subdivision 45, and the head of this subdivision, Yuri V. Skripkin, addressing the question of his employment, put him on the list of employees "subject to staff reductions". Be that as it may, Vil Sultanovich avoided this downsizing.

We think the August events contributed to that in a significant way. However, the administration had recovered from the August shock and didn't want to leave their "favorite" unpunished, especially since he had also dared to criticize them in the mass media. Finally, he encroached upon the most "sacred" item - power. He went to the Ministry of Industry of the RSFSR (Russian Socialist Federal Soviet Republic) along with Vyacheslav G. Agureev to determine if the actions of the administration were legal. He wanted to inquire how enterprises should be transferred under the jurisdiction of Russian law. He wanted to know if such a hasty transfer could save the enterprise from financial collapse, so that a person could re-appoint himself director and sign a very convenient contract with himself (violating the laws of Russia). Then the patience of our glorious management was exhausted.

The above-mentioned meeting was conducted at the request (?) of the directorate. Another farce was performed in the best traditions of the 1930s—the farce of "common censure."

(Hello, Iosif Vissarionovich Stalin! Yes, the traditions that you founded die

hard and probably they will last as long as Communist chaps like Victor A. Petrunin and Yuri V. Skripkin are at the helm. You taught them to run to the people for help, so that they could use them to get rid of disagreeable people.)

This is the whole story. This took place yesterday, in 1991, in the so-called post-Communist time, not in 1937.

Moreover, you shouldn't forget that this is no ordinary research scientist who is being persecuted, but a scientist of the highest qualification, a specialist in the analysis of micro-concentrations (in ecology). His competence and skills will not be at all superfluous to our enterprise.

So, dear workers and scientists, who will be next? Shall we continue trampling on people? Or maybe there are people at our enterprise who can stand up for the specialist, the professional as the man who wouldn't allow glastnost to be stifled? Will anyone support this person who was one of the first to start fighting against our corrupted totalitarian system?

DESPITE EVERYTHING IT SEEMS TO US THAT YOUR TIME, DEAR COMMUNISTS AND NOMENKLATURA, IS OVER!"

Annex 3

"Scandal
A Poisoned Policy

Scientists insist:
- Our country's international assurances have been and still are at variance with the real production and testing of chemical weapons.
- Moscow is threatened with poisoning.
- Generals of chemical warfare are again running high.

Today it is widely known: for many decades now chemical weapons have been developed in Moscow. True, elegant attempts have sometimes been made to reduce this work merely to the development of chemical agents with plans to use them on the battlefields somewhere "far away" from our borders. But we want to warn right now: we have already stockpiled large amounts of such agents which are said not to be toxic, which have been adopted for service and more often are not in service (existing quietly in experimental consignments) and are nevertheless particularly dangerous. The latter circumstance is also born out by the fact that in "the international talks on banning chemical weapons" (an affair of many years which is so dear to the heart of widely traveling bosses) all these "non-combat" agents figure very prominently as full-fledged objects of discussions.

Not with a vengeance upon the past it is worth recalling a statement made by Soviet scientists on May 8, 1982: "Strictly abiding by the Geneva Protocol of

1925... the USSR has never used chemical weapons and has not transferred them to other countries." It has used them, only on our own battlefields. The last time this happened in spring 1989 in Tbilisi where CS gas demonstrated its effectiveness. Preparations were also underway to envelop Russia's White House with noxious smoke in August 1991.

As a matter of fact, politically we have always sought to be "clean". As early as April 1982, SOMEONE made a statement for Der Spiegel Magazine: "There is no need for the Soviet Union necessarily to counter the escalation of chemical weapons with an escalation in the same field." That was an official rebuke to the American programme of the development and production of a new variety of chemical weapons (binary weapons). And a decade later, after yet another meeting at Geneva, SOMEONE declared that in 1987 we completely discontinued the production of toxic agents (Izvestia, August 27, 1992).

This sounds like an ode to humanism and common sense. But now let us turn to prose which cannot be done without describing our dirty reality.

A new toxic agent has been developed at a research institute of chemical technologies abbreviated in Russian as GSNIIOKhT. For its perfidy ("performance characteristics") it has considerably surpassed the well-known VX gas, an injury with it is practically incurable. In any case those who were once affected with this toxic agent have remained disabled for the rest of their lives. The new agent served as the basis on which our own binary weapons have been developed – and not only developed but also successfully completed with the manufacture of a serially produced batch, following which those involved and uninvolved in the project were lavishly decorated with government awards. Our heroes were likewise honored with the diplomas and badges of the Lenin Prize laureates.

This was done in spring 1991 personally by President Mikhail Gorbachev. By that time he had already done all he could to immortalize himself - signed the well-known Bush-Gorbachev agreement on chemical weapons and was honored with the Nobel Peace Prize. Let us recall the names of the two most remarkable recipients of that Lenin Prize: V. Petrunin, Director of GSNII-OKhT, and a certain general, deputy chief of the "chemical troops", whom we shall designate as SOMEONE (he is among those, who joined up with the project and we shall not speak about real developers because work is work, let alone dangerous work.)

However, that was not the end either. The field tests of the new binary toxic agent were completed in the first quarter of the current year 1992 but not in "exposed" Shikhany (it was too troublesome to dodge American satellites), but at the chemical test range on the Ustyurt Plateau near Nukus. On that range correspondents even met – quite accidentally - General S. Petrov, chief of the "chemical troops", and heard from the local military chief words, corresponding to the occasion, about phosphorous chemical agents - sarin, soman, and VX – used in the past, of course, whereas nothing was said about the new

State Secrets

toxic agent (Trud, April 15, 1992).

And here we come to the inevitable deliberations on the perpetual theme of who is the master in our Russia. The first industrial batch of the new toxic agent was manufactured in Volgograd, whereas the Lenin Prize was awarded in Moscow still BEFORE we had elected Boris Yeltsin the first President. However, the chemical troops carried out the field tests of the toxic agent AFTER this election and his well-known statement of January 29, 1992 ("Russia is committed to the agreement with the USA on the non-production and elimination of chemical weapons signed in 1990."). Incidentally, those tests were staged in a different state and it is by no means a fact that that state's President Islam Karimov knew anything about this.

Such is the sad result of the five years we lived through after the proclaimed termination of work in the development of chemical weapons and until the completion of testing their most powerful variety. Today we can boast of an achievement: the Russian binary weapon has proved to be more effective than its American counterpart. So what?

To begin with, let us say that GSNIIOKhT has been literally poisoning Muscovites. Because at this research institute there are practically no filters on ventilation installations and all evaporating toxic agents fly straight into Moscow's air. The decontamination of modern phosphorous chemical agents, which GSNIIOKhT has worked with until now is not as effective, as some authors of secret theses would like us to believe. Available scientific data unambiguously indicate that it is impossible to completely decontaminate either the new toxic agent – the pride of the generals - or the old ones (sarin, soman and VX). At the level of very small yet unsafe concentrations, they "live" for weeks or even months in the decontaminating solutions. This is what Muscovites have to deal with day in day out.

Incidentally, the practice of waste reclamation, accepted at GSNIIOKhT, is unsafe both for the personnel doing this job and for people in the neighborhood. Waste is kept in the open air in barrels, and then taken out as ordinary cargo by rail to Shikhany (Saratov Region) where their contents are simply emptied into a pit in the open field.

It will not be amiss to look even more deeply into the institute's history. The point is that the entire vast territory of GSNIIOKhT has been polluted with toxic agents of the yperite (mustard gas) type. All the wastes, and the toxic agents themselves, were poured right onto the ground or dug at random. But they survive for an infinitely long time in soil, slowly migrating under the impact of atmospheric fallout into subsoil waters which then mix up with deeper waters. With a high degree of probability it can be said that artesian waters here have been contaminated. Thus the chromatographic analysis of running water in Block 7, supplied from an artesian well on the institute's territory, has revealed the presence of a whole bunch of sulfur- and chlorine-containing compounds close to yperite in their structure. The institute's leadership is perfectly well aware of this, which is why earthwork on the territory is carried out at the level of combat operations with the use of gas masks. All this is being carefully hidden.

In 1990 GSNIIOKhT was visited by the First Vice-Chairman of the Moscow City Council, who was very touched by the sight of guinea pigs, promised every kind of assistance and kept his word. However, it only remains to wonder why the Muscovite's electee Sergey Stankevich, when visiting the world's largest organization for development of chemical weapons, did not try to inquire about the quantity of lethal substances which were kept in the depot at that time. Usually there are at least eight to ten kilos here, and this quantity will be enough for Moscow, should a fire or any other accident occur at the institute. Let us say that this was already four years after the Chernobyl tragedy...

Several years ago SOMEONE assured the inhabitants of Chapaevsk on oath that all gaseous waste at the plant dealing with the destruction of chemical weapons would be passed through special filters. One can only admire the courage, prudence and self-preservation instinct of the inhabitants who didn't believe him. They were right: GSNIIOKhT simply did not even envisage these filters in the project.

So ingloriously we embarked upon the road towards a world without chemical weapons, whose possessors we had become through the graces of our home-grown military-industrial complex. Instead of destroying old ones they will slip onto the development of new weapons, and they are much better in doing this. It looks as if the real masters of the military-industrial complex - generals and directors – will tolerate no stagnation in their doings. Consequently the people of Russia have no reasons whatsoever to entrust the destruction of chemical weapons to those who developed them.

At this point it is worth pondering once again over the purport of the dollar aid for which SOMEONE recently went across the ocean. Knowing our inglorious military-chemical past, it is safe to say that the 25 million dollars which the USA has initially allotted to Russia for the implementation of the chemical-weapon-elimination programme will be spent quite differently - to keep the military-industrial complex afloat, among other things, and even for carrying on the further development and improvement of new types of chemical weapons.

And recently the people of Russia were delighted by the appointment – in the post of head of the Committee on the Conventional Problems of the Chemical and Biological Weapons under the auspices of the President of Russia - of A. Kuntsevich, a "common Soviet person", a general for whom chemical weapons were developed at GSNIIOKhT, a person who in 1982 promised not to respond to the escalation of American binary weapons, a specialist who assures us that the production of toxic agents was discontinued as early as 1987, a scientist who in 1991 was honored with a Lenin Prize for the development of the world's most powerful chemical weapon, a government official who deceived the inhabitants of Chapaevsk with respect to the plant meant for the destruction of chemical weapons and, lastly, a politician who brought dollars from the USA for the continuation of chemical business. All of this is about A. Kuntsevich, an Academician and a Hero of Labor, a general and a laureate.

This appointment is not an error, but the restoration of the System. And all of us must know and know and remember this.

Vil Mirzayanov,
Lev Fedorov,
Both D.Sc. (Chemistry)"

Annex 4

Top Secret

Copy 1
To A.I. Tselikovsky,
Head of the Department for Economic Security
of the Security Ministry of the Russian Federation

October 1, 1992 N 1594 ss

The issue N. 38 of September 20, 1992 of the newspaper "Moscow News", published an article "Poisoned Policies" signed by Vil Mirzayanov and Lev Fedorov, Doctors of Chemical Science, which contains information about scientific research and experimental design work (NIOKR) that is carried out in our country in the field of chemical weapons. According to the conclusion of the Permanent Technical Commission (PDTK) at GRNIIOKhT, these publications include pieces of information, which are top secret and constitute a state secret. [The Russian language version of the Moscow News article title translates as "Poisoned Policies", while the English language edition was published as "A Poisoned Policy."]

One of the authors, Vil Sultanovich Mirzayanov, born in 1935 in the village Stary Kangysh, Djirtjuli Region, Bashkir Autonomous Soviet Socialist Republic, a Bashkir, with higher education, Doctor of Chemical Science, was an employee at GSNIIOKhT from 1965 to January of 1992. He served as the head of the Department for Foreign Technical Counterintelligence [PDITR] from September of 1986 to August of 1990, had access through Form 1 to the secret of special importance and to top secret documents of the "Foliant" program.

By virtue of his work responsibilities, Vil S. Mirzayanov was well-informed about the system of the organization, trends, and results of NIOKR work in the field of chemical weapons.

I forward to you the resolution of the PDTK of the institute and the list of functional responsibilities of Vil S. Mirzayanov, as the head of the PD ITR Department to decide whether criminal proceedings should be instituted according to Article 75 of the RSFSR Criminal Code "Disclosing state secrets."

Appendix:

1. Resolution of the PDTK, mk 1587 ss, copy 1, 2 on three pages each, top secret.
2. List of functional responsibilities of Vil S. Mirzayanov, mk 1572 ss, copy 1, 2 on three pages each, top secret.

    Director   Professor Victor A. Petrunin

Annex 5

Top Secret
Copy 1

Resolution
of the Permanent Technical Commission at GRNIIOKhT
September 25, 1992

The Permanent Technical Commission of the Russian State Scientific Research Institute for Organic Chemistry and Technology (GRNIIOKhT) consisting of Yu. I. Baranov (Chairman), Deputy Director, M.S. in Chemistry, V.G. Zoryan, Department Head, M.D., Yu V. Skripkin, Chief Chemist, M.S. in Chemistry, and V.I. Lisitsyna and German M. Mosyakin, Department Heads, following the instructions of the director of the institute, considered the question of the degree of confidentiality of the information set forth in the article "Poisoned Policies" published in Issue N. 38 of September 20, 1992 of the newspaper "Moscow News".

The commission was guided by:

- The List of Major Information that constitutes a state secret (hereafter referred to as the LMI) and the statute for establishing the degree of secrecy categories of information and for classifying information to be found in works, documents, and products approved by the Resolution N 1121-387 of the U.S.S.R. Council of Ministers dated December 3, 1980;
- The List of information subject to classification by the Office of the U.S.S.R. Ministry of Petrochemical Industry, compiled in accordance with the Resolution N 1121-387 of the Council of Ministers dated December 3, 1980 and the Order N 234-19 of the U.S.S.R. Ministry of Petrochemical Industry dated May 27, 1991 (hereinafter referred to as the List of the Ministry of Petrochemical Industry);
- The List of information that constitutes a state secret on the "Foliant" program and other information subject to classification by the U.S.S.R. Ministry of Petrochemical Industry, in accordance with the LMI and the

announced Order N 144-13 of the USSR Ministry of Petrochemical Industry dated March 25, 1991 (hereinafter referred to as the List on the "Foliant" program).

The Commission considers that the article "Poisoned Policies" published in the N 38 issue of the newspaper "Moscow News" on September 20, 1992 and signed by Vil Mirzayanov and Lev Fedorov contains the following information that constitutes a state secret.

1. "A new toxic agent has been developed at the State Scientific Research Institute for Organic Chemistry and Technology (GOSNIIOKhT). For its perfidy ("combat characteristics") it has considerably surpassed the well-known gas VX, and injury from it is practically incurable." (column 2, paragraph 1).

This information is true. GOSNIIOKhT (currently, GRNIIOKhT) did synthesize, studied, and tested a number of new chemical compounds of different classes that are considerably more potent than the VX gas (the substance that the U.S. is armed with) by a complex of combat characteristics, including difficulties of treatment. According to available information, the armies of the countries that possess chemical weapons are not armed with an equivalent of the above-mentioned agent. Equipping chemical ammunition with such compounds considerably increases its effectiveness.

Thus, information was disclosed about one of the latest achievements in the sphere of science and technology, that allows for increasing the potency of existing weapons (ammunition), which according to point 83 paragraph 2 of the LMI and point 5.3 of the List of the Ministry of Petrochemical Industry, is top secret and constitutes a state secret.

2. "...our own binary weapon was developed based on the new chemical agent" (column 2, paragraph 1)

This is also true. GRNIIOKhT developed its own binary weapons based on the new chemical agent and these weapons are currently being tested.

According to our sources, before this article was published, foreign states had no information about our country developing its own binary weapon.

Thus, information was divulged that discloses trends of promising applied research work carried out to strengthen the defense power of the country. According to point 85 from the list of major information and point 5.5 from the list of the Ministry of Petrochemical Industry, this information is top secret and constitutes a state secret.

3. "The State Scientific Research Institute of Organic Chemistry and Technology (GOSNIIOKhT) developed a new chemical agent." (column 2, paragraph 1)

"The first batch of the chemical agent was produced in Volgograd..." (column 3, paragraph 3)

"In the first quarter of the current year 1992, field testing of the new binary weapons was completed. It was not done at the "exposed" test site Shikhany, but at the chemical test site on the Ustyurt Plateau near the city of Nukus." (column 3, paragraph 2)

This information brought forth discloses the system of organization of the research aimed at developing chemical weapons. The major research Institute-designer is clearly indicated, and the locations of one of the experimental industrial bases (Volgograd) and both test sites (Shikhany and Nukus) are mentioned. That is, the author named major sites of the development of chemical weapons.

Thus, the disclosure of combined information has been revealed that divulges the cooperation of designers and manufacturers of one of the types of weapons, which, according to point 94 from the LMI and point 1.3 from the List on the Foliant program, are top secret and constitute state secrets.

The remaining information revealed in the article by Vil Mirzayanov and Lev Fedorov does not contain state secrets.

Yu. I. Baranov
V.G. Zoryan
Yu. V. Skripkin
G.M. Mosyakin
V.I. Lisitsyna

Annex 6

Top Secret
Copy 1

Ministry of Security
of the Russian Federation
Department for Economic Security

To Major General S.D. Balashov,
Head of the Investigation Department
at the RF Ministry of Security

Regarding Vil S. Mirzayanov

The Department for Economic Security at the MB RF received materials from the State Russian Science Research Institute of Organic Chemistry and Technology (GRNIIOKhT), which said that the article "Poisoned Policies" published in issue N 38 of September 16, 1992 of the newspaper "Moscow News", disclosed state secrets.

State Secrets

The article indicated is signed by Lev A. Fedorov and Vil S. Mirzayanov, Doctors of Chemical Science. The latter worked at GRNIIOKhT until January 1992 and therefore was granted access to information presented in the article, from the publication "Moscow News."

The materials were checked and the information received from GRNIIOKhT was confirmed. At the same time, it was established that the article "Inversion" by Vil S. Mirzayanov, published on October 10, 1991, by the newspaper "Kuranty" also disclosed classified information.

Additionally, as a result of technical operating measures, sanctioned by the RF Attorney General's Office, reliable information was received showing that Vil S. Mirzayanov and Lev A. Fedorov collected additional confidential information about the military-chemical potential of Russia, in order to pass it along to correspondents of the American newspaper "Baltimore Sun" and to prepare another publication in the mass media.

Mirzayanov and Fedorov also tried to persuade former and current employees of GRNIIOKhT to follow suit and to leak classified information to foreign journalists.

It was established that Edward Lyudvigovich Sarkisyan, born in 1945 in Tbilisi, a senior research scientist at GRNIIOKhT, and the former Head Physician of City Hospital 55 (permanent address: Moscow, Rossoshanky Proezd, 4, korp. 1, kv. 111), gave an interview on September 29, 1992 to the correspondent of the newspaper the "Baltimore Sun" and confirmed information published in the article "Poisoned Policies."

Taking into account everything mentioned above, that the actions of Vil Sultanovich Mirzayanov indicate a criminal offense under Clause 75 of the RSFSR Criminal Code, as well as the fact that it is necessary to prevent even greater damage to the interests of Russia, we send GRNIIOKhT's materials and results of the check on Mirzayanov for a decision on the question of instituting criminal proceedings on charges of disclosing state secrets.

Appendix:
1. The letter from GRNIIOKhT regarding the publication n/vkh N 6045 dated October 2, 1992, Top Secret, on 7 pages.
2. Non-disclosure agreement signed by Vil S. Mirzayanov n/vkh N 12290 dated January 28, 1992, open, 1 page. [*This is a shameless lie! I refused to sign it* and because of this it wasn't included in my case. V.M.]

Major General A.I. Tselikovsky, Head of the department

Vil S. Mirzayanov

Annex 7

Top Secret

TRANSCRIPT
of the interrogation of the suspect

Moscow   October 22, 1992

Captain of Jusice Shkarin, Senior Investigator of the Investigation Department of the Ministry of Security of the Russian Federation, with the participation of Leonid Grigorievich Belomestnykh, lawyer from Legal Advice Office N 150, who produced Order N 771 dated October 22, 1992, observing requirements stipulated in Articles 123, 150-152 of the RSFSR Criminal Code, interrogated the suspect, Vil Sultanovich Mirzayanov, born in 1935 in the Stary Kangysh village, Djirtjuli region, Bashkir Autonomous Soviet Socialist Republic, citizen of the Russian Federation, higher education, married, working as head of the Research Department of the joint-stock company Region-Tsentr-Vozrozhdenie, no previous convictions. Permanent address:

Moscow, Stalevarov Ulitsa, 4, korp. 4, kv. 586,
Passport presented XI-MYu N 563326
Issued on November 9, 1977

Before the interrogation began, it was explained to Vil S. Mirzayanov that, according to Articles 52, 64, 66, 70, 76, 141-1, 151, and 152 of the RSFSR Criminal and Procedural Code, the suspect has the right to defend himself; to know what he is suspected of; to give explanations; to get acquainted with transcripts of the investigation carried out with his participation, as well as the materials submitted to the court in order to confirm that he was preemptively taken into custody legally; to reject and complain about the actions and decisions of the interrogator, investigator, and prosecutor; to participate when judges are considering complaints following the procedure stipulated by Article 220-2 of the RSFSR Criminal and Procedural Code; to write testimony, ask that interrogations be recorded, to require additions and amendments be made to the transcript. It was also explained that, according to Article 47 of the RSFSR Criminal Code, the defender is allowed to participate in the case from the moment preemptive arrest was applied to me.

Vil S. Mirzayanov

The interrogation started at 12.20 P.M.
The interrogation finished at 3.30 P.M.

Vil Sultanovich Mirzayanov was notified that he was suspected of disclosing state secrets, that is of committing a crime stipulated by Article 75, Part 1, of

State Secrets

the RSFSR Criminal Code.

Question: What language would you prefer to give your testimony in?

Answer: I speak Russian fluently and don't require the services of an interpreter. I would prefer to give testimony in the Russian language.

Question: I am in charge of the preliminary investigation, according to instructions given to me, Captain of Justice Shkarin, Senior Investigator of the Investigation Department at the Ministry of Security of the Russian Federation. Do you reject the investigator who accepted the case?

Answer: I don't reject Investigator Shkarin who accepted the case. I have no basis for rejection.

Question: Were you told which crime you are suspected of, and were you informed about the suspect's rights?

Answer: I understand what crime I am suspected of and the rights of a suspect. At the same time, I claim that I request the presence of a defender at today's interrogation. I don't have any defender, so I request any lawyer be invited.

Question: To defend your interests at the preliminary investigation, you are offered the services of Leonid Grigorievich Belomestnykh, lawyer of Legal Advice Office N 150, who has been presented with order N 771 dated October 22, 1992.

Answer: I do not object to having Leonid Grigorievich Belomestnykh defend my interests at today's interrogation.

Question: What explanations can you give regarding suspicions against you?

Answer: I prepared the article "Poisoned Policies" published in issue N 38 of September 20, 1992 of the weekly "Moscow News" with a co-author Lev Aleksandrovich Fedorov, Doctor of Chemical Sciences. In this article I stated the facts, known to me from my work at the State Russian Science Research Institute for Organic Chemistry and Technology (GRNIIOKhT), that new kinds of chemical agents continued to be developed, produced, and tested, and that binary weapons were developed based on them. I worked at this institute from 1965 until January of 1992, and I was directly involved in the development of the new kinds of chemical agents that the article is talking about. I carried out analyses on them and looked through documentation necessary for conducting this analysis. This means that for the article I used trustworthy information that I knew from my work. In publishing this article, my goal was to expose the hypocrisy of the leaders of the military-chemical complex, who were violating an agreement between the U.S. and the U.S.S.R. governments in the field of chemical weapons, and their deception at the Geneva negotiations on concluding the convention on chemical disarmament, because they concealed components of the new weapons by not including them on the list of controlled substances. Additionally, I wanted to draw public attention to this problem. I realized that the Soviet, and later the Russian party, was trying to conceal the facts on the development, production, and testing of new chemical agents from the negotiators in Geneva, as well as the fact that binary weapons were being produced based on them. I knew for a fact that at the institute there was the "Foliant" program on the development of new chemical agents and that the creation of binary weapons based on them was secret; that is, information that I revealed in my article was not to be disclosed. However, I came to the conclusion that in these times concealing the facts of the development of new chemical agents and creation of binary weapons damaged the state interests of Russia, and benefited only the leaders of the military-chemical complex, since it served their narrowly selfish and extremely profitable interests.

I think that by publishing in the article "Poisoned Policies" I gave no specific information that would characterize the composition or properties of the new chemical agents or the binary weapons based on them, the location of the institute-designer, or the site of production and testing of the new chemical agents. I didn't give any concrete facts about the composition or properties of the new chemical agents. This is why I think that I didn't disclose any state secret in the above-mentioned article.

Question by the defender, Leonid G. Belomestnykh: Did you realize that by publishing the article you included information not suitable for publication, and do you think that in this way you disclosed state secrets as the investigation claims?

Answer: I presented information in the article that conceptually has to do with the strictly secret topic of the development, testing, and production of a new chemical agent and the creation of binary weapons based on it. I didn't cite a single line from classified documents in my article. This is why I think that I didn't disclose any state secrets in the article "Poisoned Policies."

I have read the interrogation transcript. It appears that my testimony has been transcribed accurately in the report. I don't want to make any corrections or additions to the report.

  Suspect   Vil S. Mirzayanov
  Defender Leonid G. Belomestnykh

The suspect was interrogated and the transcript was compiled by

State Secrets

Senior Investigator of the Investigation Department
at the MB RF,
Captain of Justice   V. Shkarin

Annex 8

Top Secret

Committee of Governmental Security [KGB] of the USSR

Report of the search

Moscow   October 22, 1992

Investigator of the Investigation Department at the MB RF, Senior Lieutenant of Justice Martynenko and Junior Investigator of the same department, Lieutenant of Justice Zenkov ---------------- with the participation of employees of the MB RF A.T. Svetin, I.V. Belyanin [former employee of GRNIIOKhT—V.M.] and A.A. Dmitriev [my former colleague at GRNIIOKhT who worked with Bogomazov—V.M.] searched the premises of Lev A. Fedorov, Moscow, ul. Profsoyuznaya, d. 8, korp. 2, kv. 83:
    1. German Mitrofanovich Mosyakin [he signed the resolution of the Permanent Technical Commission and wrote a letter about my functional responsibilities - V.M.]. Permanent address: Moscow, Orekhovy proezd, d. 39, korp. 2, kv. 342, and
    2. Ivan Ivanovich Surinsky [Deputy Chief of the Security Department at GRNIIOKhT—V.M.]. Permanent address: Moscow, ul. Sayanskaya, d. 2, kv. 54. The search was conducted on the basis of the ordinance about conducting searches dated October 20, 1992 following the requirements stipulated in Articles 169-171 of the RSFSR Criminal and Procedural Code. The search was conducted in the presence of Lev Aleksandrovich Fedorov and witnesses.
    The above mentioned people were informed that they could observe all the actions of the investigator and make statements regarding any of his actions. Witnesses were also advised that Article 135 of the RSFSR Criminal Code stipulates their obligation to attest to the fact, content, and results of the search.
(signatures)
The search started at 7.30 A.M.
    Before the search started Lev A. Fedorov was offered the chance to voluntarily submit items and documents pertaining to the case as indicated in the ordinance. After this Lev A. Fedorov produced two manuscripts in blue ink. One document is 7 (seven) pages long. The other document is 6 (six) pages long. Fedorov also produced two copies of the weekly "Moscow News" issues N 38 in Russian and N 39 in English. After this Lev A. Fedorov submitted another document that was 4 (four) pages long, a manuscript in blue ink.

Vil S. Mirzayanov

Lev A. Fedorov explained that Vil Sultanovich Mirzayanov had given him three manuscripts. Based on these documents, Fedorov and Mirzayanov prepared articles to be published in the weekly "Moscow News."
<u>After Lev A. Fedorov voluntarily produced the documents and newspapers, his apartment wasn't searched</u> [underlined by me—V.M.].

Three documents are packed in a paper envelope and sealed with stamp N 2 for documents of the Investigation Department of the KGB of the U.S.S.R., which is attested by signatures of the investigator, Fedorov, and the witnesses.

The search finished at 8.00 A.M. We_____ have read the report of the search.
The report is true and accurate.
We have no comments regarding the search and content of the report.

The person whose apartment was searched _____

(Fedorov)
Signature

The search was conducted and the report was written by
Investigator of the Investigation Department at the RF Ministry of Security, Senior Lieutenant of Justice S.M. Martynenko_____
Junior Investigator at the same department, Lieutenant of Justice I.E. Zenkov_____

Received the copy of the report of the search
October 22, 1992

Last name and signature of the person who received the last copy

Annex 9

Top Secret

TRANSCRIPT
of the interrogation of the witness

Moscow   October 22, 1992

Lieutenant Colonel of Justice Fanin, head of the Investigation Department at the Ministry of Security of the Russian Federation, in his office of the Investigation Department at the MB RF, observing requirements stipulated in Articles 72-74, 157, 158, and 160 of the RSFSR Criminal and Procedural Code interrogated the witness, Lev Aleksandrovich Fedorov, born on June 10, 1936 in Moscow, Chuvash, citizen of the Russian Federation, Doctor of Chemical Sciences,

State Secrets

Leading Research Assistant at the Institute for Geochemistry and Analytical Chemistry of the Russian Academy of Sciences (work tel. 137-49-30), married. Permanent address:
Moscow, ul. Profsoyuznaya, 8, korp. 2, kv. 83,
(home tel. 129-05-96)
Passport series XV-MYu N 608591 issued by Police Department 134, Moscow, on July 1, 1978.

It was explained to the witness that, according to Articles 73 and 74 of the RSFSR Criminal and Legal Code, he can be interrogated regarding any circumstances that have been established on the facts of a case and must give truthful evidence: produce all information known to him regarding this case and answer questions. Additionally, I was informed that, according to Articles 141-commentary and 160 of the RSFSR Criminal Code, after testifying I have the right to familiarize myself with the transcript of my testimony, to require insertions and amendments to the transcript, and also to apply to have the interrogation recorded.

I have been advised in advance about the responsibility stipulated by Article 180 of the RSFSR Criminal Code for refusing or evading giving evidence and about the responsibility stipulated by Article 181 of RSFSR Criminal Code for giving deliberately false evidence.

.... Lev A. Fedorov

The interrogation started at 9.45 A.M.
The interrogation finished at 1.50 P.M.

Witness Lev A. Fedorov was asked to give a full account of the circumstances about which he was called in for interrogation. He testified the following:

I speak Russian fluently and will testify in this language. I met Vil Sultanovich Mirzayanov two months ago. He called me, said that his name was Vil Sultanovich Mirzayanov, and asked if I had written an article for the newspaper "Sovershenno Sekretno." I don't remember the title of the article. Probably, "Delayed Death." It discussed chemical weapons the way I, a Doctor of Science, understand the problem. I confirmed that I had written this article. When Mirzayanov called me, I remembered at once that he was the author of the article "Inversion" published in autumn of 1991 in the newspaper "Kuranty." This article was interesting to me then, so I remembered its author. This is why I agreed to meet with Mirzayanov. I went to his home. When we met, Mirzayanov said that my article was interesting. Since he worked at the State Russian Science Research Institute for Organic Chemistry and Technology, we could have common interests in the area of chemical disarmament. I expressed my satisfaction with the article "Inversion." From my talk with Mirzayanov I understood that he knew the information revealed in the article "Inversion" from his work in the above-mentioned institute. During the conversation Mirzayanov stressed that the information didn't constitute state secrets. Additionally, the very fact that the article was published in "Kuranty" was evidence to me that the information written there didn't appear to be state secrets.

We talked about returning to this topic and publishing a new article, describing the negative consequences of chemical weapons production for Russia. I don't remember who came up with this suggestion. We agreed that Mirzayanov would write a rough draft and I would review it. In the middle of August of 1992 we arranged a meeting by phone and met at one of the Moscow subway stations where Mirzayanov handed me his manuscripts. From August 23 until 28 of this year I was in Finland at the international congress "Dioxin-92." At the beginning of September, I returned and started writing with notes received from Mirzayanov. I read the text through and elaborated it in such a way that it could be given to journalists for subsequent publication. I thought through and worked out the structure of the article and Mirzayanov produced the facts for me. Probably he knew this information from his work at GOSNIIOKhT. While working on the article I was certain that information it contained didn't constitute state secrets. I didn't show Mirzayanov the article after I had prepared it for publication. Then in September of this year, I gave it to Leonard Nikishin, an acquaintance of mine, a correspondent of "Moscow News", after which it was published in this newspaper issue 38 on September 20. The newspaper "Moscow News" is a weekly and it came out on Wednesday, September 16. I don't know if Nikishin changed it in any way because I didn't keep a copy of my article. If some changes were introduced, they were few and not significant. Despite the fact that I didn't familiarize Mirzayanov with the article, it had both our signatures because we had an agreement that his signature would come first.

Neither Mirzayanov, nor I have received any royalties for the article up to the present time. Literally, the day before the newspaper "Moscow News" came out, that is, on Tuesday, September 15 of this year, I visited the press center of the "Baltimore Sun" together with Mirzayanov. Knowing that the newspaper with our article would come out on September 16, we gave an interview to a correspondent of the "Baltimore Sun" on the same topic as in the article "Poisoned Policies." In particular, Mirzayanov said in the interview that a new chemical agent had been developed that surpassed in its attributed characteristics all chemical agents known up until then and that more of this substance had been produced than stipulated by the convention. I don't know what convention he was talking about. I don't remember if he said anything else about it. <u>I want to stress that I don't have access to any state secrets in my job, and I know no secrets, so I couldn't possibly disclose any such information.</u> [underlined by me—V.M.] If I remember correctly, the name of the correspondent from the "Baltimore Sun" was Will Englund. I had never met him before. We decided to visit the press center of the "Baltimore Sun" a week before the meeting, at which we had planned to discuss the dioxin problem, and then we spontaneously refocused on the article "Poisoned Policies." I called Mirzayanov and said that I

State Secrets

was meeting with a correspondent from the "Baltimore Sun" and suggested he go with me. He agreed. Since the next day the aforementioned article was supposed to come out, we touched upon issues discussed there during the conversation. Mirzayanov and I received no fee for that interview.

Two weeks ago a stranger called and introduced himself as Oleg Voldemarovich Vishnyakov, a correspondent from the magazine "Novoe Vremya." He expressed interest in the published article "Poisoned Policies" and suggested we meet and talk about this issue. I met with him in the editor's office, and I found out that he wanted to work on the topic of chemical weapons and publish an article in the magazine. I understand from him, that in the past he had worked with the issue of nuclear weapons and then had developed a parallel interest in chemical weapons. He was busy with the idea of destroying chemical weapons by nuclear explosions. I agreed to help him with an article about chemical weapons. Sometime around October 18 of this year, he called me for the second time and said that he had decided to write an article in the form of an interview. We agreed that I would come to his editor's office together with Mirzayanov and we would discuss this problem. On or around October 20, Mirzayanov and I went to his editor's office and gave an interview on the same questions that were discussed in the article "Poisoned Policies." Vishnyakov recorded the interview and <u>kept the recording</u> [underlined by me—V.M.] Recently some of my acquaintances said that the editor's office of "Argumenti i Fakty" got interested in the article "Poisoned Policies." On Friday, October 16 of this year, I called the editor's office to talk with Starkov. He wasn't there and I called him at home on October 18. I introduced myself and explained who I was. He became interested in the topic and recommended that I write an article. I started working on a new article using the information presented to me from Mirzayanov's manuscripts. By Tuesday it was ready. On October 20, after visiting Vishnyakov, I showed this article to Mirzayanov. It was called "Myths and Legends of Chemical Disarmament." He read it, corrected something, and signed it. After this I brought it to the editor's office of the newspaper "Argumenti i Fakty" where I handed it to the secretary of the Editor in Chief, Tamara Vasilievna, if I am not mistaken. In this article I used Mirzayanov's information that a new chemical agent had been developed in our country. All the remaining text is my reflections about the negative consequences of our participation in the development of chemical weapons. On the evening of October 20 this year, an employee of this newspaper called me and suggested we meet to discuss how we could agree to shorten the article. On October 21 I went to the editor's office and agreed on a new, shorter version of the article "Myths and Legends of Chemical Disarmament" with correspondent Boris Stanishnev. I signed this text. The paragraph about the development of the new chemical agent remained there. Thus, currently there are two versions of the mentioned article in the editor's office of "Argumenti i Fakty" [Don't forget this, dear Chekists!—V.M.]

Question: Today during the search in your apartment we confiscated a manuscript starting with the words "chemical sharashka..." and ending with the words "Doctors of Chemical Science Vil Mirzayanov and Lev Fedorov;" a manuscript starting with the words "on finishing the second..." and ending with the words "...survival of mankind;" a manuscript starting with the words "Dear editor..." and ending with the words "...all Russians." Whose manuscripts are these, and under what circumstances did they appear at your apartment?

Answer: All these manuscripts belong to Vil Mirzayanov. He gave them to me so that I could write articles for the press. The notes starting with the words "Chemical sharashka..." were used for the article "Poisoned Policies." Later Mirzayanov handed me the remaining manuscripts, which we planned to use for writing articles. However, up to this time, it hasn't been done.

Question: What objective did you and Mirzayanov pursue by publishing the article "Poisoned Policies" and did you take steps towards publishing similar articles?

Answer: My objective was the following. I think that the very fact that chemical weapons are being developed in our country can have grave consequences for the country. Additionally, the system of measures aimed at liberating Russia from chemical weapons adopted by official authorities doesn't, in my opinion, reflect the potential danger. Thus, I proposed publishing several articles, in which I wanted to express my attitude toward solving problems connected with the destruction of chemical weapons.

Mirzayanov, <u>if his words can be believed</u> [comrades Chekists, you know what conclusions to make, if we don't—V.M.] pursued the same objective. Mirzayanov reacted positively to the appearance of the article "Poisoned Policies." He was satisfied that it had been published.

Question: Specify for what publications Mirzayanov had given you the two remaining manuscripts that were confiscated.

Answer: On approximately September 23 of this year, in response to the article "Poisoned Policies", an article was published by of correspondent Litovkin in the evening edition of the newspaper "Izvestia." Mirzayanov and I decided to prepare another article in response to the article by Litovkin. In connection with this, Mirzayanov wrote the manuscript starting with the words "Dear editor..." and finishing with the words "...all Russians" and then gave the text to me.
 <u>In connection with this, since I had no time for a literary elaboration of Mirzayanov's text, the article wasn't prepared for us and wasn't published</u> [underlined by me—V.M.].
 The manuscript beginning with the words "on finishing the second..." and finishing with the words "...survival of mankind" was prepared by Mirzayanov

and we planned to publish it in one of the local newspapers in Volgograd, where there is a plant that produces chemical weapons, and there are plans to destroy such existing weapons there. In our opinion, chemical weapons should be destroyed where they are stored, not hauled to the production plants. However, we didn't have time to publish that article, either. Fedorov wrote: I have read the interrogation report. My testimony has been transcribed accurately in the report. I can't make any alterations or additions to the report.

Signature

Interrogator:
Head of the Section of the Investigation
Department at the MB RF,
Lieutenant Colonel of Justice   N.I. Fanin

Annex 10

Top Secret

TRANSCRIPT
of the suspect's interrogation

Moscow   October 23, 1992

Captain of Justice Shkarin, Senior Investigator of the Investigation Department of the Ministry of Security of the Russian Federation, interrogated the suspect Vil Sultanovich Mirzayanov, born on March 9, 1935 in the village Stary Kangysh, Djirtjuli Region, Bashkir Autonomous Soviet Socialist Republic (other details are to be found in the case), in his office observing the requirements stipulated in Articles 123, 150-152 of RSFSR of the Criminal Code.

The interrogation started at 2.25 P.M.
The interrogation finished at 4.45 P.M.

Question: Do you request the presence of a lawyer at today's interrogation?

Answer: I don't need the presence of a lawyer at today's interrogation.

Question: During the search of Lev Aleksandrovich Fedorov's apartment a manuscript was confiscated starting with the words "Chemical Sharashka in Moscow is Waiting for Help from America" and finishing with the words "Doctors of Chemical Sciences Vil Mirzayanov, L. Fedorov", also were confiscated - a manuscript starting with the words "After the end of the Second World War" and finishing with the words "…survival of mankind;" and a manuscript starting with the words "Dear editor…" and finishing with the words "…all Russians." What clarification can you give regarding these texts?

Vil S. Mirzayanov

Answer: I attentively examined the texts that were presented to me and I can say that I wrote all of them in the period from the end of August until the beginning of October of 1992. I wrote the text starting with words "Chemical Sharashka in Moscow is Waiting for Help from America" at the end of August 1992 for publication in the mass media. I wrote it after I read an article by L. A. Fedorov, Doctor of Chemical Science, in the paper "Sovershenno Sekretno." The article was about the problems of environmental contamination by dioxins and chemical agents. It's hard for me to remember the name of the article. It seemed to me that the questions Fedorov touched on in this article were pressing and were consistent with my own thoughts. The editor's office gave me Fedorov's telephone number. I called him and we agreed to meet. We met at some point a few days later. I wasn't acquainted with Fedorov before that time. We exchanged opinions and decided to write a joint article, in which we would elaborate on the topics I touched upon in the article "Inversion" in the October 10, 1991 issue of the newspaper "Kuranty". We agreed that I would write an article and Fedorov would then supplement it with his materials and would arrange for its publication with the editors of one of the newspapers. Over the next week or so, I wrote an article called "Chemical Sharashka in Moscow is Waiting for Help from America." and took it to Fedorov. This article was published in the newspaper "Moscow News" on September 20, 1992 under the title "Poisoned Policies" with some necessary additions and abridgements made to my version. The changes to the text concerned personal aspects and the technical side connected with the full degasification of chemical agents when they were destroyed. The information, about the creation of a new chemical agent at the Russian State Science Research Institute for Organic Chemistry and Technology, and the development of binary weapons based on it, is presented in the article in full as it was in the manuscript. In my conversation with Fedorov, I gave him the same information about the new agent and binary weapons. I have never given any additional information to anyone about new chemical agents and binary weapons, other than what was presented in the article "Poisoned Policies," either orally or in writing. I gave two other texts to Fedorov at the beginning of October of this year for further work on publications in the mass media. I did not put any information in them about the new chemical agent or binary weapons.

I read through the transcript of the interrogation. My testimony is written down correctly. I have no additions or amendments.

V.S. Mirzayanov

The suspect was interrogated and the transcript was compiled by
Senior Investigator of the Investigation Department
at the MB RF,
Captain of Justice   V.A. Shkarin

State Secrets

Annex 11

Top Secret
TRANSCRIPT
of the suspect's interrogation

Moscow   October 28, 1992

Captain of Justice Shkarin, Senior Investigator of the Investigation Department at the Ministry of Security of the Russian Federation, interrogated the suspect, VIL SULTANOVICH MIRZAYANOV, born on March 9, 1935 in the village Stary Kangysh, Djirtjuli region, Bashkir Autonomous Soviet Socialist Republic (other personal details are to be found in the case), in his office observing requirements stipulated in Articles 123, 150-152 of the RSFSR Criminal Code.

The interrogation started at 10.40 A.M.
The interrogation finished at 12.40 P.M.

Question: Do you request the presence of a lawyer at today's interrogation?

Answer: The investigator explained to me that my wife Nuria Khalitovna Mirzayanova made an agreement for my defense with Alexander Yakovlevich Asnis, a lawyer from Legal Advice Office N 10. He didn't produce a permit to work with classified documents and wasn't allowed to participate in the case. To the best of my knowledge, there are no other hindrances that prevent Alexander Ya. Asnis from participating in the case. I don't need a lawyer at today's interrogation. I decline the services of lawyer Leonid Grigorievich Belomestnykh.

Question: Did you give information about the development of chemical weapons in Russia to the mass media, apart from the editors of the newspaper "Moscow News"?

Answer: I wrote about the fact of the development of new chemical weapons in Russia in the article "Inversion" that was published in October 10, 1991 issue of the newspaper "Kuranty". I wrote that article and took it to the editor's office myself. I was under the impression that there was a victory by the Russian people in crushing the coup attempt. I foresaw then that the leaders of the military-industrial complex would continue the development, production, and testing of chemical weapons contrary to the national interests of Russia, despite the agreement concluded that year between the U.S. and U.S.S.R. governments to discontinue the development, production, and testing of chemical weapons, since those leaders didn't believe then, and don't believe now, that democratization is possible in our country. The military-chemical complex pursues its entirely selfish and profitable ends; it is still at the helm of power and feeds on the useless expenditure of people. This powerful elite is still using all its strength to try to keep the former structures together, in order to meet their above-mentioned objectives. I knew about the development of new chemical weapons in Russia, at the State Russian Science Research Institute for Organic Chemistry and Technology (GRNIIOKhT) because I worked at that institute on the problem of the development of new chemical agents. No criminal proceedings were instituted against me because of that article, and I didn't even receive a disciplinary action. Moreover, at this time two employees of the institute, who had access to even more information about the new chemical weapons, immigrated to the U.S. and to Israel. This means that the relevant authorities and administration of the institute did not protect information about the development of the new chemical weapons in Russia. In 1991 Boris Yakovlevich Libman, former chief engineer of the Volgograd Khimprom Production Association, Deputy Director for Science at the Volgograd branch of GRNIIOKhT, immigrated to the U.S. In 1992 Yefim Lazarevich Galperin, formerly Leading Research Assistant, Doctor of Chemical Science, immigrated to Israel. I don't know whether or not these people gave away information to foreign states about the development of new chemical weapons in Russia.

On September 15, 1992, I gave an interview to William Englund, a correspondent from the American newspaper "The Baltimore Sun", in which I told him about almost everything contained in the whole article "Poisoned Policy" as prepared for publication in the newspaper "Moscow News;" that is, I told the correspondent that binary weapons had been developed. In the interview I stated the fact that the new chemical agent was more potent than a similar American chemical agent. I gave this interview together with Lev Aleksandrovich Fedorov.

On October 21, 1992, I signed an article for the newspaper "Argumenti i Fakty" together with Lev A. Fedorov, about the issues of production and testing of chemical weapons in Russia, destruction of its stockpiles, as well as the related problems of ecological safety. Fedorov wrote this article himself using my version of an article, which I had given to him at the beginning of September in 1992. On the same day, that is, on October 21, Fedorov and I gave an interview to Oleg Vishnyakov, a correspondent from the magazine "Novoe Vremya". In this interview I presented my version of the nature of the new chemical agent and my version of the binary weapons that had been developed based on it. In particular, I said that about two years ago scientists from our institute had developed a new chemical agent, which by its characteristics exceeds by 5-8 times the toxicity of the currently existing chemical agents of the VX type. It causes practically incurable lesions, even if only the skin is exposed to it. Binary weapons that proved to be significantly more potent than the American binary weapons, were developed based on the new chemical agent. Each of the components of the American binary weapon taken separately is completely safe. However, one of the components of our weapon is a chemical agent.

An industrial batch of the new chemical agent was produced at the Volgograd plant. My version is based on own my intuition as a scientist who worked at GRNIIOKhT in the field of physical chemical analysis of microconcentrations of chemical agents in various media. I was never offered and never received royalties for publishing the aforementioned articles.

I have read the interrogation transcript.

My testimony has been transcribed accurately. I don't want to make any alterations or additions to the report.

Vil S. Mirzayanov

The suspect was interrogated and the transcript was compiled by
Senior Investigator of the Investigation Department at
the MB RF,
Captain of Justice
V.A. Shkarin

Annex 12

RESOLUTION

On November 2, 1992 Kalinin District Court of Moscow consisting of:

Presiding Judge A. S. Schanin, with the participation of Prosecutor V.A. Buivolov and Secretary S.V. Lebedeva considered in a closed court session a complaint about the illegality and groundlessness of the arrest of Vil Sultanovich Mirzayanov, who was born on March 9, 1935 in the village of Stary Kangysh, Djirtjuli Region, Bashkir Autonomous Soviet Socialist Republic. His permanent address is 4 Stalevarov St., Building 4, Apartment 586, Moscow. He is working as the head of the Research Department of the joint-stock company Region-Tsentr-Vozrozhdenie, Bashkir, has a higher education, married, with two children, no previous convictions, faces charges on Article 75, Part 1, of the RF Criminal Code, it is

ESTABLISHED

The court has established from the complaint of the applicant and materials that have been submitted that on October 22, 1992, V. S. Mirzayanov was detained under Article 122 of RF Criminal and Procedural Code, on suspicion of committing a crime stipulated by Article 75 Part 1 of the RF Criminal Code, and on the same day he (Mirzayanov) was taken into custody by RF Attorney General based on Articles 90-92, 96 of the RF Criminal and Procedural Code.

Having checked over the materials, and listened to the applicant and prosecutor, I consider it necessary to satisfy the complaint of V. S. Mirzayanov because, according to Article 89 of the RF Criminal and Procedural Code, there are no sufficient grounds to suppose that he will hide from the preliminary investigation or court, or hinder the restoration of the truth in the criminal case, or get involved in criminal activity. Additionally, he has a permanent place of residence in Moscow, has no previous convictions, has juvenile children dependent on him, and the deed he is charged with doesn't qualify as a serious crime.

Based on the statement above and being guided by Articles 11, 220-1, 220-2, and 331 of the RF Criminal and Procedural Code, it is

RULED:

To satisfy the complaint of Vil Sultanovich Mirzayanov and release him from custody into the court hall. To secure a written statement from V. S. Mirzayanov not to leave his permanent place of residence.

The resolution is final, not subject to appeal or protest.
Signatures of the judge and the secretary.

Annex 13

Top Secret

GENERAL
ATTORNEY'S OFFICE
of the Russian Federation
October 30, 1992 N 13/2-1040-92
Moscow

To: Ministry of Security
of the Russian Federation
For Major General S.D. Balashov,
Head of the Investigation
Department

The lawyer A.Ya. Asnis has appealed to the Attorney General's Office of the Russian Federation with a complaint about the decision of V. A. Shkarin, Senior Investigator of the Investigation Department of the Ministry of Security of the Russian Federation, according to which he wasn't allowed to participate as the defender in the criminal proceedings instituted against V. S. Mirzayanov, because he had no clearance to work with secret documents.

We think that there are no reasons to disallow A. Ya. Asnis to act as a defender in this case because, according to the criminal and procedural law, the absence of a permit to work with classified documents is not on the list of circumstances that make it possible to exclude a particular defender from taking part in the case.

At the same time, measures stipulated by Article 139 of the RSFSR Criminal and Procedural Code should be taken to prevent disclosure of secret and top secret information.

Head of the Department for Supervision of
the Implementation of the Laws on Federal Security
and International Relations,
State Justice Counselor of the Third Class   Leonid M. Syukasev

State Secrets

Annex 14

Top Secret

To The Head of the Department for Supervising
Implementation of the Laws on
Federal Security and International Relations
State Justice Counselor of the Third Class
Leonid M. Syukasev

November 4, 19926/2753

Dear Leonid Mikhailovich!

The Investigation Department of the MB RF has considered your letter N 13/2-1040-92 of October 30, 1992,. The Investigation Committee can't support the suggestion to allow the lawyer A. Ya. Asnis to act as the defender in the case of V. S. Mirzayanov for disclosing state secrets, because it contradicts the current law.

The question of allowing an individual to work with classified documents and, most of all, with documents that contain information constituting state secrets is outside the realm of the criminal and procedural law, which only determines the procedure for conducting criminal cases. The existing rules for allowing individuals to work with secrets are directed at maintaining state secrets in the interest of the national security. This is why individuals are given clearance to work with documents containing state secrets in accordance with "Instruction for maintaining the regime of secrecy in ministries, register lists, at enterprises, at institutions, and organizations of the USSR" approved by the Resolution o N 556-126 of the U.S.S.R. Council of Ministers dated May 12, 1987.

The requirements of the above-mentioned resolution are binding in Russia, according to Resolution N 51 of the RSFSR Supreme Soviet "Ratification of the Agreement on Establishing the Independent States" dated December 12, 1991, and Decree N 20 of the president of the Russian Federation "About Protecting State Secrets" dated January 14, 1992. In keeping with the above-mentioned [resolutions], the lawyer Asnis is obligated to get an appropriate permit to work with documents containing state secrets. There are conditions for this in the Moscow City Bar Association, of which he is a member.

In our opinion, if we let Asnis take part in the case without observing established requirements, the investigation will find itself in a situation where it will have to disclose information that constitutes a state secret.

Head of the Department
Major General
S.D. Balashov

Annex 15

Top Secret

ATTORNEY GENERAL'S OFFICE
THE RUSSIAN FEDERATION
December 10, 1992 N 13/2-1040-92
Moscow

to Deputy Minister of the MB RF
Major General A.E. Safonov,

The notification is written by hand:
To Comrade S.D. Balashov: Please prepare a response to the Attorney General's Office and stop violating the Law.
Signature of Safonov is correct

Dear Anatoly Efimovich!

The Investigation Department of the Ministry of Security of the Russian Federation investigating the criminal case, in which V. S. Mirzayanov is charged with committing a crime stipulated by Article 75, Part 1, of the RSFSR Criminal Code.

The lawyer A.Ya. Asnis has appealed to the RF Attorney General's Office with a complaint about the decision of Investigator V. A. Shkarin, saying that he wasn't allowed to work as the defender in this criminal case, because he had no clearance to work with classified documents.

This decision was taken in contradiction to criminal and procedural law because on the list of the circumstances excluding the participation of a certain defender in a case there is no such basis for rejecting a lawyer [underlined by Safonov—V.M.].

On October 30, 1992 the head of the Department for Supervising the Implementation of Laws on Federal Security and International Relations at the RF Attorney General's Office sent a corresponding letter to the head of the Investigation Department at the Ministry of Security of Russia, in which, in particular, it is suggested to take measures stipulated by Article 139 of the RSFSR Criminal and Procedural Code to prevent the disclosure of secret and top secret information. Investigation officers were given similar oral explanations. However, the position of the investigation remains unchanged until now, which caused well-grounded appeals of the lawyer (underlined by Safonov—V.M.) and his client to different authorities, resulting in the delay of the investigation. Please consider this question without delay, settle it according to the appropriate legal requirements, and report the results to the Attorney General's Office of the Russian Federation.

First Deputy Attorney General
of the Russian Federation.
State Justice Counselor
of the 2nd Class I.S. Zemlyanushin,

State Secrets

Handwritten Notation: for Comrade A.A. Shabunin
Handwritten Notation: for Comrade V. A. Shkarin

Please consider the question in keeping with the Criminal and Procedural Code. Signature of Balashov is correct. November 13, 1992.
Please ensure that the implementation of the instructions of the RF Attorney General's Office, in keeping with the Criminal and Procedural Code.

A. Shabunin
November 13, 1992

Annex 16

Secret

MINISTRY OF SECURITY
OF THE RUSSIAN FEDERATION
Investigation Department
October 17, 1992 N 6/2801

To: First Deputy Attorney General
of the Russian Federation
State Counselor of Justice
of the 2nd class I.S. Zemlyanushin,

We are giving notice that, according to your instructions, on November 16, 1992 the lawyer from the Legal Advice Office, Alexander Yakovlevich Asnis, was allowed to act as the defender of the accused Vil Sultanovich Mirzayanov in the criminal case *without presenting a permit to work with top secret documents* [italicized by me—V.M.].

Head of the department,
Major General

S.D. Balashov

Correct. Senior Investigator of the Investigation
Department of the RF Ministry of Security, Captain of Justice

V. A. Shkarin

Annex 17

Secret
Copy N 2

MINISTRY OF SECURITY
OF THE RUSSIAN FEDERATION

Investigation Department
To Major General V.N. Markomenko
Head of the Third Chief Department
at the Federal Agency for Government
Communications & Information (FAPSI)
under the President of Russia

November 5, 1992 N 6/02778

The Investigation Department at the Ministry of Security of the Russian Federation is investigating the criminal case filed against an employee of the State Russian Science Research Institute for Organic Chemistry and Technology (GRNIIOKhT), Doctor of Chemical Science, Vil Sultanovich Mirzayanov, who disclosed information to the mass media that constitutes a state secret about research work that was carried out in Russia in the field of chemical weapons.

In connection with that, we are asking for your instructions to check and report if FAPSI has any information about transmissions of foreign radio stations regarding Mirzayanov and the information he disclosed. If the answer is affirmative, we ask you to send us all materials that are available on this issue.

Head of the Department
Major General   S.D. Balashov

Annex 18

Secret
Copy 1

ATTORNEY GENERAL'S OFFICE
OF THE RUSSIAN FEDERATION

The Ministry of Security
of the Russian Federation
Investigation Department
To Colonel A.A. Shabunin
Head of the Department

November 6, 1992 N 13/2-1040-92
Moscow

I am sending you a Xerox copy of the article "We Waged Chemical War on

Our Own Territory" published in "Nezavisimaya Gazetta" on October 30, 1992, to check and evaluate it in the course of the preliminary investigation of the criminal case against Vil S. Mirzayanov.

Enclosure: on one page.

Senior Prosecutor of the Department for Supervising
The Implementation of Laws on Federal Security
and International Relations,
Junior Counselor of Justice V.A. Buivolov

Annex 19

Secret

ATTORNEY GENERAL'S OFFICE
OF THE RUSSIAN FEDERATION

Ministry of Security
Of the Russian Federation
Investigation Department
To Captain of Justice V.A. Shkarin
Senior Investigator

103793 GSP, Moscow, K-9
Pushkinskaya, 15-a

According to the instructions of the leadership of the RF Attorney General's Office, we are sending xeroxed copies of the article "Poison" published on January 29, 1993 in the newspaper "Trud" with an interview of V. S. Mirzayanov to be added to the materials of the criminal case against V. S. Mirzayanov and to carry out its further legal evaluation.

Senior Prosecutor of the Department for Supervising
Implementation of the Laws on Federal Security
and International Relations,
Junior Counselor of Justice V.A. Buivolov

Annex 20

Secret

THE RF MINISTRY OF SECURITY
Investigation Department

To V.A. Petrunin
Director of the State Russian Science
Research Institute for Organic
Chemistry and Technology

November 12, 1992 N 6/2835

The Investigation Department of the Ministry of Security of the Russian Federation is investigating the following criminal case, in which Vil Sultanovich Mirzayanov, a former employee of GRNIIOKhT, is charged with a crime under Article 75, Part 1, of the RSFSR Criminal Code, of disclosing the information that our country conducts scientific research work in the area of chemical weapons, in his article "Poisoned Policies" (Issue N 38 of the weekly "Moscow News" of September 20, 1992).

In connection with this, please check and inform us whether the information revealed by Mirzayanov in his article, about GRNIIOKhT being involved in the above-mentioned research, is authentic.

If the answer is affirmative, according to what normative acts was it carried out and from what sources did Mirzayanov learn this information (reading documents, taking part in meetings, etc.)?

We also ask you to send us V. S. Mirzayanov's personal file and character references.

Head of the section at the Department

A.A. Shabunin

Verified. Senior Investigator of the
Investigation Department at the MB RF,
Captain of Justice

Victor A. Shkarin

State Secrets

Annex 21

Top Secret
Copy 1

STATE RUSSIAN SCIENCE RESEARCH
INSTITUTE OF ORGANIC
CHEMISTRY AND TECHNOLOGY

To A.A. Shabunin,
Head of the section of the
Investigation Department at the
RF Ministry of Security

Moscow
November 24, 1992
N 1846 ss

In response to your inquiry N 6/2835 of November 12, 1992 we inform you that the information that Vil S. Mirzayanov, a former employee of the institute, included in his article "Poisoned Policies" about the scientific research work conducted at GRNIIOKhT aimed at the development of chemical weapons, is authentic.

Work on the creation of a new chemical agent was referred to in the above-mentioned article as follows: "The State Science Research Institute for Organic Chemistry and Technology (GRNIIOKhT) developed a new chemical agent. It significantly surpassed the well known VX by its toxicity ("battle characteristics") from which it is practically impossible to be cured...", and was developed at GRNIIOKhT in pursuance to Resolution N 3509-123 dated April 24, 1977 by the Central Committee of the C.P.S.U. and the Council of Ministers.

Also, the information that Mirzayanov reveals in the same article about the development of binary weapons at GRNIIOKhT: "...binary weapons were developed based on a new chemical agent" is true. Work on the creation of a binary weapon was carried out at GRNIIOKhT, in pursuance to Resolutions N 1584-434 of December 31, 1986 and N 844—186 of October 6, 1989 by the Central Committee of the C.P.S.U. and the Council of Ministers.

Mirzayanov knew this information through reading classified documents, participation in closed meetings, etc., in keeping with his functional duties first as Senior Research Scientist at Laboratory 29 and since 1986 as the head of the branch Department Foreign Technical Counterintelligence.

We are sending you Mirzayanov's personal files which include his character references.

Attachment: the personal file of V. S. Mirzayanov
N 10650 on 131 pages, non-confidential, to the addressee only

Deputy Director   A.V. Martynov
A.V. Martynov

Annex 22

Top Secret
Copy N 1

THE MINISTRY OF SECURITY
OF THE RUSSIAN FEDERATION
Investigation Department

To Lieutenant General V.N. Zemlyanitsyn,
Head of the 8th Department at the
General Staff Headquarters of the Armed Forces
of the Russian Federation

The Investigation Department of the Ministry of Security of the Russian Federation is investigating criminal case # 62, regarding Vil Sultanovich Mirzayanov for disclosing information to the mass media about scientific research in the area of chemical weapons.

An expert commission was appointed to determine the authenticity and degree of secrecy of the information divulged by Mirzayanov. The 8th Department at the General Staff Headquarters of the RF Armed Forces is entrusted with conducting the expertise.

We are sending the resolution dated November 10, 1992 and ask you to take charge of the expert investigation.

Appendix: -resolution dated November 10, 1992 on 6 pages, not classified
-package with the objects of research, top secret

Head of the Department,
Major General of Justice   S.D. Balashov

Annex 23

Top Secret

THE RF MINISTRY OF DEFENSE
GENERAL STAFF HEADQUARTERS
OF THE ARMED FORCES
8th Department

To Major General S.D. Balashov,
Head of the Investigation Department,
of the Ministry of Security
of the Russian Federation To Major General
Moscow

December 8, 1992
N 317/5/836
Moscow K-160

State Secrets

In Response to the letter N 6/003088 from December 1, 1992

After the 8th Department at the General Staff Headquarters of the RF Intelligence Service was re-organized, there were no specialists left who had access to [classified] works and documents on the indicated topic and who could, according to their area of specialty, evaluate the authenticity of the information presented in the materials produced, and for this reason the department can't act as an expert enterprise for conducting the expertise on this criminal case.

ACTING HEAD OF THE DEPARTMENT
Colonel G.I. Funygin

Annex 24

Secret
Copy N 2

THE MINISTRY OF SECURITY
OF THE RUSSIAN FEDERATION
Investigation Department

December 10, 1992 N 6/03240

To E.M. Primakov,
Director of the Russian Foreign
Intelligence Service
of the Russian Federation

The Investigation Department of the Ministry of Security of the Russian Federation is investigating the criminal case of the former employee of the State Russian Science Research Institute for Organic Chemistry and Technology, Vil Sultanovich Mirzayanov, who was disclosing information about scientific research in the area of chemical weapons to the mass media.

An expert commission was appointed for determining the authenticity and degree of secrecy of the information divulged by Mirzayanov.

The accused Mirzayanov wrote a petition asking to include Reserve Major General Oleg Danilovich Kalugin, a former employee of Russian Foreign Intelligence Service, in the expert commission.

In connection with this, please inform us if job responsibilities of O. D. Kalugin entailed any kind of involvement with scientific research in the area of chemical weapons. Is he a specialist in the technology of special substances or the protection of secrets in the area of scientific research aimed at the development of chemical weapons?

Head of the Department,
Major General S.D. Balashov

Annex 25

Secret
Copy 1.

OFFICE OF THE FOREIGN
INTELLIGENCE SERVICE
OF THE RUSSIAN FEDERATION
December 17, 1992 N 153/5-13265

To Major General S.D. Balashov,
Head of the Investigation Department
of the Ministry of Security of Russia

In response to N 6/03240 of December 10, 1992

Oleg Danilovich Kalugin, was born in 1934, has a higher humanitarian education, and has served in the Foreign Intelligence Services as a soldier and commander from 1958 until 1979. He was working in political intelligence, counterintelligence and supporting individuals and institutions abroad. His job responsibilities didn't entail any kind of involvement with scientific research in the sphere of chemical weapons.

Deputy Director of the RF SVR [Foreign Intelligence Service]
of the Russian Federation
Major General   V.M. Rozhkov

Annex 26

Secret

THE MINISTRY OF SECURITY
OF THE RUSSIAN FEDERATION
Investigation Department
December 10, 1992 N 6/03238

To Major General Yu. N. Lukonin,
Head of the Personnel Department
at the Ministry of Security
of the Russian Federation

The Investigation Department of the RF Ministry of Security is investigating the criminal case of a former employee of the State Russian Science Research Institute for Organic Chemistry and Technology, Vil Sultanovich Mirzayanov, who was disclosing to the mass media information about scientific research in the field of chemical weapons.

An expert commission has been appointed to determine the authenticity and the degree of secrecy of the information divulged by Mirzayanov.

State Secrets

The accused Mirzayanov wrote a petition asking to include Reserve Major General O. D. Kalugin, a former employee of the KGB, in the expert commission.

In connection with this, please inform us if the job responsibilities of Oleg D. Kalugin entailed any kind of involvement with scientific research in the sphere of chemical weapons, if he was a specialist in the technology of special substances or the protection of secrets in the area of scientific research aimed at the development of chemical weapons.

Head of the Department,
Major General   S.D. Balashov

(For some reason there are two copies of this masterpiece of the KGB in my case. On the first there are the following official handwritten notations – V.M.):

For Comrade V.N. Kazakov
Comrade Yu. V. Novoselov
Comrade Yu. I. Smirnov

E.B. Soloviev
Please prepare a response,
Lukonin
December 11, 1992

Please work through this question with the Department of the MB [Ministry of Security] for St. Petersburg and Leningrad Region and with the Foreign Intelligence Service and prepare a response.

Signature: Lukonin
December 17, 1992

To A.V. Ilyakov
Please talk it over
Soloviev
December 15

It was discussed Ilyakov December 16, 1992

To A. Kuvshinov
The signature is illegible
December 18

Annex 27

Secret
To Major General S.D. Balashov,
Head of the Investigation Department
of the Ministry of Security
of the Russian Federation

We are reporting that as a result of studying the personal file of Reserve Major General- O. D. Kalugin, which is kept in the Military-Mobilization Department of the MB of Russia for Moscow and the Moscow Region, it was established that he graduated in 1956 from the Leningrad Institute of Foreign Languages at the U.S.S.R. Council of Ministers; his major was consultant-interpreter.

There is no information that his responsibilities during this period entailed involvement with scientific research in the field of chemical weapons. The Department of the MB of Russia confirms this information for St. Petersburg and the Leningrad Region during the period of time when Oleg D. Kalugin worked at that department.

Deputy Head of the Personnel Department
of the MB of Russia.
Colonel

E. Soloviev
December 29, 1992

Annex 28

Secret
Copy N 1

THE MINISTRY OF SECURITY
OF THE RUSSIAN FEDERATION
Investigation Department
December 10, 1992 N 6/03239

To Major General A.I. Gurov,
Head of NII [the Research Institute] for
the Problems of Security
of the Russian Federation

The Investigation Department of the RF Ministry of Security is investigating the criminal case of the former employee of the State Russian Science Research Institute for Chemistry and Technology, Vil Sultanovich Mirzayanov, who was disclosing information to the mass media about scientific research in the area of chemical weapons.

An expert commission has been appointed to determine the authenticity and degree of secrecy of the information divulged by Mirzayanov.

State Secrets

The accused Mirzayanov wrote a petition asking to include Colonel of Justice Petr Segreevich Nikulin, Deputy Head of NII for Problems of Security at the MB RF, in the expert commission.

In connection with this, please inform us if the job responsibilities of Petr S. Nikulin entailed any kind of involvement with scientific research in the area of chemical weapons. Is he a specialist in the technology of special substances or a specialist in the protection of state secrets in the area of scientific research aimed at the development of chemical weapons?

Head of the Department,
Major General   S.D. Balashov

Annex 29

Secret
Copy 1

THE MINISTRY OF SECURITY
OF THE RUSSIAN FEDERATION
The Research Institute for
Matters of Security

To Major General S.D. Balashov,
Head of the Investigation Department, of
the Ministry of Security
of the Russian Federation

December 16, 1992 N 5/NII/76
Moscow

In response to your inquiry regarding the former Deputy Head of the Research Institute for Matters of Security at the RF Ministry of Security, we are giving notice that during his work at the institute, Petr Sergeevich Nikulin never performed any work in the area of chemical weapons. He is neither a specialist in the technologies of special substances, nor a specialist in protecting state secrets in the area of scientific research aimed at the development of chemical weapons. Since January 24 of this year, Nikulin has been at the disposal of the Staff Headquarters of the RF Ministry of Security and currently he is retired from active service.

Head of the Institute,
Major General   A.I. Gurov
executed by S.A. Knut
Tel. 388-91-64
N 5/NII /76

Annex 30

Secret

TRANSCRIPT OF THE INSPECTION

Moscow February 24, 1993

Captain of Justice Shkarin, Senior Investigator of the Investigation Department at the Ministry of Security of the Russian Federation, in the presence of Nikolai Aleksandrovich Kuznetsov, Deputy Director for Science of the State Russian Science Research Institute for Organic Chemistry and Technology (GRNII-OKhT), and witnesses: Valentina Ivanovna Lisitsyna, permanent address: Moscow, Ozernaya Street, Bldg. 38, and Galina Vyacheslavovna Mikhailovskaya, permanent address: Moscow, Magnitogorskaya Street, Bldg. 27, Apt. 43, being guided by the requirements stipulated in Articles 141, 178, 179, and 182 of the RSFSR Criminal and Procedural Code, in the office of the First Department of GRNIIOKhT examined Case N 73-3. The people listed above were advised that according to Article 169 of the RSFSR Criminal and Procedural Code, they have the right to observe all the actions of the investigator and to make statements to be included in the transcript of the report.

[signed]......Kuznetsov ....Lisitsyna ....Mikhailovskaya

Witnesses Valentina I. Lisistyna and Galina V. Mikhailovskaya were also informed that, according to Article 13 of the RSFSR Criminal and Procedural Code, they were obliged to witness the fact, content, and outcome of the inspection.

................./Lisitsyna/........................./Mikhailovskaya/

The inspection started at 10.35 A.M.

THE INSPECTION ESTABLISHED:

Case N 73-3, inventory number 6291, in one volume, on 260 numbered pages in the dark-blue cardboard folder. In this case there is a document on pages 160-165 with the title "Technical order for a part of the experimental and design work of "Agent A-232" based on the system of components" and the cipher "Novichok-5," stamp "Top Secret," number 2187 ss/khf. The document contains 9 clauses. (Further, all the clauses are enumerated.)

[At the bottom of the last page of the original document there is a signature and the date, April 20, 1990, in blue ink.]

During the inspection, Kuznetsov explained that Agent A-232 mentioned in the technical order was the new chemical agent in its binary version, created at GRNIIOKhT. He said Agent A-208 is a known chemical agent of the VX type;

State Secrets

Military Unit 36382 was deployed at the chemical test site in the Nukus area; signature and date, April 20, 1990. The official stamp on the document was executed by Vil Sultanovich Mirzayanov, and this means that Mirzayanov, as head of the Foreign Technical Counterintelligence Department, was responsible for the research division which concerned itself with implementation of the requirements on maintaining state and military secrecy. It also meant that Mirzayanov read this technical order and agreed with the stipulated requirements on maintaining the state and military secrecy, while carrying out experimental and design work with the new chemical agent. (Signed by the participants of the inspection.)

Annex 31

Top Secret
Copy No 2
Series "F"
According to p. 4.7 of the List

AGREED UPON Confirmed by
Chief of 4984 VP MO
E.A. Umbliya
April 27, 1990

Director of GOSNIIOKhT
V. A. Petrunin
05.04. 1990

ACCORDED
with the notes from 1244-60/chf/2T-575
Chief of 458 VP MO
N.G Ragulin
05.16. 1990

ACCORDED
with the notes from
1244-60/chf/2T-575 ss
General director of
NPO "Bazalt"
A. S. Obuchov
05.16. 1990

THE TECHNICAL ORDER
FOR THE COMPOUND PART OF
THE EXPERMIENTAL DESIGN WORK OF
Substance "A-232" ON THE BASIS OF THE
SYSTEM OF COMPONENTS

The code "Novichok-5"
"The development, manufacture and delivery of
bodies of special products (models) of the explosion
mode of operation for testing the system of
components "A-232"

2187 ss/khf

1. THE DENOMINATION, CODE AND JUSTIFICATION FOR PERFORMING THE COMPOUND OF THE OKR ["OKR" stands for

experimental design work – V.M.]

The OKR's compound part Substance "A-232" based on a system of the components, the "Novichok-5" code, "The development, manufacture and delivery of bodies of the special products (models) of the Explosion Operation Mode for Field Tests of the System of components of the substance "A-232" is being carried out following the resolution of the Authority No 844-186, adopted on 10.06.89 [*The Authority means Central Committee CPSU and the signature of it's First Secretary General M. Gorbachev this time* – V. M.], and tactical and technical assignment for the OKR.
(initial No 0076 khf of 12.07.89 of Military Unit 64518 – [*a Special Unit of Ministry of Defense on the Special Weapons* – V. M.]

2. GOAL OF CONDUCTING THE COMPOUND PART OF OKR

The provision of field tests of the system of the components of the substance "A-232" by bodies of special products (models)* of the explosive operation mode.

3. THE ASSIGNMENT OF THE COMPOUND PART OF OKR

3.1 To manufacture and deliver models of the explosion operation mode for conducting field tests of the system of components of Substance "A-232" in comparison with Substance "A-208".
3.2 To participate in field tests in Military Unit v/ch 26382. [next to the city of Nukus –V.M.]

4. THE REQUIREMENTS FOR PERFORMING THE COMPOUND PART OF OKR

4.1 A quantity of models of the explosive operation mode of complement bundles (units) for conducting field tests must be manufactured, as a result of the work necessary, and also the technical documentation for them must be presented.
Cylinders for the system of components of the substance "A-232" and the substance "A- 208" must be delivered to the equipment charging place, and also bodies and completing units must be delivered to the test polygon [test site].
4.3 The effectiveness of the mixing mechanism and functioning of the models must be confirmed by the conclusion of NPO "Bazalt" in accordance with test results.
-Tests are being conducted in simulating equipment, within the temperature interval – 30 +50 Degrees on Celsius with the application of simulators, used by NPO "Bazalt" during the development of models of drawings 243.5.586.087 and 243.5.585.820 in 1987-1988. –I-3-6(BK)

State Secrets

4.4 The manufacture, delivery of models with completing units and participation in field tests are being realized in accordance with the agreement at GOSNIIOKhT.

Within a month after the approval of this Technical Order (TZ), NPO "Bazalt" drafts and complies with the GOSNIIOKhT project-timetable for completing this work.

*Bodies of special products (models) – further referred to as models.

5. TECHNICAL REQUIREMENTS

5.1 285 models of the explosion operation mode must be manufactured, among them:

    models of draw. 243.5.586.087-02 -133 pcs
    models of draw. 243.5.586.087-12 -82 pcs
    models of draw. 243.5.585.820-02 -50 pcs
    models of draw. 243.5.585.820.12 -20 pcs

Models should have all the necessary completing parts, corresponding to drawings for each type of model, including pressure and temperature detectors, samplers and ejection valves.

5.2 The necessary number of containers must be developed and manufactured for transportation of filled and non-filled cylinders, for sets and assembled parts, as well as for bodies of all types of models. Containers should ensure the safety of their contents during shipment by rail transport to a distance up to 4,000 km, and by auto transport up to 1,000 km. The inspection can be allowed in accordance with the normative and technical documentation in effect.

5.3 Models must function properly within the range of temperature -30 +50 Degrees on Celsius.

5.4 All the necessary data on components, their mass (mass of the reaction mixture) contained in one model, and the parameters of the reaction and final substance must be provided by GOSNIIOKhT, following the request of NPO "Bazalt".

5.5 The technical description of models with the assembly manual must be delivered to Military Unit v/ch 26382 for the assembly of filled models.

5.6 Model sets should contain tackles for assembly in field conditions.

2187 ss/khf

6. STAGES OF WORK

6.1 The provision of technical documentation to GOSNIIOKhT, VF GOSNII-OKhT [Volgograd branch of GOSNIIOKhT – V.M.] and Military Unit 26382 suf-

ficient for the equipment, assembly and maintenance, and conducting of field tests.
 Term – the IIIrd quarter of 1990.
6.2 The manufacturing of 44 models, including
 models of draw.243.5.586.087-02 -32 pcs
 models of draw.242.5.585.820-02 - 8 pcs
 models of draw.243.5.585.820-12 - 4 pcs
The delivery of all types of models to VF GOSNIIOKhT, the delivery of completing units and shells of models to Military Unit v/ch 26382
 Term – the IVth quarter of 1990.
6.3 The participation in field tests in accordance with the Program.
 Term – Ist quarter of 1991 – II nd quarter of 1992.
6.4 The manufacturing of 241 models, including
 models of draw.243.5.586.087-02 – 101 pcs
 models of draw.243.5.586.087-12 – 82 pcs
 models of draw.243.5.585.820-02 – 42 pcs
 models of draw.243.5.585.820-12 – 16 pcs

The delivery of cylinders - of all types to VF GOSNIIOKhT, the delivery of completing units and shells of models – to Military Unit v/ch 26382.
 Term – May 1991
6.5 The summarization of the results of the work. The provision of a report with the results of the compound part of the OKR to GOSNIIOKhT.
 Term – September 1992
6.6 The acceptance of the compound part of the OKR.
 Term – October 1992
2187 ss/khf

7. REQUIREMENTS FOR THE DOCUMENTATION

7.1 In the work process, the technical documentation for all types of models and completing units sufficient for the charge of models in factory and field conditions, assembly and field testing must be sent to GOSNIIOKhT, VF GOSNIIOKhT, v/ch 26382:
 protocols of tests and the conclusion of the operation capability – to the address of GOSNIIOKhT;
 drawings of models – to the addresses of GOSNIIOKhT, VF GOSNIIOKhT and Military Unit v/ch 26382;
 technical description of the models with manuals on their assembly and maintenance –
  to the address of GOSNIIOKhT and Military Unit v/ch 26382;
  model cards – to the addresses of GOSNIIOKhT, VF GOSNIIOKhT and Military Unit v/ch 26382.
7.2 Report on the results of work must be printed in 4 copies, in accordance with requirements of GOST B15.110-81 and must contain:

- construction schemes of models;
- basic parameters of models;
- results of tests of operation capability.

8. ORDER OF THE ACCEPTANCE PF THE COMPOUND PART OF OKR

8.1 The consideration and acceptance of the compound part of OKR is carried out in accordance with requirements of GOST B15.204-79.

9. REQUIREMENTS ON THE PROVISIONS FOR THE PROTECTION OF STATE AND MILITARY SECRECY DURING THE EXECUTION OF THE COMPOUND PART OF OKR

9.1 Requirements on the provision of secrecy.
9.1.1 The goal and purpose of the provisions of secrecy are to conceal the fact of the test and the goals of the work from an adversary and all unauthorized persons, including employees.
9.1.2 The provision of secrecy is conducted in accordance with the instruction 1026-87, Regulations on the Foliant Problem, and other normative documents.
9.1.3 The following information is subject to the protection by the organizational and regime means:

2187 ss/khf

- the fact of conducting of the compound part of OKR on systems of components, including the concrete enterprise;
- the goal of the compound part of OKR the composition of the system of components; properties of substances; test results.

9.1.4 The access to the present TZ must be strictly limited and carried out in accordance with the permission system, functioning at the enterprise (permission lists. 9.1.5). The level of secrecy of concrete data:
the theme on the whole – top secret, series "F";
the fact of conducting OKR on the system of components,
including the concrete enterprise–
top secret, Series "F";
the real name of Substance "A-232", "A-208" – top secret, Series "F";
the real name of Substance "A-255" – secret, Series "F";
the fact of conducting the work with Substances "A-232", "A-208" and "A-255",
their physical chemical and toxicological characteristics – top secret, Series "F",
unequipped models, cylinders – not classified;
samples of imitators for the evaluation of the operation capability of models – not classified;

model, filled by imitator, after experiments in polygons of Industry and Defense Ministry – not classified.

The level of secrecy of other information and materials is being conducted in accordance with the legend "The development of models of ammunition of smoke character."

9.2 Requirements on the Technical Counterintelligence.

9.2.1 There are no requirements on the Technical Counterintelligence on the stages of the manufacturing, evaluation of operational capability in the imitating mode and delivery of models.

The present OKR is not a subject for the state register.

Head of the laboratory N. P. Fedorov
Senior researcher A.A. Savkin
Researcher N.N. Andreev

Visas (signatures)
Mosyakin   Mirzayanov
04.23.90 04.19.90   04.20.90

2187 ss/khf

Annex 32

Top secret

THE EXCERPT

from " List of Major Information Constituting State Secrets", confirmed by resolution N 1121-387 of USSR Counsel of Ministers on December 3, 1980.

Item 83. Information of the latest achievements in the area of science and technology (including discoveries, inventions, scientific and scientific technological solutions) which can be used for military purposes and have principal significance in bringing a new level of high-quality to the capabilities of arms and military machinery.

(Secrecy degree – Special Importance)

The same information allowing for the enhancement of capabilities or improving existing arms and military machinery, indicated in Item 1 and in paragraph 2 of this List.

(Secrecy degree – Top Secret)

Item 1. Information about the capacity or the creation and increase of capacities separately for the production of nuclear arms, strategic rockets, space units, units of anti-missile defense, arms with nuclear energetic units, and also for the main complete products for them disclosing the aforementioned capabilities, in the whole in the USSR, a Ministry or Departments, special important enterprise [factory].

(Secrecy degree – Special Importance)

Item 2 (paragraph 1). Information about the mobilization capabilities or the creation and increase of these capacities separately for the production of planes, helicopters, combat ships and rocket, artillery, armored, mortar-torpedo, anti-submarine arms, radio-technical units, units of hydro-location communications, infra red units, units of automatic systems of guidance, units of chemical and bacteriological defense, munitions, powders, explosive substances, liquid or solid rocket fuels, warm emitting elements for arms on the whole in the USSR, Union Republics, Ministry or Department.

(Secrecy degree – Special importance)

Item 85. Information disclosing the significance, direction [trend], initial scientific technological ideas, applicability (realization capabilities) of perspective, to be planned or conducted fundamental or applied scientific research work in the interests of country's defense.

(Secrecy degree – Top Secret)

The Extract is true. Senior investigator of
the MB RF Investigation Department
Captain of Justice   V. Shkarin
(v. 3, pp. 215, 216 of Case 62)

Annex 33

Top Secret

THE EXTRACT

from the "List of Information to be Qualified as Secret by the USSR Ministry of the Petrochemical Industry" confirmed by order N 234-19 of the USSR Ministry of Petrochemical Industry on May 27 1991.

Item 5.3. Information enhancing capabilities or leading to improvement of existing arms and military machinery for classes of strategic rockets, space units, units of anti-rocket and anti-space defense, planes, helicopters, combat ships and rocket, artillery, armored, mortar-torpedo, and anti-submarine arms.

(Secrecy degree – Top Secret)

Item 5.5. Information disclosing the significance, trend, initial scientific research ideas, application capability (realization quality) of future perspective planned or conducted fundamental or applied scientific-technical work in interests of country's defense.

(Secrecy degree – Top Secret)

Vil S. Mirzayanov

The Excerpt is true.
Senior investigator of
MB RF Investigation Department
Captain of Justice V. Shkarin

(v. 3, p. 217 of the Case 62).

Annex 34

Top Secret
Copy 1

FINDINGS OF THE EXPERT COMMISSION
Moscow March 16, 1993

The commission of experts consisting of Chairman Yuri Mikhailovich Karmishin, head of a department at the State Institute for Technology of Organic Synthesis; members of the commission: Rim Kuzmich Balchenko, M.S. in Chemical Science and Deputy Director for Science at the State Institute for Technology of Organic Synthesis, Anatoly Mikhailovich Kochetkov, chief specialist of the joint-stock company "Tyazhorgsintez," Igor Mikhailovich Gabov, leading specialist of the joint-stock company "Tyazhorgsintez," Boris Alexseevich Kuznetsov, M.S. in Chemical Science and head of the laboratory at the State Russian Science Research Institute for Organic Chemistry and Technology (GRNIIOKhT), Boris Petrovich Kosmynin, M.S. in Physical Chemistry and former senior research assistant at GRNIIOKhT, Colonel Yuri Alexeevich Klimentiev, M.S in Technical Science, military chemical engineer and chemist and head of a department at Military Unit 61469, Lieutenant Colonel Nikolai Grigorievich Pechenenko, Deputy Commander at the Military Unit 61469 for the Regime of Secrecy and Special Communications, Vadim Vasilievich Smirnitsky, engineer and chemist, head of the Representative Office on the Committee of Industrial Policy at the RF Ministry of Defense, Reserve Colonel Nikolai Iosifovich Chugunov, M.S. in Technical Science, engineer and chemist, and Reserve Colonel Arkady Egorovich Kordyukov, head of a department at Military Unit 52688; based on a resolution dated January 11, 1993, prepared by Captain of Justice Victor A. Shkarin, Senior Investigator of the Investigation Department at the MB RF, conducted an expertise commission to determine the authenticity and degree of secrecy of the information in criminal case N 62, according to Article 191 of the RSFSR Criminal and Procedural Code. The commission arrived at the following conclusion.

According to the instructions in carbon copy the following materials were at the disposal of the experts:

State Secrets

The materials are listed here.

[Also, my manuscripts and published articles are enumerated and the following two articles were also added – V.M.]:

- the article "The Binary Bomb has Exploded" published in the N 44 issue of the magazine "Novoe Vremya" in October 1992;
- the article "We Waged Chemical War on our own Territory" published in the N 210 issue of the newspaper "Nezavisimaya Gazetta" on October 30, 1992.

The decision of the experts was established based on the following questions:

a) What specific information about the research and works in the area of the development of chemical weapons did Mirzayanov disclose in his publications and interviews?

b) Does the information about the development of chemical weapons that can be found in the publications [all my manuscripts and articles are enumerated -V.M.] correspond to reality by volume and nature?

c) Is the information about the research and works in the area of the development of chemical weapons included by Mirzayanov in his articles, interviews, and manuscripts, factual? If the answer is affirmative, what is the degree of secrecy of this information? Does it constitute a state or work-related secret?

d) Did Mirzayanov's actions have any negative consequences? If yes, specifically what consequences?

THE COMMISSION IS ESTABLISHED

1. The texts of the examined documents contain information <u>about the development of the new chemical agents in our country... The indicated information is true.</u> In GOSNIIOKhT (now GRNIIOKhT) a new chemical compound has really been synthesized, studied, and tested that significantly surpasses the agent VX (a chemical agent adopted by the U.S. Army) by a complex of battle characteristics, including difficulties in curing.

<u>According to the facts available, the armies of the countries that possess chemical weapons are not armed with any compounds analogous to the abovementioned compound.</u>

In 1992 this information was top secret and constituted a state secret, and it does so presently.

2. The texts of the documents examined contain information about the direction and results of the special purpose program in the area of the development of chemical weapons... The indicated information is true. GOSNIIOKhT has developed experimental batches of binary weapons based on the new chemical agents, which were successfully tested at the test site. <u>According to the information available, foreign countries haven't possessed this information before.</u>

Clauses 2.1-2.6 contain information about the direction and resulting perspectives of long-term applied scientific research work on the development of binary weapons conducted in the interests of the defense of the country.

In 1992 this information was top secret and constituted a state secret, and it does so today.

The commission has no information (documents) at its disposal at this time about any negative consequences that Mirzayanov's actions caused.

CONCLUSIONS:

As a result of conducting the expert investigation, the commission has arrived at the following conclusions.

The excerpts from the manuscripts, publications, and interviews cited in the research part of the experts' conclusion contain information about:

1. The latest achievements in the area of science and technology (results of the scientific research in the interests of the defense of the country) that allow the increase the potential of existing weapons (ammunition).

In 1992 this information was top secret and constituted a state secret, and it is still the case at the present time.

2. The direction and the resulting perspectives of long-term applied scientific research work on the creation of binary weapons carried out in the interests of the defense of the country. In 1992 this information was top secret and constituted a state secret, and it is still so today.

The signatures of the experts follow.

Experts V. V. Smirnitsky and
N. I. Chugunov didn't sign.

Annex 35

Top secret

CONCLUSION OF THE EXPERT

Moscow   March 18, 1993

The expert Nikolai Iosifovich Chugunov, Master of Technical Science, based on the resolution dated January 11, 1993, prepared by Captain of Justice Victor A. Shkarin, Senior Investigator of the Investigation Department at the MB RF, conducted an expertise to determine the authenticity and degree of secrecy of the information in criminal case N 62, according to Article 191 of the RSFSR Criminal and Procedural Code and came to this conclusion:

According to the instructions in carbon copy the following materials were at the disposal of the expert:

State Secrets

- The article "Inversion" published in "Kuranty" October 10, 1991;
- The taped manuscript of "Inversion";
- The article "Poisoned Policy" published in "Moscow News" September 20, 1992;

There were listed 13 carbon copies of manuscripts and articles.
Further listed were the questions to be clarified by the expert:
The decision of the experts was established based on the following questions:

e) What specific information about the research and works in the area of the development of chemical weapons did Mirzayanov disclose in his publications and interviews?
f) Does the information about the development of chemical weapons that can be found in the publications [all my manuscripts and articles are enumerated -V.M.] correspond to reality by volume and nature?
g) Is the information about the research and works in the area of the development of chemical weapons included by Mirzayanov in his articles, interviews, and manuscripts, factual? If the answer is affirmative, what is the degree of secrecy of this information? Does it constitute a state or a work-related secret?
h) Did Mirzayanov's actions have any negative consequences? If so, specifically what consequences?

- The Expert conducted the investigation and established there is information about research work in the field of the development of chemical weapons.
- Further, fragments from articles and manuscripts are listed containing information about chemical weapons development.

CONCLUSION:

I can not determine whether the information listed above corresponds to reality, because I haven't had any connection with scientific research work in the field of chemical weapons since 1988, and I don't have any knowledge about the latest achievements in this area.
If the information stated is real, it can not be a state secret or a confidential business secret, because it doesn't contain any data about the structure of a new chemical agent, and revealing information about it by this way can not cause negative consequences for the military-economical potential of the country or cause other severe results for the defense capability, state security or serious damage to the state's political interests or any other damage to interests of state.

Expert   N.I. Chugunov

Annex 36

Top secret

TRANSCRIPT
of the interrogation of the expert

Moscow   April 8, 1993

Captain of Justice Shkarin, Senior Investigator of the Investigation Department of the Ministry of Security of the Russian Federation, in accordance with the requirements of Article 192 of UPK RSFSR questioned the expert Nikolai Iosifovich Chugunov in his office …..
Interrogation started at 5:10 PM
Interrogation ended at 7:15 PM
Question: In the process of the Expertise examination of the credibility and the degree of secrecy of the information set forth in the Case N 62, you came to different conclusions than those of the majority of experts, and on March 18 1993 you wrote a separate conclusion in which you pointed out that there are no state secrets in field of research work on the development of chemical weapons in the materials brought to the Expertise. Clarify, why did you come to this conclusion?
Answer: From 1959 until 1988 I was involved in work connected with the testing of new chemical agents and munitions in their charged state, research work in the field of substantiation of their major trend and the program of development of chemical weapons, and also with the substantiation of tactical-technical requirements for new chemical agents. I was also a member of all the scientific-technical and coordination counsels in the field of the creation of chemical weapons.
From 1976 up to 1982 I was an expert and later an advisor at the Soviet-American negotiations and the Committee on Disarmament in Geneva. In the last years I was working with the development of the basic direction of advancement of chemical weapons in the Defense Ministry of the USSR.
During the process of the Expertise, I analyzed all the materials presented and chose from them information which is related, as I supposed, to the field of chemical weapons. I pointed out this information in my conclusion. After evaluating this information, I concluded that it is impossible to actually derive anything about the achievements made in this area. The mention of a binary weapon, without giving the concrete components of this weapon, doesn't lend itself to judgments about its specifications of construction, of its munitions and its effectiveness. The mention of a new chemical agent without its chemical name or formula doesn't permit judgments to be made about the level of results achieved during the investigation of this kind of substance. Indicating the superiority of such a substance as 5-8 times that of a known analog is subject to a range of experimental error during the evaluation of the toxicity of all the analogs. I couldn't determinate anything about the real chemical agent created at

State Secrets

GOSNIIOKhT because of the lack of published chemical formulas and chemical names. Proceeding from this point, I came to the conclusion that the materials presented to the Expertise don't contain state secrets in the field of chemical weapons.

Q: Does the information presented to the Expertise include materials about a new chemical agent created at GOSNIIOKhT and development of a binary weapon on its basis - information about the achievement of the results of scientific research work for the defense of the country?

A: I believe that this information is not information about the results of scientific research achieved in the interests of the country's defense, because there is no information in the publications about whether this substance and its binary weapon passed through the stages of state tests with positive results.

Q: In Article 56 of "The Temporary List of Information Constituting State Secrets", of N 733-55, confirmed on September 18 1992 stated that information about results achieved in the area scientific research, conducted in the interests of country's defense is top secret and constitutes a state secret. In this article they pointed out the results, but didn't specify whether they are positive or negative. What kind of explanation could you give in connection with this?

A: I don't understand what kind of substance is discussed in the materials presented for the Expertise, what stage of testing it passed through or what kind of result was achieved. I know from experience that if the results of the state tests are positive, the degree of secrecy increases during the adoption of a tested example, and if the results are negative the degree of secrecy remains unchanged.

Q: You concluded in your conclusion of March 18 1993 that there is no work-related secret in the materials presented to the Expertise. Can you clarify this?

A: Yes. I'd like to clarify that all information which I indicated is information which constitutes a confidential business secret. I came to this conclusion on the basis of the abovementioned considerations. In my opinion it doesn't represent a state secret and the government should not protect it.

Interrogated and conducted this transcript
Senior investigator of Investigation Department of
MB RF Captain of Justice   V.A. Shkarin

Annex 37

Top secret

TRANSCRIPT
of the interrogation of the expert

Moscow   April 23, 1993

Captain of Justice Shkarin, Senior Investigator of the Investigation Department of the Ministry of Security of the Russian Federation, in accordance with the requirements of the Article 192 of UPK RSFSR questioned the expert Nikolai

Iosifovich Chugunov in his office…..

Q: In connection with the petition by the indicted, V.S. Mirzayanov, I would ask you what will be included in "the goal-oriented program of scientific research work", and is it possible to state that Mirzayanov revealed the results achieved by some concrete program of scientific research work?
A: It is necessary to understand that under the title of the goal-oriented program of scientific research would include work including the list of scientific research works confirmed by the decision of the government over the last 10 years, and the list of scientific research works each to be performed during 3-5 year periods of time. The timeframe for the completion of the concrete work doesn't have any significance. Otherwise the common goal-oriented program of scientific research work is subdivided into several separate concrete programs of scientific research work concerning the direction and problems with definition of concrete goals to be achieved as a result of fulfilling each of these programs.
It's difficult for me to answer the question as to whether Mirzayanov revealed the results of some kind of concrete program of scientific research work, because the materials presented to the Expertise don't contain any information about a concrete program of scientific research and its elements. It is mentioned that they created "a new chemical agent and on its basis a binary weapon was developed" in GOSNIIOKhT. On the basis of this, it is possible to suppose that scientific research work was performed in this institute which probably had the goal of creating new chemical agents, and on their basis developing binary systems.
Mirzayanov's reference in publications to the creation of a new chemical agent and the development of a binary system on its basis is evidence that he gave information about the generally achieved results of a program of scientific research work.
Interrogated and performed transcript:
Senior investigator of Investigation Department
Of MB RF captain of justice   V.A. Shkarin

Annex 38

Top secret

CONCLUSION OF THE EXPERT

Moscow   March 17, 1993

The expert Vadim Vasilievich Smirnitsky, the chief representative of the Defense Ministry RF to the Committee of Industrial Policy of the Government of Russian Federation, according to a resolution dated January 11, 1993, prepared

State Secrets

by Captain of Justice Victor A. Shkarin, Senior Investigator of the Investigation Department at the MB RF, conducted an expertise to determine the authenticity and degree of secrecy of the information in criminal case N 62, according to Article 191 of the RSFSR Criminal and Procedural Code and came to this conclusion.

According to the instructions in carbon copy the following materials were at the disposal of the expert:
- The article "Inversion" published in "Kuranty" October 10, 1991;
- The taped manuscript of "Inversion";
- The article "Poisoned Policy" published in "Moscow News" September 20, 1992;

There altogether were listed 13 carbon copies of manuscripts and articles.
Further listed were the questions to clarify by the expert:
The decision of the experts was established based on the following questions:

i) What specific information about the research and works in the area of the development of chemical weapons did Mirzayanov disclose in his publications and interviews?
j) Does the information about the development of chemical weapons that can be found in the publications [all my manuscripts and articles are enumerated -V.M.] correspond to reality by volume and nature?
k) Is the information about the research and works in the area of the development of chemical weapons included by Mirzayanov in his articles, interviews, and manuscripts, factual? If the answer is affirmative, what is the degree of secrecy of this information? Does it constitute a state or a work-related secret?
l) Did Mirzayanov's actions have any negative consequences? If so, specifically what consequences?

-The Expert conducted the investigation and established there is information about the research work in the field of development of chemical weapons.
- Further, fragments from articles and manuscripts are listed containing information about chemical weapons development.

CONCLUSION:

1. I can not determine if it truly does constitute information that is a state secret about research work in the area of the development of chemical weapons listed in items 1-6, because I haven't had any connection with scientific research works in the area of chemical weapons since 1980.
2. Divulging the information mentioned didn't cause any damage to the defense capabilities of the Russian Army because:
a. the information about a newly synthesized chemical agent doesn't reveal :
- the chemical or conventional name of the newly synthesized chemical agent;
- its physical or chemical properties, which are indispensable characteris-

tics of any synthesized product;
- the name and quantitative ratio of the components of the binary system;
- information about what types of ammunition the new chemical agent was intended for; or,
- information about whether the Army adopted the chemical agent as a weapon.

b. Information doesn't clarify the evaluation of toxicity in comparison with the chemical agent VX-gas (inhalation or resorption toxicity, reaction time, stability on the ground, sensitivity of indication, insured time of storage etc.).

c. The mention of the Polygon at Shikhany and in the Ustjurt Plateau isn't new information because at an early time these places were revealed in the mass-media, including in the article by Birjukov and Karpov "To beat swords into ploughshares" in *Trud,* N64 April 15, 1992.

Expert   V.V. Smirnitsky

Annex 39

Top secret

TRANSCRIPT
of interrogation of the expert

Moscow   March 22, 1993

Captain of Justice Shkarin, Senior Investigator of the Investigation Department of the Ministry of Security of the Russian Federation in accordance with the requirements of Article 192 UPK RSFSR questioned the expert Vadim Vasilievich Smirnitsky in his office .....who showed his identification card N ... of retired Major General.
Interrogation started at 10:25 PM

Q: In the process of the Expertise examination of the credibility and degree of secrecy of the information set forth in Case N 62, you came to different conclusions than those from the majority of experts and on March 18 1993 you executed a separate conclusion in which you pointed out that you couldn't determine the authenticity and degree of secrecy of the information of materials in area of chemical weapons, represented to the Expertise. Clarify, why did you come to this conclusion?

A: I couldn't determine the authenticity and degree of secrecy of the information, i.e. whether it constitutes a state secret or a work-related secret, because I don't have any information about work conducted in GOSNIIOKhT after 1980 in the area of chemical weapons.

Q: Without determining the authenticity and degree of secrecy of the information, you did nevertheless reach the conclusion that its revelation didn't cause any damage to the defense capabilities of Russian Army. How it is possible to speak out about causing damage through the revelation of information without determining its authenticity?

A: I've evaluated the damage from the perspective of causing damage to the defense capabilities of the Army.

Q: Judging by your experience, you don't assume that this information can not be authenticated?

A: No, I can not suppose so because I have no idea about it since 1980, as I pointed out.

Q: But if, let us assume, this information can not be authenticated, i.e. the mentioned works were not carried out and no new chemical agents were created, how it is possible to state no damage was caused by the revelation of information which could not be authenticated?

A: I gave a common military scientific evaluation of information related to chemical agents which could cause damage for the defense capabilities of our Army. The materials presented to the Expertise don't contain this information.

Q: There are questions to be answered, as presented in the resolution on the designation of the Expert Commission from January 11 1993, about the authenticity and degree of secrecy of information about the research work in area of chemical weapons including the question about damage caused by revelation of this information. You are speaking about a common military scientific approach for evaluating damage.

A: I am answering the concrete question of the resolution - "Did the actions of Mirzayanov cause any negative consequences? If so what are they really?"

Interrogation finished at 12:05 PM.
Interrogated and composed transcript
Senior investigator of Investigation
Department of MB RF
Captain of Justice   V.A. Shkarin

Annex 40

Top secret

TRANSCRIPT
of interrogation of the expert

Moscow   March 30, 1993

Captain of Justice Shkarin, Senior Investigator of the Investigation Department of the Ministry of Security of the Russian Federation in accordance with the requirements of the Article 192 UPK RSFSR in his office questioned the expert Anatoly Mikhailovich Kochetkov....(following personal data).

Vil S. Mirzayanov

Interrogation started at 5:15 PM
Interrogation finished at 6:35 PM

Q: You came to the conclusion in Findings of the Expertise on March 16, 1993 that the materials presented to the Expertise contain state secrets about the latest achievements in the area of science and technology (results of scientific research work in the interests of the country's defense) capable of upgrading the capabilities of existing weaponry (munitions) and also about the trend and the results perspective scientific research work on the creation of binary weapons. On what basis did you make this conclusion?
A: Since 1986 I have been a chief of the Special Technical Department of the Main Administration (GlavK) of the Heavy Organic Synthesis of the Ministry of the Chemical Industry (Minkhimprom) for the coordination of problems in area of the development and production of chemical weapons.
From the content of the materials presented to the Expertise, it follows that they mention a chemical nerve agent developed at GOSNIIOKhT which is superior in its "combat characteristics" to the known VX-gas and the development of a binary system on its basis. On the basis of this data, and proceeding from my special knowledge in the specific area of the development of chemical weapons, I came to the conclusion that in this particular case the issue is about chemical agent "A-232", created at GOSNIIOKhT by order of the USSR Defense Ministry. This substance has had a stronger toxicity than VX-gas and it is difficult to cure people poisoned with it. Because of that, I developed the conclusion that the creation of this substance was the latest achievement in field of science.
There is information in the presented materials about the development of a binary version on the basis of the new chemical agent. This information discloses the trend and the results of perspective scientific research work conducted on the creation of a binary chemical weapon. These works are perspective because they allow for the simplification of the production of the weapon and problems of its storage.
Q: What about information other than that presented in the findings?
A: Like the other members of the Expert Commission, I came to the conclusion that it doesn't constitute a state secret.
Q: Has the secrecy of scientific research work in area of the creation of chemical weapons been downgraded to a degree, due to the signing by Russian Federation of the CWC on January 13 1993?
A: From 1989 up to the present time, I have been an expert on the problems of the prohibition of chemical weapons from the chemical industry at the bilateral Russian-American negotiations and I was participating in the preparation of the Expert Conclusions for texts of the CWC. The CWC doesn't have provisions for publications of the results of scientific research work in the area of creation of chemical weapons.
In our country information about scientific research in the area of development of chemical weapons from 1974 up to the current time is a specifically protected

state secret. The CWC has provisions only for the declaration of establishments where mostly the works on the creation of chemical weapons were carried out. I'd like to remind everyone that the CWC will enter into force no earlier than January 13 1995.

Interrogated and composed transcript
Senior investigator Investigation
Department of MB RF
Captain of Justice   V.A. Shkarin

Annex 41

Top secret

TRANSCRIPT
of interrogation of the expert

Moscow   April 8, 1993

Captain of Justice Shkarin, Senior Investigator of the Investigation Department of the Ministry of Security of the Russian Federation in accordance with the requirements of Article 192 UPK RSFSR in his office questioned the expert Boris Alekseevich Kuznetsov... working in GOSNIIOKhT as chief of laboratory ...

Interrogation started at 3:10 PM
Interrogation finished at 5:35 PM

Question: In the conclusion of March 16 1993, you concluded that there is information which contains state secrets in the materials presented to the Expertise about new achievements in the area of science and technology (results of scientific research work in the interests of the defense of the country), and also about the direction and the results of perspective scientific research work for the creation of binary weapons being conducted in interests of the country's defense.
On what basis did you deduce your conclusion?
A: I have been working at GOSNIIOKhT since 1971, from 1986 on I have been the chief of a laboratory at this institute, and I was directly working on the development of the technology of production for the new chemical agents.
During the expert investigations of materials presented to the Expertise and on the basis of the fact that the production in recent years of a nerve-paralytic chemical agent which exceeds in its "combat characteristics" the well-known VX-gas as well as the development of a binary system on its basis were mentioned, I came to the conclusion that in this case the topic under discussion is the chemical agent "A-232" which was created by GOSNIIOKhT. I was directly working with this substance and I know the whole list of its properties including the difficulty of curing poisoning, which exceeds that of the known chemical

agent VX-gas. They issued patents in the course of the scientific studies of it and the technology of its production, which is evidence that it is a matter of the newest achievement in the area of science and technology, in particular, in chemistry and the technology of chemical agents. Moreover up to the present time, Russian specialists don't know whether similar substances were developed in the USA or in other countries conducting research work in area of chemical weapons. I can insist on that because I have clearance for informative materials coming to our institute and other related organizations. These research works were conducted in the interests of the defense of the country. By presenting to the Expert Conclusion proofs other than these, about the fact that the creation of this substance as the newest achievement, additional components of information about this agent could be disclosed which constitute a state secret.

There are in the materials presented to the Expertise information about the development of a new chemical agent of a binary system and its production. This information is disclosing the direction and results of perspective scientific work on the creation of a binary weapon conducted in the interests of the country's defense. These are perspective works because the binary technology of production of any chemical agent is a new step in the development of chemical weapons.

Q: What about information related to the development of chemical weapons other than information pointed out in materials presented to the Expertise?

A: During the expertise I came to the conclusion that other kinds of information about chemical weapons in materials presented to expertise doesn't constitute a state secret.

Q: Hasn't the degree of secrecy of the information about scientific research work conducted earlier in the area of the creation of chemical weapons been downgraded, due to the signing on January 13 1993 by Russian Federation of the Convention on the Prohibition of Development, Production, Stockpiling and se of Chemical Weapons and of their Destruction?

A: I was involved from 1985 on by the Ministry of Chemical Industry in the expert work on the development of the provisions of the Chemical Weapons Convention. From 1988 up to 1991, I was directly participating in the negotiations on chemical weapons in Geneva, in the staff of the Soviet delegation. Because of this I declare that information which constitutes a state secret in the materials presented to the Expertise are related to information on the development of chemical weapons. Disclosure of such information on the development of chemical weapons is not foreseen by provisions of the Convention. So, this information is a property of the state and can be divulged only with its consent.

I know exactly as a participant of the negotiations that at the state level this information was not transmitted to other states.

A: During the investigation indicted Mirzayanov declared that after the publication in the 1991 article "Inversion" in "Kuranty", an unpleasant relationship developed between him and you. How you can comment on this statement?

Q: I didn't have a relationship with Mirzayanov, due to my duties of scientific and service activities. So, we didn't have any relationship, and we were simply

acquaintances. I am not accepting Mirzayanov's accusations of Soviet experts working at the negotiations as directed towards me, because he didn't mention my last name in this publication and there were many other experts. Personally I don't have any enmity toward him.
Interrogated and composed transcript
Senior investigator of Investigation
Department of MB RF
Captain of Justice   V.A. Shkarin

Annex 42

Top secret

TRANSCRIPT
of interrogation of the expert

Moscow   April 29, 1993

Captain of Justice Shkarin, Senior Investigator of the Investigation Department of the Ministry of Security of the Russian Federation in accordance with the requirements of Article 192 UPK RSFSR questioned the expert Igor Michailovich Gabov in his office.

Interrogation started at 3:05 PM
Interrogation finished at 4:55 PM

Question: In connection with the indicted Mirzayanov's petition I'd ask you to clarify whether the conclusions of Expert Commission from March 16 conform to the formulation of Article 56 of the Temporary List of Information Constituting State Secrets?
A: During the course of the Expert examination, I came to the conclusion that materials presented to the Expertise do contain information on the results achieved of scientific research work conducted within the framework of a goal-oriented program of scientific research in interests of the country's defense.
Q: You are presented the excerpt of Resolution of the government of Russian Federation March 30 1993 N 256-16 "On making amendments and additions to the Temporary List of Information of state secrecy", in accordance with it the Temporary List of information constituting state secrets agrees with Clause 122 "Information that discloses the content of former or current works in the area of chemical or biological weapons, or the essence of those works, the results achieved, as well as information on the protocols of synthesis, production technologies, or articles of production equipment." What kind of clarification can you give us in connection with this?
A: After being familiarized with the Resolution of the Government presented, I came to the conclusion that it is directed particularly for the protection of previ-

ously achieved results of completed works in the area of chemical weapons and it is a confirmation of correctness of the conclusion of the Experts who signed a common resolution.

Interrogated and composed transcript
Senior investigator of Investigation
Department of MB RF
Captain of Justice   V.A. Shkarin

Annex 43

Top Secret

The Council of Ministers
Government of the Russian Federation

RESOLUTION

Moscow   March 30, 1993 N 256-16

On making amendments and additions to the Temporary List of Information of state secrecy.

The Council of Ministers – the Government of the Russian Federation resolves:

1. To introduce the following amendments and additions to the Temporary List of Information of state secrecy approved on September 18, 1992 by Resolution N 733-55 of the Government of the Russian Federation:

    a) To use the following wording for Sub-clause "a" of Clause 1:

OF SPECIAL IMPORTANCE

"a) nuclear ammunition, strategic missiles, rocket launching devices, military purpose space vehicles, rocket carriers for them, anti-missile and anti-space defense facilities, weapons based on new physical or other new principles or special facilities of defense from them, arms with nuclear power plants, systems for warning of a missile attack, systems of space control, military deep-water technical facilities, strategic aviation, as well as its major components within the Russian Federation on the whole, its republics, ministries, departments, enterprises with a special regime or of special importance;"

    b) To add Clause 122 that reads as follows to Section IX "Miscellaneous information":

State Secrets

"122. Information that discloses the content of former or current works in the area of chemical or biological weapons, or the essence of those works, the results achieved, as well as information on the protocols of synthesis, production technologies, or articles of production equipment."

The Ministry of Defense of the Russian Federation is giving notice that these amendments and additions are to be brought to the notice of the ministries and departments of the Russian Federation, the executive bodies of the republics within the Russian Federation, the territories, regions, autonomous districts, the cities of Moscow and St. Petersburg.

2. To the heads of the ministries and departments of the Russian Federation, to take into consideration the amendments and additions stipulated by this resolution, while developing temporary departmental lists of information subject to security classification.

The Ministry of Defense of the Russian Federation and the Ministry of Security of the Russian Federation should provide the required assistance in this work.

V. Chernomyrdin,
Chairman of the Council of Ministers
Government of the Russian Federation

Annex 44

Top Secret
Copy 2

To V. A. Petrunin, Director of the State Russian Science
Research Institute for Organic Chemistry and Technology
April 22, 1993 6/001580   111024, Moscow, 23 Shosse Entuziastov

The Investigation Department of the Ministry of Security of the Russian Federation is investigating the criminal case of Vil Sultanovich Mirzayanov, who in 1992 disclosed information to the mass media about the results of scientific research conducted at GRNIIOKhT on the creation of a new chemical agent and the development of a binary weapon based on it.

In connection with this, we ask you to inform us if the research on the creation of Chemical Agent A-232 was conducted within the framework of some specific special goal-oriented program, and if so, is the creation of the new chemical agent and the development of a binary system based on it the result of scientific research work conducted within the scope of this program? Is such research being carried out presently, and if it has been discontinued, when and on the basis of what normative act was this decision based?

We also ask you to check if this appointed program for scientific research and experimental and design work on the aforementioned chemical agent has a state standard, and if so, please tell us about it.

Head of the section at the Department   A.A. Shabunin

Annex 45

Top Secret
Copy 1

STATE RUSSIAN SCIENCE
RESEARCH INSTITUTE FOR
ORGANIC CHEMISTRY AND
TECHNOLOGY

To A.A. Shabunin, head of the
Section of the Investigation Department
at the Ministry of Security
of the Russian Federation

In response to N 6/001580 of April 22, 1993

In response to your request, we inform you that the research on the development of Agent A-232 was conducted within the framework of a special goal-oriented program under Resolution N 103-43 of the Central Committee of the C.P.S.U. and the U.S.S.R. Council of Ministers dated January 31, 1983, and declared by Decree N 131-27 of the Ministry of Chemical Industry of the USSR dated March 25, 1983.

The research work aimed at the creation of a binary system based on Agent A-232 was conducted within the framework of the special goal-oriented program under Resolution N 844-186 of the Central Committee of the C.P.S.U. and the U.S.S.R. Council of Ministers on October 6, 1989, and was declared by the Decree N 22-2 of the Ministry of Chemical Industry of the USSR dated September 11, 1989.

The development and thorough screening of the new chemical agent and the creation of a binary system based on it was the result of scientific research conducted within the framework of the indicated program.

Currently this research has concluded. Generally speaking, all scientific research work on the development of chemical weapons (works of the Foliant program) stopped on January 1, 1993, in compliance with Resolution N 518-33 of the Russian Federation dated July 24, 1992, and declared by Decree N D/12-11 of the Ministry of Industry of the Russian Federation dated September 18, 1992. The same decree prescribed that all participants of the above mentioned works take measures to protect state secrets under the Foliant program.

As a rule, the direction of the special purpose program mentioned above includes few research, experimental, and design works.

The Ministry of Defense develops a tactical-technical task specification, compiled in accordance with the State Standards V 15.101-79 for scientific research work or with State Standard V 15.201-83 for experimental and design work, for each separate work from those that are included in the program.

Deputy Director   N.A. Kuznetsov

Annex 46

Secret
Copy N 2
To Colonel General M.P. Kolesnikov,
Head of the General Staff of the
Armed Forces of the
Russian Federation

April 22, 1993 6/01584

The Investigation Department of the Ministry of Security of the Russian Federation is investigating the criminal case of V. S. Mirzayanov, who disclosed information to the mass media about scientific research in the area of chemical weapons. In connection with this development we are asking for the following necessary information.

1. Is the Temporary List of Information of state secrecy, approved by the government of the Russian Federation on September 18, 1992, by Decree N 733-55 on the whole and by Clause 56 of this list in particular, aimed at the protection of information about scientific research in the area of the development of chemical weapons in our country? Does the term "ammunition" indicated in the Sub-clause "C" of Clause 1 of the List cover ammunition equipped with military chemical agents?

2. Is the List of the Main Information of state secrecy approved by the U.S.S.R. Council of Ministers on December 3, 1980 in Resolution N 1121-387 on the whole and in Paragraph 2 of Clause 83 and Clause 85 of this List in particular, aimed at the protection of information about scientific research in the area of the development of chemical weapons in our country? Does the term "ammunition" indicated in Paragraph 1 of Clause 2 of the List cover ammunition equipped with military chemical agents?

Head of the Department,
Major General   S.D. Balashov

Annex 47

Secret
Copy N 1

GENERAL STAFF HEADQUARTERS
OF THE ARMED FORCES
OF THE RUSSIAN FEDERATION
Eighth Department

To Major General S.D. Balashov,
Head of the Investigation Department, of
the Ministry of Security
of the Russian Federation

May 12, 1993

N 317/5/0 397 in response to N 6/01584

We have considered your letter regarding the clarifications of the clauses of the Lists of Information of state secrecy. Clause 56 of the Temporary List of Information of state secrecy, approved by the government of the Russian Federation on September 18, 1992, in Decree N 733-55, provides for the determination of the degree of secrecy of the information about the goal-oriented programs, scientific research decisions or the achievements of scientific research, and experimental design work in the interests of the defense and the security of the country, including the development of weapons. The term "ammunition" covers different kinds of ammunition including ammunition equipped with military chemical agents. Additionally, Clauses 54, 55, 61, and 63 of this Temporary List are aimed at protecting the information about scientific research, including a qualitatively new level of potential for arms and military technology.

While defining the degree of secrecy of information in the area of scientific research, including the development of armaments, you can extend the explanations mentioned above to the List of the Major Information of state secrecy approved by the U.S.S.R. Council of Ministers dated December 3, 1980, in Resolution N 1121-387 and in particular by Paragraph 2 of Clause 83 and Clause 85 of this list; it was expedient to use the clarifications which are indicated above. For a more detailed interpretation of the terms and notions mentioned in the List of the Major Information of state secrecy, it is necessary to look for it from those who compiled in 1980, the MB RF.

Colonel G. Funygin,
Deputy Head of the Department

Annex 48

6/01341/April 5, 1993

Secret
Copy N 2
To Colonel General M.P. Kolesnikov,
Head of the General Staff Headquarters
of the Armed Forces of the Russian Federation

The Investigation Department of the Ministry of Security of the Russian Federation is investigating the criminal case, in which Vil Sultanovich Mirzayanov, a former employee at the State Russian Science Research Institute for Organic Chemistry and Technology (GRNIIOKhT), is accused of committing a crime stipulated by Article 75, Part 1, of the RSFSR Criminal Code.

It was established during the investigation, that in 1992 Mirzayanov disclosed information to the mass media that constitutes a state secret, about the creation of a new chemical agent and the development of a binary system based on it being created at GRNIIOKhT by order of the Ministry of Defense. In connection with this please inform us if the General Staff Headquarters of the VSRF [Armed Forces of the Russian Federation] has any information about any negative consequences to the defense capability of Russia created by Mirzayanov's actions indicated above.

Head of the Department
Major General   S.D. Balashov

Annex 49

Secret
Copy N. 1

General Headquarters
of the Armed Forces
of the Russian Federation

To Major General S.D. Balashov,
Head of the Investigation Department
at the Ministry of Security
of the Russian Federation

April 29, 1993
N 312/10/053

In response to N 6 01341 of April 5, 1993

The Ministry of Defense has considered your request for information about any kind of negative consequences for the defense capability of Russia that resulted from V. Mirzayanov's disclosure of information that constitutes a state secret.

Vil S. Mirzayanov

In his publications and interviews V. Mirzayanov discloses information about the results of our research and development work in the field of chemical weapons, which is currently not prohibited by any of the existing international agreements.

Additionally, in V. Mirzayanov's publications information is presented in such detail, which is not stipulated either by the multilateral Convention for the Prohibition of Chemical Weapons, or in the bilateral agreements on chemical weapons between Russia and the U.S. After the international agreements mentioned above come into effect, each state-participant will be required only to report "the location, character and general sphere of activity" of the sites for the development [of chemical weapons].

In this way, not one of the other countries which developed (and continue at the present time in the absence of international bans) the development of new kinds of chemical weapons will declare any such detailed information about the results of their research and development in this area, including the names of specific substances and their properties based on the results of testing.

V. Mirzayanov published ahead of the time agreed, information about the sites where chemical weapons were developed and described the nature of their activity, (In other countries this has been kept a secret up to the present time, and the question being discussed is what sites were "mainly" involved in the development and must be declared after the Convention enters into force) and he also revealed information in such detail that is not stipulated in the terms of the Convention – a comparison of the toxic characteristics and battle properties of the samples developed, the sites of their development, the accumulation of experimental batches and tests, and *conventional names of these new substances and the overall development programs* [italicized by me—V.M.]. The published information caused a negative reaction from the U.S. during the bilateral negotiations for banning chemical weapons in Geneva. This is confirmed by the fact that the American delegation accused Russia of failing to provide information at the first stage of the Wyoming Memorandum on chemical weapons, about the alleged development production and storage of a significant quantity of chemical agents (CA) in Russia, as were mentioned in Vil Mirzayanov's publications, although there are no such stockpiles of such chemical agents. At the same negotiations the American side (referring to V. Mirzayanov's indicated publications) took steps to introduce additional commitments, according to which Russia should unilaterally disclose the results of its research and development work in the field of chemical weapons. Additionally, these publications created a precedent for requesting similar commitments from Russia within the framework of the multilateral Convention, while other countries that keep such information a secret will declare only very general information regarding the nature of their activities on the development of chemical weapons after the Convention enters into force. These publications caused real political harm to Russia and undermined its authority in the international arena. A false impression was created that Russia allegedly doesn't comply with existing commitments in the area of the prohibition of chemical weapons. Thus, V. Mirzayanov's publications are currently causing military damage by unilaterally disclosing information about the results of our research and development work in the field of chemical weapons in such detail, which is not stipulated for other countries within the framework of future disclosures after the Convention for the Prohibiting of Chemical Weapons and other international agreements in this area enter into force. Additionally, a precedent was created for other countries to raise demands for Russia after the Convention enters into effect, to unilaterally give even more detailed information about the full names and detailed properties of the samples that were developed, which could be used by the states of the "third world" to meet their ends and facilitate the spread of chemical weapons.

Head of the General Staff,
Colonel General   M. Kolesnikov

Annex 50

Secret
Copy N 2

To V.P. Ivanov,
Chairman of the RF Committee for
Chemical and Petrochemical Industry

6/01342 April 5, 1993

The Investigation Department of the Ministry of Security of the Russian Federation is investigating the criminal case of Vil Sultanovich Mirzayanov, a former employee at the State Russian Science Research Institute for Organic Chemistry and Technology (GRNIIOKhT), who is charged with committing a crime under Article 75, Part 1, of the RSFSR Criminal Code. It was established during the investigation that in 1992 Mirzayanov disclosed information to the mass media that constitutes a state secret about the creation of a new chemical agent and the development of a binary system based on it being created at GRNIIOKhT, by order of the Ministry of Defense.

In connection with this, please inform us if the General Staff Headquarters of the RF Armed Forces has any information at its disposal (underlined by me— V.M.) about Mirzayanov's above-mentioned actions having any negative consequences for the defensive capabilities of Russia.

Head of the Department
Major General   S.D. Balashov

Annex 51

Secret
Copy N. 1

Russian Federation
Committee for
Chemical and Petrochemical Industry

To S.D. Balashov, Head of the
Investigation Department at the
Ministry of Security of
The Russian Federation

10185
Tsentr, ul. Myasnitskaya, 20

April 13, 1993, N 629 s in response to N 6/ 01342 of April 5, 1993

According to the evaluation of the specialists from the Committee for Chemical and Petrochemical Industry, V. S. Mirzayanov's publications in the mass media caused moral and economic damage, along with disclosing top secret information. After these publications, part of the world and the Russian public started to doubt that the production of chemical weapons had been discontinued in Russia as our government had claimed in 1987. Since the people who live in the regions where the plants are located that produced chemical weapons in the past were misinformed, it is creating a tense situation around these enterprises; in particular an example of this is the rejection of the proposal to carry out the destruction of chemical weapons on the premises of the Cheboksary PO Khimprom. As a result, this [suggested] placement threatens to disrupt Russia's fulfillment of its international agreements on the destruction of the stockpiles of chemical weapons, and also the program for the destruction of chemical weapons will entail sharply higher costs because the Cheboksary PO Khimprom can't be used for this purpose.

Concerning, evaluating the negative consequences of Mirzayanov's actions for the defensive capability of Russia, this question is outside the competence of the Committee for Chemical and Petrochemical Industry.

Chairman   V.P. Ivanov

Annex 52

Secret
Copy N 2
To G.V. Berdennikov,
Deputy Minister of Foreign Affairs of the
Russian Federation

6/01343/April 5, 1993

The Investigation Department of the RF Ministry of Security is investigating the criminal case in which Vil Sultanovich Mirzayanov, a former employee at the State Russian Science Research Institute for Organic Chemistry and Technology (GRNIIOKhT), is charged with committing a crime stipulated by Article 75, Part 1, of the RSFSR Criminal Code. It was established during the investigation that in 1992 Mirzayanov disclosed information to the mass media that constitutes a state secret about the creation of a new chemical agent and the development of a binary system based on it at GRNIIOKhT at request of the Ministry of Defense. In connection with this, please inform us if the MID [Ministry of Foreign Affairs] of Russia has any information about any kind of negative consequences to the political or any other interests of the Russian Federation that resulted from Mirzayanov's above-mentioned actions.

Head of the Department   S.D. Balashov

Annex 53

Secret
Copy N 1

The Ministry of Foreign Affairs
Of the Russian Federation
121200, Moscow, G-200
32/34 Smolensko-Sennaya Pl.
Tel. 244-16-06
May 11, 1993 N 61/drk

To S.D. Balashov, Head of the
Investigation Department at the RF
Ministry of Security

In response to 6/01343 of April 5, 1993

In connection with your inquiry into the case of V. S. Mirzayanov, the RF Ministry of Foreign Affairs can respond in the following way.

Currently it has become impossible to determine what generated a greater resonance in the country and abroad – the publications of Vil S. Mirzayanov or the fact that criminal proceedings were instituted against him on charges of disclosure of state secrets, since it was the latter that was perceived as confirmation of the information contained in these publications.

The RF MID has no information at its disposal about the authenticity of the information mentioned in the articles or about what the extent of the damage was to our national security as a consequence of the investigation of the disclosure of information about the development of binary chemical weapons.

Nevertheless, we can verify that the campaign in the Russian and foreign mass media that developed in connection with V. S. Mirzayanov's case served as the basis of the expression of concern on the part of the U.S., and requests arose for clarification of the situation. The U.S. National Academy of Sciences appealed personally to the RF President on this issue. However, no one has observed that our relations with the U.S. and other countries have become complicated so far. During the top-level Russian-American meeting in Vancouver it was noted that progress was achieved at the bilateral negotiations between Russian and U.S. on the prohibition of chemical weapons.

With respect,
Deputy Minister   G. Berdennikov

Annex 54

REPORT OF THE PRESS SERVICE OF THE PRESIDENT OF THE RUSSIAN FEDERATION

We are distributing the text of the statement of President B. N. Yeltsin of the Russian Federation on the issue of chemical weapons.

Statement made by the President of the Russian Federation on the issue of the destruction of chemical weapons

In the past few months the public in a number of regions has been seriously concerned about the issue of the destruction of chemical weapons.

In the preceding decades, tens of thousands of tons of military chemical agents have been produced and stockpiled in Russia. The world has changed, and Russia's position in the world has changed: we are not going to attack anybody. The time has come to rid ourselves of chemical weapons which we have inherited from the past legacy. This is not only Russia's view, but also the opinion shared by the one hundred and thirty eight countries which have signed the Convention on the Prohibition of Chemical Weapons this year in Paris.

We must begin the destruction of chemical weapons, proceeding from the requirements not only of international, but also of national security; as the shells and containers are steadily deteriorating and can't be stored indefinitely. These weapons were produced over the course of many years at several plants. The destruction process will be difficult and a substantial period of time will be required for its implementation. However, it has to be started. A government program for the destruction of chemical weapons is currently being prepared. It will be based upon the following principles:

- Unconditional guarantee of the safety of the life and health of the population, as well as of the condition of the surrounding natural environment;
- Unconditional fulfillment of all the social needs of the population living in the zone of influence of the chemical weapons destruction facilities;
- Use of the latest technologies, making it possible to minimize the risk and also, in cases where feasible, to extract valuable chemical substances as a result of the destruction;
- Reduction to the minimum of the volume of transportation of chemical agents, within the Russian territory.

The work on the destruction of chemical weapons will begin only after positive conclusions [have been reached] by state environmental-protection experts regarding the Program as a whole and at each individual facility. Such an expert evaluation will definitely involve the participation not only of scientists and specialists, but also of representatives of public organizations, including environmental organizations, on both the all-Russian and regional levels.

I am requesting the executive bodies of Udmurtiya, Chuvashiya, and the Saratov Region to ensure their active involvement in development of this program, in the determination of the priorities and terms of its preparation and in carrying out the work of the destruction of chemical weapons. Such participation will help transform this endeavor – an unavoidable step for Russia – into a powerful lever for the socio-economic development of significant territories of the country, while strictly ensuring the observance of guarantees for the safety of the population. A substantial part of the funds under this program will be channeled towards solving regional issues of public health protection, the protection of motherhood and childcare, as well as towards the construction of housing accommodations, social and community services, roads, and other infrastructure.

The mountains of now useless and dangerous weapons are a heavy burden inherited from the legacy of our past. Russia must be saved from it, in the interests of its own security and in the interests of the security of the whole world.

B. Yeltsin
April 20, 1993

Annex 55

Top Secret
Indictment
CONFIRMATION
Deputy Attorney General
of the Russian Federation
3^d Class State Councilor
E.G. Denisov
"25" November 1993

INDICTMENT

Concerning Criminal Case N 62, about the indictment of Vil Sultanovich Mirzayanov for committing a crime according to Part 1 of Clause 75 of the Criminal Code (UK) of the RSFSR.

This criminal case was initiated by the Investigation Department of the Security Ministry of the Russian Federation on October 19, 1992, on the basis of materials received from the Department of Economic Security of the MB RF about divulging state secrets in the article "Poisoned Policies" published in the N 38 issue of the newspaper *Moscow News* on September 16, 1992.
v. 1, p.p. 1, 18-27

On October 22, 1992 Mirzayanov was detained according to Clause 122 of the Criminal and Procedural Code (UPK); on October 24 the status was changed to that of an arrest. On November 2, 1992 by resolution of the Kalinin District Court of Moscow, his preventative arrest was changed into non-departure status.
v. 1, p.p. 166-167, 181-182, 189-190

On October 30, 1992 criminal procedures were instituted against Mirzayanov for divulging information constituting a state secret, i.e., for committing a crime according to Part 1 of Clause 75 UK of the RSFSR.
v. 1, p.p. 191-193, 229-232

The inquest established:

V.S. Mirzayanov was working during the period from 1965 up until January 1992 at different positions in GOSNIIOKhT, including the position of Head of the branch Foreign Technical Counterintelligence Department, and because of his duties he was knowledgeable about information of state secrecy concerning research work in area of development of chemical weapons.

After he was fired from the institute, in August 1992 in Moscow Mirzayanov prepared for publication in the press a manuscript titled "The Chemical Sharashka is Waiting for American Assistance" in which he included informa-

State Secrets

tion known to him in connection his duties and constituting state secrets about the latest achievements in area of science and technology (results of research work in interest of country's defense) that allowed enhancement of the capabilities of existing arms (munitions), the direction and the results of perspective scientific research work conducted in the interest of the country's defense, the applied scientific research work on the creation of binary weapons, and familiarized the leading scientist of the Institute Geochemistry and Analytical Chemistry L.A. Fedorov with them, and disclosed them by joint publication together with Fedorov in N 38 issue of the newspaper *Moscow News* on September 1992 in the article titled "Poisoned Policies".

Mirzayanov disclosed the same information, in September 1992 in Moscow, to a reporter from the newspaper the *Baltimore Sun* William Englund through whom he published it on September 16, 1992 in the aforementioned newspaper in the article "Former Scientist Says that Gorbachev's Regime Created a New Nerve Gas in 91", and in October of 1992 – to the reporter from the magazine *Novoe Vremya* O.V. Vishnyakov, and with his help it was published in the same month in the N 44 issue of that magazine in the article "'The Binary Bomb" has Exploded".

V.S. Mirzayanov refused to plead guilty to the crime as charged, because in his opinion disclosure of information about development in area of chemical weapons doesn't constitute a state secret. At the same time during the preliminary investigation, Mirzayanov pointed out that assuming GOSNIIOKhT is conducting scientific research work in the area of the development of chemical weapons in violation of Russia's international obligations, in order to focus the public attention on this problem in August-September 1992, he wrote and gave the leading scientist at the Institute Geochemistry and Analytical Chemistry, L.A. Fedorov, the text titled "The Chemical Sharashka in Moscow is waiting for American Assistance" for him to become familiarized with it and then for publication in press. In this article he presented information known to him because of his work in GOSNIIOKhT about the synthesis of a new chemical agent and the development of a binary weapon on its basis, and it was published later in the article "Poisoned Policies" in the N 38 issue of the newspaper *Moscow News* in September of 1992. The information was the same as the indicted explained, and for the same purposes he reported to the correspondent of the newspaper the *Baltimore Sun*, William Englund for the publication in September 1992, and in October 1992 – in an interview with the reporter O.V. Vishnyakov of the magazine *Novoe Vremya*.

v. 1, p.p. 169-172, 174-180, 195-200, 229-234

The guilt of Mirzayanov in committing the crime he is charged with, except for his admission of the factual circumstances of the crime, is also corroborated by:

Witnesses testimonies:

L.A. Fedorov, the leading scientist of the Institute Geochemistry and Analytical Chemistry of Russian Academy of Sciences, who stated that in August of 1992 in Moscow V.S. Mirzayanov had familiarized him with and gave him the manuscript about the development and production of chemical weapons in Russia titled "The Chemical Sharashka in Moscow is Waiting for American Assistance" for publication, and on the basis of which he (Fedorov) prepared the article, including in it information reported to him by Mirzayanov about a new chemical agent created in GOSNIIOKhT, gave this article to the reporter L.A. Nikishin and it was published in the N 38 issue of the newspaper *Moscow News* on September 20, 1992 under the title "Poisoned Policies". Moreover, as the witness pointed out, V.S. Mirzayanov reported information about the new chemical agent created in GOSNIIOKhT in his presence, in September of 1992 in Moscow in the office of the newspaper the *Baltimore Sun* to reporter William Englund, and in October 1992 in the office of the Editorial Board of the magazine *Novoe Vremya* – to the reporter O.V. Vishnyakov.

v. 1, p.p. 235-241

L.N. Nikishin, reporter for the newspaper *Moscow News*, stated that in September of 1992 L.A. Fedorov gave him an article prepared jointly with V.S. Mirzayanov for publication about the problems connected with the development of chemical weapons, which was published in the N 38 issue of the newspaper *Moscow News* on September 20 1992 under the title of "Poisoned Policies".

v.1, p.p. 267-270

O.V. Vishnyakov, reporter from the magazine *Novoe Vremya*, stated that on October 20 1992 in the building of the Editorial Office he recorded an interview with Mirzayanov in which he reported to him information about a chemical agent created in GOSNIIOKhT, after which he typed out the text and published it in the N 44 issue of the magazine *Novoe Vremya* on October 1992 as the article titled "The Binary Bomb has Exploded".

v.1, p.p. 251-253

William Englund, reporter from American newspaper the *Baltimore Sun* stated that his article "Ex Soviet Scientist Says Gorbachev's Regime Created a New Nerve Gas in 1991" which was published on September 16 1992, is written on the basis of an interview given to him on September 15 1992 by V.S. Mirzayanov and L.A. Fedorov, during which information about the creation of a new chemical agent in the USSR was reported to him by V.S. Mirzayanov.

v. 1, p.p. 292-296

A.E. Riskal who was working from 1989 until 1991 in the Foreign Technical Counterintelligence Department of GOSNIIOKhT stated that in this period of time procedures were developed in the department for the determination of the presence of the new chemical agents on objects in the environment and V.S. Mirzayanov as head of this department and as Scientific Leader was working

State Secrets

with these substances and knew their physical chemical characteristics.
v.1, p. 262

S.S. Sokolov who has been working since 1987 in the Foreign Technical Counterintelligence Department of GOSNIIOKhT stated that during 1987-89 this Department was working on the development of procedures for control of the presence of chemical agents in waste water, air and solid waste and was controlling them in those media. V.S. Mirzayanov, as head of the department and its Scientific Leader, was working directly with those substances and he knew their toxicity characteristics.
v. 1, p.p. 271-275

Material evidence:

- the typed text of the article "Poisoned Policies" handed over by L.V. Karpinsky, the Editor in Chief of the newspaper *Moscow News*, during the seizure in the Editorial Office of the newspaper, in which information is presented about the creation of a new chemical agent and the development of a binary weapon on its basis, in GOSNIIOKhT.
v.1, p.p. 97-105, v.2., p.p. 303-312

- two manuscripts titled "The Chemical Sharashka in Moscow is Waiting for American Assistance" seized during the search V.S. Mirzayanov's and L.A. Fedorov's apartments, and also the N 38 issue of the newspaper *Moscow News* on September 20 1992. They were seized from Fedorov, and in them there is information about the creation of a new chemical agent in GOSNIIOKhT and the development of a binary weapon on its basis.
v.1, p.p. 134-153, v.2, p.p. 198-219
v.1, p.p. 29-34, 48-53, v.2, p.p. 1-9, 92-97

- the typed text of an interview given by V.S. Mirzayanov and L.A. Fedorov, given to the investigation by A.B. Pumpyansky the Editor in Chief of the magazine *Novoe Vremya*, during the seizure in the Editorial Board of the magazine, from which it follows that Mirzayanov, while answering the reporter's questions, told him about the creation of a new chemical agent in GOSNIIOKhT and the development of a binary weapon on its basis.
v.1, p.p. 116-131, v.2, 287-302

- a carbon copy of the article "Ex Soviet Scientist Says Gorbachev's Regime Created a New Nerve Gas in 91" published in the newspaper the *Baltimore Sun*, seized during the search V.S. Mirzayanov's and L.A. Fedorov's apartments which contains information about the highest level secret highly lethal chemical nerve agent created in the USSR in a binary form.
v.1, p.p. 29-34, 57-62, v.2, p.p. 1-9, 101-104

Vil S. Mirzayanov

- the Technical Order for the compound part of the system of components N 2187 ss/khf, delivered from GOSNIIOKhT as evidence of conducting field tests of the new chemical agent. As established by the Investigation, Mirzayanov was familiarized with this document on April 20 1990.

v.3, p.p. 272-277, v.2, p.p. 262-264

- the compact cassette with a recording of part of Mirzayanov's interview published in the N 44 issue of the magazine *Novoe Vremya* on October 1992 as the article "The Binary Bomb has Exploded" presented by the witness O.V. Vishnyakov on October 22, 1992, in which he reported to the reporter of that magazine information about a new chemical agent created in GOSNIIOKhT.

v.1, p.p. 254-257, v.6, p.p. 55-57,
v.2, p.p. 250-261, v.5

Transcripts of the survey of material evidence:

- of the N 44 issue of the magazine *Novoe Vremya* on October 1992 from which it follows that in this magazine the interview of Mirzayanov titled "The Binary Bomb has Exploded" is published. In this interview Mirzayanov answered a question of the reporter, giving information about the new chemical agent and the development of the binary weapon on its basis created in GOSNIIOKhT.

v.2, p.p. 287-302

- the personnel file of V.S. Mirzayanov from which it follows that Mirzayanov was an employee of GOSNIIOKhT from 1965 up until January of 1992, and from September 1986 up until August 1990 he performed the duties of the Chief of the Foreign Technical Counterintelligence Department (Department 11) of the Branch.

v.3, p.p. 1-140

Documents:

- A report (N 1494 ss) from October 1 1992 and reference (N 1572 ss) from GOSNIIOKhT about the functional duties of the Chief of the Foreign Technical Counterintelligence Department on September 29, 1992 which shows that Vil Sultanovich Mirzayanov was well-informed about the system of organization, the trend and the results of scientific research and experiment design work (NIOKR) in the area of chemical weapons.

v.1, p.p. 20-21, 25-26

- The signed obligation of V.S. Mirzayanov dated August 23, 1976 not to disclose information constituting state secrets and secret information entrusted to him or which became known to him in connection with his work.

v.1, p. 27

State Secrets

- Reports of GOSNIIOKhT (N 1846ss from 11.14.92 and N 357ss from 04.27.93) showing that this institute had conducted scientific research works on the creation of new chemical weapons and the development of binary systems on their basis in accordance with resolutions of the USSR Counsel of Ministers.

v.3, p.p. 268-269, 279-280

- A report of the General Staff of Russian Federation Defense Ministry (N 312/10/053 from 04.29.93) that the scientific research work in the area of the development chemical weapons is not prohibited by any acting international agreements, which refutes the reasons claimed by Mirzayanov for his publications of the abovementioned information in mass media.

v. 3, p.p. 262-264

Resolutions of the Experts:

- N 120 from April 12, 1993, that the signature and the date on page 6 of the Technical Order for the Compound Part of the Experimental Design Work on the basis of the system of the components N 2187ss/khf were executed by V.S. Mirzayanov.

v.3, p.p. 149-151

- N 31 from February 9, 1993, that the two manuscripts seized in the apartments of L.A. Fedorov and V.S. Mirzayanov titled "The Chemical Sharashka in Moscow is Waiting for American Assistance" were executed by V.S. Mirzayanov.

- N 6/00999 from March16, 1993, that in the manuscripts titled as "The Chemical Sharashka in Moscow is waiting for American Assistance" seized in the apartments of V.S. Mirzayanov and L.A. Fedorov, in the typed text of the article "Poisoned Policies" seized during the seizure in the Editorial Office of the newspaper *Moscow News*, in the article "Poisoned Policies" published in the newspaper *Moscow News* N38 on September 20, in the interview of V.S. Mirzayanov and L.A. Fedorov seized in the Editorial Office of the magazine *Novoe Vremya*, in the article "Binary Bomb has exploded" published in the N44 issue of the magazine *Novoe Vremya* on October 1992, in the article "Ex Soviet Scientist Says that Gorbachev's Regime Created a New Nerve Gas in 91" published in newspaper the *Baltimore Sun* on September 16, 1992, disclosed top secret information constituting state secrets about the latest achievements in the area of science and technology (the results of scientific research work in interests of country's defense), which permits the enhancement of the capabilities of existing arms (munitions), the direction and the results of perspective works, conducted in the interests of the country's defense - applied scientific research work on the creation of a binary weapon.

v.3, p.p. 206-237

Vil S. Mirzayanov

Mirzayanov's illegal actions are qualified according to Part 1 of Clause 75 UK of the RSFSR.

No aggravating or mitigating circumstances are found in the amenability of Mirzayanov.

On the basis of all that is here expressed, the following is indicted:

Vil Sultanovich Mirzayanov, DOB 1935, native of village Stary Kangish of Djurtjuli District Bashkir ASSR, Bashkir, citizen of the Russian Federation, higher education, married, with two dependent children with DOBs 1980 and 1988, pensioner, permanent resident at: Moscow, Stalevarov Street, House 4, Bldg. 4, Apt. 586,

that he: when he was working at GOSNIIOKhT from 1965 until 1992 including from 1986 until 1990 in the capacity of Chief of the branch's Foreign Technical Counterintelligence Department, he had clearance for top secret information constituting a state secret about research works conducted in the institute in the area of development of chemical weapons.

After being fired from the institute in August-October 1992 in Moscow for disclosure in the mass media information reported to a number of people and published in the press information known to him through his work in GOSNIIOKhT about the creation in this institute of a new chemical agent and the development of a binary weapon on its basis, disclosed by this top secret information constituting a state secret about latest achievement in the area of science and technology (the results of scientific work in the interest of the country's defense), which permitted the enhancement of the capabilities of existing arms (munitions), and also about the trend and the results of applied scientific research work on the creation of a binary weapon in interest of country's defense:

- in August 1992 – to leading the scientist at the Institute of Geochemistry and Analytical Chemistry of Russian Academy of Sciences L.A. Fedorov, published jointly with him this information on September 16 1992 in the N 38 issue of the weekly newspaper *Moscow News* in the article "Poisoned Policies";

- in October 1992 – to the reporter O.V. Vishnyakov from the magazine *Novoe Vremya* and with his assistance published in the N 44 issue of his magazine *Novoe Vremya* the article "The Binary Bomb has Exploded";

- in September 1992 – to the reporter William Englund of the American newspaper the *Baltimore Sun* and through him published this information in that paper on September 16, 1992 in the article "Ex Soviet Scientist Says Gorbachev's Regime Created a New Nerve Gas in 1991" , that is to say this is the commission of a crime stipulated for Part 1, Clause 75 UK RSFSR.

The Indictment was composed November 17, 1993 in Moscow.

Senior investigator of
MB RF Investigation Department
Major of Justice   V.A. Shkarin

Annex 56

Letter of U.S. Senator Bill Bradley to Strobe Talbot the Ambassador Plenipotentiary to Russia and Special Advisor on issues of the Newly Independent States, October 14, 1993.

Dear Strobe:
I am writing regarding the case of Vil Mirzayanov, the Russian chemist charged with divulging state secrets for disclosing the existence of a secret Russian chemical weapons production plant.

I am concerned by reports that Dr. Mirzayanov has been charged according to an unpublished list of state secrets drawn up after the publication of Dr. Mirzayanov's articles, in Moscow News, in violation of Article 66 of the Russian criminal code. I am also concerned that he has not had access to the prosecutor's evidence, some of which may have been falsified. It is also important that Dr. Mirzayanov's trial be open to the public, in accordance with Russian law.

Dr. Mirzayanov's allegations also have important implications for Russia's adherence to its chemical weapons commitments. It is important that the Administration follow up on the information Dr. Mirzayanov has provided.

I would encourage you to raise these concerns with the Russian government at a senior level. It is important for the development of Russia's democratic institutions that it respect the human and legal rights of people like Dr. Mirzayanov.

I look forward to your prompt response.

Sincerely,
Bill Bradley

Annex 57

Letter of John Conyers, Jr., Chairman of the Congressional Legislation and National Security Subcommittee of the Committee on Government Operations, to Warren Christopher, the U.S. Secretary of State, October 19, 1993.

"Dear Mr. Secretary,

I am writing today regarding Dr. Vil Mirzayanov, former researcher at the State Union Scientific Research Institute for Organic Chemistry and Technology in Moscow, Russia, who was arrested in October 1992 and charged with divulging state secrets. Dr. Mirzayanov recently received a Special Recognition Award for Moral Courage from the Cavallo Foundation, and his case has been the concern of numerous human rights committees.

Dr. Mirzayanov's arrest resulted from an article he co-authored which discussed a secret institute for research and development of a new generation of powerful binary chemical weapons, and the danger posed to the public from leakage of toxic chemicals by the institute into the environment. Concerned that the Institute's activities created serious health dangers to Moscow's civilian population, Dr. Mirzayanov courageously revealed that the Russian government's public call for the elimination of chemical weapons was deceptive, since new chemical weapons research was being secretly funded.

I am concerned about the charges brought against Dr. Mirzayanov -- the first person to be accused of violating Communist-era secrecy laws since the August 1991 coup -- and the actions of the Yeltsin administration. As you know, Soviet law covering state secrets became invalid when Russia became an independent state. Yet, it appears that Russian security forces continue to suppress public discussion of vital government policies.

Thus, the arrest of Dr. Mirzayanov appears to serve as a warning to other reform-minded individuals who may be contemplating exercising their newly established "democratic rights" of freedom of expression. Additionally, Dr. Mirzayanov's detention without access to an attorney and the restrictions placed on his access to evidence violate internationally accepted standards of due process.

The persecution of Dr. Mirzayanov stands in direct contradiction of the Clinton Administration's commitment to strengthen democratization efforts in the former Soviet Union, and halt the proliferation of weapons of mass destruction. I am confident that you share my deep concern over the treatment of this courageous scientist, and I call on you to personally appeal for his release.

As the only remaining super power and the leading proponent of democracy in the world, the United States is in a unique position of influence. With Dr. Mirzayanov's trial likely to begin in November, time is growing short. Please have your staff contact Ms. Randy Katsoyannis at 225-5147 to schedule a briefing on the State Department's plan to assist Dr. Mirzayanov.

I appreciate your attention to this vital matter.
Sincerely,
John Conyers, Jr.
Chairman
Legislation and National Security Subcommittee"

Annex 58

Letter of U.S. Senator Daniel Patrick Moynihan to the Secretary of State Warren Christopher, December 23, 1993.

Dear Chris:

State Secrets

I am writing to express my deep concern regarding Dr. Vil Mirzayanov, a Russian chemist who has been arrested for publishing an article in *Moskovski Novosti* (Moscow News) alleging that the Soviet Union developed and that Russia subsequently tested a new class of organophosphorous nerve gases, which are highly toxic and when are absorbed through the skin or lungs shut down the nervous system, for use as chemical weapons. This matter was brought to my attention by David Wise, a journalist of distinction and friend of thirty years, who met with Mirzayanov last month while in Moscow researching a documentary program for FRONTLINE.

In the September 16, 1992 article, Dr. Mirzayanov asserts the new nerve gasses, gas known as Novichok (Newcomer) were developed at the State Union Scientific Research Institute for Organic Chemistry and Technology in Moscow between 1987 and 1991. Dr. Mirzayanov also asserts that the chemicals have been weaponized and that they were tested in 1992. Recent articles by Vladimir Uglev, a senior researcher from the Institute have corroborated Dr. Mirzayanov's account.

As a result of his article, Dr. Mirzayanov was arrested on October 22, 1992. He has since been released but is awaiting trial on charges of divulging state secrets. However, I am informed that his work on chemical weapons was not classified until after his arrest. Specifically, I understand that on March 30, 1993 the Council of Ministers issued a decree signed by Prime Minister Victor Chernomyrdin to classify all previous work on chemical and biological weapons.

This case is particularly disturbing because the administration has just sent the Chemical Weapons Convention to the Senate Foreign Relations Committee for its ratification. Agreement was reached on this treaty on September 3, 1992, less than two weeks before Dr. Mirzayanov's article was published. His allegations are serious. If true, it means Russia may have disingenuously negotiated and signed a treaty on chemical weapons which does not prohibit its newly developed weapon because it is not listed on the detailed schedules appended to the convention.

Before the Chemical Weapons Convention is considered by the committee I think it would be appropriate for the administration to make its position on this matter clearly known to us and to report on any efforts it has made, both with regard to Dr. Mirzayanov's case and the broader more serious allegations concerning Russia's chemical weapons program. In particular, it would be important to know on what legal grounds the United States or the international community could take action to address this problem, if Dr. Mirzayanov's assertions are found to be credible.

President Clinton will be meeting with President Yeltsin in January. Would you not think it appropriate to raise this issue at that time? I look forward to hearing your views.

Sincerely,
Daniel Patrick Moynihan"

Annex 59

Letter of Dr. Wolfgang Hirschwald a professor of Berlin Free University, on behalf of the International Network of Engineers and Scientists for Global Responsibility (INES), the largest association of scientists in Germany and Western countries to Frederico Mayor, the Director General of UNESCO, December 27, 1993.

Dear Mr. Mayor,

On behalf of the German Scientists Initiative "Responsibility for the Peace" e.V. I should like to inform you about the situation of a russian colleague. It is the chemist, <u>Dr. Vil Mirzayanov</u>, who worked for the Government Research Center for Organic Chemistry and Technology (GOSNIIOKhT) in Moscow until end of January this year. Dr. Mirzayanov informed in 1991 the Lord Mayor of Moscow and thereafter in 1992 the russian public (via the journal Moscow News) about research on and development of highly toxic binary chemical weapons (8 to 10 times more toxic than the US nerve-poison VX!) in his institute and about testing of these weapons in two test areas (Saratov and Uzbekistan). Dr. M. also pointed out in his publication, that the amount of this supertoxic nerve-poison stored in his institute constituted a high danger for the environment and for the citizens of Moscow.

In October 1992 Dr. M. was arrested by the Russian Ministry of Security (former KGB), imprisoned for 11 days in the Lefortovo-Prison in Moscow and interrogated there all the time. On November 1st, 1992 Dr. M. was released from the Lefortovo-Prison, but since he has to report to the Ministry of Security frequently, he is not allowed to leave the City of Moscow, criminal proceedings are initiated against him - being charged with "divulging state secrets" - and he is examined since then nearly every day. At the end of January this year, Dr. M. was dismissed from his job at the Moscow Institute.

The trial will probably start in December 1993 or in January 1994. It will be, most probably, <u>a closed trial</u>. But what is even more severe is the fact, that the judgment and accusation will be based on an ordinance, issued on March 30, 1993, i.e. five months <u>after</u> the prosecution was initiated! (see enclosure I).

This is in contradiction to any legal procedure in democratic states. From both facts one must expect, that this trial will not be a fair and legal trial based on the principles of the Charter of the United Nations.

So, we ask the UNESCO and its Commission on Human Rights to send a protest to the Russian Government and to the General Prosecutor of Russia, Mr. Alexei Kazannik (address: see enclosure II) with respect to the procedure and ask them to quash the whole trial.

Furthermore we want to stress, that Dr. M. did <u>not</u> publish any chemical or technical details concerning the composition of the new chemical weapons nor the production process. So, he did <u>not</u> divulge any state secrets!

State Secrets

In view of the UN Convention on Chemical Weapons (CWC), signed in Paris January of 1993, Dr. M. informed the international public, that in Moscow research is still performed on super-toxic binary chemical weapons (these facts were denied by the Russian Government) and that the CW's as well as and their precursors are not listed in any of the three schedules of chemicals attached to the final draft of the Chemical Weapons Convention, nor are they included in the list of chemicals prohibited for export from Russia (again, he gave no chemical or technical details!).

From these facts one must question the seriousness of the Russian Government to fulfill the CWC, and two dangerous developments of international dimension and importance arise:

1) the possibility to circumvent the CWC,
2) the enhanced probability of CW proliferation.

We, nearly one thousand scientists of the Initiative in Germany and more than one hundred thousand international colleagues of the International Network of Engineers and Scientists for Global Responsibility (INES) are deeply concerned about this situation. We are firmly convinced, that Dr. Mirzayanov acted highly responsible and in full agreement with the UNESCO-Recommendations on the Status (in jail) would constitute a severe violation of human rights.

So, again we ask you to observe the development and to intervene in favor of Dr. Vil Mirzayanov and in order to consolidate of the CWC.

Thank you!
Sincerely,
Prof. Dr. Wolfgang Hirschwald

P.s. Facts and details submitted here do not only stem from the press, but were confirmed by Dr. Mirzayanov and his wife personally. Members of the Initiative visited Dr. M. three times this year in Moscow and his wife stayed in Germany for one week with our Initiative in October this year.

Annex 60

Letter of the American Association for the Advancement of Science to the President Boris Yeltsin, March 30, 1993

Dear Mr. President:

On behalf of the Committee on Scientific Freedom and Responsibility of the American Association for the Advancement of Science (AAAS), I am writing to express our deep concern about the situation of Russian chemist Vil Mirzayanov. Dr. Vil Mirzayanov and a colleague, Lev Fedorov, also a chemist,

Vil S. Mirzayanov

wrote an article, which was published in *Moscow News* on 20 September 1992, revealing information about the development of chemical weapons in Moscow and the possible environmental hazards posed to the local population by such research. The two men also participated in an interview published in the *Baltimore Sun*, a U.S. newspaper. Following these events the two men were arrested and their apartments were searched. Although Dr. Fedorov was released after questioning, Dr. Mirzayanov faces prosecution for allegedly divulging state secrets and violating an agreement not to reveal secret information that he signed at his place of employment, the State Union Scientific Research Institute for Organic Chemistry and Technology.

According to information the Committee has received, neither Dr. Mirzayanov nor his lawyer has been allowed to see the formal charges against Dr. Mirzayanov. This appears to violate Article 10 of the Universal Declaration of Human Rights, which states that "Everyone is entitled in full equality to a fair and public hearing by an independent and impartial tribunal, in the determination of his rights and obligations and of any criminal charge against him."

Our Committee believes that Dr. Mirzayanov, as a scientist with special knowledge about the hazards of chemicals released into the environment, has acted in a manner consistent with his professional responsibility to bring forth information about the potential or real dangers of such research. Furthermore, given the Russian participation in negotiations for a Chemical Weapons Convention, the prosecution of Dr. Mirzayanov for revealing information about the development of a binary nerve gas would appear to contradict the spirit of the Convention. The recent corroboration of another chemist, Vladimir Uglev, of Dr. Mirzayanov's account lends weight to the seriousness of Dr. Mirzayanov's report.

We urge your government to consider carefully the merits of Dr. Mirzayanov's case and Russia's obligations under the Convention. In the event that this matter cannot be resolved without bringing Dr. Mirzayanov to trial, we ask that foreign observers be allowed to attend the trial and that all legal safeguards are accorded Dr. Mirzayanov, as provided under international human rights law.

The AAAS, with 296 affilated scientific societies and 134,000 individual members, is the largest organization of natural and social scientists in the United States and the world's largest federation of scientific associations. The AAAS publishes Science magazine and concerns itself not only with substantive issues of science but also with the role of science in the world and the rights and responsibilities of scientists. The AAAS Committee on Scientific Freedom and Responsibility, formed in 1976, focuses on this latter concern and seeks to defend the professional and human rights of scientists everywhere.

Sincerely,
C.K. Gunsalus
Chair, AAAS Committee on Scientific
Freedom and Responsibility

State Secrets

cc: His Excellency Vladimir Petrovich Lukin
Mr. James F. Collins, Charge d'Affaires
Matt Bryza, Department of State
Eric Schultz, Department of State

Annex 61

Letter of the Committee of Concerned Scientists in the U.S to President of Russia Boris Yeltsin, October 25, 1993.

Dear Mr. President,

Troubled by word that the chemist Vil Mirzayanov is still slated for trial on charges of revealing state secrets, we appeal to you once again to intervene so that the case may be dismissed.

As we stated in our July 16 letter to you, the charges against Mirzayanov are based on a new list of state secrets decreed by the Council of Ministers on March 30, 1993. This list includes chemical weapons previously not so categorized. But, Mirzayanov's alleged offense stems from an article he co-authored six months earlier in Moscow News of September 16, 1992, concerning an ongoing chemical weapons development program and its impending environmental danger. Evidently, this decree is being applied retroactively in Mirzayanov's case.

We firmly believe that the positive resolution of this case is crucial to the development of the democratic society you are laboring to achieve. We therefore urge you in the strongest possible terms to see that the case is dismissed without further delay.

With best wishes for your success in establishing democracy in the Russian Federation and in contributing to world peace,

Sincerely yours,
Co-chairman Joel L. Lebowitz
Co-chairman Paul H. Plotz

Annex 62

Letter of New York Academy of Science to President of Russia Boris Yeltsin, August 25, 1993.

Dear Mr. President,

On behalf of the 39,000 members of this Academy, we are writing to express our concern for the chemist Vil Mirzayanov, who has been indicted for allegedly divulging information about "the overall thrust of research in the interests of the country's defenses" (the development of binary weapons). These charges were initiated as a result of an article he co-authored with Dr. Lev Fedorov in Moscow News of September 16, 1992, about an ongoing chemical weapons development program and its impending environmental danger.

The accusation is reported based on a new list of "state secrets" drawn up on March 30, 1993 and signed by Prime Minister Chernomyrdin. This new list includes chemical weapons previously not so categorized, and efforts have been made to make the list apply retroactively to the case. Thus it appears that his accusers are attempting to make our colleague's action retroactively illegal.

We call upon you to intervene so that the charges against Dr. Mirzayanov may be dropped and his diplomas be restored in order for him to continue his professional employment so that he may again contribute to the advancement of the human condition.

The speedy termination of this case should be looked upon at this time as an opportunity to bring about improved international and internal relations. Mutual trust between the U.S. and Russia and increasing openness will be an essential part of the disarmament and verification process.

Thank you for giving this matter your attention.

Sincerely,
Dr. Cyril Harris
cc: Procurator General of Russia V.G. Stepankov, Chairman of the Human Rights Committee Dr. Sergei Kovalev

Annex 63

Letter of the president of the Academy, Nobel Prize Laureate Joshua Lederberg to the Executive Director of the newspaper "The New York Times" Max Frankel. December 6, 1993

Dear Mr. Frankel,

Michael Gordon's December 1 article referred briefly to the arrest of Russian scientists who maintain that Russia developed a new class of deadly nerve gases.

I would like to call your attention to the central importance of the case of one of these scientists, Dr. Vil Mirzayanov, a chemist and a whistleblower who was arrested in October of 1992 presumably for allegedly revealing state secrets. At that time, no Russian law existed which had any legal bearing on his case. There was no basis for his prosecution: a secret decree was passed by the Council of Ministers on March 30, 1993, which classified all previous work on chemical and biological weapons a state secret. This decree is being used to prosecute the case retroactively, and the case was assigned to the Russian Supreme Court on Nov. 25th.

Since it is doubtful that Mirzayanov revealed any state secrets by merely mentioning this program and, furthermore, that unpublished legal norms have no legal standing, it is highly advisable that the case be promptly dismissed by either the General Procurator's office or the judge assigned to the case by the Supreme Court.

Otherwise we must conclude that Mirzayanov was telling the truth and a whole new class of deadly binary chemical weapons was created and that the Russian government is reverting to the old Soviet-style practice of persecuting dissident scientists.

Best regards,
Dr. Joshua Lederberg
President of the New York Academy of Sciences
University Professor, the Rockefeller University

Annex 64

The statement of the Andrei Sakharov Foundation in the United States on September 15, 1993.

On January 24 the trial of Dr. Mirzayanov will start in Moscow. In a throwback to old discredited practices the trial will be a closed one without independent observers allowed. Dr. Mirzayanov will be tried for disclosing information about a dangerous type of chemical weapons. The charges against him are based on law applied retroactively to cover his actions, and it seems the law was specifically designed for the purpose. These and other extremely questionable decisions by the prosecution should be sufficient for dismissal of the case for procedural grounds. But there are also important human rights principles involved.

Dr. Mirzayanov followed his conscience in making public important information. He did not pursue personal gain. The information that he released about chemical weapons was, possibly damaging to the state or, at least, to the image of some powerful governmental bodies. His actions were not illegal at the time (hence, retroactive application of the law) but they certainly pushed the envelope of things discussed publicly in Russia. If Russia is to become a fully democratic open society, there will be many other instances when the public will have a vested interest in open discussion of problems. If Dr. Mirzayanov is convicted would it mean that every time the state agencies find it unpleasant to have certain issues raised, there will be a new law adopted to retroactively punish disseminators of information? It seems that the intent of forces pushing for the prosecution of Dr. Mirzayanov is to intimidate the public and possible future dissenters. These forces within the Russian "power ministries" are afraid that they will be obligated to change their practices to more open forms suitable for democratic society, and hence relinquish old privileges that allowed, back in the days of the Soviet Union, the power structures to pursue their objectives and administrative policies free from any interference from the public or supervision by the law.

In many respects, Dr. Mirzayanov's case is a test of the ability of the "old guard" to check the democratization of Russian society and institutions. The Andrei Sakharov Foundation (USA) hopes that the legitimate interest of the state in protecting state secrets will not be used as an excuse to stifle freedom of information which is of such paramount importance in the development of Russian democracy. We urge the court to act as a truly independent branch of the Russian government and not to succumb to pressure. We hope Dr. Mirzayanov will be cleared of all charges.

signed by Alexey Semyonov [son of Elena Bonner]

Annex 65

Sergei Alexeev, Georgi Arbatov, Yuri Afansiev, Vitali Goldansky, Tatiana Zaslavskaya, Len Karpinsky, Viktor Loshak, Alexander Pumpyansky, and Grigory Yavlinsky, Mirzayanov will Face a Secret Trial, *Moscow News*, January 2, 1993.

In Moscow a closed trial process is beginning for the scientist and chemist Vil Mirzayanov. He is charged with disclosing state secrets, connected with the creation of a new kind of chemical weapon in the former USSR, to the mass media (for example, to *MN* and the magazine *Novoe Vremya*.)

During the whole period of the investigation the public was trying to stop the persecution of Vil Mirzayanov, who was saying nothing at all in the press about the technical or other secrets of the new weapons, though he only spoke out about the danger posed to the world by the double standards which were involved in their development, which has continued, even after the Soviet and Russian politicians were mouthing off that work in this area had been terminated.

It seems as though the international convention that Russia signed in January of 1993, that bans the development, production, stockpiling, and use of chemical weapons should mean that all of the charges against Mirzayanov, which are based on "sub-legal and departmental norms" and were adopted under a different regime, would automatically be dropped. However, this never happened.

The April 20, 1993 statement of the Russian Federation president reads, "The mountains of now useless and dangerous weapons are a heavy burden inherited from the legacy of our past". Then what will Vil Mirzayanov be prosecuted for?

Bitterness and bewilderment are aroused, not only by the fact of such a trial process, but also because it will be a closed one, in a country which was establishing the principles of democracy.

Far-fetched charges and a secret trial - these are the symbols of an epoch that has passed. Silence in such a situation will mean supporting lawlessness. We demand that the persecution of Vil Mirzayanov be stopped. It would be natural for the Attorney General's Office to drop the charges and thus put a full stop to the dishonest game of the groups that still yearn for their omnipotence of the past.

Annex 66

The Statement the Chairman of the U.S. Congress Committee on Government Operations, John Conyers, January 4, 1994.

"I am deeply troubled by reports that the Russian government intends to proceed with a closed trial this week in the case of Dr. Vil Mirzayanov.

Dr. Mirzayanov was a researcher who worked in the State Union Scientific Research Institute for Organic Chemistry and Technology in Russia who was arrested for divulging state secrets. His arrest resulted from an article he co-authored, which revealed that the Russian government's public call for the elimination of chemical weapons was deceptive, since new chemical weapons research was being secretly funded. Recently, he received a Special Recognition Award for Moral Courage from the Cavallo Foundation.

Secret Star Chamber proceedings are completely inconsistent with the open democratic society that Russia claims it is in the process of building. The continuation of closed and secret trials in Russia is very disturbing, especially on the eve of the upcoming Summit. Indeed, the treatment of Dr. Mirzayanov stands in stark contrast to the most important purpose of the upcoming summit – the strengthening of Russia's democratic institutions...I have asked Secretary of State Christopher to personally appeal for the release of Dr. Mirzayanov. Whistleblowers on both sides of the now defunct Iron Curtain deserve protection, not prosecution.

I have asked Secretary of State Christopher to personally appeal for the release of Dr. Mirzayanov. Whistleblowers on both sides of the now defunct Iron Curtain deserve protection, not prosecution. I know that the Clinton Administration shares my concern, and is working to see that justice is served in the Mirzayanov case."

Annex 67

Letter of the the American Association for the Advancement of Science (AAAS) to the Attorney General of Russia, Aleksei Kazannik, January 13, 1994.

Dear Attorney General Kazannik,

We understand that the trial of Dr. Vil Mirzayanov on criminal charges of having revealed state secrets has been scheduled to begin on the Moscow City Court on the morning of January 24, 1994. We further understand that an initial determination has been made that these proceedings will not be open to the public.

As the largest scientific organization in the United States, with 138,000 individual members and 296 affiliated scientific groups, the American Association for the Advancement of Science (AAAS) wishes to express serious concern about the charges that have been brought against Dr. Mirzayanov, and to strongly encourage you to permit foreign observers to witness his trial.

Our concerns are based on the fact that Dr. Mirzayanov, in making public information on chemical weapons development, storage and leakage in the Moscow region, was acting pursuant to his professional and ethical responsibilities as a scientist, and under the protection of international treaty standards regarding human rights and the regulation of chemical weapons production. Under the terms of a number of international instruments to which Russia is a party, including the Convention on the Prohibition of the Development, Production and Stockpiling of Bacteriological and Toxic Weapons, the Declaration on the Prohibition of Chemical Weapons, and the bilateral Agreement Between the United States and the U.S.S.R. on Destruction and Non-Production of Chemical Weapons, the production and storage of the chemical agents in question may well have been in violation of international law. This fact, plus the very real environmental and health hazards posed by the production and storage of these chemical agents near Moscow, placed a clear obligation on Dr. Mirzayanov to make public the information available to him on this matter, consistent with his ethical and professional responsibilities as a scientist working on the project.

Russia also is bound by a number of international human rights instruments whose provisions would apply to the Mirzayanov case, including assurances against arbitrary arrest and prosecutions, and the guarantee of a fair and <u>public hearing,</u> in Articles 9 and 10 of the Universal Declaration of Human Rights, and Articles 9 through 14 of the International Covenant on Civil and Political Rights.

The fact, thankfully, that Russia and the nations of the West are no longer in a state of "cold war" adds a powerful practical reason why "state secret" laws should not be applied in this case. Holding the criminal proceedings against Dr. Mirzayanov in secret only adds to the concern that standards of international human rights and justice are not being properly observed. The criminal prosecution and the holding of the trial with closed proceedings are inconsistent with the new spirit of openness and cooperation between our two countries that most recently is demonstrated by the visit of President Clinton to Russia that is taking place this week. Nothing would be a more appropriate follow-up to this visit, and the cordial meetings between Presidents Clinton and Yeltsin that are now taking place, than to permit U.S. observers at the trial, or better still, dropping all charges against Dr. Mirzayanov. Over the past few years, Russia has made substantial forward strides in releasing its political prisoners and eliminating the past practice of secret trials. The Mirzayanov prosecution and secret trial is an unfortunate and very surprising throwback to past practices under the totalitarian regime.

We would appreciate any efforts and assistance you can provide in bringing this petition and the guarantees to a public trial in the Universal Declaration and the Civil and Political Rights Covenant to the attention of the appropriate prosecutors and judges dealing with the Mirzayanov case. Please let us know as soon as possible if it is decided to open the trial to foreign observers, so that we can make the necessary arrangements for a representative to attend.

Sincerely,
C.K. Gunsalus, Chair
AAAS Committee on Scientific
Freedom and Responsibility

Annex 68

Letter of the Federation of American Scientists to the Attorney General of Russia, Aleksei Kazannik, January 14, 1994

Dear Sir:

As the attached resolution shows, the Federation of American Scientists, founded in 1945 by Manhattan Project atomic scientists, has been concerned about the Mirzayanov case for more than a year.

We appeal to you to ensure that he receives a fair trial. Our letter is prompted by our learning that the trial would be a closed one. And we have been advised that the statute under which he is to be tried is one that did not exist at the time the crime is alleged.

The Mirzayanov case is a famous one now in the American scientific community and has been discussed, as we understand it, at the highest levels of our two Governments. For these reasons, we do hope that it can be resolved in a way that maintains the respect of all concerned.

Thank you in advance for any help or advice you can provide to Mirzayanov or to us.

Sincerely,

Jeremy J. Stone
President

Annex 69

Letter of the U.S. National Academy of Science to President Yeltsin, January 19, 1994.

Excellency:

We write to you on behalf of the Committee on Human Rights of the U.S. National Academy of Sciences which is deeply concerned about the plight of scientific colleague Vil Mirzayanov, a Russian chemist who will reportedly be brought to trial on January 24, 1994, in a closed session at the Moscow City Court. Dr. Mirzayanov has been charged with violating state secrets by making public statements about ongoing research and development of chemical weapons in Russia.

According to information available to the committee, Dr. Mirzayanov revealed only nontechnical information about chemical weapons, and he took such action in an effort to inform the Russian people and others about a clear danger. The committee also understands that revealing information about chemical weapons research and development was not illegal at the time that Dr. Mirzayanov made his public statements. The Russian Federation added chemical weapons research and development to its unpublished list of state secrets on March 30, 1993 --more than five months after charges had been brought against Dr. Mirzayanov. The new of Russian Constitution does not permit laws to be used retroactively.

We appeal to the Russian government to drop the charges against Dr. Mirzayanov because they are in clear violation of the Russian Constitution.

If the charge is not dropped, we would expect the Russian government to grant Dr. Mirzayanov a fair trial, and we would appeal that it be open in accordance with the U.N. Universal Declaration of Human Rights. Dr. Mirzayanov acted on the dictates of his conscience and, if accorded due process, he would be exonerated on the grounds that he exercised his right to the free speech and did not reveal information that was, at the time, officially recognized as a state secret.

Sincerely yours,

Bruce Alberts
President

James B. Wyngaarden
Foreign Secretary

Annex 70

Letter of the President of New York Academy of Science Joshua Lederberg to the Attorney General of the Russian Federation Alexei Kazannik, January 20, 1994.

The New York Academy of Sciences has received notification that Dr. Vil Mirzayanov will be brought to trial for actions protected under international agreements and required under ethical standards of scientific responsibility.

We ask that charges against Dr. Mirzayanov be dropped and that international observers be permitted to attend the trial on January 24, 1994.

The freedom of scientists to call the attention of the world to possible transgressions by elements of their government is an elementary part of the scientific freedom. The abuse of that freedom undermines the foundations of confidence in the trustworthiness of governments in their international relations.

Joshua Lederberg, Ph.D.
President
New York Academy of Sciences

Annex 71

Letter of the Committee of Concerned Scientists appealed to Attorney General Alexei Kazannik, January 19, 1994.

Dear Sir:

As an organization dedicated to the protection and advancement of the human rights and scientific freedom of colleagues around the world, we are dismayed to learn that a closed trial beginning January 24 is planned in the case of the chemist Vil Mirzayanov.

We ask you to do all in your power to avert it. A closed trial only compounds the injustice of the fact that this case is being prosecuted retroactively based on a new list of state secrets.

If this trial takes place in camera, it will suggest that Russia has indeed created a new group of binary chemical weapons. We therefore urge in the strongest possible terms to stop this prosecution lest it cast a pall on your country's declared intent to join with other nations in banning the development of chemical weaponry.

Sincerely yours

Co-chairman   Joel L. Lebowitz
Co-chairman   Paul H. Plotz

Annex 72

Letter of Academician Roald Sagdeev to the Attorney General of Russia Aleksei Kazannik. January 21, 1993 to Mr. Alexei Kazannik, Procurator General of Russia
(copy to Academician Y. Osipov, President of the Russian Academy of Sciences.)

Esteemed General Procurator:

Let me appeal to You, as Your colleague from the Congress of Peoples Deputies of the former USSR. As one of the most memorable episodes of that time, I remember your noble act, which enabled Boris Yeltsin to become a leader of Democrats in the Supreme Soviet.

Now, when democracy seems to be a winner, Your urgent intervention is needed again, -this time in a different case – in a trial against the scientist-chemist Vil Mirzayanov.

I would not go into details of allegations against Mirzayanov, who is accused in the breach of secrecy. If we were able to defeat the cold war and start the complete destruction of chemical weapons what kind of secrets should be hidden from the world public? The very fact of continuation of further research and development of new types of chemical warfare?

In the eyes of the international community, the trial of Mirzayanov can only bring irreparable damage to the politics of Russian leadership and to the very cause of peace.

It is not so much a guilt, but a tragedy of a whole generation of scientists and engineers forced to spend their talents in making the weapons of mass destruction. The voice of Mirzayanov - the voice of the conscience of a whole generation – must be heard and not strangled.

Academician Roald Sagdeev,
University of Maryland

Annex 73

Letter of the Lawyers Committee for Human Rights of the U.S. to the President of Russia.
January 21, 1994

Dear President Yeltsin,

The trial of Dr. Vil Mirzayanov, a former researcher with the State Union Scientific Research Institute for Organic Chemistry and Technology in Russia, is scheduled to begin on January 24th. The Lawyers' Committee for Human Rights is concerned by the conditions and procedures surrounding the upcoming trial.

First, according to information we have received, Mr. Mirzayanov's arrest resulted from an article he co-authored, which asserted that the Russian government continues to fund chemical weapons research.

Mr. Mirzayanov will be tried for disclosing information about Russian chemical weapons production. These charges are based upon a law that did not exist at the time he wrote the article. He is charged with a violation of resolution # 256-16 of March 30, 1993. Under that provision the Council of Ministers made changes to the "Temporary List of Categories of Data Considered State Secrets," which was adopted by the Government of the Russian Federation on September 18, 1992 in resolution # 733-55.

Hence, the law is being applied retroactively, denying Mr. Mirzayanov the basic right to be notified and adequately informed of the charges against him. Article 15 of the International Covenant on Civil and Political Rights, of which Russia is a signatory, states that: "No one shall be held guilty of a criminal offence on account of any act or omission which did not constitute a criminal offence, under national or international law, at the time when it was committed."

Ex post fact prosecution is also prohibited by Article 15 of the Russian Constitution. In paragraph 3 stated that, "Unpublished laws shall not be applicable." Additionally, Article 54, paragraph 1 of the new Constitution stated: "The law instituting or aggravating the liability of a person shall have no retroactive force."

We are disturbed to learn of the Russian government's intention to hold a secret trial closed to all observers. Secret proceedings are inherently inconsistent with the open democratic society Russia is ostensibly committed to building. We request therefore that the Russian government permit independent Russian and international observers to attend the trial.

Mr. Mirzayanov's case is an important test of the Russian government's commitment to respect human rights and build just legal institutions. We urge you to ensure that the courts act as a truly independent branch of government, according to the rule of law and free from government pressure.

Sincerely,
Michael Posner
Executive director

Annex 74

Letter of the Physicians for Social Responsibility to the Alexsei Kazannik, General Procurator of the Russian Federation. January 21, 1994

Dear Procurator General,

I understand that the closed trial of Dr. Vil Mirzayanov is scheduled to begin on Monday, 24 January in Moscow City Court.

During my visit to your country last year, I was fortunate to be able to meet with Dr. Mirzayanov and we had a number of long talks together. At the time I made his acquaintance, I was very impressed by his sincerity, his integrity and his strong love of his country. It was not selfish motivation, but Dr. Mirzayanov's deep patriotism and his true concern for the welfare of his fellow Muscovites that prompted him to act, to try to draw attention to and to correct environment environmentally dangerous practices of his institute and the chemical-military complex. I personally feel a strong common bond with this courageous man, recognizing that his motives are the same as those that led me to release the Pentagon Papers.

Fortunately for all of us, we are living in different times now, the beginning of a post-Cold War Era. We must recognize however, that for the arms control agreements we are forging to have any real meaning, it is essential that they be verifiable by citizens. In Stalinist times, Dr. Mirzayanov would have been considered an enemy of the state. Now he should be recognized for what he is, a pioneer in creating a new, needed international norm of citizen responsibility, a man on the cutting edge of reform and democracy in your country. Silencing Mirzayanov and others like him will not help your country solve environmental problems or reduce the threat posed by chemical accidents that could happen at any time. Silencing them will serve to reduce the world's confidence in Russia's stated intentions to comply with international accords. And it will reduce Russian citizen's confidence in their government's ability to change or be honest about mistakes of the past which directly threatened the lives of many people.

One of your officials has mentioned to some people in our country that the Mirzayanov trial is a small thing, something of little importance. Instead, I think you will find that the Mirzayanov case is of critical importance to us, at the center of much that we value and honor most in our culture - freedom of speech, the of the scientist to disclose information to prevent a greater danger, the official who recognizes a loyalty to the constitution and to his countrymen that is more important than the rules of his agency, the ecologist against the polluters, anyone who rallies against weapons of mass destruction, a man who has exposed the corruption and incompetence of more powerful people.

The Mirzayanov case is an immediate legal litmus test of emerging Russian democracy. He is an individual in the true tradition of Andrei Sakharov, a man persecuted under the former regime for telling the truth, but now, rightfully, universally honored. I urge you to take the high road and use your authority to have the case dismissed immediately. There a number of statutes of the new Russian Constitution that can be referenced as grounds for dismissal. Furthermore, I would urge you to call for an intensive investigation by your office into the allegations Dr. Mirzayanov and others have made about secret chemical weapons programs and unsafe practices in the chemical military.
With respect,

Daniel Ellsberg

Annex 75

Letter of the American Physical Society to the President of Russia, Boris Nikoloyevich Yeltsin.
January 24, 1994

Dear President Yeltsin:

The Committee on the International Freedom of Scientists (CIFS) at the American Physical Society, a 43,000 member organization of physicists, is charged with monitoring the human rights situation of physicists and other scientists around the world, and advocating for those requiring assistance.

It has come to our attention that Dr. Vil Mirzayanov, a Russian chemist who publicized information concerning production of binary nerve gases in the Moscow vicinity, will be brought to trial on criminal charges concerning this publicity on January 26, 1994. Further, it is our understanding that Dr. Mirzayanov's trial will not be open to foreign observers.

It is troubling that Dr. Mirzayanov will be brought to trial for acting in accordance with at least two international treaties to which the Russian Federation is a signatory nation, the Convention on Chemical Disarmament and the Declaration on the Prohibition of Chemical Weapons, which both specifically prohibit chemical weapons production. We respectfully request that Dr. Mirzayanov's trial be open to international observers and that the charges against him be dropped.

Thank you for your attention to this matter. We look forward to your reply.

Sincerely yours,
Fang Lizhi,
Chair
Committee on the International Freedom of Scientists

Annex 76

The Extract from the Congressional Record – Senate. (February 1, 1994. S.S.543-544). *Library of Congress*. http: //thomas.loc.gov/cgi-bin

Mr. DeConcini: Mr. President, I would like to call to the attention of my colleagues today a closed trial that opened in Moscow last Monday, January 24. A Russian scientist named Vil Mirzayanov is being tried on charges of exposing state secrets.

As chairman of the Senate Intelligence Committee, I most assuredly believe a nation has a right to preserve certain secrets related to national security. But let's look at the particulars of this case.

Dr. Mirzayanov is a Moscow scientist and chemist who in 1992, on the basis of his work in a secret laboratory in Moscow, disclosed in the Russian and Western press that Russia was continuing to test chemical weapons despite having signed international agreements banning such tests. Subsequently, Dr. Mirzayanov was arrested and briefly held in custody in October 1992. He was then kept under house arrest until January 24, 1994, when his trial convened.

What Dr. Mirzayanov did must have infuriated some influential members of the Russian military-industrial complex, although it was apparently not illegal under Russian law at that time. Therefore, authorities prevailed upon Prime Minister Chernomyrdin to sign a retroactive secret decree in March 1993 to make Mirzayanov's allegations a crime. It hardly seems likely that a government supposedly commited to rule of law would hold a citizen liable for violating a decree not made public. Incidentally, the new Russian Constitution quite sensibly forbids using secret decrees as basis for criminal charges.

Human rights activists and members of the scientific community have come to

Dr. Mirzayanov's defense, both in terms of the legality of his trial and with respect to the substance of Dr. Mirzayanov's allegations that Russia is continuing chemical weapons testing. Dr. Joshua Lederberg, president of the New York Academy, has called for the charges against Dr. Mirzayanov to be dropped. "Otherwise", he notes, "we must conclude that Mirzayanov was telling the truth and a whole new class of deadly binary chemical weapons was created and that the Russian Government is reverting to the old Soviet-style practice of presecuting dissident scientists." I would note also that the respected Russian scientist and academic Roald Sagdeev has written that "the trial of Mirzayanov can only bring irreparable moral harm to the policies of the Russian Government and indeed the entire cause of peace."

The administration has also been following this case closely. Ambassodor Pickering in Moscow has called it "more than strange and more than usual that someone could be either prosecuted or persecuted for telling the truth about an activity which is contrary to a treaty obligation of a foreign government." I'd say that's putting it mildly, considering the nature of the treaty obligations.

The Mirzayanov trial involves more than the fate of one man. It is foreboding indication of the direction toward which Russia may be heading in the post-cold war era. Who is in charge here, civilians operating under the rule of law, or a military-industrial complex that can pull secret regulations out of a hat when challenged?

I hope that good will, common sense, and the rule of law prevail in Moscow. Many conscientious Russians, in and out of government, are seeking justice for Dr. Mirzayanov. The Commission on Security and Cooperation in Europe, of which I am pleased to serve as chairman, is proud to join in their efforts. Along with Commission co-chairman Representative Steny Hoyer, I have written to Ambassador Lukin and asked him to convey our deepest concerns about the Mirzayanov trial to President Yeltsin. I hope that others will join us. *Library of Congress.* http://www.thomas.loc.gov/cgi-bin

Annex 77

RESOLUTION

on the termination of the criminal case

Moscow   March 11, 1994

A.N. Ilyushenko Acting Attorney General of the Russian Federation has considered the materials of criminal case No 62-92 that were sent from the Moscow City Court for conducting an additional investigation,

Vil S. Mirzayanov

IT IS ESTABLISHED:

From 1965 until January 1992 V. S. Mirzayanov held various scientific positions at the State Russian Science Research Institute for Organic Chemistry and Technology (GRNIIOKhT), and from 1986 until 1990 he was head of the Department for Foreign Technical Counterintelligence. According to his job responsibilities he was informed about the system of organization, the major trends, and some of the results of the scientific-research and the experimental-design work in the area of the development of chemical weapons.

After he was dismissed from the institute in January 1992 due to staff reductions, Mirzayanov made an attempt to draw the attention of the public to the possible ecological danger of the utilization of chemical agents. With this goal in mind, he prepared materials for publication and gave interviews to the various members of the mass media about the problems of the development of toxic chemicals in Russia.

According to the materials of the criminal case, on September 16, 1992 issue 38 of the weekly newspaper *Moscow News* and the American newspaper the *Baltimore Sun*, as well as issue 44 of October 1992 of the magazine *Novoe Vremya* published articles and the interview of Mirzayanov "Poisoned Policies," "Former Soviet Scientist Says that the Regime of Gorbachev Created a New Paralytic-Nerve Agent in 1991," and "The Binary Bomb has Exploded," in which it was reported that a new chemical agent had been created in the former Soviet Union and new binary weapons had been developed based on it.

These articles served as a basis for criminal proceedings charging Mirzayanov with a crime stipulated by Part 1, Article 75 of the RSFSR Criminal Code.

During the preliminary and court investigations Mirzayanov pleaded not guilty to disclosing state secrets and explained that he had only intended to warn the public, by way of a general outline, of the threat and possible consequences of the creation of chemical weapons.

According to the conclusion of the expert commission-specialists dated March 16, 1993, which was presented in the preliminary investigation, information published in the articles constituted state secrets, according to "List of Major Information of state secrecy" approved by the Resolution No 1121-387 of the U.S.S.R. Council of Ministers dated December 3, 1980.

At the same time, during the repeated examination in court, the specialists V.V. Smirnitsky and N.I. Chugunov explained that the analysis of normative documents allowed these questions to be studied in more detail. In the opinion of these experts, not one of the publications based on the materials presented by Mirzayanov or his interview contained specific information that constituted state secrets. Concepts and terms: chemical weapons, chemical agents, binary weapons, their development and production were excluded from the list of state secrets in 1984. In the publications nothing specific was disclosed about the newest achievements in this area of science and technology, or the factual data about the results of scientific research, experimental-design work, or field testing of the samples of chemical weapons, information which really constitutes state secrets, according to the above-mentioned "List..."

Thus, Mirzayanov appeared as a bearer of secret information, but didn't disclose specific information of state secrecy and can't be criminally responsible, according to Part 1, Article 75 of the RSFSR Criminal Code.

Moreover, according to Articles 15 and 29 of the Constitution of Russia, unpublished normative acts, which "The List..." refers to, and due to the absence of federal law "about the lists of information of state secrecy" the legal basis for Mirzayanov's possible criminal responsibility for communicating information about the development of new chemical weapons is precluded.

Under such circumstances, the resolution of the panel of judges for criminal cases at the Moscow City Court dated February 14, 1994 about returning the current criminal case for conducting an additional investigation doesn't entail the necessity of fulfilling any additional investigation procedures, because the absence of grounds for attaching criminal responsibility to V. S. Mirzayanov has been established with sufficient completeness by the preliminary and court investigations.

Based on the aforementioned and being guided by Clause 2, Article 5, Part 1, Article 208, and Article 209 of the RSFSR Criminal and Procedrual Code,

IT IS RULED:

1. To dismiss the criminal case, according to which Vil Sultanovich Mirzayanov born on March 9, 1935 was charged with committing a crime stipulated by Part 1 Article 75 of the RSFSR Criminal Code, because of the absence of corpus delicti in his actions and to inform the interested people.
2. To cancel the preventive detention [house arrest]- a written pledge not to leave Moscow - executed by the Kalinin District People's Court of Moscow on November 2, 1992.
3. To return the passport of Vil S. Mirzayanov to its owner.

Acting Attorney General
of the Russian Federation A. N. Ilyushenko

Annex 78

U.S. Senate (Congressional Record. Proceedings and Debates of the 103d Congress, First Session. Vol.140, No. 28. Washington, Tuesday, March 15, 1994.) Senator Patrick Moynihan read as follows:

"Mr. Moynihan: Madam President, on March 11, good news was heard from Moscow. All charges were dropped against a courageous Russian scientist, Dr. Vil Mirzayanov who, 2 years ago in a Moscow News article, revealed to the world that the Soviet Union had secretly developed a powerful binary nerve gas. For this, Dr. Mirzayanov was jailed twice, and placed on trial.

David Wise, who brought this case to my attention, is a noted and respected author who has written extensively about the dangers of excessive secrecy and about the operations of intelligence agencies. Mr. Wise spoke at great length with Dr. Mirzayanov in Moscow last November. Upon his return he contacted me. I was proud to add my voice to that of the many scientific and human rights organizations that have worked to free Dr. Mirzayanov. In particular, I would like to commend the efforts of two individuals, Gale M. Colby and Irene Goldman.

As Mr. Wise points out, although Dr. Mirzayanov no longer faces criminal charges, important questions remain about Russia's intentions in the field of nerve gas production. This case is particularly disturbing because agreement was reached on the chemical weapons convention in Geneva less than 2 weeks before Dr. Mirzayanov published his article.

In his article, David Wise wrote that it was a moral realization that gave Dr. Mirzayanov the courage to speak out. We can do no less. I trust that these questions will continue to be carefully pursued by our Government and the Senate as ratification of the chemical weapons convention is considered.

Madam President, at this time I ask that David Wise's article from the March 12, 1994, *New York Times* be placed in the Record.

There being no objection, the article was ordered to be printed in the Record, as follows.

Index

A-262, 145
Abdrazakov, Ildar, 30
Academy: of Chemical Defense, 41, 49, 66, 68, 90, 108, 120, 128, 131, 133, 137, 147, 162, 179, 215, 216, 243, 302, 425; of Sciences, National (USA), 373, 408; New York, 3, 366, 373, 408, 447; of U.S.S.R. (Russia), 11, 40, 60, 62, 63, 67, 91, 107, 111-113, 120, 126, 146
Activated carbon, 67, 188
Adsorbent, 67, 157, 187; inorganic, 200
Afanasiev, Yuri, 240, 367
Agence France Presse, 405, 408
Aglyamova, Sag'dat, 29
Agureev, Vyacheslav, 253
Aida, by G. Verdi, 37
Ames, Aldrich, 2, 3
Ak-ebi, 16, 17
All-Russia Channel Two, 372
All-Tatar Public Center, 332, 339
Alekseev, Sergei, 250, 302, 367
Aluminum oxide, 200, 201
Amendola, J., 319
America, United States of, 2, 15, 98, 109, 133, 261, 262, 367; Voice of, 24-28, 309
American (-s), 357, 359, 425, 429, 431, 447; agent, 128, 237; Association for the Advancement of Science, 365, 372; bank, 278; binary weapon, 126; Chemical Society, 318, 366, 408; chromatograph, 139; correspondent, 261, 429; defoliant, 163; democracy, 305; dollar (-s), 13, 133; edition, 418; glass sample, 161; intervention, 235; Information Press Center, 386, 390; intelligence community, 222; invention, 139; journalist, 343, 389, 431, 426; law, 227, 308; legislators, 316; manufacturer, 189; military chemists, 123, 235; organization, 374; people, 2, 227; Physical Society, 374, 408; position, 405; public, 372, 386, 407; radio, 24; satellite, 136; scientists, 122, 317; scientific equipment, 133, 196; soldiers, 237; specialists, 222; troops, 27, 236; version, 139; VX gas, 303
Angarsk, 51
Arabic alphabet, 8
Arbat Street, 356, 359
Arbatov, Georgi, 312, 313, 367
Aral Sea, 438
Arkhipova, Irina, 37
Argumenti i Facti, 272
Arnold, Andrei, 287, 346
Aum Shinrikyo, 2, 281

Asnis, Aleksander, 113, 255, 256, 284, 286, 291, 299, 300, 302, 307, 311, 315, 321, 323, 337, 363, 364, 368, 376-390, 403, 404, 406, 407, 412, 420, 423, 428, 434-436, 442, 444-446
Associated Press, 405, 442
Attorney, defense, 270, 280, 286, 293, 294, 300, 369, 379, 406, 412; General, 299, 318-320, 363, 366, 372-374, 376, 388, 389, 408, 434, 440, 443, 445; Deputy of, 300, 320; General's Office, 298-300, 308, 344, 345, 362-364, 379, 381, 426, 440, 442, 444, 446
Azatlyk, Tatar broadcast, 369
Ayala, Dr. Francisco J., 2, 4

Baghdad, 19
Baika, 9
Bainazarova, Irene (Ira), 33-35
Balashov, Sergei, 299, 309, 342
Baltic republics, 240 436, 438, 439
Baltimore Sun, 150, 261, 265, 267, 425, 430, 442
Baranaev, Michael, 162
Barannikov, Victor, 266, 301, 360
Baranov, Lev, 446
Baranov, Yuri, 106
Baranovskoe, 247, 350, 359
Barrer, R.P., 68
Basalt, NPO (Scientific Industrial Association), 126, 166, 167
Bashkir (-s), 6-8, 25, 32, 330, 418; music, 24
Bashkirov, Andrey, 49, 51-53, 68
Bashkortstan, 6, 8, 9, 25, 26, 51, 102, 351, 367
Batova, Elena, 209
Baturin, Yuri, 408, 418
Bayanov, Madkhat and Favaris, 26
BBC, 251, 309, 333
Beketovka, 125, 201

Belarus, 159, 330
Belaya River, 8, 11, 21, 31, 399
Belgorod, 52
Belikov, Valeri, 180, 188
Belomestnykh, Leonid, 270, 284
Belousov, Rem, 46, 47
Beregova, Tamara, 170
Beresnev, Aleksei, 75, 76, 79, 90, 95, 139, 154, 170, 172-176, 182, 194
Berezkin, Victor, 75
Beria, Lavrentii, 28, 36, 45, 160, 161
Bethel, N., Lord, 444
Bettini, V., 319
Binary, 164, 246, 262; agents, 262, 265; bomb, 124, 340; chemical agent, 125; compound, 246; components, 125, 325; device, 167; form, 325; nerve agents, 220; program, 270, 271; reactor, 123; rocket, 166, 167; system, 340; tests, 262; variant, 262; version, 122; weapon (-s), 119, 123, 126-128, 139, 140, 142, 149-151, 167, 192, 211, 220, 221, 261, 271, 272, 277, 283, 303, 304, 310, 322, 325, 327, 335, 336, 373, 428, 429
Biological Weapons, 141, 207, 217, 342,
"Blue-8", 123
Bogdanov, Nikolai, 159, 160, 242
Bogomazov, Yevgeni, 84, 147, 169, 179, 180-183, 185-193
Bolshoi Theatre, 37, 38
Bonner, Elena, 409
Borai, 18
Boranes, 55, 60-63, 158; di-, 56, 58, 60
Bradley, Bill, 365, 408
Braun, Reiner, 360
Breher, Ch., 319
Brezhnev, Leonid, 190
Brovkin, Lev, 94, 95, 104, 132, 155
Buasier, B., 319

Bugrov, Yuri, 104, 105
Bujnitski, Yuri, 61
Buivolov, Vladimir, 294, 309, 344, 364
Burganov, Agdas, 319
Buzaev, Vladimir, 234
BZ, western hallucinogen, 128

Cathedral of Ivan the Great, 354
Caucasus, 8, 248, 394, 397;
Caucasian, 45
Cassidy, Joseph, 128-130
Cavallo, Michael, 434; Foundation, 2, 356, 357, 359
Central Committee of CPSU, 41, 46, 48, 49, 98, 101, 109, 113, 126, 143, 150, 151, 167, 180, 188, 207, 209, 210, 210, 233, 310, 347
Chapaevsk, 153
Chechen, 333, 351; leader, 354; Republic, 354
Chefir, 395, 398, 402
Chekist (-s), 28, 76, 92, 206, 209, 230, 235, 245, 250, 251, 266, 267, 272-274, 276-278, 283, 286, 295, 299-301, 308, 312, 315, 335, 336, 342, 349, 358, 372, 376, 389, 411, 430, 431
Chemical (-s), 87, 89, 136, 141, 148, 149, 154, 162, 167, 170, 197, 201, 220, 231, 263, 402, 409, 426; agent (-s), 42, 43, 61, 67, 75, 76, 80, 83, 87, 88, 92-95, 99, 102, 104, 112, 119, 123, 125-129, 131,132, 135, 138, 139, 142, 144, 146-148, 150-154, 158, 160, 162-164, 166, 167, 169, 179-181, 183, 185-188, 191-193, 195, 198-202, 204-206, 215, 219-223, 229-233, 235-237, 243, 252, 265, 271, 272, 277, 303-305, 310, 322, 323, 325-327, 336, 338 341, 355, 375, 381; A-230, 190, 192; A-232, 147, 219, 341; analysis, 104; arms, 163, 228, 237, 294; battalion, 46, 132, 164; binaries, 271; career, 63; college, 109; complex, 112, 149, 154; composition, 122, 236, 350; compound (-s), 98, 125, 136, 178, 183, 196, 213, 219, 236, 250; constants, 42; defense, 41, 42, 66, 68, 90, 108, 111, 120, 126, 128, 131, 133, 136, 137, 147, 162, 179, 215, 216, 243, 302, 338, 425; defoliation, 163; destruction, 236; disarmament, 140, 150, 325; engineers, 152; engineering, 52; formula (-s), 83, 84, 322; industry, 48, 49, 61, 88, 95, 98, 102, 104, 107, 108,113-115, 126, 153,156, 158, 190, 200, 203, 206, 207, 211, 212, 214, 216, 217, 232, 243, 253, 338; information, 423; Institute, 62, 67, 132; laboratory, 79; name, 84; notation, 83; officer, 198; plant, 36, 51, 52, 61, 103, 122, 164, 190, 202, 220, 272, 329; precursors, 243; poisoning, 149; products, 51, 102, 219; properties, 96, 121, 237; science (-s), 66, 97, 128, 129, 133, 140, 152, 154, 164, 254, 400; "sharashka", 232; shells, 326; specialist, 237; solvent, 75; Technical Institute, 99, 206; technology, 153; troops, 108, 123, 132, 140, 147, 164, 180, 189, 220, 302, 340; war, 237; warfare arsenal, 191; weapons, 49, 51, 96, 97, 105, 106, 109, 110-112, 123, 129, 130, 137, 140, 141, 148, 150, 163, 167, 182, 183, 187, 207, 214, 215, 217, 220, 225, 227, 234, 235, 237, 243-246, 249, 250, 259-263, 265, 266, 271, 274, 277, 282, 287, 288, 302, 304, 305, 308, 310, 316-319, 322, 323, 325-329, 337-346, 349, 351-356, 358, 362, 365, 366, 373, 375, 418, 422, 425, 428-430, 439
Chemical and Engineering News, 375, 442
Chemical Weapons, 137, 148, 214, 215, 225, 277, 294, 303, 305, 309,

325, 343, 345
Cheredilov, A.M., 274
Chernomyrdin, Victor, 342
China, 52, 53, 374
Chinese, 374, 393
Chizhov, Evgeni, 128, 311
Cholinesterase, 136, 170, 191, 203, 204, 216
Chlorine, 201, 229
Christian Science Monitor, 442
Chromatography, 64-67, 71, 93-95, 132, 173, 187, 191, 193, 217; Laboratory, 79
Chromatographic, analysis, 64, 71, 184, 185, 196; instruments, 93, 94, 133; isolation, 129; methods, 93-95, 102, 123, 133, 151, 164, 170, 202; peaks, 184; problems, 92; research, 71 Chromatograms, 184
Chromatograph, 64, 93, 95, 98, 99, 125, 132, 139, 155, 182, 183, 186, 188-190, 196, 217, 241
Chromatomass-spectrometers, 98, 178, 213, 217, 235, 241, 242
Christopher, Warren, 365, 368
Chugunov, Nikolai, 324, 336, 338-340, 379, 424, 425
Churchill, Winston, 27
CIA, 347
Civil war, 18, 163, 351
Clinton, Bill, 318, 365, 366, 387
CNN, 360
Colby (Mirzayanov), Gale, 287, 315, 342, 347, 350, 356, 359, 372, 404, 421, 432, 435, 441, 447
Commission for Human Rights in the European Parliament, 444
Committee for Conventional Problems of Chemical and Biological Weapons, 207, 217, 302, 329, 352, 354, 358
Committee for Ecology, 328
Committee for Radio and Television, 353
Committee of Concerned Scientists, 366, 373, 408
Committee of Constitutional Supervision, 320, 321
Committee of Emergency Situations, 410
Committee of Government Operations, 365, 368
Committee of the International Freedom of Scientists, 326
Committee on Legislative Matters, 321, 322
Communist(-s), 6, 7, 9, 10, 19, 23, 47, 48, 129, 217, 248, 334, 349, 350-353, 376, 437; balalaika, 92; convictions, 385; deputies, 350; friendship, 91; ideals, 114; kingdom, 46; leader (-s), 330, 332, 411; morals, 48; newspaper, 286; opposition, 360; Party, 19, 41, 63, 100, 167, 188, 317; power, 240; regime, 248, 370, 376, 403; reporter, 367; tyrants, 414
Convention for the Prohibition of Chemical Weapons, 137, 148, 214, 215, 225, 277, 294, 303, 305, 309, 325, 343, 345
Conyers, John, 338
Corpus delicti, 315, 391
Cossack, 5

Danilin, Michael, 128
DeConcini, Dennis, 418
Demin, Yuri, 301, 302, 342
Demidyuk, Valeri, 129
Democratic Russia Movement, 101, 239, 249, 254, 255, 261, 311
Demon, by A. Rubinshtein, 37
Dengiran, M.-M., 319
Denisenko, V., 320
Diffusion in and through Solids, 68
Directorate of the, Chief of Chemical Troops (UNKhV), 123, 132, 140, 147, 183; institute, 68, 69
Djirtjuli, 8, 18, 21, 29, 30
Djuzhev-Maltsev, Valerij, 144, 147,

170, 172, 193
Dmitriev, Aleksander, 179, 182, 184
Dmitriev, German, 311
Dmitriev, Victor, 159, 246
Dobrianski, Vsevolod, 92
Drozd, Georgi, 121, 122, 126, 137-141, 163, 170, 194
Drell, Efim, 195, 196
Dubin, Boris, 125, 153, 155,156
Dubinin, Michael, 66, 67, 179
Dubov, Semyon, 176-178, 181, 182, 187
Dudaev, Dzhochar, 334
Duka, Nikolai, 207
Dukhovich, Felix, 128
Duma, 165, 301, 367, 376, 445

Echo Moskva, 325
Efron, Soni, 371
Eliel, Ernst, 318
Ellsberg, Daniel, 226, 227-228, 302, 357, 358, 374, 386, 441
Eltsov, Yu., 320
Emelianenkov, Aleksander, 357
Englin, Michael, 92, 93, 131, 132, 136, 137, 179
Englund, William, 260-262, 265, 267, 342, 343, 358, 425, 429, 430, 431, 433
ENITI, 186, 187
Ernst, B., 319
Ermakov, Yuri, 62
Evstafeev, Igor, 132, 136, 137
Evtushenko, K., 320
Evzirikhin, Evgeni, 127
Expert Commission, 169, 216, 218, 282, 307, 309-312, 315, 322, 324, 335, 337, 339, 340, 344, 346, 364, 376, 379, 380, 432

Fanin, Nikolai, 272
Faust, by Ch.Gounod, 38
Federal Agency for Government Communications and Information (FAPSI), 309
Federation of American Scientists (FAS), 316, 372, 408
Fedorov, Lev, 140, 259, 260-262, 264-266 272- 274, 276, 283, 284, 308, 327, 358, 359, 422, 427-430
Fedyachkin, Michael, 92
Filatov, Sergei, 352, 353
Filippova, Maria, 29
Fokin, Evgeni, 92, 126
Florichi, 43
Foliant, secret program, 138, 169, 181, 186, 190, 209
Forov, Vladimir, 104
Frankel, Max, 367
Funygin, G., 345
Furtseva, Ekaterina, 47

Gabov, Igor, 156, 219, 308, 340, 345
Gabsatarov, Minkamal (grandfather), 18
Gaidar, Egor, 257, 258
Galimov, Rifkat, 318
Garipov, Nur, 318
Galperin, Efim, 180
Gas mask, 43, 45, 56, 59, 129, 136, 179, 182, 186, 187, 197, 198, 201; filters, 42, 93, 131, 132, 136, 153, 158, 179, 183-185, 187, 188, 190
Gdlyan, Telman, 240
Gelperin, Nisson, 41
General Staff Headquarters, 311, 324, 341, 344, 344-346
Geneva, 137, 183, 218-220, 237, 239, 308, 424, 444; negotiations, 205, 308
Gerey, 14
German (-s), 18, 20, 22-24, 51, 160, 230; armies, 110; fighters, 160; mortar fire, 23; officers, 230; prisoners, 79; samples, 161; scientific society, 408; shepherds, 419; technology, 51; territory, 23; troops, 20, 79, 230
Germany, 19, 27, 51, 212, 261, 319, 359, 366

Gevorkyan, Natalia, 413
Gilyarovskaya, Minna, 51
Ginsburg, Vsevolod, 129-131
Giprosynthesis, Institute, 155
Gitel, Pavel, 130
Gladstein, Boris, 120
Goal-oriented program, 340
Godovikov, Sergei, 120
Godzhello, Natalia, 152, 153, 322
Gogol, Nikolai, 134
Goldansky, Vitali, 367
Goldman, Irene, 315, 359, 372, 404, 432, 441
Gololobov, Yuri, 127
Golosov, Nikolai, 101
Golubkov, Sergei, 104, 200, 203, 232
Golubeva (Kulbeda), Olga, 154
Gorbatova, Elena, 128
Gorbunov, Yuri, 133
Gordeyev, Alexander, 425
Gorelov, V., 320
Gorelov, Foma,111, 112
GOSNIIOKhT (GRNIIOKhT), 49, 60, 62, 68, 79, 81-90, 93, 94, 97-100, 105-110, 112-114, 119-123, 127, 128, 130, 133, 137, 139, 141, 144, 146-148, 150, 153-156, 160, 162-170, 172, 175, 177, 178, 181, 186, 187, 189, 191-193, 197-201, 203-205, 207, 209-211, 213-215, 218-220, 223, 225, 226, 230-232, 234, 239-241, 243-246, 252, 253, 257, 261-263, 265, 268, 270, 308, 310, 311, 324, 335, 424, 425; Department of Analytical Chemistry, 91, 104; Computer Center, 211, 212; Department for Medical and Biological Research (MB), 127; Department RP, 136, 159, 160; Department of Technology of Organic Synthesis TOS, 102; Director, 112, 113, 117, 127, 137, 138, 140, 146, 148, 149, 152, 155, 160, 166, 172, 173, 190, 193, 194, 203, 206, 207, 215, 234, 241, 245, 246, 249, 253, 266, 326, 426; Directorate, 108, 142, 234; Deputy Director, 106, 108, 166, 204, 206, 213, 218, 229, 234, 244; Dzerzhinsk and Borislavl branches, 109; Decontamination (Degasification) Department D, 195, 200, 230; Engineering Department 151, 180; Experimental Plant, 97, 101, 128, 156, 160, 223; First Department, 80-82, 85, 138, 173, 175, 186, 211, 217, 309; Foreign Technical Counterintelligence (PD ITR) Department, 205-218, 221, 239; Main Laboratory Building (GLK), 78-80, 139, 204; Medical Department, 100; Party Committee, 99, 100, 188, 218, 239, 240, 242; Physical Chemistry Department, 177, 180, 181, 193, 213, 216; Permanent Technical Commission, 140, 265, 337; Science Council, 106, 108, 138, 146, 169, 172, 173, 181, 250; Volgograd Branch, 124, 148, 149, 216; Volsk (Shikhany) Branch, 110, 115, 117, 124, 126, 128, 129, 143, 144, 148, 149, 154, 193, 216, 309, 325, 327; Scientific Technical Department, 111
Greenpeace, 350
Greenshtein, Evgeni, 183
Gref, F., 319
Grigoriyants, Sergei, 302, 329
GRU (General Intelligence Directorate), 127, 128, 131, 178
Gulag (s), 27, 67
Gulf War veterans, 235
Gun, R., 319
Guskov, Konstantin, 94, 96, 99, 101-106, 114, 122, 124, 125, 155, 157, 158, 166, 172, 200, 204, 206, 208, 214, 215, 222, 232-234

Hafez Assad, Syrian President, 140

State Secrets

Heitler and London (wave function), 67
Hiatt, Fred, 386
Higher Attestation Commission (VAK), 169, 171, 172, 176
Highway of Enthusiasts, 55, 76, 79, 139, 268
Hirshwald, Wolfgang, 366
Hippel, von, Frank, 315-317
HIV/AID test, 399
Human Rights Watch, 367
Hydrochloric acid, 200, 201, 227
Hunt, Kathleen, 368, 389
Iakimets, Vladimir, 315
Idel-Ural, 330
Illesh, Andrei, 283
Ilyushenko, Aleksey, 445
Imprisonment, 218, 283, 285-289, 322, 335, 343-347, 364, 375, 379, 382, 383
Indictment, 195, 251, 253-256, 283, 294, 300-303, 316, 317, 327, 331, 334
Institute, 36-38, 41, 46-50, 55, 60, 62-64, 68-70, 76, 77, 81-84, 86, 90-92, 96, 98-100, 104, 107-109, 112, 114, 115, 123, 126, 127, 132, 134, 138, 139, 148, 151, 152, 154, 155, 159-161, 165, 166, 169, 171-176, 178, 181, 186, 205-207, 209, 213, 215, 217, 220, 225, 226, 229, 231, 239, 241, 243, 245, 250-252, 257, 265, 305, 307, 309-311, 322, 411; at the General Intelligence Directorate (GRU), 178; of the Chlorine Industry, 229; Complex Automation of the Oil and Gas Industry (VNIKANeftGas), 71, 75; Elemental Organic Compounds, 107, 120; Fine Chemical Technology (MITKhT), 36; KGB, 130, 210; Nuclear Geophysics and Geochemistry, 64; Organic Silicon Compounds Technology, 60; Petrochemical Synthesis, 11, 40, 49, 60, 63, 64, 78; Physical Chemical, 61,67; Physiologically Active Compounds, 111, 121; Toxicology in Kiev, 132; Toxicology and Professional Pathology, 201; for, Chemical Defense of Plant Life (VNIISKhZR), 126; Legal Expertise, 380; Problems of Security of the KGB, 312
International Covenant on Civil and Political Rights, 379
International Network of Engineers and Scientists for Global Responsibility (INES), 408
Inversion, 250, 254, 259, 288, 308
Ishan, 10, 11, 14, 15
Islam, 11, 19
Isler-Begen, M.-A., 319
Israel, 106, 227, 228
ITAR-TASS, 408, 419
Ivan the Terrible, 7, 331
Ivanov, Aleksei, 37
Ivanov, Aleksander, 207
Ivin, Sergey, 108, 119-121, 123, 126-128, 137, 162
Izvestia, 282, 283, 300, 304, 324, 369, 388, 389, 404-406, 412, 426, 435

Kabachnik, Michael, 107, 120
Kagan, Yuli, 52, 53
Kagarmanov, Khabel, 20
Kalugin, Oleg, 130, 312, 313
Kamalov, Mirkasim, 9, 16, 19
Kandaurov, Aleksei, 284, 301
Kanifa-apa, Bayanova, 26
Kara-Kalpakia, 147, 191
Karavanov, Konstatin, 96
Karimov, Islam, 262
Karimova, Nazifa, 368
Karmishin, Yuri, 304
Karpinsky, Len, 367
Katanyan, Constantine, 250
Kazakhstan,148, 208
Kazakov, clan, 5
Kazakov, Mirzazhan, 5
Kazakov, Nazhmetdin, 11
Kazan, 5, 7, 24, 332, 333, 335, 352, 367; plant, 51, 99, 102, 151; train station,

595

132, 413; University, 29
Kazannik, Aleksey, 362, 366, 372-374, 388, 389, 408, 434, 442, 444, 445
Kazhdan, Henri, 49, 151, 152
KGB, 1, 2, 28-30, 36, 67, 81, 83, 84-86, 98, 130, 138, 141, 150, 152, 159-161, 172, 207, 208, 210, 211, 213, 214, 216-218, 221, 228-231, 235, 243, 244, 250, 251, 259, 266-268, 270, 278-280, 283, 284, 286, 291, 299, 300, 302, 309, 311, 312, 315, 326-329, 332, 337, 341, 342, 349, 351, 360, 363, 364, 399, 411, 418, 426, 440
Khadi Taktash, 29
Khandozhko, General, 46
Khasanbikov, Mirkasim, 9
Khasanyanov, Salikh, 12-15
Khasbulatov, Ruslan, 320, 328, 333, 350, 351, 360, 367
Khimavtomatika, 190
Khokhlova, lecturer, 48
Khoryok, 107, 124, 149
Khotimskaya, Minna, 69
Khrulev, Yu., 320
Khrushchev, Nikita, 114, 257
Kirpichev, Petr, 110, 126, 142-146, 309, 326
Kishlaks, 153
Klin, 22, 61
Klochkov, Aleksander, 180
Knight, Amy, 426
Knunyantz, Ivan, 91, 110
Kolyada, Olga, 196, 197
Kochetkov, Anatoly, 216, 340, 342, 345
Kolovertnov, Gena, 62
Koltsov, Nikolai, 426
Komarov, Victor, 128
Komchatov, V., 320
Komsomol, 28, 33, 35, 46, 96, 243, 246, 262, 272, 443; Lenin's national policy, 330; room, 45, 48

Komsomolskaya Square, 369
Kondratiev, Yuri, 126, 162
Kopeiko, A., 320
Korean, prisoner, 394
Korneva, Zoya, 412
Koshelev, Aleksander, 436, 438, 439
Koshelev, Sergey, 144
Kostenko, Gennady, 162-164, 170
Kostikin, Leonid, 156, 174, 175
Kostin, Aleksei, 396, 416
Kovalev, Sergei, 320
Kozlovski, Ivan, 37
Krasheninnikov, Victor, 208, 209, 211, 216, 217
Kryuchkov, Vladimir, 250, 332, 411
Kuibyshevski Special Design Bureau, 134
Kuibyshevski Miliary District, 166
Kulikov, Mikhail, 160-162
Kuntsevich, Anatoly, 132, 140, 141,198, 207, 220, 221, 243, 246, 304, 305, 352, 358
Kuranty, 250, 254, 288, 442
Kurdish, citizens, 235; village, 236
Kurochkin, Vladimir, 110, 152, 176, 178, 181, 206, 244, 246, 287
Kuwait, 235
Kuznetsky Most (Bridge), 363
Kuznetsov, Boris, 218, 219, 308, 340, 342, 425
Kuznetsov, Nikolai, 166, 167, 192
Kvmpstrop, E., 319

Langer, A., 319
Lannoi, P., 319
Laricheva, Valentina, 378, 379, 383, 385
Lawyers Committee for Human Rights, 374, 408
Lebedev, Valeri, 123
Lefortovo, Investigation Department, 323, 325, 350, 360, 425; Prison, 140, 150, 221, 261, 267-269, 272-274, 276, 278-281, 283, 289, 295, 297, 360, 361,

367, 369, 398, 399, 401, 402, 423, 425
Lemeshev, Sergei, 32
Lenin, 10, 20, 27, 46, 47, 77, 99, 107, 333, 364, 411; Leninism, 41, 46, 63, 248; Leningrad, 30, 109,188; Prospect, 389; Prize, 61, 105, 107, 141, 159, 167, 221, 246, 262, 272
Lermontov, Michael, 29
Levina, Faina, 30
Lewisite, 142, 153, 303
Lipasov, Leonid, 221
Lisitsian, Pavel, 37
List of chemical agents, 148
List of employees, 226, 336
List of information of state secrecy, 226, 338, 339, 345, 375, 378
List of Major Information (LMI), 343, 378
List of experts, 308, 309
Listov, Vladimir, 115, 126
Los Angeles Times, 371
Loshak, Aleksander, 367
Luchinsky, Yu., 320
Lukiyanov, Aleksei, 302
Lukiyanov, Anatoly, 410
Luzhkov, Yuri, 190
Luzhniki, 240
Lyuberetskaya gang, 436

Maleykin, Sergei, 137
Markov, Georgi, 130
Martins, K., 319
Maslov, Nikolai, 207
Maslov, Victor, 435
Mayak, 275, 281, 372
Mayor, Frederico, 366
Mecca, 6, 19
Medvedev, Boris, 100
Medvedev, R., 319
Meissner, Dieter, 360
Meizel, U., 319
Melandri, E., 319
Melik-Pashaev, Aleksander, 38
Merzabekova, Natalia, 129

Military Unit 61469, 123, 132, 134, 135, 143, 147, 163, 198, 324, 328, 329
Milyutin, Michael, 208
Ministry of Atomic Energy, 159
Ministry of Geology, 69, 70
Ministry of Chemical Industry, 61, 95, 102, 104, 113, 114, 156, 158, 172, 207-209, 211, 212, 214, 216, 219, 232, 253, 378
Ministry of Defense, 180, 324
Ministry of Foreign Affairs, 344
Ministry of Foreign Trade, 133
Ministry of Health, Third Chief Administration, 165
Ministry of Industry, 253
Ministry of Mineral Fertilizers, 207
Ministry of Security of the Russian Federation (MB RF), 267, 282-284, 299, 301, 324, 345, 369, 381, 389, 425, 430
Mintyukov, Aleksei, 322
Minyamal, Grandmother, 6
Mironov, Andrei, 261, 267, 273, 343, 369, 389, 407, 426, 430, 431, 432, 442
Mirzayanov, Akhmetziya, 8
Mirzayanov, Fazliakhmet, 6
Mirzayanov, Iskander, 257, 279, 297, 298, 390
Mirzayanova Lisa, 26
Mirzayanova, Nuria, 267, 268, 276, 278
Mirzayanov, Sultan, 9, 10
Mirzayanov, Sultan V., 257, 276, 298, 387, 390, 391, 398
Mirzayanova (Skibko), Rita, 52, 55, 59, 75
Mirzayanova, Vaziga, 10, 18
Mitkova, Tatiana, 404, 405, 423
Mohammed, Prophet, 11
Molodezhny Kanal (Youth), 372
Molostvov, M., 320
Morozov, Nikolai, 52

Morris, 319
Moscow, 1. 13, 22, 31, 32, 35, 36, 39-41, 46, 47, 50, 55, 57, 58, 65, 75, 79, 109, 111, 114-116, 121, 126, 133, 153, 177, 190, 200, 231, 232, 245, 247, 260, 265, 282, 295, 317, 328, 332, 335, 350, 351, 352, 357, 359, 372, 376, 383, 392, 394, 405, 406, 415, 422, 426, 438, 444; air, 139; Bauman High Technical School in, 32, 36; 284, 298, 357-360, 387, 390, 391; Burdenko Military Hospital, 127; City Committee of the CPSU, 98, 100; City Committee for Ecology, 242; City Court, 364, 368, 369, 387, 406, 412, 413, 415, 419, 423, 413, 416, 439; City District Council, 243; City Duma, 165; City Prosecutor's Office, 371; City Fire Brigade, 139; City sewage system, 198; district courts, 92; Frunze Naberejnaya, 132; Highway of Enthusiastov in, 55, 76, 79, 139, 268; jails, 292, 413, 416, 437; Kalinin District Peopl's Court in, 293; Karpov Physical Chemical Institute, 62, 67; Khlebny Pereulok, 385, 389; Lenin State Library in, 64; Mayor of, 190, 249; media, 367; Mendeleev Chemical Technical Institute of, 101; newspaper, 250, 423; Police Department 387; press, 418; Radisson-Slavyanskaya Hotel in, 1, 447; River, 41; State University, 57, 153, 176, 210, 249, 428; Yaroslav Train Station, 76
Moscow News, weekly, 204, 221, 260-262, 265, 268, 274, 283, 284, 296, 316, 366, 367, 383, 407, 412, 419, 422, 435, 446
Moscow Times, 425
Moscow Tribune, 442
Mostovshchikov, Sergei, 388, 389, 390, 406
Moynihan, Daniel, 365, 387

Mufti, 11
Mukhamadiev, Renat, 333
Mujahedeen, 350
Murashev, Arkady, 243, 244
Muratov, Rishat, 32
Murov, 26
Musa Dzhalil, 23, 24
Musin, A., 319
Muslim pilgrims, 19
Myshko, Nikolai, 47, 48

Nabrerezhnich, Rudolf, 132, 136
Nasokhin, A., 320
Nasirov, Colonel, 28
Nazarov, Ivan, 38
Nazarov, Vladimir, 442
Nazi war criminals, 182
Nefedov, Oleg, 113
Nelep, Georgi, 37
Netrebko, Anna
Newman, E., 319
New York Academy of Sciences, 2, 3, 366, 373, 408, 447
New York Times, 302, 315, 405, 442
New York Metropolitan Opera House, 30
Nikishin, Leonard, 262, 422, 423
Nikolaev, K.M., 68
Nikulin, Peter, 312, 313
Nim, Naum, 386
Nizhny Novgorod, 43
Nixon, Richard, 227
Nobel Prize, 167, 316; laureate, 3, 318, 366, 447
Novichok, chemical agent, 2, 138, 140, 142, 149, 233, 237, 238, 261, 341, 447
Novikov, Yuri, 93
Novocheboksary, 61, 103-107, 119, 122, 128, 154, 155, 158, 167, 190, 203, 204, 220, 221, 226, 303
Novocherkassk, 19, 51
Novodvorskaya, Valeria, 369, 377, 382

Novoe Vremya, weekly, 150, 263, 266, 274, 292, 312, 323
NTV, Russian Channel, 372, 404, 423
Nuclear magnetic resonance (NMR), 98, 178
Nukus, 147, 148, 166, 191, 237, 259, 267, 277
Nuremberg trials, 182

Olympic Games, 440
OMON, 387, 388, 390-393
Onesta, J., 319
Ordzhonikidze, Sergo, 65
Orenburg, 5, 6, 31
Orlov, Count, 115
Orlov, Oleg, 389
Orlova, Elena, 389, 411
Ostapchuk, 230
Ottoman Empire, 19
OVIR, 359
Ovchinnikov, Yuri, 113

Pacific Ocean, 53
Pagel, R. Heinz, 2, 391
Pankratov, Leonid, 323, 329-331, 333, 338-340, 368, 369, 373, 375, 380, 381, 386
Patrushev, Grigroy, 79, 99-101, 110, 128, 146, 152, 157, 168, 184
Pavlodar, 129
Pavlov, Valentin, 290, 360
Pentagon Papers, 201
Perestroika, 170, 208
Perkin Elmer GC, 163, 173
Permanent Technical Commission, 234
Persian Gulf, 208, 209, 210
Pesticide (s), 83, 148, 170, 203, 220
Petrunin, Victor, 115-117, 140, 141, 143, 144, 146, 147, 149, 154, 155, 166, 167, 188, 190-193, 203, 207, 215, 226, 232-234, 238, 239, 241-246, 253, 266, 340, 426, 427
Physicians for Social Responsibility, 374
Phosphoorganic, chemical agents (POCA), 99, 127, 129, 135, 138, 148, 170, 236; chemicals, 148; compounds, 130, 201; radicals, 130
Phosphorous chloride, 200
Pickering, Tomas, 405, 408, 418
Plekhanov, Yuri, 300, 410, 411
Pikalov, Vladimir, 164
Pikovaya Dama, by P. Tchaikovsky, 37
Plisetskaya, Maya, 38
Plushch, Oleg, 159, 164, 165
Politburo of the Central Committee of the CPCU, 47, 126, 233
Poltoranin, Michael, 353
Polyakov, Victor, 141, 242, 245
Polyani, Michael, 66
Ponomarenko, Felix, 123, 124
Ponomarev, Lev, 254-256, 320
Popov, Gavriil, 249
Pravda, 254
Proceedings of the USSR Academy of Science, 66, 91
Princeton, 350, 433, 447; University, 1
Prison, 361; prisoner, 18, 22, 23, 27, 36, 56, 65, 79, 225, 276, 279, 280, 281, 289, 291-293, 295, 350, 360, 361, 369, 393-398, 400-402, 404-406, 410, 412, 413, 416-418, 423, 426, 436, 437, 439, 442, 494
Privezentsev, Yuri, 106, 107
Pugachev, Emiliyan, 6
Pushkin, Aleksander, 29, 376; Street, 446
Pushkinskaya, metro, 266
Pumpyansky, Aleksander, 367
Putsch, 248, 367, 376

Radio, 21, 23, 24, 27, 30, 247, 275, 277, 278, 281, 292, 325, 352, 353, 375, 390, 411, 416; radioactive, 159, 164, 215, 216; Radio Azatliq 369; Committee for, 358; National

Public, 368; "Mayak", 275, 281, 371; monitoring, 309; Radio Station Vozrozhdenie, 302; Echo Moskva, 325, 371; Radio Stations - The Voice of America, Freedom, BBC, and others, 309; Youth Channel, 383, 271, 324; *National Public*, 321; *Echo Moskva*, 284, 324; *Liberty*, 321; *Azatltk*, 321
Radisson Hotel, 1
Rafflin, J.P., 319
Razuvanov, R.F., 134
Red Army, 14, 152
Revelsky, Igor, 172, 173, 194
Reznik, Henri, 300
Reznik, Semeyon, 432
Richardson, Bill, 304, 305
Ricin, 129, 130
Rossiskaya Gazetta, 303, 304
Rot, K., 319
Rudnev, Valery, 300, 346, 426, 442
Russia, 3, 7, 8, 11, 16, 19, 22, 27, 28, 96, 97, 104, 129, 141, 146, 150, 165, 187, 192, 217, 239, 240, 244, 248, 254, 255, 257, 258, 260, 262, 265, 277, 279, 289, 293, 294, 301, 303, 304, 309, 310, 311, 313, 317, 319, 330, 331, 333, 334, 339, 341, 342, 344, 347, 350-356, 358, 360-362, 364-368, 372, 373, 375, 377, 381, 383, 386, 391, 392, 405, 407, 408, 414, 447
Russian, 1, 2, 6-8, 13, 15, 24, 26, 32-35, 46, 68, 263, 270, 281, 282, 331, 335, 342, 343, 351, 359, 374, 423; Academy of Sciences, 113, 409, 435; affairs, 335; Air Force General, 361; American International Press Center, 386, 390, 405, 418; Attorney General of, 300, 318, 319, 372, 445; 6; authorities, 124, 284, 357, 367; authorities, 141, 325, 408, 419; autocracy, 4, 7; Binary Weapons, 119, 283; captives, 19; carriage, 115; chauvinism, 7; -Chechen war, 333, 334; chemical weapons, 5, 226; chemist,365; citizens, 317; Committee for Conventional Problems of Chemical and Biological Weapons, 207, 217; Constitution, 361, 373, 375, 377, 384, 386, 390, 409; correspondents, 298, 358, 377; Criminal Code, 270, 379; delegation, 414; democratic figures, 311; Deputy Attorney General, 266; Deputy Prime Minister, 140; economy, 141; Empire, 7, 330, 331, 332, 334; expansionism 7; Federation, 266, 308, 320, 332, 354, 378, 384; folk songs, 115, 281; foreign policy, 345; gentry, 6; Government, 303, 341, 358, 365, 373, 374, 405, 408; historians, 91; Industry, 253; journal, 316; landlady 33, language, 29, 30, 32, 35; law, 257, 365; literature, 29; magazine, 150; mass-media, 431; military authorities, 262; military-chemical complex, 344; military specialists, 226; Muslims, 19; nation, 335; newspaper, 266; Novichok program, 2; officials, 367; pass, 330; patriotism 316; people, 7, 8, 333, 361; poets, 29; politicians, 368; President, 119, 207 302, 303, 316, 318, 335, 354, 362, 374, 385, 439; reform, 418; revolution, 19; reporters, 434; romance, 115; scientist (s), 66, 67, 435; school, 32, 39; secret-bearer, 447; soldiers, 334; State Library, 248; troops, 332; tsar, 6; Vice President, 328; villages, 15; VX gas, 119; words 33, 394
Russia's Choice, 407
Ryurikov, Dmitry, 358
Ryskal, Anatoly, 422

Saddam Hussein, 427
Sammaruga, Cornelio, 444

State Secrets

Safonov, Anatoly, 300
Sagdeev, Roald, 373, 400
Sakharov, Andrei, 317, 367, 373, 374, 408, 409
Salie, M., 320
Samara, 167
Saratov, 64, 109, 132, 163, 198; military chemical college, 109; region, 352, 356; regional Party Committee, 115; University, 66
Sarin, 58, 72, 82-84, 92, 106, 123-125, 158, 67, 84, 94, 96, 105, 123, 141, 143, 179, 183, 186, 197, 198, 201-203, 217, 222, 232, 236, 237, 281, 303, 449
Sarkisyan, Edward, 240, 261, 267
Sazonov, Nikolai, 364, 369-371, 378, 379, 383-385, 390, 420-423, 425, 428, 429, 436, 446, 442
Shchekotikhin, Alexander, 89-91, 94, 131, 132, 137, 165
Scientific and Technical Department (NTO), 175
Secretary of State, 365, 368
Semyonov, Aleksei, 367
Sergievski, Igor, 105, 106
Schanin, Aleksander, 292-295
Shabad, A., 320
Shaimiev, Mintimer, 332, 333
Shakhrai, Sergei, 249
Shakhrai, Volodya, 75
Sharashka, 79, 225, 226, 232, 260
Shargorodsky, Sergei, 442
Sharia, 17
Sharipova, Gaishagar, 30
Shiekh-Gali, 335
Sheinis, V., 320
Shelakova, Iya, 119-121
Sheluchenko, Vladislav, 92-94, 96, 132
Shestov, S., 320
Shkarin, Victor, 140, 213, 269, 270-272, 274, 276-278, 280, 282, 284-287, 291, 292, 299, 307, 308, 315, 322-324, 332, 335-337, 340, 341, 343, 346, 349, 361, 363, 369, 375, 425, 431, 434
Sholokhov, Michael, 23
Shumeiko, Vladimir, 140
Shikhany, 109, 114, 117, 123, 124, 126, 128, 141-143, 153, 164, 167, 188, 233, 277, 302, 328, 329; Polygon, 132, 136; test site, 132, 147, 163, 263, 326
Shikhany-2, 132, 136
Siberian Branch of the Academy of Sciences, 62
Simeoni, M.., 320
Simonov, Aleksei, 386, 390
Simonov, Konstantin, 23
Sirotkin, S., 320
Sitdikov, Ravil, 423
Slavgorod, 155
Sloan, Wendy, 442
Smirnitsky, Vadim, 324, 337, 339, 379, 424, 425
Smirnov, Aleksander, 48, 49, 151
Smirnov, Sergei, 153-155, 158, 159
Smirnov, Vladimir, 186, 187, 194
Shoko Asahara, 281
Soborovsky, Leonid, 108, 127
Sokalski, Georgi, 137
Sokolov, Boris, 435
Sokolov, Leonid, 106, 137, 176
Sokolov, Vasili, 64-66, 68-70, 72, 75
Sokolov, Svyatoslav, 210, 218, 322, 336
Solow, Robert, 316
Solzhenitsyn, Alexander, 130, 225, 227
Soman, 67, 84, 94, 105, 123, 140, 141, 143, 179, 180, 183, 184, 186, 197, 198, 200-203, 217, 222, 232, 233, 261, 303
Sorochkin, Ivan, 205, 206
Soros, George, 2, 408, 447
Sovershenno Secretno, 259, 260
Soyuzorgsynthesis, 61, 102, 104, 156, 207, 216, 219
Soviet, 2, 32, 49, 105, 129, 134, 206,

601

230, 243, 244, 246, 251, 255, 286, 312, 313, 319, 333; Academy of Sciences, 409; agents, 230, 237; - American joint venture, 410; - American negotiations, 324; analogue, 84; administration, 18, 48; Army, 43, 45, 128, 144, 148, 149, 167, 178, 185, 191, 198, 237, 272, 303, 304; 352, 353, 359, 368, 418, 423 arsenal, 167; binary weapon, 149; bureaucracy, 95, 114, 134; bureaucrat, 174; camp, 27; chemical weapons, 237; concentration camps, 329; deceptions, 233; delegation, 137, 308, 324; disarmament policy, 229; "economists", 248; elite, 48; era, 61; Labor Code, 77; justice, 376, 382; jewry, 408; power, 8; regime, 28; state, 28, 47; system, 25, 65, 72, 77; times, 5, 372, 393; troops, 27; Union, 41, 63, 65, 85, 109, 148, 150, 167, 237, 317, 333, 365, 366, 381; war captives, 24, 27

Staes, P., 319

Stalin, Josif, 20-23, 28, 36, 41, 47, 90, 91, 105, 110, 114, 225; -ist, 27, 226, 228

Stalingrad, 21

Stary Kangysh, 10, 11, 17, 18, 20-22, 55

Steklenyova, Nadezhda, 193

Stockholm International Peace Research Institute, 429

Stone, Jermy, 316

Stroganov, Sergei, 207, 210

Substance 33, 61, 84, 94, 100-109, 119, 121-125, 127, 128, 139, 141, 143, 145, 147, 151, 167, 190, 197, 204, 215, 216, 221, 226, 227, 237, 261, 272, 303-305, 310, 327

Substance 78, 128

Substance 84, 142

Supreme, Court, 369, 364; Soviet, 241, 243, 244, 251, 255, 312, 313,
319-321, 328, 333, 334, 350, 352, 362, 410

Surinski, Ivan, 218

Surkov, N., 320

Syria, 140

Syrian, government, 140, 141; Syrians, 140, 141; President, 140

Talbot, Strobe, 365

Tammelin, L.E., 119

Tarasovka Settlement, 76

Tatar, 5-8, 13, 23-27, 29, 30, 32-34, 51, 90,

Tatarstan, 332, 359, 38, 418, 423

Tearing agent (lachrymator), 6, 83, 153

Technical Order, 336

Tiananmen Square, 374

Timmermans, 24

Tkachenko, Ivan, 208, 211, 216

Tokyo's subway, 281

Trans-Ural, 8

Tsar, 6-8, 19, 20, 307, 331, 353

Tsar-Cannon, 354

Tsvet, Micahel, 66, 155, 184, 189, 190

Tugan Tel, 319

Tula Special Design Bureau of Automation (OKBA), 215

Turkeltaub, Nusselt, 63-66

Turkey, 19, 154

Tver, 161

Uglev, Vladimir, 111, 143, 265, 325-327, 340, 382

Ukraine, 27, 109, 330, 335

UNKhV, 108, 123, 124, 132, 147, 159, 183, 187, 199, 220

Umetskaya, S., 319

UNESCO, 366

United Nations, 342

United States, 2, 15, 98, 109, 132, 261, 262, 366

Universal Declaration of Human Rights, 373, 378

State Secrets

Urazhtsev, V., 320
USA, 213, 217
U.S., Congressional Committee on Government Operations, 368
Uzbekistan, 147, 153, 191, 240, 259, 262, 272

Valitovs, 6
Van-Dyke, N., 319
Vanunu, Mordechai, 228, 229
Varlaam, monk, 308
Varov, V., 320
Varshavski, Semion, 105, 106
Varukhin, V., 320357, 358, 368, 372
Vasiliev, Igor, 140, 149, 246
Vasiliev, lawyer, 286, 291
Veremchuk, V., 320
Versen, F., 319
Vershinin, N, 320
Vietnam, 163, 227, 302
Vishnevskaya, Galina, 37
Vitchenko, Antonina, 175
Vlasov, general-traitor, 23
Vlasov, Nikolai, 243
VNIIKANeftGas, 76, 77
Volga, car, 104, 112; River, 115, 163, 164, 201, 203;
Volgograd, 109, 123, 126, 148, 149, 155, 159, 200-203, 233, 262, 322; Industrial Association VPO Khimprom, 203, 204, 216, 222, 223, 232, 262, 308, 322; plant, 200, 202, 203, 261, 308, 322
Volkova, Evgenia, 165
Volkov, V.,320
Volsk, 109, 110, 115, 126, 128, 129, 147, 149, 154, 160, 163, 166, 193, 216, 309, 325, 327
Vorontsov, Nikolai, 406
Vozrozhdenie, island, 438
VX gas, 99, 108, 119, 121-123, 221, 237, 262, 265, 303, 304

Wall Street Journal, 407, 418
Waller, J. Michael, 407
Washington Post, 386
Watson, James, 447
Whistleblower, 368
White Army, 8
Workshop, 17, 55, 56, 59, 61, 151, 200, 217, 222, 223, 308
World War I, 5, 133
World War II, 16, 55, 67, 68, 141, 144, 151, 232, 291
Wyoming Memorandum, 150, 222, 250

Yablokov, Aleksei, 354
Yakov, Valery, 435
Yakunin, Gleb, 240, 254
Yarovenko, Nikolai,128
Yavitsky, Aleksander, 278, 281, 287, 289
Yavlinsky, Grigory, 368
Yeltsin, Boris, 140, 188, 234, 240, 247, 248, 249, 251, 262, 266, 283, 303, 313, 316, 318, 332, 350-354, 356, 358, 360, 362, 366, 373, 407, 419, 423, 435
Yudin, Victor, 378, 379, 383, 420, 421, 423
Yushenkov, Sergei, 320, 352, 353

Zadonsky, G., 279
Zalygin, Sergei, 381
Zaozerov, Adolph, 145, 146
Zaritovsky, colonel, 384
Zaslavskaya, Tatiana, 320
Zaslavsky, Victor, 215
Zasukhin, S., 279
Zefirov, Nikolai, 100
Zemlyanishin, Ivan, 235, 246, 263, 279
Zhakov, Alfred, 137, 224
Zheleznyakov, Andrei, 130, 131, 149-150, 233, 281, 297, 380

Zhiguli, 268
Zhiguli-luxe, 135
Zhirinovsky, Vladimir, 376
Zhukhovitsky, Aleksander, 64, 66, 67, 69, 71
Zilyaev, Gali, 25
Zoryan, Vladimir, 92
Zuberbiller, Olga, 41

Printed in the United States
209847BV00001B/196-204/P